ARMY HISTORICAL SERIES

THE ROLE OF
FEDERAL MILITARY FORCES
IN DOMESTIC DISORDERS
1877–1945

by

Clayton D. Laurie

and

Ronald H. Cole

MILITARY INSTRVCTION

CENTER OF MILITARY HISTORY
UNITED STATES ARMY
WASHINGTON, D.C., 1997

Library of Congress Cataloging-in-Publication Data

Laurie, Clayton D. (Clayton David), 1954–
  The role of federal military forces in domestic disorders, 1877–1945 / by Clayton
D. Laurie and Ronald H. Cole.
      p. cm. — (Army historical series)
  Includes bibliographical references and index.
    1. United States. Army—History—19th century. 2. United States. Army—
History—20th century. 3. Riots—United States—History. 4. Insurgency—United
States—History. 5. Internal security—United States—History.
I. Cole, Ronald H., 1943– . II. Title. III. Series.
UA25.L28   1997
363.3'2'0973—dc20   94–13148
                                                                                    CIP

First Printing—CMH Pub 30–15

For sale by the U.S. Government Printing Office
Superintendent of Documents, Mail Stop: SSOP, Washington, DC 20402-9328
ISBN 0-16-048983-0

Army Historical Series

Jeffrey J. Clarke, General Editor

Foreword

Though the turmoil of the cold war focused the Army on the challenges of conventional and nuclear conflict, the Army has a rich legacy of conducting domestic support operations. These have included activities from disaster relief to managing Indian reservations, military government in the post–Civil War South to supporting domestic law enforcement. This study focuses on the use of federal troops in domestic disorders from 1877 through 1945. These operations are not only an important part of our Army's past, but they portend lessons for the future. As the U.S. Army enters its third century of service to the nation, it faces an era in which it will undoubtedly be called on again to conduct domestic support operations at home and stability and peace operations overseas.

This work, the second of three volumes on the history of Army domestic support operations, encompasses a tumultuous era, the rise of industrial America with attendant social dislocation and strife. It begins with the first major U.S. Army intervention in a labor dispute, the Great Railway Strike of 1877, and concludes with War Department seizures of strike-plagued industries during World War II. The evolution of the Army's role in domestic support operations, its strict adherence to law, and the disciplined manner in which it conducted these difficult and often unpopular operations are major themes of this volume.

Throughout these troubled times presidents came to rely on the U.S. Army to provide units for civil disturbance duty. The national leadership began to tap the Army for units as a first, not last, resort. Army units not only enforced federal authority, but also aided local and state officials in maintaining law and order, protecting lives and property, and preserving social and political stability. The Army responded promptly and decisively to unrest, exercising disciplined responses that quelled disorders within legal boundaries. Army forces employed effective nonlethal tactics, techniques, and procedures during a time when the nation was buffeted by the greatest number of labor and race-related disturbances in its history, and local authorities often demonstrated far less forbearance.

Though this is a study of the U.S. Army's experience at a specific time in U.S. history, the issues it addresses offer broader perspectives. Similar challenges may be faced by active and reserve Army units both in the United States and overseas. In particular, U.S. forces may be called on to participate in peace operations, especially in countries confronting social unrest resulting from ethnic tensions and rapidly changing economies. Lessons gleaned from this chapter in our Army's past include the value of highly disciplined soldiers, careful operational and logistical planning, flexibility, and initiative at the lowest levels of command. These hallmarks of a trained and ready force apply not only to domestic support, but also to the full range of military operations the United States may face in the twenty-first century.

Washington, D.C.
8 November 1996

JOHN W. MOUNTCASTLE
Brigadier General, USA
Chief of Military History

v

The Authors

Clayton D. Laurie received a B.A. in history at the University of Northern Iowa in 1977 and taught American history and government in Council Bluffs, Iowa, until 1984. He earned an M.A. in history at the University of Nebraska in 1982 and the degree Doctor of Philosophy in history at the American University in 1990. Since joining the U.S. Army Center of Military History in 1986 he has taught at the American University and the University of Maryland in Baltimore County. In addition to this volume, he has published over twenty-five articles on military history topics and is the author of *The Propaganda Warriors: America's Crusade Against Nazi Germany*. He is also the author of the forthcoming Center of Military History publication The U.S. Army and Psychological Warfare Operations, 1918–1945, and has edited The Emergency Operation of Private Industrial Facilities by the War Department During World War II, written by former Assistant Secretary of Defense John H. Ohly. He is now working on several volumes for the Center, including a volume describing the medical and disaster relief missions of the U.S. Army. Dr. Laurie was awarded a Secretary of the Army Research and Study Fellowship in 1994 and began writing a history of the War Department Military Intelligence Division during World War II and a history of the Allied Intelligence Bureau in the Southwest Pacific.

Ronald H. Cole received the degree Doctor of Philosophy in history from the University of Maryland. He has taught for that university and the Ohio University. After completing a tour as military intelligence officer with the Eighth U.S. Army in Korea and finishing his doctorate, he joined the U.S. Army Center of Military History in 1975. While at the Center Dr. Cole wrote chapters for the official U.S. Army in Vietnam series and coauthored the present volume. Since 1983 he has been writing for the Joint History Office of the Joint Chiefs of Staff. In addition to writing chapters for The History of the Joint Chiefs of Staff and National Policy series, he has coauthored the *History of the Chairmen of the Joint Chiefs of Staff*, as well as the revised edition entitled *The Chairmanship of the Joint Chiefs of Staff*, and *The History of the Unified Command Plan, 1946–1993*. Dr. Cole wrote *Operation Just Cause: The Planning and Execution of Joint Operations in Panama, February 1988–January 1989*, and *Urgent Fury: The Role of the Joint Chiefs of Staff in Planning and Executing Rescue and Combat Operations in Grenada, 1983*, a forthcoming publication. He has also written classified studies of past and recent joint operations, and is currently doing research for a study on joint operations in Haiti in 1994–1995 (Uphold Democracy) and coauthoring a volume on the role of the Chairman, Joint Chiefs of Staff, and the Joint Staff in the Persian Gulf War.

Preface

This second of three volumes on the use of federal military forces in domestic disorders deals with the period between 1877 and 1945, a time when the nation was wracked by the greatest number of violent labor and race-related disturbances in its history, many that required the intervention of federal military forces to quell. This period of American history was unique, and the causes and nature of domestic disorders changed significantly from those of the antebellum years discussed in volume one. During that earlier period major constitutional and nation-building issues had prompted presidents to initiate federal military interventions in numerous crises between 1789 and 1877, stemming from such issues as the right of the federal government to tax and police or demand military service from its citizens to questions of whose laws, federal or state, took precedence. The U.S. Army served as the only significant law enforcement agency capable of major operations available to the national government during this time and ensured that federal authority was respected and its laws followed. Most of the issues of governance that divided Americans during the first century of the nation's existence were finally resolved by the end of the Civil War, although significant disagreements requiring a continued domestic role for the federal military remained well into the Reconstruction era.

Between 1877 and 1945 the Army was called to intervene domestically for far more mundane and less abstract purposes, primarily to assist legally constituted local, state, and federal civil authorities maintain or restore order, to protect the lives and rights of foreign and racial minorities, and to maintain social and political stability where it was threatened by labor disputes or racial tensions. The impact of the industrial revolution and the rapid growth of industrial combines and labor unions, as well as new racial tensions caused by post–Civil War civil rights legislation intended to benefit black Americans, saw the federal executive rely increasingly on the U.S. Army as a peacekeeping constabulary of first resort to enforce its authority and maintain law and order. The U.S. Army thus came to serve as a brake on rapid, uncontrolled, and potentially destabilizing social and political change in a tumultuous time and served successive presidents as the only disciplined and reliable body available as a bulwark against what were perceived as sinister forces of anarchy and chaos.

The changing domestic role of the U.S. Army, and the restrained nature in which the Army carried out this difficult and unpopular mission, is a major theme of this volume. Further attention is devoted to the development of a doctrine to fit the increased domestic role of the Army and the attention paid by the military and the federal government to constitutional and legal processes. Finally, the gradual evolution of thoughts and attitudes of the government, the public, labor and management, and the Army toward strikes, labor unions, racial minorities, and the roles of government and the Army in labor-management relations, and in social and racial affairs, are other central themes of this volume.

This volume opens with the first major federal military intervention in a labor dispute, the Great Railway Strike of 1877, and ends with the final War Department interventions in labor affairs during World War II when strike-plagued war industries were seized largely through administrative means without employing large numbers of combat troops. The volume thus encompasses those years in American history when a major role of the U.S. Army was dealing with violence associated with nineteenth and twentieth century national urbanization, modernization, industrial growth, and social change.

Any study of broad scope and of long duration leaves its authors with significant debts of acknowledgment. This volume is no exception. Foremost the authors want to acknowledge the contributions of Dr. Robert W. Coakley and Dr. Paul J. Scheips, formerly of the U.S. Army Center of Military History, who developed the idea for a series detailing the history of the Army's civil disorder mission. Dr. Coakley, the author of the first volume in this series, was helpful in providing suggestions on this volume. Attention is also called to the crucial role of Dr. Scheips, the author of the third volume in this series, whose general knowledge of the entire field of American civil-military relations is unparalleled.

A similar debt of appreciation is owed to successive Chiefs of Military History: Brig. Gen. James L. Collins, Jr. (Ret.), Brig. Gen. Douglas Kinnard (Ret.), Maj. Gen. William A. Stofft (Ret.), Brig. Gen. Harold W. Nelson (Ret.), and Brig. Gen. John W. Mountcastle, who maintained the Center's commitment to produce this series. Chief and Acting Chief Historians Dr. David F. Trask, Mr. Morris J. MacGregor, and Dr. Jeffrey J. Clarke also deserve credit for keeping the civil disorder project active.

The authors further wish to thank the archivists of the Modern Military Reference Branch of the National Archives and Records Administration in Washington, D.C., in particular George Chalou and Edward Reese. Similar gratitude is due the many employees of the Library of Congress in Washington, D.C., especially those in the Main Reading Room, Manuscript and Law Libraries, and the Prints and Photographic Division.

Our appreciation goes to the following members of the Center's Office of Production Services: John W. Elsberg, Catherine A. Heerin, and Arthur S. Hardyman; the late Rae Todd Panella edited the book, Barbara Harris Gilbert copy edited, and Diane Sedore Arms, Joycelyn M. Canery, Diane M. Donovan, and Scott Janes assisted; S. L. Dowdy compiled the excellent maps; Howell C. Brewer, Jr., obtained the many photographs; John Birmingham designed the paperback cover; and Beth MacKenzie designed the book layout. The CMH Librarians James B. Knight and Mary L. Sawyer obtained hundreds of books and articles, including many obscure and forgotten memoirs, legal treatises, and manuals that were all vital to our research.

Those who aided in researching, writing, and critiquing portions of the various drafts of this work include Dr. Paul C. Latowski, Ricardo Padron, and Dr. John Ray Skates. Col. William T. Bowers (Ret.), Maj. James Currie, Col. James W. Dunn (Ret.), Dr. Stanley Falk, Col. Michael Krause (Ret.), Col. Richard O. Perry (Ret.), Col. John Price, Col. Robert Sholly (Ret.), Col. Joseph W. A. Whitehorne (Ret.), and Dr. Robert K. Wright, Jr., made many helpful suggestions on the various draft manuscripts. A special debt of gratitude is owed to Dr. Jerry M. Cooper of the University of Missouri in St. Louis, whose seminal work, *The Army and Civil Disorder* (1980), served as a valuable guide and research tool and whose long-term interest in the Center's civil disorder project and in this volume in particular is much appreciated.

Special thanks also goes to Dr. Albert E. Cowdrey, the former chief of the Center's Conventional Warfare Studies Branch, whose insightful and pertinent criticisms and numerous useful suggestions on style and organization helped to improve the final product. Susan Carroll prepared the index.

As always, the authors accept the responsibility for any errors that may be found.

Washington, D.C.   CLAYTON D. LAURIE
8 November 1996   RONALD H. COLE

Contents

Maps

Illustrations

xvi

THE ROLE OF
FEDERAL MILITARY FORCES
IN DOMESTIC DISORDERS
1877–1945

Introduction

During the months of July and August 1877, over 3,700 federal troops were deployed throughout the East and Midwest to quell disorders arising from the country's first nation-wide railroad strike. Although these forces restored order in a matter of weeks without bloodshed, Maj. Gen. Winfield Scott Hancock, commander of the U.S. Army's Division of the Atlantic, wrote to Maj. Gen. John M. Schofield that "this thing [labor-related civil dis-order] will appear again, and . . . I judge from the passions I have seen outcrop, society may be shaken to its foundations." Few prominent people within the federal government, the Army, or society at large initially shared either his alarm or his distaste at the prospect of using federal military forces as "a police force for the state" or as "an instrument for deciding internal political and social struggles." Yet Hancock's words often proved prophetic during the following seven decades. The nation was undergoing fundamental changes, and "the thing" of which Hancock wrote reappeared with such frequency that federal military forces were repeatedly called to quell domestic disorders.[1]

The civil disturbance role of the U.S. Army changed significantly between 1877 and 1945. Unlike the earlier role of federal troops in domestic disorders, which arose large-ly from the political issues of nation building and questions concerning the extent and power of federal authority, the post-Reconstruction use of the Army involved primarily industrial disputes and social and racial tensions. These disorders were a direct result of the modernization of the United States. In the post–Civil War period, however, new destabilizing factors were introduced to the national scene—a large influx of immigrants from ethnic groups and world regions previously unrepresented in American society; the organization of labor unions, some radical in action and thought; and the shift of eco-nomic and political power from local to national levels amid rapid and uncontrolled industrialization and urbanization.

For much of the period the small U.S. Army was the only reliable force of adequate size available to the federal executive to maintain public order. Although the military was ostensibly nonpartisan, many conservative Americans regarded the Regular Army as the sole force standing between social stability and chaos. Despite the experience gained dur-ing the antebellum period, the Army was still unprepared for the types of disturbances encountered after the Civil War. Soldiers became involved in disorders stemming from extraordinarily complex economic and social issues of which they had little understanding or applicable professional experience and, initially, no guiding doctrine.

---

[1] Quotes from Jerry M. Cooper, *The Army and Civil Disorder: Federal Military Interventions in Labor Disputes, 1877–1900* (Westport: Greenwood, 1980), p. 83, and David M. Jordan, *Winfield Scott Hancock: A Soldier's Life* (Bloomington: Indiana University Press, 1988), p. 249, respectively.

The Army's primary mission was to defend the nation's borders against foreign enemies and to protect the rapidly expanding western frontier. The service did not possess a clearly defined internal mission, which only evolved over the course of several decades through a series of precedent-setting domestic operations. Beginning in the 1890s, the first attempts to create a doctrine reflected harsh contemporary public and government views of immigrants, labor organizations, radicals, and minority groups—indeed, of any group that threatened the status quo. Both Army doctrine and public opinion initially sanctioned the use of overwhelming force and firepower. Paradoxically, however, such measures were never necessary in practice and were never used. Army domestic interventions were always restrained and rarely resulted in bloodshed. By the later years of the period, its interventions became infrequent as other agencies capable of maintaining order were created at the state and local levels. Meanwhile, the thinking of the Army changed with its experience. Its leaders came to see domestic interventions fundamentally as noncombat functions rather than as incipient civil wars that might necessitate the use of deadly force. By the early 1940s, Army civil disturbance doctrine had evolved along with public attitudes and those of the federal government and reflected in word what had always been true in deed.

There was, however, another side to the story. Even though the Army's domestic interventions were largely nonviolent and mostly conducted in a neutral and nonpartisan fashion, such duty by its nature cast the Army as the defender of wealthy property owners and political power holders. To many the service appeared to be the shield of an unjust status quo and the enemy of outsiders—political dissidents, workers, immigrants, minority groups, and the poor—without regard to the justice of their demands for change. As Reconstruction duty had entailed the ill will of many white Southerners, duty in labor disturbances brought decades of resentment on the part of radical leaders, moderate as well as radical labor unions, and ordinary working men and women who clearly saw federal military interventions as antilabor in nature and intent. Similarly, Army involvement in activities against aliens and political dissidents during World War I and in the immediate postwar years prompted further charges that the nation was threatened by militarism and reaction. Such charges struck a nerve with many citizens whose perennial concern about military infringement upon and domination of civil affairs dated back to the American Revolution.

Though the Army sought direction from its civilian superiors throughout the period, the federal government initially failed, or was slow, to provide detailed policies, or even guidelines, directly applicable to the Army's conduct in domestic interventions. Until late in the period the Army was left largely on its own and consequently dealt with most civil disturbances ad hoc, in ways that took advantage of standard military tactics, training, and organization. In the vast majority of cases, however, the service worked within a loose structure of statutes governing its domestic use. Military officers, despite personal feelings and prejudices, were mostly pragmatic and evenhanded in their use of federal military power.

In striking contrast to contemporary Europe, the United States was never threatened by a military coup during times of crisis, and officers were clearly deferential (perhaps too much on occasion) to their civilian counterparts and superiors. They followed the orders and mirrored the thoughts and attitudes of the public and leaders in the White House, cabinet, or War Department, who likewise hesitated to use military force and did so only as a last resort when all other options and resources had been exhausted. The massive slaughter of civilians by government military forces experienced by Russians in 1905, for example, or by Frenchmen in 1832, 1848, or 1871, was unknown in the United States because of the restraint shown by Army commanders at the scenes of disorder. When civilian leaders stressed neutrality, nonviolence, and adherence to legal principles, and when civil authorities were closely involved in dealing with disorders, Army interventions reflected the same characteristics. When local civilian leaders were prejudicial, discriminatory, biased, or distracted by other events, or were otherwise uninvolved, as was often the case, Army interventions sometimes drew justified criticism as being partisan, excessive, or even illegal. Yet in almost every instance order was maintained or quickly restored constitutionally by the use of minimum force. Army restraint, as much as Army responsiveness and discipline, proved critical in maintaining public order until changing attitudes and democratic processes had slowly transformed the nation's response to the crises of industrialization and modernization.

CHAPTER 1

The Forces of Order in a Disordered Era: The U.S. Army and Late Nineteenth Century America

The Army is not an enemy of labor or a friend of capital. It is simply an instrument of popular power.

—Col. Thomas A. Anderson.

Look carefully through the ranks of the soldiers, scan well the forms and faces of the men who defend . . . the property of the millionaires, and you will find no millionaires or sons of millionaires. They are all workingmen, sons of workingmen and merchants. Do not enlist in either the state militia or regular army.

—Terence V. Powderly of the Knights of Labor.

In the decades following the Civil War the United States underwent a massive transformation caused by the onset of the industrial revolution, which was similar in many ways to earlier transformations in Europe. American growth was largely unregulated and accompanied by a high degree of economic change and social upheaval, often manifested in violent labor disputes and, in the opening decades of the twentieth century, by racial disturbances. In some areas, small local police and state militia forces existed to maintain law, order, and authority during these times of instability, but the United States Army was the sole professional force available to the federal executive to quell any domestic disorders that arose on a regional or national scale, and to aid state and local forces overwhelmed by events. Although the United States Army was neither large nor particularly well equipped to deal with the civil disturbance mission that fell to it by default when state and local forces lost control, it represented to many Americans the one reliable and disciplined bulwark between order and anarchy in a troubled time.

To the average American of the late nineteenth century the changes occurring domestically were both fascinating and troubling. The magnitude of American economic expansion was unprecedented. Industries were created where none had existed before. The total value of manufactures in the twenty years preceding the Civil War increased fourfold in nearly all areas from textiles to heavy machinery. But by 1914 the total value of industrial production had increased twelvefold to $24 billion annually, and the work force expanded fivefold to 7 million workers. As the United States matured as an industrial power, it began to supplant many nations as world suppliers of low-cost industrial goods, rapidly surpassing such European industrial giants as Great Britain, Germany, and France. The American economy showed every sign of increased vitality and future growth providing employment for millions.[1]

Concomitant with industrial expansion, the population of the United States grew to 75 million by 1900, double its 1860 figure. A significant and to some an alarming trend was the great population growth occurring in the burgeoning industrial cities of the northern Midwest and northeast. These cities, to most urban and rural conservatives of the middle and upper classes, embodied all the evils of contemporary society: immorality, poverty, rootlessness, irreligiousness, labor and political radicalism, and a general disregard for what were perceived as traditional American values. Everything that was wrong with the nation, many believed, could be traced to the cities and urban growth. Although the rural population of the United States doubled between 1860 and 1910, the urban population increased sevenfold. This growth was accompanied by a shift in power and status from small rural communities to the state and then to the national level, a trend causing a further sense of uncertainty and uneasiness among people who saw the nation changing, with the majority of the changes being made in places and by people beyond their control.[2]

Immigration accounted for a sizable portion of the nation's population growth. Fourteen million people entered the United States between 1860 and 1900, three times the number that had entered prior to 1860. Unlike the pre–Civil War period when the majority of immigrants came from the British Isles and northern Europe, an increasing majority of immigrants in the postwar period came from southeastern Europe (the Austro-Hungarian Empire, the Balkan States, Italy) and from the Russian Empire. Smaller numbers of Orientals arrived in the Pacific northwest. These new immigrants, especially Orientals, were greeted with hostility by many Americans of previous immigrant groups, property owners and laborers alike, and were regarded as a threat to the American way of life. While laborers feared immigrant job competition, property owners and businessmen feared the radical political, economic, and social philosophies reputedly held by immigrants and the negative influences these revolutionary ideas could have on labor and American society. By the later years of the century, antiradical nativism, in the words of one historian, "had become an American perennial."[3]

Yet many immigrants were merely sojourners, intending to stay temporarily in the United States; the rest were too busy seeking work and shelter and otherwise adjusting to a new society to be involved in radical labor politics. Moreover, the pool of generally docile labor that they provided was a boon to rapidly growing industries.

---

[1] John A. Garraty, *The New Commonwealth, 1877–1890* (New York: Harper & Brothers, 1968), pp. 78–84, 89; see also Sigmund Diamond, ed., *The Nation Transformed: The Creation of an Industrial Society* (New York: George Braziller, 1963).

[2] John A. Garraty, ed., *Labor and Capital in the Gilded Age* (Boston: Little Brown, 1968), p. viii.

[3] Quote from John Higham, *Strangers in the Land: Patterns of American Nativism, 1860–1925* (Westport: Greenwood Press, 1955), pp. 45–52; Alan Kraut, *Huddled Masses: The Immigrant in American Society, 1880–1921* (Arlington Heights, Ill.: Harlan Davidson, 1982), pp. 20–21, 150–51, 155–56; Nell Irving Painter, *Standing at Armageddon: The United States, 1877–1919* (New York: W. W. Norton, 1987), pp. xxviii–xxxiii.

The immigrants entered the lower levels of an increasingly complex class structure. American urban society in general had been clearly divided into a relatively small, wealthy upper class and an enormous working class, although neither was monolithic in attitude, identity, or action. The urban middle class of clerical workers, salespersons, government employees, technicians, and salaried professionals was growing rapidly during the period, from approximately 800,000 in 1870 to 5,609,000 by 1910. Although it formed only a small proportion of the 1910 national population of 75 million, this group rapidly adjusted to the emerging new order of society and provided the impetus for reforms during the Progressive era of the first part of the twentieth century. As early as the 1880s its influence was already being felt on the local and state level.[4]

For the wealthy and powerful, about 1 percent of American families, huge fortunes could be made from a multitude of new inventions and new industries. The names of the leaders of huge industrial combinations became household words, synonymous with wealth, political power, and often conspicuous consumption, greed, and corruption as well. Thomas A. Scott reportedly received $175,000 annually as president of the Pennsylvania Railroad, a salary by no means considered large for a railroad magnate. Cornelius Vanderbilt, shipping baron and owner of the New York Central Railroad, reputedly possessed a fortune of $105 million in 1877—also the same year in which he died—and bequeathed $90 million to his son William. Jay Gould's fortune was valued at $77 million on his death in 1892, while that of Henry Clay Frick was estimated at $150 million in 1919. Most corporate leaders could boast annual incomes in the tens of thousands or even in the tens of millions of dollars. By 1892 over 4,000 Americans claimed millionaire status, all beneficiaries of the post–Civil War economic expansion.[5]

The leaders of industry generally opposed any sort of change that threatened their economic positions and life-styles. They claimed that their positions of wealth and prominence were due to their own hard work, acquisitiveness, and thrift—the Puritan work ethic—or, as was so often claimed in that era of social Darwinism, to an inherent or inbred physical and intellectual superiority to those who lived and labored beneath them. Personal fortunes were seen as rewards for competence. Those who were less fortunate were either lazy, profligate, or unintelligent.[6]

The political, economic, and social conditions that prevailed in the United States in the late nineteenth century reflected the views of the wealthy and well established and put a high value on the acquisition of individual wealth. Above all, law and tradition emphasized the sanctity of private property—not only physical property of individuals and corporations, but intangible property such as profits and capital. This had been true since the

---

[4] Samuel P. Hays, *The Response to Industrialism, 1885–1914* (Chicago: University of Chicago Press, 1957), pp. 73–76; Robert H. Weibe, *The Search for Order, 1877–1920* (New York: Hill and Wang, 1967), pp. 111–32.

[5] Robert V. Bruce, *1877: Year of Violence* (Indianapolis: Bobbs Merrill, 1959), p. 25; J. A. Dacus, *Annals of the Great Strike* (Chicago: L. T. Palmer, 1877; reprint, New York: Arno, 1969), p. 20; Painter, *Standing at Armageddon*, pp. xxviii–xxix; Weibe, *The Search for Order*, pp. 8–9, 18.

[6] David K. Burbank, *Reign of the Rabble: The St. Louis General Strike of 1877* (New York: Augustus M. Kelley, 1966); "The Late Riots," *Nation* 25 (2 August 1877):68–69. One study of three hundred industrialists showed "that the typical leader came not from a log cabin or tenement, but from an upper or middle class family of English stock, Congregational, Presbyterian, or Episcopalian in religion; already in business." Most "usually graduated from an academy or college and almost never went to work before the age of eighteen." See Bruce, *1877*, p. 25.

founding of the Republic in the previous century, itself based on the ideas of inalienable rights to life, liberty, and property dating from the Enlightenment of the eighteenth century. As in Europe, supply and demand—the natural laws of classical economics—determined wages and the value of labor, not workers' demands.[7] Laws created by conservative middle and upper class legislators supported these views of property, and many firmly believed that society, indeed civilization itself, rested on them.

The system was designed for stability and preservation of the status quo. Workers who banded together to take collective action against employers to effect changes were usually swiftly condemned by conservative property owners and the press as threats to society and stability (and as subversives, radicals, anarchists, Communists, or Socialists). Strike activities were interpreted as thinly veiled attempts by radical workers, alleged to be of foreign origin, to rob industrialists of their justly earned profits. One such radical group, the Molly Maguires, became the stereotype of a subversive labor organization imported from abroad. Made up of Irish-immigrant coal miners, the Molly Maguires sought a rough justice and revenge in the coal fields of Pennsylvania for grievances real and fabricated through the practice of intimidation, robbery, vandalism, and murder. Their ruthless methods were matched by those of Pinkerton-trained company forces and local and state officials, who destroyed the organization in the late 1870s. The radical and brutal activities of the Molly Maguires were later automatically and falsely attributed to all labor and immigrant organizations. Even less violent labor actions, such as strikes, were routinely condemned as preludes to social revolution.[8] In addition, and from a practical standpoint, employers regarded work stoppages as simply illogical and wasteful, a violation of natural social and economic laws. Few strikes, prior to the creation of the first national labor organizations in the 1860s, were successful in doing anything but furthering the impoverishment of strikers.

Industrialization created an environment that necessitated the organization of labor and collective action. Strikes were legally recognized in 1842, and unions, especially those resembling fraternal or social organizations, were acceptable to some employers but were rarely recognized when seeking to dictate wages, hours, and hiring practices.[9] Employees, according to the prevailing industrial philosophy, were free to leave their jobs over real or alleged grievances but were forbidden to picket, to intimidate nonstriking workers, or to interfere with plant operations by nonunion men or strikebreakers. Damage to company property or striker-induced violence was perceived by owners as tantamount to social revolution and was usually condemned as such. Employers had the right to fire strikers, to hire

---

[7] Cooper, *The Army and Civil Disorder*, p. 4; Garraty, *New Commonwealth*, pp. 145–46; Louis P. Galambos, *The Public Image of Business in America, 1880–1940* (Baltimore: Johns Hopkins University Press, 1975); Herbert Gutman, "Work, Culture, and Society in Industrializing America, 1815–1919," *American Historical Review* 78 (June 1973):531–88.

[8] David B. Davis, ed., *The Fear of Conspiracy* (Ithaca, N.Y.: Cornell University Press, 1971), p. 150; Arthur A. Ekirch, Jr., *The Civilian and the Military: A History of the American Anti-Militarist Tradition* (Colorado Springs: Ralph Myers, 1972), pp. 117–18; Richard D. Lunt, *Law and Order vs. the Miners* (Hamden: Archon, 1979), p. 112; Wayne G. Broehl, Jr., *The Molly MaGuires* (Cambridge: Harvard University Press, 1964); Walter J. Coleman, *The Molly Maguire Riots: Industrial Conflict in the Pennsylvania Coal Region* (Washington, D.C.: Catholic University, 1936; reprint, New York: Arno, 1969); John Laslett, *Labor and the Left: A Study of Socialist and Radical Influences in the American Labor Movement, 1881–1924* (New York: Basic Books, 1970). For a contemporary view, see Waldo L. Cook, "Wars and Labor War," *International Journal of Ethics* 18 (April 1908):328.

[9] *Commonwealth* v. *Hunt*, 4 Metcalf 111 (Mass. 1842).

strikebreakers, and to continue operation during strikes, as well as to combine with other companies to thwart the demands of labor before, during, or after a work stoppage. Private armed guards were often hired, and county sheriffs were called upon to enforce company authority, to protect company property, or to break strikes. Further antiunion devices, such as the blacklist and the yellow-dog contract (forbidding union membership as a condition of employment), remained legal until well into the twentieth century.[10]

In this unregulated atmosphere that revered private property and discouraged collective action by workers, labor organized slowly. The power and increasingly impersonal nature of the corporations, most led by distant managers ignorant of or unconcerned about their workers' conditions, induced workers who had previously dealt directly with employers to organize. Unions and collective action were seen by growing numbers as the only way to impress employers and to improve working and living conditions. If industrial magnates could combine against the interests of the worker, labor leaders reasoned, workers could similarly organize against management. In spite of an environment that favored corporations over workers, laborers began to organize local craft and trade unions early in the nineteenth century. Due to their small size, however, they wielded little power and commanded even less company respect.[11]

During the final quarter of the nineteenth century most laborers, skilled and unskilled, working an average ten-hour day and a six-day week, considered themselves poorly paid. In 1900 the federal government considered workers who received less than $600 per year to be making less than a living wage, and 48 to 51 percent of males above the age of sixteen failed to exceed this figure. As many as 10 million people may have lived in poverty.[12] Reformers estimated that of wages received, three-fifths were spent by the worker for shelter and a further one-fifth for food. Little remained for clothing, health care, education, or recreation. It was often necessary for the entire family, including children, to work to survive. Numerous contemporary accounts describe the miserable conditions under which countless thousands lived in the teeming slums of the urban northeast and Midwest. Reformers claimed these conditions existed because the wealth of the nation was becoming concentrated in too few hands.[13]

Labor's first attempts to federate workers into national organizations capable of confronting management took place in 1866, when William H. Sylvis founded the National

---

[10] Cooper, *The Army and Civil Disorder*, pp. 5–6; Edwin E. Witte, *The Government in Labor Disputes*, (New York: McGraw Hill, 1931; reprint, New York: Arno, 1969), pp. 208–13; Lindley Clark, "The Present Legal Status of Organized Labor in the United States," *Journal of Political Economy* 13 (March 1905):174–75; Garraty, *New Commonwealth*, pp. 145, 149–50.

[11] For an overview, see Melvyn Dubofsky, *Industrialism and the American Worker, 1865–1920* (Arlington Heights, Ill.: Harlan Davidson, 1985); Hays, *Response to Industrialism*; Irwin Yellowitz, *Industrialization and the American Labor Movement, 1850–1900* (Port Washington, N.Y.: Kennikat Press, 1977).

[12] John A. Ryan, "The Underpaid Laborers of America," *The Catholic World* 81 (May 1905):143–47; Garraty, *New Commonwealth*, pp. 129–32, 136–37.

[13] Ryan, "Underpaid Laborers," pp. 149–50, 156. Wages in late-nineteenth century America are still a controversial subject. See Paul H. Douglas, *Real Wages in the United States, 1890–1925* (New York: Houghton Mifflin, 1930); Stanley Lebegott, "Wage Trends, 1800–1900," in National Bureau of Economic Research, *Trends in the American Economy in the Nineteenth Century* (Princeton: Princeton University Press, 1960); Clarence D. Long, *Wages and Earnings in the United States, 1860–1890* (Princeton: Princeton University Press, 1960); Robert F. Martin, *National Income in the United States, 1799–1938* (New York: National Industrial Conference Board, 1939); John F. McClymer, "Late Nineteenth Century American Working Class Living Standards," *Journal of Interdisciplinary History* 17 (Autumn 1986):379–88.

Labor Union and in 1869 when Uriah S. Stephens formed the secret Noble Order of the Knights of Labor.[14] The National Labor Union failed in 1872, but the Knights of Labor thrived. Its program, however, was vague, and the organization provided little immediate relief for its members, initially eschewing direct action. The Knights chose to endorse long-range idealistic goals requiring sweeping economic and social reforms. By 1886, under the leadership of Terence V. Powderly, the Knights of Labor had grown to 700,000 members, a size that was unprecedented for an American labor group. Powderly, nevertheless, lost control of the organization to undisciplined and militant locals, whose members felt that strikes were the only way to improve the workers' conditions. Although successful in a few instances, the Knights lost more disputes than they won. In addition, there was a growing public perception of an association of the union with anarchism and radical leaders. The perceived link was furthered by the 1886 Chicago Haymarket Square Bombing, where an explosion at a rally, generally believed to have been perpetrated by anarchists, killed and injured many people. The incident tarnished the public image of all labor groups and caused the rapid decline of the Knights of Labor after 1886. By 1900 its membership had dropped below 100,000.[15]

Even before the Knights' decline, a rival union based on an entirely new concept emerged. In 1881 several craft unions joined to form the Federation of Trade and Labor Unions of the United States and Canada. In 1886 it took the name American Federation of Labor (AFofL) under the leadership of Samuel Gompers. Over the next generation the AFofL became the dominant union in the country, representing the interests of all skilled workers in its federated structure. Founded as a politically moderate organization, its primary goal, unlike that of either predecessor, was to secure for labor a greater share of capitalism's material rewards. The federation repudiated all ideas of changing the economic system of the nation, of effecting long-term reforms, or of creating a working-class political party. It concentrated instead on immediate objectives such as securing improved working conditions, a shorter workday, and higher wages. Like its predecessors, the AFofL hoped to meet its goals by collective bargaining rather than by strikes, but it did not preclude work stoppages should employers fail to bargain with its members.[16] Despite AFofL intentions and the relative weakness of unions in comparison to industry, strikes did occur. Between 1881 and 1900, 22,793 strikes affecting 117,509 establishments and involving 6,105,694 workers took place, with an average duration of 23.8 days.[17]

---

[14] Foster R. Dulles, *Labor in America* (New York: Thomas Crowell, 1960), pp. 100–107; Gerald N. Grob, "Reform Unionism: The National Labor Union Movement," *Journal of Economic History* 14 (1954):126–42.

[15] Dulles, *Labor in America*, pp. 128, 133, 137–38, 141, 144–47; Leon Fink, *Workingmen's Democracy: The Knights of Labor and American Politics* (Urbana: University of Illinois Press, 1983); Gerald N. Grob, "Terence V. Powderly and the Knights of Labor," *Mid-America* 39 (1957):39–55; idem, "The Knights of Labor and the Trade Unions, 1878–1886," *Journal of Economic History* 18 (1958):176–92; idem, "The Knights of Labor, Politics, and Populism," *Mid-America* 40 (January 1958):3–21; William C. Birdsall, "The Problem of Structure in the Knights of Labor," *Industrial and Labor Relations Review* 6 (1953):532–46.

[16] Richard J. Hinton, "American Labor Organizations," *North American Review* 140 (January 1885):62; Stuart B. Kaufman, *Samuel Gompers and the Origins of the American Federation of Labor, 1848–1896* (Westport: Greenwood Press, 1967). For the growth of organized labor, see Leo Troy, *Trade Union Membership, 1897–1962* (New York: Columbia University Press, 1965).

[17] Strike statistics from Cooper, *The Army and Civil Disorder*, p. 3. See also P. K. Edwards, *Strikes in the United States, 1881–1974* (Oxford: Oxford University Press, 1981); U.S. Department of Labor, "Strikes in the United States, 1880–1936," Bulletin no. 652 by Florence Peterson (Washington, D.C.: Government Printing Office, 1938).

Union organization, collective bargaining, and strikes were viewed by most workers as a fundamental right of free citizens and free labor. The views of labor and capital, however, were at opposite philosophical extremes, and management regarded such activities as being subversive in nature and intent. As a result, compromise was rarely considered by any of the groups concerned, including the federal government, in the labor disputes of the late nineteenth century.

During these times of rising labor-management tensions, the three branches of the federal government held the attitude that interventions in private economic and commercial matters were not legitimate government functions. Congress passed little positive labor-related legislation; the judiciary was openly antilabor; and, until well into the twentieth century, the federal government failed to mandate or fund any sort of social welfare system. Similarly, federally sponsored mediation of labor-management disputes was not seriously considered until the end of the nineteenth century.[18] Concerning labor disputes, unions and industry were left to work out their own relationships free from government interference, as long the participants broke no laws, threatened or challenged no legally constituted authority, and destroyed no private or public property.

The Private and Local Forces of Order

Rarely did strikes escalate to the point of uncontrolled mob violence or massive property destruction that was beyond the power of company officials to quell by the use of privately hired armed guards, their usual first recourse. Railroad and coal companies, especially, routinely employed private police, who often managed through political connections to acquire all the powers of a sheriff or constable. If local guards were unobtainable, private security firms, such as the Pinkerton Detective Agency, provided guards who functioned as strikebreakers with full powers of arrest. The men hired by such agencies were effective strikebreakers, and their intervention frequently caused violent confrontations with labor. Union leaders viewed them with bitterness. Socialist Eugene Debs described the Pinkertons as "a motley gang of vagabonds mustered from the slums of the great cities, pimps and parasites, outcasts, abandoned wretches of every grade . . . cut-throats who murder for hire, creatures in the form of humans but heartless as stones."[19]

Industrialists claimed that they hired private guards because municipal police forces were either nonexistent or incompetent and usually made matters worse. In practice, however, both private guards and municipal police forces caused an increase in violence, leading to frequent appeals by company managers and owners to state officials for the dispatch of militia forces, the primary force available to the states to maintain order and local authority.[20]

---

[18] Goldwin Smith, "The Labor War in the United States," *Contemporary Review* 30 (September 1877):540; Samuel Rezneck, "Distress, Relief, and Discontent in the United States During the Depression of 1873–1878," *Journal of Political Economy* 58 (December 1950):494–512; idem, "Unemployment, Unrest, and Relief in the United States During the Depression of 1893–1897," *Journal of Political Economy* 61 (August 1953):324–25.

[19] Between 1877 and 1892, the Pinkerton Agency suppressed over seventy strikes. See Cooper, *The Army and Civil Disorder*, pp. 8–9; James D. Horan, *The Pinkertons: The Detective Dynasty That Made History* (New York: Crown, 1967).

[20] Cooper, *The Army and Civil Disorder*, pp. 8–9.

The National Guard and Labor Disputes

The 1792 Calling Forth Act for the Militia and the Uniform Militia Act made all free, white American males from the ages of eighteen to forty-five liable for federal service in times of national emergency as part of state militia forces. Until "called forth" by the national government, these units, later known as the unorganized militia, were under state control and maintained by state revenues. This militia system proved unreliable, however, and by the mid-nineteenth century was gradually replaced by a better-administered volunteer militia system. The new scheme, although more efficient, implied the virtual abandonment of universal service, which in theory had guaranteed that all state militia units consisted of a cross section of the adult population.

The militia served the federal government on many occasions during the first half of the nineteenth century, including a limited role during the Civil War, but declined rapidly after 1865 because of war-weariness, antimilitarism, and the feeling that the nation was secure. Federal support for state militia forces had always been minimal. In spite of constant prodding from the War Department and proponents of a nationwide, standardized "national guard" force, militia reform and appropriation bills repeatedly foundered in Congress because of apathy, Southern memories of Reconstruction, and antimilitarism. By the late 1860s, two-thirds of the states had no organized militia force whatever.[21]

By the early 1870s many states began to reexamine their needs and revive volunteer militias. The war-weariness of the immediate post–Civil War period had diminished, and many now considered such service a romantic and patriotic duty. These units also served as social organizations within the large and otherwise impersonal industrial cities of the northeast and Middle West.[22] Their revival was spurred further by the increased industrial violence and conservative middle and upper class fears of revolution that resulted. The most heavily industrialized states—Massachusetts, Connecticut, New York, Pennsylvania, Ohio, and Illinois—developed the largest, best-funded, and highest quality forces, which became collectively known as the National Guard.

Throughout the 1877–1945 period the National Guard intervened in far more labor-related disorders than the U.S. Army. Inevitably, many labor organizations, labor leaders, and working men viewed the National Guard as a partisan, antilabor tool created and perpetuated by property owners and industrialists. Samuel Gompers of the American Federation of

---

[21] Some of the more important works on the National Guard are as follows: John K. Mahon, *A History of the Militia and National Guard* (New York: Macmillan, 1983); Martha Derthick, *The National Guard in Politics* (Cambridge: Harvard University Press, 1965), pp. 16–19; Walter Millis, *Arms and Men: A Study in Military History* (New York: G. P. Putnam's Sons, 1956), pp. 143–45; William H. Riker, *Soldiers of the States: The Role of the National Guard in American Democracy* (Washington, D.C.: Public Affairs Press, 1957), pp. 21, 41–61; Jim Dan Hill, *The Minute Man in Peace and War: A History of the National Guard* (Harrisburg: Stackpole, 1964), pp. 124–29, 135; Louis Cantor, "The Creation of the Modern National Guard: The Dick Militia Act of 1903" (Ph.D. diss., Duke University, 1963), pp. 48–49; Barton Hacker, "The United States Army as a National Police Force: The Federal Policing of Labor Disputes, 1877–1898," *Military Affairs* 33 (April 1969):259; Joseph J. Holmes, "National Guard of Pennsylvania: Policemen of Industry, 1865–1905" (Ph.D. diss., University of Connecticut, 1971), pp. 88–90, 94, 180.

[22] Among those works citing the social reasons for the revival of the National Guard are Donald M. Douglas, "Social Soldiers: The Winona Company and the Beginnings of the Minnesota National Guard," *Minnesota History* 45 (April 1976):130–40; Roy Turnbaugh, "Ethnicity, Civic Pride, and Commitment: The Evolution of the Chicago Militia," *Journal of the Illinois State Historical Society* 72 (February 1979):111–27.

Labor referred to the guard as "a machine of monopolistic oppression against labor," and one labor journal claimed that "if the Pinkertons were shut out, it seems the militia steps in . . . to overawe and shoot the men into abject submission."[23] Although the contention that the National Guard was revived as an antilabor, strikebreaking force is still disputed, strike duty became one of its major functions. Militia units acquired the image of an industrial police force to both management and labor. Between 1877 and 1892 a minimum of 30 percent of National Guard duty involved strikes; the actual figure was probably much higher, for states euphemistically referred to strikebreaking duties as "suppression of riots," or "repression of mobs."[24]

Labor's suspicion of the National Guard was increased by the way the force was funded. In an era when the federal government did not allocate substantial revenue for the militia, most guard units supplemented small state appropriations with funds from private sources, usually well-to-do unit members and corporations. To some labor leaders the ranks of the militia appeared to be composed of rich businessmen or those determined to be representative of the "better classes." Some National Guard supporters agreed. As one stated, "The militia man to be good for anything must be a business man, a skilled artisan, a property-holder, somebody having a stake in the country." Many units were formed according to these principles. Thus, Chicago formed a battalion of five companies of cavalry after the riots of 1877, "hastily organized," as a colonel declared, "among our business men who had seen cavalry service during the war." It was not, however, equipped by the state. Although it belonged to the National Guard, the Chicago cavalry "was equipped and uniformed completely by the Citizen's Association of the City of Chicago," an "association . . . composed of businessmen, who look after the best interests of our city.[25] Yet both labor and business misrepresented the true makeup of the National Guard. Labor leaders cited fragmentary evidence as definitive proof that the guard was antilabor, but few confronted the facts that only the rich had sufficient financial resources to support such units, and that many of the labor movement's own rank and file belonged to it by choice.

Labor groups initially called for the abolition of the National Guard and, when that failed, waged a continuous campaign to keep workers from joining. To union leaders, guard service and union membership were incompatible. Many unions went so far as to adopt charters forbidding members to join the militia and sanctioned expulsion of those who did join. Although such policies were judged illegal by courts at all levels, many unions continued the practice well into the twentieth century. Despite union efforts, however, working-class men joined militia units, always forming the bulk of the enlisted ranks. In 1880, workers formed 60 percent of Wisconsin's National Guard and over half of New Jersey's in 1896.[26]

---

[23] Cooper, *The Army and Civil Disorder*, pp. 13–15; Allen Millett and Peter Maslowski, *For the Common Defense: A Military History of the United States* (New York: Free Press, 1984), p. 249.

[24] Mahon, *History of the Militia and National Guard*, pp. 112–19; Hill, *Minute Man in Peace and War*, p. 126; Derthick, *National Guard Politics*, pp. 16–17; Hacker, "U.S. Army as National Police," p. 259; Riker, *Soldiers of the States*, pp. 51–55; Alexander Winthrop, "Ten Years of Riot Duty," *Journal of the Military Service Institution of the United States* 19 (July 1896); Millett and Maslowski, *For the Common Defense*, pp. 248–49; Painter, *Standing at Armageddon*, pp. 22–23; Russell F. Weigley, *History of the United States Army* (New York: Macmillan, 1967), p. 282.

[25] Derthick, *National Guard Politics*, p. 17. See also "Rioters and the Army," *Nation* 25 (9 August 1877):85.

[26] Cooper, *The Army and Civil Disorder*, pp. 14–15. See also "Labor Unions and the National Guard," *Outlook* 72 (22 November 1902):674.

To the National Guard members and supporters, labor claims of bias were ludicrous. One supporter stated that "there is no evidence . . . the guard . . . has been used for illegal purposes, or to aid capitalists or employers against labor unions, or to coerce men into work which they do not wish to undertake, or to shoot down unarmed and innocent persons. The National Guard has simply been employed to protect persons and property against violence."[27] Another guard officer, Col. Thomas Wilhelm, believed that the guard was an absolute necessity in times of nationwide domestic crises to augment the Army as "it is not safe to ignore the fact that we have a population from abroad within our borders impregnated with a tendency to foster opposition to law and order. This class forms a great part of the labor unions and must be held with wisdom and firmness in the grip of the restraining power."[28]

Many critics who had no connection with organized labor attacked the guard on grounds of inefficiency, not of bias. One wrote that "no esprit de Corps, the life and soul of a volunteer organization, can possibly be infused into men who do not meet often enough to know their officers or to feel that they are either learning or doing anything of value to themselves or others." Others claimed that "the militias at best are a clumsy substitute either for a military or a police establishment." Few congressmen believed that expansion beyond current levels was necessary.[29]

As late as 1900 critics were voicing the same complaints and criticisms, often accompanied by demands for reform. As one critic wrote, the faults of the guard were caused by a lack of money, equipment, discipline, instructional facilities, effective liaison with the Regular Army, regular inspections, and standardization; there was no system to select and advance officers according to merit rather than by political connections. At this time momentum was growing for an overhaul of the National Guard system. During the Gilded Age, however, the guard was the principal answer of the states to violent labor or race-related civil disorder.[30]

At the federal level, with the exception of the 1794 Whiskey Rebellion, the militia had not been called upon for service in the domestic disturbances of the pre–1877 period. The same was true after its transformation into the National Guard in the 1870s. Even though the Regular Army was small, it became the force of first resort when the federal government intervened to enforce laws and restore state or federal authority. Although legally empowered to do so, between 1867 and 1957 no president chose to call forth the militia in a domestic disturbance.[31] Guard forces came to be regarded by decision makers on the federal level (and sometimes at the state level) as inefficient, ill led, ill equipped, and undisciplined. Invariably when the guard was called to quell a disturbance, bloodshed and casualties resulted. One journal stated that the guard forces "are not to be relied on for serious emergencies."[32] Regular Army units were believed inherently nonpartisan, more reliable,

---

[27] "National Guard and Trade Unions," *Outlook* 73 (7 March 1903):511–12.

[28] Thomas Wilhelm, "National Guard and Its Value," *Overland Monthly* 38 (December 1901):496–97.

[29] "Rioters and the Army," *Nation* 25 (9 August 1877):85; T. R. Lounsbury, "The Militia in the United States," *Nation* 4 (4 January 1867):72–73.

[30] Charles S. Clark, "The Future of the National Guard," *North American Review* 170 (May 1900):730–31.

[31] Robert W. Coakley, "Federal Use of Militia and National Guard in Civil Disturbances," in Robin D. Higham, ed., *Bayonets in the Streets* (Manhattan: University of Kansas Press, 1969), pp. 26–27.

[32] "The Late Riots," p. 68.

and more efficient. Perhaps the primary reason the Army became the first recourse of successive presidents in cases of civil disorder is that this force was always under the direct control of the federal executive and his delegated representatives.

The President and Civil Disorder

The National Guard was called by state and local authorities to restore order in the majority of domestic disturbances during the nineteenth century when military force was required. However, during massive nationwide or regional outbreaks of mob violence, general strikes, and destruction of property, business and civil officials turned to the president to provide military aid. The president was empowered by the Constitution and by federal legislation to commit federal troops to aid civil officials, but only under certain conditions and in accord with legally defined procedures.[33]

The United States Constitution laid the basis for the use of federal military force in civil disorders. Article I, Section 8, empowered Congress "To provide for calling forth the militia to execute the Laws of the Union, suppress insurrections, and repel invasions," as well as "to raise and support Armies, . . . provide and maintain a Navy [and] . . . provide for organizing, arming, and disciplining the Militia." Two other articles, although not specifically calling for the use of military force, also applied to domestic disturbance intervention. Article II, Sections 2 and 3, provided that "the President shall be Commander in Chief of the Army and Navy of the United States, and of the Militia of the several States, when called into the actual Service of the United States [and] . . . shall take care that the Laws be faithfully executed." Article IV, Section 4, provided that "the United States shall guarantee to every State in this Union a republican form of government, and shall protect each of them against invasion, and on application of the legislature, or of the executive (when the legislature can not be convened), against domestic violence."

The legislature, therefore, was responsible for maintaining a military force to be used to enforce the law by a civilian chief executive. Although the Constitution did not specifically delegate responsibility, in actual practice Congress and the president were together charged with ensuring the existence of republican governments within the Union and with taking appropriate actions to guarantee that state governments were not altered in other than the "regularly prescribed manner, which is in accordance with the wishes of the governed."[34] In addition to the authority granted to the president under the Constitution, from 1792 to 1872 Congress passed enabling legislation that broadened executive powers.

---

[33] For a general discussion, see Robert W. Coakley, *The Role of Federal Military Forces in Domestic Disorders, 1789–1878*, the first of three such volumes (Washington, D.C.: U.S. Army Center of Military History, 1988), ch. 1; Samuel J. Raphalides, "The President's Use of Troops in Civil Disorders," *Presidential Studies Quarterly* 8 (1978):180–87; Douglas A. Poe, "The Use of Federal Troops to Suppress Domestic Violence," *American Bar Association Journal* 54 (February 1968):180–87; David E. Engdahl, "Soldiers, Riots, and Revolution: The Law and History of Military Troops in Civil Disorder," *Iowa Law Review* 57 (October 1971):35–72; idem, "The New Civil Disturbance Regulations: The Threat of Military Intervention," *Indiana Law Review* 49 (Summer 1974):581–617.

[34] Coakley, *Role of Federal Military Forces*, ch. 1; 20 *U.S. Statutes at Large, 1881–1883*; Frederick T. Wilson, *Federal Aid in Domestic Disturbances, 1787–1903, With Supplement, 1903–1922* (Washington, D.C.: Government Printing Office, 1922), pp. 1–7; Cassius M. Dowell, *Military Aid to the Civil Power* (Fort Leavenworth, Kans.: General Service School, 1925), pp. 203–04.

The first Congress, in passing the Calling Forth Act for the Militia in 1792, delegated to the president the power to call state militia forces into federal service to enforce the laws of the union against "conspiracies too powerful to be overcome by the ordinary course of judicial proceedings" or to answer state calls requesting aid in quelling insurrection or, as stated in the Constitution, domestic violence. In each case the president was required to issue a "cease and desist" proclamation to rioters before acting. In 1795 this act was broadened and renewed. In 1807 the executive was empowered to use U.S. regular forces for similar ends, subject to the same restrictions. The process of committing federal forces outlined by these acts provided part of the legal basis for subsequent legislation. Other laws, in the form of neutrality acts, empowered the president to use military force to prevent expeditions mounted in America against nations at peace with the United States. Under these specific legal authorizations successive presidents used federal military forces on several occasions between 1788 and 1861 to enforce federal laws or to aid state and local forces to keep the peace.[35]

At the outset of the Civil War in 1861, President Abraham Lincoln's initial call for troops was issued under the revision of the Calling Forth Act in 1795 dealing with domestic disorders. The war, however, quickly developed into a contest between what were in reality sovereign nations, a situation which rendered the 1795 law inapplicable. The president secured more power with the Lincoln Law of 1861, which combined certain provisions of the 1795 and 1807 laws. In the North during the Civil War, military responsibility for law enforcement was taken for granted and was exercised without reference to the provisions of the 1795, 1807, and 1861 laws. The War Department dealt with draft riots during the war years without Lincoln's specific direction, participation, or prior approval.[36]

During Reconstruction, 1865–1878, federal troops in the South were the main instruments of federal authority responsible for preserving law and order as well as for enforcing new laws securing the civil rights of emancipated slaves. Under various dispensations—the laws against conspiracies, the Reconstruction Acts and the Ku Klux Act of 1871—troops were routinely used for law enforcement duties by the War Department and the president. Many of these Army activities in support of civil authority in the South were accomplished through a revival of the 1856 Cushing Doctrine, which stated that all military personnel were subject to duty as a *posse comitatus* to aid civil law enforcement officials.[37]

The entire body of federal law was codified in the 1874 *Revised Statutes* (RS). Four of these statutes, RS 5297, RS 5298, RS 5299, and RS 5300, dealt with federal aid to civil authorities and insurrections against either state or federal authority. RS 5297 reflected the laws of 1795 and 1807 regarding state requests: "In case of an insurrection in any state against the government thereof it shall be lawful for the President, on application of the legislature of such states, or of the executive when the legislature cannot be convened, to call forth such number of the militia of any state or states, which may be applied for as he deems

---

[35] These situations are covered in Coakley, *Role of Federal Military Forces*.

[36] For the Civil War years, see ibid., chs. 11 and 12. See also Mark E. Neely, Jr., *The Fate of Liberty: Abraham Lincoln and Civil Liberties* (New York: Oxford University Press, 1991).

[37] For the Reconstruction period, see Coakley, *Role of Federal Military Forces*, chs. 13–15, and for the Cushing Doctrine, see pp. 132–33.

sufficient to suppress such insurrection, or, on like application, to employ for the same purposes, such part of the land or naval forces of the United States, as he deems necessary."

To invoke federal aid under this statute, state officials first had to attempt to quell the disturbance by using police or militia (that is, National Guard) forces under their control. Failing in that, the governor could convene the state legislature and request legislation calling for federal aid. If the legislature could not be called in time to prevent serious damage or bloodshed, the governor might request federal aid without prior legislative consultation or approval.[38]

The second statute applicable to domestic disorders, RS 5298, was also derived from the laws of 1795 and 1807, as revised by the Lincoln Law of 1861. (Most antebellum federal interventions had been initiated under the predecessors of RS 5298.) The new statute read:

Whenever, by reasons of unlawful obstructions, combinations or assemblage of persons, or rebellion against the authority of the Government of the United States, it shall become impracticable, in the judgement of the President, to enforce by the ordinary course of proceedings the laws of the United States within any State or Territory, it shall be lawful for the President to call forth the militia of any or of all the States, and to employ such parts of the land and naval forces of the United States as he may deem necessary to enforce the faithful execution of the laws of the United States or to suppress such rebellion in whatever State or Territory thereof the laws of the United States may be forcibly opposed or the execution thereof forcibly obstructed.

RS 5298, like RS 5297, was intended to uphold civil government and to combat forces opposing federal authority, but unlike RS 5297, RS 5298 applied to situations in which federal authority was being defied, federal laws had been broken, or where federal property was threatened or destroyed. RS 5298 was to be frequently invoked to allow military intervention when the writs of federal courts could not be served by federal marshals or when federal court orders and injunctions were ignored.[39]

The third law, RS 5299, had been passed in 1872 as part of the Ku Klux Act and involved civil rights enforcement:

Whenever conspiracies in any State so obstruct or hinder the execution of the laws thereof and of the United States as to deprive any portion or class of the people of such state of any of the rights, privileges, or immunities of the protection named in the Constitution and secured by the laws for the protection of such rights, privileges, or immunities and the constituted authorities of such state are unable to protect or from any cause fail in or refuse protection of the people in such rights, such facts shall be deemed a denial by such state of the equal protection of the laws to which they are entitled by the Constitution of the United States, and in all such cases, whenever any such insurrection, violence, unlawful combination or conspiracy opposes or impedes or obstructs the due course of justice under the same, it shall be lawful for the President, and it shall be his duty, to take such measures, by the employment of the militia or the land and naval forces of the United States, or of either, or by other means, as he may deem necessary for the suppression of such insurrection, domestic violence, or combinations.

RS 5299 could be applied in cases where minority or immigrant groups encountered hostile racist sentiment or were subjected to racial attack that denied them civil or legal rights guaranteed by the federal government. RS 5299 could be invoked by the federal

---

[38] Dowell, *Military Aid to the Civil Power*, pp. 204–05.
[39] Ibid., p. 205.

executive without a state's request or approval, if its civil and military authorities were unable or unwilling to act on their own, or they, themselves, opposed the execution of federal laws or acted to repress the civil rights of individuals.[40]

Other laws that permitted the president to commit troops under the authority granted in RS 5298 and 5299 included acts like that approved on 2 July 1890, intended to "protect trade and commerce against unlawful restraints and monopolies," and the Railway Acts of 1 July 1862, 2 July 1864, and 27 July 1866. These laws promised federal aid to ensure the safe, unhindered operation of the major transcontinental railroad routes by declaring them to be "military roads" and "post routes," vital to national security.[41]

In all cases covered by RS 5297, 5298, and 5299, after making the decision to intervene, the president was required to issue a proclamation calling on insurgents or lawless elements to disperse. The relevant statute, RS 5300, derived from the 1792 Calling Forth Act, and read that "Whenever in the judgement of the President, it becomes necessary to use the military forces under this title, the President shall forthwith, by proclamation, command the insurgents to disperse and retire peaceably to their respective abodes, within a limited time."[42] The intent of RS 5300 was to inform lawless elements of federal intervention and the impending arrival of troops and to allow sufficient time for lawless elements to disperse before the government took stringent steps to restore order.

If lawless elements failed to disperse after the first proclamation, the president could then issue a second proclamation, under RS 5301, declaring a state of nonintercourse. RS 5301 declared that whenever "the inhabitants of a state, or a portion of a state are in a state of insurrection; and thereafter, while the condition of insurgency continues, all commercial intercourse directed to or from the designated territory is unlawful." Goods in transit were subject to seizure by, and forfeiture to, the government. This second proclamation, however, was not to be issued until after state and federal troops had already been deployed and had attempted to quell the disturbance.[43]

In addition to the revised statutes that applied to insurrections against state and federal authority, the president could also commit regulars under other federal laws, although these were rarely invoked in the major disturbances of the late nineteenth and early twentieth centuries. In addition to the Neutrality Act of 1837 (RS 5296) and subsequent revisions (RS 5286, 5287), the president could intervene under RS 1984, 1989, and 1991, dealing with the enforcement of civil rights legislation; RS 2147, 2150, 2151, 2152, dealing with the enforcement of laws concerning American Indians, Indian lands, and federal reservations; RS 2460, dealing with the protection of public lands; RS 4792, dealing with the public health; and RS 5275, concerning protection of foreign prisoners bound over to the United States as a result of extradition to or from foreign nations.[44]

The last piece of relevant federal legislation was the Act of 18 June 1878, commonly known as the Posse Comitatus Act. This law, passed at the insistence of Southern con-

---

[40] Ibid.

[41] Frederick T. Wilson, *Federal Aid in Domestic Disturbances, 1787–1903* (Washington, D.C.: Government Printing Office, 1903), pp. 9–10. This was updated with a supplement in 1922. Unless otherwise noted, all citations are from Wilson's 1922 work.

[42] Dowell, *Military Aid to the Civil Power*, p. 205.

[43] Ibid., pp. 207–08.

[44] Wilson, *Federal Aid in Domestic Disturbances*, pp. 5–8.

gressmen disturbed by the widespread and relatively uncontrolled use of regulars during Reconstruction, prohibited the employment of federal troops as posses to enforce laws at the request of local and state officials or federal marshals without the prior, explicit approval of the president. Even then, the chief executive could act only after all civil authorities had completed the legal process outlined by the Constitution and by Congress in RS 5297, 5298, 5299, and 5300. The ramifications of the Posse Comitatus Act were extensive. The act did not, however, prohibit the use of federal troops under any of the legal provisions cited above if executive approval was received prior to the commitment of regulars, and if the necessary proclamation was made as required by RS 5300.[45]

In spite of flexible enabling legislation governing the use of troops in aiding civil authorities, it was often difficult for state and federal authorities to determine quickly which statute applied in the many unusual situations in which federal military assistance was requested. In numerous cases between 1877 and 1945, presidents dispatched troops to the proximity of a disturbance without seeking any specific state request or statutory justification for doing so. All civil authorities clearly understood that the mere threat of federal military intervention, or the presence of regular troops in a disturbed area, often restored order without those same authorities having to undertake the slow formal process that allowed direct federal military intervention.

The Army in the Gilded Age

Despite the existence of pertinent legislation, federal action was inhibited by another consideration: late nineteenth century presidents did not have a sizable force of Army regulars available to aid civil officials. Within six months of the end of the Civil War, 800,000 of the 1 million men in the Union's Grand Army of the Republic were mustered out of federal service. This enforced decline continued until 1875, when the permanent strength of the Army leveled off at 25,000 officers and enlisted men. Army strength thereafter did not exceed 28,000 men at any time until the outbreak of the Spanish-American War in 1898, despite the efforts of military leaders to convince a skeptical and essentially antimilitary public to augment the nation's standing Army.[46]

The Army was not only reduced in numbers but also scattered throughout the continental United States, primarily on the western frontier. By the end of Reconstruction, most of the Army, including all the cavalry forces and three-fourths of the infantry, had moved

---

[45] For an extensive discussion of the act, see Coakley, *Role of Federal Military Forces*, especially pp. 344–47; see also Wilson, *Federal Aid in Domestic Disturbances*, p. 5; Dowell, *Military Aid to the Civil Power*, p. 203; H. W. C. Furman, "Restrictions Upon the Use of the Army Imposed by the Posse Comitatus Act," *Military Review* 7 (January 1960):85–129.

[46] Unless otherwise stated, the following account is drawn from Edward Coffman, *The Old Army: A Portrait of the American Army in Peacetime, 1784–1898* (Oxford: Oxford University Press, 1986), pp. 215–372 passim; and Robert M. Utley, *Frontier Regulars: The United States Army and the Indian, 1866–1891* (New York: Macmillan, 1973), pp. 12–69. For works on the Army of this period, see Millett and Maslowski, *For the Common Defense*, pp. 233–34; Ekirch, *The Civilian and the Military*, pp. 112–14; William A. Ganoe, *The History of the United States Army* (New York: Appleton Century, 1943), pp. 306–07; Weigley, *History of United States Army*, pp. 266–67; Jack D. Foner, *The United States Soldier Between Two Wars: Army Life and Reforms, 1865–1898* (New York: Humanities Press, 1970), p. 1; Jerry M. Cooper, "The Army's Search for a Mission, 1865–1890," in Kenneth J. Hagan and William R. Roberts, eds., *Against All Enemies: Interpretations of American Military History From Colonial Times to the Present* (Westport: Greenwood, 1986), pp. 173–95.

west of the Mississippi River to battle hostile Indians and otherwise police the frontier. The majority of artillery units were posted along either the Great Lakes or the Atlantic seaboard. This dispersion had serious ramifications when it became necessary to gather federal troops to quell civil disorders. Although military officials usually responded within hours to requests to aid civil authorities, it often took days if not weeks for the necessary forces to be gathered and transported by rail to trouble spots sometimes thousands of miles distant. In the soldier's view, moreover, quelling hostile Indians and maintaining peace on the frontier were the Army's top priorities and the main factors determining deployments, not riot duty in the urbanized east. As late as 1892, 70 percent of the Army remained west of the Mississippi River, occupying ninety-six posts. Although the negative aspects of spreading federal forces so thin were recognized by many, the situation persisted well into the twentieth century. In 1911 Secretary of War Henry L. Stimson complained that units, usually of company size, were still stationed in over thirty states and territories in forty-nine posts.[47]

Leading this small military force was a correspondingly small officer corps, a relatively conservative and closed caste into which entrance was difficult and subsequent advancement slow. By 1871, after the most severe force reductions were completed, only 2,105 officers of all ranks remained. This figure did not vary by more than 100 men until the end of the century. Between 1865 and 1898, 3,598 men received commissions, the majority entering the officer corps during years 1865–1867. Initially, the overwhelming number of new commissions went to volunteer officers with Civil War service (1,360), but during the above period as a whole, 76.4 percent of commissions went to West Point graduates, 13.6 percent to civil appointees, and the remaining 10 percent to men who had risen from enlisted ranks. By 1897, 60 percent of the officer corps were graduates of West Point, 30 percent were civil appointees, and the remaining 10 percent were former rankers. Like former enlisted men, blacks and other minorities never made up a large segment of the officers corps. Only 8 blacks received commissions between 1866 and 1898, 5 being commissioned as chaplains and 3 as cavalry lieutenants. Although the number of military academy graduates indicated an increased professionalism in the Army, the preponderance of West Point–educated officers raised concern among many that the nation was fast approaching the creation of a military aristocracy, spurning its volunteer heritage, and failing to draw its military, especially its officer corps, from a cross section of the American population. Civil War–era volunteer officers, however, continued to dominate the upper ranks of the officer corps until well after the turn of the century.[48]

Promotion was tortuously slow and occurred only through death, retirement, or resignation. Few officers resigned. Between 1874 and 1897, the largest number of officers to resign in one year was 28 in 1889, while only 7 left in 1895. Overall, in seventeen of twenty-four years, less than 1 percent of the officer corps resigned annually. Even taking into account casualties in the Indian Wars, few vacancies occurred through combat. Many officers remained in the same grade for decades while steadily growing older. Lt. Gen. Nelson A. Miles wrote in 1889 that some 110 officers had not been promoted in twenty

---

[47] Coffman, *Old Army*, p. 215; and Cooper, *The Army and Civil Disorder*, p. 26; Hacker, "U.S. Army as National Police Force," p. 256; Weigley, *History of United States Army*, p. 267; Foner, *United States Soldier*, p. 2.

[48] John A. Logan, *The Volunteer Soldier of America* (Chicago: R. S. Peale, 1887), pp. 461–75, 578–80. On Blacks, see Foner, *United States Soldier*, pp. 127–48.

years, including 57 infantry captains. In 1885 more than 30 percent of the officer corps (753) were between forty-one and fifty-two years of age with 52, or 2 percent, being age sixty-one or older. The situation was so serious that Brig. Gen. Oliver Otis Howard commented in 1890 that most infantry and artillery captains were too old for any duty that involved marching on foot or drill that required continuous quick movements. By 1893 the average captain, at fifty, was only four years younger than the average general. Civil War–era officers dominated the officer corps until the beginning of the twentieth century, with 26 of 40 regimental commanders having seen service as Civil War generals. As late as 1895, 271 company-grade officers were veterans and 9 Civil War generals remained as regimental commanders.

In view of these statistics, it could be said that the late nineteenth century Army officer corps was relatively unchanging, not only in size and composition, but in all probability in the social and political attitudes of its members, since most officers who held commissions at the end of the 1860s still had those positions twenty, if not forty, years later. Although the Army underwent substantial and significant advances in the professional status, development, and training of officers in the last quarter of the century, pre–Civil War and Civil War volunteer officers continued to dominate the service.

Previously, studies have held that Army officers were cut off physically and intellectually from the society around them, by choice and by public antimilitary attitudes.[49] Although the officer corps did display values that were generally more conservative than the society around it and showed a disdain for individualism, liberalism, commercialism, politics, and mass democracy, one later study suggests that some qualification of this critique is necessary. New interpretations suggest that "The Army officer corps was not isolated physically, or in attitudes, interests, and spirit from other institutions of government and society and, indeed from the American people. Officers did not lead a 'semi-cloistered' existence that remained outside the mainstream of civil life." The annual reports of the Army adjutant general, for example, show that between 1867 and 1897, "from 17 percent to 44 percent of all officers present for duty in established Army commands . . . were serving in the Department of the East . . . living in the most settled region of the United States, often on the Atlantic seaboard." Indeed, most officers spent all, or at least part, of their careers in the urbanized east. Even those officers on extended duty on the western frontier were often near major urban areas. In 1871 two-thirds of the officers in the Department of California were in or near San Francisco, and almost all were there by 1896.[50]

With access to urban settings, officers generally took full advantage of available civilian educational and social opportunities wherever they were stationed and enjoyed widespread contact with civilians. Yet the late nineteenth century Army officer corps intermingled only with the dominant minority, the conservative upper and middle classes. Officers, as a result, clearly reflected traditional, conservative viewpoints that favored the status quo. This was true from the beginning of a potential officer's career at West Point. As one historian writes:

---

[49] Samuel P. Huntington, *The Soldier and the State: The Theory and Politics of Civil-Military Relations* (Cambridge: Harvard University Press, 1957), pp. 254–69.

[50] John M. Gates, "The Alleged Isolation of United States Army Officers in the Late Nineteenth Century," *Parameters* 10 (September 1980):33–34.

The process for selection of cadets entering West Point worked to insure that the vast majority of officers would come from families with better than average incomes, connections, or both. Successful applicants needed political pull or, at the very least, acceptability in the eyes of their home community's political elite. The hurdles that preceded a young man's entry into West Point required a certain degree of prior socialization of a nonmilitary sort which would have occurred most often in the nation's middle and upper classes.[51]

Not only did the vast majority of officers come from the conservative upper and middle classes, they also were inclined to be a reflection of that segment of society, and "were overwhelmingly native-born, of northern European ethnic heritage, and protestant."[52] Of even greater significance than the social background of the officer corps was the fact that "many of the civilians with whom officers interacted were extremely well placed, often the political, economic, and intellectual leaders of the nation." This meant that officers "had more in common with the ruling elite than with any other societal group in the nation." In the 1880s General Schofield could count among his friends such wealthy, powerful, and influential businessmen as Marshall Field, George M. Pullman, and George A. Armour. Schofield was so influential, and moved so comfortably within Chicago business and social circles, that when he proposed to a dinner party of businessmen in 1887 that they purchase a plot of territory near the city for gratis presentation to the federal government as the site of a proposed Army post (the future Fort Philip Sheridan), they quickly and enthusiastically followed his suggestion.[53]

Although Schofield's annual salary of $7,500 as a major general or William Sherman's salary of $13,500 as commanding general seemed paltry in comparison to the fortunes possessed by their civilian friends, their incomes were far above those of the average working-class Americans. Army officers did not share the extravagant wealth of the upper classes, but they did share similar views on political, economic, and social issues, which often led to allegations of Army partisanship during interventions in labor disputes. Such officers "considered themselves above the sharp practices and values of the business world," but they were nonetheless "part of the middle class and thus had essentially the same values as did community leaders." Officers of all grades "associated with the leading figures in the business world," or "moved in similar circles."[54] According to T. Bentley Mott, aide-de-camp to General Wesley Merritt, "when the General was in Chicago they took their meals at 'the famous Round Table' with 'Marshall Field, George Pullman, Potter Palmer, John Clark, Robert Lincoln, and all the rest.'" After moving to New York, Merritt and Mott renewed their acquaintances "with 'the Sloanes, the J. P. Morgans, the Hamilton Fishes, and other New York people.'"[55]

---

[51] Quotes from ibid., pp. 33–34, 36–37. See also William B. Skelton, "The Army Officer as Organization Man," in Garry D. Ryan and Timothy K. Nenninger, eds., *Soldiers and Civilians: The U.S. Army and the American People* (Washington, D.C.: National Archives and Records Administration, 1987), pp. 62–64; Cooper, *The Army and Civil Disorder*, pp. 29–30.

[52] Cooper, *The Army and Civil Disorder*, pp. 29–30.

[53] There was relatively little government or public concern about conflict of interest in the late nineteenth century as evidenced by Schofield, who often controlled federal troops deployed in labor disputes, while simultaneously owning stock in five railroads, the Pullman Company, and a sugar refinery. See Coffman, *Old Army*, p. 266.

[54] Quotes from Coffman, *Old Army*, pp. 247, 264–65.

[55] Quote from Gates, "Alleged Isolation," pp. 35, 38. See also Jerry M. Cooper, "The Army and Industrial Workers," in Ryan and Nenninger, *Soldiers and Civilians*, p. 148.

Thus, although officers shared the political, social, and economic views of civilian society, their opinions were inclined to be those of the conservative middle and upper classes to which many officers belonged and with which they clearly identified.

Any sympathy that Army officers may have had for the "'idle, suffering and desperate' in times of depression" was more than offset by the threat these same people, with whom officers shared so little, posed to their way of life.[56] Although most were

"reluctant to condemn laborers as a group," Army officers opposed extreme solutions to problems caused by industrialization and rejected "socialism, anarchism, and 'its kindred fallacies.'" The Army officer corps was "imbued with middle class values concerning the sanctity of property and the necessity of social order." It "readily identified itself with the propertied classes and negated any opportunity for the Army to appear as a third party."[57]

Some officers took strong exception to the charges of labor leaders, unions, and workers that the Army was a partisan of the nation's wealthy corporate and political elite. As Col. Thomas A. Anderson wrote in the fall of 1892, "The Army is not an enemy to labor or a friend to capital. It is simply an instrument . . . of popular power." Anderson, like many officers, however, was not totally blind to the nation's troubles nor ignorant of who was truly responsible. The *Army and Navy Journal* later editorialized that mob violence would increase in the United States "in exact proportion to the increase in the unreasoning classes and to the tendency of wealth to accumulate in comparatively few hands."[58]

Despite personal views, Army officers, professionals as they were, carried out the orders of the civilian president and enforced the laws that the civilian Congress had enacted for the nation. They neither made the laws, interpreted them, nor questioned them—although they agreed overwhelmingly with these laws and with the intentions of those making them. As General of the Army Ulysses S. Grant had stated in 1875 in reference to the legal problems associated with Reconstruction, "the Army is not composed of lawyers capable of judging at a moment's notice just how far they can go in the maintenance of law and order." To the Army officer during the years 1877 to 1945, as before and after, "subordination to the will of the President was their single most important commitment."[59] One historian has written that the Army developed the image of "the country's general servant, well-disciplined, obedient, performing civil functions"; it behaved as "a vast, organic machine, blindly following orders from on high . . . but an instrument in the hands of a superior will . . . passive to the exercise of other government functions." The officer of the late nineteenth century Army shared the views of those who dominated American society, but in spite of what many termed as harsh and inflexible views on the social, political, racial, and economic issues of the day, officers believed, above all else, in the constitutional system, in the virtues of stability, law, order, and authority, and in loyalty to the civilian chief executive.[60]

---

[56] Coffman, *Old Army*, pp. 247–48.
[57] Gates, "Alleged Isolation," p. 42.
[58] Coffman, *Old Army*, pp. 247–48.
[59] See Coakley, *Role of Federal Military Forces*, p. 314, and Cooper, *The Army and Civil Disorder*, p. 36, respectively.
[60] Huntington, *The Soldier and the State*, pp. 254–69; Edward M. Coffman, "The Army Officer and the Constitution," *Parameters* 17 (September 1987):2–12.

The enlisted ranks of the late nineteenth century Army, unlike the officer corps, were highly representative of the lower classes of American society and were generally filled by men of mediocre intelligence and limited experience. Enlisted men, as in the antebellum period, were predominantly immigrants and urban workers recruited from the industrialized states of the North and Midwest, where "the floating population is the greatest . . . where the lower haunts of dissipation abound." According to an adjutant general survey in 1880, 27.3 percent of all Army recruits came from either Boston or New York City. A further 21.1 percent came from elsewhere in New York State, and 14 percent from Pennsylvania. Only 3 percent of the recruits came from the seven states of the Deep South, indicating the strong Southern feeling against federal service dating from the Civil War and the Reconstruction period.[61]

Since most enlisted men came from the urban, industrialized North and Midwest, a sizable number were foreign-born or recent immigrants. In the decade after the Civil War, over 50 percent of recruits were foreign-born, compared to 34.5 percent for the eighteen-year period 1880–1897. Men of Irish and German background predominated. In 1881, men from these two nations made up 65.5 percent of all volunteers; the figure dropped, as immigration from those two nations fell, until 1895 when Irish and German recruits formed less than 18 percent of the Army's enlisted ranks. The Noncommissioned Officer Corps always contained a majority of native-born Americans, approximately 57.1 percent in 1890, although sizable numbers of Irish and German soldiers held noncommissioned officer ranks, 16.3 percent and 13.3 percent, respectively, in 1890. The predominance of foreign citizens or men of foreign birth in the Army continued until 1894, when Congress passed legislation requiring that all men enlisting for the first time be either American citizens or immigrants who had declared their intention to become citizens. In addition, Congress mandated that all new recruits demonstrate the ability to read, write, and speak English. Thereafter, the number of foreign-born, immigrant, and noncitizen soldiers in the Army continued to decline, dropping from 30 percent of the total enlisted ranks in 1894 to 25 percent within two years.[62]

The term of service for an enlisted man was set at five years in 1869 until a three-year term was adopted in 1894. There was no subsequent reserve or militia obligation once active duty was completed. Unlike the officer corps, the enlisted ranks were relatively young. Until 1895 the Army took recruits between the ages of 16 and 35 years of age, and after 1895 took only those between 21 and 30 years of age. In 1893 the average age of an Army enlisted man was 25.9. The number of available recruits and the numbers accepted by the Army varied with the economic health of the nation. In good economic times, recruits were scarce, and the Army was forced to accept more men with substandard profiles to maintain strengths. During economic downturns, especially those accompanied by high unemployment rates, the Army could afford to be more selective and take only recruits with the highest qualities. During the 1880s, for example, a period of high employment and economic growth, the Army accepted 26 percent of those recruited, but after the Panic of 1894 and the subsequent depression, the Army took only 17 percent.

---

[61] Coffman, *Old Army*, p. 330.
[62] Millett and Maslowski, *For the Common Defense*, p. 261.

To many enlisted men, Army service was a financial necessity rather than a patriotic duty. Stationed at remote frontier outposts, many soldiers felt underpaid, overworked, poorly fed, lonely, and abused by their noncommissioned officers. The rate of enlisted pay did not vary between 1872 and 1898, but according to a report of the Army inspector general in 1884 "a great difference exists in favor of the soldier when compared with the civilian laborer." An enlisted man could count on food, shelter, clothing, and transportation at government expense, while these items took all or most of the civilian's income.[63] Nonetheless, many enlisted men chose to end their military careers prematurely and unilaterally by deserting.

Desertion was the major problem of the Army during the late nineteenth century. Between 1 January 1867 and 30 June 1891, a total of 88,475 desertions, an average annual rate of 14.8 percent, was recorded in an Army that never exceeded 28,000 men. The peak years for desertion were 1871 and 1872 when, according to Army statistics, nearly 30 percent of the Army deserted in each of those years. Like recruitment levels, desertion rates were closely connected to national prosperity and the availability of civilian jobs, as well as service conditions, especially on the frontier. In 1873, a year of predicted continued economic growth, 33.5 percent of the enlisted men in the Division of the Atlantic deserted. The financial panic of that same year, however, caused massive unemployment that reduced the desertion rate in the Division of the Atlantic to 5.1 percent by 1877.[64]

In spite of the composition of its ranks, the perceived low pay, loneliness, poor food, ill treatment, boredom, and the consequent high desertion rate, the enlisted ranks, like the officer corps, provided reliable service during labor and racial disturbances. Unlike the state militia, the loyalty and discipline of the enlisted ranks of the U.S. Army were never in doubt, in spite of indications that many had more in common with working-class Americans, immigrants, and striking workers than with their officers, with civilian employers, or with conservative middle- and upper-class property owners.[65] No incidents were ever reported of regular troops joining mobs, engaging in mutiny, or in other duty-related conflicts between officers and enlisted men, as frequently occurred with state militia forces. That many soldiers could and did sympathize with striking workers and generally found riot duty distasteful did not interfere with their obedience to the orders of their superiors or hinder them in the performance of their duty. This adherence to duty, as well as the applicability and adequacy of existing civil disturbance legislation and the ability of the president and the Army to aid civil officials effectively to suppress a major labor disorder, was initially tested during the nation's first general strike, the Great Railway Strike of 1877.

---

[63] Quote from Coffman, *Old Army*, pp. 348, 346–50; Foner, *United States Soldier*, especially pp. 13–30.
[64] Edward M. Coffman, "Army Life on the Frontier, 1865–1898," *Military Affairs* 20 (Winter 1956):193–201; Foner, *United States Soldier*, pp. 6–10.
[65] Foner, *United States Soldier*, pp. 59–76.

CHAPTER 2

The Great Railway Strike of 1877

When the governor of a State has declared his inability to suppress an insurrection and has called upon the President . . . from that time commences a state not of peace but of war, and . . . although civil local authority still exists, yet the only outcome is to resort to force through Federal military authorities . . . that can be only through a subordination of the State authorities for the time being and until lawful order is restored.

—Maj. Gen. Winfield Scott Hancock, 1877.

The March 1877 inauguration of Rutherford B. Hayes ended Reconstruction in the South and saw the climax of an economic depression that started with the Panic of 1873. Over the next twenty-seven years the nation experienced economic swings between boom and bust. This economic instability exacerbated tensions between labor and capital and resulted in serious social unrest that brought federal military intervention to restore order. The first intervention occurred during the railway strike of 1877.[1]

The Depression of the 1870s

The panic that initiated the depression of the 1870s began with the failure of the banking concern of Jay Cooke and Company, which had overextended itself financially in railroad construction and had failed to gain long-term investors to support continued expansion. Troubles in the railroad industry were indicative of similar problems facing many corporations that had grown too fast following the Civil War. Because the depression that followed the panic touched all facets of the economy, the public widely perceived the railroads, the first industry affected, and the reputed greed of their owners as the major causes of the nation's distress. In the strike of 1877 many Americans initially believed the railroads were receiving their just reward for plundering the nation.

Already the single biggest business interest in the nation, railroad companies had built a total of 30,000 miles of track by 1860 and, due to generous postwar federal grants of land and money, had constructed over 70,628 miles of track by 1873. Railroad construction was largely unplanned and unregulated, in many cases bearing no relationship to commercial

---

[1] For the panic and depression, see Samuel Rezneck, *Business Depression and Financial Panics: Essays in American Business and Economic History* (Westport: Greenwood Press, 1968); Arthur G. Auble, "The Depressions of 1873 and 1882 in the United States" (Ph.D. diss., Harvard University, 1949).

or transportation needs. Cutthroat competition, monopolistic combinations, rate variations and abuses, stock manipulations and fraud, and railroad-related political corruption increased the instability of the companies and tarnished their image in the eyes of an increasingly resentful public. When the railroad industry suffered its first financial set-backs in late 1873, the resulting depression shook the nation, leading many from the president to the average worker to question the apparent pervasive grip the railroads had on the country's economic well-being.[2]

In the four years following 1873 nearly one-quarter of the American working population, an estimated 1 to 3 million people, became unemployed. Businesses failed by the thousands, and many corporations, facing serious threats to their survival, either fired workers or demanded repeated wage reductions and longer workdays. Laborers in all industries and trades saw their wages reduced. Even those fortunate enough to have jobs could not count on full employment, and 2 out of 5 worked no more than six to seven months of the year, while less than 1 out of 5 was regularly employed. Of those out of work, 1 in 5 became permanently unemployed.[3]

The depression reduced the ranks of organized labor. The nation's fledgling unions—small, disunited, and internally divided—could do little to aid members and their families, or to halt mass firings and wage reductions. Many members were out of work, and those still employed lacked the means to support union activities or pay dues. Of the thirty national unions in existence in 1873, only nine still functioned by 1877. Of all workers, railroad employees saw themselves as the worst hit by the depression and wage reductions.[4]

Railroad workers' resentment was exacerbated when, although they were forced to endure repeated wage cuts, company officials took no similar liberties with the salaries of managers or with stockholders' dividends. The Baltimore and Ohio Railroad continued to pay a 10 percent dividend annually during the depression, and the New York Central paid 8 percent. Thomas Scott's Pennsylvania Railroad stock dividend rate dropped only 2 percent between 1874–1876. In spite of the professed need for wage reductions, many railroads were still fiscally sound, earning large surpluses and increasing the value of stock shares. To railroad workers such disclosures were proof that wage cuts were not for reasons of financial necessity, but for purposes of maintaining the high rate of profits and dividends, views shared by many influential newspapers including the *Baltimore American* and the *Boston Herald*.[5]

Such actions of company officials enraged many Americans, who hated the railroads for a long catalog of perceived abuses: unfair rates that discriminated against individuals,

---

[2] Weibe, *The Search for Order*, p. 1; Garraty, *New Commonwealth*, pp. 85–87, 109–13; Philip A. Slaner, "The Railroad Strikes of 1877," *Marxist Quarterly* 1 (April–June 1937):216. For railroad growth, see Alfred D. Chandler, Jr., *The Railroads: The Nation's First Big Business* (New York: Harcourt Brace & World, 1965).

[3] Bruce, *1877*, p. 19; Philip S. Foner, *History of the Labor Movement in the United States*, 8 vols. (New York: International Publishers, 1947–88), 1:439, 442; Garraty, *New Commonwealth*, pp. 157–58; Slaner, "The Railroad Strikes of 1877," p. 217; Reznek, "Distress, Relief, and Discontent in the United States During the Depression of 1873–1878," pp. 494–512.

[4] Foner, *History of the Labor Movement*, pp. 439–40; Garraty, *New Commonwealth*, pp. 156–57; Bruce, *1877*, pp. 19, 44–46; Slaner, "The Railroad Strikes of 1877," pp. 214, 217; Samuel Bernstein, "American Labor in the Long Depression, 1873–1878," *Science and Society* 20 (1956):59–83; Clifton K. Yearly, Jr., "The Baltimore and Ohio Railroad Strike of 1877," *Maryland Historical Magazine* 51 (September 1956):195.

[5] Slaner, "The Railroad Strikes of 1877," pp. 217–18, 224, 230.

companies, or communities; stock manipulation; bribery; political corruption; and the wholesale plunder of the public domain. Throughout the nation, farmers, grain dealers, mine operators, common workmen, and even stockholders evidenced outrage and anger.[6]

Railroad magnates responded to criticisms vigorously. President Scott of the Pennsylvania Railroad stated that "every important industry in the country has been compelled to practice the closest and most rigid economies, in order to escape marketing its products at an absolute loss." The railroads, unlike other industries, kept workers on at reduced wages instead of firing them altogether. Collectively the owners claimed that they had suffered in the business decline just as everyone else had, and, although some railroads paid dividends, many others faced financial ruin. Indeed many lines, especially those in the West, paid no dividends at all or did not survive. A total of seventy-six railroads went bankrupt or into federal receivership in 1876 alone.

Other factors, in addition to mounting debts and falling revenues, added to the woes of owners. The cost of doing business was increased by the wage demands of workers who were members of unions in the coal, iron-mining, smelting, and steel-rolling industries, which raised the cost of materials vital to railroad operation. In the opinion of railroad owners, the rail workers were better off than most workers in the country and, like their employers, had to suffer the consequences of hard times like everyone else. If workers were dissatisfied with their wages, railroad owners stated, they were free to leave. Others could be found to work for their wages or for even less.[7]

President John Garrett of the Baltimore and Ohio Railroad expressed that he "realized wage cuts added to workingmen's hardships," but that he also knew previous "strikes had been easily broken and the men easily replaced." Garrett stated that "Labor lacked unity and was, thanks to the depression, amenable to company discipline." In early July 1877 he announced another 10 percent wage cut, following the lead of the other eastern railroads that announced similar reductions the previous month.[8]

In response, on 16 July 1877, rail workers struck the Baltimore and Ohio in Baltimore, Maryland, and in Martinsburg, West Virginia. Within a week spontaneous strikes spread north and west, soon halting all rail traffic east of the Mississippi River. Fourteen major rail centers in seven states and ten railroad companies controlling two-thirds of the nation's total track mileage were affected. During the strike masses of rail workers, unemployed men, desperate women, and thrill-seeking youths, most with little or no connection to the railroads or the labor action itself, flocked around the railroad stations to support the strikers and violently vent their frustrations at the railroads and the hard economic times, thereby destroying the workers' initial public support. Mobs paralyzed train traffic, disrupted commerce, and attacked nonstriking workers in Baltimore, Pittsburgh, Chicago, St. Louis, Philadelphia, Harrisburg, Scranton, Reading, and a dozen other smaller communities. When the strike had ended, more than 100 people were dead; countless hundreds had sustained

---

[6] E. H. Heywood, "The Great Strike," *Radical Review* 1 (1877):561–62; Yearly, "The Baltimore and Ohio Railroad Strike," pp. 188, 193.

[7] Bruce, *1877*, 33, 51–52. Quote from Thomas A. Scott, "The Recent Strikes," *North American Review* 125 (September–October 1877):353, 355. See also W. M. Grosvenor, "The Communist and the Railway," *International Review* 4 (1877):585–87, 590–96.

[8] Quotes from Yearly, "Baltimore and Ohio Railroad Strike," p. 193. See also Cooper, *The Army and Civil Disorder*, p. 43; Slaner, "The Railroad Strikes of 1877," pp. 217–18.

injuries, and property damage amounted to the tens of millions of dollars. For the first time, property owners of the conservative middle and upper classes faced fears of revolution and equated the strike to the Paris Commune of 1871.[9]

As the strike and related violence spread, the press, the public, and the railroad magnates pressured state governors to employ force to end the upheaval, which many saw as a class war. Police and state militia forces quickly proved unable to handle large mobs, and the governors of several states turned to the president for federal troops. In the case of some midwestern states, federal judges and U.S. marshals requested permission to employ federal troops in nearby garrisons to protect federal property, including railroads under federal receivership.[10]

President Hayes initially considered the possibility of federalizing state militia forces to deal with the disturbances, but finally decided he must rely on the Regular Army as a more disciplined and efficient force. However, a major problem confronted him that could have had potentially disastrous results. Congress had deadlocked over the Army's appropriations bill for the fiscal year starting 1 July 1877, exactly fifteen days before the strike began, and the Army was serving without pay.[11] Under such circumstances Hayes and his advisers naturally wondered whether troops already risking their lives out on the frontier against outlaws and hostile Indians could "also be expected to kill their fellow Americans in defense of property rights." But in the end Hayes set a critical post–Civil War precedent by using regulars as the first resort, beginning in West Virginia.[12]

West Virginia and Maryland

The first crisis of the strike took place in Martinsburg, West Virginia, on 16 July, when hundreds of Baltimore and Ohio Railroad workers halted freight trains moving through much of that state and western Maryland. When Martinsburg's police force under Mayor A. P. Shutt failed to clear the tracks or put the operators back to work, Baltimore and Ohio Railroad Vice President John King, Jr., urged West Virginia Governor Henry M. Mathews to send the state militia.[13]

The request for state troops raised immediate difficulties. Two years earlier the West Virginia legislature had placed membership in the state militia on an all-volunteer basis.

---

[9] Yearly, "Baltimore and Ohio Railroad Strike," p. 188; Cooper, *The Army and Civil Disorder*, pp. 42–45; Bennett M. Rich, *The President and Civil Disorder* (Washington, D.C.: Brookings Institution, 1941), p. 72; Gerald G. Eggert, *Railroad Labor Disputes: The Beginnings of a Federal Strike Policy* (Ann Arbor: University of Michigan Press, 1967), p. 24; Bruce, *1877*, pp. 27, 65, 271–72; Weibe, *The Search for Order*, p. 10.

[10] For the first reactions to the strike, see Riker, *Soldiers of the States*, pp. 44–46; Coakley, "Federal Use of Militia and the National Guard in Civil Disturbances," pp. 26–27; Eggert, *Railroad Labor Disputes*, pp. 50–51; Bruce, *1877*, p. 213.

[11] Bruce, *1877*, pp. 88–89. For Hayes, see Harry Barnard, *Rutherford B. Hayes and His America* (Indianapolis: Bobbs-Merrill, 1954), pp. 445–47; Kenneth E. Davison, *The Presidency of Rutherford B. Hayes* (Westport: Greenwood Press, 1972), pp. 145–53; Harry T. Williams, ed., *Hayes: The Diary of a President, 1875–1881* (New York: David McKay, 1964), pp. 87–91. For the deadlock over Army appropriations, see Coakley, *Role of Federal Military Forces*, pp. 343–44.

[12] Quote from Rich, *President and Civil Disorder*, pp. 83–84. See also U.S. War Department, *Annual Report of the Secretary of War, 1876* (Washington, D.C.: Government Printing Office, 1876), pp. 4–5 (hereafter cited as *Secretary of War Report, 1876*). Hayes' decision to use regulars and not federalized militia set the pattern for future use, which culminated in the provision in the 1903 Dick Act that gave preference to the use of regulars.

[13] Eggert, *Railroad Labor Disputes*, p. 26. King was Garrett's son-in-law.

When the strike erupted, Mathews had only four companies of volunteers at his disposal, one company thirty-eight miles from the railroad, two near Martinsburg, and a fourth in reserve to protect the state capital. He sent the two companies at Martinsburg to the scene of the strike on 17–18 July. But when the members of the Martinsburg Berkeley Light Guard and the Mathews Light Guard from Wheeling proved too undisciplined and too sympathetic to the strikers to be of any use, King telegraphed agents of the Baltimore and Ohio Railroad to apprise the secretary of war that Governor Mathews might request federal troops.[14]

GEORGE W. MCCRARY

King had correctly anticipated the governor's final recourse. On 18 July Mathews' adjutant, Col. Robert M. Delaplain, reported that the entire population of Martinsburg stood ready to join the strikers in forcibly resisting attempts by the militia to escort freight trains through the junction. Without confirming the accuracy of Delaplain's estimate, Mathews sent a telegram to President Hayes that same day stating that "unlawful combinations and domestic violence now existing at Martinsburg" made it impossible to execute the laws of the state and that the legislature could not be summoned promptly. He requested that 200 to 300 men be sent under an officer who would consult with Colonel Delaplain before taking action.[15]

Dissatisfied with the brevity of the request, Hayes asked for a more complete explanation of the state's inability to end the reported rioting. Mathews responded that of the four volunteer companies at his disposal, only one company of 40 men could be relied upon to face the Martinsburg mob, which numbered 800. Another volunteer force would take ten days to form, during which time the mob could inflict considerable property damage and loss of life. President Hayes accepted this explanation without any independent verification and ordered Secretary of War George W. McCrary to dispatch troops under authority of RS 5297. Hayes then issued the appropriate proclamation.[16]

To obtain the necessary forces, McCrary turned to Maj. Gen. Winfield Scott Hancock's Division of the Atlantic. Under Hancock, Col. Thomas H. Ruger commanded the Department of the South, and Brig. Gen. Christopher C. Augur commanded the Department of the Gulf. The northern states of the division made up the Department of the

---

[14] Wilson, *Federal Aid in Domestic Disturbances*, p. 189; Eggert, *Railroad Labor Disputes*, pp. 26, 29–30; Bruce, *1877*, pp. 77–80.

[15] Quote from Wilson, *Federal Aid in Domestic Disturbances*, p. 189, see also pp. 190, 315; Eggert, *Railroad Labor Disputes*, pp. 27, 84–85; Bruce, *1877*, pp. 84–85.

[16] Rich, *President and Civil Disorder*, p. 73; Eggert, *Railroad Labor Disputes*, pp. 29–30, 50. For Hayes' 18 July proclamation and legal justification, see Wilson, *Federal Aid in Domestic Disturbances*, p. 190.

WINFIELD SCOTT HANCOCK

East, commanded by Hancock himself from his joint divisional and departmental headquarters in New York City. When McCrary ordered Hancock to aid Mathews, the general had less than 3,300 officers and men available in his entire division, most of whom were wholly unprepared for duty of this sort.[17]

Hancock reacted quickly. On 18 July he ordered the commander of the Washington Arsenal, Col. William H. French, 4th Artillery, to equip as infantrymen all 212 men at his disposal, plus 120 artillerymen from the 2d Artillery stationed at Fort McHenry, and to transport them by rail to Martinsburg. On arrival French was to consult with Mathews on how best to deploy the regulars, but was to delay any further action until a reading of President Hayes' proclamation to disperse had taken place, as required by RS 5300. The troops boarded trains at 2200 and traveled as far as Harper's Ferry, West Virginia, where reports of sabotage to the track farther west forced them to stop overnight.[18]

Reaching Martinsburg after dawn, French found more than 100 engines and 1,500 freight cars standing idle and blocking every approach to town, although strikers were allowing passenger and mail trains to move without interference. While he conferred with local officials on various measures to start all trains moving again, deputy sheriffs and city police distributed copies of Hayes' proclamation calling on "all persons engaged in said unlawful and insurrectionary proceedings to disperse and retire peaceably to their respective abodes on or before 12 o'clock noon of the 19th day of July."[19]

When the strikers ignored Hayes' admonition, on 20 July French issued one more warning: "Strikers impeding the passage of United States troops in any manner whatsoever, do so at their own peril." During the next two days he placed escorts aboard the trains with orders to arrest anyone interfering with their operation. Sympathetic to the plight of the railroad workers, coal miners and boatmen from the Chesapeake and Ohio Canal swarmed around the depot at Martinsburg during the next two days and joined strikers in stoning passing trains. In one incident, escorting federal troops halted their train and

    [17] *Secretary of War Report, 1877*, pp. 5–6, 86, 405. For Hancock's life and strike role, see Jordan, *Winfield Scott Hancock: A Soldier's Life*, pp. 242–50.
    [18] Bruce, *1877*, pp. 93–94; *Secretary of War Report, 1877*, p. 87; Wilson, *Federal Aid in Domestic Disturbances*, pp. 190, 316–17.
    [19] Quote from Telg, French to AG, 20 Jul 1877, Record Group (RG) 94, Records of the Office of the Adjutant General, U.S. Army, Consolidated File 4042 (Strike Papers), National Archives and Records Administration (NARA), Washington, D.C.; Bruce, *1877*, p. 82.

formed into ranks. In the face of rocks and insults hurled by the mob, they prepared to fire while the boatmen quickly dispersed.[20]

By nightfall on 20 July all trains were moving again through West Virginia. Pleased with this success, Colonel French sent strong detachments to stations farther west, as far as Keyser, West Virginia. After complimenting Governor Mathews and Colonel Delaplain for their "able and energetic assistance," he wired Washington that without any additional troops he could open the Baltimore and Ohio Railroad all the way to the Ohio River.[21]

While French restored rail traffic along the Baltimore and Ohio line in West Virginia, rioting erupted in Baltimore, Pittsburgh, and Chicago. Mobs of strikers, unemployed men, and even women and children battled local police. The governors of Maryland, Pennsylvania, and Illinois hesitated to concentrate their small militia forces at any one place for fear of leaving any locale vulnerable. In addition, the prolabor sympathies of many militiamen, and the negative political consequences of firing on voters, compelled these governors to seek federal troops.

Rioting in Maryland first erupted at Cumberland and then at Baltimore. By 20 July Baltimore and Ohio Railroad President Garrett had persuaded Maryland Governor John Lee Carroll to send militiamen to Cumberland. Later that same day, 400 men of the 5th and 6th Regiments of the Maryland militia left their armories for Baltimore's Camden Station for the trip west. As they marched through the streets of the city, angry crowds numbering up to 15,000 stoned the militiamen. The 5th Regiment was the first to encounter the wrath of the mob, and 10 soldiers were injured before the unit found refuge in the depot. The 6th Regiment was not as fortunate. After being besieged in their armory for several hours by a mob numbering in the thousands, part of the regiment attempted to begin the march to Camden Station. In the ensuing confusion and chaos, and amid a hail of debris, several militiamen opened fire into the crowd without orders, beginning a running fight between the militia and the mob lasting the entire distance to Camden Station. At least ten people in the mob were killed and scores were wounded before the 6th Regiment also found refuge in the depot. Enraged, the mob failed to disperse. Unable to storm the roundhouse occupied by heavily armed militia, the rioters set fire to nearby railroad cars and equipment and prevented firemen from quenching the blaze. Rumors abounded that the mobs planned to raze all Baltimore and Ohio Railroad property and much of the city as well.[22]

In a telegram to President Hayes, Governor Carroll explained that his militia could not disperse the rioters and that the legislature could not convene in time to meet the emergency. He called upon the president "to furnish the force necessary to protect the State against domestic violence." The following day, 21 July, Secretary McCrary notified Carroll that federal troops, and possibly militiamen from adjacent states, would certainly be sent to Baltimore under authority of RS 5297. The secretary, however, only took steps to obtain federal forces and directed Brig. Gen. William F. Barry, the commander of Fort McHenry, to send the remaining fifty-six men of his command not already in Martinsburg to Baltimore. After further consultation with Hancock and Secretary of the

---

[20] Telg, French to AG, 20 Jul 1877, RG 94; Bruce, *1877*, p. 96.
[21] Telg, French to AG, 20 Jul 1877, RG 94.
[22] Bruce, *1877*, pp. 100–10.

Navy Richard W. Thompson, who placed all units in his control under the secretary of war, McCrary succeeded in obtaining three additional companies of regulars from New York Harbor to reinforce Barry and a detachment of marines from the Washington Navy Yard under command of Bvt. Lt. Col. Charles Heywood. All units were immediately dispatched to Baltimore. Before the arrival of these troops, President Hayes issued another proclamation warning all persons engaged in domestic violence against the Baltimore and Ohio Railroad, or otherwise obstructing the laws of Maryland, to retire peaceably to their homes before noon on 22 July.[23]

Arriving at Camden Station just before midnight on 21 July, 135 marines immediately reported to Governor Carroll, who directed them to capture over 100 mob ringleaders. For the next few hours, as a show of force to preclude further violence, marines, joined by police and detectives, marched through the most unstable sections of the city. Later the marines linked up with an Army battery from Fort McHenry and escorted it to Camden Station, finally relieving the still-besieged militiamen.[24]

Hancock reached Baltimore early the next day. After consulting with Carroll, he deployed the marines at Camden Station and other key points through the city. By noon three companies of Army regulars, about 360 men from New York and New England, also entered Baltimore. Hancock used these men to reinforce the marines and to relieve the militia at both Camden Station and the 6th Regiment Armory. When federal troops en route to President Street Station under command of Brig. Gen. Henry Abbott encountered a rock-throwing mob, Abbott ordered his men to halt, turn about, and fix bayonets. Before the command was even finished, the mob had scattered.[25]

While federal forces restored order in Baltimore, hundreds of strikers in Cumberland, Maryland, a major stronghold of the strike, threatened to impede the passage of trains and to damage rail cars. Carroll telegraphed Hayes requesting federal troops, putting his state in competition with West Virginia for the services of a limited number of regulars. After Hancock repeated the request, the War Department directed Colonel French to leave Martinsburg for Cumberland and place his command under the orders of Carroll. A second telegram from Hancock to the colonel, instructing French to move his headquarters from Martinsburg to Cumberland and remain there, arrived after he had departed.[26]

French quickly and efficiently carried out Hancock's original orders. After restoring calm, he attempted to return to West Virginia, ignorant of Hancock's second telegram ordering him to stay in Cumberland. At this point two men began to exert pressure on French to concentrate all his troops at Cumberland and to adopt a hard line toward the strikers: Thomas R. Sharp, a Baltimore and Ohio Railroad official and former Confederate Army colonel, and Col. H. Kyd Douglas, Governor Carroll's top military aide. French, who lacked sympathy for the plight of the railroads and who believed their woes were largely

---

[23] Telg, McCrary to AG, 21 Jul 1877, RG 94, File 4042, NARA; *Secretary of War Report, 1877*, p. 87. For the proclamation of 21 July, see Wilson, *Federal Aid in Domestic Disturbances*, p. 193, and pp. 317–18. See also H. C. Cochrane, "The Naval Brigade and the Marine Battalions in the Labor Strikes of 1877," *United Service Magazine* 1 (January 1879):123–24; Bruce, *1877*, p. 110.

[24] Cochrane, "Naval Brigade," pp. 124–25; Telg, McCrary to Adj Gen Vincent, 21 Jul 1877, in Wilson, *Federal Aid in Domestic Disturbances*, pp. 192–93, 318–19.

[25] Telg, Hancock to AG, 22 Jul 1877, RG 94, File 4042, NARA; *Secretary of War Report, 1877*, pp. 87–88; Bruce, *1877*, p. 113.

[26] Bruce, *1877*, pp. 214–15; Wilson, *Federal Aid in Domestic Disturbances*, p. 319.

MARYLAND 6TH MILITIA REGIMENT FIRES ON A MOB DURING THE B&O RAILROAD STRIKE. *A woodcut engraving from* Frank Leslie's Illustrated Newspaper.

self-inflicted, bristled at the overbearing manner of both men. He was determined to keep full tactical control of his troops and would have preferred to keep his force in West Virginia in pursuance of his original plan to reopen the railroad from Martinsburg to Wheeling. When Sharp, who had orchestrated the original order to bring troops to Cumberland, refused to provide transportation on the Baltimore and Ohio Railroad, French lost his temper and allegedly cursed him and threatened him with arrest in front of many witnesses and newspaper correspondents. He was quoted as saying, "I am not going to be under control and orders of that man Sharp. He is a damned old rebel as he was during the war." In telegrams to the secretary of war and the adjutant general, French complained that Sharp's behavior had injured the prestige of his command and threatened to undo the bloodless reopening of the Baltimore and Ohio Railroad, so far accomplished. He made clear that, if he had to suffer any further meddling by petty railroad officials, he preferred to be relieved and replaced by an officer "less objectionable to that corporation."[27]

More influential in Washington than Colonel French, King complained to Hancock that French had verbally and physically attacked Sharp in a raging fit of intoxication. In view of this allegation, the colonel's telegrams, and his earlier failure to carry out the second order to go to Cumberland, Hancock recommended replacement of the mercurial

---

[27] Quotes from Bruce, *1877*, pp. 214–16. See also Telgs, French to McCrary, 22 Jul 1877, and to AG, 23 Jul 1877, both in RG 94, File 4042, NARA.

officer. The secretary of war agreed, and Hancock substituted Col. George W. Getty, 3d Artillery. During the next few days Getty took command from Cumberland and apportioned French's 200 men between that city in Maryland and Martinsburg, Keyser, and Grafton, West Virginia.[28]

Within five days Colonel Getty and General Barry had removed all impediments to rail traffic in the Cumberland and Baltimore areas. Carroll then decided to reopen the lines connecting the two cities by means of federally escorted freight trains. Getty willingly cooperated with Carroll's requests for troops on trains eastbound from Cumberland, but Barry hesitated to provide comparable escorts from Baltimore at the risk of leaving that city open to new rioting.[29]

Secretary McCrary assuaged Barry's fears by ordering an additional force of marines to Baltimore. Commanded by Bvt. Lt. Col. James Forney, the 2d Marine Battalion left the Washington Navy Yard on 29 July and reported to Barry later that same day. First he ordered Forney to join Bvt. Maj. Gen. R. B. Ayres, 3d Artillery, at Camden Station, but later instructed him to detach seventy-five marines from his force to guard a convoy of twenty-five freight trains preparing to leave for Martinsburg.[30]

After posting two marines on each locomotive and the remainder among the cars, Forney instructed his men to fire at any man attempting to desert a locomotive or interfere with a train. On 30 July a marine detachment under the command of Capt. J. J. Bishop led the convoy to Martinsburg without incident. The next day the marines performed the same service on eastbound trains and continued to escort convoys both ways until ordered back to the Washington Navy Yard on 15 August. By that date the combined actions of Colonel Getty, General Barry, and Colonel Forney, and their respective Army and Marine Corps commands, had effectively broken the strike along the Baltimore and Ohio Railroad, ending the worst unrest in West Virginia and Maryland. Elsewhere, however, the strike still raged.[31]

The Strike in Pennsylvania

On the same day that strikes erupted in Maryland and West Virginia, Robert Pitcairn, an official of the Pennsylvania Railroad, quite unwisely announced a new and untimely company policy of using two locomotives per train on the Pittsburgh to Philadelphia run. Saving labor costs by adding cars to the overall length of each train without increasing the crew, a practice known as doubleheading, drastically increased both the danger to and work load of railroad brakemen. When twenty-six employees, already disgusted with wage reductions, refused to handle the enlarged trains they were fired. On 19 July, the day the new policy was to take effect, the Trainmen's Union ordered Pennsylvania Railroad workers throughout the region out on strike.[32] The strike caused an immediate outbreak of mob violence in the major rail and industrial centers of the state.

The violence in Martinsburg and Baltimore soon paled in comparison to that in Pittsburgh. Within three days, angry crowds of thousands of strikers, unemployed men, and

---

[28] Telg, Hancock to AG, 22 Jul 1877, RG 94.
[29] Telg, Getty to Hancock, 28 Jul 1877, RG 94, File 4042, NARA.
[30] Cochrane, "Naval Brigade," pp. 618–19.
[31] Ibid., pp. 620–23.
[32] Bruce, *1877*, pp. 73, 115–16, 125–26, 138–58.

RIOT IN PITTSBURGH AT THE UNION DEPOT OF THE PENNSYLVANIA RAILROAD. *As seen by artists of* Frank Leslie's Illustrated Newspaper.

curious women and children began to mill around city streets, eventually gathering at the Pennsylvania Railroad's 28th Street Crossing. When the mob refused to heed the call of the local sheriff to disperse, Pennsylvania's adjutant general, James W. Latta, sent for the militia. Under the command of Maj. Gen. Alfred L. Pearson, 600 Pittsburgh-area militiamen of the 6th Division of the Pennsylvania National Guard entered the city on 20 July. They were followed the next morning by another 650 militiamen of the 1st Division of the Pennsylvania National Guard from Philadelphia, commanded by Maj. Gen. Robert M. Brinton. Lack of discipline and sympathy for the strikers and their fellow Pittsburgh citizens caused many of Pearson's men to ignore the muster and to join the milling crowd of spectators. Brinton's men from Philadelphia, although equally undisciplined, did not share these local sympathies and single-handedly attempted to clear the 28th Street Crossing on 21 July, immediately after arriving in the city.[33]

Brinton's command formed a square on the tracks near the crossing under a hail of stones, taunts, and insults from the mob. The situation rapidly deteriorated as the fatigued militiamen began to fall victim to the hot sun and missiles thrown by the crowd. Finally, when unknown members of the mob fired several scattered shots, the militiamen replied, without orders, with ten minutes of random musket fire. An estimated 10 to 20 of the rioters died and

---

[33] Ibid.

60 to 70 were wounded. Included in the casualties were men, women, children, and, ironically, several members of the Pittsburgh militia.

The crowd initially dispersed in panic and shock. Brinton's men retreated and barricaded themselves in the Pennsylvania Railroad roundhouse where they were soon besieged as the mob returned, now blindly enraged and strengthened by many members of the Pittsburgh militia. The Philadelphians managed to hold off their assailants until the next morning, then the militiamen retreated from the burning rail yard to the outskirts of the city. Meanwhile, Pittsburgh was subjected to a wild orgy of arson, vandalism, and looting. All Pennsylvania Railroad property in sight was destroyed, including the machine shops, 2 roundhouses, 125 locomotives, over 2,000 loaded freight cars, and most of the buildings belonging to the railroad to the value of $8 to $10 million. On the next day, Sunday, the mob proceeded to destroy the offices and property of the Cincinnati and St. Louis Railroad, the Panhandle Railroad, the Adams Express Company, and the Pullman Railcar Company, as well as other private businesses and structures. The destruction was unopposed by either the Philadelphia or the Pittsburgh militias.[34]

Pennsylvania officials determined that federal military intervention was needed to restore order and avert further bloodshed and destruction. The carnage attributed to the actions of the Pennsylvania militia also served to strengthen the belief in Washington that committing the Regular Army was a better answer, a vindication of Hayes' decision several days earlier to use federal troops rather than federalized state troops to quell disorder. During the initial stages of the strike, Pennsylvania Governor John Hartranft was vacationing in Wyoming at Thomas A. Scott's expense. In his absence the state's adjutant general and the secretary of the commonwealth asked President Hayes for sufficient military force to suppress disorder and protect persons and property against violence. Although properly phrased, the request failed to meet constitutional requirements as set forth in RS 5297 that such a request originate with either the governor or the legislature. Hayes further suspected that Pennsylvania officials had failed to exhaust state peacekeeping resources before calling for federal military aid. He ignored the request.[35]

Yet Hayes did not intend to let the disorder spread. When the mayor of Philadelphia requested troops to replace militiamen of the 1st Division sent to Pittsburgh, the president directed the War Department to use regulars to protect Philadelphia's numerous federal buildings and facilities. Although he realized that a municipal official did not have the authority to ask for troops without a formal request from the governor, Hayes also knew that something had to be done immediately to aid distressed local officials. Therefore the president used the pretext of protecting federal buildings and property in Philadelphia to intervene, hoping that the mere presence of regulars would not only protect property, but would also intimidate any groups threatening civil authority. This action set a precedent that was used frequently in the next few weeks by Hayes, and in the coming decades by presidents who, after the passage of the *Posse Comitatus Act*, viewed the protection of federal property as an inherent responsibility of the federal executive implicitly authorized by RS 5298. Under subsequent orders from Secretary McCrary, Hancock left Baltimore for

---

[34] Ibid.; Wilson, *Federal Aid in Domestic Disturbances*, p. 195.

[35] Eggert, *Railroad Labor Disputes*, p. 31; Bruce, *1877*, pp. 134, 195–96; Wilson, *Federal Aid in Domestic Disturbances*, p. 195; Telg, Adj Gen to Hancock, 22 Jul 1877, RG 94, File 4042, NARA; *Secretary of War Report, 1877*, p. 88.

Philadelphia on 22 July. Simultaneously, Secretary of the Navy Thompson ordered the battalion of marines in Baltimore to accompany the general. Hancock further telegraphed troop trains en route from New England and New York to Baltimore to divert to Philadelphia, and by midnight on 23 July he had collected 125 marines, 450 infantrymen, and a light artillery battery in the city.[36]

Meanwhile, Governor Hartranft had learned of the crisis and started home from Wyoming. Just as Hancock was leaving for Philadelphia, Hartranft asked President Hayes for military aid "to assist in quelling mobs within the borders of the state of Pennsylvania" and suggested that the president obtain troops by calling up volunteers or by federalizing the militias of adjacent states. Hayes refused to act because Hartranft's request had omitted the phrase "domestic insurrection" as prescribed by RS 5297. The next day Hartranft sent a telegram from Nebraska with the appropriate wording: "domestic insurrection exists in Pennsylvania which State authorities are unable to suppress, and the legislature is not in session and cannot be convened in time."[37]

Hayes finally consented to the governor's petition under authority of RS 5297, and on the same day issued a proclamation as required by RS 5300, ordering the "insurgents to disperse and retire peaceably to their abodes . . . on or before 12 o'clock noon on the 24th day of July."[38] His action marked his third intervention in a state disorder. In the name of law and order, and according to the applicable and prevailing legal, social, and political philosophy of the time, Hayes took the only course open to him. The rail strike had careened out of what little control it ever had and deteriorated into a series of senseless mob actions, causing widespread public revulsion.[39]

As disorders continued through the East and Midwest, on 23 July McCrary granted Hancock direct authority over all Army forces and installations in the Atlantic Division so that he could respond to threats more quickly with federal military aid. In addition to the power to move men without higher executive authority anywhere in the division, Hancock enjoyed direct command over Army organizations usually controlled by Washington bureaus, including engineer and medical posts, recruiting depots, and arsenals. When emergencies arose, he could immediately commandeer and dispatch supplies or garrisons throughout the eastern United States.[40]

Hancock arrived in Philadelphia on 23 July and immediately exerted his authority by redeploying companies to incipient trouble spots and alerting troops in the South and Gulf Departments to prepare for possible riot duty in Baltimore, Washington, D.C., or Pennsylvania. By concentrating substantial numbers of troops at key trouble spots, he could periodically dispatch sizable detachments to open all local rail lines or clear away threatening mobs. In his view, the use of battalion-size units minimized the possibility of being overwhelmed by mobs, as had already happened to several militia units. He believed

---

[36] Telg, AG to Hancock, and reply, 22 Jul 1877, both in RG 94; *Secretary of War Report, 1877*, p. 88; Cochrane, "Naval Brigade," pp. 126–27.

[37] Quotes from Bruce, *1877*, pp. 217–18; Eggert, *Railroad Labor Disputes*, pp. 32, 50; Rich, *President and Civil Disorder*, pp. 75–76.

[38] Proclamation cited in Wilson, *Federal Aid in Domestic Disturbances*, p. 168. See also Coakley, *Role of Federal Military Forces*, p. 20n.46.

[39] Eggert, *Railroad Labor Disputes*, pp. 50–51.

[40] *Secretary of War Report, 1877*, p. 5.

the Army's reputation for strict discipline, awesome firepower, and invincibility more than compensated for its lack of numbers.[41]

Assured by the War Department of tactical autonomy in Pennsylvania, Hancock initially accepted the concept that civil supremacy required placing his men under state control. In West Virginia and Maryland, Hayes had delegated authority over federal forces to state governors. Regarding the force ordered to Philadelphia to protect federal property, McCrary had ordered Hancock to prepare to turn over federal units to local police for use as a riot-quelling *posse comitatus*. In all three cases, however, precedent restricted civil authorities to directing unit commanders to take their men to specific sites. Actual command of the men and their tactical deployment at the sites remained with the officer in charge.[42]

However, after witnessing the ineffectiveness of the militias in West Virginia, Pennsylvania, and Maryland, and especially after the debacle at Pittsburgh, Hancock began to question even nominal control of federal forces by state authorities. In a lengthy communique to McCrary he explained his position:

When the governor of a State has declared his inability to suppress an insurrection and has called upon the President . . . under the Constitution . . . from that time commences a state not of peace but of war; . . . although civil local authority still exists, yet the only outcome is to resort to force through the Federal military authorities, . . . that can only be through a subordination of the State authorities for the time being and until lawful order is restored; otherwise there can be no complete exercise of power in a military way within the limits of the State by the Federal officers.[43]

McCrary responded that federal civil officials, not military commanders, determined in each case whether regular troops should be placed under state authorities, since this was a civil and not a military decision. If necessary, however, Hayes was willing to let Hancock "take command of all troops suppressing domestic violence within the State of Pennsylvania, including both United States forces and forces furnished by the State" even if the state troops were not federalized.[44]

Although Hayes agreed with the general and was prepared to concentrate all state and federal military forces under him, subsequent events rendered the question moot. When Hartranft returned on 25 July he convinced Hancock of the efficacy of a plan to end the strike. Seeing Pittsburgh as the focal point of the disturbances, he believed that a strong military demonstration there would have a ripple effect elsewhere. By the time he reached the state, disorders involving striking rail workers, coal miners, and the unemployed had been reported, among other places, in Erie, Bethlehem, Sunbury, Reading, Meadville, Altoona, Johnstown, Harrisburg, Mauch Chunk, Scranton, and Wilkes-Barre. Hartranft therefore proposed to lead a sizable combined force of state militia and federal regulars to Pittsburgh the very next day.[45]

---

[41] Telg, Hancock to AG and McCrary, 23 Jul 1877, RG 94, File 4042, NARA; Cooper, *The Army and Civil Disorder*, pp. 49–50; Coakley, *Role of Federal Military Forces*, p. 348.

[42] Telg, Hancock to AG, 24 Jul 1877, RG 94, File 4042, NARA.

[43] Quote from Wilson, *Federal Aid in Domestic Disturbances*, pp. 322–23; Bruce, *1877*, pp. 285–86.

[44] Quote from Telg, McCrary to Hancock, 25 Jul 1877, RG 94, File 4042, NARA. See also Wilson, *Federal Aid in Domestic Disturbances*, p. 324.

[45] Wilson, *Federal Aid in Domestic Disturbances*, pp. 197–98; Bruce, *1877*, pp. 285–86; Joseph A. Dacus, *Annals of the Great Strikes* (New York: L. T. Palmer, 1877; reprint, New York: Arno, 1969), pp. 143–53.

Impressed by the governor's courage and determination to regain control of the state from lawless elements, Hancock urged McCrary to let Hartranft try to reestablish his authority with the understanding that if he failed, Hancock would assume command over both federal and state forces. When McCrary approved Hartranft's plan, Hancock ordered Maj. John Hamilton, 1st Artillery, to leave Philadelphia on 26 July and place his 577 officers and men under the governor's control. By arrangement with Hartranft, Hamilton's men were to occupy the first of two trains bound for Pittsburgh.[46]

Following Hamilton's force was a second train carrying Hartranft and 2,000 state troops commanded by militia Maj. Gen. James A. Beaver. Hartranft directed that Beaver's men, upon arriving in Pittsburgh, were to deploy in small groups, each holding its fire until all other methods of crowd dispersal had failed and an appropriate warning to disperse had been given. Firing was to be effective and to continue until the mob dispersed. All persons attempting to dissuade regulars or militiamen from doing their duty were to be arrested.[47]

Despite the boldness of Hartranft's instructions, Hamilton discerned hesitancy in Beaver's preparations. He decided therefore to place his men on both trains and proceed alone, expecting Beaver's force to follow later on another train. When Hamilton's trains stopped at Altoona, the crowd, which had been harassing all rail traffic passing through the city for several days, forcibly removed the engineers and firemen. Hamilton impressed replacements from among the strikers and prepared to move on. Frightened at the prospect of being left to the mercies of a fully aroused mob, railroad officials tried to delay his progress for several hours by refusing the extra engines needed to haul the two trains up the Allegheny Mountains. When Hamilton threatened to detain three passenger trains in Altoona by taking the locomotives from them, the railroad officials relented and his force proceeded.[48]

The mob at Johnstown showed even less restraint than that at Altoona. As Hamilton's lead train throttled down to go through town, the crowd threw rocks, injuring some of the soldiers. Hamilton ordered the engineer to stop the train and reverse direction, but the train jumped the tracks, which had been sabotaged, injuring Hamilton and several of his men. With one hand supporting a broken rib, he ordered part of his men to form around the train, while a second group arrested a hundred members of the mob. All but fourteen were released the following day. When the second train pulled into Johnstown, Hamilton placed soldiers in each car of both trains with instructions to protect the crewmen and fire upon the mob if they threw any more missiles.[49]

News of the imminent arrival of federal troops and the mob's spent fury convinced strikers in Pittsburgh to come to terms with railroad officials on 27 July. Hamilton's force entered the city the next day and moved unopposed to the U.S. arsenal. Beaver's force of militia arrived later the same day and likewise moved unimpeded to their encampment. Within three days normal railroad traffic resumed. Without once being

---

[46] Telg, Hancock to McCrary, 26 Jul 1877, RG 94, File 4042, NARA.

[47] Cochrane, "Naval Brigade," p. 618.

[48] Cooper, *The Army and Civil Disorder*, pp. 54–55; Bruce, *1877*, p. 286; Dacus, *Annals of the Great Strikes*, p. 145.

[49] Cooper, *The Army and Civil Disorder*, pp. 54–55. The arrests of mob members by federal troops in this incident violated the doctrine of *Ex Parte Milligan* set down in 1866. This highly unusual action did not violate the terms of the Posse Comitatus Act, however.

called for actual riot duty, Hamilton's men remained at the arsenal for two weeks before returning to Philadelphia.

Although their withdrawal from Pittsburgh marked the end of the railroad strike throughout the state, sympathy strikes of ironworkers and coal miners required the further deployment of federal troops to protect mining companies and railroad property in Scranton, Wilkes-Barre, Mauch Chunk, Reading, and Easton, Pennsylvania.[50] To meet these new labor troubles, McCrary deployed six companies of the 22d Infantry to eastern Pennsylvania on 4 August to join state troops and other federal regulars previously gathered by Hancock. The federal forces aided local authorities as a *posse comitatus* to protect coal companies and rail lines in federal receivership and to escort coal, freight, and passenger trains. Although the combined state and federal forces quickly restored order, the striking miners were determined to remain off the job, and state and company officials were equally determined to keep federal forces on the scene until the strike had ended.

Hancock became increasingly disturbed at such duty, which appeared to be little more than intimidation of otherwise peaceful strikers. While the strike dragged on, the coal and rail companies attempted to starve the strikers into submission. The general reported that almost 100,000 men were idle and that they and their families lived on potatoes, wild blackberries, and whortleberries. Although the strikers attempted in vain to elicit sympathy from Army officers, Hancock was concerned that enlisted men, many of whom were of foreign and working-class origins, would be subject to strikers' entreaties and ordered that Army encampments be moved well away from their neighborhoods. Despite repeated requests to have his troops relieved from this increasingly odious duty, the regulars stayed in eastern Pennsylvania until the coal strike collapsed in mid-October 1877.[51]

Chicago, Illinois

With the outbreaks of strikes and rioting in the east, as early as 22 July military authorities in Illinois prepared for trouble in Chicago. On that date Maj. Gen. Arthur C. Ducat, commanding two regiments of the Illinois militia, put all Chicago armories on alert and advised private companies in the city to comply with orders from Chicago Mayor Monroe Heath to arm loyal employees. At the same time, Secretary McCrary began redeploying federal forces in the Military Division of the Missouri for possible service in the Chicago area. Convinced that Chicago, the nation's major midwestern crossroads, lay at the heart of the nationwide strike, McCrary planned to concentrate more troops in that city than in any other and, as in Pennsylvania, to place them under the governor's command.[52]

Lt. Gen. Philip Sheridan's Division of the Missouri encompassed four departments and over 15,000 men, most of whom were stationed in the western states and territories dealing with outlaws and hostile Indians. At the outbreak of the strike, Sheridan was in Montana supervising the reinterment of Custer's command at the Little Big Horn battlefield, and the commander of the Department of the Missouri, Brig. Gen. John Pope, was

---

[50] Wilson, *Federal Aid in Domestic Disturbances*, p. 198; Cooper, *The Army and Civil Disorder*, pp. 77–80.

[51] Cooper, *The Army and Civil Disorder*, pp. 77–80; see also *Secretary of War Report, 1877*, p. 97.

[52] Bruce, *1877*, p. 237.

ILLINOIS MILITIAMEN FIRE ON A MOB IN CHICAGO

at his headquarters in Fort Leavenworth, Kansas, too far removed to control events. During the strike, Col. Richard C. Drum, Sheridan's adjutant general, became the de facto commander of federal troops in Chicago.[53]

Although no major strikes or riots had yet occurred in the area, and without presidential action, McCrary directed Drum to build up an antiriot force from six companies of the 22d Infantry, whose 226 officers and men were at Detroit on their way to new assignments. Drum immediately summoned two companies into Chicago, but kept the remaining four outside the city in reserve. During the next two days McCrary shifted several more companies composed of 218 officers and men of the 9th Infantry, from Omaha, Nebraska, to the Rock Island Arsenal 150 miles southwest of Chicago. The 9th Infantry was to provide support for the 22d, but only if requested to do so by the Chicago mayor through the Illinois governor or by the governor himself. Thus far, however, no such requests had been received from either Mayor Heath or Governor Shelby M. Cullom.[54]

Tensions in the city increased as the Workingman's Party of the United States, a Marxist organization, held well-attended rallies urging all Chicago workers to organize and strike. With this encouragement, railway workers throughout the city, and soon throughout the region, left their jobs on 24 July. Mobs of strikers took to the streets inviting, and sometimes

---

[53] *Secretary of War Report, 1877*, pp. 5–6, 56; Cooper, *The Army and Civil Disorder*, p. 56.

[54] Bruce, *1877*, pp. 237–41; Cooper, *The Army and Civil Disorder*, p. 57; Wilson, *Federal Aid in Domestic Disturbances*, pp. 200–201.

JOHN POPE

forcing, laborers in other industries to join them. Attempts to enforce the strike caused frequent street battles between mobs of strikers, nonstrikers, and the Chicago police. Rioting in Chicago peaked on 25 July. Police indiscriminately clubbed and shot members of the mob and innocent bystanders and urged on the 2d Illinois Militia as it drove spectators indoors at bayonet point. Confrontations between the police and rioters continued during the remainder of the day at various points throughout the city, leaving at least three people dead and nine wounded. Now regretting his earlier decision not to seek federal aid, Mayor Heath asked Drum for troops and government stocks of weapons to arm citizen volunteers guarding private property. Colonel Drum lent rifles to the city, but arming private citizens only contributed to the anarchy and violence. Sensing that the situation was escalating beyond the control of local officials and state militia, Governor Cullom asked Hayes to order Drum to move the 9th Regiment from Rock Island to Chicago.[55]

In anticipation of presidential approval, General Pope recommended that Drum order such infantry to Chicago as he thought General Sheridan would approve. Under pressure from Heath, Drum took Pope's advice and summoned all 6 companies from the 9th Infantry at Rock Island, 4 companies of the 5th Cavalry from Fort McPherson, Nebraska, 2 companies from the 4th Infantry at Omaha Barracks, Nebraska, and 3 companies from Fort Randall, Dakota Territory, totaling 650 men. At the urging of Cullom, he also requested six Gatling guns from the Rock Island Arsenal. McCrary approved his request and further informed him that President Hayes had approved the use of federal troops under the orders of Governor Cullom to suppress rioting in Chicago.[56]

For reasons not evident from surviving documents, however, the president suddenly reversed his policy of allowing state officials to control federal troops, starting with Governor Cullom.[57] On 27 July Hayes withdrew Cullom's authority to deploy and direct Drum's command, ostensibly because the governor had failed to request federal military aid formally through the state legislature and to request a presidential proclamation ordering the Chicago mobs to disperse as required by RS 5297 and RS 5300. A more likely

[55] Bruce, *1877*, pp. 237–39, 243–47; Cooper, *The Army and Civil Disorder*, p. 57; Telg, Cullom to Hayes, 25 Jul 1877, RG 94, File 4042, NARA.

[56] Telgs, AG to Drum, and reply, 25 Jul 1877, and AG to Drum, 26 Jul 1877, all in RG 94, File 4042, NARA; see also Telg, AG to McCrary, 25 Jul 1877, Rutherford B. Hayes Papers, Rutherford B. Hayes Memorial Library, Fremont, Ohio.

[57] Cooper, *The Army and Civil Disorder*, pp. 57–58.

explanation is that after his experiences with the governors of West Virginia, Maryland, and Pennsylvania, Hayes realized that most state officials were requesting federal troops without having fully exhausted state and local peacekeeping resources. Calling out local forces to disperse mobs of potential voters was not only politically and strategically risky for mayors and governors, but was also expensive. These two factors led many officials to exaggerate the intensity of civil disturbances and to call quickly for outside federal aid, which was politically safe and charged to federal revenues. Whatever Hayes' reasoning, he replaced Drum's mandate to serve under Cullom for state purposes with orders to defend U.S. property, execute federal court processes, and display the troops for moral effect, which could be justified under RS 5298 if necessary. The procedure was legal because the president at this time was still able to use federal troops as a *posse comitatus*.[58] His action, undertaken without invocation of RS 5298, and without the issuance of a proclamation, placed regulars in Chicago, where they could intimidate mobs by their presence, while ostensibly protecting federal interests, and indirectly aid state officials but without being under their control.

Hayes' action, and the overwhelming presence of large numbers of regulars, had the desired calming effect. On 27 July Drum wrote McCrary that no emergency had yet arisen requiring operations against the mob, but he recommended against withdrawing troops prematurely. He believed a great potential for violence existed among the 25,000 unemployed people of Chicago who were dominated by "what is generally termed here the communistic element, unquestionably capable of almost any act of disturbing the public peace." The next day, however, he noted more optimistically that the "excitement here has calmed down . . . the presence of U.S. troops has given great confidence."[59]

Two days later General Sheridan had returned to his Chicago division headquarters and found the city quite peaceful because of the presence of the regulars. From 15 to 19 August, he withdrew the remaining 13 companies from Chicago.[60]

After somewhat precipitate decisions to aid the first three governors who requested troops under RS 5297, Hayes, wary of providing military aid to others, restricted the troops to the role of supporting federal marshals as a *posse comitatus*. In Indiana, Missouri, and Illinois, where the railroads were in federal receivership, U.S. judges and marshals played the paramount role in calling for federal military intervention. The receiverships had been created when several bankrupt railroads had turned over their assets and effective control of their operations to federal courts, to avoid liquidation by creditors after the Panic of 1873. Successive federal judges identified the survival of such railroads with the public welfare, and often appointed as receivers the same company officials who had driven the lines to bankruptcy. When strikers halted the traffic of companies in receivership and obstructed lines that had been designated "military roads" and "postal routes" under the Pacific Railway Acts, judges charged contempt of court and interference with the enforcement of federal law and court orders to keep the lines open.[61]

Under RS 5298, whenever it became impracticable in the judgment of the president, to enforce by the ordinary course of judicial proceedings the law of the United States, the

[58] Telg, Sheridan to AG, and reply, 30 Jul 1877, RG 94, File 4042, NARA.
[59] Quotes from Telgs, Drum to AG, 27 and 28 Jul 1877, respectively, RG 94, File 4042, NARA.
[60] Wilson, *Federal Aid in Domestic Disturbances*, p. 202; *Secretary of War Report, 1877*, p. 97.
[61] Eggert, *Railroad Labor Disputes*, pp. 34–35; Bruce, *1877*, p. 287.

A CAVALRY UNIT CHARGES THE MOB DURING THE CHICAGO RIOTING

president could authorize federal military intervention. Once marshals armed with court orders, but with few reliable deputies, had failed to reopen the lines, the judges turned to the president for federal troops. Hayes could either send troops under authority of RS 5298 or dispatch troops without a proclamation to act as a *posse comitatus*, to aid federal marshals to enforce the law and court orders. Using troops in this way, to enforce court injunctions against striking unions, was a landmark in the annals of the labor movement and in the history of civil disorders.[62]

Indiana

The first use of troops to enforce court orders and, in effect, to break a strike occurred in Indiana. From 20 to 24 July, strikers at Indianapolis halted all rail traffic. To prevent the possibility of mobs storming the federal arsenal, the Army sent a token force to Indianapolis and to nearby Louisville, Kentucky. But this force lacked the authority to intervene in the strike. Meanwhile, the receiver for the St. Louis & Southeastern, James H. Wilson, persuaded Judge Thomas Drummond, Seventh U.S. Circuit Court in Chicago, to order federal protection for railroads in receivership. On 24 July Drummond ruled that anyone obstructing a federally controlled railroad was in contempt of court. Following the lead of the circuit court, Judge Walter Q. Gresham of the U.S. District Court in Indianapolis directed the U.S. marshal for Indiana, Benjamin Spooner, to arrest strike leaders in that city.[63]

Unable to form a reliable posse among citizens predominantly sympathetic to the strikers, Spooner and Gresham asked the U.S. attorney general to obtain military aid.[64] Now the commander of the detachment guarding the federal arsenal in Indianapolis notified Hancock's headquarters on 24 July that "it is the opinion of the Governor, Judge Gresham, General Harrison and leading citizens that a force of three or four hundred troops ought to be sent . . . to save the city from a repetition of the Pittsburgh affair. The State militia consists of only three or four organized companies scattered over the State, and I do not think they are to be relied on."[65]

Following such reports, which indicated the situation was far worse than Washington previously believed, Gresham sent a "calculatedly frantic telegram" to Hayes on 25 July, declaring that "the situation here is most critical and dangerous. The state authorities are doing nothing, and the mob is the only supreme authority in the state at present. . . . There is so much sympathy with the strike and so much distrust of local authorities that I regard it impossible to get up [a posse]."[66]

Gresham's words, followed by an informal request for assistance from Governor James D. Williams on 27 July, moved Washington to action, although Hancock apparently had already dispatched Lt. Col. Henry A. Morrow, 13th Infantry, with two companies, to Indianapolis to protect the arsenals and, "if duly called upon [to act] as a *posse comitatus*, to preserve the peace."[67] Hayes approved Hancock's actions two days later, saying that "in cases where troops should be called by United States courts, they might be furnished." He warned that such employment of troops did not preclude officer's retaining

[62] Eggert, *Railroad Labor Disputes*, pp. 34–35; Bruce, *1877*, p. 287; Wilson, *Federal Aid in Domestic Disturbances*, pp. 9–10, discusses the federal railway acts.

[63] Bruce, *1877*, p. 287; Wilson, *Federal Aid in Domestic Disturbances*, p. 199.

[64] Telgs, Spooner to and Gresham to Atty Gen, both 24 Jul 1877, RG 60, Records of the Department of Justice, Source Chronological File: Indiana, NARA.

[65] Telg, Arnold to Hancock, 24 Jul 1877, RG 94, File 4042, NARA.

[66] Telg, Gresham to Hayes, 25 Jul 1877, Hayes Papers.

[67] Telgs, Hancock to Morrow, 26 Jul 1877, and McCrary to Hancock, 28 Jul 1877, both in RG 94, File 4042, NARA.

full tactical control over their men or first commanding the insurgents to "disperse and desist before making any arrests."[68] Later that same day Marshal Spooner asked for fifty men to serve writs to strikers blocking the Ohio & Mississippi Railroad in receivership in Vincennes, Indiana. Morrow sent two companies, commanded by Capt. John H. Page, to join Spooner's *posse comitatus*. The mere appearance of the soldiers ended the riot and, under the direction of the marshal, soldiers arrested strikebreakers who had ignored federal court orders.[69]

Following the success in Vincennes, Governor Williams asked Morrow for 600 regulars to end rioting in Terre Haute. When Williams inquired whether Morrow was authorized to grant such a request, the colonel realized for the first time that the president had never officially authorized military aid to Indiana state officials. While delaying action on the Terre Haute matter, Morrow telegraphed the commander of the Department of the Gulf, Col. Thomas H. Ruger, for additional instructions. The equally uninformed Ruger relayed the message to Hancock. After consultation with the War Department, Hancock informed Ruger that Morrow's original instructions remained in effect, but that in no case were federal troops to serve directly under Governor Williams. Since the anticipated Terre Haute action would not contradict his instructions, Captain Page, with Marshal Spooner, went from Vincennes to Terre Haute, where the mob of 3,000 to 4,000 strikers dispersed immediately upon their arrival, effectively ending the strike in Indiana.[70]

St. Louis General Strike

As in areas farther north and east, rail workers in East St. Louis, Illinois, went on strike on 21 July, and within hours virtually controlled the city. Shortly thereafter, across the Mississippi River, rail and other strikers in St. Louis, Missouri, under the leadership of a Socialist Workingman's Party (with Lasallean and Marxist factions) initiated the nation's first general strike. St. Louis railroad workers immediately met in convention to discuss goals and tactics. Although most speakers deprecated violence, they vowed to strike until management restored wages to former levels and inaugurated an eight-hour working day. In a burst of bravado one faction resolved to ask Congress for an appropriation of two or three hundred million dollars to be applied for the benefit of the working people.[71] Directed by a Central Executive Committee, the Workingman's Party nearly succeeded in supplanting civil authority, causing local officials to liken the job action to the Paris Commune of 1871. Even more so than elsewhere, the strikers in St. Louis enjoyed the support and sympathy of unemployed citizens who were not connected with the railroads.

While none of the bloodshed and property damage that characterized strikes in Pittsburgh, Baltimore, and Chicago marred the St. Louis area, the general strike, with its

---

[68] Wilson, *Federal Aid in Domestic Disturbances*, p. 200.

[69] Ibid., pp. 200, 327; Rich, *President and Civil Disorder*, pp. 78–79.

[70] Telgs, Morrow to HQ, U.S. Troops, Scranton, Pa., 26 Jul 1877; Hancock to McCrary, 29 and 30 Jul 1877; Hancock to AG, 30 and 31 Jul 1877; all in RG 94, File 4042, NARA. Wilson, *Federal Aid in Domestic Disturbances*, p. 200.

[71] Telg, Sgt Finn, Signal Corps, St. Louis, to Chief Signal Officer, WD, 24 Jul 1877, Hayes Papers; Russell M. Nolen, "The Labor Movement in St. Louis From 1860 to 1890," *Missouri Historical Review* 34 (1940):157–81.

themes of class struggle and social revolution, frightened property owners there much more than elsewhere. The St. Louis militia was intimidated and extremely weak, and the 360 local policemen "remained strangely inert during the upheaval."[72] By 21 July rail traffic and business in general were at a standstill. Federal receivers and Secretary of the Interior Carl Schurz, urged McCrary to intervene. Schurz wrote that "no United States Marshal, unless backed by Federal troops, can restore order or protect men willing to work . . . the presence of Federal troops will form a rallying point and do much to restore order."[73]

Swayed by this appeal, McCrary directed General Pope to protect railroads in receivership and promote peace by the judicious show of force, the same tactic applied elsewhere under the authority of RS 5298. Until the president agreed to a formal request for such aid from the governor of Missouri, however, Pope was to take no part in suppressing insurrection against state laws. The general thereupon wired Col. Jefferson C. Davis, 23d Infantry, to take six companies from Fort Leavenworth and proceed to St. Louis to protect federal property, the only legal means at that point for dispatching troops to the city without a request for aid from state officials. He also arranged, during the next two days, for six companies from the 16th and 19th Infantry regiments to leave posts in Kansas, Colorado, and the Oklahoma Indian Territory to join Davis. Two of the new companies brought Gatling guns.[74]

Leaving immediately, Davis and his six companies, "all bronzed and hardy looking," entered St. Louis on 24 July without resistance. After announcing to the crowds that his troops would merely protect government and public property, not quell the strikers or run the trains, Davis' force encamped at an old arsenal two miles south of the business district. Three more companies arrived later that day, followed by three more the next day, bringing the total to 42 officers and 410 men.[75] Although under explicit orders to protect only federal property, Davis saw other opportunities to help local and state officials. He was perhaps the only officer during the strike who encouraged civilians to take arms and enforce state laws being violated by strikers. Restrained from direct action in St. Louis, he met with the mayor and a citizens' committee of safety, promised federal arms, and urged the civilians to exhaust their own resources before calling upon the federal government for troops. The mayor and the committee accepted his offer and from 24 to 28 July, 3,000 federally armed vigilantes, aided by the frequent appearance of Army units, began to bring the strikers under control, primarily through armed intimidation, for they encountered no substantial resistance.[76] Davis' unilateral and unauthorized intervention and his provision of federal arms to private citizens did not elicit any sort of reaction or comment from his superiors, probably because it reduced the need for federal intervention.

Meanwhile, events across the Mississippi River in East St. Louis required Davis' attention. On 26 July rioters in East St. Louis, Illinois, had seized the Eads Bridge spanning the Mississippi River and the tracks of two railroads in federal receivership, the Ohio

---

[72] Bruce, *1877*, pp. 258–59.

[73] Ibid. See also Burbank, *Reign of the Rabble*, pp. 1–2.

[74] Telg, AG, Dept of the Missouri, Ft. Leavenworth, to Davis, 23 Jul 1877, RG 94, File 4042, NARA; *Secretary of War Report, 1877*, p. 97; Cooper, *The Army and Civil Disorder*, p. 59.

[75] Telg, Sgt Finn to Chief Signal Officer, 24 Jul 1877, Hayes Papers.

[76] Telg, Davis to AG, 30 Aug 1877, RG 94, File 4042, NARA; Cooper, *The Army and Civil Disorder*, pp. 65–66; Burbank, *Reign of the Rabble*, pp. 60, 158.

& Mississippi and the St. Louis & Southeastern. In response to a request from St. Louis federal Judge Samuel Treat to reopen the roads, the War Department had Davis and his men report for duty as a *posse comitatus* of the deputy U.S. marshal.[77]

Illinois Governor Cullom, silent on the subject of East St. Louis since the troubles began there, now requested federal military aid, admitting that the Illinois National Guard was "inchoate and almost entirely without military equipment." Suspecting that he had not exhausted state resources, Hayes refused the request and confined Davis' troops to enforcement of the mandates of the federal courts and the protection of federal property. After consultation with the marshal, Davis crossed the Mississippi River to the Pittsburg landing at East St. Louis on the same day. Under the command of Lt. Col. R. I. Dodge, all eight companies of the 23d Infantry marched to their field headquarters at the local relay depot. Under Col. C. E. Smith, companies of the 16th and 19th Infantry subsequently landed at the eastern end of the St. Louis bridge and marched off to join the 23d Infantry.[78]

Though part of the *posse comitatus*, Davis' command still took orders from a chain of command extending to Washington. President Hayes directed General Pope to have Davis station his men in East St. Louis in the vicinity of apprehended trouble and display force for moral effect. Beyond the protection of federal property and the enforcement of federal court orders, he was to do nothing else. In a pressing emergency, he was to telegraph for further orders but could act immediately if the conditions permitted no delay.[79]

The appearance of 400 heavily armed regulars intimidated the strikers, who did not resist. As in St. Louis, the strike in East St. Louis had been conducted without bloodshed or property damage. Federal marshals arrested 27 strikers, releasing all but 2 the following day. The "moral effect" of the federal troops on the city convinced strikers to begin talks with railroad officials about resolving the work stoppage, and on 29 July the strike ended. Within a day freight trains resumed movement, and by 2 August business returned to normal. One week later Pope ordered Davis to retire the companies on a staggered schedule. The last units in Illinois and Missouri returned to their stations by 20 August 1877. Their departure marked the end of the nationwide strike.[80]

Little changed in the aftermath of this violent upheaval. Nationwide, the violence and destruction had severely frightened business, political, and military leaders. Although urban riots were not new to the United States, never before were federal troop deployments required on so broad a scale or over so wide a territory. Many viewed the riots as the beginning of class warfare, nurtured by aliens and by Socialist and anarchist teachings from abroad. Citizens called upon state legislatures and Congress to expand state militias and the U.S. Army to deal more effectively with the threat of social revolution.[81] Now more so than ever before, businessmen began to see both the Regular Army and the militia as allies

---

[77] Telg, Treat to Hayes, 27 Jul 1877, RG 94, File 4042, NARA.

[78] Quote from Burbank, *Reign of the Rabble*, p. 153; Telg, Davis to AG, 30 Aug 1877, RG 94.

[79] Telg, McCrary to Pope, 28 Jul 1877, RG 94, File 4042, NARA.

[80] Telg, Davis to AG, 30 Aug 1877, RG 94; Wilson, *Federal Aid in Domestic Disturbances*, p. 203; Burbank, *Reign of the Rabble*, pp. 153–54; Dacus, *Annals of the Great Strike*, p. 364.

[81] Mortimer D. Leggett, "The Military and the Mob," *Sketches of War History, 1861–1865: Paper Before the Ohio Commandery of the Military Order of the Loyal Legion of the United States* (Cincinnati: Robert Clark, 1888), 1:192–93; Cooper, *The Army and Civil Disorder*, p. 144; Garraty, *New Commonwealth*, pp. 159–60. The National Guard Association is a private organization that was formed in 1879 to promote the National Guard.

in future strikebreaking operations. In Congress, friends of the Army argued for increased appropriations to support its new mission as a peacekeeping constabulary.

Secretary of War McCrary quickly acted upon this favorable opinion to attempt to break congressional limitations on Army manpower. In his annual report he argued that in an age of increasing unrest among the unemployed or impoverished urban masses "the Army is to the United States what a well-disciplined and trained police force is to a city."[82] He recommended granting to the president emergency powers to expand the size of Army companies from 30 to 100 men and proposed establishment of garrisons near each industrial city.

McCrary's words were echoed by the soldiers themselves. James H. Wilson, a railroad man and former general, wrote: "It will be remembered that the very foundations of government were threatened, and that order gave place to anarchy, till the federal courts called the regular Army to assist . . . in enforcing obedience to the law." The Army, he continued, "has been instrumental in saving the government in more than one great emergency." Once order was restored, General Hancock reflected that federal troops had done an outstanding job of restoring the peace without bloodshed and without firing a shot. "The troops," he stated, "have lost the government no prestige." In a letter to General Schofield, however, he predicted later that "'this thing' will appear again, and at that time, it will be necessary that the states have a well organized militia, of force and power, that it be used promptly, or that the Federal Government shall have the means of commanding—or the next time this comes, I judge from the passions I have seen outcrop, society may be shaken to its foundations."[83] Efforts to enlarge the Army ran counter, nonetheless, to prevailing sentiment among Southern critics of Reconstruction. The Democratic majority in the House voted instead to restrict the Army to its existing size. Until the next great nationwide strike in 1894, Congress left the burden of handling labor disturbances to the police and the state militias, providing no additional funds to the Army for dealing with such disputes.[84]

The Army itself did little to prepare for the future conflagration Hancock and others predicted. Although officers had learned a number of tactical lessons from strike duty and wrote of those experiences in contemporary military journals, no official doctrine developed. Army intervention in labor disputes was considered by many military officers to be such a rare and extraordinary duty that it did not require specific doctrine or tactics. Col. Elwell Otis expressed the problem when he stated that riot duty was unpleasant "not because of the details in themselves, which it [the Army] was actually required to perform, but because of the exceeding delicacy of the duty, and the vagueness of expressed law to guide action under circumstances that were liable at any time to arise." A civil disturbance doctrine would not begin to emerge until a further rail strike paralyzed the nation in 1894.[85]

---

[82] *Secretary of War Report, 1877*, pp. v–vi.

[83] Initial quote from James H. Wilson, "Size and Organization of Armies," *International Review* 5 (January–February 1878):515; all other quotes from Cooper, *The Army and Civil Disorder*, pp. 61, 82–83.

[84] *Secretary of War Report, 1877*, pp. v–vi; Ekirch, *The Civilian and the Military*, pp. 116–18.

[85] Elwell S. Otis, "The Army in Connection With the Labor Riots," *Journal of the Military Service Institution of the United States* 5 (1884):311. Among the more pertinent works are E. L. Molineaux, "Riots in Cities and Their Suppression," *Journal of the Military Service Institution of the United States* 4 (1883):355–70; Richard W. Young, *Legal and Tactical Considerations Affecting the Employment of the Military in the Suppression of Mobs Including an Essay on Martial Law* (New York: Public Service Publishing, 1888); Leggett, "The Military and the Mob."

On the federal executive level, the outbreak of strikes and riots in several states initially caught Hayes' administration unprepared. The president and his advisers had to resolve by trial and error questions involving the legal bases for intervention, command and control, civil-military relations in the states, and the necessary degree of military force to be used. Considering the lack of any applicable precedent in labor disputes, Hayes' response was restrained, moderate, and legal.

The administration committed federal troops under three legal justifications: to aid state officials (West Virginia, Maryland, and Pennsylvania) to suppress "domestic violence" or insurrection, as authorized in Section 4, Article IV, of the Constitution and Revised Statute 5297; to protect federal property (Philadelphia, Chicago, St. Louis, and Indianapolis), a right recognized as an executive responsibility under RS 5298; and to aid federal marshals (Indiana, Pennsylvania, Missouri, and Illinois) as a *posse comitatus*, enforcing the faithful execution of the laws of the United States, in this case the orders of federal courts acting for railroads and other properties in federal receivership as authorized by RS 5298. Few could question the legal authority of the president in committing the troops. Army intervention in the strike of 1877 was legally justified and supportable.

Yet Hayes, though he committed federal troops to suppress riotous strikers and the unemployed, was aware of the need to solve the causes of the strikes. He believed that the federal executive treated the symptoms of unrest and not the disease itself. "Shall the railroads govern the country, or shall the people govern the railroads?" he asked later. Leaving no doubt as to how he felt, he stated that "this is a government of the people, by the people, and for the people no longer. It is a government of corporations, by corporations, and for corporations. How is this? . . . The governmental policy should be to prevent the accumulation of vast fortunes, and monopolies, so dangerous in control, should be held firmly in the grip of people. . . . Free government cannot long endure if property is largely in a few hands and large masses of people are unable to earn homes, education, and support in old age."[86] But significant changes in attitudes concerning wealth, property, and business-labor relations were still decades away.

Besides the broad questions of law and policy, the strikes raised practical issues of command and control. Since the Great Railway Strike of 1877 disrupted railroad and telegraphic communications, the Hayes administration could not always exercise timely control over events. Messages to the cabinet bearing intelligence on the various strikes often arrived too late to be acted upon. Hayes consequently entrusted federal forces to state governors in some areas (West Virginia, Maryland, Pennsylvania) and to regional federal military commanders in others (Hancock). In the beginning Hancock hesitated to put his command under Governor Hartranft of Pennsylvania. Influenced by Hancock's argument that governors forfeited their authority when they requested outside aid, Hayes gave Hancock supreme authority in the Department of the East. But in Pittsburgh Hartranft proved that at least one governor could effectively marshal state and federal forces to restore order. Hayes nonetheless changed his mind about turning federal troops over to state officials and in the Midwest refused to allow federal forces to be put under state control. Instead, federal troops were sent to protect federal property and to aid federal marshals to enforce court orders, thereby attempting to avoid the

---

[86] Quote from Weibe, *Search for Order*, p. 45. See also Bruce, *1877*, p. 320.

thorny, legally murky civil-military issues involved in putting federal military forces under state civil authorities.

The main goal of the Hayes administration was to restore order as quickly as possible with a minimum of violence or bloodshed, not to end the railroad strike or to operate the railroads. Troops were not intentionally committed to act as strikebreakers, and in most cases served Hayes' purpose by their mere presence. By the time federal troops reached the scenes of tumult in the wake of militias, crowd violence had largely abated. Already exhausted by bloody struggles with militiamen, crowds gave up new efforts at violence when confronted by fresh, disciplined, and heavily armed professional soldiers. That federal troops were few in number, relative to the militia, did not minimize the effectiveness of their moral influence. Regulars were a symbol of the nation's determination to end lawlessness.

Acting under precise orders, commanders did not compromise the moral force of federal troops by overusing them or placing them in situations where they might be overwhelmed. Showing maximum restraint, officers generally committed their men in sizable contingents and confined their activities to protecting railways in receivership, confronting mobs only when police or militia were unable or unwilling to do so. The regulars never fired into crowds during the 1877 riots, and the U.S. Army, unlike the various militias and police forces, killed no rioters. Army intervention produced a quick and relatively nonviolent end to the strike, as Hayes had hoped. It also established an Army internal defense mission and a firm precedent for the future domestic use of regular federal military forces in labor disputes and civil disorders.

CHAPTER 3

Lawlessness in the Trans-Mississippi West, 1878–1892

In the new and sparsely populated regions of the West, to say to robbers and thieves that they shall not be taken on writ unless the sheriff and his local posse is able to capture them without aid from soldiers, is almost to grant them immunity from arrest. In these regions the Army is the power chiefly relied upon by the law-abiding people for protection.
—Secretary of War George W. McCrary, 1878.

A second region where federal troops were employed to control domestic disorder was the trans-Mississippi West. The end of the Civil War and the construction of transcontinental railroads opened the Great Plains and foothills of the Rockies to a dramatic influx of people. For twenty-five years the legendary "Cattle Kingdom" flourished in this area until superseded by advancing farm and mining frontiers in the 1880s and 1890s. The forces of law and order were spread thin among this population of farmers, ranchers, and miners, who often took the law into their own hands. There were frequent and bloody clashes between organized groups of cattlemen, sheepherders, and farmers. Cattle barons attempted to monopolize grazing lands and water sources, hiring gunmen to subdue smaller ranchers and farmers who opposed them. Mining and railroad magnates attempted to keep profits high, workers unorganized, and wages low, often through the use of violent methods, and by importing Oriental labor. In addition, roving bands of outlaws infested many areas, robbing and killing at will.

Law enforcement rested in the hands of territorial governments that lacked the resources to deal with these problems in the vast, sparsely populated West. The normal law enforcement machinery consisted of federal marshals, responsible for serving the writs of federal judges, and of county sheriffs, responsible for enforcing territorial laws. Federal and local officials were few and could not cope with outbreaks of organized violence or the depredations of outlaw gangs. Civilian posses were seldom effective, territorial militias were virtually nonexistent, and marshals came to rely on the nearest federal military posts for aid. Commanders in the West, prior to 1878, often responded to requests for assistance by lawmen under the Cushing Doctrine of 1854 and provided troops without reference to higher authority. As posse members, federal troops remained under the orders and command of their officers, who acted on the request or advice of local lawmen.

The situation changed with the passage of the Posse Comitatus Act in June 1878, which specifically repudiated the Cushing Doctrine. This legislation was formulated because of Southern resentments stemming from the use of federal troops to enforce the many laws created by Radical Republicans in Congress during Reconstruction. Often, it was believed, federal troops had been misused in the south during the 1860s and 1870s by federal and state authorities, especially in policing elections and enforcing civil rights laws. It was also the contention of many congressmen that federal troops were still being used by local officials whose authority to do so was dubious and that if these practices were not halted by specific legislation they would escalate in number. The Posse Comitatus Act was an attempt by the federal legislative branch to control more tightly the powers of the executive to use the Army as a law enforcement agency and to ensure that "troops could not be used on any lesser authority than that of the president" acting in accordance with the Constitution and laws created by Congress. Attached to the Army appropriations bill, Section 15 of the Act of Congress, 18 June 1878, read: "From and after passage of this act it shall be unlawful to employ any part of the Army of the United States as a *posse comitatus*, or otherwise, for the purpose of executing the laws, except in such cases and under such circumstances as such employment of said force may be expressly authorized by the Constitution or by act of Congress."[1]

Any person violating this law was subject to a $10,000 fine, two years imprisonment, or both. The act sought to define legal responsibilities for the use of federal troops and to determine the extent of tactical control under civil officials. The act clearly delineated and prohibited policies previously implied under the Judiciary Act of 1789 (as well as the Militia Acts of 1792, 1795, and 1807; Section 3, Article II of the Constitution; the Cushing Doctrine of 1854; and the Civil Rights Acts of 1866, 1870, and 1871), namely "that the marshal appointed for a judicial district 'shall have the power to command all necessary assistance in the execution of his duty,'" including, if necessary, federal troops. From 1878 on, each legal intervention of federal troops had to be expressly authorized by Congress or justified under existing statutes.[2]

The immediate effect of the act in the West was that local commanders could no longer dispatch federal troops for law enforcement purposes on their own authority. If territorial officials wanted military aid, they were required to request it from the president. Although most territorial governors were unaware of it, they were not authorized aid under the provisions of the Constitution and federal statutes that guaranteed states protection against domestic violence (RS 5297). Territories were not states, but the president could legally use regulars in territorial law enforcement under RS 5298, dealing with rebellions against federal authority "too powerful to be overcome by the ordinary course of judicial proceedings"; RS 1984, RS 1989, and RS 1991, dealing with civil rights protections; and under the Acts of 1 July 1862, 2 July 1864, and 27 July 1866, protecting transcontinental rail routes from interference as "military roads" and postal routes.[3]

---

[1] For the Cushing Doctrine and Posse Comitatus Act, see Coakley, *Role of Federal Military Forces*, pp. 132–33, 342–43; see also 20 *U.S. Statutes at Large*, 152; Dowell, *Military Aid to the Civil Power*, p. 203.

[2] Attorney General Charles Devens, who reviewed President Hayes' response in the Great Railway Strike, determined that his use of federal troops conformed to the Posse Comitatus Act. For a detailed explanation of the laws that existed before the *U.S. Revised Statutes of 1874* affecting civil disturbance interventions, see Coakley, *Role of Federal Military Forces*.

[3] Wilson, *Federal Aid in Domestic Disturbances*, pp. 5–10.

Yet the whole procedure of requesting aid was complex and time consuming, making the impact of the Posse Comitatus Act greater in the West than elsewhere. In effect it required federal commanders to acquire through civilian and military channels specific authorization to act, meaning in many cases that they were unable to offer timely and needed assistance. When combined with the perennial lack of manpower and the need to control hostile Indians, the new act interfered with the Army's ability to support local and territorial law enforcement officials.

Lincoln County, New Mexico, 1878–1879

The effects of the new law were first evident in Lincoln County, New Mexico. In 1878, several months before its passage, two factions, each accurately claiming a degree of legal and moral justification, had begun vying for economic hegemony using hired gunfighters. Initially, the Army entered this extraordinarily complex struggle with little knowledge of the situation or its background. Instead of interposing federal troops between the warring factions as a neutral force, successive commanders supported those factions the positions of which they regarded as the most lawful or, in their eyes, the most just. Passage of the new law ended this subjective use of troops and left peacekeeping in Lincoln County to inept sheriffs. The reputation of the local sheriffs, and the Army's apparent paralysis, produced chaos and anarchy that soon attracted outlaws from neighboring counties and from Texas and Mexico.

The dispute, known as the Lincoln County war, had begun when two ranchers, cattleman John Chisum and an Englishman named John Tunstall, challenged the well-established economic monopoly of the "House of Murphy" in Lincoln County.[4] Through connections with the "Santa Fe Ring," the dominant political and economic force in the territorial capital, Lawrence G. Murphy and his associates John J. Dolan and James H. Riley established a monopoly over all trade, including beef contracts with the Army, and nearly every other mercantile enterprise, in Lincoln County. When Chisum and Tunstall set up a rival general store in the county seat of Lincoln, Dolan resorted to political connivance, legal harassment, and physical force to preserve his monopoly. This campaign culminated in the shooting death of the 24-year-old Tunstall on 18 February 1878, by a deputized posse of Dolan employees, acting under the authority of Lincoln County Sheriff William Brady.[5]

To prevent retaliation by Chisum and Tunstall's lawyer, Alexander McSween, Dolan prevailed upon Brady to ask the commander at nearby Fort Stanton, Lt. Col. George A. Purington, 9th Cavalry, to send a detachment into Lincoln for a few days to keep the peace, as was customary in the days before the Posse Comitatus Act.[6] In the meantime, however, McSween convinced the local justice of the peace to swear out murder warrants for the posse members, including Dolan, and a larceny warrant for Brady, who, McSween

---

[4] For Tunstall, see Frederick Nolan, ed., *The Life and Death of John Henry Tunstall* (Albuquerque: University of New Mexico Press, 1965).

[5] For Brady, see Donald Lavash, *Sheriff William Brady: Tragic Hero of the Lincoln County War* (Sante Fe: Sunstone Press, 1986).

[6] For McSween, see Robert M. Utley, *Four Fighters of Lincoln County* (Albuquerque: University of New Mexico Press, 1986), pp. 1–19.

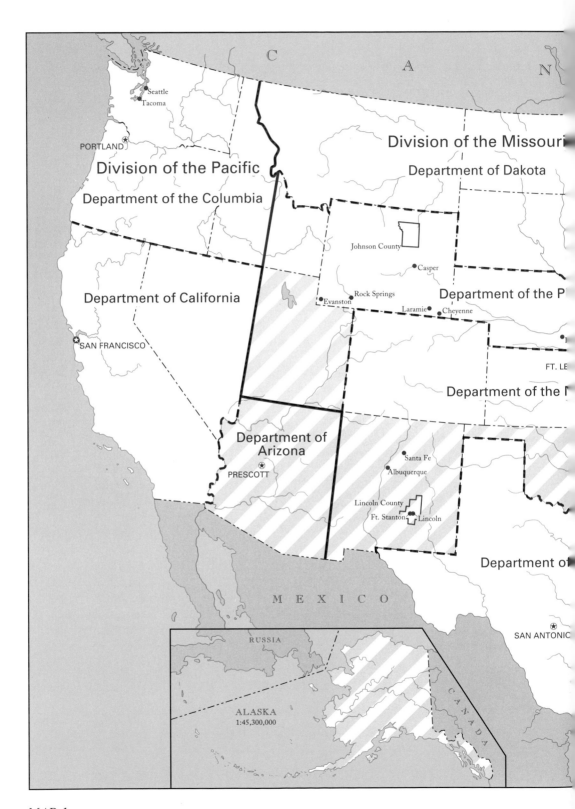

MAP 1

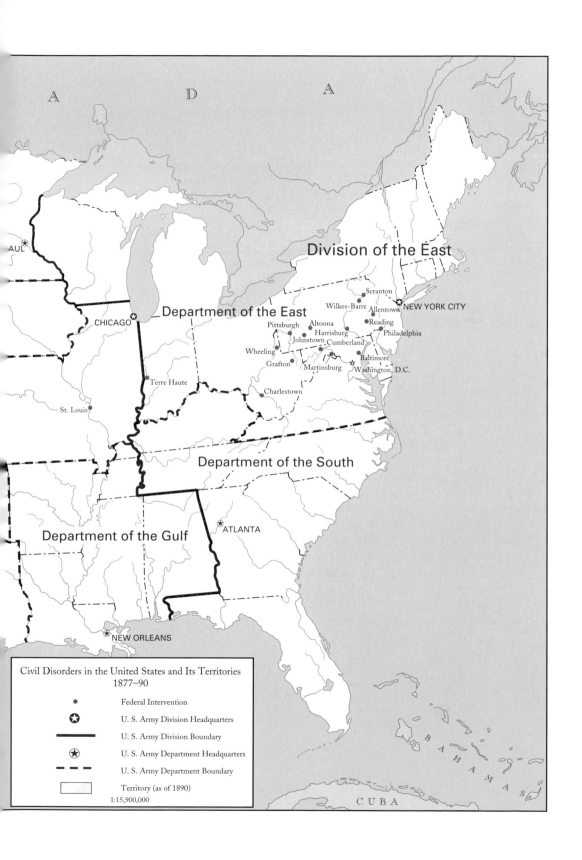

Division of the East

Department of the East

Department of the South

Department of the Gulf

Scranton
Wilkes-Barre   Allentown   NEW YORK CITY
Pittsburgh   Altoona   Reading
Harrisburg   Philadelphia
Johnstown   Cumberland
Wheeling   Baltimore
Grafton   Martinsburg   Washington, D.C.
Charlestown

CHICAGO

Terre Haute

St. Louis

AUL

ATLANTA

NEW ORLEANS

A   D   A

BAHAMAS

CUBA

Civil Disorders in the United States and Its Territories
1877–90

- • Federal Intervention
- ✪ U. S. Army Division Headquarters
- —— U. S. Army Division Boundary
- ✪ U. S. Army Department Headquarters
- --- U. S. Army Department Boundary
- ▢ Territory (as of 1890)

1:15,900,000

FORT STANTON, NEW MEXICO TERRITORY, c. 1878

claimed, had stolen property from Tunstall. Thus both factions claimed legal justification for their subsequent actions.[7]

Random interventions by federal troops failed to end the troubles, which recurred whenever they withdrew and persisted until they returned. Hence, the Dolan faction turned to territorial Governor Samuel B. Axtell, who asked Purington's superior, Col. Edward Hatch, 9th Cavalry, and commander of the District of New Mexico, for a permanent garrison of federal troops for Lincoln. When Hatch declined to approve such long-term aid without orders from the secretary of war, based on an official request to the president, Axtell wrote to Hayes on 4 March 1878. With Hayes' permission, Secretary McCrary sent orders instructing that Purington's troops remain in Lincoln for as long as needed. With these orders, Purington continued to support Sheriff Brady, who, although a Dolan partisan, was the only legally recognized law enforcement official of any significant authority. Purington even provided military escorts when Brady removed pro-McSween officials from local office, though he made no similar effort to arrest men suspected of murdering Tunstall.[8]

---

[7] Robert M. Utley, *High Noon in Lincoln: Violence on the Western Frontier* (Albuquerque: University of New Mexico Press, 1987), pp. 54–55; Ltr, Brooke Herfore to Lt Gen Philip H. Sheridan, Div of the Missouri, 4 Apr 1878, sub: Factional Strife in Lincoln County, and Telg, Purington to AG, USA, HQ, Dist of New Mexico, Santa Fe, 6 Mar 1878, RG 94, File 1405 AGO 1878: Lincoln County War, NARA.

[8] Telgs, Axtell to Hayes, 4 Mar 1878; McCrary to Sherman, 5 Mar 1878; Sherman to Sheridan, 5 Mar 1878; Purington to AG, HQ, Dist of New Mexico, 29 Mar 1878. All in RG 94, File 1405, NARA. See also Maurice G. Fulton, *History of the Lincoln County War* (Tuscon: University of Arizona Press, 1968), pp. 162–64, 171. For territorial politics, see Calvin Horn, *New Mexico's Troubled Years: The Story of Early Territorial Governors* (Albuquerque: Horn & Wallace, 1963).

These actions enraged Tunstall's supporters, who formed a group known as the Regulators, which included William H. Bonney, alias "Billy the Kid."[9] Shortly thereafter, the Regulators entered Lincoln, then ambushed and killed Brady. At the request of Deputy Sheriff George A. Peppin, soon to become Brady's successor, Purington returned and helped to arrest McSween's men as suspects, while his troops, without warrants, searched McSween's house for evidence. This action prompted Dr. Montague P. Leverson, a friend of both McSween's and President Hayes', to write several letters of complaint to Secretary of the Interior Carl Schurz, the federal official responsible for the administration of federal territories. Meanwhile, the British embassy in Washington, D.C., also pressed the Hayes administration for an investigation into Tunstall's death, since he was a British subject.[10]

NATHANIEL A. DUDLEY

Irritated by McSween-faction allegations of Purington's partisanship, Hatch replaced him on 5 April 1878 with Lt. Col. Nathaniel A. ("N. A. M.") Dudley, 9th Cavalry. The new commander was a 23-year veteran of Army service who had faced disciplinary action on several occasions and had recently been court-martialed and relieved of command at Fort Union. He has been described by one historian as a man who suffered "from muddled thought and bad judgement, the result of mediocre endowments impaired by years of dissipation," who "compensated for his deficiencies with pomposity, bellicosity, petty despotism, and an extraordinary aptitude for contention." Strangely, considering the allegations of partisanship against Purington, Dudley accepted the political realities in Lincoln at face value without further investigation of the merits or issues of the conflict. He replicated Purington's actions and began to support the Dolan faction soon after his arrival. From April until July, his men repeatedly aided deputies in arresting McSween supporters, even though "the Army's Judge Advocate General had written an opinion holding Dudley's activities . . . to be unconstitutional." When these activities were reported to Army Commanding General William T. Sherman, Hatch was immediately ordered to withdraw all federal troops from the town. Governor Axtell interceded, however, and prevailed upon Sherman to delay the removal. In the meantime, Dudley's men continued to aid the sheriff by serving arrest warrants and by conducting searches. Impatient with the sheriff's slow

---

[9] For Bonney, see Robert M. Utley, *Billy the Kid: A Short and Violent Life* (Lincoln: University of Nebraska Press, 1989); Utley, *Four Fighters of Lincoln County*, pp. 21–39.

[10] Telgs, Axtell to Hayes, 4 Mar 1878; McCrary to Sherman, 5 Mar 1878; Sherman to Sheridan, 5 Mar 1878; Purington to AG, HQ, Dist of New Mexico, 29 Mar 1878; all in RG 94. Fulton, *Lincoln County War*, pp. 162–64, 171; Utley, *High Noon in Lincoln*, p. 74.

pace, Dudley allegedly browbeat Justice of the Peace D. M. Easton into making him a "special constable" with power to have his men make arrests entirely on their own.[11]

On 18 June, the day Congress enacted the Posse Comitatus Act, Sheriff Peppin asked Dudley for a military posse to pursue a party of McSween men taking refuge near San Patricio, a small town about six miles southeast of Lincoln. The men were wanted on charges of having killed a Dolan man while he camped on a federally protected Indian reservation. Unaware of the Posse Comitatus Act, Dudley, according to standard procedure, sent a detachment of thirty-five men in pursuit. Several weeks later, as the cavalrymen approached the fugitives in the mountains outside San Patricio, word of the new law reached Hatch in the form of General Order 49 of 7 July 1878, and he ordered Dudley to recall the posse immediately and to cease further aid to civil officials without specific permission from higher authority.[12]

Although the Posse Comitatus Act precluded Dudley from providing men for Peppin's posses, he intervened one last time to aid the Dolan faction during the "Five Days Battle" of 15–19 July. McSween, weary of the chase by Peppin's posse and Dolan's gunmen, decided to confront both in Lincoln. On 15 July, sixty of his men entered town, half taking positions in McSween's well-barricaded house and the remainder occupying smaller buildings nearby. A three-day gunfight ensued, characterized by sporadic firing throughout the town. Knowing that he was outnumbered, Peppin rode to Fort Stanton to seek federal military help. When he asked for a mountain cannon to dislodge the McSween party, Dudley responded that "you are acting strictly within the provisions of the duty incumbent upon you" and if he were not encumbered by the Posse Comitatus Act, he "would most gladly give you every man and material [sic] at my post to sustain you in your present position believing it to be strictly legal."[13] Peppin, however, returned empty handed to Lincoln.

Dudley soon changed his mind, having realized that Peppin lacked the firepower needed to dislodge the McSween men and to restore order. In consultation with his officers, he decided to send a large force to Lincoln to protect property and the lives of women and children. Dudley then led an estimated fifty regulars into Lincoln on 19 July, the fifth and final day of the battle, and set up temporary headquarters in Wortley's Hotel. There he explained to Peppin that the troops could neither take sides nor make arrests, but would protect women and children. Then he announced that if either side fired shots at his men, he would demand surrender of the guilty parties. Refusal would be met with return fire to include rounds from a mountain howitzer and a Gatling gun.[14]

Accounts of Dudley's ensuing actions conflict, depending upon the observers. His supporters, including subordinate officers and members of the Dolan faction, maintained

---

[11] Quotes from Utley, *High Noon in Lincoln*, pp. 66–67, 84. See also Telgs, Sherman to Sheridan, 15 Apr 1878; Pope to Hatch, 23 and 24 Apr 1878; Thomas Dale and G. W. Smith to Dudley, 1 May 1878; D. M. Easton to Dudley, 1 May 1878; Hatch to Dudley and reply, 4 May 1878. All in RG 94, File 1405, NARA. Fulton, *Lincoln County War*, pp. 208, 228–29. For Dudley, see Utley, *Four Fighters of Lincoln County*, pp. 41–59.

[12] Affidavit of Sheriff G. W. Peppin, Special Deputy U.S. Marshal, 15 Aug 1878, RG 94, File 1405, NARA; Fulton, *Lincoln County War*, pp. 232–35; Larry D. Ball, *The United States Marshals of New Mexico and Arizona Territories, 1846–1912* (Albuquerque: University of New Mexico Press, 1978), p. 91.

[13] Quote from Utley, *High Noon Lincoln*, p. 93; Court of Inquiry Into Case of Lt Col N. A. M. Dudley (Lincoln County War), 15 Oct 1879 (hereafter cited as Dudley Inquiry), RG 153, File QQ 1284, Box 1923, Exhibit 49, JAG Office, 1812–1938, NARA.

[14] Dudley Inquiry, pp. 538, 883, RG 153; Fulton, *Lincoln County War*, pp. 258–61.

that without provocation McSween's men opened fire on a three-man military patrol recon-noitering the town to determine the safety of their nearby campsite. Mrs. McSween and other witnesses, however, maintained that as soon as Dudley arrived he immediately went to the aid of Peppin's forces and that federal troops escorted Peppin's deputies close to the McSween house, providing covering fire while they piled up combustible materials near the building to burn out McSween and his men. Moreover, Mrs. McSween claimed that when she visited Dudley to protest the partisan actions of his men, he was insulting and made veiled threats to bombard the house with his howitzer if the occupants dared to fire at any of his men. In addition, he had refused to intervene as a neutral intermediary or to consider allowing McSween's party to surrender to him rather than to Peppin.[15]

It is unknown whether McSween's men provoked the final round of firing, but Peppin's force began shooting into the house. When the blaze they had ignited finally forced the defenders out into the open, Peppin's deputies opened fire, killing McSween and four others. Billy the Kid and several more men escaped. The next day members of the posse and Dolan's supporters looted the Tunstall store after Dudley's troops left.

The role of federal troops in the actual firing of the McSween House and killing of McSween is unclear, although his followers later testified that Dudley's troops not only aided in setting fire to the house, but also lent covering fire during the final attack. This is not corroborated, although Dudley's mere presence in Lincoln and his refusal to attempt to defuse the situation without bloodshed seem to indicate that his sympathies clearly lay with the Peppin-Dolan faction. Dudley steadfastly maintained that his activities indicated nothing but impartiality and strict neutrality. The death of McSween and the ensuing destruction of the Tunstall-McSween holdings virtually ended the feud. After the Five Days Battle, when Peppin reported the death of McSween, Dudley allegedly replied, "Thank God for that . . . if it weren't for me, you would not have succeeded in your undertaking."[16]

In spite of the appearance of calm, Billy the Kid had escaped to regroup McSween's followers. In addition, about 200 outlaws from Texas and Mexico, having heard of the anar-chy in Lincoln County, soon arrived in search of opportunities for plunder. Except for the unique situation of the Five Days Battle, when Dudley contrived a pretext for intervention, the Posse Comitatus Act prevented him from rendering military support to combat these new lawbreakers. Taking advantage of the Army's paralysis, outlaws adopted hit-and-run tactics against peaceful Indians, isolated ranchers, and unsuspecting travelers. Highway robbery, arson, rape, and murder prevailed from August to October 1878—a powerful tes-timony to the need for a territorial militia to enforce the law once the Posse Comitatus Act forbade such actions by federal troops.[17]

A candid report written by Dudley's surgeon at Fort Stanton summarized the new trou-bles in New Mexico and the Army's helplessness under existing restraints, stating that

---

[15] Dudley Inquiry, pp. 216–32, 262–63, RG 153; Utley, *High Noon Lincoln*, p. 100.

[16] Quote from Dudley Inquiry, pp. 258–61; see also ibid., pp. 283–85, 320–21, RG 153; Utley, *High Noon in Lincoln*, pp. 107–10.

[17] Affidavit of Peppin, 15 Aug 1878, RG 94; Telgs, Dudley to Axtell, 15 Aug 1878, and Axtell to Hayes, 20 Aug 1878, both in RG 94, File 1405, NARA; Ltr, AG, HQ, Dist of New Mexico, to Dudley, 15 Aug 1878, RG 393, Records of the United States Army Continental Commands, 1821–1920, Ltrs Sent, Dist of New Mexico, NARA; Wilson, *Federal Aid in Domestic Disturbances*, pp. 207–08; Fulton, *Lincoln County War*, p. 294.

the war is no longer the . . . war of Dolan versus McSween, but seems . . . confined to depredations and murder by a band of miscreants who have probably been attracted from all parts of the country by the knowledge of the inability of the authorities, civil or military, to afford protection. . . . There is also a strong feeling against the military authorities for failing to afford protection, and it is hard to convince . . . citizens . . . that there is any necessity in keeping a strong military post almost within gunshot of the scenes of the disturbances without raising a hand for their protection."[18]

Federal officials acknowledged that the Posse Comitatus Act, by prohibiting the use of regulars by civil officials without presidential authorization, had made law enforcement difficult in Lincoln County and throughout the West. Maj. Gen. John Pope, commander of the Department of the Missouri, lamented that under the act "soldiers had to stand by and see houses containing women and children attacked," while Hayes noted in his diary that "the Government is a good deal crippled" by prohibitions on the use of the Army as a *posse comitatus* to aid U.S. officers.[19] The situation was such that even Axtell finally requested aid from Hayes. After stating that he had no authority to call for volunteers and that the territorial legislature could not be convened in time to act, Axtell summed up the crimes transpiring daily: "Many men have been murdered and several women and young girls, mere children, have been ravished. . . . One of the bandit leaders, on being asked from where he came replied, 'We are devils, just come from hell.'"[20]

While Hayes contemplated Axtell's request, Dudley complained to Hatch about a group of outlaws from Texas known as Wrestlers who robbed and killed citizens regardless of factional allegiances. Dudley wanted to protect stagecoaches carrying the mails and to arrest or kill outlaws caught attacking them. In addition, he requested permission to mount punitive expeditions anywhere in the territory.[21]

But it was Secretary McCrary who responded to the general deterioration of law enforcement throughout the western territories. In an order issued on 1 October 1878, he reiterated the restrictions of the Posse Comitatus Act but also allowed some leeway for the emergency use of troops as posses under military control. He wrote:

If time permits a detailed application will be forwarded to the President; but in cases of sudden and unexpected invasion, insurrection, or riot *endangering public property of the United States*, or in cases of *attempted or threatened robbery or interruption of the United States mails, or other equal emergency*, officers, if they think a necessity exists, may take action before receipt of instructions from the seat of the Government. In every case they will report circumstances and their actions to the Adjutant General for information of the President."[22]

He stopped short of authorizing systematic campaigns against outlaws, however, and by the requirement that emergency actions be reported he sought to avoid abuse of that elastic term by local commanders.

Word of a new Wrestlers' outrage so angered Dudley that he sought much broader power. On 27 September an outlaw band raided Bartlett's Mill on the Rio Bonito, eleven

---

[18] Telg, Lyon to AG, Ft. Stanton, 1 Oct 1878, RG 94, File 1405, NARA.
[19] Quotes from Wilson, *Federal Aid in Domestic Disturbances*, p. 207, and Williams, *Hayes*, entry for 30 Jul 1878, p. 155, respectively.
[20] Telg, Axtell to Hayes, 20 Aug 1878, RG 94.
[21] Ltr, Dudley to Hatch, 29 Sep 1878, RG 94, File 1405, NARA.
[22] GO 71, 1 Oct 1878; emphasis added.

miles from Fort Stanton, abducted the wives of two mill employees, and repeatedly raped them. On learning of the crime, Dudley sent twenty men to "afford necessary protection" to ranches in the vicinity. In a report sent to Hatch for retroactive approval he called for imposition of martial law as the only course to end the reign of terror.[23]

By this time Hayes was convinced that Axtell's known links with the Santa Fe ring had compromised his ability to act impartially in restoring peace in Lincoln County. Already, it appeared, he had taken steps that placed federal troops in a position supporting one faction against another, instead of acting as an entirely neutral force.[24] On 1 October Hayes replaced him with Lew Wallace, the colorful Civil War general who was soon to be famous as the author of *Ben Hur.* The president directed the War Department to provide Wallace with suitable military escorts during a fact-finding reconnaissance of southern New Mexico.[25]

LEW WALLACE

Assuming freer use of troops at a later date should civil procedures fail, Wallace formulated a seven-point contingency plan that he hoped would pacify Lincoln County within sixty days. The plan called for (1) concentration of all available troops in New Mexico near Fort Stanton and other sites in Lincoln and adjacent Dona Ana Counties; (2) military forays to break up outlaw camps in both counties; (3) arrests of any people found in possession of stolen property; (4) detention of suspected outlaws in military custody until civil courts could dispose of their cases; (5) identification and safekeeping of stolen goods for future reclamation; (6) release of any prisoners whom officers determined to be innocent; and (7) strictest avoidance of interference with the activities of peaceful, law-abiding citizens.[26]

Reaching New Mexico on 5 October 1878, Wallace learned from U.S. Marshal John Sherman and Judge Warren Bristol of New Mexico's Third Judicial District that ordinary means of law enforcement, even if administered by a conscientious governor, were

---

[23] Telg, Dudley to Actg AG, Dist of New Mexico, 3 Oct 1878, RG 94, File 1405, NARA; Fulton, *Lincoln County War,* pp. 295–96.

[24] Utley, *High Noon in Lincoln,* pp. 118–19.

[25] Telgs, McCrary to Hatch, 4 Oct 1878, and Hatch to AG, Dept of the Missouri, 17 Feb 1879, both in RG 94, File 1405, NARA; Fulton, *Lincoln County War,* pp. 298–300. For Wallace, see Robert E. and Katherine M. Morsberger, *Lew Wallace: Militant Romantic* (New York: McGraw Hill, 1980), especially pp. 258–64; Okah L. Jones, "Lew Wallace: Hoosier Governor of Territorial New Mexico, 1878–1881," *New Mexico Historical Review* 70 (April 1965):129–58; Utley, *Four Fighters of Lincoln County,* pp. 61–77; Lew Wallace, *Lew Wallace: An Autobiography,* 2 vols. (New York: Harper & Bros., 1906).

[26] Ltrs, Wallace to Hatch, 26 Oct 1878, and to Actg AG, Dist of New Mexico to CO, Ft. Stanton, 27 Oct 1878, both in RG 393, Ltrs Sent, Dist of New Mexico, NARA; Fulton, *Lincoln County War,* pp. 298–300.

inadequate for pacifying Lincoln County. Lawlessness had not only prevented Sherman from recruiting posses to execute warrants but had also stopped Bristol from convening court sessions. Noting the lack of a territorial militia, Sherman recommended that Wallace exercise his option to seek federal military aid.[27]

But when Wallace did request federal aid, he mistakenly cited RS 5297, which was applicable only to state requests. He wrote Hayes that since "regular troops were fixed to their posts . . . by the *Posse Comitatus* Act," the president should declare Lincoln County to be in a state of insurrection, place it under martial law, suspend habeas corpus, and appoint a military commission to try all offenders. In his request, he made the mandatory statement that the territorial legislature was not in session and could not be convened in time to act.[28]

Instead of returning the improper request, Hayes consulted with Secretary McCrary on the best mode for intervention. McCrary in turn queried the judge advocate general, who advised him that even in a territory the Posse Comitatus Act restricted federal troops to the provision of refuge at local posts and to the defense of stagecoaches carrying mail. The judge advocate concluded, however, that in western areas sheriffs and local posses, terrorized as they were by large bands of outlaws, could not operate without the help of the Army, "the power chiefly relied upon by law-abiding people for protection and the power chiefly feared by the lawless classes." McCrary added that "the inability of the officer in command to aid in making arrests was one of the principal causes which led to the most disgraceful scenes of riot and murder, amounting in fact, to anarchy."[29]

These conclusions may have suggested the proper course to the president. Quoting RS 5298, the appropriate statute for acting in a territory, Hayes issued a proclamation on 7 October 1878 announcing that "unlawful obstructions, combinations, or assemblages of persons . . . against the authority of the United States make it impracticable . . . to enforce, by the ordinary course of judicial proceedings, laws of the United States within the Territory of New Mexico." He therefore authorized the use of federal military force to ensure "faithful execution of the law." He concluded the proclamation with the order that all armed bands in Lincoln County disperse and retire peaceably to their respective abodes on or before 13 October 1878, as required by RS 5300. Though falling short of Wallace's request to impose martial law or to appoint a military commission, the proclamation conformed closely to the relevant laws and provided Hatch with adequate power to drive most of the outlaws from the district.[30]

Following the proclamation McCrary ordered General Sherman to notify Generals Sheridan and Pope—commanders of the Division and the Department of the Missouri, respectively—and Hatch that after the 13 October deadline the troops in the District of New Mexico were to disperse all known gangs of outlaws and, "so long as resistance to the laws shall continue," aid the governor and other territorial authorities to keep the peace and enforce the law. None of these orders from Hayes and McCrary, however, gave Wallace the

---

[27] William A. Keleher, *Violence in Lincoln County, 1869–1881* (Albuquerque: University of New Mexico Press, 1957), pp. 184–89.

[28] Ibid.

[29] Memo, JAG for McCrary, WD, c. 6 Oct 1878, RG 94, File 1405, NARA; Wilson, *Federal Aid in Domestic Disturbances*, p. 210.

[30] Wilson, *Federal Aid in Domestic Disturbances*, p. 208; Keleher, *Violence Lincoln County*, p. 190.

power over federal troops exercised by the territorial governor of Kansas in the 1850s, indicating a significant change in federal policy.[31]

Two weeks later Pope's instructions were forwarded to Dudley for implementation. They roughly paralleled Wallace's contingency plan of early October and allowed troops to act lawfully as a *posse comitatus*. Upon receiving proper writs, Dudley was to furnish soldiers either to the federal marshal or to the territorial sheriffs for the purpose of arresting persons "lately engaged in murders, robberies, and resistance to civil authorities." His men were further ordered to disperse and disarm bands of outlaws and to turn over any recovered property to the nearest authorities for restoration to the owners. Any prisoners captured during the raids were to be held until authorities requested their transfer to territorial jails.[32]

As for robberies, murders, or thefts of livestock committed after 27 October, Pope authorized Dudley to pursue perpetrators at once, without awaiting action by a deputy sheriff or marshal. Pope did, however, add the important qualification that, before pursuing anyone, Dudley was to satisfy himself beyond a reasonable doubt as to the identity and guilt of the people involved. Moreover, while enforcing federal laws in New Mexico, he was to avoid detaining good citizens or quartering troops in their homes. "The entire object for which the troops are required is to enforce the laws, preserve the peace, and give to the residents . . . absolute security in their lives and property."[33]

During the next few weeks Dudley sent numerous reports to Hatch indicating that he had largely restored peace and quiet to Lincoln County, using the new policy. Taking Dudley at his word Wallace issued a proclamation on 13 November urging peaceful citizens to return to their homes and occupations with the assurance that "ample measures . . . now are, and will be continued, in force to make them secure in person and property." To expedite a return to normalcy and to avoid imposing unbearable case loads upon the territorial courts, Wallace magnanimously offered a general pardon for all bona fide residents of Lincoln County, including Army officers, guilty of misdemeanors and other minor offenses committed since Tunstall's murder in February 1878.[34]

Dudley, who believed he had done nothing wrong during his service in Lincoln County, was angry at this proclamation and "blasted Wallace for the implication of guilt." In an open letter described as "both a grave official impropriety and a personal insult to the governor of the territory," he wrote: "There can be but one construction placed upon the language of the proclamation. It virtually charges myself and the officers of the Army who have been on duty here since February 1st with having violated the laws of the territory, and then proceeds to pardon us, classing one and all of us with murderers, cattle thieves, and outlaws."[35] Wallace, who already had doubts about Dudley's impartiality during events dating from the time of his arrival at Fort Stanton, was more convinced than ever

---

[31] Ltr, McCrary to Sherman, 8 Oct 1878, RG 94, File 1405, NARA; GO 74, 8 Oct 1878. For the powers of the territorial governor in Kansas, see Coakley, *Role of Federal Military Forces* , pp. 145–93.

[32] Ltr, Actg AG, Dist of New Mexico, to Dudley, 27 Oct 1878, RG 393, Ltrs Sent, Dist of New Mexico, NARA.

[33] Ibid.

[34] Dudley Inquiry, pp. 69–70, 74, RG 153; quote from Proclamation, Wallace to Citizens of Lincoln County, RG 94, File 1045, NARA.

[35] Quotes from Utley, *High Noon in Lincoln*, p. 127. See also Fulton, *Lincoln County War*, p. 307.

after reading the letter, in spite of Dudley's continued professions of innocence, that he needed to be replaced.

In the month following Wallace's announcement that "ample measures" would be taken to protect law-abiding residents, violence erupted sporadically in various parts of the county. Hatch blamed county authorities for failing to institute speedy trials and administer exemplary punishments. Wallace, however, attributed the lack of progress to Dudley's strict adherence to the orders of 8 and 27 October and a lack of enthusiasm for Wallace's leadership. During late December 1878 and January 1879, Dudley provided troops to the marshal and sheriff, but only to capture armed bands roving through the county. Wallace insisted, however, that outlaws constituted only part of the problem. Brawling townsmen who had taken sides during the Dolan-McSween feud represented a major obstacle to true pacification, causing him to recommend strongly to Hatch and Dudley that they distribute small numbers of troops to towns through Lincoln County to assist local constables in keeping the peace.[36]

Dudley responded that compliance with Wallace's proposal violated General Order 71 and amounted to de facto martial law, with the Army assuming the full-time role of a police force. Hatch agreed with his assessment that the War Department's directive limited the Army to the pursuit of outlaw gangs, not to the enforcement of town ordinances against barroom brawling.[37] In St. Louis, General Pope wrote that under Wallace's proposal local law enforcement officials would be likely to call on the military in every circumstance, no matter how trivial, and that civilians would not feel any responsibility to serve in posses. As a result, military posses would be substituted for civilians, an illegal action uncalled for by presidential proclamation. McCrary and Sherman agreed with Pope's position that troops should not be used as requested by Wallace.[38]

While Wallace argued with the commanders over policy, the widow of Alexander McSween and her lawyer, Huston I. Chapman, conducted a four-month-long campaign to have Dudley relieved for his allegedly partisan role during the Five Days Battle. In vitriolic letters to Wallace, Chapman denounced Dudley and his officers for harassing Sue McSween and her supporters. Persuaded by these accounts and his own experiences and observations, Wallace determined that Dudley's effectiveness had been compromised and asked Hatch to dismiss the contentious officer. Although Hatch thoroughly disliked Dudley, after a decade-long personal quarrel with him, he deferred punitive action—knowing through experience that Dudley had powerful friends in the War Department.[39]

Wallace's next effort to oust Dudley came in early March 1879. About one month earlier Mrs. McSween, on the advice of Chapman, had sworn in an affidavit accusing Dudley of complicity in the murder of her husband and the subsequent looting and burning of his property. Before any further legal action could take place, however, Dolan and several

---

[36] Ltrs, Wallace to Hatch, 14 Dec 1878 and 14 Feb 1879; Hatch to Pope, 17 Dec 1878 and 17 Feb 1879; all in RG 94, File 1405, NARA.

[37] Telg, Hatch to Wallace, 21 Feb 1879, RG 393, Ltrs Sent, Dist of New Mexico, NARA.

[38] Pope Endorsement, 24 Feb 1879, to Ltr, Wallace to Hatch, 14 Feb 1879; Telg, AG to CO, Dept of the Missouri, 15 Mar 1879; both in RG 94, File 1405, NARA.

[39] Ltrs, Chapman to Wallace, 24 Oct, 25 Nov, and 29 Nov 1878, Exhibits 4, 24, 25, respectively, all in Dudley Inquiry, RG 153; Fulton, *Lincoln County War*, pp. 311–17; Keleher, *Violence in Lincoln County*, p. 179; Ltr, Wallace to Hatch, 7 Dec 1878, RG 94, File 1405, NARA.

other men murdered the unarmed Chapman in cold blood on the night of 18 February 1879. During commission of the crime, and in the presence of several witnesses, they boasted of having fulfilled a promise made to Dudley. In view of these disturbing events, Judge Ira E. Leonard, Chapman's friend and counsel for Sue McSween, filed charges against Dudley with the War Department for the murder of McSween, the burning of the McSween home, and the looting of the Tunstall store. A newspaper account of Chapman's murder that implicated Dudley was enclosed with the letter, but no charges connecting him with that crime were made. Alarmed by this apparent sudden turn for the worse in Lincoln County, Wallace visited the county seat to investigate the homicide personally.[40]

In private conversations with the governor, several citizens accused Dolan and his men of killing Chapman. Fearing that Dudley could not be relied upon to protect them against reprisals, several witnesses initially refused to sign affidavits needed to arrest the suspects. On 7 March, appealing to Hatch for the removal of Dudley, Wallace explained: "He is so compromised by connection with the troubles . . . that his usefulness is utterly gone. Intimidation . . . by Dudley prevents me from getting sworn statements. . . . Dread is not irrational. In general terms Dudley has been charged with responsibility for the killing of McSween . . . and is also suspected of a part in the Chapman killing."[41]

On 8 March Hatch acted by forwarding all allegations to General Pope. Without awaiting a response, he removed Dudley from his command and, having little choice, reappointed Purington as acting commander of Fort Stanton—the same man he had removed in April 1878 for partisanship. Perhaps believing that the penalties of the Posse Comitatus Act and more strict control by Wallace and himself would render Purington more effective, he instructed him not to interfere in civil matters beyond his instructions should Wallace declare martial law.[42]

Observing the letter of Army regulations and War Department guidelines, Wallace made vigorous use of Hatch's men during early 1879. A writer for the Mesilla, New Mexico, *Independent*, serving as a correspondent at Fort Stanton, observed that "the troops of this post are nearly tired out; not a day passes but two or three squads are following some deputy of Governor Wallace in making *ex parte* arrests." The troops never moved, however, until Wallace first requested their use from Hatch. Not content with that procedure, in late March Wallace created a company of militia from residents living in or near the town of Lincoln and grandiosely named them the Lincoln County Rifles. Captained by Juan B. Patron, a graduate of the University of Notre Dame and a former McSween supporter, the militia served several months without pay, pending an appropriation from the territorial legislature.[43]

Upon being relieved Dudley demanded a court of inquiry. On orders from General Pope, the court convened at Fort Stanton, and from early May to mid-July heard testi-

---

[40] Quote from Ltr, Leonard to McCrary, 4 Mar 1879, RG 94, File 1405, NARA. See also Fulton, *Lincoln County War*, pp. 331–34; Dudley Inquiry, p. 257, RG 153; Utley, *High Noon in Lincoln*, pp. 151–52.

[41] Quote from Ltr, Wallace to Hatch, 7 Mar 1879, Exhibit 1, RG 153, Dudley Inquiry; Fulton, *Lincoln County War*, pp. 331–32.

[42] Ltr, Hatch to Pope, 8 Mar 1879, RG 393, Ltrs Sent, Dist of New Mexico, NARA; Special Order (SO) 2, HQ, Dist of New Mexico, 8 Mar 1879, and Ltr, Actg AG, Dist of New Mexico, to Purington, 19 Mar 1879, both in RG 94, File 1405, NARA.

[43] Quote from Fulton, *Lincoln County War*, pp. 339–42; Ltr, AG, Dist of New Mexico, to CO, Ft. Stanton, 28 Apr 1879, RG 393, Ltrs Sent, Dist of New Mexico, NARA.

mony from both sides on charges that Dudley had violated the Posse Comitatus Act and had taken sides in the Lincoln County war. Under the second charge, Wallace's lawyer accused Dudley of assisting the Dolan faction on many occasions, while simultaneously abusing Mrs. McSween and Chapman. The charge of violating the Posse Comitatus Act stemmed from Dudley's use of troops during the Five Days Battle to screen Peppin's men from gunfire, and from the use of troops on two other occasions to protect Dolan partisans from reprisals.[44]

The court of inquiry excluded many of Wallace's witnesses on the grounds that their testimony established a conspiracy to kill Chapman, an accusation not included in the charges. Without these witnesses the court dismissed all other evidence as hearsay, a decision that Wallace referred to as a "whitewash." Although the court faulted Dudley on many counts, it found that he had violated no laws nor had he committed any crime. On his actions during the Five Days Battle the court concluded that he intervened "for the most humane and worthy motives and of good military judgement under exceptional circumstances." When word of Dudley's exoneration and a transcript of the inquiry reached Pope, he rejected its findings as a travesty of justice and recommended that Judge Advocate General Brig. Gen. William M. Dunn institute a court-martial.

Dunn disagreed. He ruled that a court-martial would turn up the same complex and contradictory evidence raised by the court of inquiry, concluding that sufficient evidence was not available to find Dudley guilty beyond a reasonable doubt.[45] Dunn excused Dudley's behavior on the grounds that he had probably supported the more lawful of the two factions and sent troops into Lincoln to protect innocent civilians. Dunn reasoned a court-martial would serve no purpose and could only garner more adverse publicity for the Army. He believed Dudley had already been punished sufficiently for any indiscretions by the loss of his command. Secretary McCrary concurred.

With great success, Pope also tried to end military involvement in Lincoln County and to restore his troops to their primary function of Indian fighting. "As matters now stand," he wrote early in 1880, "anyone who commits a crime expects to be shielded from the vengeance of those whom the crime has incensed in the asylum of a military post, or the civil authorities expect their prisoners to be guarded for them."[46] Soon after, a new secretary of war, Alexander Ramsay, decided to remove the troops from Lincoln County, and when Pope received word that Wallace had formed a territorial militia he issued the necessary orders for withdrawal. On 28 February 1880, the commander at Fort Stanton officially ended seventeen months of federal military intervention in New Mexico.

---

[44] Dudley Inquiry, pp. 1–12, 58–62, 69–70, 74, 80–81, 106–09, 160–67, 957–62, RG 153; Ltrs, JAG, Dept of the Missouri, to AG, Dept of the Missouri, 23 Sep 1879; Pope to Sheridan, 27 Sep 1879; Pope to AG, 15 Oct 1879; Dunn to McCrary, 22 Oct 1879; Hatch to AG, Dept of the Missouri, 3 Feb 1880; Pope to AG, 13 Mar 1880. All in RG 94, File 1405, NARA. Fulton, *Lincoln County War*, pp. 356–58; Keleher, *Violence in Lincoln County*, pp. 226–27; Wilson, *Federal Aid in Domestic Disturbances*, pp. 210–11.

[45] Quote from Utley, *High Noon in Lincoln*, p. 153; Dudley Inquiry, pp. 1–12, 58–62, 69–70, 74, 80–81, 106–09, 160–67, 957–62, RG 153; Ltrs, JAG, Dept of the Missouri, to AG, Dept of the Missouri, 23 Sep 1879; Pope to Sheridan, 27 Sep 1879; Pope to AG, 15 Oct 1879; Dunn to McCrary, 22 Oct 1879; Hatch to AG, Dept of the Missouri, 3 Feb 1880; Pope to AG, 13 Mar 1880. All in RG 94, File 1405, NARA. Fulton, *Lincoln County War*, pp. 356–58; Keleher, *Violence in Lincoln County*, pp. 226–27; Wilson, *Federal Aid in Domestic Disturbances*, pp. 210–11; Morsberger and Morsberger, *Lew Wallace: Militant Romantic*, pp. 277–78.

[46] Wilson, *Federal Aid in Domestic Disturbances*, p. 210.

Despite the personal failings of Purington and Dudley, the Lincoln County war helped clarify the impact of the Posse Comitatus Act on western law enforcement. Although the act made partisan intervention by the Army more difficult by requiring local commanders to await orders from supposedly unbiased higher authority, it also exacerbated existing problems by slowing federal military responses in all but emergencies. Wallace was one of the first territorial governors to realize that a militia answerable directly to the executive was a necessary alternative to inadequate civilian posses and to federal troops that were only obtainable after a lengthy, cumbersome request procedure. Yet disorders were frequently necessary to convince legislatures to fund militias. In the interim, federal military intervention based on RS 5298 offered the best remedy for territorial lawlessness when presidents could be persuaded to authorize them.

Yet Dudley's actions also provided a precedent of sorts for direct action. While the Posse Comitatus Act virtually ended the routine use of troops in minor disturbances, in more serious cases, when time was considered of the essence, local commanders henceforth either found other reasons to intervene without waiting for formal approval or intervened under the emergency authorizations of General Order 71. After troops suppressed disorders, authorities in Washington either issued belated reprimands or justified intervention based on the extraordinary nature of the emergency. A process so disorderly and unpredictable confused both soldiers and civilians, as exemplified by the case of Hastings, Nebraska.

Hastings, Nebraska, 1879

In 1878 Isom Pierce ("Print") Olive, a prominent cattleman in southern Nebraska, exerted his considerable economic and political influence in Custer County to be elected sheriff. Shortly thereafter his brother Robert, acting as deputy sheriff, was killed in a gunfight when he tried to arrest two homesteaders for shooting Olive cattle that had strayed onto their farm. Olive summoned a posse, captured the homesteaders, and lynched both on the spot. The bodies were then doused with whiskey and burned. This incident caused such a scandal that state authorities issued murder indictments for Olive (who had gained the sobriquet "manburner") as well as the members of his posse. A trial was convened in Hastings, the Adams county seat. Before the conclusion of the trial, however, the special prosecutor learned that a gang from Plum Creek, sympathetic to Olive, planned to storm the courthouse and free the defendants. While the prosecutor and judge appealed to the Nebraska state adjutant general for military protection, the county sheriff turned to Governor Albinus Nance for aid.[47]

In response to a request from the Nebraska adjutant general, Brig. Gen. George Crook, commanding the Department of the Platte, took immediate emergency measures to meet the alleged threat. On 11 April, after advising Nance to make a formal request to President Hayes for military aid, on his own authority Crook ordered Capt. Andrew S. Burt, 9th Infantry, to take two companies from Fort Omaha to Hastings to defend the court and town

---

[47] Merrill J. Mattes, *Indians, Infants, and Infantry: Andrew and Elizabeth Burt on the Frontier* (Denver: Old West, 1960), pp. 239–40; George Crook, *General George Crook: His Autobiography* (Norman: University of Oklahoma Press, 1946), pp. 230–31; Telg, Nance to Hayes, 14 Apr 1879, and Ltr, Crook to AG, Div of the Missouri, 14 Apr 1879, both in RG 94, File 2165, AGO 1879: Disorder at Hastings, Nebr, 1879, NARA.

GEORGE CROOK

against attack. He remarked later that "knowing the desperate character of the Olive gang and their friends . . . there was a great danger of their injuring many persons and perhaps of their burning the town."[48]

Nance meanwhile wired Hayes requesting permission to use federal troops as a *posse comitatus* to maintain order during the trial, if necessary, because the state lacked an organized militia. The next day Secretary McCrary replied on behalf of the president that the Act of June 1878 forbade the use of troops as a *posse comitatus* before an actual, demonstrable need existed; therefore troops could not be sent for the purposes described. He did note, however, that regulars could be so stationed "as to exercise a moral influence and in the case of domestic violence can be employed to keep the peace after a regular call for aid from the President."[49]

That same morning Burt led a detachment of ninety-two men and a Gatling gun into Hastings, deploying opposite the courthouse. The show of force exerted the desired moral effect, and the trial proceeded without interruption, ending in a conviction of Olive and the other defendants. Shortly after Burt's intervention Crook notified Sheridan of his actions, as required by General Order 71, seeking retroactive approval. Sheridan, however, reproved him for his actions and for breaching the Posse Comitatus Act, ordering the immediate withdrawal of Burt's men. Crook, according to Sheridan, had unnecessarily committed federal troops before any violation of the law had taken place and before appropriate orders had come from the president. He concluded that, although Crook and McCrary thought otherwise, the evidence presented was not of a serious enough nature to warrant the intervention of troops under General Order 71, and that Crook's hasty intervention had precluded a calm assessment of the true nature of the situation. Burt's detachment left Hastings on 12 April.[50]

Sheridan's rejection of Crook's actions made other commanders reluctant to act quickly in emergencies for fear of reprimand from their superiors. Although the immediate dispatch of Burt's detachment to Hastings had probably prevented a bloody shoot-out, when faced with more serious disorders in 1882 and 1885, Bvt. Maj. Gen. Orlando B. Willcox and Col. Alexander McDowell McCook hesitated to take similar risks and

---

[48] Crook acted under the emergency powers granted by General Order 71 of 1 October 1878. Quote from Ltr, Crook to AG, Div of the Missouri, 14 Apr 1879; see also Telg, AG to Sheridan, 12 Apr 1879; both in RG 94, File 2165, NARA; Mattes, *Indians, Infants, and Infantry*, pp. 240–41; Crook, *His Autobiography*, p. 231.

[49] Quote from Telg, McCrary to Nance, 12 Apr 1879; see also Telg, Nance to Hayes, 11 Apr 1879; both in RG 94, File 2165, NARA.

[50] Telg, McCrary to Nance, 12 Apr 1879, RG 94.

delayed action for several months, pending guidance from higher headquarters. The resultant delays, caused by commanders' fears of the negative legal and professional ramifications of misusing troops under the Posse Comitatus Act, prolonged lawlessness in Arizona and Utah.

Arizona, 1881–1882

In late 1881 and early 1882 lawlessness in Cochise County, Arizona Territory, compelled another commander to act under the emergency powers of General Order 71, this time, however, after a delay of several months. In addition to gangs of outlaws, the citizens of Arizona had to contend with Apaches who frequently left their reservation and, from sanctuaries in the Mexican Sierra Madre Mountains, conducted raids on settlers. The anarchy in Cochise County prompted Governor John T. Cooper to call on the residents of Tombstone to organize vigilance committees. On 6 December 1881, President Chester A. Arthur, acting on Cooper's advice, recommended that Congress enact a new law making it a federal crime for marauding gangs of outlaws or Indians to cross territorial or national boundaries. He further proposed that Congress repeal or modify the Posse Comitatus Act to allow troops to aid sheriffs. When Congress failed to act, the new territorial governor, Frederick Tritle, asked Arthur to request $150,000 to organize a mounted Arizona territorial militia that could restore order in conjunction with federal troops.[51]

While these ideas were pending, in April 1882 a band of Chiricahua Apaches led by Geronimo entered the Warm Springs Reservation at San Carlos and coerced a local Apache band into joining them for raids upon ranchers and settlers. Cries of alarm and outrage from residents inundated Washington. Responding to the new crisis, Arthur repeated his proposals of the previous December to Congress. The Senate Judiciary Committee, however, on 1 May stated that no further legislation was necessary because existing laws, such as RS 5286 and RS 5298, could be broadly interpreted to permit military intervention. All that Arthur needed to do in either case, the committee explained, was first to issue a cease and desist proclamation (RS 5300). He did so the same day.[52]

Meanwhile, impatient with the progress of politicians and generals in Washington, Tritle decided on a course of action. On 1 May he informed the commander of the Department of Arizona, General Willcox, that he was deputizing citizens to end lawlessness, giving them authority to arrest both outlaws and Indians. Fearing the results of

---

[51] Henry P. Walker, "Retire Peaceably to Your Homes: Arizona Faces Martial Law, 1882," *Journal of Arizona History* 10 (Spring 1969):1–2; Oliver L. Spaulding, *The United States Army in War and Peace* (New York: G. P. Putnam & Sons, 1937), p. 371; Dan L. Thrapp, *The Conquest of Apacheria* (Norman: University of Oklahoma Press, 1967), chs. 17–18; Jay J. Wagoner, *Arizona Territory, 1863–1912: A Political History* (Tucson: University of Arizona Press, 1969), pp. 191–96; Ltrs, Cooper to Secy of the Interior Samuel J. Kirkwood, 29 Nov and 19 Dec 1881; and Kirkwood to Arthur, 20 Jan 1882, in U.S. Congress, House, *Lawlessness in Parts of Arizona*, 47th Cong., 1st sess., 1882, Exec. Doc. 58; see also U.S. Congress, House, *Message From the President of the United States on Relations to Disorders and Lawlessness in Arizona, April 2*, 47th Cong., 1st sess., 1882, Exec. Doc. 188.

[52] Wagoner, *Arizona Territory*, pp. 198–99; Msg, Arthur in U.S. Congress, House, *Message . . . in Relations to Disorders and Lawlessness in Arizona*; Resolution, House of Reps to Secy of War, 28 Apr 1882, and Ltr, AG to Secy of War, 2 May 1882. Both in RG 94, File 1749, AGO 1882: Papers Relating to Violence in New Mexico and in Arizona by Chiricahua Apaches, Apr 1882–May 1885, NARA; U.S. Congress, Senate, "Finding of the Senate Judiciary Committee," *Congressional Record*, 47th Cong., 1st sess., 13:3457–58.

violent incursions into federal Indian reservations by hordes of undisciplined and venge-ful "deputies," Willcox warned Tritle that any such action would be resisted by military force. Then, acting under the emergency authority of General Order 71, Willcox ordered the commanders of all posts in Arizona and New Mexico to pursue and capture any bands of lawbreakers wherever found.[53] On 3 May President Arthur issued a superfluous proclamation calling for all unlawful "obstructions, combinations, or assemblages" to disband no later than 15 May. Since American and Mexican soldiers had eliminated the Apache menace for the time being, peace returned to Cochise County and no further action was required to implement the proclamation.[54] Even before the disturbances in Arizona were quelled, however, congressional action was setting the stage for a further violent confrontation between the federal government and the Mormon settlers of Utah.

Utah, 1885

The unorthodox beliefs of the Mormons and their rigid control of political affairs in Utah had long been a source of contention and conflict with other American religious groups and the federal government. Contemporary journals abounded in articles criticiz-ing all aspects of Mormon life.[55] On 22 March 1882, Congress enacted a bill sponsored by Vermont Republican Senator George File Edmunds "to extirpate polygamy in Utah," which made polygamy a misdemeanor and provided for the disenfranchisement of offend-ers. Even though the act became law in 1882, its rigorous enforcement was not attempted until nearly three years later. When it was enforced, Mormon indignation culminated in the Flag Riots in Salt Lake City on 4 July 1885.

When mobs of irate Mormons protested enforcement of the anti-polygamy statute by turning American flags upside down in Salt Lake City on Independence Day, groups of non-Mormon veterans forcibly righted the colors, precipitating riots and assaults by Mormons upon federal officials and their homes. Civil authorities were either unwilling or unable to contain or quell this violence with the forces at their disposal. After ten days of mayhem, Col. Alexander McCook, 6th Infantry, sought permission from Brig. Gen. Oliver O. Howard, commander of the Department of the Platte, Omaha, to dispatch one of his ten companies from Fort Douglas to Salt Lake City, three miles away, to protect property under emergency regulations. Howard relayed the request to the War Department.[56]

Categorizing the violence as too minor to justify federal intervention, and perhaps hoping to avoid a wider conflict, on 15 July Secretary of War William C. Endicott refused the request. Governor Eli Murray made a similar request to the president the next day, but Cleveland refused aid for the same reason. The disorders continued. Three months later Murray renewed the recommendations made earlier by General Sherman and President

---

[53] Telg, Tritle to Willcox, 1 May 1882, RG 94, File 1749, NARA.

[54] *Secretary of War Report, 1882*, p. 148; Wilson, *Federal Aid in Domestic Disturbances*, p. 214.

[55] For example, see J. R. McBride, "Utah and the Mormons," *International Review* 181 (12 February 1882):183. For earlier disputes, see Coakley, *Role of Federal Military Forces*, pp. 106–09, 194–226.

[56] McCook intended to act under authority of Section 823 of *Army Regulations of 1881* concerning "cases of sudden and unexpected . . . insurrection, or riot," a codification of *General Order 71* issued in 1878. Telgs, Schofield, Div of the Missouri, to AG, 14 Jul 1885, and Murray, Utah Territory, to Cleveland, 16 Jul 1885, both in RG 94, File 3913, AGO 1885: Mormon Disorders, 1885, NARA.

Arthur that the Posse Comitatus Act either be revised to deal with the extraordinary situations as found in the West, or be rescinded altogether.[57] Instead, Washington authorities asked McCook for a candid reassessment of the situation. He replied that the Mormon-dominated legislature and constabulary were unwilling to punish fellow Mormons in Salt Lake City. To provide a rallying point for federal officials and law-abiding citizens, he asked permission to send one company of regulars to Salt Lake and requested one battery of light artillery from Omaha for moral effect.[58]

In the time between his request and War Department approval, McCook assured Governor Murray that troops at Fort Douglas stood ready to enter the city in case of danger to lives and federal property under Section 853 of the *Army Regulations of 1881*.[59] Even after federal troops had helped with the arrests of several Mormons who were considered ringleaders, McCook reported that conditions were still unsettled. Many other Mormons wanted for violation of the Edmunds Law were still at large, inciting their followers to resist the federal government.[60]

Danger of new and potentially more serious trouble arose two months later. On 16 February 1886, a U.S. marshal arrested the first president of the Mormon Church at Promontory, Utah, about sixty miles northwest of Salt Lake City. Fearful of an attempted rescue while en route to trial at Salt Lake, the deputy marshal joined Murray in requesting a military escort from McCook. Without clearing the request at higher headquarters, but acting under authority of Section 853 of *Army Regulations of 1881*, McCook sent a 26-man detachment under Capt. Charles B. Penny to escort the marshal and his prisoner. News of the federal military involvement produced a scathing editorial in the Mormon-owned *Deseret Daily News* on 17 February, denouncing the Army's apparent assumption of control over the marshal's posse as unlawful and provocative.[61]

Accusations of illegal use of federal military force leveled by the Mormon press prompted an inquiry. When questioned, McCook insisted that he had neither displaced the marshal in command of the posse nor permitted the use of troops as a subordinate part of that body, actions prohibited by the Posse Comitatus Act. Standing by McCook's assertion that regulars had merely provided an escort, Howard defended McCook's actions by citing Section 853 of *Army Regulations of 1881* dealing with "cases of sudden and unexpected . . . insurrection, or riot, . . . or other equal emergency." Howard's superiors accepted this legal interpretation. Cleveland's apparent willingness to support McCook's activities and attempts to aid the U.S. marshal with the full force of the federal government rapidly defused Mormon resistance and ended the three-year-long crisis.[62]

---

[57] Telgs, AG to Schofield, Div of the Missouri, 16 Jul and 17 Oct 1885, in *Report of the Governor of Utah Territory*, 1885, RG 94, File 3913, NARA; Wilson, *Federal Aid in Domestic Disturbances*, p. 214.

[58] Telgs, AG to McCook, 2 Dec 1885; Murray to Cleveland, 3 Dec 1885; McCook to AG, 3 Dec 1885; AG to Howard, Dept of the Platte; and AG to McCook, 4 Dec 1885. All in RG 94, File 3913, NARA.

[59] Telg, McCook to AG, 3 Dec 1885, RG 94.

[60] Ltr, McCook to AG, 13 Dec 1885, and Telg, Howard, Dept of the Platte, to AG, 14 Dec 1885. Both in RG 94, File 3913, NARA.

[61] Ltr, Vandencook to McCook, 16 Feb 1886; Telg, McCook to AG, 18 Feb 1886; SO, McCook to Penny, 16 Feb 1886. All in RG 94, File 3913, NARA. "The Soldiers, the Prisoner, and the People," *Deseret Evening News*, Salt Lake City, Utah Territory, 17 Feb 1886.

[62] Rpts, McCook to Div of the Missouri, and to AG, 18 Feb 1886; Quote from Telg, Howard to Div of the Missouri, 23 Feb 1886. Both in RG 94, File 3913, NARA.

The Johnson County War, 1892

The 1890 United States Census declared that the trans-Mississippi West, long considered an inexhaustible expanse of cheap land, was settled to the extent that a frontier as such no longer existed. This phenomenon—later characterized by historian Frederick Jackson Turner as the closing of the frontier—produced a strong psychological effect, if no other, increasing tensions as farmers and ranchers, large and small, sought to expand their holdings in areas where they believed land would soon be at a premium.

This was especially true of large cattle ranchers in Wyoming, who sought to protect grazing lands and water sources while expanding their range holdings and herds at the expense of smaller rivals. In 1884 the large Wyoming Stock Growers Association (WSGA), whose membership roster was a Who's Who of state's rich and influential, passed a "maverick law" in the territorial legislature. Henceforth any cattle found without brands after spring roundups—which could be legally conducted only by the WSGA—automatically became the association's property. Many small farmers and ranchers without herds large enough to brand still used the open range and interpreted the law as a license for big cattlemen to steal their stock and drive them out of business. For several years thereafter, especially in northeastern Wyoming, small ranchers retaliated by rustling back their own cattle, frequently adding a few head as interest. In 1892 a small group of ranchers announced their intentions to conduct a May Day roundup in advance of the WSGA and without its participation or approval. The WSGA decided to act. To end rustling permanently, to curtail economic competition, and to maintain their land and cattle monopoly, a hundred members of the association organized and funded a punitive expedition of hired gunfighters and cattlemen to carry out an invasion of Johnson County, the area most affected. Suspected rustlers were placed on blacklists indicating that they were either to be driven from Wyoming or killed.[63]

In many ways the so-called Johnson County war resembled the earlier troubles in Lincoln County. In both altercations, conflicting factions resorted to violence, with one side enjoying widespread political influence at territorial and federal levels. To end the disturbance, territorial authorities employed the resources of the federal government. But one aspect of the Johnson County war was new: partisanship and factionalism prevented a sheriff from raising effective posses. The absence of posses and a territorial militia and the inability of a sheriff to call on federal troops paradoxically made military intervention inevitable. In Johnson County the sheriff and local citizens formed one faction, and the state governor and influential cattlemen residing outside the county formed the other. When a sheriff's posse attempted to subdue invading gunfighters, the governor—favoring the faction that had hired the gunfighters—requested federal military aid, not to help the sheriff but to circumvent his authority and impede the performance of his legal duties.

By the spring of 1892, politicians and western military commanders fully realized how the Posse Comitatus Act restrained federal military intervention. Local military commanders no longer dared to offer aid to local officials without having first referred all such

---

[63] Frank N. Schubert, "The Suggs Affray: The Black Cavalry in the Johnson County War," *Western Historical Quarterly* (January 1973):53, 58–59; Helena Huntington Smith, *The War on Powder River* (Lincoln: University of Nebraska Press, 1967), pp. 192–93, 214, 223–24; Paul Trachtman, *The Gunfighters* (New York: Time-Life Books, 1974), pp. 206–10.

STEPHEN B. ELKINS

FRANCIS E. WARREN

requests to higher authorities. Similarly, the president and secretary of war agreed that federal military aid should be the last resort used only after all other methods had failed.

The expedition of WSGA-hired gunfighters from Texas and Wyoming, known as the Regulators or Invaders, traveled by rail from Cheyenne to Johnson County under the leadership of Frank Wolcott. Soon after arriving, they cut the telegraph wires leading into the county. On the next day, 7 April, they killed two cowboys, Nate Champion and Nick Ray, who were summarily judged to be rustlers, at the KC Ranch near the North Fork of the Powder River. Alerted by witnesses to the murders, the citizens of Johnson County fought back. Led by local Sheriff W. E. "Red" Angus, a posse of 200 to 300 enraged citizens tracked down and besieged the Regulators in a house on the TA Ranch on Crazy Woman River. Shooting started soon after dawn on 11 April, with the posse determined to blast or burn out the Regulators. On the second day of the siege, Johnson County officials notified Governor Amos W. Barber that an illegal armed force had invaded Johnson County, that the invaders had killed two settlers, and were now resisting arrest by the sheriff and a posse. The officials requested that the governor summon federal troops from nearby Fort McKinney. Barber, who had advance knowledge of the WSGA plot and counted many friends and supporters among its members, delayed acting on the request until he had heard from the association.[64]

Word of the plight of Wolcott's Regulator force arrived from the Stock Growers Association later that same day, and Barber immediately requested federal military aid,

---

[64] Trachtman, *The Gunfighters*, pp. 214–18.

describing the Angus' posse to President Benjamin Harrison as a mob in insurrection against state authority. Because Wyoming had been a state since 1890 he cited RS 5297. Barber's actions and the pleas of Wyoming Senators Francis E. Warren and Joseph M. Carey convinced Harrison to grant their request. He ordered Secretary of War Stephen B. Elkins to send troops from Fort McKinney to protect Wyoming against domestic violence and to cooperate with state authorities.[65]

Within hours the order worked its way through the chain of command. Concerned with maintaining Army neutrality, Maj. Gen. John M. Schofield, commanding general of the Army since 1888, ordered Brig. Gen. John R. Brooke, commander of the Department of the Platte, to prevent conflict between the opposing parties and to preserve the peace with prudence and firmness. Brooke forwarded Schofield's message to Col. J. J. Van Horn, 8th Infantry, who commanded 351 troops at Fort McKinney on Clear Fork Creek, strongly emphasizing the need to prevent further bloodshed and to ensure that neither party prevailed over the other. For this mission Brooke directed Van Horn to prepare two 25-man detachments. At Brooke's request Barber sent his aide-de-camp, Capt. C. H. Parmelee, to act as liaison. They made no contact with Sheriff Angus before the troops arrived.[66]

Although most outside civil authorities considered Johnson County citizens at fault for the disturbance, military men at the scene, with firsthand knowledge, were convinced that the vigilante actions of the Regulators had earned the just wrath of local citizens. Putting aside these personal convictions, however, Van Horn led his command to the TA Ranch where the Regulators were still under siege. Accompanied by 6th Cavalry Maj. Edmond G. Fechet and Captain Parmelee, Van Horn met with Angus behind a knoll some 800 yards from the Regulators. He asked Angus to order a cease-fire and allow Wolcott's party to surrender to the Army. After receiving assurances from Van Horn that the Regulators would be handed over to civil authorities for trial, Angus complied.[67]

Flanked by Fechet, Parmelee, Angus, and Sam Clover, a correspondent of the *Chicago Herald*, Van Horn rode under a makeshift truce flag to the ranch house. Wolcott strode forward to meet them. When Van Horn explained that he had come by order of the president to prevent further loss of life, Wolcott responded that he would surrender to the Army but never to Angus. Wolcott and forty-three of his men were immediately surrounded by the troops of cavalry, who escorted them toward Fort McKinney, past the sullen but restrained members of Angus' posse. Angus doubted whether justice would be done, commenting to the press: "These people came in here with murder and destruction in their hearts and hands. They have murdered and burned and defied the law, and it was my duty to arrest them. They were mine. I had them in my grasp and they were taken from me." On return to Fort McKinney, Van Horn sought further instructions from General Brooke on the care of the prisoners. Brooke responded that Wolcott and his men should

---

[65] Telgs, Col J. J. Van Horn, CO, 8th Infantry, Ft. McKinney to AG, Dept of the Platte, 11–13 Apr 1892, and Schofield to Brooke, 13 Apr 1892, RG 393, File 3739: Corres Johnson County Disturbances, Apr–June 1892, NARA. Schubert, "The Suggs Affray," p. 58; Smith, *War on Powder River*, pp. 192–93, 214, 223–24.

[66] Telgs, Schofield to Brooke, 12 Apr 1892; Brooke to Barber, 12 Apr; Brooke to Van Horn, 13 Apr; and Barber to Brook, 13 Apr 1892. All in RG 393, File 3739, NARA. Smith, *War on Powder River*, pp. 224–25.

[67] Rpt, Van Horn to AG, Dept of the Platte, 13 Apr 1892, RG 393, File 3739, NARA; Smith, *War on Powder River*, pp. 206, 225–26.

pay for rations, bedding, and animal forage, but if this was not possible essentials should be provided temporarily.[68]

Several days later the people of Buffalo, Wyoming, viewed the bullet-riddled, charred remains of Champion and Ray, the murdered cowboys. Outraged and still in possession of a murder warrant for Wolcott and the others, Angus demanded that Van Horn surrender the perpetrators. Van Horn refused on the grounds that those named in the warrant were "held under instructions from the President of the United States through the Departmental Commander until further instruction."[69]

Realizing that the Army could not hold Wolcott's party indefinitely and fearing the results of a trial in Johnson County, Barber sought a change of venue to Cheyenne. On 15 April Brooke consented to the request and ordered Van Horn to escort the defendants to Douglas, Wyoming, midway between Fort McKinney and Cheyenne. Leading 150 cavalry troopers, Hotchkiss gunners, and hospital corpsmen, Major Fechet of the 6th Cavalry traveled to Douglas in seven days through blizzards and subfreezing temperatures, arriving two days behind schedule. He transferred the prisoners to the custody of Maj. Harry C. Egbert, 17th Cavalry, who had traveled with his command of 177 men by train from Cheyenne on 21 April. Egbert's detachment returned to Cheyenne with the prisoners in private railway cars provided by the WSGA later the same evening.[70]

At the request of Governor Barber, Secretary Elkins authorized Brooke to make empty Army barracks available for the prisoners until they could be relocated in state facilities. In the interim Brooke was to have either Wyoming or the prisoners pay for incarceration. Barber forwarded the necessary funds and promised a trial as soon as a change of venue was obtained. Eight months later, in January 1893, Wolcott and his men came to trial in Cheyenne, the headquarters of the WSGA, on charges of murder. All charges were dropped because of lack of evidence resulting from the disappearance of the only two prosecution witnesses to the murders at the KC Ranch.[71]

Meanwhile, however, anticipating the trial and expecting the demise of WSGA influence in Johnson County, rustlers looted properties of absentee stock growers. Vengeful WSGA members sought to punish them, demanding that the federal government declare martial law and authorize the Army to take over the civil government. In this they failed. Presidential imposition of martial law had not taken place since the Ku Klux Klan disturbances in South Carolina during the 1870s. A weapon of last resort, it was used only in cases of widespread insurrection or persistent violence to life and property, as during the Civil War and Reconstruction under authority of the Ku Klux Act. Even then its provisions dealing with martial law expired after a year, with the remaining portions becoming the

---

[68] Quote from Trachtman, *The Gunfighters*, p. 222. See also Telg, Van Horn to AG, Dept of the Platte, and reply, 13 Apr 1892, RG 393.

[69] Writ Calling for Release of Prisoners to Sheriff of Johnson County, 13 Apr 1892; quote from Telg, Van Horn to AG, Dept of the Platte, 15 Apr 1892. Both in RG 393, File 3739, NARA.

[70] Telgs, Brooke to Schofield, 14 Apr 1892; AG, Dept of the Platte, to Van Horn, 15 Apr 1892, and reply, 18 Apr 1892; Fechet to AG, Ft. McKinney, 2 May 1892; AG, Dept of the Platte, to Egbert, 17 and 19 Apr 1892, and replies, 21 and 22 Apr 1892; Rpt, Egbert to AG, Dept of the Platte, 28 Apr 1892. All in RG 393, File 3739, NARA.

[71] Telgs, Barber to Brooke, 20 Apr and 9 May 1892; Elkins to Brooke, 21 Apr 1892; all in RG 393, File 3739, NARA. The two witnesses had been bribed by the Wyoming Stock Grower's Association to prevent their testimony; see Trachtman, *The Gunfighters*, p. 223.

basis for RS 5299. In Harrison's view the sporadic looting of stock growers' properties failed to justify such a remedy.

Unprepared to relinquish property rights in Johnson County, WSGA leaders now prevailed upon Senator Carey to urge Elkins to replace Fechet's command with troops "whose sympathy is with us." Alleging that Fechet's command was sympathetic to Angus and the rustlers, the stock growers specifically requested troops from the black 9th Cavalry regiment at Fort Robinson, Nebraska, who they believed had no sympathy for the white rustlers. Although the evidence shows that Fechet's command exercised complete neutrality during its tenure, this in itself was unsatisfactory to the WSGA members, who hoped that Army intervention could be used to destroy their economic competitors and other enemies in Johnson County.[72]

In the wake of Senator Carey's request for the black regiment, General Schofield asked Brooke's opinion on the need for a semipermanent peacekeeping force in northern Wyoming. He advised Brooke that once established, such an encampment could be employed in peaceful times as a site of tactical instruction. Brooke immediately warmed to the idea and recommended establishment of two camps, north and south of Johnson County in Coverse County, between Douglas and Casper, and in Sheridan County where the Burlington & Missouri Railroad crossed the Powder River. Schofield authorized him to act on the plan.[73]

Sensing the need to respond with overwhelming federal force to prevent further lawlessness, on 4 June Brooke ordered the commanding officers of the 6th and 9th Cavalry regiments at Forts Niobara and Robinson, Nebraska, to Wyoming. Numbering over 300 men in six troops, each regiment was to bring field equipment, 200 rounds of ammunition per man, 2 Hotchkiss guns, 1 medical officer, and hospital corpsmen.[74] He also ordered Col. Eugene A. Carr's 6th Cavalry to old Fort Fetterman and Maj. Charles S. Ilsley's 9th Cavalry to the Powder River rail crossing thirty-five miles northwest of Buffalo, Wyoming. He cautioned the commanders to avoid involvement in other than emergencies without receiving instructions. In the meantime, both were to collect and forward to Omaha coded intelligence reports on outlaws and participants in any local disorders.[75]

In less than a week, Senator Warren sought to use these recently stationed troops for posse duty. On 10 June he informed General Brooke that the U.S. marshal for Wyoming was preparing to issue criminal warrants against some twenty men in Johnson County for burning and stealing federal property and for obstructing the process of the federal court. But when he asked Brooke to provide the necessary troops, the general refused, stating that the president alone can take the action desired. Brooke did not interpret his instructions to mean providing soldiers for posses proscribed by the Posse Comitatus Act.[76]

If the big cattlemen were disappointed, the citizens of Johnson County were exhausted by the recent conflicts and impressed by the cavalry. Residents complied with

---

[72] Smith, *War on Powder River*, pp. 206–61; Schubert, "The Suggs Affray," pp. 59–60. For black troops in the West, see William H. Leckie, *The Buffalo Soldiers: A Narrative of the Negro Cavalry in the West* (Norman: University of Oklahoma Press, 1967).

[73] Telg, Schofield to Brooke, 3 Jun, and reply, 4 Jun 1892, RG 393, File 3937, NARA.

[74] Telg, AG, Dept of the Platte, to COs, Fts. Niobara and Robinson, 4 Jun 1892, RG 393, File 3937, NARA.

[75] Ibid.

[76] Telg, Warren to Brooke, 10 Jun 1892, and reply, 13 Jun 1892, RG 393, File 3937, NARA. Senator, and later governor, Francis E. Warren, a veteran of Wyoming and federal politics, was the future father-in-law of General of the Armies John Joseph Pershing.

a proclamation issued by President Harrison at the end of July that called on all persons to disperse and retire peaceably to their homes. During the remainder of the summer the 9th Cavalry at Camp Bettens performed ordinary garrison duty. On 26 September four troops of cavalry returned to Fort Robinson, followed a month and a half later by the remaining two troops, as relative calm returned to Johnson County.[77]

Despite the restrictions posed by the Posse Comitatus Act, the Army was used extensively to control disorders in the western states and territories between 1878–1892. The Army, however, was never truly effective in its new police role, due to the restrictions of the act and the scarcity and wide dispersal of troops. One problem developed in the territories. Denied federal troops for posse duty, beleaguered territorial law enforcement officials and governors requested military aid from the federal government to suppress domestic disorders, only to find that existing laws permitted such requests only from states. When requests were made under applicable laws, Presidents Hayes, Arthur, Cleveland, and Harrison all initially hesitated to use regulars to enforce laws in the territories, but eventually consented, to save lives and buy time for local legislatures to raise militia forces capable of restoring law and order.

On occasions when presidents temporized about providing aid, local military commanders, for better or for worse, often stretched Army regulations to allow flexibility and sent troops to troubled areas in advance of formal approval. Such action, however, occasionally revived the worst features of the days during Reconstruction, before the Posse Comitatus Act, including the tendency of certain officers to use troops under their command in a partisan manner to support one faction against another. Most frequently, though, the local military commanders supported the recognized and legal wielders of economic, legal, and political power, whether or not they were morally justified. Just as the Posse Comitatus Act inhibited military support of western law enforcement, it also hampered potentially partisan activities on the part of local military commanders. It prevented neither completely.

---

[77] Smith, *War on Powder River*, p. 262.

CHAPTER 4

The Anti-Chinese Riots of 1885–1886

Is it not a . . . damnable disgrace to see a rich and powerful corporation . . . claiming and receiving the assistance of American soldiers to enforce the employment of leprous aliens? . . . Why even the soldiers themselves curse the duty that compels them to sustain the alien against Americans. Let the demand go up from one end of the Union Pacific to the other, "The Chinese Must Go."
                                                                          —Rock Springs *Independent*, 1885.

While the Army dealt with range wars, roving bands of outlaws, and hostile Indians, several racial disturbances requiring federal military intervention occurred also throughout the West. Especially severe outbreaks in Wyoming, Washington, and New Mexico territories resulted directly from the influx of thousands of Chinese immigrants in the years prior to 1885. Although immigrants from Asia formed a very small percentage of the nearly 24 million foreigners who entered the United States between 1880 and 1919, most were densely concentrated on the West Coast in California and Washington Territory.[1] Popular prejudice against them resulted in riots that gave the Army its first experience with race riots in the post-Reconstruction period.[2]

Americans and Chinese Immigration

The first Chinese immigrants arrived on the Pacific coast after the 1848 California gold discoveries and initially were welcomed as a solution to labor shortages. In the 1860s Oriental laborers, known as coolies, were imported by firms who in turn were under contract to railroad and mining companies, despite an 1862 congressional ban on their importation. During construction of the first transcontinental railroads the Chinese gained a reputation for being extraordinarily diligent workers, willing to labor long hours under miserable and dangerous conditions for less pay than Caucasians. In spite of the protests

---

[1] Immigration figures between 1880 and 1919 show a total of 383,304 Asians entered the United States. See Kraut, *Huddled Masses*, pp. 20–21; Rose Hum Lee, *The Chinese in the United States of America* (Hong Kong: Oxford University Press, 1960), pp. 12–13, 21; Willard A. Heaps, *Riots, U.S.A., 1765–1970* (New York: Seabury Press, 1970), p. 61. For population statistics and a study of the regions Chinese, see Robert E. Wynne, *Reaction to the Chinese in the Pacific Northwest and British Columbia, 1850–1910* (New York: Arno Press, 1978), pp. 492–99.

[2] For race riots associated with the Civil War draft riots and Reconstruction, see Coakley, *Role of Federal Military Forces*, chs. 12–15, especially pp. 340–41.

of local labor unions and white residents of the Pacific coast, in 1868 the United States signed the Burlingame Treaty with China, facilitating the immigration of Chinese laborers and providing them with "most favored nation" rights, privileges, and protections. Under the treaty, the Chinese did not need to declare their intention of becoming citizens to reside or work in the country. The treaty did, however, preserve the American right to regulate, limit, and suspend the admission of Chinese laborers, or else absolutely prohibit their entry.[3] Increasing racial differences and economic competition and what the whites perceived as the presence of overwhelming numbers of Chinese soon aroused racial nativism.

Examples of racial and economic discrimination toward the Chinese by whites were evident from the outset. American society until the mid-nineteenth century was predominantly white, Anglo-Saxon, and Protestant. The United States was an extension of Western civilization, which dominated world affairs. To many Americans, China represented a primitive culture and a strange, backward society; its people were supposedly racially inferior heathens who threatened to pollute the Caucasian race and challenge Western predominance. They were believed to be incapable of assimilation and of participation in the American way of life.[4]

The proclivity of the Chinese for various reasons to live in segregated "Chinatowns" led to additional accusations of moral depravity and racial degeneration. E. W. Gilliam deemed Californians "the most competent judges, and their opinions, excepting some interested manufacturers," are "intense and unanimous" against the Chinese. The effect of Oriental immigration on the state was described as "vile." A widely quoted July 1885 special committee report of the San Francisco Board of Supervisors claimed that the twelve blocks of the Chinese quarter were indescribably filthy and contained 30,000 men and 1,385 women, 567 of the women were supposedly prostitutes.[5]

By the 1870s and 1880s Oriental immigrants came to represent a vaguely defined but nonetheless insidious threat, later characterized as the "yellow peril." The Chinese image changed from that of the harmless "coolie" to that of an evil, opium-addicted mandarin devil. They allegedly ate rats and snakes; they were cunning, crafty, mysterious, dishonest,

---

[3] Lee, *Chinese in the U.S.A.*, pp. 11–12; Heaps, *Riots, U.S.A.*, pp. 61–62; Paul Crane and Alfred Larson, "The Chinese Massacre," *Annals of Wyoming* 12 (1940):52. For histories of the Chinese in America, see Gunther Barth, *Bitter Strength: A History of the Chinese in the United States, 1850–1870* (Cambridge: Harvard University Press, 1964); Stuart C. Miller, *The Unwelcome Immigrant: The American Image of the Chinese, 1785–1882* (Berkeley: University of California Press, 1969); Roger Daniels, *Asian America: Chinese and Japanese in the United States Since 1850* (Seattle: University of Washington Press, 1989); Betty Lee Sung, *Mountain of Gold: The Story of Chinese in America* (Detroit: Wayne State University Press, 1972); Ronald Takaki, *Strangers From a Different Shore: A History of Asian Americans* (Boston: Little Brown, 1989); Cheng-Tsu Wu, ed., *Chink!: A Documentary History of Anti-Chinese Prejudice in America* (New York: World, 1972); James A. Halseth and Bruce A. Glasrud, "Anti-Chinese Movements in Washington, 1885–1886: A Reconsideration," in James A. Halseth and Bruce A. Glasrud, eds., *The Northwest Mosaic: Minority Conflicts in Pacific Northwest History* (Boulder: Pruett, 1977), pp. 118–21.

[4] Walter MacArthur, "Opposition to Oriental Immigration" *Annals of the American Academy of Political and Social Sciences* 34 (September 1909):22–23, 239; W. W. Stone, "The Knights of Labor on the Chinese Situation" *Overland Monthly* 7 [new series] (March 1886):226–27; A. A. Sargeant, "The Wyoming Anti-Chinese Riot" *Overland Monthly* 6 [new series] (November 1885):509; E. W. Gilliam, "Chinese Immigration," *North American Review* (July 1886):28–32; Bryan J. Church, "The Chinese in America," *American Catholic Quarterly* 9 (January 1886):60–61.

[5] Quotes from Gilliam, "Chinese Immigration," pp. 32–33; Church, "Chinese in America," p. 66.

inscrutable, without souls or nerves; and they lusted after Caucasian women, seducing them with opium. "Agitators and demagogues," writes a historian, "evoked hordes of Chinese 'coolies' invading the United States and 'conquering' it by sheer numbers if barriers were not erected."[6] Although most Orientals did not settle permanently in the United States and posed no real threat to American racial purity or economic security, these facts did not disarm the critics. Foes of the Chinese claimed that the transients were "draining the wealth of the nation" by sending wages home, and that every dollar paid to the Chinese was lost to Americans.[7]

Labor, Business, and the Chinese

By the late 1870s the combination of racial prejudices and job competition caused the troubles among Americans, European immigrants, and Chinese to become inextricably intertwined with the ongoing struggle between capital and labor.[8] Western mine owners and other corporate leaders believed that limitless numbers of Orientals could be used to minimize labor costs, maximize profits, and frustrate the growth and demands of budding labor unions. Hence corporations helped speed the flow of Chinese into the mining, railroad, and lumber industries. According to accepted business philosophy of the time, these policies made good economic sense. Corporations further used their wealth and influence, from the state and territorial to the federal level, to support legislation that assured continued Chinese immigration and protected immigrants from the wrath of Americans in general and labor unions in particular. Having a vested interest in unrestricted immigration and favorable Sino-American relations, business leaders gave exaggerated testimonials to Chinese industry, thrift, morality, honesty, and cleanliness that contradicted the equally exaggerated claims of nativists, working-class leaders, and union racists.[9]

The conflict that developed between white and Oriental workers was fundamental and bitter. Labor unions composed of white Americans and European immigrants were struggling for mere recognition of their organizations, as well as for higher wages and improved living and working conditions. Chinese immigrants were either forbidden to join unions or refused to do so, and by not supporting striking whites they threatened the hard-fought, hard-won gains of the whites. Labor unions therefore joined ranks with nativists in demanding restrictions on Chinese immigration and the exclusion of Chinese laborers from the logging, railroad, and mining industries. The Knights of Labor, the American

---

[6] Lee, *Chinese in the U.S.A.*, pp. 357–62; Gilliam, "Chinese Immigration," p. 27; Church, "Chinese in America," p. 62.

[7] Lee, *Chinese in the U.S.A.*, p. 358. For favorable views, see George F. Seward, "Mongolian Immigration," *North American Review* 134 (June 1882):562; H. Shewin, "Observations on Chinese Labor" *Overland Monthly* 7 [new series] (January 1886):91–99; Francis E. Sheldon, "The Chinese Immigration Discussion" *Overland Monthly* 7 (February 1886):113–19; John S. Hittell, "Benefits of Chinese Immigration" *Overland Monthly* 7 (February 1886):120–21; "The Other Side of the Chinese Question," *Nation* 42 (April 1886):272–73.

[8] See Alexander Saxton, *The Indispensable Enemy: Labor and the Anti-Chinese Movement in California* (Berkeley: University of California Press, 1971).

[9] Lee, *Chinese in the U.S.A.*, p. 358; Seward, "Mongolian Immigration," p. 562; "The Other Side of the Chinese Question," pp. 272–73; Herbert Hill, "Anti-Oriental Agitation and the Rise of Working-Class Racism," *Society* 10 (1973):43–54.

Federation of Labor, and other unions not only urged economic arguments against the Chinese but also endorsed other nativist themes.[10]

The voices of nativists and labor unionists were making themselves heard in Washington, D.C., by 1880. On 31 October the United States modified the Burlingame Treaty requiring China to recognize and accept the American right to limit or suspend unilaterally, although not absolutely to prohibit, Chinese immigration. This effort, strongly supported by business interests as preferable to outright exclusion, did not end demands for stronger restrictions and exclusions. With the subsequent passage of the 1882 Exclusion Act, however, labor demands were partially met. Congress suspended the immigration of Chinese laborers for ten years, made all Chinese ineligible for citizenship, and closed certain industries (mining for example) to Chinese labor. The Exclusion Act was to be reviewed each decade and renewed or amended as necessary. However, the United States—to the chagrin of nativist and labor movements— promised as it had in 1880 to protect the 105,000 Chinese already working and residing in America:

If Chinese laborers, or Chinese of any other class, now either permanently or temporarily residing in the territory of the United States, meet with ill-treatment at the hands of any other persons, the government of the United States will exert all its power to devise means for their protection, and to secure to them the same rights, privileges, amenities, and exemptions as may be enjoyed by the citizens or subjects of the most favored nation, and to which they are entitled by treaty.[11]

Union frustrations over the lack of comprehensive restrictive legislation and widespread corporate evasion of the prohibitory statutes now took an ugly turn. Anti-Chinese violence was not new in the West; outbreaks had occurred as early as the 1860s. In 1871 massive anti-Chinese riots in Los Angeles and San Francisco had resulted in the deaths of twenty-one Chinese. Six years later, during the Great Railway Strike, in San Francisco mobs had burned twenty-five Chinese business establishments. New anti-Chinese disturbances had followed in Denver in 1880.[12]

During these upheavals corporate and territorial authorities, in spite of professions to the contrary, seemed either unwilling or unable to protect the Chinese from mobs. Immigrant brokers fueled the unrest by smuggling Chinese workers into the West where they were still hired promptly. The commanding general of the Division of the Pacific, Brig. Gen. John Pope, asserted that this illicit trade made the Chinese population a conspicuous

---

[10] Isabella Black, "American Labor and Chinese Immigration," *Past and Present* 25 (1963):59–76; Roger Daniels, "American Labor and Chinese Immigration," *Past and Present* 27 (1964):113–15; Philip Taft, *The American Federation of Labor in the Time of Gompers* (New York: Harper Brothers, 1957), pp. 304–07.

[11] Article III cited in E. P. Clark, "The Boycotting of the Chinese Is Illegal," *Nation* 42 (13 May 1886):397. See also Lee, *Chinese in the U.S.A.*, pp. 12–13, 21–22, 33–34, 254–55; U.S. Department of State, *Papers Relating to the Foreign Relations of the United States, 1881* (Washington, D.C.: Government Printing Office, 1882), pp. 318–37; 20 *U.S. Statutes at Large, 1881–1883*, pp. 58–61, 826–27; Taft, *A. F. of L. in Time of Gompers*, pp. 11–12, 302–03; Thomas Bailey, *A Diplomatic History of the American People*, 3d ed. (New York: F. S. Crofts, 1946), pp. 430–31; Heaps, *Riots, U.S.A.*, p. 70; Crane and Larson, "The Chinese Massacre," pp. 51–52; John Higham, "Origins of Immigration Restriction, 1882–1897: A Social Analysis," *Mississippi Valley Historical Review* 39 (1952):77–88.

[12] Kraut, *Huddled Masses*, p. 157; Heaps, *Riots, U.S.A*, pp. 61–71; Higham, *Strangers in the Land*, pp. 150–51. For the Los Angeles riot, see Richard O. Hofstadter and Michael Wallace, eds., *American Violence: A Documentary History* (New York: A. A. Knopf, 1971), pp. 324–29; Wu, *Chink*, pp. 146–48.

THE START OF THE ROCK SPRINGS ANTI-CHINESE MASSACRE. *As depicted in a woodcut engraving in* Harper's Weekly.

part of the small, previously all-white, inland towns, where juries probably could not be found to punish anyone guilty of attacks upon the Chinese.[13]

In response to the continued hiring of Chinese workers, the Knights of Labor began a campaign for more effective and vigorous enforcement of the Exclusion Act. However, with their confidence in legal methods shaken, and under the influence of inflammatory racist labor and nativist rhetoric, which claimed that Chinese immigrants illegally in the United States were not entitled to legal protection, many white citizens and union members were determined to take law enforcement into their own hands. By 1885 a major outbreak of anti-Chinese racial violence was only a matter of time. The first occurred in Rock Springs, Wyoming, in September.[14]

Rock Springs, Wyoming, 1885

Located halfway between Rawlins and Evanston in Sweetwater County, Wyoming Territory, Rock Springs was a small mining community of 1,000 inhabitants, most of

---

[13] Ltr, Pope to Sheridan, U.S. Army, Commanding, 13 Nov 1885, RG 94, Records of the Office of the Adjutant General, United States Army, File 5820, AGO 1885: Papers Relating to an Attack on Chinese Workers of the Union Pacific Railroad on 2 Sep 1885 at Rock Springs, Wyoming; the Other Violations of Chinese in the Western United States, 1885–1887, Ltrs Received by the Adjutant General's Office, NARA.

[14] Taft, *A. F. of L. in the Time of Gompers*, p. 10.

whom worked for the Union Pacific (U.P.) Railroad's coal mines.[15] Until 1875 the mines had been worked exclusively by whites, but in that year a strike for higher wages prompted the Union Pacific to fire the striking workers and replace them with 150 Chinese immigrants. According to a U.P. spokesman "if the white men will not dig the company's coal for pay, who will blame the company for hiring yellow, black, or red men, who are ready and willing to do what white men will not do?" At least 150 white miners lost their jobs to Chinese workers, while 50 other whites returned to work for previous wages.[16]

By August 1885 the Union Pacific in Rock Springs employed 842 workers: 552 Chinese and 290 predominately European whites. The Chinese did not live among the white miners, but in settlements in remote areas "where law and authority are feeble and where race prejudice may be precipitated on the slightest pretext."[17]

With racial tensions growing locally and nationwide, white hatred toward the Chinese miners festered during the summer of 1885. More Chinese were hired for wages lower than those paid to whites and steadfastly refused to join the Knights of Labor or support anticipated labor actions. Rumors were rife among whites that the Chinese received special treatment from "pit bosses," who often accepted bribes to hire them. The *Rock Springs Independent* reported that "white men had been turned off . . . and hundreds could not get work while the Chinese were shipped in by the carload and given work." Although company officials insisted that the Chinese received similar pay, worked under the same regulations, and were not meant to supplant white miners, the company's privately contracted labor agent confirmed that the Chinese miners were paid one dollar less per day than whites.

Union Pacific officials were undaunted by the rising racial tensions, and later claimed that they were unaware of any problems. About the company right to hire Chinese they were adamant. In the summer of 1885 one official stated that "when the company can be assured against strikes and other outbreaks at the hands of persons who deny its owners the right to manage their property, it may consider the expediency of abandoning Chinese labor; but under all circumstances and at any cost or hazard it will assert its right to employ whom it pleases and refuse to ostracize any one class of its employees at the dictation of another."[18]

Anti-Chinese resentment climaxed on 2 September 1885. Fighting between Caucasian and Chinese miners in the pits was followed at 0600 by the stoning of startled

---

[15] George B. Pryde, "The Union Pacific Coal Company, 1868 to August 1952," *Annals of Wyoming* 25 (July 1953):191–205.

[16] Crane and Larson, "The Chinese Massacre," pp. 52–53. For a history of Rock Springs, see Robert B. Rhodes, *Booms and Bust on Bitter Creek: A History of Rock Springs, Wyoming* (Boulder: Pruett, 1987), especially pp. 44–63. See also Clayton D. Laurie, "Civil Disorder and the Military in Rock Springs, Wyoming; The Army's Role in the 1885 Chinese Massacre," *Montana: The Magazine of Western History* 40 (Summer 1990):44–59.

[17] Quote from "Special Report Concerning Chinese Labor Troubles (1885)," *Report of the Governor of Wyoming to the Secretary of the Interior, 1885* (Washington, D.C.: Government Printing Office, 1886), p. 102 (hereafter cited as *Rpt of Gov of Wyoming*). For Rock Springs before the massacre, see Paul J. Scheips and Mary L. Haynes, Anti-Chinese Disturbances in the Western Territories of Wyoming and Washington, 1885–1886, MS in U.S. Army Center of Military History, pp. 10–12a; Telg, Bayard to Cheng Tsao-Ju, 18 Feb 1886, in U.S. Department of State, *Foreign Relations of the United States, 1886* (Washington, D.C.: Government Printing Office, 1887), pp. 158–68.

[18] Crane and Larson, "The Chinese Massacre," pp. 51–55.

Chinese workers leaving the mines by a group of white youths. At noon seventy miners, joined by an equal number of the unemployed, left local saloons armed for action. The mob sent three men to warn the Chinese miners to leave town in one hour. Impatient lest their quarry elude them completely, the whites reached the Chinese area a half-hour early. The mob burned and plundered dwellings, causing an estimated $140,000 worth of damage. In all, twenty-eight Chinese perished in their burning homes or at the hands of the mob; fourteen were severely injured; and the remainder, thoroughly panic-stricken, fled to the surrounding hills. After the mob disbanded, company officials collected the frightened survivors and placed them on a train for Evanston in Uinta County, just west of Sweetwater.[19]

Shortly thereafter, D. O. Clark, the assistant superintendent of Union Pacific's coal mining department, and Joseph Young, the sheriff of Sweetwater County, wired Governor Francis E. Warren for military aid. Warren forwarded the request to Brig. Gen. Oliver Otis Howard, commander of the Department of the Platte, suggesting that one or more companies of federal troops be sent to Rock Springs from Fort D. A. Russell. Howard, in turn, sent the request to General Schofield at the Division of the Missouri headquarters in Chicago.[20]

Anticipating a slow response through military channels, S. R. Callaway of the Union Pacific's Omaha office convinced Warren to telegraph Secretary of War William C. Endicott also. Warren stated that an "armed mob of white men" had attacked Chinese miners, that county authorities were powerless, and that the territory lacked a militia to end the crisis. He asked the federal government to "afford military protection to life and property at Rock Springs." During the following days Charles Francis Adams, president of the Union Pacific, descendant of two former U.S. presidents, and former ambassador to the Court of St. James, wrote the War Department, repeatedly asking for military intervention and declaring that the Union Pacific had no intention of negotiating with the miners until order had been restored. The messages reached Adjutant General Richard C. Drum, who located the vacationing secretary at Salem, Massachusetts. Endicott advised Drum to consult Attorney General A. H. Garland on a course of action. Garland, however, was out of town also, and Drum referred the messages to Secretary of State Thomas F. Bayard.[21]

While Drum sought a responsible federal official, Warren, in the company of several Union Pacific officials, visited Sweetwater County to investigate the riot. In a conference with Sheriff Young he learned that widespread hatred of the Chinese made assembly of

---

[19] Isaac H. Bromley, *The Chinese Massacre at Rock Springs, Wyoming Territory, September 2, 1885* (Boston: Franklin Press; Rand, Avery, 1886), pp. 48–52; Wilson, *Federal Aid in Domestic Disturbances*, p. 215; John W. Caughey, *Their Majesties the Mob* (Chicago: University of Chicago Press, 1960), pp. 101–02; Scheips and Haynes, Anti-Chinese Disturbances, pp. 12a–15b, 16–19; U.S. Congress, House, *Providing Indemnity to Certain Chinese Subjects*, 49th Cong., 1st sess., 1885, Exec. Doc. 2044, pp. 31–41.

[20] "Special Report Concerning Chinese Labor Troubles," *Rpt of Gov of Wyoming*, pp. 109–11; Murry L. Carroll, "Governor Francis E. Warren, The United States Army, and the Chinese Massacre at Rock Springs," *Annals of Wyoming* 59 (Fall 1987):16–27.

[21] Telgs, Kimball to Warren, and reply, 2 Sep 1885; Endicott to Drum, 3 and 4 Sep 1885, and reply; Adams to Endicott, 7 and 8 Sep 1885. All in RG 94, File 5820, NARA. See also Telg, Warren to Endicott, 2 Sep 1885, in *Rpt of Gov of Wyoming*. Cleveland was also away from Washington, see Scheips and Haynes, Anti-Chinese Disturbances, pp. 19ff.

OLIVER OTIS HOWARD   WILLIAM C. ENDICOTT

reliable posses to track down the perpetrators of the massacre impossible. Later at the county seat of Green River, Warren received a telegram from Sheriff J. J. Le Cain of Uinta County stating that the Chinese who had fled to Evanston had now regrouped and armed themselves. Thronged with hundreds of armed and angry men of two races, Evanston was threatened with becoming the scene of even more bloodshed than Rock Springs. Warren, still lacking a response about federal military aid, urged Le Cain to swear in as many deputies as possible, but his efforts raised only twenty men.[22]

The imminent spread of open racial warfare in southwestern Wyoming left Warren with no recourse but to make a direct appeal to President Grover Cleveland. In a 3 September telegram he repeated what he had told Endicott, adding that immediate assistance was imperative to preserve life and property. Uncertain as to how the Constitution or federal statutes concerning domestic disturbances applied to a federal territory and crimes against foreign nationals, Warren first omitted any reference to either. However, Generals Schofield and Howard urged him to correct his omission. The next day he appropriately cited RS 5298 and informed Cleveland that "unlawful combinations and conspiracies exist among the coal miners and others in Uinta and Sweetwater Counties which prevent individuals and corporations from enjoyment and protection of their property and obstruct execution of territorial law." He described the situation at Rock Springs as an "open insurrection" and sheriffs as powerless to prevent further violence without organized bodies of armed men. Since Wyoming lacked a territorial militia, he requested

---

[22] Telg, Le Cain to Warren, and reply, 3 Sep 1885, *Rpt of Gov of Wyoming*, pp. 111–12; Bromley, *The Chinese Massacre at Rock Springs*, p. 52.

federal regulars "to support civil authorities until order is restored, criminals arrested, and the sufferers relieved."[23]

Meanwhile, Bayard conferred with Drum and the two agreed that regulars should be deployed in Sweetwater County "to prevent any interruption to the United States mail or the routes over which they are received," but not to protect the Chinese or Union Pacific property. The decision to commit troops under the Act of 2 July 1864 and Act of 27 July 1866, which allowed for federal protection of transcontinental rail lines as "military roads" and "post routes," may appear strange. Regulars could have been committed under the provisions of the treaties with China, which guaranteed federal protection to Chinese in the United States, enforceable under the provisions of RS 5298. Probably Bayard's decision was motivated by the hope that calm could be restored rapidly without sending federal troops to protect an unpopular minority against working-class whites and citizens. His primary motivation, however, was probably a desire to avoid setting the precedent of committing troops to quell what could become widespread anti-Chinese rioting in the West, which the Army lacked the manpower, time, and resources to suppress. And certainly in the weeks following the incident, anti-Chinese violence broke out in at least thirty towns and cities along the West Coast, primarily in California.

Secretary Endicott endorsed their plan, and on 4 September Schofield authorized Howard to send troops to Rock Springs and any other place in Wyoming where their presence might deter anti-Chinese violence. Howard ordered two companies of the 7th Infantry at Fort Steele, under Lt. Col. Henry L. Chipman, and two companies of the 9th Infantry at Fort D. A. Russell, under Lt. Col. Thomas M. Anderson, to travel on the Union Pacific to Rock Springs and Evanston. The troops arrived the following day.[24] By then violence had subsided, and Sheriff Young began to arrest men suspected of being involved in the anti-Chinese attacks on the pretext that their actions interfered with the proper operation of the Union Pacific as a federal military road and mail route. Meanwhile, Anderson's forces in Evanston also prevented violence, but the colonel predicted more trouble as soon as Chinese workers returned to the mines. To meet that exigency, Anderson asked for a ten-man Gatling gun detachment from Fort D. A. Russell, which arrived on the afternoon train.[25]

But the situation remained tense. In the face of this continued unstable situation, Warren telegraphed Cleveland that

unlawful organized mobs in possession of coal mines . . . will not permit Chinamen to approach their own homes, property, or employment. . . . From the nature of outbreak sheriff of county cannot rally sufficient posse and Territorial government cannot sufficiently aid him. Insurrectionists know

---

[23] Telgs, Warren to Cleveland, 3, 4, and 5 Sep 1885, *Rpt of Gov of Wyoming*, pp. 113–14; Wilson, *Federal Aid in Domestic Disturbances*, pp. 184–85. Prompted by Drum, Warren submitted a third request on 5 September, adding the phrase that the "legislature of Wyoming is not in session and cannot be convened in time to provide for the emergency." This was irrelevant since he was not asking for aid under RS 5297—the statute covering state requests—but for enforcement of federal laws under RS 5298.

[24] Telgs, Endicott to Drum, and reply, 4 Sep 1885; Drum to Warren, 4 Sep 1885; SO 86, HQ, Dept of the Platte, 4 Sep 1885; Telgs, Schofield to AG, 5 Sep 1885; Drum to Endicott, 5 Sep 1885. All in RG 94, File 5820, NARA. See also *Secretary of War Report, 1885*, pp. 88–97; Scheips and Haynes, Anti-Chinese Disturbances, pp. 26–27.

[25] Returns of 7th, 9th, 21st Infantry Regiments for Sep 1885, RG 94, Returns from Regular Army Regiments, 1821–1916, NARA; see also Telgs, Drum to Endicott and Schofield, and reply; Schofield to Drum, 6 Sep 1885; Drum to Endicott, 7 Sep 1885; and Breck to AG, Div of the Missouri, 6 and 7 Sep 1885. All in RG 94, File 5820, NARA. *Rpt of Gov of Wyoming*, p. 114.

FEDERAL TROOPS OF THE 7TH AND 9TH INFANTRY ARRIVE IN ROCK SPRINGS

through the newspapers and dispatches that troops will not interfere under present orders and moral effect of presence of troops is destroyed. If troops were known to have orders to assist sheriff's posse in case driven back, I am quite sure civil authorities could restore order without actual use of soldiers; but unless U.S. Government can find a way to relieve us immediately, I believe worse scenes than those at Rock Springs will follow and all Chinamen will be driven from the territory.

Adams repeated Warren's requests, emphasizing the importance of protecting county authorities guarding mines and nonstriking workers.[26]

The urgency of Anderson's request for a Gatling gun and the continued pleas of Warren and Adams convinced Schofield to expand the Army role in Wyoming. Lacking a presidential proclamation under RS 5298, he decided to act under the authority granted by Congress in the Acts of 2 July 1864 and 27 July 1866. Schofield argued that the breakdown of any portion of the Union Pacific's transportation system jeopardized the nation's communication and strategic links to the West Coast and urged Drum to extend protection to all trains, rails, and coal mines held by the Union Pacific.[27]

Diplomatic considerations added weight to the efforts of Warren, Adams, and Schofield. President Cleveland also believed it to be imperative to honor Article III of the

---

[26] Telg, Warren to Cleveland, 7 Sep 1885, *Rpt of Gov of Wyoming*, pp. 114–15; Telgs, Adams to Endicott, 7 Sep 1885, and to Endicott, 8 Sep 1885, both in RG 94, File 5820, NARA.

[27] Telg, Schofield to AG, 7 Sep 1885, RG 94, File 5820, NARA.

Burlingame Treaty of 17 November 1880, protecting all resident Chinese, although he had hoped to do so without the use of troops. With soldiers already committed, however, now he ordered the Army also to protect Chinese laborers at points of threatened or actual violence. He further authorized that Schofield aid civil authorities and "if necessity actually exists" to arrest "those committing offenses against the laws." To ensure that troops did not fall under direct control of the governor or other civil officials, however, he insisted that field commanders be encouraged to confer directly with Schofield.[28]

Once the president had made this decision, Schofield informed his field commanders at Rock Springs and Evanston, through Howard, that the president had ordered the Army to protect Chinese laborers. In detailed guidance the next day, he cautioned that, in protecting the Chinese and aiding civil authorities, commanders were to limit their actions to the necessary measures of defense. Further action such as arrest and confinement of offenders, or other aid to civil authorities was to be taken in each case only upon Schofield's express orders. He explained that he would authorize arrest and confinement only after local commanders had received an application for aid, investigated the case, and related the facts to him. Further, Chipman and Anderson were to make daily situation reports through department headquarters to division headquarters. He instructed them that they "must bear in mind and caution their troops that it is no part of their duty to punish offenders, but rather to prevent, so far as possible, any commission of the specific offense apprehended and to protect those in danger of attack in the absence of civil protection." In a separate message to Warren, Schofield enclosed a copy of the instructions of 8 September and urged him to inform local commanders fully of any facts that might justify an appeal for troops to arrest or confine federal offenders.[29]

Howard, believing 4 companies inadequate to carry out this expanded mission, ordered the commander of Camp Murray, Utah, to dispatch 6 companies to Evanston. Leading a detachment composed of 3 companies of the 9th Infantry, 1 of the 6th Infantry, and 2 of the 21st Infantry, Capt. Alfred Morton reached the Wyoming town on 9 September. After leaving 2 companies with Anderson, Morton and the remaining units escorted several hundred Chinese to Rock Springs by rail. All entered town without incident, and Morton placed his detachment under command of Chipman. Warren conveyed his appreciation for such prompt assistance to Drum, predicting that the show of force would preclude further hostility.[30]

The sudden reappearance of hundreds of Chinese, accompanied by 4 additional companies of federal regulars, convinced white miners that the Union Pacific, with federal military aid, intended to oust white miners in favor of the Chinese. The Rock Springs *Independent* wrote that the "action of the company in bringing back the Chinese means that they are to be set to work in the mines and that American soldiers are to prevent them from again being driven out. It means that all (white) miners at Rock Springs, except those absolutely required, are to be replaced by Chinese labor. It means that the company intends

---

[28] Telg, Drum to Schofield, 7 Sep 1885, and copies to Sheridan, Endicott, Warren, 8 Sep 1885, all in RG 94, File 5820, NARA. See also Scheips and Haynes, Anti-Chinese Disturbances, pp. 34–37.

[29] Telgs, Schofield to Breck, AG, Dept of the Platte, and reply, 7 Sep 1885; AG, Div of the Missouri, to CO, Dept of the Platte, 8 Sep 1885; and Ltr, Schofield to Warren, 8 Sep 1885. All in RG 94, File 5820, NARA.

[30] Telgs, AG, Dept of the Platte, to McCook, 8 Sep 1885, and Warren to Drum, 8 Sep 1885, both in RG 94, File 5820, NARA.

CHINESE MINERS DRIVEN FROM ROCK SPRINGS STAND BY UNION PACIFIC BOXCARS

to make a 'Chinatown' out of Rock Springs. . . . Let the demand go up from one end of the U.P. to the other, 'The Chinese must go.'" Other anti-Chinese newspapers in Wyoming similarly denounced federal intervention.

Workers, inflamed by the rhetoric of a union lawyer, passed a resolution declaring that "the presence of Federal bayonets at Rock Springs and Evanston . . . [were unnecessary to protect] either life or property, but a power wielded solely in the interest of a grasping corporation . . . to force a revolting system of slave labor upon the country."[31] The miners, however, were intimidated by the presence of Chipman's command and made no attempt to harm the Chinese during the daytime. The situation was different after nightfall. To escape the vengeance of the whites, the frightened Chinese huddled together for safety in railroad boxcars guarded by federal troops.[32]

Despite union protests, railroad officials were determined to return the Chinese to the mines as rapidly as possible. The Chinese, on the other hand, balked at any talk of returning to work until troops stood guard over every mine shaft. When Chipman proved reluctant to provide troops for this purpose, company officials complained to Howard, who issued the necessary orders for Chipman to comply with after consultation with Schofield. To provide the required reinforcements, on 17 September Howard decided to summon another company of the 21st Infantry from an instructional camp at Goose

---

[31] Quoted in Bromley, *The Chinese Massacre at Rock Springs*, pp. 15–17; for further newspaper commentary, see pp. 7–10, 83–86.
[32] Telgs, Schofield to Drum, 10, 11, and 15 Sep 1885; Drum to Endicott, 11 Sep 1885; Howard to AG, Div of the Missouri, 12 Sep 1885. All in RG 94, File 5820, NARA. Crane and Larson, "Chinese Massacre," pp. 50–51.

Creek, Wyoming. Drum, however, overruled both officers the next day when he declared that preemptive deployment of troops at the mines, prior to an actual need for soldiers to quell a specific outbreak of disorder, exceeded the instructions issued by Schofield nine days before.[33]

As Howard reinforced the troops at Rock Springs, the Chinese government prepared to investigate the events of 2 September. Upon receiving War Department approval, Cheng Tsao-Ju, the Chinese minister to the United States, sent two consular officials from San Francisco to Wyoming. Under Army protection, they interrogated witnesses and company officials for eight days. Their report, read with great interest by Imperial Chinese officials, stated among other things that the attackers, like the victims, were aliens and not citizens of the United States. Despite this, the Chinese government claimed that the United States was legally and morally responsible for protecting Chinese residents under treaty obligations or, failing that, to indemnify the Chinese government for property damage and the abuse of its subjects.

The Chinese claim provoked an unseemly effort by the federal government to evade responsibility. In spite of explicit treaty obligations that affirmed the Chinese view, the Cleveland administration initially denied that the United States owed anything either to the Chinese government or to the Chinese in Rock Springs. After the position of the government was soundly and publicly condemned by many Americans, however, President Cleveland, without any admission of national guilt or responsibility, saw to it that Congress approved a sum of $147,748.74 for payment to the Chinese government.[34]

During the fall investigation, Schofield informed Drum that he intended to go to Rock Springs for a firsthand look. Apparently these plans leaked out. The Knights of Labor, who now viewed the Army as a partisan supporter of the Chinese and Union Pacific against the workingman, ordered a walkout along the rail line west of Nebraska to disrupt his visit. Speaking off the record during the stopover at Omaha, Schofield warned the union that any tampering with the operation of a "military road," in violation of the Acts of 2 July 1864 and 27 July 1866, would be treated as an "act of war" against the government. The walkout never materialized.[35]

Other issues that had to be considered by Schofield during his troubled journey included McCook's warning to Howard that any attempt by civil authorities to punish those involved in the riots was a waste of time, in view of public prejudice against the Chinese. A Sweetwater grand jury had already convened and interviewed witnesses, but had failed to return any indictments, finding that "whatever crimes may have been committed, the perpetrators thereof have not been disclosed by evidence before us." Reflecting local sympathies, the grand jury concluded: "there appears to be no doubt of abuses existing that should have been promptly adjusted by the railroad company and its officers." In view of the local situation, McCook recommended creating a military

---

[33] Bromley, *The Chinese Massacre at Rock Springs*, pp. 69–70; Telgs, Howard to AG, Div of the Missouri, 12 Sep 1885; Schofield to Drum, 16 Sep, and reply, 18 Sep 1885; last three in RG 94, File 5820, NARA.

[34] For this dispute, see Telgs, Cheng Tsao-Ju to Bayard, 11 Sep 1885, and reply, *U.S. Foreign Relations, 1885*, pp. 187–91; Crane and Larson, "Chinese Massacre," pp. 157–60; E. L. Godkin, "A Strange Doctrine Indeed," *Nation* 42 (11 March 1886):206–07; Clark, "Boycotting of Chinese Is Illegal," pp. 396–97.

[35] Telgs, Schofield to Drum, 19, 22, and 25 Sep 1885, RG 94, File 5820, NARA; John M. Schofield, *Forty-Six Years in the Army* (New York: Century, 1897), pp. 509–10.

commission to try the accused and cited as precedent the commission that tried the Modoc Indians in 1873.[36]

Following Schofield's arrival on 21 September, the Union Pacific reopened its mines. But when 100 Chinese entered the shafts, protesting union workers ceased the operation of weighing and loading machines. The company, seeking to rid its operations of troublesome union workers, immediately replaced them, as it had in the 1870s, with more Orientals and Mormon strikebreakers from Utah. Confident that the idle miners would make no further trouble as long as troops remained in the vicinity, Schofield dismissed McCook's highly unusual recommendation for a military commission to try civilian offenders. He did, however, order another company of the 21st Infantry from Fort Sidney, Nebraska, bringing the total number of companies in Rock Springs to eight. He left Rock Springs the next day for a visit to Cheyenne to reassure Warren that the Army was firmly in control and that peace would prevail.[37]

The buildup of federal forces in southwestern Wyoming peaked on 25 September with 203 regulars occupying Rock Springs and 120 occupying Evanston. By 4 October Schofield was convinced that withdrawals could begin. Orders from Howard eleven days later reduced Chipman's command to two companies of the 7th Infantry and the Gatling gun crew of the 21st Infantry. At Evanston, Howard reduced the force to one company of the 9th Infantry. These substantial reductions worried Warren, who asked Howard to retain the last three companies for several more months. Howard consented, and on 20 October ordered construction of semipermanent encampments at Rock Springs and Evanston, named Pilot and Medicine Butte respectively. As a direct beneficiary of the Army's peace-keeping mission, the Union Pacific agreed to pay for and construct the buildings at both posts by the end of November 1885.[38]

With the federal government firmly committed to a modest military presence in Wyoming for purposes of keeping the peace and protecting both the Union Pacific and the Chinese, the company proceeded to break the miners' union and rid the area of its influence. Although no indictments had been handed down for the massacre, and no concrete evidence existed according to the grand jury to prove that the Knights of Labor were in any way involved with the racial violence, the Union Pacific fired forty-five Caucasian miners whom they believed to be participants in the riot. Company officials offered to allow the other miners to return to work under the same conditions that had existed before the outbreak. Those who chose not to return to the mines with Chinese workers, primarily union members and their sympathizers, were offered free rail transportation out of Wyoming. When the majority refused to return to work in the vain hope of forcing concessions, company officials brought a further 120 Chinese laborers into Rock Springs to replace them, raising the number of Chinese miners to 457.

-----

[36] Quotes from Crane and Larson, "Chinese Massacre," pp. 48–49. See also Bromley, *The Chinese Massacre at Rock Springs*, p. 77; Scheips and Haynes, Anti-Chinese Disturbances, pp. 40–62 passim.

[37] Bromley, *The Chinese Massacre at Rock Springs*, pp. 72–76, 87; Telgs, Schofield to AG, Div of the Missouri, and to AG, 2 Oct 1885, both in RG 94, File 5820, NARA. Returns of 21st Inf, for Sep 1885, RG 94, NARA.

[38] SO 103, HQ, Dept of the Platte, 15 Oct 1885; Telgs, Schofield to AG, and reply, 15 Oct 1885; SO 105, HQ, Dept of the Platte, 20 Oct 1885; Telg, Howard to AG, Div of the Missouri, 1 Nov 1885. All in RG 94, File 5820, NARA. See also *Rpt of Gov of Wyoming*, pp. 46, 117.

By December 1885 only eighty-five white miners remained as the mines returned to full production without a union and with Chinese labor. Company officials claimed that after the mines were cleared of union influence coal output climbed from 1,450 tons mined in August 1885 to 1,610 tons in December 1885, implying that Chinese miners rather than new and recently installed drilling equipment was the reason. The Union Pacific had succeeded in using the anti-Chinese violence and federal military aid to break the Knights of Labor in the Rock Springs area and gain a cheaper, more malleable, nonunion work force.[39]

Federal troops remained in southwestern Wyoming for fourteen years after the riots of 1885. The last company of the 17th Infantry stationed at Camp Medicine Butte left the Evanston area in April 1887. After several garrison changes at Pilot Butte, the last company of the 24th Infantry left for Fort Assinniboine, Montana, in March 1899. During these years of garrison duty the regulars had little to occupy them beyond countless marches and rifle practice. Concerted anti-Chinese violence erupted on only one occasion, in 1896, when a group of Caucasians, allegedly including a few soldiers, assaulted five Chinese miners.[40] Otherwise peace reigned in the region.

Anti-Chinese Rioting in Washington Territory, 1885–1886

The same could not be said of other regions in the West. The failure of civil authorities at Rock Springs to punish rioters encouraged anti-Chinese violence in Washington Territory. As in Wyoming, white immigrant workers in Tacoma and Seattle fiercely resented the Chinese who were displacing them in area mines. Here, however, local politics and class friction added fuel to the anti-Chinese riots, and the local federal military commander, unlike his Wyoming counterparts, was unfamiliar with the restraints imposed by the Posse Comitatus Act.[41]

On 20 September 1885, the presence of over 3,200 Chinese miners, concentrated along the Tacoma-Seattle corridor bordering Puget Sound, led to a meeting of disgruntled workers in Tacoma. Rallying to the slogan "The Chinese must go," these workers considered exerting legislative and social pressures to harass the Chinese and deny them jobs. Many, however, favored more direct action—forcible expulsion, as at Rock Springs.

Under the auspices of the Knights of Labor, a second meeting, now including workers from Seattle as well as Tacoma, was held on 28 September. R. Jacob Weisbach, Tacoma's mayor, presided as the participants resolved to rid the territory of all "Chinese slave labor" by asking employers to discharge the Chinese and by having local committees

---

[39] Bromley, *The Chinese Massacre at Rock Springs*, p. 86.

[40] Returns of Camps Medicine Butte, 1885–1887, and Pilot Butte, Wyo., 1885–1899, RG 94, AGO, Returns for Regular Army Regiments, 1821–1916, NARA.

[41] Jules Alexander Karlin, "The Anti-Chinese Outbreaks in Seattle, 1885–1886," *Pacific Northwest Quarterly* 39 (April 1948):103–09. See also B. P. Wilcox, "The Anti-Chinese Riots in Washington," *Washington Historical Quarterly* 20 (January 1929):204–12; Clayton D. Laurie, "The Chinese Must Go: The United States Army and the Anti-Chinese Riots in Washington Territory, 1885–1886," *Pacific Northwest Quarterly* 81 (January 1990):22–29; Alexander H. Meneely, "The Anti-Chinese Movement in the Northwest" (M.A. thesis, University of Washington, 1922). For background, see Karen C. Wong, *Chinese History in the Pacific Northwest* (Seattle: University of Washington Press, 1972).

order them to leave Tacoma and Seattle by 1 November. If necessary, the white workers would use force.[42]

Between the two gatherings a group of middle-class Seattle citizens conducted their own meeting on 23 September, chaired by Mayor Henry L. Yesler and attended by territorial Governor Watson C. Squire. Although sympathetic to workers' desires to expel the Chinese, Yesler and his supporters abhorred violence. Aside from humanitarian considerations, this group hoped to avoid any trouble that could complicate Sino-American foreign relations or impede progress toward Washington statehood.[43]

Through early October the miners of Tacoma and Seattle worked at cross purposes with the middle-class citizens of Seattle. The "Puget Sound (Workers) Congress" elected a fifteen-member subcommittee to order the Chinese to depart Seattle no later than 1 November. In the meantime, 600 supporters of Yesler met on 3 October in the Seattle Opera House and agreed to serve as deputies should the sheriff need help quelling mobs who were trying to evict the Chinese. Seattle Sheriff John H. McGraw planned to divide Seattle into twenty districts, assigning his volunteers accordingly.[44]

The proposed ultimatum for the Chinese to depart Seattle alarmed the Imperial Chinese vice consul in San Francisco and the Washington territorial chief justice in Seattle. Having visited Rock Springs, Consul Frederick Bee knew what a racist mob could do. On 4 October he asked Governor Squire whether he could protect the Chinese and, if not, whether he would arrange for federal military protection. Although Squire assured him that local and territorial authorities would suffice, Chief Justice Roger S. Greene declared that, "while the presence of Chinese is an evil," any effort to drive them out "by lawless violence is suicidal."[45]

Ignoring Judge Greene's warning, however, the Committee of Fifteen issued their ultimatum on 10 October. Five days later Squire asked Pierce County Sheriff Lewis Byrd if the situation in Tacoma was as tense as that in Seattle. Byrd answered yes and predicted large-scale rioting and arson in Tacoma unless the Chinese evacuated by 1 November. He promised, nevertheless, to strengthen his force of deputies as a deterrent. During the next two weeks thousands of anti-Chinese demonstrators conducted raucous, yet nonviolent, torchlight processions in both cities.[46]

Violence erupted first in Tacoma on 2 November. Unopposed by local authorities, a mob of nearly 300 whites, many of them armed, forced some 200 Chinese to leave in

---

[42] Carlos A. Schwantes in "Protest in the Promised Land: Unemployment, Disinheritance, and the Origin of Labor Militancy in the Pacific Northwest, 1885–1886," *Western Historical Quarterly* 13 (October 1982):373–90, puts the anti-Chinese riots in the larger context of unemployment and labor troubles.

[43] Murry C. Morgan, *Puget's Sound: A Narrative of Early Tacoma and the Southern Sound* (Seattle: University of Washington Press, 1979), pp. 212–53; Kent D. Richards, "Insurrection, Agitation, and Riots, the Police Power and Washington Statehood," *Montana: The Magazine of Western History* 37 (Autumn 1987):10–21.

[44] John H. McGraw, "The Anti-Chinese Riots of 1885," *Washington State Historical Society Publications* (Olympia: State Historical Society, 1915), II:388–97.

[45] Clarence B. Bagley, *History of Seattle From the Earliest Settlement to the Present Time*, 3 vols. (Chicago: S. J. Clarke, 1916), 2:461.

[46] *Report of the Governor of Washington Territory to the Secretary of the Interior, 1886* (Washington, D.C.: Government Printing Office, 1886), pp. 14–15 (hereafter cited as *Rpt of Gov of Washington Territory*). On rioting in Tacoma, see Jules A. Karlin, "Anti-Chinese Outbreaks in Tacoma, 1885," *Pacific Historical Review* 23 (August 1954):271–83. For the press role in inflaming anti-Chinese prejudices, see Howard H. Shuman, "The Role of Seattle's Newspapers in the Anti-Chinese Agitation of 1885–1886" (M.A. thesis, University of Washington, 1968).

wagons. During a drive in pouring rain to Lake View Station, where the Chinese were to board a train for Portland, several Chinese suffered ill effects from exposure and died soon after.[47]

Yet it was in Seattle that federal intervention took shape. Yesler first met with 3 members of the Knights of Labor, 3 civic leaders, and 5 Chinese "bosses." The labor spokesmen and civic leaders persuaded the bosses to evacuate their people at once. Between 4 and 14 November, 150 Chinese fled Seattle by boat and train.[48] Meanwhile, on 4 November Yesler wrote Squire, expressing concern for the safety of those still in Seattle. In response, Squire issued a proclamation urging the citizens of the Puget Sound area to exercise self-restraint and resist that "spirit of lawlessness which is destructive alike to immigration, to labor, and to capital." Local officials were directed to treat any riot or breach of the peace inciting others to riot as flagrant violations of federal law. He explained that if the sheriff and his deputies were unable to protect the Chinese, Tacoma and Seattle could expect "speedy interference of United States troops." Secretary of the Interior Lucius Q. C. Lamar subsequently approved Squire's proclamation, but urged him to make every effort to settle the crisis without federal military intervention. He assured Squire that any expense incurred by local forces would be reimbursed by federal funds.[49]

Despite Lamar's wishes, Squire quickly lost confidence in McGraw's ability to enforce the proclamation. On 6 November he requested troops from President Cleveland and notified the commander of the Department of the Columbia, Brig. Gen. John Gibbon, to expect orders from Washington, D.C. Gibbon commanded 1,800 troops at Vancouver Barracks, 130 miles south of Seattle on the Columbia River. Anticipating Cleveland's actions, he ordered Col. Isaac DeRussy of the 14th Infantry to ready six companies at Vancouver Barracks for action in Seattle.[50]

Cleveland's decision to send federal troops under RS 5298 came the same day. Secretary of War Endicott directed Gibbon to send regulars to Seattle to execute a presidential proclamation to be issued on 7 November. Gibbon immediately dispatched DeRussy with ten companies, totaling 18 officers and 300 enlisted men, by steamer and rail to Seattle. At Tenino, fifty miles south of Seattle, Squire boarded DeRussy's train. Following the president's orders, Gibbon also made preparations to go to Seattle by train the following day.[51]

Cleveland's proclamation clearly stated the reasons for military intervention: the governor had reported the existence of domestic violence caused by unlawful obstructions, combinations, and assemblages of "evil-disposed persons," that made impracticable the

---

[47] *Rpt of Gov of Washington Territory*, pp. 23–24; Karlin, "Anti-Chinese Outbreaks in Seattle," pp. 111–12; Schwantes in "Protest in the Promised Land," p. 227, claims two Chinese died of exposure, as do Halseth and Glasrud in "Anti-Chinese Movements in Washington," p. 126.

[48] *Rpt of Gov of Washington Territory*, pp. 23–24; Karlin, "Anti-Chinese Outbreaks in Seattle," pp. 111–12.

[49] "Proclamation by the Governor of Washington Territory, 4 November 1885," in Wilson, *Federal Aid in Domestic Disturbances*, pp. 341–42.

[50] Telgs, Squire to Gibbon, 6 Nov 1885; McClearn to HQ, Dept of the Columbia, 6 Nov 1885; 2d Cavalry to HQ, Dept of the Columbia, 6 Nov 1885; Secretary of War to Gibbon, 6 Nov 1885. All in Register of Letters Received, Department of the Columbia, Part I: 1885–1886, RG 393, Records of the U.S. Army Continental Commands, 1821–1938, NARA. *Report of the Secretary of War, 1886* (Washington, D.C.: Government Printing Office, 1886), pp. 84–95.

[51] Ibid.; for the proclamation, see Wilson, *Federal Aid in Domestic Disturbances*, pp. 218–19.

JOHN GIBBON

enforcement by the ordinary course of judicial proceedings of federal law in Seattle and elsewhere. Although the proclamation was irrelevant to a territorial request under RS 5298, it cited a criterion of RS 5297: that the legislature could not be assembled in time. The proclamation concluded with the admonition that all citizens desist, disperse, and retire peaceably to their abodes on or before noon on 8 November.[52]

Squire and DeRussy arrived in Seattle at 0100, 8 November. Unable to locate suitable quarters, DeRussy's men slept in their rail cars until later that morning. By the time the residents of the city awoke, the soldiers had posted the proclamation throughout Seattle. Combined with the presence of the troops, it produced the desired effect. Confident that fewer soldiers were needed now, Squire telegraphed Gibbon, still at Vancouver Barracks, and recommended

that two companies be sent to Tacoma, three companies kept at Seattle, and the remainder returned to Vancouver Barracks. DeRussy, however, deferred any withdrawals until Gibbon arrived.[53]

The troops enjoyed friendly relations with Seattle residents. Military discipline had become so lax that several intoxicated soldiers reportedly assaulted some Chinese. Visiting Chinatown on the night of 9 November, one group of soldiers extorted a "special tax" amounting to $150. The *Seattle Call* noted sardonically that citizens "will (soon) be called upon to protect the Chinese against the troops."[54]

The only event that marred Gibbon's otherwise quiet entry into Seattle was his own inadvertent violation of the Posse Comitatus Act. As four companies prepared to go to Tacoma, the U.S. marshal gave them custody of twenty-seven prisoners bound for trial in a Vancouver federal court for complicity in assaults on the Chinese. Restoration of civil order, however, deprived the regulars of authority to arrest or detain civilian prisoners. Unaware of the act's provisions, Gibbon approved the custody and authorized Capt. G. E. Carpenter to request steamship transportation to Vancouver Barracks. Tersely the War Department informed Gibbon of his error: "Troops at Seattle not to be used as a *posse*

[52] Wilson, *Federal Aid in Domestic Disturbances*, pp. 218–19; James D. Richardson, *A Compilation of the Messages and Papers of the Presidents, 1787–1897* (Washington, D.C.: Library of Congress, 1900), 8:311–12.

[53] Telgs, DeRussy to HQ, 8 Nov 1885; Squires to Gibbon, 8 Nov 1885; both in Register of Ltrs Rec'vd, Dept of the Columbia, RG 393, NARA.

[54] It is not known if these soldiers were ever reprimanded for this alleged incident, see Karlin, "Anti-Chinese Outbreaks in Seattle," p. 114; *Seattle Post Intelligencer*, 10 Nov 1885; *Seattle Call*, 10 Nov 1885. See also Telg, DeRussy to HQ, 10 Nov 1885, Register of Ltrs Rec'vd, Dept of the Columbia, RG 393, NARA.

comitatus for arrest and detention of offenders unless necessary to suppress domestic violence." On 10 November Carpenter returned the prisoners to the marshal's custody before departing for Vancouver Barracks.[55]

Gibbon thereafter limited his men to garrison duties and himself to investigating the causes of the recent disorders. In an open letter to Mayor Yesler, Gibbon blamed the banishment of 200 Chinese on 4 November to a lack "of a proper and efficient organization for protecting society against turbulent elements." He lectured Yesler further on the importance of upholding U.S. treaty obligations, because attacks upon Chinese nationals not only lowered the prestige of Seattle, but imperiled the safety of Americans living in China and portrayed Americans generally as lawbreakers. Yesler diplomatically sidestepped these criticisms and thanked the general on "behalf of the citizens for the interest taken in their welfare."[56]

On orders from Gibbon, DeRussy's six remaining companies left Seattle on 17 November, without having performed any action since their arrival. Their nine-day stay discouraged any overt hostilities toward the Chinese, but did not preclude further racial outbreaks. As DeRussy suggested, the troops may have given the Chinese a false sense of security, encouraging them to remain in Seattle when it was unsafe to do so.[57]

In his annual address to Congress on 8 December 1885, President Cleveland voiced deep concern that "the bitterness of feeling against the Mongolian race on the Pacific slope may find vent [elsewhere] in lawless demonstrations [similar to those in Wyoming and Washington]" and promised to exert all government power "to maintain the amplest good faith toward China in the treatment" of its nationals. He noted that the lawlessness stemmed from the racial prejudice "of men not citizens of the United States [European immigrants] engaged in competition with Chinese laborers." Despite professed sympathy for the Chinese, however, he advocated a solution that restrained the victims rather than the victimizers by proposing that Congress legislate tighter controls over the influx of Chinese immigrants. In fact, the following months saw anti-Chinese disturbances in Colorado, Oregon, Montana, Idaho, Utah, Arizona, and New Mexico.[58]

Meanwhile, in Washington Territory, advocates of legal action to expel the Chinese demonstrated how little they could do in face of U.S. treaty obligations, federal laws, and constitutional guarantees that protected them. Efforts by the Seattle City Council and the territorial legislature to discriminate against Orientals proved unsuccessful. Although the lower house passed bills prohibiting aliens incapable of becoming citizens from acquiring land, operating laundries, and holding jobs in public or private enterprises, the upper house rejected all but the landowning measure. The failure of anti-Chinese legislation and the acquittal of those indicted for the November assaults revived the movement for direct action.

---

[55] Karlin, "Anti-Chinese Outbreaks in Seattle," p. 114; Telg, Carpenter to HQ, Dept of the Columbia, Register of Ltrs Rec'vd, Dept of the Columbia, RG 393, NARA; Telg, Pope, Div of the Pacific, to AG, 11 Nov 1885, RG 94, File 5820, NARA.

[56] Ltr, Gibbon to Yesler, reported in *Seattle Daily Chronicle*, 14 Nov 1885, RG 94, File 5820, NARA; Telg, Yesler to Gibbon, 14 Nov 1885, Register of Ltrs Rec'vd, Dept of the Columbia, RG 393, NARA.

[57] Telg, DeRussey to HQ, 16 Nov 1885, Register of Ltrs Rec'vd, Dept of the Columbia, RG 393, NARA.

[58] Richardson, *Messages and Papers*, 8:329. For other outbreaks, see Halseth and Glasrud, "Anti-Chinese Movements in Washington," pp. 123–24. Only New Mexico's governor requested troops, but they were not sent because violence had not yet occurred and did not. See Telgs, Ross to Cleveland, 14 Jan 1886, and Endicott to Ross, 16 Jan 1886, both in RG 94, File 5820, NARA.

Citizens meeting at Seattle's Bijou Theater on the evening of 6 February 1886 passed resolutions calling for economic and social boycotts of any firms still employing Chinese. Residents charged a six-man committee with delivering an ultimatum to the Chinese demanding that they leave the city. At daybreak, dozens of "committees" forced their way into Chinese homes. After demanding that inhabitants pack their belongings and report to the steamship *Queen of the Pacific* at 1300, each committee left one man behind to enforce compliance. By late morning the committees had assembled a number of wagons in Chinatown to haul luggage to the pier. After a thorough search for hold-outs, the committeemen marched 350 Chinese to the dock.[59]

In response to this incident, Seattle U.S. Attorney W. H. White tried to arouse the forces of law and order. He prompted Sheriff McGraw to organize a force of deputies and urged the police to halt the expulsion. In sympathy with the rioters, neither force took any action other than preventing physical injury to the Chinese en route to the *Queen of the Pacific*. Governor Squire, who was visiting Seattle, ordered the release of the hapless Chinese and dispersal of the mob. Guarded by thirty deputies, the U.S. marshal read Squire's proclamation at noon, but stood helplessly by as the crowd hooted, jeered, and shoved the Chinese along to the pier.[60] Meanwhile, Squire ordered the local militia, the "Seattle Rifles," to arm themselves and support McGraw. Not waiting to test the reliability of this force, he also requested troops from both General Gibbon and Secretary Endicott to stop an "immense mob" from ousting the Chinese. Gibbon alerted his troops, but refused to move without a presidential directive.[61]

While the forces of law and order slowly organized, confusion developed at the Seattle dock. Advocates of the expulsion of the Chinese had raised funds to book passage for only 97 of the 350 Chinese. Upon complaint from a Chinese merchant that his countrymen were being held against their will, Justice Greene issued a writ of habeas corpus requiring the ship captain to produce the Chinese for a court hearing the next day at 0800. At midnight McGraw and two militia companies blocked attempts to transfer the 253 remaining Chinese from the pier to the railroad station, where the mob leaders planned to put them on the next train for Tacoma, the only destination to which their collective funds could transport them. To discourage any confrontation between the mob and the militia, McGraw ordered the train to depart before the crowd could reach the station.[62]

After daybreak McGraw and his collected forces escorted the passengers from the *Queen of the Pacific* to the territorial court. A mob tried to block the way, forcing him to arrest 8 ringleaders. In court, Greene informed the Chinese that they had a legal right to remain in Seattle. Though assuring them that law enforcement officials would make every effort to protect them, he stopped short of guaranteeing their safety. Only 16 elected to stay, while the remainder returned under escort to the ship. By late morning the mob had raised enough money for 115 more Chinese to board, and the ship set sail. After the departure of the *Queen of the Pacific*, McGraw negotiated with mob ringleaders to allow

---

[59] Karlin, "Anti-Chinese Outbreaks in Seattle," pp. 117–20.

[60] Wilson, *Federal Aid in Domestic Disturbances*, pp. 219–22.

[61] Telg, Squire to Gibbon, 7 Feb 1886, Register of Ltrs Rec'vd, Dept of the Columbia, RG 393, NARA; *Secretary of War Report, 1886*, p. 185.

[62] Karlin, "Anti-Chinese Outbreaks in Seattle," pp. 121–22.

the remaining 154 Chinese to stay until money could be raised to arrange transport on the *George W. Elder.*[63]

Word of this arrangement, however, failed to reach all of Seattle. Irate over the earlier arrest of 8 ringleaders, a new mob formed at noon and blocked McGraw as he escorted the Chinese to their homes. The sheriff's party included 81 deputies, the Seattle Rifles, and cadets from the University of Washington. Using rifle butts, they clubbed their way through the mob. When some of the mob tried to wrest rifles away from McGraw's men, 1 or more of the militiamen opened fire. More shots of unknown origin followed. The firing stopped only after 2 militiamen and 3 members of the mob had been seriously wounded.[64]

The crowd backed off, allowing McGraw time to regroup his force into a hollow square with the Chinese in the center. As the mob prepared to charge, another company of militia appeared, causing the crowd to mill about in confusion long enough for McGraw to mount a platform and attempt to address them. He was shouted down. Finally, a mob leader climbed onto the same platform and explained that the Chinese would be leaving on the next steamer. The crowd dispersed after McGraw promised that the militiamen responsible for the shooting would be prosecuted.[65]

Soon thereafter, a group of Seattle workers appeared before Justice Greene and tried to swear out warrants for the arrest of the militiamen who had opened fire during the demonstration. Greene refused the warrants on the grounds that the militiamen had acted in the capacity of officers of the court and were immune to prosecution. When a mob subsequently threatened the lives of the accused militiamen, Greene advised Governor Squire to declare martial law. Squire concurred, suspending operations of the court and appointing militia Col. Granville O. Haller provost marshal with power to close all saloons and impose a citywide curfew from 1900 to 0500. Haller promptly posted sentinels to enforce the order.[66]

By this time the members of the Seattle Rifles, university cadets, and militia began to show signs of strain. Renewed violence seemed likely as miners from nearby areas streamed into Seattle after their shifts. Neither Greene nor Squire was confident that martial law could be enforced without federal aid. Greene therefore notified Attorney General William M. Evarts that Seattle was under martial law to combat a state of insurrection and that Squire, on Greene's advice, had wired President Cleveland for federal troops.[67]

For a time the government hesitated. On Cleveland's behalf, Secretary Endicott urged Squire to enforce martial law by territorial means and advised the governor to convene the legislature and to keep the War Department informed of any further deterioration. Expecting the worst, however, he alerted General Gibbon to prepare for a new civil disturbance mission in Seattle. Eight companies from Vancouver Barracks went aboard a steamship for quick transport to the scene of the trouble.[68]

---

[63] Ibid., p. 102.

[64] Ibid., pp. 122–23; *Secretary of War Report, 1886*, pp. 187–88.

[65] Ibid.

[66] Ibid.; Rpt, Gibbon to Drum, 17 Feb 1886, RG 94, File 5820, NARA.

[67] Telg, Squire to HQ, Dept of the Columbia, 8 Feb 1886, Register of Ltrs Rec'vd, Dept of the Columbia, RG 393, NARA; Wilson *Federal Aid in Domestic Disturbances*, p. 342.

[68] Wilson, *Federal Aid in Domestic Disturbances*, p. 220; Telg, AG to HQ, Dept of the Columbia, 8 Feb 1886, Register of Ltrs Recv'd, Dept of the Columbia, RG 393, NARA; *Secretary of War Report, 1886*, p. 185.

Soon after, reports of renewed mob agitation reached Cleveland. In a replay of November 1885, he issued another proclamation ordering the insurgents to disperse by 1800 on 10 February. The War Department authorized Gibbon to send Colonel DeRussy's 14th Infantry to Seattle "to suppress domestic violence and aid the civil authorities in overcoming other obstructions to the enforcement of federal law." Again Adjutant General Drum directed Gibbon to visit Seattle after troop deployment and report on conditions.[69]

But the anti-Chinese fury was spent for the time being, and all rioting ceased before the president's deadline. Martial law, Cleveland's proclamation, and the return of the 14th Infantry to Seattle for the second time in three months convinced the rioters that a stronger will than theirs would ultimately prevail. When DeRussy's eight companies arrived on 10 February, they found Seattle devoid of noticeable traces of the previous three days' rioting. Only the periodic appearance of pairs of sentinels, one militiaman and one deputy sheriff, and the uncharacteristic quiet of the local saloons betrayed the city's previous tumult.[70] If the militia and police had continued to enforce martial law, Gibbon's command would have had little to do. However, Squire was eager to return citizen-soldiers and university cadets to their usual endeavors and transferred full responsibility for implementation of martial law to Gibbon. Hence, federal troops patrolled the city streets, enforced saloon closings, and checked civilians for passes to travel through Seattle after curfew in the name of the territorial governor.[71]

Initially Gibbon gave his troops great leeway in how they assisted civil authority. By allowing his men to arrest a number of suspected mob ringleaders, place them under guard, and eventually transfer custody to the U.S. marshal, for the second time in three months Gibbon encroached upon the Posse Comitatus Act. In this case he overlooked the distinction between martial law declared by the governor and that declared by the president; only the latter case, theoretically, could justify the use of federal troops to carry out police functions.[72]

Word of this violation surfaced in a message from Governor Squire to Secretary Endicott. On 13 February 1886, Squire informed Endicott that, despite the president's proclamation, residents in Olympia, Puyallup, Sumner, Coronado, and Snohomish had tried to expel local Chinese with some degree of success. Then, perhaps as an afterthought, he mentioned the "arrests of leaders [in Seattle] being made by General Gibbon."[73] Gibbon received word of Endicott's displeasure three days later: "troops [are] not to be used as a posse to do work of local magistracy. . . . [You have] not clearly comprehended the purpose for which troops were sent . . . they are to preserve peace, give security to life and property, and prevent obstruction to the enforcement of laws. Only if civil authorities were prevented by violence from operating could military assume their functions."[74]

Gibbon tried to justify the arrests his command had made. In a report to Endicott he explained that his instructions had been to support civil authority and noted that when

[69] Telg, AG to HQ, Dept of the Columbia, 9 Feb 1886, Register of Ltrs Rec'vd, Dept of the Columbia, RG 393, NARA.

[70] Telg, Wisser to HQ, Dept of the Columbia, 11 Feb 1886, Register of Ltrs Rec'vd, Dept of the Columbia, RG 393, NARA; *Secretary of War Report, 1886*, pp. 186–88.

[71] *Secretary of War Report, 1886*, p. 186.

[72] Telg, Squire to Endicott, 13 Feb 1866, RG 94, File 5820, NARA; *Secretary of War Report, 1886*, pp. 187–88.

[73] Telg, Squire to Endicott, 13 Feb 1886, RG 94.

[74] Telg, Drum to Gibbon, 16 Feb 1886, RG 94, File 5820, NARA.

DeRussy's regiment arrived in Seattle, the governor represented the only functioning civil authority. Gibbon maintained that he knew of no means of supporting Squire other than by having his men arrest and guard troublemakers, thereby preventing them from inciting further riots. He contended that the prevalence of anti-Chinese hostility made effective law enforcement by police or deputies unlikely and that only martial law could keep the peace.[75] His rationale overlooked the success of the territorial militia and quasi-military forces prior to his arrival, taking no notice of the distinction between shielding civil officials and replacing them.

The need for martial law slowly diminished. Cooperation between Seattle residents and federal troops prompted Gibbon to reopen saloons, withdraw guards from various buildings, and lift the curfew. Following the general's recommendations, Squire publicly repealed martial law and restored local civil control over the city on 23 February. But as a precaution he asked the president to leave two companies of federal troops in Seattle for several months. Between 25 February and 1 April Cleveland ordered six companies back to Vancouver Barracks, but retained the last two companies in Seattle for four more months.[76]

During April and May 1886, Governor Squire, Mayor Yesler, and General Gibbon disagreed on the necessity of retaining these last units. On 20 April the War Department had directed Gibbon to ask the two politicians if federal regulars could be relieved. Fearing new riots in June, when members of the anti-Chinese mobs went on trial, both wanted DeRussy's troops to remain one more month. Gibbon protested that Seattle had taken substantial advantage of the presence of federal troops to reduce the size of its police force—in his view, a disgusting dereliction of civic duty. Civil officials, however, were not the only Seattle residents who were loath to see the troops go; even anti-Chinese spokesmen implored Cleveland to retain troops in Seattle until after the July 1886 local elections. These men claimed that Yesler and McGraw, both up for reelection, were training private bands of armed men—three companies of militia and nearly eighty deputy sheriffs—to coerce voters into renewing their terms of office. Seemingly, the opportunities for entanglement in local politics were endless.[77]

Yet in the end the citizens solved their own problems in their own way. In June 1886 a Seattle grand jury failed to return indictments against seven persons accused of leading the anti-Chinese outrages, but indicted six others for trial in September. (All were later acquitted.) During the July elections the citizens of Seattle unseated Yesler and McGraw in a resounding show of support for anti-Chinese forces. The crisis had ended. Most of the Chinese had left the Seattle area, and the officials who attempted to protect them had been ousted from office. All agreed that the need for troops had passed. On 19 August the last units boarded a train for the first leg of the journey back to Vancouver Barracks. At no time during the previous seven months had Gibbon's troops encountered any resistance from the people of Seattle.[78]

The anti-Chinese riots at Rock Springs caught the Cleveland administration by surprise and demonstrated government confusion about the objectives of military intervention

---

[75] Telg, Gibbon to Drum, 17 Feb 1886, RG 94, File 5820, NARA; *Secretary of War Report, 1886*, pp. 187–88.

[76] *Secretary of War Report, 1886*, p. 188; Telg, Squire to Cleveland, 23 Feb 1886, RG 94, File 5820, NARA.

[77] Telg, Gibbon to Drum, 22 Apr 1886; SO 67, HQ, Dept of the Columbia, 23 Apr 1886; Petition to Cleveland from Citizens of Seattle, 28 Apr 1886; Telg, Drum to Gibbon, 4, 5 May 1886. All in RG 94, File 5820, NARA.

[78] *Secretary of War Report, 1886*, p. 188; Karlin, "Anti-Chinese Outbreaks in Seattle," p. 128.

and how to bring intervention about.[79] At the outset, Adjutant General Drum agreed with Secretary of State Bayard and Secretary of War Endicott that troops might be used in advance of a presidential proclamation to protect the mails and the railroads over which they were carried. Later, General Schofield suggested broadening protection to include all rails of any transcontinental line designated by Congress as a "military road." To those objectives President Cleveland later added protection of the Chinese, in fulfillment of federal obligations under Article III of the Burlingame Treaty of 17 November 1880.

Occasionally overstepping the bounds set by the Posse Comitatus Act, the troops of Generals Howard and Gibbon succeeded in suppressing violence and property damage to railroad and mining company property. To a lesser extent they intervened also to prevent further violence against Chinese immigrants and to ensure their safety. The Army accomplished all these civil disturbance missions without violence. But prolonged military presence—fourteen years in the case of Rock Springs—contributed to the destruction of labor organizations in the region. Exploiting the presence of the troops, railroad and mining companies prevented union activity by importing more Chinese laborers, who spurned all organization efforts.

Although anti-Chinese violence requiring federal military intervention diminished following 1885–1886, the struggle between organized labor and management over the importation and widespread use of Chinese labor continued for the next four decades. In retrospective comments on the violence in Wyoming, Terrence V. Powderly, leader of the Knights of Labor, clearly placed the blame for racial violence on Congress when he stated:

The recent assault upon the Chinese at Rock Springs is but the outcome of the feeling caused by the indifference of our law-makers to the just demands of the people . . . no blame can be attached to organized labor for the outbreak perpetrated at Rock Springs . . . if Congress had listened to union organizations about Chinese, if Congress had penalized those breaking immigrant laws, if Congress had not "winked" at violations, and refused to listen to those wronged, men at Rock Springs would not have had to take the law into their own hands.[80]

In response to popular feeling against Chinese labor, pressures from labor groups, and desires to avoid further outbreaks of violence, Congress produced a flurry of legislation in the years following 1886. In addition to the restrictions of the Exclusion Act of 1882, which was renewed in 1892 and again in 1902, Congress added restrictions in the Scott Act of 1887 that prohibited the immigration of all Chinese laborers and accepted only teachers, merchants, students, and tourists. The Scott Act was broadly defined to include any Chinese, whether or not they were nationals, and prohibited reentry of laborers if they left the United States. When the act went into effect, 20,000 laborers, most with property and families in the United States, were permanently denied readmission. Legislation was finally passed in 1924 that permanently restricted all immigration, not just Chinese. Its impact was notable; during the decade following its passage, only 4,928 Chinese were admitted to the United States, compared to 29,907 admitted in the prior ten years.[81]

---

[79] Cooper, *The Army and Civil Disorder*, pp. 86–87.
[80] Stone, "Knights of Labor," p. 230.
[81] Lee, *Chinese in the U.S.A.*, pp. 11–13, 21; Kraut, *Huddled Masses*, pp. 161–62; Heaps, *Riots, U.S.A.*, pp. 61–62, 70–71.

With each additional piece of restrictive legislation, the number of Chinese immigrants entering the country diminished. Concomitant with this fall in immigration, fewer and fewer racial incidents were reported. Through legislative means the United States solved what many had termed the *Chinese problem*, precluding any further use of federal troops to quell anti-Chinese violence.

CHAPTER 5

Industrial Armies and the Western Pullman Strike

The laboring men of this country—I mean the honest ones . . . firmly believe the powers of Government have been perverted to their injury in the interests of the rich.
—Secretary of State Walter Q. Gresham, 1894.

It seems at least probable that many of the "Commonwealers" are only actuated by the laudable desire to get out of a country where they are no longer able to obtain subsistence. Would it not be better to let them go quietly, slowly, and laboriously make their way wither they wish to go.
—Maj. Gen. John M. Schofield, 1894.

Between the anti-Chinese riots in 1886 and the spring of 1894, civil authorities called upon the Army only once to quell disorder stemming from a labor dispute. Although violent labor disorders continued unabated during this period, state and federal civil officials thought none, other than the 1892 intervention in Coeur d'Alene, Idaho, serious enough to warrant federal military intervention. Privately hired company guards, local police, and state National Guard forces quelled the disorders that did occur. In 1894, however, massive, nationwide social and labor unrest again compelled the president to call upon the Army to bolster beleaguered civil authorities attempting to restore and maintain order.

As in 1877, a new economic depression caused the social and labor unrest of 1894. The 1880s had witnessed an economic boom resulting in industrial overexpansion, led by railroad construction. Combined with this overexpansion were sharp declines in agricultural prices, exports, and investments in the United States, themselves caused by a similar economic depression that had swept western Europe in 1890.[1] A panic occurred in May 1890, the effects of which were even more severe than those of 1873. Within six months, over 8,000 businesses failed, 156 railroads went into federal receivership, and over 400 banks, including 141 national banks, suspended operations. Farm prices, already depressed, plummeted even further, and an estimated 1 to 3 million workers, at least 20 percent of the work force, were out of jobs. Those who remained employed saw their

---

[1] On the panic, see the following: Charles Hoffman, *The Depression of the Nineties: An Economic History* (Westport: Greenwood Press, 1970); Frank B. Latham, *The Panic of 1893: A Time of Strikes, Riots, Hobos, Coxey's "Army," Starvation, Withering Droughts, and Fears of "Revolution"* (New York: Franklin Watts, 1971); William J. Lauck, *The Causes of the Panic of 1893* (Boston: Houghton Mifflin, 1907); Frank P. Weberg, "The Background of the Panic of 1893" (Ph.D. diss., Catholic University of America, 1929).

wages and work hours drastically reduced. As in 1877, private corporations and the federal government, in keeping with the philosophy of the times, failed to do anything to lessen the effects of this economic downturn on millions of the unemployed, and no widespread or comprehensive public or private social welfare system had been created to meet their needs.[2]

Now, however, many workers were members of established national and local labor and trade unions, which had organized and grown steadily in strength, numbers, and assertiveness since 1873. These unions became more vocal during the 1880s, and in the economic crisis of 1893–1894 were determined to prevent massive firings and wage reductions like those of the 1870s. Corporate leaders, many politicians, and the conservative urban upper and middle classes came to view the stronger and more vocal unions as a major threat, not only to propertied interests, but to social order and political stability. The activities of legitimate, nonradical labor unions, such as the Knights of Labor, the American Federation of Labor, and the American Railway Union were increasingly equated with the sometimes vicious and violent activities of nonlabor-affiliated mobs and of radical labor, political, and social groups. These groups, following ideologies of socialism, anarchism, nihilism, or communism, seemed to threaten the basic tenets of American society and appeared bent on fomenting revolution under the guise of social and economic justice. The result was an increased number of strikes and work slowdowns combined with revolutionary rhetoric.

In turn the strong reaction against such groups and their rhetoric by the propertied classes prompted federal action and, within weeks, Army intervention. The unemployed and strikers involved in the disorders of 1894, however, enjoyed more public sympathy than their 1877 predecessors, especially among Populist, farm, and labor groups who resented the power and control of monopolistic corporations and the railroads. Many other Americans were disturbed by the "'fact that the spirit of discontent and despair should have so far saturated large masses of our people of our country as to make such things possible.'" In the depression following 1893, thousands of the unemployed were forced to leave their homes and families to seek work elsewhere in the nation. These armies of unemployed placed the blame for their miseries on the "plutocrats," who allegedly controlled the wealth of the nation, and on the federal government, which did nothing to prevent this control.[3]

Combined with the increased power of the unions was the creation of the People's, or Populist, Party in 1892. Composed primarily of farmers and workers, the new party grew rapidly and challenged the political monopoly held by the traditional Republican and Democratic Parties. Strongest in the Midwest, Rocky Mountain states, and South, Populists wanted a broad expansion of government powers combined with a more direct control by the people. Many Americans, especially in the urban, middle and upper social

---

[2] Painter, *Standing at Armageddon*, pp. 116–17; Cooper, *The Army and Civil Disorder*, pp. 99–100; Rezneck, "Unemployment, Unrest," pp. 324–28; H. Leibowitz, "Unemployment Relief During the Depression of 1893–1894" (M.A. thesis, Columbia University, 1936).

[3] Quote from Cooper, *The Army and Civil Disorder*, p. 100. For social conditions, see Davis, *The Fear of Conspiracy*, pp. 151, 161–62, 168–76; Norman Pollack, *The Populist Response to Industrial America* (Cambridge: Harvard University Press, 1962), pp. 51–54; Rezneck, "Unemployment, Unrest," pp. 334–35; Rich, *President and Civil Disorder*, p. 87.

and economic strata of society, considered the Populist program wildly radical and threatening as any foreign ideology. The party's first platform, developed in Omaha, did little to assuage these fears. The Populists called for the free and unlimited coinage of silver; government ownership of rail, telephone, and telegraph systems; a graduated income tax; government-run postal savings banks; a flexible national currency; an eight-hour workday; restricted immigration; the nationwide use of the secret or Australian ballot; direct, popular election of senators; and the introduction of the political initiative and referendum. When the Panic of 1893 developed into the depression of 1894, the Populists had already elected 1,500 candidates, including 3 governors, 5 senators, and 10 representatives, spokesmen for the views of millions who sincerely believed the United States had been ruled and plundered by the wealthy few for too long. Together, populism and strong unionism transformed the context of federal intervention in domestics disorders.[4]

The Coal Strike of 1894

The social and labor unrest of 1894 began on 21 April, when the United Mine Workers (UMW) of America, a union of the AFofL, called a strike affecting coal fields in eight states. Although strikers were initially peaceful, company attempts to introduce strikebreakers precipitated violence, compelling governors to call out their respective National Guards. These state forces, especially in the urbanized East, were better led, better disciplined, and better equipped than their 1877 counterparts and performed more effective service. Federal military forces were dispatched on only one occasion. On 19 May troops from Fort Leavenworth, Kansas, under Lt. Col. John N. Andrews, were ordered to the Oklahoma Indian Territory to evict striking miners from federal lands. The coal mines were in a unique legal situation. Privately operated, they were owned by Indians and supervised by the Department of the Interior. The coal companies quickly persuaded the Interior Department to reclassify the strikers as unemployed, thereby making them guilty of trespassing and settling illegally on a federal Indian reservation. On 15 June federal troops began evicting striking miners and their families from their homes in the Indian Territory and continued to do so until the nationwide coal strike ended in July 1894.[5]

The Coxeyites and the Industrial Armies

Yet even as the coal strike continued, a more unusual form of industrial protest occurred: the creation of industrial armies of the unemployed and discontented. The first such army was named after its leader, Jacob S. Coxey—who also called it the "Commonweal of Christ"—and was formed less than a year after the Panic of 1893. Coxey, a 40-year-old Massilon, Ohio, quarry owner and self-styled social reformer, announced a campaign to

---

[4] For the Populists, see Painter, *Standing at Armageddon*, pp. 98, 115–16; Cooper, *The Army and Civil Disorder*, p. 98; Garraty, *New Commonwealth*, p. 53; Pollack, *Populist Response*; John D. Hicks, *The Populist Revolt* (Minneapolis: University of Minnesota Press, 1931); "Platform of the Populist Party, 4 July 1892," doc. 325, in Henry S. Commager, ed., *Documents of American History*, 2 vols. (Englewood Cliffs, N.J.: Prentice-Hall, 1973), 1:593.

[5] According to RS 2118 and RS 2147; Cooper, *The Army and Civil Disorder*, pp. 100–101; Wilson, *Federal Aid in Domestic Disturbances*, p. 6.

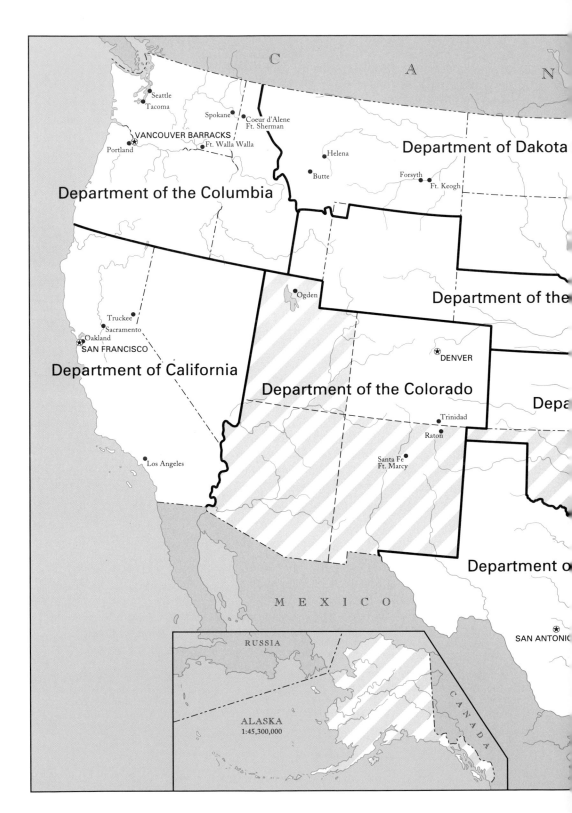

Seattle
Tacoma
Spokane
Coeur d'Alene
Ft. Sherman
VANCOUVER BARRACKS
Ft. Walla Walla
Portland
Helena
Butte
Forsyth
Ft. Keogh

Department of Dakota

Department of the Columbia

Ogden

Department of the

Truckee
Sacramento
Oakland
SAN FRANCISCO

⊛ DENVER

Department of California

Department of the Colorado

Trinidad
Raton

Los Angeles

Santa Fe
Ft. Marcy

Depa

Department o

M E X I C O

⊛ SAN ANTONIO

RUSSIA

C A N A D A

ALASKA
1:45,300,000

MAP 2

A   D   A

Ft. Brady

UL
APOLIS

Ft. Sheridan
CHICAGO   Hammond
Spring Valley   Massilon
Danville
Decatur
St. Louis

NEW YORK CITY

Washington, D.C.

the Missouri   Department of the East

Cairo

New Orleans

BAHAMAS

Civil Disorders in the United States and Its Territories
1894

•   Civil Disorder

⊛   U. S. Army Department Headquarters

▬▬▬   U. S. Army Department Boundary

▭   Territory

1:15,900,000

CUBA

organize a large number of the unemployed for a march on Washington, D.C. He believed a peaceful, Christian, and democratically inspired "petition in boots" converging on Congress would force the government into circulating cheaper money and hiring thousands of the unemployed for a program of federally funded public works he had devised to solve the economic crisis. "General" Coxey's unorthodox scheme had great popular appeal, especially among Populists and the unemployed of the Midwest and West.[6]

While Coxey slowly formed his industrial army in Massilon, other, larger and more radical industrial armies formed on the Pacific coast and in the Rocky Mountain states. The members of these western armies, entirely unconnected with Coxey's movement and his fiscal ideas, soon began to demand free passage on the nation's railroads to Washington, D.C. If passage was not granted, trains were simply commandeered. The flood of publicity surrounding Coxey, however, soon led the public to associate all the industrial armies with the Commonweal of Christ, and to name them "Coxey Armies."[7]

To the Cleveland administration and urban property owners, especially on the east coast, the approach of a predicted 100,000 unemployed people from the Midwest and West caused considerable uneasiness and distress. The publicity surrounding the industrial armies was certain, many believed, to attract large gangs of tramps and other undesirables, who would seek to enrich themselves by crime and looting. Even the participants in the industrial army movement were suspect. Leading and respected national journals such as *Harper's Weekly*, *Nation*, *Literary Digest*, and *Independent* all ran articles portraying the participants and goals of the industrial armies in a negative light. In an age when most middle-class Americans still equated the working classes and labor unions with subversion and worker agitation with social revolution, the industrial armies convinced many that catastrophe was imminent.[8]

Preceded by these dire omens, Coxey and more than 300 followers began their trek from Ohio to Washington, D.C., on 25 March, arriving in the capital on 1 May 1894. Alarmed that the marchers represented the vanguard of up to 10,000 workers, gangsters, bums, and tramps intent on vandalizing and looting the city, local police and federal authorities were determined to deal quickly and decisively with his band. Coxey received a parade permit, but the District of Columbia police chief warned him that a recently passed federal statute prohibited holding rallies or displaying banners on the Capitol grounds, and further prohibited political addresses from being delivered from the steps of

---

[6] Gerald G. Eggert, "Coxey's March on Washington," *American History Illustrated* 12 (October 1977):22–23; Painter, *Standing at Armageddon*, pp. 117–21; Donald L. McMurry, *Coxey's Army: A Study of the Industrial Army Movement of 1894* (Boston, 1929; reprint, Seattle: University of Washington Press, 1968), pp. xiii–xix, 25–32, 44–45; Carlos A. Schwantes, *Coxey's Army: An American Odyssey* (Lincoln: University of Nebraska Press, 1985); Commager, *Documents of American History*, doc. 332, 1:605.

[7] Painter, *Standing at Armageddon*, p. 120; McMurry, *Coxey's Army*, pp. 127–29, 147–58; Pollack, *Populist Response*, pp. 51–52. One such army included future writer Jack London.

[8] Cooper, *The Army and Civil Disorder*, pp. 106–07; McMurry, *Coxey's Army*, p. 106; Eggert, "Coxey's March," p. 26. See the following for contemporary accounts: S. P. Austin, "Coxey Crusade," *Review of Reviews* 10 (July 1894):63–67; "Coxeyism: Character Sketch and Marching Itinerary," *Review of Reviews* 10 (July 1894):47–59; E. L. Godkin, "Organized Tramp: Coxey's Army," *Nation* 58 (12 April 1894):306; "March of the Miserable in America: Coxey's Army," *Spectator* 72 (28 April 1894):572–74; R. P. Skinner, "Coxey-Browne Crusade," *Harper's Weekly* 38 (31 March 1894):308; R. Ogden, "Vagabond's Disease," *Nation* 58 (12 April 1894):266; J. V. Tracy, "Mission to Coxey's Army," *Catholic World* 59 (August 1894):660–80; O. O. Howard, "The Menace of Coxeyism," *North American Review* 158 (June 1894):687–96.

the Capitol building. Coxey believed this a direct infringement of his First Amendment rights of free speech and assembly, and he was undaunted.[9]

On May Day, while an estimated 15,000 to 30,000 curious spectators lined Pennsylvania Avenue, Coxey's army, now approximately 500 strong, paraded toward Capitol Hill. A reinforced squadron of waiting police moved into position at the east front of the Capitol, while 30 more policemen stationed themselves throughout the building. In addition to the police, 1,350 federal soldiers were put on alert in the Baltimore-Washington area, although they played no part in the action that followed. As soon as Coxey and 2 of his followers entered the Capitol grounds they were arrested for trespassing. When angry spectators surged forward in protest, mounted police pushed them back with nightsticks, injuring 50 persons before the crowd dis-

JACOB COXEY

persed. For all practical purposes, Coxey's movement was over. The remnants of the "army" quietly retreated to the District-Maryland border, where it encamped for several weeks before its dispirited but still law-abiding ranks drifted back to their homes. Coxey and his two colleagues were sentenced to twenty days in the District jail and fined $5.00.[10]

For all of its comic aspects, the much-publicized arrest of Jacob Coxey was part of a concerted federal campaign to curb the western industrial armies, which had already involved the U.S. Army for more than a week. Responding to the concerns of business interests and property owners, President Grover Cleveland urged Attorney General Richard Olney to make an example of the Coxeyites before more industrial armies either seized trains or otherwise descended upon Washington. Looking beyond train seizures, many politicians saw the potential in the industrial armies for a recurrence of the violence and destruction of the Great Strike of 1877. Secretary of State Walter Q. Gresham "regarded the armies as lawless bands infected with anarchist doctrines who portended much trouble," while Olney foresaw in the industrial armies "the first symptoms of impending industrial revolution." Both Republicans and the conservative Democrats who controlled Congress largely agreed.[11]

---

[9] McMurry, *Coxey's Army*, pp. 113–14; Eggert, "Coxey's March," p. 26.

[10] McMurry, *Coxey's Army*, pp. 114–16; Eggert, "Coxey's March," pp. 29, 31. For Army preparations, see Schwantes, *Coxey's Army*, pp. 167–68, and also "Coxey in Washington," *Harper's Weekly* 38 (12 May 1894):436. Coxey later served as mayor of Massillon; after, he ran unsuccessfully for Congress from Ohio in 1894, 1938, and 1942, for Ohio governor in 1897, and for U.S. president in 1936. He eventually delivered the speech he intended to give in 1894 from the Capitol steps in a similar, less-publicized march on Washington in 1914. He died at age 97 in 1951.

[11] Quotes from Eggert, "Coxey's March," p. 26. See also Horace S. Marrill, *Bourbon Leader: Grover Cleveland and the Democratic Party* (Boston: Little Brown, 1957), pp. 44–45; Eggert, *Railroad Labor Disputes*, pp. 137–39.

A railroad lawyer and staunch defender of law and order, Olney was sympathetic to these concerns. Although train theft was normally a state and not a federal crime, most railroads west of the Mississippi River were in federal receivership as a result of the depression. Olney initially proposed using U.S. marshals to arrest members of the industrial armies seizing trains, citing violations of federal court orders that guaranteed continued and unobstructed operation of railroads vital to the national security. (Olney commented later "that the train stealing was not only stopped but also 'very large numbers of almost desperate men who would otherwise have found their way to Washington were compelled to remain at home.'")[12] At the outset of the movement, however, providing a marshal force capable of arresting leaders and physically restraining industrial armies numbering up to 1,500 men proved to be a problem. Apparently Olney realized that local and state law enforcement personnel and the U.S. marshals and federal posses alone could not halt the train thefts. As he and his marshals discovered, many citizens, even civil authorities, either sympathized with the industrial armies or feared reprisals from them and therefore shunned posse duty or any interference with Coxeyite activities or their eastward progress. The western railroads, more so than those in the East, had long been a symbol of greed, corruption, and power resented by many westerners. In addition, the costs to the Justice Department for raising posses, which were often of dubious quality, was unacceptably high. Obtaining federal military intervention became Olney's primary goal. Olney met any difficulties created by the Posse Comitatus Act through use of precedents that President Hayes had set during the Great Strike of 1877.[13]

When an industrial army seized or threatened to seize a train belonging to a railroad in federal receivership, Olney sought an injunction from the nearest federal judge forbidding the action. If the industrial army ignored the federal writ, as it usually did, federal marshals made a pro forma attempt to arrest the leaders for contempt of court. Greatly outnumbered by their adversaries and facing largely unsympathetic crowds, such attempts usually failed. Armed with telegrams from federal court officials stating their inability to enforce court orders, Olney then prevailed upon Cleveland to order Secretary of War Daniel S. Lamont to intervene with troops under the authority of RS 5298 to "enforce the faithful execution of the laws of the United States . . . in whatever State or Territory thereof the laws of the United States may be forcibly opposed, or the execution thereof forcibly obstructed."[14]

Under Lamont's supervision, the task of enforcing federal injunctions devolved upon Commanding General of the Army John M. Schofield. The 63-year-old Schofield had had a long and varied military career that included both combat service and civil affairs duty. An 1853 graduate of the U.S. Military Academy with a law degree from the University of Chicago, he saw active duty in the Third Seminole War, and commanded volunteers in the Civil War at Atlanta, Franklin, and Nashville. Following the war, he helped implement Reconstruction programs in the South and served briefly as the secretary of war and as commandant of West Point. A highly educated man, Schofield taught natural philosophy

---

[12] Cooper, *The Army and Civil Disorder*, p. 107.

[13] Rich, *President and Civil Disorder*, p. 88; Eggert, *Railroad Labor Disputes*, pp. 139–40; Edwin S. Corwin, *The President: Office and Powers, 1787–1948*, 3d ed. (New York: New York University Press, 1948), p. 156. See ch. 2 on Hayes' actions in 1877.

[14] Eggert, *Railroad Labor Disputes*, pp. 145–46.

at West Point and, for a brief period, physics at Washington University in St. Louis. Unlike most officers of his generation, he had broad experience in civil-military relations gained in a variety of posts where he had served in daily contact with government workers and society at large. Now within two years of mandatory retirement, he faced a series of unequaled domestic disturbances.[15]

In 1894, as in 1877, the Army numbered approximately 28,000 officers and men, divided among various regional commands. Since 1877, however, the War Department had eliminated the top echelon in the regional hierarchy, that of the geographical divisions. In 1894, Schofield had direct access to the eight departmental commanders, whose 1877 predecessors had borne the brunt of responsibility for the nearly daily quelling of labor-related disorders. Decisions on troop deployments rested squarely on Schofield, who was determined to exercise direct control of military movements. Yet his troops supported marshals most frequently in the states of the West and Northwest, at a great distance from his headquarters.[16]

To those in the federal government, as to most Americans, industrial armies seemed to be forming everywhere during the spring of 1894. Two groups began to travel toward Washington from Los Angeles and San Francisco. The first, led by Lewis C. Fry, included 850 men who had organized in February 1894 and adopted a formal constitution. The group called on the government to create jobs, to ban all immigration for a decade, and to end the right of aliens to own property. Fry's army seized trains and left on 15 March. Meanwhile, a larger army of 1,500 formed in San Francisco under the leadership of Charles T. Kelly. His group, embracing similar ideas on how the government could halt unemployment, began seizing and boarding trains in early April. By late that month, other contingents numbering from 400 to 850 began gathering in Montana, Washington, and Oregon, demanding free transportation on the Northern Pacific Railroad to St. Paul, Minnesota.[17] From there these industrial armies intended to board eastbound lines for Washington. Here, as in California, if free transportation was not provided, trains were hijacked. At the direction of President Cleveland, Schofield ordered troops in the Northwest to retake stolen trains and to protect bridges, tunnels, and other railroad property from harm, while capturing those interfering with railroad operations as authorized under RS 5298. His orders were neither preceded by nor followed by a presidential proclamation calling for the Coxeyites to cease and desist.[18]

On 20 April, in Brig. Gen. Wesley Merritt's Department of the Dakota, 500 unemployed miners, led by William E. Hogan, entered Butte, Montana, to seize trains of the Northern Pacific for transport to St. Paul. The U.S. marshal for Montana, William McDermott, tried to stop "Hogan's Army" at Butte, and later at Billings, but with only 78 deputies, his force had little effect. Within four days McDermott and federal Judge Hiram Knowles telegraphed Olney, requesting that troops from Fort Keogh, Montana, detain Hogan's army for arrest.

---

[15] See Schofield's autobiography, *Forty-Six Years in the Army*.

[16] U.S. War Department, *Annual Report of the Secretary of War, 1894* (Washington, D.C.: Government Printing Office, 1895), p. 82 (hereafter cited as *Secretary of War Report, 1894*).

[17] Thomas C. Clinch, "Coxey's Army in Montana," *Montana* 15 (October 1965):2–11; Herman Voeltz, "Coxey's Army in Oregon, 1894," *Oregon Historical Quarterly* 65 (September 1964):263–95.

[18] Telg, McNaught to Olney, 24 Apr 1894, RG 60, Records of the Department of Justice, File 4017, 1894: Correspondence, NARA; see also Eggert, "Coxey's March," p. 25.

WESLEY MERRITT

Knowles explained that McDermott could not collect and organize a sufficient posse and that Populist Governor G. E. Rickards refused to call in the state National Guard. Convinced by Olney that only regulars could start the trains moving again, Cleveland directed Merritt and his forces to capture and detain the Coxeyites under RS 5298. The following day, 25 April 1894, Rickards made a belated request for aid to suppress "insurrection" under RS 5297, but the superfluous request was ignored.[19]

In anticipation of further requests to provide military support to other marshals, Schofield asked Olney to draft suitable instructions for Merritt's command that could be reissued to other commanders on demand as necessary. Olney complied, submitting the following generic order reflecting executive authority to commit federal forces to aid civil authorities as defined by RS 5298:

By direction of the President, you are hereby instructed to aid United States Marshal with such military force as may be necessary to enable him to execute process of United States Courts, now obstructed by forcible resistance, beyond the power of the United States Marshal and deputies to overcome. Put yourself in communication at once with Marshal.[20]

While Merritt was on a temporary leave of absence, his second in command, Col. P. T. Swaine, carried out the directive. He ordered Lt. Col. John H. Page to take six companies of the 22d Infantry from Fort Keogh, Montana, and intercept Hogan's army where the Northern Pacific Railroad passed the fort. The miners, however, evaded Page's force and continued on toward Forsyth, where Page finally arrived at midnight on 26 April. Surprising Hogan's party as they slept, the regulars took the miners into custody pending McDermott's arrival. Despite rumors that Hogan's army was heavily armed, Page's force confiscated only three pistols.[21]

When McDermott arrived, with many federal writs but few posse members, he requested that Page escort the 331 prisoners to Helena, where they would be held for

---

[19] Telgs, McDermott to Olney, 24 Apr 1897, and Knowles to Olney, 24 Apr 1894, both in RG 60, File 4017, NARA; see also Eggert, *Railroad Labor Disputes*, pp. 142–43; McMurry, *Coxey's Army*, pp. 203–05; Rich, *President and Civil Disorder*, p. 89.

[20] Ltr, Olney to Schofield, 28 Apr 1894, RG 94, Records of the Office of the Adjutant General, U.S. Army, 1890–1917, File 6370, 1894 (Coxey's Army), NARA.

[21] Cooper, *The Army and Civil Disorder*, pp. 108–09; Rich, *President and Civil Disorder*, pp. 89–90; McMurry, *Coxey's Army*, pp. 204–05; Eggert, *Railroad Labor Disputes*, p. 143; Schwantes, *Coxey's Army*, pp. 154–65.

FEDERAL TROOPS ON ESCORT DUTY IN MONTANA DURING THE NORTHERN PACIFIC
RAILROAD STRIKE. *At center right is the legendary Calamity Jane.*

trial. Page initially hesitated to grant this request, which placed federal troops in violation of the Posse Comitatus Act, but after receiving approval for action from Schofield
under RS 5298, he complied. On arrival in Helena, the soldiers converted an old race-
track into a makeshift stockade and settled down to occupation duty. Page's men did not
actually perform guard duty, but their presence helped to forestall any jailbreaks that
might have been attempted by the sympathetic citizens of Helena. Two weeks later
Knowles found all Hogan's followers in contempt of court, but released everyone except
Hogan and 40 others. Hogan was sentenced to six months' imprisonment and each of the
others to thirty days'.[22]

The most widespread disorders occurred in the Department of the Columbia, where
Populist governors and state guardsmen were sympathetic to the unemployed. In late April
1894, confident that the governors could not or would not interfere, hundreds of so-called

---

[22] Telgs, McDermott to Olney, 26, 27, 28 Apr 1894, RG 60, File 4017, NARA; Telgs, Swaine to Schofield,
26, 28 Apr 1894, RG 94, File 6370, NARA; McMurry, *Coxey's Army*, pp. 204–05; Rich, *President and Civil
Disorder*, pp. 89–90.

Coxeyites gathered in Portland, Oregon, and in Tacoma, Seattle, and Spokane, Washington. Brig. Gen. Elwell S. Otis, commanding the Department of the Columbia, concluded that U.S. marshals, without the aid of state militias, could not protect the Union Pacific, the Northern Pacific, or other lines in federal receivership. Therefore, on 25 April he alerted the commanders of Forts Walla Walla and Spokane, both in Washington, and Fort Sherman, Idaho, to have forces ready for possible intervention.[23]

When nearly 500 Coxeyites seized an engine and some boxcars of the Northern Pacific in Portland on 28 April, Governor Sylvester Pennoyer chose to dismiss pleas from the county sheriff to deploy the state National Guard. Realizing that state officials tacitly supported the industrial armies, U.S. District Court Judge Charles B. Bellinger ordered U.S. Marshal H. C. Grady to warn the Coxeyites not to interfere with a railroad in federal receivership. The marshal's warning was ignored. Powerless to enforce the injunction, Grady and Bellinger asked Olney to appeal to President Cleveland to send federal military aid.[24]

By order of the president, Schofield instructed General Otis to assist Grady. When Otis reached Grady, he requested that two troops of the 4th Cavalry at Fort Walla Walla, commanded by Col. Charles E. Compton, be sent to Umatilla Junction to detain Coxeyites until he arrived. The troops successfully carried out Grady's plan, and Otis ordered Compton to escort the 507 prisoners to Portland to stand trial. On arrival, he detailed an officer and 25 men to help federal deputies guard the prisoners.[25]

On the morning of the trial, 30 April 1894, unruly crowds sympathetic to the Coxeyite defendants threatened Grady as he prepared to lead the prisoners to the courthouse. Ignoring the procedure for requesting troops through Otis, Grady directly ordered the regulars guarding the jail to march the prisoners to the courthouse. Irate at Grady's ignorance or disregard of the Posse Comitatus Act and Army policies that forbade civilians from controlling federal troops, Otis promptly chastised the unwary Compton for allowing the marshal to take command of even a small detachment of his regulars, explaining that "troops must act as a body when aiding civil authorities and under the immediate orders of yourself or one of your officers." Compton promptly recalled his men. In the ensuing trial the court failed to convict any of the Coxeyites, who were released on 1 May. This action sufficiently quieted Portland's residents, and federal troops departed the following day.[26]

Meanwhile, disturbances had become widespread in Washington and Idaho. Although no specific authorization had arrived from the president to commit troops to act against the industrial armies, Otis nonetheless took the initiative and dispatched soldiers to Spokane on 29 April to exert a "moral force" in the area. On that same day, U.S. Marshal James C. Drake of Tacoma and U.S. District Judge Cornelius Hanford requested troops from Col. Thomas M. Anderson, 24th Infantry, Vancouver Barracks, to enforce federal injunctions against Coxeyites at Puyallup, just outside Tacoma. When Anderson passed on the request, Otis reminded the federal officials of the provisions of the Posse Comitatus Act and of RS 5298.

[23] *Secretary of War Report, 1894*, p. 152; Rpt, Otis to Schofield, 1 May 1894, RG 94, File 6370, NARA.

[24] *Secretary of War Report, 1894*, p. 152; Telgs, Grady and Bellinger to Olney, 28 Apr 1894, RG 60, File 4017, NARA.

[25] Rpt, Otis to Schofield, 1 May 1894, RG 94; Telg, Grady to Olney, 30 Apr 1894, RG 60, File 4017, NARA.

[26] Rpt, Otis to Schofield, 1 May 1894, RG 94; Cooper, *The Army and Civil Disorder*, p. 111.

Repeating his instructions from Schofield, he added that, for each case in which military support was necessary, a marshal or federal judge must request aid from the president through the attorney general.[27]

Hence Drake telegraphed Olney that "it seems hardly possible [for deputies] to prevent the capture [of Northern Pacific trains in Puyallup]. Railroad officials think and I concur that it would be advisable to have U.S. troops on the ground." In turn, Olney persuaded Cleveland to authorize military assistance under RS 5298. Otis sent troops on 12 May to guard railroad property and patrol the tracks, but no further incidents of theft or violence occurred. By 31 May Otis was able to report that "Affairs in the Department have assumed accustomed quiet and all detached troops have joined their permanent stations."[28]

ELWELL S. OTIS

Although Schofield personally favored the policy of assisting U.S. marshals, he refused to allow his troops to be used to harass Coxeyites who had not stolen trains or otherwise broken the law. On one occasion he instructed commanders that "no action of the troops shall tend to aggravate the difficulty or prevent an amicable adjustment between the contending parties."[29] He even spoke on behalf of the industrial armies on one occasion. In May President James J. Hill of the Great Northern Railroad wrote Secretary Lamont, asking that military commanders in Montana and the Dakotas turn back any train of Coxeyites attempting to travel east through military posts or federal Indian reservations.[30] In a memorandum to Lamont, however, Schofield, who realized the extent of the misery being endured by the unemployed, argued that those in the industrial armies had "the same right as others to the use of public highways, even though those public highways cross a military or Indian reservation," and that in his opinion it was more prudent to let them go quietly and slowly on their way while ensuring that they did not break the law than to hunt down every group and arrest every Coxeyite. Agreeing with Schofield, Lamont turned down Hill's request.[31]

---

[27] Ibid.; Telg, Schofield to Otis, 30 Apr 1894, RG 94, File 6370, NARA.

[28] Quotes from Telg, Drake to Olney, 29 Apr 1894, RG 60, File 4017, NARA, and Cooper, *The Army and Civil Disorder*, p. 111, respectively. See also Eggert, *Railroad Labor Disputes*, pp. 144–45.

[29] Rich, *President and Civil Disorder*, p. 90.

[30] This was legal under RS 2147 and RS 2150, which authorized the government to remove lawbreakers or stolen property from federal land. See Coffman, *Old Army*, p. 254.

[31] Quote from Memo, Schofield for Lamont, 18 May 1894, RG 94, File 6370, NARA. See also Rich, *President and Civil Disorder*, p. 90; Wilson, *Federal Aid in Domestic Disturbances*, p. 6. Daniel Lamont, a railroad attorney like Olney, was a staunch supporter of railroad interests. In 1897 he became a vice president of the Northern Pacific Railroad. See Coffman, *Old Army*, p. 254.

Sensitive to the need to keep the Army free of control by contending parties, Schofield reinforced the provisions of the Posse Comitatus Act with an order of his own. On 25 May he declared that

the troops are employed as a part of the military power of the United States, and act under the orders of the president . . . and his military subordinates. They cannot be directed to act under the orders of any civil officer. The commanding officers of the troops so employed are directly responsible to their military superiors. Any unlawful or unauthorized act on their part would not be excusable on the ground of any order or request received by them from a marshal or any other civil officer.[32]

Federal troops were always to remain under the command and direct control of their officers and could not be commanded or subjected legally to the direct orders or control of sheriffs, marshals, mayors, or governors. Officers could take advice and consult with local officials on the best means of deployment, but subsequent deployment and tactical control always remained with the military officer. General Order 15 implied further that military officers were liable to military disciplinary action and civil or criminal prosecution should their actions violate the order, even if the concerned officer was following the instructions of civil officials. This was in substance the view of General Hancock during the Great Railway Strike of 1877 and now became an official part of Army civil disturbance doctrine. Although issued during the now rapidly fading Coxeyite movement, General Order 15 had greater significance later in the summer of 1894 and in the decades beyond.

Army deployments throughout the West helped to end the illegal seizure of trains, which in turn deflated the Coxeyite movement as Olney had intended. Only small groups of Kelly's or Fry's armies finally reached Washington, D.C., long after Coxey had been arrested and served his prison term. Subsequent groups of stragglers had no more positive influence on the federal government than the original Coxey marchers. By mid-June 1894 most who had attempted to commandeer trains were in prison. Those few who had succeeded in reaching the eastern states found that Coxey's, as well as most Populists', political appeals were less enthusiastically received there and that both the public and the civil authorities were clearly inhospitable. The industrial armies did, however, leave one durable legacy: the practice by which federal courts used injunctions or writs to prevent or frustrate labor organization and strike activities. With the eruption of nationwide railroad strikes in July 1894, Olney's basic strategy was employed again.[33]

The Western Pullman Strikes

No sooner had federal civil and military officials finished dealing with the last vestiges of the coal strike and industrial armies in the West than a new, more widespread and serious civil disturbance began. The Pullman Strike had started in late May 1894 in the small town of Pullman, Illinois, and had remained a localized affair until the cause of the strikers was taken up in June by the American Railway Union (ARU) under Eugene Debs. The General Managers' Association (GMA), a group of corporate leaders representing

---

[32] *Secretary of War Report, 1894*, pp. 57–59; Cooper, *The Army and Civil Disorder*, pp. 104–05. The Army incorporated GO 15 verbatim into *Army Regulations of 1895* as paragraph 490, Article 52.

[33] McMurry, *Coxey's Army*, pp. 225–26, 244–45; Eggert, *Railroad Labor Disputes*, pp. 150–51.

twenty-four railroads either based in or operating from Chicago, supported the position of George Pullman and the railroad corporations. When the ARU announced a boycott of trains pulling Pullman cars, the strike was enthusiastically joined by thousands of railroad workers nationwide, who promptly tied up rail traffic coast to coast. The strike eventually affected nearly 41,000 miles of track in twenty-seven states. The Army's response varied from region to region; in the Midwest the Army worked with state guardsmen, deputy federal marshals, and city police to restore order; in the West, it played the dominant role because no other large and capable law enforcement organizations existed.[34]

Colorado and New Mexico

The Department of the Colorado, commanded by Brig. Gen. Alexander McDowell McCook, experienced the first convulsion of the Pullman Strike west of the Mississippi River. The department itself was crisscrossed by four transcontinental railroads, including the Atchison, Topeka, & Santa Fe. On 30 June 1894, striking railroad workers and coal miners blocked trains attempting to haul Pullman cars between Trinidad, Colorado, and Raton, New Mexico.[35]

At Raton on 30 June, 500 strikers of the Atchison, Topeka, & Santa Fe, and 300 coal miners threatened bodily injury to any strikebreakers or nonstriking workers attempting to operate trains. Because the New Mexico legislature had failed to fund the territorial militia, Governor W. T. Thornton lacked forces to protect the train crews. Moreover, a prounion sheriff and his deputies threatened to block any efforts by U.S. marshals to intervene. But when Thornton asked the secretary of war for federal troops to reopen the lines, Lamont responded that regulars could not be deployed until a marshal and either a federal attorney or a judge indicated that court injunctions could not be enforced, bringing the situation under the coverage of RS 5298.[36]

These conditions were soon met. When the local sheriff prevented U.S. Marshal E. L. Hall and his force of 85 deputies from entering Raton on 2 July to serve their warrants, the marshal and a territorial judge requested 200 federal regulars from Olney. Cleveland agreed with Olney's assessment of the situation and began the process that resulted in Schofield's ordering McCook to have Col. E. P. Pearson of the 10th Infantry, at Fort Marcy near Santa Fe, take two companies to Raton. Arriving on 4 July, Pearson's force of 150 men escorted all trains for the next week. Intimidated by this show of force, the strikers offered little resistance.[37]

While Hall and his deputies were approaching Raton, U.S. Marshal J. A. Israel sent 52 deputies to Trinidad, Colorado, to escort the strike-encumbered trains of three railroads in federal receivership: the Atchison, Topeka, & Santa Fe; the Union Pacific; and the Denver and Gulf. Before the governor could send the state National Guard to aid the federal

[34] *Secretary of War Report, 1894*, pp. 4, 11, 57–58.

[35] Almont Lindsey, *The Pullman Strike: The Story of a Unique Experiment and of a Great Labor Upheaval* (Chicago: The University of Chicago Press, 1942; reprint, 1967), p. 246.

[36] Telg, Thornton to Lamont, and reply, 1 Jul 1894, Rpt on the Chicago Strike of Jun-Jul 1894 by the U.S. Strike Comm, RG 94, File 10, NARA.

[37] Telgs, Seeds to Olney, 2 Jul 1894; Hall to Olney, 16 Jul 1894, *Annual Report of the Attorney General for 1896* (Washington, D.C.: Government Printing Office, 1896), Appendix.

deputies in these duties, however, 300 strikers assaulted and disarmed the small marshal force. With the approval of Schofield, McCook sent five companies from Fort Logan, near Denver, under the command of Maj. Charles C. Hood, 7th Infantry. Reaching Trinidad on Independence Day, Hood's men accompanied Israel's deputies as they arrested 48 strike leaders for transport to the Denver jail, ending resistance in the region.[38]

The Dakota Territory and the Northwest

In General Merritt's Department of the Dakota, as in New Mexico and Colorado, President Cleveland authorized federal military intervention under RS 5298 to enforce laws meant to safeguard "military roads," in this instance the Northern Pacific Railroad, and sent troops "to secure the safe and speedy transportation of the mails, troops, munitions of war, and public stores."[39] Between 27 June and 6 July, however, strikers along the rail line from St. Paul, Minnesota, to Puget Sound, Washington, interfered with rail traffic, including trains carrying payrolls, supplies, and mail bound for several Army garrisons west of Fargo, North Dakota. Following complaints from Merritt that the Army posts along the Great Northern Railroad were literally at the mercy of the strikers, Olney declared him free to use whatever force he believed necessary to reopen the route.[40]

On 6 July Schofield ordered Merritt and General Otis, commanding the Department of the Columbia, to reopen and protect the Northern Pacific by placing federal troops on trains going to and from St. Paul and Puget Sound. Both men were also to assign deputy federal marshals to each train to make any necessary arrests. Between 7 and 9 July 1894, 1,000 men of Merritt's 3d Infantry guarded tunnels and bridges or escorted trains of the Northern Pacific from the east to Idaho. Once in Idaho, troops from the Department of the Columbia replaced them for the remainder of the trip to the Pacific coast. The process was then reversed for trains going from west to east. Army activities were soundly condemned by strikers and their sympathizers, who cursed and jeered at the troops as they traveled through many rail towns. The Army's popularity decreased further when it became public knowledge that many of the trains under federal military escort were carrying strikebreakers from the East.[41]

One notable confrontation occurred at Livingston, Montana, on 10 July. As Capt. Benjamin C. Lockwood led a company of the black 24th Infantry into town on two Northern Pacific trains, a mob of 600 people became particularly violent, profane, and abusive, hurling insults as well as stones. After the trains halted, Lockwood deployed his troops on both sides of the platform and ordered the crowd to disperse. When the crowd refused to move, even under prodding of bayonets and rifle butts, and a local leader of the American Railway

---

[38] Telgs, Israel to Olney, 1 Jul 1894, and McCook, Dept of Colorado, to Lamont, 5 Jul 1894, both in RG 94, File 10, NARA; *Secretary of War Report, 1894*, pp. 136–37.

[39] RS 5298 was invoked to enforce Section 3, Act of 2 July 1894 (13 *Stat.* 365), the statute cited in this particular case. See also Telgs, Merritt to AG, 3 Jul 1894, and Olney to Lamont, 5 Jul 1894, *Rpt of Atty Gen, 1894*; Telg, Merritt to Lamont, 6 Jul 1894, RG 94, File 10, NARA.

[40] Telgs, Merritt to AG, 3 Jul 1894, and Olney to Lamont, 5 Jul 1894, *Rpt of Atty Gen, 1894*; Telg, Merritt to Lamont, 6 Jul 1894, RG 94, File 10, NARA. Olney's role in the strike was far greater than his position as attorney general suggested; he was sort of a "deputy president" dealing with labor unrest by Cleveland's permission and subsequently usurped many presidential prerogatives concerning federal troop use and deployment.

[41] Telgs, McNaught to Olney, 6 Jul 1884, and Schofield to Merritt, 7 Jul 1894, *Rpt of Atty Gen, 1894*; Cooper, *The Army and Civil Disorder*, p. 122.

Union defiantly pushed one soldier, an angry Lockwood struck the man on the head with the flat of his saber and cursed him. As one eyewitness later testified, "it was not an occasion for the exercise of Chesterfieldian politeness or drawing room etiquette." This slight show of force, however, was sufficient to calm the crowd, and Lockwood, after posting a detachment of 4 officers and 90 men in the town, left Livingston.[42]

The incident caused a public outcry against the Army. The next day Montana Governor J. E. Rickards sent a formal note of protest and a petition from the citizens of Livingston to President Cleveland demanding that Lockwood be punished. In response, the War Department sent Capt. E. F. Glenn to investigate. After Glenn had concluded his investigation and issued his report on 6 August, the judge advocate general cleared Lockwood of any wrongdoing, noting that his actions in relation to the mob conformed to the recently issued General Order 23 of 9 July 1894, which stated that troops should make their "blows so effective as to promptly suppress all resistance." Schofield and Merritt agreed with the decisions, Merritt adding that Lockwood's use of force was justified, although his use of profanity while carrying out his duty was not.[43]

California

With the exception of Chicago, the greatest turmoil of the strike occurred in California, where large numbers of citizens deeply resented the commercial and political monopoly held by the owners of the Central and Southern Pacific Railroads and, even more than elsewhere in the country, sympathized with the strikers. Many also resented the use of the Sherman Anti-Trust Act by the federal government against labor unions and the dispatch of troops to enforce it.[44] But deputy marshals and state National Guard forces in California lacked the manpower or the willingness to reopen paralyzed railroads. Without waiting for a request from the governor of California, Olney initiated federal military intervention for enforcing federal laws and court injunctions, as authorized by Congress under RS 5298, and for protecting the mails, interstate commerce, and military roads as defined by the various federal railway acts.[45]

On the evening of 1 July Schofield ordered the commander of the Department of California, Brig. Gen. Thomas H. Ruger, to "send a sufficient military force from San Francisco to Los Angeles with orders to enforce the mandates and warrants of the United States Court and to prevent any obstruction of the United States mails."

[42] Quote from Cooper, *The Army and Civil Disorder*, pp. 122–24, see also Telg, Lieber, Actg JAG, to AG, 3 Oct 1894, sub: Lockwood Incident, RG 94, File 10, NARA.

[43] Cooper, *The Army and Civil Disorder*, p. 124; W. Thomas White, "Boycott: The Pullman Strike in Montana," *Montana* 29 (Autumn 1979):3–13.

[44] The Sherman Anti-Trust Act (*U.S. Statutes at Large*, vol. 26, 209) was passed on 2 July 1890. It was the first federal act attempting to regulate trusts. Originally intended to control business trusts and corporations, the act did not clearly define the terms *trust*, *monopoly*, or *restraint*, nor did it make clear whether it applied to combinations of labor as well as of capital. See Commager, *Documents of American History*, doc. 320, 1:586; for its use as an antilabor tool, see doc. 326, "U.S. vs. Workingmen's Amalgamated Council of New Orleans, et. al.," 1:596, and doc. 335, "U.S. vs. Debs, et. al.," 1:612.

[45] Telg, Call to Olney, 18 Jul 1894, *Rpt of Atty Gen, 1894*; Cooper, *The Army and Civil Disorder*, pp. 114, 118; Rich, *President and Civil Disorder*, p. 104; Schofield, *Forty-Six Years in the Army*, pp. 46, 507–12; Wilson, *Federal Aid in Domestic Disturbances*, pp. 9–10; Thomas R. Bacon, "The Railroad Strike in California," *Yale Review* 3 (November 1894):241–50.

THOMAS H. RUGER

Schofield recommended that Ruger send the 1st Infantry, under the command of Col. William R. Shafter, and instruct him, upon his arrival, to consult with U.S. District Attorney George J. Denis.[46]

The next day, Shafter had six companies board trains and travel from San Francisco's Angel Island and Benicia Barracks to Los Angeles. After the regulars reached their destination two days later, Olney telegraphed Denis concerning the restrictions on the use of these troops as defined by the Posse Comitatus Act and RS 5298, explaining that "the troops are not under the marshal nor part of the marshal's force or posse, but are a substitute therefor and are under the command of the officer in charge who will use the force at his disposal . . . to execute orders of the court, to prevent obstruction of the mails, and interference with interstate commerce."[47]

Within forty-eight hours after Shafter had deployed his troops to guard and escort mail, freight, and passenger trains of the Southern Pacific, traffic began moving again without interference. Deputy marshals resumed serving the injunctions previously issued by the federal courts. Before Shafter's arrival, threats of violence by strikers had dissuaded nonunion men from operating trains. The presence of troops, however, intimidated the strikers, allowing the railroad to convince nonstriking crewmen that it was safe to return to work. With rail service bloodlessly restored, Schofield ordered Ruger to withdraw Shafter's men on 16 July 1894. The last federal troops left Los Angeles on 28 July 1894.[48]

Strikers farther north in California, however, were not very willing to tolerate outside intervention. Hostile activities by strikers and the unemployed against the Central Pacific Railroad peaked in the Sacramento–San Francisco area between 4 and 12 July. As the month began, 3,000 strikers and their supporters disrupted mail service and interstate commerce in Sacramento. Unable to enforce federal laws concerning the unobstructed flow of mail and commerce, U.S. Marshal Berry Baldwin asked the governor to send state guardsmen to aid him as a *posse comitatus*. Three regiments soon arrived from San Francisco. These troops were useless: they lacked rations, uniforms, and other equipment necessary to perform effective service; in addition they sympathized with the strikers. When Baldwin directed them to

---

[46] Telg, Schofield to Ruger, 1 Jul 1894, RG 94, File 10, NARA; *Secretary of War Report, 1894*, p. 11.

[47] Telg, Olney to Denis, 5 Jul 1894, *Rpt of Atty Gen, 1894*, Appendix.

[48] Telgs, Shafter to Lamont, 5 Jul 1894, and Denis to Olney, 6 Jul 1894, *Rpt of Atty Gen, 1894*; see also *Secretary of War Report, 1894*, p. 111; Cooper, *The Army and Civil Disorder*, p. 118. For Shafter's life and strike role, see Paul H. Carlson, *"Pecos Bill": A Military Biography of William R. Shafter* (College Station: Texas A&M University Press, 1989), pp. 155–58.

move against strikers in a round house, the guardsmen simply refused. A San Francisco paper later explained that "the strikers know personally everyone in the front ranks of the troops. . . . Many of the militiamen were railroad hands themselves."[49]

In view of the inability and unwillingness of the National Guard to intervene effectively, Charles A. Garter, the U.S. attorney in San Francisco, wired Olney that "there is no doubt as to open insurrection at Sacramento," that state authorities and federal marshals had failed to remove interference to the mails and interstate rail traffic, and that federal troops were needed at once.[50]

Because the Central Pacific had been a "military road" since passage of the Act of 1 July 1892, and was entitled to federal military protection, President Cleveland ordered Schofield to reopen the rail line from Ogden, Utah, to Sacramento. Schofield ordered Ruger to coordinate the operation

JOHN R. BROOKE

with Department of the Platte Commander Brig. Gen. John R. Brooke. After consultation, Ruger and Brooke decided to repeat the shuttle tactic used so successfully to reopen the Northern Pacific, selecting an east-west rendezvous point at Truckee, California, on the Nevada-California border.[51]

Compliance with Schofield's order, however, left Ruger with only 400 regulars to maintain order in the entire San Francisco–Sacramento area. On 8 July, therefore, he requested permission to take command of the 500 marines stationed at San Francisco's Mare Island. Having commanded sailors and marines in Washington, D.C., during the Great Railway Strike of 1877, Schofield anticipated no interservice problems and forwarded the request to the president. On that same date, Cleveland ordered the secretary of the Navy to comply.[52]

Adequately reinforced, Ruger began to reopen the Central Pacific line on 10 July. He ordered the commandant of the Presidio of San Francisco, Col. William M. Graham, to move to Sacramento with 5 batteries of the 5th Artillery, 1 squadron of the 4th Cavalry, 1 company of infantry from Benicia Barracks, and 1 battalion of marines from Mare Island, a force totaling 26 officers and 516 men.[53] Graham's expedition reached Sacramento the next day. While the cavalry squadron advanced through town with drawn sabers, the infantry, artillerymen,

[49] Quote from Cooper, *The Army and Civil Disorder*, p. 118. See also *Secretary of War Report, 1894*, p. 112; Winthrop Alexander, "Ten Years of Riot Duty," *Journal of the Military Service Institution of the United States* 19 (July 1896):46–47.

[50] Telg, Garter to Olney, 5 Jul 1894, *Rpt of Atty Gen, 1894*.

[51] Telgs, Schofield and Ruger to Brooke, 7 Jul 1894, *Rpt of Atty Gen, 1894*, p. 112.

[52] Telgs between War and Navy Depts, 8 Jul 1894, RG 94, File 10, NARA.

[53] *Secretary of War Report, 1894*, p. 113.

and marines swept through the rail yards clearing them of strikers and members of the mob. Gatling guns were set up to protect the offices of the Central Pacific. Meanwhile, the governor placed the 900 men of the state's 1st and 2d National Guard Regiments under Graham's command, the only such instance of federal control over nonfederalized state National Guardsmen during the entire 1865–1957 period. Facing more than 1,400 federal and state troops, the strikers quickly submitted, and the troops restored Sacramento to order.[54]

Deep resentments still remained. Unable to combat Graham's forces openly, several of the strikers or their sympathizers turned to sabotaging railroad property. At a trestle two miles south of town, unknown persons removed spikes and fish joints from the tracks, which caused the rails to spread. On 11 July a train guarded by a detachment from the 5th Artillery derailed, killing both engineers and three soldiers and injuring many others. The wreckage temporarily disrupted rail traffic between Sacramento and San Francisco and dramatically increased the antipathy between Army regulars, strikers, and state National Guardsmen, with the guardsmen's true loyalties greatly in doubt. Three days later, as federal troops on escort duty attempted to clear tracks of strikers and their sympathizers at bayonet point, the mob responded by throwing rocks. Without orders, the regulars opened fire into the crowd and killed two people. The shocked and confused crowd dispersed, and Sacramento returned again to order.[55]

Ruger's deployment in Sacramento left both San Francisco and Oakland vulnerable to strike and mob activities. To protect federal property against potential violence, Ruger, acting on his previous authorization to use naval personnel, asked the commander of Mare Island Naval Station to provide sailors and marines from the warships *Charleston*, *Monterey*, *Thetis*, and *Independence*, which were docked in the San Francisco Bay. In response, 370 sailors and marines under the command of Lt. Comdr. W. H. Reeder reported to Ruger, who presented them with two Gatling guns. Reeder marched this mixed force to the Central Pacific's "Oakland Mole" terminal to aid 1,500 California National Guardsmen, who were already present, in clearing railroad yards and guarding trains and other railroad property. Although trains resumed normal schedules on 14 July, Reeder's force remained under Army control for another two weeks before returning to Mare Island.[56]

Satisfied with the stability created in the Bay area, Ruger proceeded with the second phase of his mission, the link-up with Brooke's force at Truckee. At Sacramento on 13 July Graham ordered Lt. Col. Francis L. Guenther, 5th Artillery, to take two companies by rail to Truckee and place guards at bridges and tunnels along his route. Guenther reached Truckee the next day and was met two days later by four companies from the Department of the Platte under Colonel J. S. Poland, 16th Infantry. With the protection of this combined force, trains resumed their regular Ogden to San Francisco traverse without interference. The railroad strike in Sacramento ended on 22 July 1894.[57]

---

[54] Telg, Ruger to Schofield, 10 Jul 1894, RG 94, File 10, NARA; see also *Secretary of War Report, 1894*, p. 115; Cooper, *The Army and Civil Disorder*, pp. 119–20.

[55] Telgs, Ruger to AG, 10 Aug, 3 Sep 1894, and AG to Ruger, 16 Aug 1894, all in RG 94, File 10, NARA. See also *Secretary of War Report, 1894*, pp. 113–14, 116; Telg, Ruger to Schofield, 11 Jul 1894, *Rpt of Atty Gen, 1894*; Cooper, *The Army and Civil Disorder*, pp. 120–21; Coffman, *Old Army*, p. 252.

[56] *Secretary of War Report, 1894*, p. 114; Telg, Ruger to Schofield, 14 Jul 1894, RG 94, File 10, NARA.

[57] *Secretary of War Report, 1894*, p. 113; Telgs, Brooke to Schofield, 12, 13 Jul 1894, RG 94, File 10, NARA; Cooper, *The Army and Civil Disorder*, p. 121.

With the restoration of calm in northern California, the upheavals caused by the industrial armies and the Western Pullman strike came to an end. Unlike the civil disorders in the East where the Army aided local officials, the Army quelled disturbances in the West alone, without significant aid from federal or local law enforcement officials, or state or territorial National Guard forces, with the exception of California guardsmen, and without the sympathy of the majority of local residents. Nonetheless, the Army did manage, with relatively little bloodshed, to restore order in the West and to protect property while maintaining legally constituted civil authority. In Chicago, however, near the original center of the strike, the Army was experiencing greater difficulties.

CHAPTER 6

The Chicago Pullman Strike

In the opinion read by the learned justice, the inherent power of the government to execute the powers and functions belonging to it by means of physical force through its official agents, and on every foot of American soil, was amply vindicated by a process of reasoning simple, logical, unhampered by fanciful distinctions, and absolutely conclusive.

—President Grover Cleveland.

There is ample proof sufficient to make it clear . . . that the United States government . . . was at the beck and call of the railroad corporations . . . and that these corporations, with the Federal Courts and troops to back them up, had swarms of mercenaries sworn in as deputy marshals to incite violence as a pretext for taking possession of the headquarters of the ARU by armed force, throwing its leaders into prison without trial and breaking down the union . . . maligning, brow-beating, and persecuting its peaceable and law-abiding members, and putting the railroad corporations in supreme control.

—Eugene Victor Debs.

The Pullman Strike in the West grew from disorders that began in May 1894 in the company town of Pullman, Illinois, twelve miles south of Chicago. The magnitude of events there and in nearby localities quickly dwarfed the western disorders. The resulting turmoil brought about one of the largest deployments of federal military troops for riot duty to that time and prompted the Army's first attempt to develop a specific doctrine on civil disturbances to guide its officers in such disturbances.

In all probability the labor dispute that caused the Pullman Strike would have remained a local affair had it not been for the intense rivalry of two larger trade organizations that escalated the conflict into one of nationwide proportions. On one side was the American Railway Union of 150,000 members, including 4,000 Pullman employees, which Eugene Victor Debs formed in June 1893. In opposition to the union was the General Manager's Association, founded in 1886, consisting of the Pullman Company and twenty-four railroads, among them the giants of the rail industry. The hard and uncompromising attitudes held by both groups assured violence that eventually required federal military intervention to restore order.[1]

---

[1] For Debs, see Ray Ginger, *The Bending Cross: A Biography of Eugene Victor Debs* (New Brunswick: Rutgers University Press, 1949; reprint, New York: Russell and Russell, 1969). On the ARU and GMA, see Paul A. Varg, "The Political Ideas of the American Railway Union," *The Historian* 10 (1948):85–100; Donald L. McMurry, "Labor Policies of the General Manager's Association of Chicago, 1886–1894," *Journal of Economic History* 13 (1953):160–78; Lindsey, *Pullman Strike*, p. 113; Eggert, *Railroad Labor Disputes*, pp. 147–48.

Origins of the Pullman Strike

Pullman, Illinois, was founded in 1880 by entrepreneur George M. Pullman as a model town and the site of the Pullman Palace Car Company. The town was intended to be a worker's paradise where the 12,000 inhabitants lived in strict accordance with George Pullman's paternalistic policies under close company control. With the firm supposedly providing all possible worker needs, company officials considered labor organizations unnecessary and viewed them with hostility.[2]

In the year following the Panic of 1893 the Pullman Company reduced average employee wages without similar reductions in rents and prices that the company charged in Pullman, or in the salaries of managers or superintendents. Although citing the depression as the cause for these measures, the company continued to pay stock dividends as it had each year since its founding in 1867 and succeeded in amassing a surplus of $25 million. When workers protested company actions the company fired them, and when workers threatened to strike in May 1894 George Pullman declared a lockout, effectively closing the plant. Stalemate ensued; worker attempts to seek a negotiated settlement failed, as did the American Railway Union when it interceded on the workers' behalf. After management had rebuffed all attempts at a compromise, the union presented the company with an ultimatum: unless the company's representatives agreed to arbitration by 26 June, the union would begin a nationwide rail strike and boycott any train carrying a Pullman car. Since most major railroads used Pullman cars, nationwide paralysis of the rail system would result. When Pullman ignored the union's ultimatum, in effect calling its bluff, the strike began.[3]

The General Manager's Association quickly came to the defense of the Pullman Company. Railroad lawyers called for court injunctions against the strike and placed Pullman cars on as many trains as possible, calculating that widespread disruption of passenger, freight, and mail traffic would provoke a public outcry, cause federal intervention, and tarnish the image of the Railway Union. For the same reasons, the association avoided calling on municipal authorities or the Illinois state militia between 26 June and 2 July to break what was initially a peaceful and well-ordered strike, hoping instead for decisive federal actions.[4]

The railroads had a powerful friend and ally in U.S. Attorney General Richard Olney. Prior to, even during, his tenure at the Justice Department, Olney served as a director or legal adviser to several railroads whose officials were members of the General Manager's Association. At the same time that he earned an annual salary of $8,000 as attorney general, the Chicago, Burlington, & Quincy Railroad was paying him more than $10,000 a

---

[2] On Pullman, Ill., see Samuel Yellen, *American Labor Struggles, 1877–1934* (New York: Monad, 1936), pp. 101–10; William H. Carwardine, *The Pullman Strike* (Chicago: Charles Kerr, 1894; reprint, New York: Arno, 1969), pp. 15–26.

[3] Yellen, *American Labor Struggles*, pp. 101–10; Lindsey, *Pullman Strike*, pp. 32, 94–96, 100; Heaps, *Riots, U.S.A.*, pp. 85–87; Allan Nevins, *Grover Cleveland: A Study in Courage* (New York: Dodd, Mead, 1966), pp. 611–13; "The Strike at Pullman: Statements of George Pullman and Second V.P. Wickes Before the U.S. Strike Commission," in Carwardine, *The Pullman Strike*, pp. 3–4, 8–13; "The Pullman Company and Its Striking Workmen," *Harper's Weekly* 38 (21 July 1894):677, 684–89.

[4] Yellen, *American Labor Struggles*, pp. 113–15, 118–19; Eggert, *Railroad Labor Disputes*, pp. 149–50, 156–57; Lindsey, *Pullman Strike*, pp. 131–37, 142–43; Nevins, *Grover Cleveland*, p. 613.

year as a retainer for legal services. Olney agreed that the Railway Union constituted not only an implacable foe of business to be curbed by any method necessary, but was also a radical and revolutionary threat to federal authority. Even though strikebreaking was incidental to making the railroads operational again, "in Chicago Olney consciously worked to break the strike and the power of the ARU and remove Eugene Debs from the leadership of the outbreak."[5]

The first step in Olney's campaign to involve the federal government in the strike entailed the appointment of Attorney Edwin Walker as Special Counsel and Strike Adviser to the U.S. District Attorney for the Northern District of Illinois, Thomas E. Milchrist. As a former railroad lawyer and GMA's choice to lead antistrike efforts Walker, like Olney, was well suited for the task ahead. Olney's next step was to convince President Cleveland of the need to act. Although the president was troubled by the events in Chicago, he hesitated to commit federal troops until their presence was absolutely necessary. As Olney pointed out, however, he had the legal authority to intervene militarily under RS 5298 and the various federal railroad acts to protect the mails and interstate commerce, without awaiting court action. While Cleveland hesitated, Olney directed Walker and Milchrist to initiate court injunctions as the first recourse to start rail traffic moving.[6]

With the industrial armies that spring, Olney had used injunctions to protect railroads in federal receivership. But in July 1894 this familiar gambit no longer worked, because few eastern railroads were financially insolvent. Instead, he used two other justifications for federal injunctions: to prevent interference with the mails or with interstate commerce. During an earlier strike against the Great Northern Railroad in April, Olney's solicitor general had determined that any train hauling at least one mail car was officially a mail train. By extrapolation, Olney reasoned that efforts to remove the mail car, or any other car on the same train, constituted interference with the United States mail. On 28 June he instructed Walker to obtain federal court injunctions so that "passage of regular trains carrying U.S. mails in the usual and ordinary way . . . [would not be] obstructed." As an added antistrike measure, the General Manager's Association pressed the attorney general to invoke the Sherman Anti-Trust Act as a further basis for federal intervention. Olney readily complied.[7]

Having selected protection of the mails and interstate commerce, with antitrust legislation as grounds for intervention, Olney sought a blanket injunction citing all three justifications that would render ARU interference with rail traffic in the Chicago area virtually impossible. Although neither Chicago nor Illinois authorities had yet requested his assistance, or believed federal aid to be necessary during what had thus far been a peaceful strike, U.S. Circuit Court Judge William A. Woods and U.S. District Court Judge Peter S. Grosscup issued an injunction on 2 July, at Olney's behest, of such

---

[5] Quote from Cooper, *The Army and Civil Disorder*, p. 144. For Olney, see Schwantes, *Coxey's Army*, p. 162; Lindsey, *Pullman Strike*, pp. 147–50; Eggert, *Railroad Labor Disputes*, pp. 163–64; Nevins, *Grover Cleveland*, p. 615.

[6] Lindsey, *Pullman Strike*, pp. 153–54; Eggert, *Railroad Labor Disputes*, p. 162; Nevins, *Grover Cleveland*, p. 616.

[7] Quote from Eggert, *Railroad Labor Disputes*, pp. 149, see also pp. 158, 164–66, 171–72, 271n.51; Yellen, *American Labor Struggles*, 123–24; Lindsey, *Pullman Strike*, pp. 150–51, 158–61; Wilson, *Federal Aid in Domestic Disturbances*, pp. 9–10. For a contemporary view, see L. Abbot, "The Legal Aspects of the Disorder at Chicago," *Outlook* 50 (14 July 1894):54–55.

EUGENE V. DEBS   RICHARD OLNEY

breadth that labor leaders bitterly denounced it as a "Gatling gun on paper." It prohibited ARU members from interfering with mail trains or those engaged in interstate commerce and further forbade union members to attempt to persuade others to join the strike
or to encourage those already engaged in the boycott. If Debs complied, the American
Railway Union would cease to exist. The injunction, however, as Olney and the GMA
executives understood, meant little without the power to enforce it.[8]

Federal marshals had already been unsuccessful at controlling what little disorder
existed, that primarily caused by unemployed persons unconnected with the strike and the
union, and now appeared to be unable to enforce the injunction. Under Olney's orders,
since 26 June U.S. Marshal John W. Arnold had deputized 3,000 men in the Chicago area.
Many were white-collar or nonstriking railroad workers volunteered by their companies,
but the vast majority were thugs, drunks, and other disreputable persons who made need-
less arrests, brutalized citizens, and, in some cases, plundered the very property they were
hired to protect. The association paid, armed, and deployed these deputies, even though
Walker complained to Olney "that the marshal is appointing a mob of deputies that are
worse than useless." Rather than assuring law and order, the federal deputies guaranteed
the opposite, provoking the strikers and unemployed to violence.[9]

---

[8] Lindsey, *Pullman Strike*, pp. 161–62; Rpt on the Chicago Strike of Jun–Jul 1894 by the U.S. Strike Comm,
pp. 41–42, RG 94, Records of the Office of the Adjutant General, U.S. Army, File 10, 1894: Chicago Strike,
NARA.

[9] Quote from Cooper, *The Army and Civil Disorder*, p. 145. See also Rpt on the Chicago Strike of Jun–Jul
1894 by the U.S. Strike Comm, pp. 41–42, RG 94, File 10, NARA; Lindsey, *Pullman Strike*, p. 167; Nevins,
Grover Cleveland, p. 622.

The apparent failure of deputies—and of local police—to maintain law and order left only two other alternatives: the state militia or federal troops. At the outset of the boycott, Illinois prolabor Governor John P. Altgeld had deployed portions of the state's 4,774-member National Guard at trouble spots in Danville, Decatur, and Cairo; but, as conditions appeared to worsen, he prepared to concentrate the entire force near Chicago. Despite his readiness to attempt to restore order, Altgeld was unsympathetic to the railroads, believed that the cause of the Pullman strikers was just, and was entirely unwilling to put state forces in the position of strikebreakers in support of the Manager's Association. Local and federal officials had long distrusted Altgeld because of his immigrant, working-class background, his perceived Populist leanings, and his past support for radical causes. Railroad owners in Chicago, therefore,

JOHN PETER ALTGELD

had little trouble convincing Walker and Milchrist that if Altgeld used state troops they would be restricted to restoring order and not to breaking the strike.[10]

Despite Altgeld's uncooperative nature, earlier actions against the industrial armies had eroded Olney's confidence in the state guardsmen and in the law enforcement capabilities of his own force of marshals. From the beginning of the Pullman boycott Olney had wanted to employ federal troops as a first resort, but he needed to demonstrate to the president, as required by RS 5298, that it had become impracticable "to enforce the law by the ordinary course of judicial proceedings," with the Justice Department's own resources.[11]

Olney's first opportunity to persuade Cleveland to send troops came on 1 and 2 July 1894. When a mob of 2,000 strikers who had gathered at Chicago's Blue Island Rail Yard defied Arnold's orders to disperse, the federal marshal wired Olney to say that it was "impossible," even when he was accompanied by a force of 125 deputies, "to move trains here without having the 15th Infantry from Ft. Sheridan ordered here now." Although the press reports, the Chicago chief of police, and Mayor John Hopkins all later testified that no significant disturbances had taken place at Blue Island before or took place anywhere in Chicago after 2 July, Olney used Arnold's telegram to convince Cleveland of the need for federal military intervention. In anticipation of presidential orders, General Schofield alerted the Department of the Missouri to prepare to move the entire garrison of infantry, cavalry, and artillery at Fort Sheridan, by steamer or rail, to Chicago's Lake Front Park. Despite the pleas of Olney and

---

[10] Lindsey, *Pullman Strike*, pp. 179, 181, 185. For Altgeld, see Harry Barnard, *Eagle Forgotten: The Life of John Peter Altgeld* (Secaucus: Lyle Stuart, 1938).

[11] Quote from Lindsey, *Pullman Strike*, pp. 164–65, 246. See also Cooper, *The Army and Civil Disorder*, p. 145.

DANIEL S. LAMONT

Arnold and Schofield's preparations, Cleveland "deemed it best to follow strictly the precedent observed during the Coxey episode and not to move [troops] until satisfied that he must do so by overwhelming proof, preferably a joint statement from the marshal, the United States attorney, and the federal judge."[12]

Therefore, on 3 July Olney instructed Walker to forward a request for troops signed jointly by Milchrist and Grosscup. With that statement he persuaded Cleveland to commit federal forces and summoned Schofield to the White House. After locating the vacationing department commander, General Miles, Schofield accompanied him to a White House conference with President Cleveland, Secretary of State Walter Q. Gresham, and Secretary of War Daniel S. Lamont. After discussing the Chicago situation, Miles and Gresham balked at sending federal troops to the city on the grounds that they were unnecessary and might provoke further violence. Olney convinced the other members of the conference by reportedly waving Arnold's telegram as proof of the existing danger, overruled both Miles and Gresham, and convinced the president that immediate federal military aid was crucial.[13]

However, the conference brought to the fore a long-standing rivalry between Generals Miles and Schofield that was to have an enervating effect on federal intervention in Chicago. Their respective memoirs differ sharply on the sequence of events at the conference, but they do indicate some of the subtle hostility the two had long held toward one another. Miles claims he "happened to be on important duty in the east" when the crisis erupted, but Schofield writes that Miles' "staff officers didn't know his whereabouts nor did the Adjutant General of the Army." Miles also claims that he favored sending troops to Chicago immediately to put down what he perceived as a radical revolution, while Schofield pictured Miles as "not having anticipated any emergency which would require or justify . . . use of troops in his department." According to Schofield, "in [Miles'] opinion the U.S. troops ought not be employed in the city of Chicago at that time."[14]

---

[12] Lindsey, *Pullman Strike*, pp. 163–64; Telg, AG, Dept of the Missouri, to CO, Ft. Sheridan, 2 Jul 1894, Letters Sent, Department of the Missouri, 1894, RG 393, Records of the United States Army Continental Commands, 1821–1920, NARA; Rich, *President and Civil Disorder*, pp. 96–97; Nevins, *Grover Cleveland*, pp. 619–20; Schofield, *Forty-Six Years in the Army*, pp. 493–97.

[13] Rich, *President and Civil Disorder*, pp. 96–97; Cooper, *The Army and Civil Disorder*, pp. 145–46; Nelson A. Miles, *Serving the Republic: Memoirs of the Civil and Military Life of Nelson A. Miles* (New York: Harper Brothers, 1911), pp. 252–54; Schofield, *Forty-Six Years in the Army*, pp. 493–97.

[14] See Miles, *Serving the Republic*, pp. 252–54; Schofield, *Forty-Six Years in the Army*, pp. 493–97.

Miles' view that troops were unnecessary upset Schofield, who already considered him derelict in his duty for not returning to Chicago earlier in the crisis. The two generals had already clashed on several occasions concerning Miles' slowness in responding to orders from Schofield, and Miles' proclivity either to change or to ignore orders altogether. Earlier in the spring, during the coal strike in Indian Territory, Miles had taken nearly a month to respond to Schofield's order to send troops to aid with evictions of miners from coal pits on federal property.[15]

Their strained relations reflected both a personality clash and policy differences over the role of the Army in civil disorders. Miles, fifty-five years old in 1894, was a hardened combat veteran with little experience in civil-military affairs. As a commander of volunteers he had seen action in many major campaigns of the Civil War and had

JOHN M. SCHOFIELD

won the Medal of Honor for gallantry at Chancellorsville, where he had been severely wounded. By age twenty-five, Miles, known as one of the "boy generals," had commanded a corps of 26,000 men. Following the Civil War his active combat service continued on the western frontier, where he had engaged the Comanche, Kiowa, Nez Perce, Arapaho, Sioux, Cheyenne, and Apache between 1866 and 1894. Unlike Schofield, he had little formal education but could count on valuable family, military, and political contacts, for his wife was a niece of both Ohio Senator John Sherman and General William T. Sherman, the former commanding general of the Army. Accustomed to the independence of frontier commands and sure of his authority, connections, powers, and capabilities, Miles grew restive under Schofield's attempts to control directly the federal military intervention in Chicago. Schofield, convinced that a rapid and decisive military response was needed and similarly convinced of his own command capability, overruled his strong-willed subordinate and issued orders to effect troop deployments in the Midwest.[16]

After personally putting Miles on the next train for Chicago, Schofield sent orders to Miles' adjutant, Lt. Col. James P. Martin, instructing him to concentrate all the forces

---

[15] Cooper, *The Army and Civil Disorder*, p. 146; Schofield, *Forty-Six Years in the Army*, pp. 493–97.

[16] For Miles, see *Who Was Who in American History: The Military* (Chicago: Marquis' Who's Who, 1975), p. 383; *Webster's American Military Biographies* (Springfield: G. C. Merriam, 1978), p. 283; Virginia W. Johnson, *The Unregimented General: A Biography of Nelson A. Miles* (Boston: Houghton Mifflin, 1962); Miles, *Serving the Republic*; Nelson A. Miles, *Personal Recollections and Observations of General Nelson A. Miles* (Chicago, 1896; reprint, New York: DaCapo, 1969); Louise C. Wade, "Hell Hath No Fury Like a General Scorned: Nelson A. Miles, The Pullman Strike, and the Beef Scandal of 1898," *Illinois Historical Journal* 79 (Autumn 1986):165–67; Robert M. Utley, "General Nelson A. Miles," *By Valor and Arms* 3 (March 1978):47–50.

THE 15TH INFANTRY CAMPS ON LAKE FRONT PARK

from Fort Sheridan at Lake Front Park. As soon as the encampment at Lake Front was complete, the commander, Col. Robert E. A. Crofton, 15th Infantry, was to confer with Arnold and the government's two attorneys, Milchrist and Walker, on the details of how best to deploy troops for enforcement of federal laws and how best to facilitate transport of the mail.[17]

Early on the evening of 3 July Crofton entered Chicago with 8 companies of the 15th Infantry, 2 troops of the 7th Cavalry, and 1 light battery of the 1st Artillery. Upon consultation with Arnold, Colonel Martin, Milchrist, and John M. Egan, GMA chairman (but ignoring both Chicago and Illinois civil and military authorities), Crofton decided to deploy his men throughout the city, instead of concentrating them at Lake Front Park. He sent 4 companies of infantry to the Blue Island Rail Yards, 2 companies to Union Stock Yards, and 2 companies to Grand Crossing. The next morning he reinforced the regulars at the stockyards with 2 cavalry troops and an artillery battery. Then he set up headquarters downtown, where he could take advantage of telegraph and telephone facilities.[18]

At Arnold's recommendation, Crofton subsequently broke up these large troop formations into scores of small detachments of 10 to 20 men, assigning them to work beside police squads and marshals' posses throughout the city. Edwin Walker then advised Arnold that "certain divisions of the U.S. Army are detailed for special duty of assisting you . . . if necessary, in making arrests. You should have a force of deputies where the officers and

[17] Telg, Schofield to Martin, Dept of the Missouri, 3 Jul 1894, Ltrs Recv'd, Dept of the Missouri, RG 393, File 2611, NARA.

[18] Rpt of Crofton, 28 Jul 1894, Ltrs and Telgs Recv'd Concerning the Chicago Riots, Dept of the Missouri, RG 393, File 2611, NARA; Schofield, *Forty-Six Years in the Army*, pp. 493–95.

soldiers of the Regular Army are stationed, as the army officers will expect you or your deputies to arrest offenders."[19]

By deploying federal military forces in small detachments to work with police and deputies, Crofton showed a lack of appreciation for Schofield's policy (and that of General Hancock in 1877) that troops always remain in large formations under exclusive military control. In General Order 15, issued on 25 May 1894, Schofield had told department commanders explicitly that federal regulars were to operate only as cohesive tactical units under the direct orders of their military superiors, not as reinforcements integrated into the posses of federal and local law enforcement agencies. Such integration that put federal troops under orders of municipal and civil authorities, instead of their own officers, constituted a direct violation of the Posse Comitatus Act. Like Hancock, he believed

NELSON A. MILES

that civil authorities, in asking for military aid, confessed their own inability to restore order and should therefore stand aside.[20]

There were also sound tactical reasons not to use scattered detachments. On 4 July the sight of small numbers of federal troops accompanying policemen and deputy marshals failed to intimidate the Chicago mobs. That evening crowds numbering 10,000, consisting of strikers, the unemployed, youths, and thrill seekers, roamed the rail yard at Blue Island and the stockyards, tampering with signal lights, overturning rail cars, and setting fires. Restrained by Miles' standing orders not to fire unless directly threatened with assault, federal troops attempted to disperse the mobs from railroad property by using rifle butts and bayonets during that time and the following day.[21]

Meanwhile, Miles had entered Chicago and returned to the Department of the Missouri headquarters in the Pullman Building at Michigan Avenue and Adams Street. Several troubling issues awaited him, the first concerning troop deployments. The legal questions raised by Crofton's assignment of federal troops as reinforcements for posses did not concern Miles as much as the potential danger of scattered federal military units' being overwhelmed by mobs that might take advantage of the restrictions placed upon the troops' use of lethal force. Even more troubling to him, Miles was forced to confront newspaper

[19] Quote from Telg, Walker to Arnold, 5 Jul 1894, Ltrs and Telgs Recv'd, Dept of the Missouri, Chicago Strike Rpt, RG 393, File 2611, NARA. See also Eggert, *Railroad Labor Disputes*, p. 173; Cooper, *The Army and Civil Disorder*, p. 147.

[20] GO 15, HQ of the Army, AGO, Washington, D.C., 25 May 1894; Schofield, *Forty-Six Years in the Army*, p. 508; Rich, *President and Civil Disorder*, p. 102.

[21] Schofield, *Forty-Six Years in the Army*, p. 498; Lindsey, *Pullman Strike*, pp. 205–06.

reporters, labor groups, and Governor Altgeld, who increasingly criticized federal actions and charged the Army with protecting the Pullman Palace Car Company and the railroads. Miles explained that the soldiers were present to aid federal marshals, to protect federal property, to reopen interstate commerce and mail service, as authorized under RS 5298, and, if requested to do so, to aid state militia and local police forces when they were in danger of being overtaken. Thus far, however, neither state nor local officials had requested that federal troops come to Chicago, nor had they asked them to restore order, this being a task of local and state forces. The strikers and the crowds were convinced that the federal military deployments were directed at them. Hostility toward the federal troops was intense, the officers receiving reports that "time and again, troops were met with boos, jeers, and curses." One Army officer stated that his "men bore patiently the vilest abuse and vilification," while a newspaper correspondent wrote that the strikers "seemed to take it as a personal insult that the soldiers were there."[22]

Learning that mobs were converging upon federal military units along the Rock Island line at Blue Island and at the stockyards, Miles authorized Crofton to disperse them by warnings, pickets, and guards—and, if these methods failed, by firearms. Although such measures enhanced the security of his troops, they did little to reopen blocked roads. Without directly menacing the troops and thus risking federal firepower, large mobs continued to obstruct the tracks and destroy railroad property. On 5 July the regulars at the stockyards repeatedly removed some of the estimated 2,000 to 5,000 rioters from the tracks, but were unable to move the trains and soon withdrew. At Blue Island, the attempts of regulars to clear the tracks and start trains moving again were thwarted as well.

Needing reinforcements, Miles sent for 7 companies from Fort Leavenworth, Kansas, and Fort Brady, Michigan. On 5 July he telegraphed Schofield that "the injunction of the United States Court is openly defied and unless the mobs are dispersed by action of police or fired upon by U.S. troops [whether menaced or not], more serious trouble may be expected. Mob is increasing and becoming more defiant. Shall I give the order for troops to fire on mobs obstructing trains?" To prepare for any eventuality and to enhance his firepower, Miles ordered the commander of Fort Riley, Kansas, to send 1 battery of Hotchkiss revolving guns and 3 batteries of artillery.[23]

Schofield's response indicated a growing dissatisfaction with Miles' handling of affairs in Chicago, especially his failure to halt Crofton's tactic of dividing federal forces into small detachments to aid civil authorities. In his haste to reproach Miles, he temporarily ignored the question of firepower: "troops should not be scattered or diverted into small detachments nor should they attempt to perform service in several places at the same time." Schofield reminded Miles further that his first duty was to protect federal property. The preservation of private property and restoration of public order was the mission of

---

[22] Quote from Cooper, *The Army and Civil Disorder*, p. 148. See also Ltrs, Miles to Hopkins, 14 Jul 1894, and to Pullman Palace Car Co., 16 Jul 1894, Ltrs Sent, Dept of the Missouri, RG 393, File 2611, NARA; Yellen, *American Labor Struggles*, p. 119; Pollack, *Populist Response*, pp. 52–54; Wade, "Hell Hath No Fury," p. 168.

[23] Ltr, HQ, Dept of the Missouri, to Crofton, 4 Jul 1894; Telg, Miles to CO, Ft. Leavenworth, 4 Jul 1894; Telg, Miles to CO, Ft. Brady, 4 Jul 1894; quote from Telg, Miles to AG, 5 Jul 1894; Telg, Martin, Dept of the Missouri, to CO, Ft. Riley, 5 Jul 1894. All in Ltrs Recv'd, Dept of the Missouri, RG 393, File 2611, NARA. See also Ltr, Insp of Artillery to HQ, Dept of the Missouri, 5 Jul 1894, Ltrs Sent, Dept of the Missouri, RG 393, File 2611, NARA. Cooper, *The Army and Civil Disorder*, pp. 147–48.

state and local authorities. Schofield later commented that "it was difficult to believe that a major general of the Army could be so ignorant of the duty devolved upon the troops when ordered by the president to enforce the laws of the United States."[24]

Miles ignored Schofield's instructions for another day. Even after 5 companies of regulars from Fort Leavenworth and 2 companies from Fort Brady arrived on 6 July, he continued to deploy federal forces, now numbering 930 officers and men, in company-size or smaller detachments throughout Chicago. In addition to assigning 2 companies to guard the federal building at Adams and Jackson streets, he sent a detachment to each of the city's six major rail depots. These detachments escorted deputy marshals to make arrests and rail crews to repair tracks within the city.[25] He hoped these efforts would clear the major lines of communication of rioters and obstructions. Since most of the tracks traversed Chicago's working-class residential areas, success was limited and of short duration. As soon as trains bearing troops passed, mobs of residents, strikers, and the unemployed reappeared and swarmed over the tracks. Realizing the futility of these tactics, Miles belatedly complied with Schofield's order to reconcentrate federal forces. Late on 6 July he redeployed 8 companies of infantry, 1 battery of artillery, and 1 troop of cavalry to Lake Front Park to reinforce the other 7 companies of infantry and 1 cavalry troop still active downtown.[26]

While Miles was rearranging his troops and seeking freer use of their firepower, the destruction of railroad property reached a peak. On 6 July, when an agent of the Illinois Central Railroad shot two rioters, an angry mob of 6,000 went on a rampage and burned nearly 7,000 cars in the 50th Street Panhandle Yards, causing an estimated $340,000 worth of damage, as compared to an average of $4,000 for each of the previous days of the strike. Elsewhere mobs destroyed other railroad property, forced nonstriking railroad workers to flee from job sites, and even burned six large buildings on the site of Chicago's World Columbian Exposition, which had opened the previous year. It was now obvious to all, especially to Debs and other union leaders, that what had started as an orderly and relatively peaceful attempt by the union to aid the Pullman strikers had now become a wild, uncontrolled spree involving thousands of strikers and Chicago's unemployed, a spree that even federal troops were finding difficult to quell. Critics in the media, particularly the reporters of the *Chicago Times*, and in groups representing both labor and capital, were quick to point out, much to the chagrin of Olney and the association, that the troops under Miles had failed to clear the tracks, ostensibly the main reason for summoning that force to the city. After all, impatient businessmen complained, John Egan had predicted that the presence of regulars "would bring peace with a short sharp jerk." Instead, violence and disorder had now escalated to alarming levels. Distressed at the inability of police, U.S. marshals, or federal troops to quell the violence and destruction, and aware of press reports

---

[24] Quote from Cooper, *The Army and Civil Disorder*, p. 150. See also Telg, Schofield to Miles, 5 Jul 1894, Ltrs Recv'd, Dept of the Missouri, RG 393, File 2611, NARA.

[25] Rpt of Crofton, 28 Jul 1894, Ltrs and Telgs Recv'd, Dept of the Missouri; Telgs, Miles to AG, to Arnold, to Lamont, all 6 Jul 1894; Telgs, AG, Dept of the Missouri, to Crofton and Ovenshine, 15th Infantry, 6 Jul 1894, and Miles to AG, 8 Jul 1894, Ltrs Sent, Dept of the Missouri. All in RG 393, File 2611, NARA.

[26] Cooper, *The Army and Civil Disorder*, p. 147; Rpt of Crofton, 28 Jul 1894, Ltrs and Telgs Recv'd, Dept of the Missouri, and Telg, Miles to Lamont, 6 Jul 1894, Ltrs Sent, Dept of the Missouri, both in RG 393, File 2611, NARA; Wade, "Hell Hath No Fury," pp. 168–71.

that the mob was conducting a veritable reign of terror in the city, Mayor Hopkins finally asked Governor Altgeld to intervene with state troops.[27]

Altgeld had waited for Hopkins' call since 4 July, growing increasingly angry with the federal government and the city. He had protested vigorously that the situation did not call for federal troops nor did he want them, especially since neither local authorities nor Olney had encouraged him to commit state forces. Although not wanting to appear to be turning a blind eye to lawlessness or to be helping either the strikers, with whom he sympathized, or the association, he continued to be one of the loudest critics of federal involvement. In a strongly worded telegram to Cleveland on 5 July he protested the unilateral and gratuitous commitment of federal troops to the city without his knowledge, consent, or participation. He contended it was a lack of public sympathy that caused the railroad's inability to hire enough nonstriking workers to run the trains, and not the interference of strikers or of unruly mobs. Altgeld added that the restoration of order was his responsibility, not the federal government's, and that, if either Cook County or the railroad owners had requested state aid, he could have promptly provided 3 regiments of infantry, 1 troop of cavalry, and 1 battery of artillery.

To Altgeld's arguments Cleveland tersely replied that he had ordered federal troops to Chicago in strict accordance with the Constitution and federal statutes and had issued, somewhat belatedly, a cease and desist proclamation to the rioters. Every action was perfectly legal and, under the circumstances, justified. Events in Chicago, Cleveland maintained, were nothing more than simple issues of law and order. Altgeld, nonetheless, remained convinced that federal actions constituted an illegal usurpation of state prerogatives.[28]

Determined to assert gubernatorial authority in a situation rapidly moving out of state control, on 6 July Altgeld answered Mayor Hopkins' request for aid by sending 4,000 Illinois National Guardsmen to the city—a fourth force (after federal troops, federal marshals, and local police) operating independently to restore order. Repeating Crofton's earlier error, however, Hopkins gave directions that scattered the Illinois guardsmen in small units to clear tracks and protect railroad property at key points throughout the city. This encouraged confrontations between militiamen and the mob with tragic results. On the afternoon of 7 July, while furnishing protection to a utility train on the Grand Trunk line at 49th and Loomis streets, Company H of the 2d Regiment of the Illinois National Guard became involved in the bloodiest encounter of the strike. As the train stopped to raise an overturned car, the crowd cursed and threw stones at escorting guardsmen. The junior officer commanding the company ordered the mob to disperse and his men to load their rifles. The mob thinned out as many women and children left. Reduced to its most militant members, the mob grew more threatening and

---

[27] Lindsey, *Pullman Strike*, pp. 207–08; Yellen, *American Labor Struggles*, pp. 122–23; Nevins, *Grover Cleveland*, p. 623.

[28] Federal troops had already been in Chicago for six days before Olney noticed this oversight and encouraged Cleveland to issue the appropriate cease and desist proclamation on 9 July 1894. For the proclamation, see Wilson, *Federal Aid in Domestic Disturbances*, pp. 230–31. See also Lindsey, *Pullman Strike*, pp. 188–89, 221–22; Rich, *President and Civil Disorder*, p. 101; Colston Estey Warne, ed., *The Pullman Boycott of 1894: The Problem of Federal Intervention* (Boston: D.C. Heath, 1955), pp. 52–63; Ekirch, *The Civilian and the Military*, p. 118. Altgeld's antifederal stand during the strike brought an end to his political career.

continued throwing rocks. The officer then ordered a bayonet charge that wounded several people. When the crowd retaliated by throwing more rocks, one struck the officer on the head. Fearing for the safety of his men and despairing of receiving reinforcements, he then ordered his command to fire at will and make every shot count. After firing 100 rounds in several volleys that killed or wounded a minimum of twenty people, the mob began to mill about in confusion until the Chicago police arrived, and using revolvers and clubs, made a series of charges that finally dispersed the crowd.[29]

The intensity of the mob violence on 7 July prompted Miles once again to scatter his forces, contrary to orders, to protect the railroads from threatened attacks. By now he had become convinced that Chicago was on the verge of revolution, the result of a labor conspiracy led by the Railway Union and involving heavily armed Socialists and anarchists. He was convinced further that only federal forces could save the city from a bloodbath and notified Schofield that "the masses want peace but the agitators [are] very ugly and say they must have civil war."[30] On Miles' orders Crofton sent 2 companies to the Dearborn Station, 2 to Union Depot, and 1 each to depots of the Illinois Central, Rock Island, Grand Central, and Chicago & Northwestern Railroads. His orders directed subordinates to accompany, support, and assist, if necessary, United States marshals in arresting trespassers and men engaged in obstructing or destroying lines of communication along mail and interstate commerce railways. If the crowds fired on trains, or even threw rocks and pieces of iron, the soldiers were to open fire.[31]

At one point on 7 July Miles sent a small detachment of regulars to protect the warehouses of two whiskey companies after Milchrist informed him of the likelihood of their being looted by the mob. Miles was persuaded because, as the owners of the Calumet and Riverdale Whiskey Companies owed the federal government $149,215.50 in taxes upon the sale of whiskey then in stock, the federal government had a proprietary interest in protecting company warehouses. Motivated by Milchrist's logic and by an equally strong desire to deny an already volatile populace any additional fuel, he sent Lt. F. H. Sargent, 7th Infantry, and 25 men to protect the property.[32]

By late evening on 7 July Chicago was an armed camp containing 13,430 men sworn to protect property or uphold local, state, or federal law: 3,500 Chicago police, 5,000 U.S. marshals and deputies, 930 federal troops, and 4,000 Illinois National Guardsmen. Between 6 and 10 July, 1,000 additional federal troops arrived in Chicago, including infantry, cavalry, and artillery from Fort Leavenworth and other western posts, and the 9th Infantry from Madison Barracks, New York. Initially, each group charged with law enforcement or riot control operated independently, with only slight efforts at coordination between city police and state guardsmen, or between U.S. marshals and federal regulars. Throughout 7 July several of these forces responded to the same disturbances, often simultaneously, but without common leadership, goals, or plan of action. Seeing the folly of such efforts, Arnold placed his deputies at the disposal of Miles and the federal troops. The

---

[29] Heaps, *Riots, U.S.A.*, pp. 95–96; Nevins, *Grover Cleveland*, p. 623; Wade, "Hell Hath No Fury," pp. 170–71.
[30] Cooper, *The Army and Civil Disorder*, pp. 150–51.
[31] Rpt of Crofton, 28 Jul 1894, Ltrs and Telgs Recv'd, Dept of the Missouri; Telgs, Miles to Lamont, 7 Jul 1894, and AG, Dept of the Missouri, to Crofton, 7 Jul 1894, Ltrs Sent, Dept of the Missouri. All in RG 393, File 2611, NARA. Miles, *Serving the Republic*, pp. 253–54.
[32] Rpt of Crofton, 28 Jul 1894, RG 393.

two men then arranged a division of responsibility with troops protecting deputies as they made arrests.[33]

Disappointed at the slow pace of police, deputies, and troops acting separately to end the rioting, the association sent Chairman John Egan, the strike manager, to consult with Hopkins and Miles about consolidating all forces under one federal commander. Although Hopkins declined the proposal, Miles nonetheless informed his officers that if state and local governments fail to maintain peace and good order within the territory of their juris-diction, military forces would assist them, but not to the extent of leaving unprotected property belonging to or under the protection of the United States. On 10 July, however, Mayor Hopkins finally agreed that it was best to coordinate efforts and have Chicago's police and Illinois' guardsmen concentrate on restoring order, while federal forces reopened rail traffic. Each force remained under the command of its own respective civil or military leader.[34]

In light of the persistent refusal of city police and state guardsmen, prior to this time, to share intelligence on mob activities with each other or with federal forces, Miles turned to Egan for assistance. Egan organized a network of informants to report on the activities and plans of the union and a central intelligence agency to disburse information on all strike-related incidents and activities. Whenever beleaguered railroad officials needed fed-eral troops to prevent or quell mob activity, looting, or vandalism, he informed Miles, who on almost every instance sent troops to support deputy marshals as they arrested mob or strike ringleaders threatening railroad property. Army deployments and Miles' own reports on the Chicago strike clearly reflected the information and ideas gathered and provided by Egan and his informants.[35]

As Egan developed the intelligence framework needed for operational planning, Schofield issued a seminal general order that became the foundation of Army civil distur-bance doctrine and for the first time laid down tactical guidelines for operations against mobs. Soon incorporated into Army regulations, the general order remained virtually unchanged until 1937. Issued on 9 July 1894, General Order 23 read:

A mob, forcibly resisting or obstructing the execution of the laws of the United States, or attempting to destroy property belonging to or under the protection of the United States is a public enemy.

Troops called into action against such a mob are governed by the general regulations of the Army and military tactics in respect to the manner in which they shall act to accomplish the desired end. It is purely a tactical question in which manner they shall use the weapons with which they are

---

[33] Telg, Lamont to Miles, 7 Jul 1894, Ltrs Recv'd, Dept of the Missouri, and Telg, Miles to AG, 8 Jul 1894, Ltrs Sent, Dept of the Missouri, both in RG 393, File 2611, NARA; Cooper, *The Army and Civil Disorder*, p. 149. For contemporary views, see Frederick Remington, "Chicago Under the Mob," *Harper's Weekly* 38 (21 July 1894):680–81; J. D. Sherman, "The Situation in Chicago," *Harper's Weekly* 38 (14 July 1894):665–67.

[34] Schofield, *Forty-Six Years in the Army*, pp. 503–04; Miles, *Serving the Republic*, pp. 255–56; Ltr, Hopkins to Miles, 10 Jul 1894, Ltrs Recv'd, Dept of the Missouri, RG 393, File 2611, NARA; Cooper, *The Army and Civil Disorder*, pp. 149–59.

[35] Cooper, *The Army and Civil Disorder*, pp. 151, 161n.31. See also Ltr, Crofton to HQ, Dept of the Missouri, 11 Jul 1894, Ltrs Recv'd, Dept of the Missouri, RG 393, File 2611, NARA. Miles later denied in testimony before the U.S. Strike Commission that he had had any such contact with Egan or that he acted on GMA orders, but doc-uments in the files of the Department of the Missouri proved that he was in almost daily contact with Egan by memo and telephone.

armed—whether by the fire of musketry and artillery or by the use of the bayonet and saber, or by both, and at what stage of operations each or either mode of attack shall be employed.

This tactical question must necessarily be decided by the immediate commander of the troops, according to his best judgment of the situation and the authorized drill regulations.

In the first stage of an insurrection, lawless mobs are frequently commingled with great crowds of comparatively innocent people, drawn there by curiosity and excitement, and ignorant of the great danger to which they are exposed.

Under such circumstances the commanding officer should withhold the fire of his troops, if possible, until timely warning has been given to the innocent to separate themselves from the guilty. Under no circumstances are the troops to fire into a crowd without the order of the commanding officer, except that single sharpshooters, selected by the commanding officer, may shoot down individual rioters who have fired upon or thrown missiles at the troops.

As a general rule the bayonet alone should be used against mixed crowds in the first stages of a revolt. But as soon as sufficient warning has been given to enable the innocent to separate themselves from the guilty, the action of the troops should be governed solely by the tactical considerations involved in the duty they are ordered to perform. They are not called upon to consider how great may be the losses inflicted upon the public enemy, except to make their blows so effective as to promptly suppress all resistance to lawful authority, and to stop the destruction of life the moment lawless resistance has ceased. Punishment belongs not to the troops but to the courts of justice.[36]

Miles was in full agreement with the contents of General Order 23. Strongly supportive of the railroads, federal authority, and law and order, he was now convinced that labor unions, especially the Railway Union, were synonymous with anarchists, Communists, and Socialists. When Egan's spies reported that Eugene Debs was orchestrating a general strike in Chicago, Miles was certain that this was the expected bloody revolution that had as its primary goal the overthrow of the federal government. In reality, however, the now desperate Debs was seeking the support of Chicago's gas, electric, and other utility workers whose absence from their jobs would effectively shut down the city. He reasoned that this condition of paralysis could then be used as a negotiating point to have state and federal troops withdrawn from the city.[37]

Debs' general strike never occurred. The increasingly desperate economic situation of the Pullman and other rail strikers forced them to submit. More important, Debs and the other top ARU leaders had ignored the 2 July federal court injunction, which would have destroyed the union if they had complied, and were arrested on charges of contempt of court, conspiracy, and interference with the mails—all prohibited by the Sherman Anti-Trust Act. Denied leadership, the American Railway Union, on the advice of AFofL President Samuel Gompers, ended the Chicago strike. Labor and labor-related disputes in the city had cost the railroads, local, state, and federal governments an estimated $685,308 in direct damages and costs for law enforcement. Strikers lost an estimated $1,400,000 in wages. In human terms, at least 13 people were killed, 53 were wounded, and 190 were arrested by federal officials. None of the deaths or serious injuries was caused by federal troops, indicating that the harsh instructions of General Order 23 were not followed literally.[38]

---

[36] GO 23, HQ, USA, AGO, 9 Jul 1894; *Army Regulations of 1895*, sec. 491, subsequent regulations to, and including, *AR 500-50*, par. 8, 6 Jun 1923; *AR 500-50*, par. 7, 5 Apr 1937.

[37] Telgs, Miles to Schofield, 9 Jul 1894, and to Lamont, 10 Jul 1894, both in RG 94, File 10, NARA; Miles, *Serving the Republic*, p. 255.

[38] Lindsey, *Pullman Strike*, pp. 214, 278–81; Wilson, *Federal Aid in Domestic Disturbances*, pp. 231, 236–37; Heaps, *Riots, U.S.A.*, p. 96.

Shortly after Debs' arrest, Schofield directed Miles to confer with Arnold and other local, state, and federal officials to determine the necessity of a continued federal military presence in the city. Miles was instructed further to inquire whether Hopkins and Altgeld could substitute police and state militia for regulars protecting federal courts trying strikers arrested for obstruction of the mails. Miles, however, vigorously and repeatedly protested these steps leading to what he determined was a dangerously premature withdrawal of troops from a city on the verge of open rebellion. Although Walker and Arnold agreed initially that troops could be withdrawn safely, pressure from the General Manager's Association forced them to change their opinion, and they agreed with Miles. Nonetheless, after an explicit telegram from Secretary Lamont ordering a withdrawal, and a further telegram from Schofield directly ordering Miles to act, he acquiesced. On 18 July the withdrawal of the 9th Infantry to Madison Barracks and the removal of all other troops temporarily to nearby Fort Sheridan ended the federal military intervention.[39]

Hammond, Indiana

Meanwhile, in Hammond, Indiana, a major railroad junction twenty miles east of Chicago, federal troops had been involved in clashes with mobs of strikers and the unemployed, as violent as any in Chicago. When the boycott began on 26 June, thousands of Indiana railroad men and unemployed workers halted trains to uncouple Pullman cars. Within three days larger and more violent mobs had formed that attacked nonstriking workers, derailed locomotives and rolling stock, and on 7 July seized the telegraph office. As apparent anarchy descended upon Hammond, the helpless local sheriff began pleading with Indiana Governor Claude Matthews either to send in the state National Guard or to call for federal troops. Matthews initially refused these calls, just as he had earlier requests on 29 June, believing that the events of recent days in Hammond were not serious enough to justify the use of state or federal forces. In the meantime, the U.S. marshal for Indiana and his deputies succeeded in arresting a few strikers on charges of interfering with the mails, but these actions only angered the crowd more.[40]

Emboldened by agitators from South Chicago, on 8 July the mob, now numbering 3,000, continued their rampage. In Indianapolis the U.S. marshal, a federal judge, and the U.S. district attorney jointly requested that Olney obtain federal military aid. Olney urged Matthews to make a formal request under Article 4 of the Constitution for troops to protect the state against domestic violence. When to Olney's dismay, Matthews refused, Secretary Lamont instructed Miles to send forces to Hammond to remove obstructions to the mails and interstate commerce under the same authorization that had guided his actions in Chicago.[41]

---

[39] Telgs, Schofield to Miles, 14, 17, 18 Jul 1894, RG 94, File 10, NARA; Wilson, *Federal Aid in Domestic Disturbances*, p. 231; Cooper, *The Army and Civil Disorder*, p. 154. See also Frederick Remington, "Chicago Under the Law," *Harper's Weekly* 38 (28 July 1894):703–05, and "Withdrawal of the United States Troops," *Harper's Weekly* 38 (11 August 1894):748–49.

[40] Wilson, *Federal Aid in Domestic Disturbances*, pp. 231–32; Lindsey, *Pullman Strike*, pp. 259–60; Cooper, *The Army and Civil Disorder*, pp. 151–52.

[41] This was RS 5298. See Wilson, *Federal Aid in Domestic Disturbances*, pp. 231–32; and Lindsey, *Pullman Strike*, pp. 259–60.

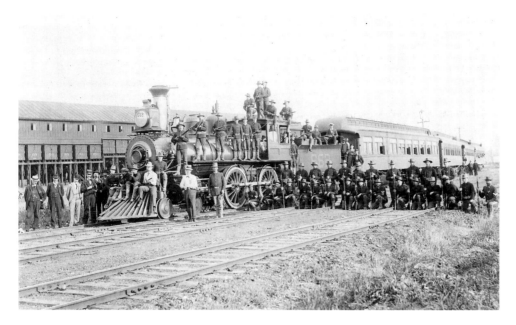

SOLDIERS OF THE 15TH INFANTRY SHORTLY AFTER THE COLLAPSE OF THE PULLMAN STRIKE

On 8 July Miles ordered Colonel Crofton to send three companies to clear the rail line between Chicago and Hammond. He was ordered further to allow deputy marshals to accompany the units and noted that "if the mob insists on obstructing the road, you may fire at their feet first and then raise fire if you want to." Matthews, relieved of the burden of requesting federal aid, still termed Hammond "a dangerous point on the state border that federal troops could control more completely," but nonetheless now dispatched 700 state guardsmen to the city to reinforce Crofton.[42]

Late in the afternoon the federal force reached Hammond aboard the Illinois Central Railroad. One company of this force, under Capt. W. T. Hartz, immediately became involved in a fatal incident with the Hammond mob. After learning that a crowd was preparing to block a section of the Louisville, Chicago, & New Albany Railroad with an overturned Pullman car, Hartz personally led 17 men to the site. While still 300 yards away, several soldiers riding in the engine saw the mob attempting to overturn a rail car directly in their path. To avert a collision and disperse the crowd, several soldiers, without orders, indiscriminately fired an estimated thirty rounds before Hartz could order a cease-fire. The shots wounded 12 to 15 people and killed Charles Fleischer, an innocent bystander and father of four, who was at the scene searching for one of his sons.

Federal reinforcements arrived by 9 July and the presence of 4 companies of federal regulars, supported by 16 companies of Indiana National Guardsmen, fully intimidated the mob

---

[42] Rpt of Crofton, 28 Jul 1894, Ltrs and Telgs Rec'd, Dept of the Missouri; see also Telgs, Miles to Lamont, 8 Jul 1894, and Matthews to Miles, 8 Jul 1894, Ltrs Sent, Dept of the Missouri. All in RG 393, File 2611, NARA.

and restored order to Hammond. Still irate over the death of Charles Fleischer, however, Hammond citizens pressed for a coroner's inquest, which concluded that Fleischer "came to his death by accident, caused by soldiers of Company D, 15th Infantry Regiment, United States Army, shooting wantonly and carelessly into a peaceable crowd." Both the mayor and the local ARU representative protested the dispatch of federal troops to the city and the shootings that followed. Citizens held public meetings on 9 and 16 July to protest President Cleveland's decision to send troops, and the local magistrate swore out warrants for the arrest of the regulars involved in the shooting. Given the nature of the provocation that led to the shooting and Hartz's men having previously endured four days of exhausting riot duty in Chicago, the Army did not press for a court-martial and ignored the civil charges.[43]

The Aftermath

After considerable monetary and property losses on both sides, the Railway Union ended the strike on 5 August 1894. The loss of effective union leadership after the arrest of Debs and his chief lieutenants and the crippling effect of the omnibus injunctions best explain the ARU's decision. Under escort of federal troops, deputy marshals had arrested scores of strike leaders and mob members for contempt of court, while state guardsmen similarly aided city police and deputy sheriffs to arrest 515 more strikers and mob members on charges of murder, arson, burglary, assault, intimidation, riot, conspiracy, and incitement to riot. On 14 December 1894, five months after the strike ended, the U.S. Circuit Court for the Northern District of Illinois found ARU President Eugene Debs guilty of conspiracy to restrain interstate commerce in violation of the Sherman Anti-Trust Act of 1890. Following an unsuccessful Supreme Court appeal, Debs served a six-month prison term.[44]

In the landmark decision of 27 May 1895, *in re Debs*, the U.S. Supreme Court denied Debs' petition for a writ of habeas corpus, ruling that even without the permission of state governments "the strong arm of the National Government may brush aside all obstructions to the freedom of interstate commerce or the transportation of the mails. If the emergency arises, the Army of the nation and all its militias, are at the service of the nation to compel obedience to its laws." This precedent-setting decision authorized and confirmed the president's power to use federal military force, even with the restrictions of the Posse Comitatus Act, in any strike involving either the transportation of the mails or the movement of interstate commerce.[45]

---

[43] Quote from Cooper, *The Army and Civil Disorder*, pp. 151–52. Cooper, on p. 152, and Coffman, *Old Army*, p. 252, cite a further fatal shooting involving the 15th Infantry in Spring Valley, Illinois. See also Ltrs, Morlock to HQ, Dept of the Missouri, 14 Jul 1894, Ltrs Rec'd, Dept of the Missouri, Entry 2611, RG 393, NARA. Lindsey, *Pullman Strike*, pp. 259–60. The troops involved in the Hammond shootings, having fired without orders, were liable to prosecution under both military and civil law. They could have been charged and tried for murder and armed assault had Hammond or Indiana officials pressed their case. Such an event, however, was unprecedented and according to one constitutional law authority "In no instance has an . . . American jury allowed an officer or soldier to suffer for acts done with any shadow of right to repel invasion or quell a mob." See Dowell, *Military Aid to the Civil Power*, pp. 210–14, quote on p. 211.

[44] Yellen, *American Labor Struggles*, pp. 130, 134–35; D. M. Means, "Principles Involved in the Recent Strike," *Forum* 17 (August 1894):633–34; E. W. Bemis, "The Chicago Strike of 1894," *Review of Reviews* 12 (October 1895):466.

[45] *In re Debs*, 158 U.S. 564 (1895); see also Yellen, *American Labor Struggles*, pp. 124–25, 132; Eggert, *Railroad Labor Disputes*, pp. 202–03; Commager, *Documents of American History*, docs. 335 and 336, 1:612–16.

In late July 1894 President Cleveland appointed a three-man commission to investigate the causes of the strike and to offer suggestions for the prevention of future railroad upheavals. Labor praised the U.S. Strike Commission's controversial findings, issued in November 1894, but railroad interests soundly condemned them. The commission found that the Pullman Company was unduly harsh in its relations with its laborers, that the Manager's Association practiced an illegal usurpation of civil power, and that the association's refusal to arbitrate its differences with the Railway Union was largely responsible for the strike. The commission recommended that railroad companies recognize unions, which were already in existence and unlikely to disappear, and ban all labor contracts forbidding union membership. A final recommendation of the commission called for enactment of some form of compulsory negotiation and arbitration in labor disputes that would prevent violent labor upheavals. Although the commission recommendations initially were ignored, in 1898 a Railroad Arbitration Act was passed, the first of a number of pieces of legislation intended to prevent future rail strikes. Richard Olney was its author.[46]

The effectiveness of the federal military response to the disorders associated with the Pullman Strike had varied widely from place to place. In Chicago Miles concentrated the efforts of his men on guarding federal buildings and railroad depots, while Illinois guardsmen and city police crushed riotous mobs and broke the strike. In the West, the Army assumed a dual role as guardians of private, state, and federal property, and as effective strikebreakers by their mere presence on the trains and in the cities. Troops were repeatedly deployed to guard bridges, clear tracks, and aid deputy marshals in arresting union leaders for conspiracy to interfere with the mails, interstate commerce, or military roads, as authorized under RS 5298. Much more conscientious in following Schofield's orders and advice than Miles, the commanders of the western departments consistently kept units under the military chain of command and successfully coordinated operations with state and local civil and military officials, avoiding violations of the Posse Comitatus Act and maintaining the spirit of General Orders 15 and 23. In addition, in California Brig. Gen. Thomas H. Ruger demonstrated great competence and ability in leading a command of combined services including units of the Navy, Marine Corps, and California State National Guard.

In 1894 riot and strike duty significantly affected the Army's image, organization, and doctrine. Federal military intervention confirmed labor's suspicions, held since the disturbances of 1877, that both the Army and various state National Guard forces were sympathetic to and willing partners of big businesses, if not outright tools under direct control of American corporations. Many commanders who shared the beliefs of business and civic leaders found railroad officials most generous in furnishing transportation, lodging, supplies, and intelligence for operational planning. By contrast, President Cleveland's intention to commit federal troops was solely to uphold federal laws and to remove obstructions to the federal mails and railroads under federal receivership. In reaching these goals, however, federal troops were deployed at a time and in such a manner by the attorney general as to prevent the union from conducting their strike successfully, and in effect the Army

---

[46] Rezneck, "Unemployment, Unrest," pp. 336–37; Lindsey, *Pullman Strike*, pp. 350–58; Witte, *The Government in Labor Disputes*, p. 236. Commission findings are in Warne, *Pullman Boycott*, pp. 7–25, 31–32. For contemporary reaction, see R. Ogden, "Report on the Chicago Strike," *Nation* 59 (22 November 1894):376; H. Robinson, "The Humiliating Report of the Strike Commission," *Forum* 18 (January 1895):523–31.

unconsciously aided the association in breaking the strike and the union. The inability of the union to prevent disorder unleashed by the strike was a critical factor in enabling Attorney General Olney to persuade the president to intervene. The strikes were in no sense peaceful and mob violence, by whatever groups, gave Olney the opportunity he sought to secure military forces to break the strikes and the Railway Union, a group he considered revolutionary.[47]

As with their predecessors in 1877, Secretary of War Lamont and General Schofield quickly took advantage of the Army's new popularity with the conservative urban middle and upper classes in asking Congress to finance the establishment of 2 artillery and 2 cavalry regiments as a force to secure the cities and railroads against future labor unrest. But Congress, as in 1877, and for the same reasons, refused to augment the size of the Army. Most congressmen preferred to fund an improved state National Guard system rather than a larger standing Army. Critics of the Army cited the example of Chicago, when Miles' troops protected trains and federal property, while Altgeld's state National Guard actually broke the strike and suppressed the mobs. Congress continued to vote appropriations to maintain the Army at 28,000 men.[48]

Denied funds for expansion, the War Department increasingly relied on consolidation of existing units to meet the demands of future missions, including labor disorders. By the end of 1894 the Army, as part of an ongoing process, reduced the number of posts from 95 to 80. By 1900, 16 garrisons of regimental strength, 22 of from 4 to 7 companies each, and 14 posts of 2 companies each existed. The experiences of 1877 and 1894 convinced the Army further that large garrisons should be located near urban centers and railroad junctions, readily available to quell any future labor-related violence.[49]

But consolidation of their very limited manpower near critical urban areas failed to reassure the Army leadership. In an era when the fear of social revolution was strong, General Schofield inaugurated a major shift in civil disturbance tactical doctrine. Although during the Whiskey Rebellion of 1794 President Washington had directed a massive show of force to intimidate rioters, a practice used frequently after 1877, Schofield and his successors began to frame Army regulations to emphasize a greater reliance on firepower. General Order 23 of 9 July 1894 and its variations published over the next half-century treated the use of sabers, bayonets, rifles, and artillery as purely tactical questions, and mobs of rioting citizens as public enemies "beyond the pale of protection against military violence accorded to the general public."[50] Paradoxically, this emphasis on firepower and overwhelming force when dealing with domestic disturbances was actually accompanied by an increasing policy of restraint that characterized most federal military interventions. The first test of this new doctrine, however, did not take place in a labor dispute in the streets of an industrial metropolis as anticipated by military leaders, but in the Idaho mountains of the Coeur d'Alene region during recurring violence involving hard-rock miners.

---

[47] Yellen, *American Labor Struggles*, p. 132; Cooper, *The Army and Civil Disorder*, pp. 155–56.

[48] *Secretary of War Report, 1895*, pp. 4, 58–59, 72; Cooper, *The Army and Civil Disorder*, pp. 217–18. For a soldier's view, see Capt. J. J. O'Connell, lst Infantry, U.S. Army, "The Great Strike of 1894," *United Service Magazine* 15 (April 1896):299–316.

[49] *Secretary of War Report, 1894*, pp. 9–11, 60, 74–82.

[50] Paul J. Scheips, Some Aspects of the Federal Response to Civil Disorder, MS in CMH files, pp. 45–48.

CHAPTER 7

The Army and Labor Radicalism in Coeur d'Alene, 1892–1899

Investigations of violent intents of miners claimed by operators is not supported by the facts. Certain parties wish Federal Government to believe the anarchy of 1892 still exists. That is false. Arrival of troops was not the cause of peace. People were capable of handling matters before troops or without them.

—Capt. J. Milton Thompson, 24th Infantry, 1894.

From 1892 to 1899 three violent labor struggles occurred in Coeur d'Alene, Idaho. As mining corporations sought mineral wealth, mine workers' unions sought recognition of the right to recruit members and to engage in collective bargaining for the improvement of wages and working and living conditions. Company efforts to break strikes by bringing in strikebreakers and using armed guards caused violent reactions. Strikers dynamited company property and assaulted and shot strikebreakers and nonunion men. When state and local law enforcement officers failed to restore order out of the disorder caused by those they had labeled "labor radicals," they sought and received federal military aid as other state and local officials had in previous labor disturbances.

More so than in previous Army interventions, the federal military involvement in the Coeur d'Alene disturbances raised serious questions among members of the labor organizations and other critics of the military regarding the neutrality of state and federal civil officials and of Army personnel on the scene. The Coeur d'Alene disturbances were glaring examples of the partisan use of federal military units as an antilabor strikebreaking force.

The Background of Coeur d'Alene Troubles

Located in Shoshone County in northern Idaho, the mountainous Coeur d'Alene District encompasses the river of the same name, running from the Montana-Idaho border to the eastern border of Washington. The Coeur d'Alene Mountains effectively separated Idaho from Montana until the two states were connected by the Northern Pacific Railroad near Mullan, Idaho, in the early 1890s. That rail line extended westward from Mullan six miles to Wallace, Idaho, in the center of the mining district. In the western part of Idaho a line of the Oregon Railway & Navigation Company followed the Coeur d'Alene River eastward to Wardner and then about twelve miles farther to Wallace. After connecting with the Northern Pacific line in Wallace, the Oregon line continued north up Cannon Creek, six miles through the small mining communities of Gem, Mace, and Burke. In winter heavy snow usually limited travel in and out of the region to those two rail lines.[1]

Silver and lead mining conducted by large corporations dominated the economy of the region. Most company owners lived in major urban centers on the east and west coasts and rarely if ever visited the mining camps. Managers also shunned the rough conditions of the mining towns for more convivial accommodations in nearby Spokane, Washington, or Butte, Montana. Both groups remained isolated from the miners' physical and economic conditions and were largely ignorant of their grievances. Miners in the Coeur d' Alene District consequently organized a union in Wardner in 1887. A series of subsequent mine accidents increased resentment of the camp owners and helped union organization efforts to spread throughout the region under the auspices of the Butte Miner's Union (BMU), founded in 1878.

Although it was a loose confederation, the unions under the BMU experienced success in many confrontations with the mine companies. As a result, in 1893 fourteen unions, representing 10,000 western hard-rock miners, met in Butte, Montana, and formed the Western Federation of Miners (WFM). The federation grew rapidly to 200 unions and 50,000 members by 1902, affiliated first with the American Federation of Labor, and then with the Industrial Workers of the World (IWW), ultimately becoming one of the toughest, most militant, and most aggressive labor organizations ever faced by American corporations. Most mine owners viewed these organizations and activities with alarm, forming the Mine Owners' Association to hinder union organization efforts and to protect company interests against the attacks of what they saw as radical labor organizations.[2]

Outbreaks of labor violence in Chicago in 1886 and in Homestead, Pennsylvania, in 1892, had made successive Idaho governors wary.[3] Realizing the dependence of the state's economy on the mining industry and the threat posed to the state's prosperity by union-led strikes, most of these strikes allegedly due to alien radical agitation, state officials allied with the mine owners against the increasingly militant Miner's Union, the later Western Federation of Miners, and their Coeur d'Alene locals. The state tacitly supported company efforts to fire and harass union organizers and to hire strikebreakers and nonunion

---

[1] *Annual Report of the Secretary of War, 1899* (Washington, D.C.: Government Printing Office, 1889), p. 29 (hereafter cited as *Secretary of War Report, 1899*); D. E. Livingstone-Little, "An Economic History of North Idaho: Part V, Discovery and Development of the Coeur d'Alene Mines," *Journal of the West* 3 (July 1964):318–54; Clayton D. Laurie, "The U.S. Army and the Labor Radicals of Coeur d' Alene: Federal Military Intervention in the Idaho Mine Wars of 1892–1899," *Idaho Yesterdays* 37 (Summer 1993):12–29.

[2] Cooper, *The Army and Civil Disorder*, p. 167; Robert W. Smith, *The Coeur d'Alene Mining War of 1892* (Corvallis: Oregon State College, 1961), pp. 13–22, 110–14. For western labor organization, see Melvyn Dubofsky, "The Origins of Western Working Class Radicalism, 1890–1905," *Labor History* 7 (1966):131–54; Richard Lingenfelter, *The Hardrock Miners: A History of the Mining Labor Movement in the American West, 1863–1893* (Berkeley: University of California Press, 1974); Mark Wyman, *Hard Rock Epic: Western Miners and the Industrial Revolution, 1860–1910* (Berkeley: University of California Press, 1979); D. G. Thiessen and Carlos A. Schwantes, "Industrial Violence in Coeur d'Alene Mining District: The Visual Record," *Pacific Northwest Quarterly* 78 (July 1987).

[3] On the Homestead Strike, see Leon Wolff, *Lockout: The Story of the Homestead Strike of 1892* (New York: Harper & Row, 1965).

workers. Union leaders retaliated by encouraging the rank and file to abuse and destroy company property and to harass company guards and strikebreakers. Open warfare resulted in 1892, 1894, and 1899.[4]

Both sides were well armed, determined, and prone to take extreme measures. In clashes between the companies and unions, however, freedom of movement and cover provided by hilly terrain enabled strikers to concentrate their forces and dynamite whatever buildings afforded company guards some measure of protection. County sheriffs hesitated to arrest lawless strikers because the miners made up a large segment of the local population and were courted by local politicians, who often sympathized with their grievances. To halt the destruction of company property and to protect nonunion and nonstriking miners, company managers requested military help, first from the Idaho governor, and then from the president.[5]

The First Coeur d'Alene Intervention, 1892

When the Northern Pacific Railroad raised freight rates in late 1891, the increased costs passed on to Coeur d'Alene mining corporations drastically cut profits and forced owners to close their mines until a solution to the fiscal crisis was found. The railroad then rescinded its increase, but mine officials announced in the spring of 1892 that a cut in miners' wages was necessary to resume operations and to keep their companies profitable. Protesting miners walked off the job on 1 June. In response, company managers locked out all workers and imported up to 800 unemployed eastern miners. When the unionized Coeur d'Alene workers began to harass the strikebreakers and interfere with operations, company officials obtained a federal court injunction. Although union members initially complied, the continued importation of strikebreakers precipitated further violence. Company officials then turned to Idaho Governor Norman B. Willey, who issued a weakly worded proclamation on 4 June "ordering an end to unlawful assembly, interference with private property, and intimidation of nonunion men."[6]

When the miners ignored the governor's order, Willey asked Idaho Senator George L. Shoup to use his influence at the War Department to obtain federal aid and to appeal directly but informally to President Benjamin Harrison. Harrison declined to commit troops on the grounds that their premature dispatch might only aggravate existing problems, recommending instead that local and state officials use their own resources to restore state control.[7]

Meanwhile, three events served to strengthen the strikers' resolve: on 5 July the *Boise Statesman* published a letter from Senator Shoup, telling Willey not to expect federal military aid. On the same day in Homestead, Pennsylvania, striking steel workers captured 300 Pinkerton detectives who had been hired to reopen the mill by force. Finally, on 9 July members of the local miners' union at Gem, Idaho, learned that their own recording secretary, Charles A. Siringo, alias C. Leon Allison, was a Pinkerton detective employed as a company spy. Enraged by this discovery and emboldened by the

---

[4] Melvyn Dubofsky, *We Shall Be All: A History of the IWW* (New York: Quadrangle, 1969), pp. 19, 37–39, 58.
[5] Ibid., pp. 37–38.
[6] Quote from Cooper, *The Army and Civil Disorder*, p. 166. See also Smith, *Coeur d'Alene Mining War of 1892*, pp. 30–37, 41–49 passim; Lingenfelter, *Hardrock Miners*, pp. 196–218.
[7] Cooper, *The Army and Civil Disorder*, p. 166.

refusal of the federal government to intervene, union leaders determined to seek a violent solution to their disputes with the mining companies.[8]

On 11 July miners in Gem decided to drive away strikebreakers at two local mines, the Helena-Frisco and the Gem. At five in the morning the miners opened fire on the first mine from the surrounding hillsides. After three and a half hours of sporadic shooting that produced no casualties, the miners sent a charge of dynamite down a sluice into a four-story wooden building. The ensuing explosion destroyed the building, and falling timbers crushed one of the nonunion occupants. The remaining nonunion workers surrendered to their attackers and were imprisoned in the Miners' Union Hall in Gem.[9]

More intense fighting at the Gem Mine resulted in the deaths of five people—three union men, one company guard, and a nonunion employee. The company spy, Charles Siringo, took advantage of the confusion caused by the gun battle and sawed a hole in the floor of a building in which he was hiding and, crawling underneath a wooden sidewalk, fled to the hills. Less resourceful company men surrendered and traveled under armed striker escort to the union hall at Gem, which by the end of the day held 150 prisoners. Later the union miners put the prisoners on a train to Wallace with orders to draw their pay and leave the county.[10]

The fighting took company, local, and state officials completely by surprise. Willey instructed Shoshone County Sheriff Richard A. Cunningham to form a posse and stop the disorder at all costs. Despite his own prolabor sympathies, Cunningham tried to form a posse by issuing subpoenas to 300 men known to favor the cause of the mine owners. When none responded, he notified the governor of the county officials' helplessness and subsequently confined himself to urging moderation on both sides.[11]

Willey, who had already taken steps to call out the Idaho National Guard, wired Harrison from the state capital at Boise and for a second time requested federal aid, explaining that "this morning riot and bloodshed by the miners in the Coeur d'Alene District commenced. The mill was blown up by dynamite and many men were killed and injured." He declared further that

Inspector-General Curtis, Idaho National Guard, informs me that 400 or 500 armed men constituted the mob. The legislature is not in session and cannot be promptly convened. The civil authorities of the county and State are wholly inadequate to maintain peace. The immediate military force of the Idaho National Guard numbers only 196 men, which is, in my opinion far too few to successfully cope with the mob, though I will at once order it into the field. In this emergency I deem it necessary to call for the assistance of the Federal troops. I therefore request that a sufficient force be detailed from Fort Sherman [Idaho] or elsewhere to act in concert with State authorities in maintaining public order.[12]

Satisfied that Willey's telegram met the criteria established by Section 4 of Article IV of the Constitution and by RS 5297 for intervening on behalf of a state facing lawlessness, insurrection, and domestic violence, Harrison ordered Secretary of War Elkins to direct

---

[8] Wilson, *Federal Aid in Domestic Disturbances*, p. 222; Rich, *President and Civil Disorder*, p. 110; Smith, *Coeur d'Alene Mining War of 1892*, pp. 61–64. Victory for the Homestead strikers was short-lived, for Pennsylvania National Guardsmen soon reclaimed Carnegie's property and freed the Pinkertons.

[9] Smith, *Coeur d'Alene Mining War of 1892*, p. 65.

[10] Ibid., pp. 64–67.

[11] Ibid., pp. 74–75.

[12] Wilson, *Federal Aid in Domestic Disturbances*, p. 223.

U.S. ARMY SOLDIERS BIVOUAC IN COEUR D' ALENE, 1892

Maj. Gen. John M. Schofield to send an "adequate force of troops from the nearest station under an officer of rank and discretion with orders to cooperate with the civil authorities in preserving the peace and protecting life and property."[13] The president inexplicably neglected, however, to issue a formal cease and desist proclamation at this time.

The nearest Army units were in Brig. Gen. Thomas H. Ruger's Department of the Columbia, which included 1,500 troops distributed among seven posts in Oregon, Washington, Alaska, and Idaho. In addition to elements of the 14th Infantry stationed at Ruger's headquarters, the garrison forces nearest to Coeur d'Alene included the 4th Infantry at Fort Sherman, Idaho, and the 4th Cavalry at Fort Walla Walla, Washington.[14]

Following Harrison's orders, Schofield directed Ruger to send four companies of the 4th Infantry at Fort Sherman—168 men in all—to Wardner. He ordered further the Department of the Dakota commander, Brig. Gen. Wesley Merritt, to prepare three companies of the black 24th Regiment at Fort Missoula, Montana, for travel to Mullan, Idaho. Schofield was to be informed immediately if Ruger needed more troops.[15]

To save time, Schofield also authorized Willey to communicate directly with Ruger about using federal troops. On receipt of the message, Willey immediately sent a wire requesting more regulars from Fort Walla Walla and Fort Spokane on the grounds that the Bunker Hill and Sullivan Mine in Wardner was being attacked by one thousand armed men.[16] In this Willey exaggerated, but only in terms of numbers. After the attacks on the

---

[13] Telg, Harrison to Schofield, 12 Jul 1892, RG 94, Records of the Office of the Adjutant General, U.S. Army, Principal Record Division 34728: Consolidated File on the Army's Activities During the Coeur d'Alene Strike, NARA; Rich, *President and Civil Disorder*, p. 111.

[14] *Secretary of War Report, 1892*, pp. 77–86.

[15] Telgs, Schofield to Ruger, Carlin, Merritt, 12 Jul 1892, RG 94, File 34728, NARA.

[16] Telg, Schofield to Willey, and reply, 12 Jul 1892, RG 94, File 34728, NARA.

Helena-Frisco and Gem mines, 500 miners had gone to Wardner, where they took over the concentrator apparatus and threatened to destroy it, supposedly with dynamite, unless the company discharged its strikebreakers and nonunion workers within forty-eight hours.[17]

Meanwhile, Col. William P. Carlin led four companies of the 4th Infantry from Fort Sherman to Coeur d'Alene City, where they boarded a steamer for Harrison, arriving late on 12 July. James T. Curtis, inspector general of the Idaho National Guard, greeted them with the warning that the miners were armed and fully prepared to fight. He recommended a one-day stay at Harrison to await the expected arrival of six National Guard companies. Carlin agreed, and, fearing the worst, wired General Ruger for 300 reinforcements.[18]

On receipt of Carlin's communication, Ruger requested that Schofield dispatch three companies of the 25th Infantry, totaling 155 men. Under Capt. Washington I. Sanborn, the troops left on 12 July and arrived at Mullan the next day. Because the tracks leading farther west had been blown up in two places, Sanborn on Carlin's orders returned to Missoula and took an alternate route to Wardner by way of Coeur d'Alene City. Carlin explained later that he was afraid that the force might "be badly cut up or driven back," and because it was "of the utmost importance that the United States troops should not meet with defeat or even a check," he ordered the return to Missoula.[19]

Ruger apparently shared Carlin's concern that federal troops might be checked by superior numbers; so after ordering the 25th Infantry to Mullan, he directed three companies of the 4th Infantry, commanded by Lt. Col. Henry C. Cook at Fort Spokane, and five companies of the 14th Infantry, commanded by Lt. Col. Hugh A. Theaker at Vancouver Barracks, to Wardner. On 13 July, with the approval of Schofield, he asked Merritt for additional reinforcements from the 22d Infantry at Fort Keogh, Montana. Merritt sent five companies under the command of Lt. Col. John H. Page. Between 12 and 14 July approximately twenty companies, nearly 1,000 federal troops, converged on the Coeur d'Alene.[20]

While Ruger assembled a force large enough to overawe the miners, Carlin led four companies to Cataldo, Idaho. Three hours later the six companies of the National Guard promised by Willey arrived under the command of Curtis. Although Curtis outranked Carlin and had served as a colonel in the Union Army during the Civil War, he gave no orders to him. Instead, the two men formed a cooperative joint command, with guardsmen remaining in state service and under state control.[21] However, action was delayed again when the manager of the Bunker Hill & Sullivan Company persuaded Carlin to wait until the rioting miners released the nearly 200 nonstrikers being held prisoner at Wardner. Carlin agreed that a premature advance might lead to a massacre of the prisoners and demolition of mine property.[22] Then a slow and arduous advance began with the

---

[17] Smith, *Coeur d'Alene Mining War of 1892*, pp. 68–70. A concentrator is a large device that separates waste materials from silver ore by using water and gravity. The concentrated silver ore is then smelted.

[18] Rpt, Ruger to AG, 5 Sep 1892, sub: Coeur d'Alene (hereafter cited as Ruger Rpt), RG 94, File 34728, NARA; *Secretary of War Report, 1892*, p. 110.

[19] Ruger Rpt; Returns From Regular Army Infantry Regiments, Rpt of 25th Infantry, July 1892; Rpt, Carlin to AG, Dept of the Columbia, 26 Jul 1892. All in RG 94, File 34728, NARA.

[20] Telg, Ruger to AG, 12 Jul 1892, RG 94, File 34728, NARA; *Secretary of War Report, 1892*, p. 107.

[21] *Secretary of War Report, 1892*, p. 110; Smith, *Coeur d'Alene Mining War of 1892*, pp. 77–78.

[22] Ruger Rpt, and Telg, Heyburn to Dubois, 13 Jul 1892, both in RG 94, File 34728, NARA; Smith, *Coeur d'Alene Mining War of 1892*, pp. 68–70, 77–78.

troop train stopping at every trestle to permit a search for explosives. At last the train arrived in Wardner at 0920. Carlin established his headquarters, while Curtis continued on to Wallace.[23]

Over the next several days, reinforcements from the 4th, 14th, 22d, and 25th Infantry regiments entered Shoshone County, bringing the total number of state and federal troops to 1,200, the large majority being Army regulars. Keeping the bulk of their forces in the vicinity of Wardner and Wallace, Carlin and Curtis placed companies of regulars and guardsmen together at Osburn, Gem, Burke, and Mullan. The military concentration, despite the predictions of Willey, caused the miners to disperse peacefully.[24]

Although relative calm now prevailed, on 13 July the governor declared martial law, citing a "state of insurrection and rebellion" in Shoshone County. Two days later, Curtis received broad powers as provost marshal to protect life and property and to meet force with force in protecting the mines, railroads, and telegraph lines. Guardsmen were empowered to arrest and imprison all persons engaged in violence or in efforts to prevent nonstrikers from working. Moreover, guardsmen could shoot any person caught in the act of dynamiting or otherwise damaging either railroad or mine property. On 15 July Curtis ordered members of the union to surrender their arms to their local guard officer and instructed railroad officials to refuse passage to anyone not bearing a special pass. Then he removed Sheriff Cunningham from office and replaced him with the county coroner, Dr. W. S. Sims, who was less sympathetic to the cause of labor.[25]

Acting in support of state efforts to reestablish law and order in the region, on 17 July Secretary of War Stephen B. Elkins ordered Ruger to issue a presidential proclamation, as a measure of precaution intended to "allay excitement," as required by RS 5300, that commanded all persons in Shoshone County "in insurrection and in resistance to the laws to disperse."[26] That the proclamation was legally supposed to precede the deployment of federal military forces and was now being issued four days after the regulars had arrived was overlooked. Nonetheless, acting on their instructions to enforce the proclamation, federal troops over the next four days escorted and protected deputies while the latter arrested 350 miners who ignored the order and remained armed and at large. In some cases, however, federal troops exceeded their instructions, and based upon information provided by civil officers or "law-abiding citizens," made arrests directly without civil officers being present. After making these arrests, the regulars maintained a guard over their prisoners to prevent rescue attempts, and protected nonstrikers as work in the mines resumed.[27]

In addition to aiding in the roundup of lawless elements in Shoshone County, Colonel Carlin interpreted his instructions to include apprehending lawbreakers in other locales as well. When he was alerted on 19 July by Curtis that ninety armed miners were in the hills above Mullan on the Montana side of the state line, Carlin telegraphed Montana Governor Joseph K. Toole requesting permission to pursue them across the border. Without waiting

[23] *Secretary of War Report, 1892*, p. 111; Telg, Carlin to Schofield, 14 Jul 1892, RG 94, File 34728, NARA.
[24] Telg, Carlin to Schofield, 14 Jul 1892, RG 94; Smith, *Coeur d'Alene Mining War of 1892*, p. 79; Wilson, *Federal Aid in Domestic Disturbances*, pp. 223–24.
[25] Smith, *Coeur d'Alene Mining War of 1892*, pp. 78–81.
[26] Wilson, *Federal Aid in Domestic Disturbances*, p. 224.
[27] Telg, Merritt to AG, 18 Jul 1892, RG 94, File 34728, NARA; *Secretary of War Report, 1892*, p. 112.

FEDERAL TROOPS ENTER WALLACE, IDAHO, 1892

for a reply, he sent two companies into Montana. The miners, however, had already escaped. On his return the next day, Carlin received a telegram from Toole refusing his request unless a similar appeal came from Governor Willey.[28]

These improper procedures and apparent violations of the Posse Comitatus Act received official sanction when a deputy marshal asked Carlin for troops to guard prisoners at Wardner and to escort them to Boise for trial. Ruger telegraphed Carlin that "instructions so far received did not provide for use of troops as a *posse comitatus*, or to guard the United States Marshal for that purpose, and if the United States civil officers concerned expected such service as a necessity there, application should be made to Washington."[29] Then he referred the question of the propriety of guarding and escorting prisoners to President Harrison. On 2 August the president ordered Elkins to inform Ruger that the aid of the troops in the Coeur d'Alene region in Idaho will be given to the United States marshal in guarding the prisoners in his custody, and, if necessary, in transit to Boise City, or wherever they may be taken for trial. The attorney general will give instructions to the marshal to relieve the troops by civil guards at the earliest practicable moment. Federal troops were therefore authorized for use as a *posse comitatus* if so requested by civil officials and were

---

[28] *Secretary of War Report, 1892*, p. 112; Smith, *Coeur d'Alene Mining War of 1892*, pp. 85–86.

[29] Telg, Ruger to Schofield, 31 Jul 1892, RG 94, File 34728, NARA; Telg, Carlin to HQ, 30 Jul 1892, Register of Letters Received, Department of the Columbia, RG 393, Records of the U.S. Army Continental Commands, 1821–1920, Entry 714, NARA.

instructed to provide such aid by Washington.[30] Shortly thereafter Carlin moved his head-quarters to Wallace and ordered his men to perform escort duty. The largest shipment of prisoners took place on 23 August, when three companies of the 4th Infantry escorted 135 prisoners by rail to Coeur d'Alene City. The last group of prisoners under federal military escort left Wallace for Coeur d'Alene City on 9 September.[31]

The Army, however, had no desire to protract the troops' stay. The question of with-drawal came up first on 21 July, after Carlin helped arrest 350 of the most troublesome strikers. Schofield advised Ruger that most of the troops in Idaho should return to their sta-tions as soon as they are no longer needed. He further directed Ruger to confer with Willey and Carlin on when all troops could be withdrawn safely.[32] Fearful of miners' vengeance against the companies and nonstrikers when Idaho guardsmen were returned to civilian status on 29 July, Willey advocated retaining federal troops in Coeur d'Alene for two years. Carlin, however, called for an immediate return of the eight companies from the Department of the Dakota to Montana, to be followed, once the jailed miners had been conducted to Boise for trial, by the return of the nine companies from the Department of the Columbia. For the period after the trials, both Carlin and Ruger recommended keeping three companies in Coeur d'Alene for three weeks.[33] The War Department refused Willey's request to establish a garrison in Coeur d'Alene, Secretary Elkins informing him on 23 July that "troops were placed at your disposal only temporarily and upon your statement that you were powerless to execute the laws and suppress disorder. The President does not desire that the troops shall remain under your orders longer than absolutely necessary to assist you to restore peace and order."[34]

The guardsmen soon followed the Army's withdrawal. Despite uncertainty over the future of federal military forces in his state, Willey succumbed to financial and political pressures to return the guardsmen to their families and regular civilian occupations after two weeks of military duty. On 26 July he dismissed five companies, but kept the sixth in Coeur d'Alene until it relinquished custody of the prisoners to federal troops on 29 July.[35]

On 25 July Schofield ordered Ruger to return Merritt's eight companies to Montana but to retain such force as may be necessary to assist the civil authorities in preserving peace and restoring order. Two days later Ruger released the troops from the Department of the Dakota, and they returned to Fort Missoula and Fort Keogh. He made no further withdrawals until 14 September when Colonel Theaker returned his five companies to Vancouver Barracks. On 21 July two companies of Carlin's original force returned to Fort Sherman, and another company of the 4th Infantry returned the next day to Fort Spokane, leaving four companies of the 4th in the Coeur d'Alene.[36]

---

[30] Telgs, Harrison to Elkins, 2 Aug 1892, and Schofield to Ruger, 3 Aug 1892, both in RG 94, File 34728, NARA.

[31] Telgs, Carlin to HQ, 10, 20 Aug, 13 Sep 1892, all in Register of Ltrs Recv'd, RG 393, Entry 714, NARA. For a contemporary view, see J. R. Reavis, "The Coeur d'Alene Trouble," *Harper's Weekly* 36 (30 July 1892):734.

[32] Telg, Schofield to Ruger, 21 Jul 1892, RG 94, File 34728, NARA.

[33] Telgs, Willey to Elkins, 22 Jul 1892, Carlin to Schofield, 22 Jul 1892, Ruger to Schofield, 23 Jul 1892, all in RG 94, File 34728, NARA; *Secretary of War Report, 1892*, p. 112.

[34] Telg, Elkins to Willey, 23 Jul 1892, RG 94, File 34728, NARA.

[35] Smith, *Coeur d'Alene Mining War of 1892*, pp. 82–83; Cooper, *The Army and Civil Disorder*, pp. 294–95.

[36] Ruger Rpt, RG 94, File 34728, NARA; Telgs, Schofield to Ruger, 25 Jul 1892, HQ, Dept of the Columbia, to Carlin, 20 Sep 1892, both in Ltrs and Telgs Sent, RG 393, Entry 714, NARA.

THE 4TH INFANTRY CAMPS IN WALLACE

After Carlin's departure Cook placed 2 companies in Wardner, 1 in Wallace, and 1 in Gem. For the next several weeks troops at these locations had little to do other than fraternize with townsfolk, attend picnics, play baseball, and frequent saloons. On 10 November Ruger notified Schofield that "a state of quiet prevails in Coeur d'Alene region. Colonel Carlin reports that the civil authorities are now able to protect life and property." Five days later, at the direction of the president, the last four federal companies left, followed by state National Guardsmen. Willey lifted martial law on 18 November and a fragile peace prevailed.[37]

During four months of strike duty in Coeur d'Alene the Army had assisted civil authorities and the state National Guard to maintain order and to arrest and guard nearly 600 miners for alleged participation in the crimes committed on 11 July. From Carlin's 14 July arrival in Wardner until the final federal withdrawal on 15 November, striking miners made no further efforts to harass nonunion strikebreakers, or to damage mine or railroad property, or to resist local, state, or federal authorities.

Willey's establishment of martial law had prompted the arrest of almost every union member in the Coeur d'Alene District, most of whom were quickly released and thereafter fled Shoshone County. No convictions were obtained against any of the participants in the

---

[37] Quote from Telg, Ruger to AG, 10 Nov 1892; Telg, Atty Gen to Ruger, 11 Nov 1892, both in RG 94, File 34728, NARA; Cooper, *The Army and Civil Disorder*, p. 169.

Frisco mill raid. Under state-imposed martial law the Posse Comitatus Act fared poorly. Federal troops cooperated with state authorities, escorting deputy sheriffs as they made arrests and guarding the prisoners until civil authorities could reassert their power. Troops acted, however, under the command of their military superiors, and orders came from the highest levels. Schofield approved federal escort duty, and Harrison himself ordered Carlin to provide federal guards for prisoners. No recorded instance exists in which deputy sheriffs assumed direct command over regulars. There were, although, rare occasions when federal troops did arrest and detain miners pending the arrival of civil law enforcement personnel.

On the whole, the government appeared to have responded to violence with acts of justifiable legality. Federal military intervention was the fundamental reason for the failure of the miners' strike and decreased union activity that followed. Although peace returned to the mining regions by late 1892 and work resumed largely with nonunion miners, the tensions that caused the unrest were still unresolved. The consequence was another federal military intervention in 1894.[38]

Coeur d'Alene, 1894

New disorders began in the region during the 1894 Pullman Strike. Repeating the events of 1877, when miners struck from sympathy for striking railroad workers, the miners of Coeur d'Alene coordinated their attacks against the mines with the strike of workers along the Northern Pacific Railroad. Mine owners and Idaho Governor W. J. McConnell sought federal military aid, ostensibly to end lawlessness and to guarantee residents of Shoshone County their constitutional rights to equal protection under the laws. The evidence shows, however, that the Army was used by mine owners and the governor, who took advantage of the railroad strike and the proximity of federal troops to attempt the destruction of the Western Federation of Miners and to establish a garrison in the region to prevent further union activity.[39]

Violence associated with the Pullman Strike in the West spread to Coeur d'Alene and impelled Schofield on his own initiative to take measures in Idaho, as he had done elsewhere, to reopen the railroad for the mails, for interstate commerce, and for usage as a "military road under RS 5298, the Sherman Anti-Trust Act, and various federal Railway Acts."[40] In response to his orders, the new commanding general of the Department of the Columbia, Brig. Gen. Elwell S. Otis, detailed 700 men from Vancouver Barracks, Fort Walla Walla, Fort Sherman, and Fort Spokane, Washington, to clear the Northern Pacific tracks. On 7 and 8 July, infantry moved to trouble spots at Takoma, Spokane, and Davenport, Washington, where they patrolled rail lines and inspected trestles for explosives. For the most part the troops encountered no resistance or other signs of hostility.[41]

---

[38] Cooper, *The Army and Civil Disorder*, pp. 168–70.

[39] Wilson, *Federal Aid in Domestic Disturbances*, p. 233; Rich, *President and Civil Disorder*, p. 113; Cooper, *The Army and Civil Disorder*, pp. 170–71.

[40] Quote from Rich, *President and Civil Disorder*, p. 113; see also Telg, Schofield to Otis, CG, Dept of the Columbia, 7 Jul 1894, RG 94, File 10, NARA. On 2 July 1894, Congress declared the Northern Pacific Railroad to be a post route and a military road worthy of federal protection. Reports on the Coeur d'Alene riots of 1894 were included as an appendix to the commanding general's report on the Pullman Strike.

[41] *Secretary of War Report, 1894*, pp. 155–56; Telg, Otis to Schofield, 8 Jul 1894, RG 94, File 10, NARA.

But tranquility stopped short of Coeur d'Alene. Here miners, taking advantage of the railroad strike, resorted to violence to settle old scores. On 3 July 1894, a group of forty masked men shot and killed John Kneebone, a principal witness against the union miners who had been tried in the 1892 disturbances. During the next few days miners abducted a mine superintendent and attempted to blow up the powerhouse of the Bunker Hill & Sullivan operation at Wardner. Local law enforcement officials made no attempt to restore order, and Governor McConnell made no attempt to call up state troops. Instead, on 9 July, under pressure from mine officials with whom he sympathized, he requested federal military aid from President Cleveland under RS 5297 and RS 5299, claiming that domestic violence threatened not only property, legal authority, and order, but the equal protection under the laws guaranteed the citizens of Idaho by the U.S. Constitution.[42]

A note of ingenuity was added by McConnell's appeal to RS 5299. Originally drafted as the Ku Klux Act to protect blacks from Southern white vigilantism, the law was applied to a labor dispute upon the view that strikebreakers were a class of citizens being deprived of their civil rights and equal protections as required by the Fourteenth Amendment of the Constitution. Although Cleveland hesitated to commit troops to the Coeur d'Alene area for a second time, pressure from Idaho's congressmen forced his acquiescence on 9 July. Cleveland, however, authorized deployment based on RS 5297, the statute dealing with insurrections against a state, deeming the Ku Klux Act inapplicable.[43]

Acting on presidential orders, Schofield directed Otis to send a company of regulars to Coeur d'Alene to protect the Northern Pacific Railroad, not to intervene in the mining dispute. Apparently the Army lacked knowledge of the true purpose of the Idaho governor's request—to deal with the mine strikes. When Otis sent an infantry company from Fort Sherman to Wardner, the infantrymen encountered no resistance or disorder. All trains were moving without interference by 17 July. However, when the mine owners learned three days later that Otis intended to recall the company, they petitioned their congressmen "to have United States Troops permanently stationed in Shoshone County, for the purpose of putting down lawlessness in that section, in order that the business interests of the citizens . . . may be improved." McConnell likewise urged Idaho's senators to persuade Secretary of War Lamont to station two companies in Coeur d'Alene indefinitely "to protect property against the Miners' Union which is controlled by Molly McGuires."[44]

On 26 July Otis, still under the impression that federal troops were in Coeur d'Alene on railroad protection duty, reinforced the company already in Wardner with a second from

---

[42] Wilson, *Federal Aid in Domestic Disturbances*, p. 233; Cooper, *The Army and Civil Disorder*, p. 171; U.S. Dept of Justice, *Annual Report of the Attorney General of the United States, 1896*, Appendix, pp. 214–18.

[43] The Ku Klux Act of 1871 required the president to step in when a state was either unable to protect, or failed, or refused to protect the civil rights of its citizens. No action under RS 5299 was taken after Reconstruction. For the act and its ramifications, see Coakley, *Role of Federal Military Forces*, pp. 344–47.

[44] Telgs, Schofield to Otis, 9, 17 Jul 1894; Petition, Citizens of State of Washington to Senator Watson C. Squire and Representatives John L. Wilson and Witt Doolittle, 20 Jul 1894 (most of the affected mine owners lived in Spokane, Wash.); Telg, McConnell to Shoup Dubois, 25 Jul 1894; all in RG 94, File 10, NARA. *Secretary of War Report, 1894*, p. 156; Telg, Otis to Hall, 9 Jul 1894, Register of Ltrs Sent, Dept of the Columbia, RG 393, Entry 714, NARA; Cooper, *The Army and Civil Disorder*, p. 171. For the Molly Maguires, see Wayne G. Broehl, Jr., *The Molly Maguires* (Cambridge: Harvard University Press, 1964); Walter J. Coleman, *The Molly Maguire Riots: Industrial Conflict in the Pennsylvania Coal Region* (Washington, D.C.: Catholic University of America, 1936; reprint, New York: Arno, 1969). McConnell's charge had no basis in fact. The Molly Maguires were destroyed by the late 1870s.

Fort Sherman. He instructed the commander of the 133 soldiers to "remove all unlawful and forcible obstructions from Wardner to Missoula. . . . In fact to keep that line open for passage of its mail and interstate commerce trains . . . you will furnish such escorts as may be necessary. You will also upon request assist the civil executive authorities acting under the orders of the United States court to protect the property of said railroad cooperating with them in the execution of your duty."[45]

Otis' detailed instructions proved unnecessary, for the commander at Wardner found the trains unimpeded. Considering the Army's mission completed, on 3 August Otis requested Schofield's permission to withdraw all regulars from Shoshone County. Political strings, however, tied Schofield's hands. The two senators from Idaho had prevailed upon Attorney General Richard Olney to intercede with the president to keep federal troops in Coeur d'Alene until further notice.[46]

In early August the commander of the troops at Wardner warned Otis that the pretext given for the intervention was not true; that "all difficulties [had] been adjusted" before federal troops arrived, that the mines were operating, and that local officials were in control of events.[47] Otis made one last effort to remove troops from Coeur d'Alene. After noting that the Northern Pacific was in full operation and that he expected no hostile interruption or demonstration, he argued that even if the governor had requested troops in Coeur d'Alene because of the state's inability to govern there, the section could now be given back to state and local authorities.[48] The Cleveland administration, however, ignored his assessment again. Otis and Schofield now suspected that the true purpose in sending troops to Coeur d'Alene was not to reopen the railroads or to aid state and local officials maintain order, but to assist in destroying the WFM at the behest of state and mine company officials. By September 1894 even a lieutenant serving in Coeur d'Alene discerned that the motive for retaining troops in the district had little to do with reopening railroads. He stated, "There was no disorder, and I could see no reason for our presence except to overawe the striking miners." Federal troops had little to do in Wardner, for the miner-initiated violence had ended long before the regulars arrived.[49] The miners avoided any provocative behavior that could justify placing a federal garrison in Coeur d'Alene, avoided any conflicts with local, state, and federal authorities, and did nothing that could jeopardize public sympathy for their cause.

Results justified their passive tactics. State and mine company officials, faced with a now pacific, seemingly law-abiding union, reluctantly ended their campaign against the Western Federation of Miners, and on 8 September Secretary Lamont granted Otis permission to send the regulars back to Fort Sherman.[50] The federal occupation of Coeur d'Alene ended the following day. The unresolved conflict between the unions and the mine owners, however, only went underground to erupt with greater force five years later.

---

[45] Telg, Otis to Thompson, 28 Jul 1894, Register of Ltrs Sent, Dept of the Columbia, RG 393, Entry 714, NARA.

[46] Telgs, Otis to AG, 3, 10 Aug 1894, Register of Ltrs Sent, Dept of the Columbia, RG 393, Entry 714, NARA; Cooper, *The Army and Civil Disorder*, pp. 171–72.

[47] Telg, Thompson to Otis, 9 Aug 1894, quoted in Telg, Otis to AG, 10 Aug 1894, RG 393.

[48] Telg, Otis to AG, 10 Aug 1894, RG 393.

[49] Cooper, *The Army and Civil Disorder*, pp. 171–72.

[50] Telg, Otis to Thompson, 8 Sep 1894, Register of Ltrs Sent, Dept of the Columbia, RG 393, Entry 714, NARA.

Coeur d'Alene, 1899

Following the troop withdrawals in 1894, the Western Federation of Miners success-fully unionized the miners in every Coeur d'Alene firm except the Bunker Hill & Sullivan Company. The largest company in the region, it had resisted all attempts at unionization and refused to recognize the federation or bargain with its members. By arrangement with Idaho Governor Frank Steunenberg, the firm organized its nonunion employees into two National Guard companies and stored their weapons and munitions in private vaults on company property. In 1898, however, Idaho's National Guard entered federal service for duty in the Philippines, thus depriving the governor of the force that he had been using to support mine owners. Despite the loss of what amounted to a private army, the mine com-panies continued to resist unionization by means of privately hired armed guards, labor spies, and blacklists.

In early 1899 company recalcitrance prompted the federation to organize its mem-bership for the third and most significant clash of the decade with mine owners, partic-ularly targeting the Bunker Hill & Sullivan operation. In April local union leaders met secretly in Mullan, Burke, Gem, and Wardner to plan strategy.[51] On 29 April the union leadership distributed firearms and masks to their members. Over 200 miners then seized a Northern Pacific train at Burke and moved southwest along Canyon Creek to Gem and Wallace, where another 400 miners climbed aboard. This small army proceed-ed west along the Coeur d'Alene River to Wardner, where they used 3,500 pounds of dynamite to blow up the Bunker Hill & Sullivan's ore concentrator, an enormous piece of equipment valued at $250,000. After the explosion, a gunfight between the miners and company mine guards took place among the rubble, resulting in death for two guards and wounding for another.[52]

The coordinated and methodical execution of the miners' attack led subsequent inves-tigators living outside the region to conclude that there existed in Coeur d'Alene a "wide-spread, deep-seated and thoroughly organized conspiracy." Shoshone County officials, however, held working class sympathies and sided with the miners and the federation against the owners. The miners had twice elected a sympathetic sheriff, James D. Young, who reciprocated their support by riding with the mob on the train to Wardner on the day of the attack.[53]

The complicity of Sheriff Young and the absence of most of the National Guard com-pelled Governor Steunenberg to ask President William McKinley for federal military aid. In a message to the president he noted, as was required by RS 5297, that the legislature was not in session and could not be convened in time to take action "to suppress insurrec-tion in Shoshone County." He requested 500 regulars. McKinley agreed to intervene but, being either unaware or unconcerned about statutory requirements, failed to issue the proclamation required by law, which would have legalized all subsequent Army actions.[54]

---

[51] U.S. Congress, House, *Coeur d'Alene Labor Troubles*, House Report (H.R.) 1899, 56th Cong., 1st sess., 1900, p. 1 (hereafter cited as H.R. 1899); Wilson, *Federal Aid in Domestic Disturbances*, p. 247; Cooper, *The Army and Civil Disorder*, pp. 172–73.

[52] H.R. 1899, p. 1.

[53] Ibid., p. 12; Cooper, *The Army and Civil Disorder*, p. 173.

[54] Wilson, *Federal Aid in Domestic Disturbances*, pp. 247–48.

Mustering a force of 500 federal troops, however, challenged the ingenuity of the administration and the War Department. Of an Army totaling 100,000 men, the occupation of Cuba, Puerto Rico, and the Philippines had left a mere 17,000 troops available for duty throughout the continental United States. In addition, to compensate for the dispatch of general officers overseas, the War Department had combined several military departments under a single commander. The need to preside over several departments, muster out volunteers, and simultaneously prepare new units for overseas duty severely taxed the commanders who remained. In April 1899 Maj. Gen. William R. Shafter commanded both the Department of California and the Department of the Columbia, the latter encompassing Coeur d'Alene. To free Shafter to help prepare troops for Philippine service, Commanding General of the Army Maj. Gen. Nelson A.

FRANK R. STEUNENBERG

Miles assigned Brig. Gen. Henry C. Merriam, commander of the Departments of the Colorado and the Missouri, the difficult task of bringing peace to Idaho.[55]

Miles' decision affected significantly the course of the subsequent intervention. Shafter, sixty-four years old, was a Civil War veteran and Medal of Honor winner, who had also performed riot duty during the 1894 Coxeyite affair and the Pullman Strike.[56] Merriam's service was more traditional: a Civil War veteran like Shafter, he had also won a Medal of Honor and seen action at Antietam, Fredericksburg, and Port Hudson. Following the war, he served on the frontier in campaigns against Mexican bandits and hostile Indians, including the Nez Perce and Sioux. Lacking experience with civil disturbances, however, the 62-year-old Merriam, like most officers with a great deal of frontier service, had not been sufficiently exposed to the 1894 Schofield doctrine, which established the principle that Army officers were subject only to their own officers and, ultimately, to their commander in chief. Merriam apparently believed that McKinley intended his troops to be directly subordinate to Governor Steunenberg for riot and police duty in Coeur d'Alene, as a force supplementing state and local law officials.[57]

Merriam's belief was not entirely unwarranted. Temporary state control over federal forces was not without precedent. The issue had been raised but had not been entirely settled

---

[55] By the Act of 2 March 1899, Congress increased Army strength to 65,000 regulars and 35,000 volunteers. See *Secretary of War Report, 1899*, vol. 1, pt. 3, pp. 7, 14–17; Cooper, *The Army and Civil Disorder*, p. 175. Miles became commanding general of the Army in 1895.

[56] For Shafter, see Carlson, "Pecos Bill."

[57] Gen H. C. Merriam, CB 1866, Appts, Comms, Pers Br, AGO, RG 94, AGO Files: Merriam, Henry C., NARA.

RUINS OF BUNKER HILL & SULLIVAN COMPANY ORE CONCENTRATOR IN KELLOGG

during the Railway Strike of 1877 and continued to confuse military and civilian officials for several decades afterward. In 1892 a former judge advocate of the Department of the Columbia, Maj. William E. Birkhimer, had added to the confusion by his book, *Military Government and Martial Law*, in which he declared that the president defined the rights, duties, and obligations of commanders called to suppress an insurrection and maintained that the president upon occasion could authorize a commander to place his troops under the authority of a governor, as Hayes had done in 1877 in West Virginia, Maryland, and Pennsylvania.[58] This interpretation, however, ran contrary to Schofield's subsequent General Order 15 of 12 May 1894, prohibiting the command of federal troops by any state or local civil official. Included in paragraph 490 of *Army Regulations of 1895*, Schofield's views had become official doctrine.[59]

Although General Order 15 set official Army policy over command and control of troops in a civil disturbance situation, knowledge of it and its implications spread very slowly through the officer corps. The order had existed for five years, but many officers, apparently including Merriam, were unfamiliar with its content, practical application, and in

[58] William E. Birkhimer, *Military Government and Martial Law* (Washington, D.C.: Chapman, 1892), pp. 403–07.

[59] U.S. War Department, *Regulations of the Army of the United States, 1895* (Washington, D.C.: Government Printing Office, 1895), art. 52, p. 69.

some cases its very existence. Furthermore, the degree to which a military subordinate adhered to regulations depended to a great extent on what his civil superiors ordered him to do and on the degree of vigilance and supervision they provided. In 1899 neither Secretary of War Russell A. Alger nor Commanding General Nelson Miles was unduly concerned with enforcing Merriam's strict adherence to paragraph 490. When not feuding with each other, Alger and Miles shared McKinley's preoccupation with the Philippine Insurrection and the reorganization of the Army. The Coeur d'Alene disturbances were simply not a top priority. The only official who tried to supervise military affairs in Idaho was Henry C. Corbin, the Army adjutant general. Corbin enjoyed close personal relations with McKinley and was a proved high-level administrator, but like his civil and military contemporaries, he was also distracted by other more impor-

HENRY C. MERRIAM

tant duties and events. Hence Merriam—murky on the laws and regulations governing federal military aid to civil authorities and lacking riot-duty and civil-military relations experience—found himself left largely to his own devices.[60]

Merriam's mission in Coeur d'Alene began with a vaguely worded order from Corbin to "repair at once to [Boise], and after conference with the authorities thence to the seat of the action, calling to your aid such troops as may be most convenient regardless of department lines."[61] Even after conferring with Steunenberg at Glenn's Ferry near Boise on 1 May, Merriam was uncertain whether the governor intended to declare martial law. To prevent the escape of the saboteurs of the Bunker Hill complex, Merriam, on his own initiative, decided to impose a limited form of martial law and on 2 May notified Corbin of his intent: "Troops concentrating at Wardner and Mullan will control outlets from mining camps. If not disapproved, I will direct them to scrutinize travel outward and detain suspected passengers. This is martial law, but no other course likely to secure rioters."[62] McKinley approved Merriam's actions after the fact, even though his audacious move was a clear violation of both *Ex Parte Milligan* and the Posse Comitatus Act, as well as an illegal usurpation of a presidential prerogative. The general then called upon two troops of the 4th Cavalry and six companies of the 24th Infantry. Half of this force moved to Wardner from Boise Barracks and three other forts in Washington state, while the remaining regulars traveled from posts in Montana, Wyoming, and Utah to Mullan. Merriam arrived in

---

[60] Cooper, *The Army and Civil Disorder*, pp. 174–75; Graham Cosmas, *An Army for Empire* (Columbia: University of Missouri Press, 1971), pp. 62–64, 71.

[61] *Secretary of War Report, 1899*, vol. 1, pt. 3, p. 28.

[62] Quote from ibid., pp. 30–31; Rich, *President and Civil Disorder*, pp. 209–10.

THE 4TH CAVALRY ARRIVES IN WARDNER, IDAHO, MAY 1899

Wardner on 3 May. Apparently McKinley still did not believe that a proclamation calling upon lawless elements to disperse, as required by RS 5300, was necessary prior to intervention because Merriam reported no sign of organized resistance on his arrival.[63]

Idaho officials, however, acted the following day. After studying conditions in Shoshone County, State Auditor Barton Sinclair persuaded the governor to proclaim also a state of martial law. Evidence suggests that Steunenberg and Sinclair based their decision upon the existence of sporadic violence since 1892, not the current lawlessness, and upon the unwillingness or inability of the county's "incompetent and corrupt" officials to raise a posse and arrest the lawbreakers before they could flee Idaho.[64]

To prevent the escape of those guilty of participating in the crimes of late April, the governor and his auditor ordered mass arrests in Shoshone County. With nearly 500 federal troops at their disposal, they planned to enforce martial law by having soldiers help special constables arrest and detain, without the formality of warrants, all union members and their sympathizers. After state officials screened the prisoners, Steunenberg intended to release those who, for lack of evidence, were unlikely to be convicted. The rest of the

---

[63] U.S. Congress, House, *Report of the Industrial Commission on the Relations and Conditions of Capital and Labor Employed in the Mining Industry*, H. Doc. 181, 57th Cong., 1st sess., 1901, p. 92 (hereafter cited as H. Doc. 181); Rich, *President and Civil Disorder*, pp. 114–15.

[64] H. Doc. 181; *Secretary of War Report, 1899*, vol. 1, pt. 3, pp. 30–31; Rich, *President and Civil Disorder*, p. 114; Wilson, *Federal Aid in Domestic Disturbances*, pp. 248–49.

prisoners he intended to incarcerate until the return of Idaho's National Guard regiment ensured that the miners remained peaceful after the departure of the regulars. By these means, authorities could break the WFM union once and for all and prevent a recurrence of the troubles of the last seven years. According to Idaho Attorney General Samuel H. Hays, "we have the monster by the throat and we are going to choke the life out of it. No halfway measures have or will be adopted. It is a plain case of the state or the union winning, and we do not propose that the state shall be defeated."[65]

Initially Merriam hesitated to endorse the policy of mass arrests. On 3 May, when Steunenberg ordered him to "have all trains stopped and suspicious persons returned," he directed his officers at Mullan and Wardner to rely on common sense and "to arrest all persons attempting to leave the mining region . . . unless fully satisfied that they are not implicated in the riots."[66] In practice, however, commanders of detachments accompanying constables apprehended and detained all persons pointed out by the constables, who were not very selective. Army detachments became military posses, the commanding officers of which interpreted constable recommendations as orders for immediate execution without prior approval through normal channels.[67]

Escorted by federal troops, the constables arrested not only suspected criminals but also union members and even nonminers, including Sheriff Young and three members of the Shoshone County Board of Commissioners. A reporter for *Harper's Weekly* described one such sweep: "The town stretches out for about a mile at the bottom of a steep canyon. Guards were stationed on the walls of the gorge to prevent escape . . . then the soldiers made a house to house search. At the shafts other soldiers were detailed to seize the miners as they came off shift." During the first two weeks of May 1899 special constables aided by federal troops arrested 700 men who were incarcerated in Wardner.[68]

With troops standing guard, the constables put the first 150 prisoners, primarily union miners, into a two-story grain warehouse soon to be named the "Bull Pen." Beginning on 5 May and continuing over the next few days, constables placed another 200 prisoners into railroad boxcars, for the Bull Pen had been filled beyond capacity. Official reports understated the privations suffered by the prisoners in the boxcars: "Although an abundance of hay was furnished . . . it is probable the men so confined were less comfortable than those in the warehouse, yet they were not obliged to sleep on the ground, as did the troops who were guarding them." By 7 May over 1,000 miners had been arrested and incarcerated in Wardner.[69] The imprisoned miners complained bitterly about their treatment at the hands of the soldiers. They claimed that they were prodded and nicked by bayonets on their way from the mines to the Bull Pen and boxcars. Rations were characterized as horrible.

---

[65] Quote from Cooper, *The Army and Civil Disorder*, p. 178. See also H. Doc. 181, pp. 93–95; "Herded in by Negro Troops," *Spokesman Review*, Spokane, 4 May 1899, Scrapbook, Dept of the Columbia, RG 393, NARA; Telg, AG to Merriam, 18 Oct 1899, Register of Ltrs Recv'd, Dept of the Columbia, RG 393, Entry 714, NARA; Ltr, Steunenberg to Root, 10 Oct 1899, RG 94, File 231071, NARA.

[66] *Secretary of War Report, 1899*, vol. 1, pt. 3, p. 31.

[67] H. Doc. 181, pp. 93–95; Cooper, *The Army and Civil Disorder*, pp. 176–77; "Herded in by Negro Troops," RG 393.

[68] *Harper's Weekly* 43 (30 May 1899), quoted in Cooper, *The Army and Civil Disorder*, p. 176; H.R. 1899, pp. 76–77; H. Doc. 181, pp. 93–95.

[69] Quote from Wilson, *Federal Aid in Domestic Disturbances*, pp. 250–51. See also Cooper, *The Army and Civil Disorder*, p. 177.

THE BULL PEN AT WARDNER, IDAHO

Witnesses claimed that some soldiers, especially the blacks from the 24th Infantry, used abusive language and forced prisoners to sit on wet manure or outside in the rain.[70]

Increasingly concerned about the unsanitary prison conditions in Wardner, Merriam urged Steunenberg to expedite the screening and release of those miners against whom the state could not establish a *prima facie* case. Steunenberg, however, failed to approve prisoner releases. In response, Merriam permitted prisoners' families to provide bunks, blankets, overcoats, and stoves, while he authorized the provision of an exercise yard. In a report to Corbin in June, he claimed that the prisoners at Wardner were, in many cases, better housed and better fed than his own troops.[71]

Not content with the arrests made along the railroad line from Mullan to Wardner, Merriam was determined to prevent fugitives from escaping by foot into Montana. In 1892 Colonel Carlin's unauthorized foray into Montana had met with the disapproval of that state's governor. To avoid a second encroachment upon state sovereignty, Merriam arranged through Steunenberg's office to get prior approval from Montana Governor Robert B. Smith for cross-border incursions. Smith agreed, provided that Montana authorities assisted in making any arrests.[72]

Yet some problems with the Montana press resulted. Merriam assigned the task of escorting constables into the state to collect prisoners detained by Montana authorities to Lt. H. G. Lyons, Company D, 24th Infantry. When the press learned of Lyons' presence in

---

[70] H. Doc. 181, pp. 95–98.
[71] Telg, Merriam to Corbin, 12 Jun 1899, RG 94, File 231071, NARA; *Secretary of War Report, 1899*, vol. 1, pt. 3, p. 58.
[72] *Secretary of War Report, 1899*, vol. 1, pt. 3, p. 58.

Montana, it concluded hastily that he was imitating Carlin's 1892 practice of hunting fugitives without first obtaining aid or permission of Montana law enforcement officers. On 12 May Smith confronted Merriam, stating that "It must not be assumed that the civil authorities of this state will silently permit even federal troops to disregard the civil law or the process of civil authorities." With copies of his orders to Lyons in hand, Merriam assured Smith that local Montana officials were not being ignored.[73]

Despite his best efforts to maintain good relations with local and state civil officials, Merriam soon opened the Army to further controversy and criticism by becoming involved in a work permit system devised by the state and mining companies. On 8 May Governor Steunenberg announced that all miners wishing to return to work first had to obtain a permit from the local sheriff. Requirements to obtain the permit included an oath that the miner had not participated in the riot at the Bunker Hill & Sullivan Mine on 29 April, a denunciation of the Western Federation of Miners for its role in causing that and other disturbances, and an agreement to renounce membership in that organization. Although it was unnecessary under the circumstances, the governor forbade mining companies to employ miners without permits.[74]

At best the permit system violated the Idaho law against yellow-dog contracts—the practice of requiring individuals to promise not to join a union as a condition of employment—this was clearly an illegal union-busting arrangement. Steuenberg justified the measure as a part of state martial law necessary to break the cycle of violence, military aid, military withdrawal, and renewed violence that had afflicted Coeur d'Alene since 1892. Sinclair characterized the miners' union as a criminal organization, the destruction of which was necessary for the restoration of law and order.[75]

After recommending that members of "innocent unions" receive permits, Merriam endorsed Steunenberg's work permit scheme with the words, "Examined and Approved. H. C. Merriam." The governor's permit proclamation, with apparent Army approval, was published in newspapers and posted on broadsides throughout the state. Merriam later contended that his endorsement in no way constituted approval of the work permit system, only his willingness to enforce a measure of martial law deemed necessary by the governor.[76] Nevertheless, much of the local press seized upon this issue. During the summer, labor unions and prolabor newspapers had been demanding the recall of the "political" general in Idaho, before he carried his "antilabor persecutions" any further. Now the federation went further and charged Merriam with initiating the permit system. Even moderate critics accused him of giving moral force to a virulent and highly controversial antilabor practice. In August 1899 Terrence V. Powderly of the Knights of Labor, and subsequently McKinley's commissioner general of immigration, warned the president to renounce Merriam's actions or face the criticisms of aroused Democrats.[77]

Reacting to the pressure, McKinley directed the War Department to straighten out the "misguided" and "embarrassing" commander. On 26 May Corbin sent Merriam an order to

---

[73] Ibid., pp. 31–33.
[74] Ibid., p. 35.
[75] H.R. 1899, pp. 109–10; H. Doc. 181, pp. 99, 545–47, 557–61.
[76] Ibid.; *Secretary of War Report, 1899*, vol. 1, pt. 3, p. 35.
[77] Cooper, *The Army and Civil Disorder*, pp. 181–83; *Secretary of War Report, 1899*, vol. 1, pt. 3, p. 57; Memo, Powderly for McKinley, Aug 1899, RG 94, File 231071, NARA.

RUSSELL A. ALGER WITH HENRY C. CORBIN

correct any impression that the Army was out to destroy the miners' union or endorsed the work permit system. Merriam maintained stubbornly that he was simply carrying out his mission to support state authorities. His feigned innocence was perceived as such and drew a stern rebuke from Secretary of War Alger, who on 31 May ordered Merriam to ensure that local commanders in Coeur d'Alene eschew any part of the work permit system. Although the actions of Corbin and Alger convinced labor organizations that the federal government did not endorse the system at the national level, federal actions did little to stem the flow of criticism of Merriam on the local level. In addition, miners in the Coeur d'Alene area refused absolutely to submit to the permit system. Shortly after the 18 May deadline for all miners to have permits had passed, mines throughout the region closed for lack of labor. Swarms of unemployed workers now joined union members previously denied work in the region.[78]

While the controversy over the work permit system continued, Merriam prepared to leave the Coeur d'Alene for his departmental headquarters. Maj. Allen Smith, 1st Cavalry, received command of troops in Wardner, and Merriam left Idaho on 25 May 1899, convinced he had done his duty in a fair and impartial manner, seemingly unaware of the depth of feeling elsewhere in the nation.[79]

At the end of the summer nearly 200 miners still remained in military custody at Wardner. The approach of winter worried federal commanders, whose troops lacked suitable clothing or housing. The prisoners also dreaded the thought of spending the winter in the drafty Bull Pen or in railroad boxcars. In desperation several prisoners attempted to

---

[78] Telg, Alger to Merriam, 31 May 1899, Ltrs Recv'd, Dept of the Columbia, RG 393, Entry 714, NARA; *Secretary of War Report, 1899*, vol. 1, pt. 3, pp. 38–39; Rich, *President and Civil Disorder*, pp. 115–16; Cooper, *The Army and Civil Disorder*, p. 179.

[79] Cooper, *The Army and Civil Disorder*, p. 180.

tunnel out of the Bull Pen in late September. After being recaptured, they refused to return to confinement and had to be forced back to the Bull Pen. To restore discipline, the new officer in charge of the makeshift prison, Capt. F. A. Edwards, 1st Cavalry, placed all prisoners, except the sick, on bread and water rations for eight days.[80]

In response, Edward Boyce, president of the Western Federation of Miners, lodged a strong protest with McKinley on 27 September, stating that the treatment of prisoners had "of late been so brutal that some are contemplating suicide rather than longer endure such misery." New Secretary of War Elihu Root asked Steunenberg and Merriam to investigate. Steunenberg labeled Boyce's charge as "base falsehood in every particular," while Merriam argued that Captain Edwards was a man of experience and excellent character who only resorted to such measures when it was absolutely necessary to maintain prison discipline.[81] In the ensuing congressional investigation, a majority of the Republican investigators shared Merriam's assessment that "the punishments . . . were not excessive and that treatment of the prisoners . . . was humane and considerate." The Democrats thought otherwise.[82]

Nevertheless, the furor over the "bread and water" treatment prompted Secretary Root to seek an early withdrawal of the remaining 200 troops. He telegraphed Steunenberg, asking whether the insurrection had been suppressed and whether the troops could be withdrawn, expressing his dissatisfaction that federal troops were still being used to guard citizens who had little prospect of speedy trials. If Idaho officials were going to continue this incarceration they were to replace federal troops with civilian guards.[83] But Steunenberg replied that the release of troops before 1 November would foster a campaign of terror and revenge by the miners against all who had cooperated with either the owners or the civil authorities. Then he stated his antipathy to the WFM union: "It should be understood that this is not a conflict between labor and capital nor a question of wages, but it is a conflict between the State of Idaho and certain criminal organizations which seek to cloak themselves under the cover of Labor organizations."[84]

Unconvinced, Root gave Steunenberg until 20 October to take custody of the 24 miners still in the Bull Pen. The remainder of the 200 prisoners were released for lack of evidence. Of the 1,000 men originally arrested, only 14 ever went to trial, and of that number 11 were convicted. Increased public outcry, especially from labor unions and their leaders, did much to prod Secretary Root toward seeking an early withdrawal of troops. In a personal visit to Washington, D.C., however, Steunenberg persuaded him to postpone the transfer of prisoners until the end of October when a returning company of the Idaho National Guard could take custody. Root assured him that Merriam would issue orders keeping troops in nearby camps in readiness for any new emergency.[85]

After October most regulars in the Coeur d'Alene returned to their stations. A troop of 1st Cavalry from Fort Robinson, Nebraska, and a detachment of 200 dismounted troopers

[80] Ltr, Merriam to Corbin, 7 Sep 1899, and Telg, Merriam to Corbin, c. 28 Sep 1899, Register of Ltrs Sent, Dept of the Columbia, RG 393, Entry 174, NARA.
[81] *Secretary of War Report, 1899*, vol. 1, pt. 3, pp. 64–65.
[82] Quote from H.R. 1899, p. 2; see also Telg, Merriam to Corbin, c. 28 Sep 1899, RG 393.
[83] Telg, Root to Steunenberg, 28 Sep 1899, RG 94, File 231071, NARA.
[84] Ltr, Steunenberg to Root, 10 Oct 1899, RG 94, File 231071, NARA.
[85] Telg, Corbin to Merriam, 18 Oct 1899, Register of Ltrs Recv'd, Dept of the Columbia, RG 393, Entry 714, NARA.

from the 6th Cavalry, Fort Riley, Kansas, however, set up winter quarters respectively in Osburn and in Wallace. In May 1900 a company of the 7th Infantry from the Department of the Columbia replaced the two cavalry units. When new Governor Frank Hunt ended martial law on 11 April 1901, the last federal troops were withdrawn.[86]

Three months after Root began pressing for troop withdrawals, the House of Representatives opened an investigation into the legality of the Army's presence and subsequent conduct in Coeur d'Alene. In February 1900 the Committee on Military Affairs traveled to the mining region and initiated a four-month examination of eyewitnesses, including labor union spokesmen, state officials, Merriam, and his officers. Composed of Republicans who wanted to protect McKinley on the eve of an election year and Democrats who wanted to destroy him, the committee submitted two sharply divergent and heavily politicized reports in June 1900.[87]

The Democratic minority faulted President McKinley for sending troops to suppress what they categorized as a nonexistent insurrection: rioting ceased after 29 April, state courts continued to function, a coroner's inquest was in progress, a grand jury had been impaneled, and local law officials encountered no interference in the performance of their duties. Claiming that such facts disproved the existence of an insurrection, the minority report then singled out Merriam for "slavishly" helping Steunenberg to perpetrate an unwarranted state of martial law that violated due process and the civil rights of miners.

To the Republican majority the collusion of the sheriff and county commissioners with the miners' union had established a self-evident example of insurrection that fully justified a state imposition of martial law and the dispatch of federal military aid to state authorities. Having determined the legality of the Army's presence in Coeur d'Alene in their own minds, the Republicans then considered charges that the Army had overstepped its authority by making arrests and guarding prisoners. The majority dismissed the charge of usurping the state's responsibility on the grounds that, until 31 October, the governor lacked national guardsmen to perform these functions. Without military guards, the prisoners, guilty and innocent, might have fled, some of them to wreak new violence against the mining companies.[88]

Sensitive to journalistic accusations that to protect McKinley they intended to make Merriam the scapegoat for any wrongdoing, the Republican committeemen tersely defended the general. They concluded that his telegrams to Steunenberg and Alger calling for improved prison living conditions and early release of the majority of prisoners showed humanitarian concern. They denied the existence of proof that he had engaged in a war against labor by endorsement of the work permit scheme. In their view he had simply tried to ferret out persons who had used the union to cloak crimes of sabotage and murder. The administration agreed with the findings of the Republican majority report and took no action against Merriam.[89]

---

[86] *Secretary of War Report, 1899*, vol. 1, pt. 3, p. 41; Cooper, *The Army and Civil Disorder*, p. 195.

[87] H.R. 1899, p. 127.

[88] Ibid.

[89] Ibid.; "Hiding Behind Merriam," *Rocky Mountain News*, Denver, 25 Jun 1899, Scrapbook, Dept of the Columbia, RG 393, NARA. Merriam commanded the Department of the Colorado until his retirement after thirty-nine years of active service in 1901. He was advanced to the rank of major general on the retired list and died in Portland, Maine, in 1912. See *Who Was Who in American History: The Military*, p. 380; *Webster's American Military Biographies* (Springfield: G. C. Merriam, 1978), pp. 280–81.

Conclusion

The report of the congressional majority in 1900 was interpreted by some workmen and labor groups as further proof that the federal government was not functioning as a neutral broker in the ongoing struggle between labor and capital. During both the railroad strikes of 1877 and 1894 and the Coeur d'Alene disturbances of 1892 and 1894, three presidents had dispatched troops to end violence or prevent its recurrence. Such intervention was justified by the need to reestablish law and order, to safeguard private and government property, and to protect interstate commerce and transportation of the mails. Such objectives were not in and of themselves antilabor. The tactics of implementation, however, especially when they resulted in the protection of strikebreakers, the arrest of strikers, and the occupation of company property and working class communities, effectively deprived the strikers of leverage at the negotiating table and doomed most strikes, even those that were nonviolent, to failure.

During the Coeur d'Alene disturbance of 1899, organized labor believed that the federal government had knowingly sent the Army to join with state officials in destroying local branches of the Western Federation of Miners rather than to restore peace and maintain state authority. No proof exists to show such a conspiracy by federal civil and military officials, at least on the national level. Though certainly probusiness in orientation, the McKinley administration appeared too preoccupied with the Philippine War and upcoming national elections to orchestrate the demise of the WFM union in Idaho. The major lack of the federal government and, by association, of the Army, was its failure to interfere with the wholesale denial of civil rights by Idaho state authorities and to prevent active and publicly declared strikebreaking intentions of state officials.

Nonetheless, feuding within the War Department between Alger and Miles and the resultant demands upon Corbin as the de facto head of the War Department make it clear that, if the actions of the civil and military high command harmed the labor movement, the harm was not intentional. They clearly failed to provide the local commander with the necessary guidance to assure that he did not exceed his mission of preventing renewed mob violence and of restoring order. In addition, the War Department failed to act when Merriam violated principles set down in *Ex Parte Milligan*, failed to correct his violations of the laws excepted by the Posse Comitatus Act once they were discovered, and failed to take adequate measures to prevent future transgressions. Lacking civil disturbance experience, effective supervision, and a thorough knowledge of Army regulations and federal laws governing military aid to civil authorities, Merriam misinterpreted his mission, ignored General Order 15, and placed his men at the disposal of Steunenberg and Sinclair. Under civilian direction, his men joined state authorities in making mass arrests and incarcerating hundreds of miners in violation of their constitutional rights. He participated further in Steunenberg's assault on the WFM union by inadvertently endorsing the work permit system. Confusion pervaded the federal intervention.

The record of blunders in Coeur d'Alene made Merriam's cooperation in the war against the WFM union a watershed in the history of civil disturbances. The Army, when compared to the National Guard, had just begun to earn a modest reputation for impartiality during the Great Railway Strike of 1877 and the labor upheavals of the early 1890s. At the dawn of the twentieth century, however, the Army found itself being castigated as the enemy of organized labor like the National Guard. In Congress, friends of the labor movement campaigned against all efforts to expand and modernize the Army, or to increase the pay of its men. Others saw the recent actions during the Coeur d'Alene troubles and the Spanish-American War as proof of the need for widespread reform in the military.

Meanwhile, the rapid decline of the WFM affected radically many western hard-rock miners, who later joined more militant and aggressive organizations like the Industrial Workers of the World (IWW). Indeed, the ill feelings remaining from the Coeur d'Alene troubles claimed one last victim in the early years of the twentieth century. On 30 December 1905, now-retired Governor Steunenberg was fatally wounded by a bomb set to explode when he opened a gate at his home in Caldwell, Idaho. In spite of the state's contention that the leaders of the WFM were behind the assassination, a subsequent trial failed to convict any union members. Nonetheless, the fear of labor radicals among conservative upper- and middle-class Americans and business leaders apparently was becoming a self-fulfilling prophecy.[90] Despite such portents, however, as the United States entered the twentieth century a new, and more modern, progressive attitude toward labor, business, government, and society was becoming evident. It would affect the Army's future civil disturbance role.

---

[90] Rich, *President and Civil Disorder*, pp. 118–20; Cooper, *The Army and Civil Disorder*, pp. 191–96; Dubofsky, *We Shall Be All*, pp. 96–105. On Steunenberg's death, see Hofstadter and Wallace, *American Violence*, pp. 423–25.

CHAPTER 8

Army Interventions in Labor Disputes During the Progressive Era 1901–1913

The Troops are not sent to take the part of either side in a purely industrial dispute, as long as it is kept within the bounds of law and order. They are to be neither for nor against either the strikers or the employers. They are to prevent riot, violence and disorder, under and in accordance with the Constitution and the laws of the land. . . . Better twenty-four hours of riot, damage, and disorder than illegal use of troops.

—President Theodore Roosevelt, 1907.

During the first sixteen years of the twentieth century, the Army undertook significant and far-reaching internal reforms that affected its size, structure, and doctrine. The Regular Army of 1916 was better trained and funded, more professional in makeup and outlook, more modern technically and scientifically, better organized and deployed, and better able to fulfill its mission of defending the nation from enemies at home and abroad than its late nineteenth-century counterpart. The transformation of the Army, however, did not take place in a vacuum. Military reforms closely reflected similar changes already taking place in civilian institutions. Collectively, these reforms had a substantial impact on federal attitudes and policies concerning labor disputes and on the Army's role in dealing with labor-related civil disturbances.

As the twentieth century began, the United States had just completed twenty-five years of rapid growth amid considerable social upheaval, typified by the labor disputes of the period. Concomitant with this rapid physical transformation was an increased sense of uneasiness and uncertainty among large segments of the population concerning the future of the nation and the ability of its institutions to cope with the changes that had already taken place, as well as with those expected in the new century. Centers of production, power, politics, and wealth had long ago moved from small communities, where the majority of Americans had lived, to sizable urban centers dominated by large formal labor, industrial, social, and political organizations. Many believed that these new urban forces were beyond the average citizen's influence or control, and that the inhabitants of the cities were politically radical, vice ridden, materialistic, corrupt, faceless, and cold. To Americans of traditional views, including members of the urban middle class who still espoused older rural and agrarian values, the nation was in need of fundamental and sweeping reforms—in essence a new order to replace the old.[1] Although individuals and groups of citizens and soldiers had begun to adapt to the changes caused by industrialization on local and state levels as early as the late 1880s, these efforts at reform were not uniformly evident until the turn of the century, culminating in a nationwide movement known as progressivism.

During the Progressive era the liberal idea of modernization, peaceful reform, and evolutionary change gripped the nation as never before. In the century's first decade and a half, nearly every American institution experienced some reform despite steadfast conservative opposition. Among the more noticeable changes were increasing public antipathy for large, impersonal corporations that had combined into trusts or holding companies, and decreasing public fears of workers and labor unions (although the activities of the unions were increasing and were still viewed with some suspicion). Calls for government regulation of industry and for acceptance of unions as a necessary balance to unchecked corporate power were expressed at all levels. As a result, federal civil and military leaders exhibited a more tolerant attitude toward organized labor and a corresponding reluctance to use force as the first resort in settling labor disputes. This growing forbearance was especially apparent during the presidencies of Theodore Roosevelt and Woodrow Wilson. The trend of military intervention in labor disputes during the Progressive era was toward an irreproachable neutrality in both policy and action—a pattern that endured until World War I.[2]

Theodore Roosevelt and the Square Deal

With Theodore Roosevelt's presidency, progressivism became a national force. Convinced of the necessity for more government involvement in the social and business affairs of the nation, he encouraged a legislative course aimed at reforming the monetary system, reducing the tariff, regulating the railroads, and controlling the trusts. He believed that labor and industrial groups, like individuals, should strive to behave in an honest, honorable, and moral manner in all dealings at all times. If they did this, "they would be left alone and the function of coordination 'would be performed by the natural forces which seemed to work in the past.'"[3] If they did not do this, however, regulation and control were

---

[1] Weibe, *The Search for Order*, pp. 44, 76–80, 133–34, 153–54, 165–74; Louis Galambos, "The Emerging Organizational Synthesis in Modern American History," *Business History Review* 44 (Autumn 1970):280, 287; Samuel Hays, "The Social Analysis of American Political History, 1890–1920," *Political Science Quarterly* 80 (September 1965):388–91; Alfred D. Chandler, Jr., and Louis Galambos, "The Development of Large-Scale Economic Organizations in American History," *Journal of Economic History* 30 (March 1970):202–05; Robert D. Cuff, "American History and the Organizational Factor," *Canadian Review of American Studies* 4 (Spring 1973):22.

[2] For progressivism, see John G. Sprout, *The Best Men: Liberal Reformers in the Gilded Age* (New York: Oxford University Press, 1968); Garraty, *New Commonwealth*; Hays, *Response to Industrialism*, p. 76; Lawrence Goodwyn, *Democratic Promise: The Populist Movement in America* (New York: Oxford University Press, 1976). For the trusts, see David G. Bunting, *Statistical View of the Trusts: A Manual of Large American Industrial and Mining Corporations Active Around 1900* (Westport: Greenwood, 1974); Galambos, *The Public Image of Business in America*.

[3] Chandler and Galambos, "The Development of Large-Scale Economic Organizations," p. 209; George E. Mowry, *The Era of Theodore Roosevelt, 1900–1912* (New York: Harper & Row, 1958), pp. 94–96, and *Theodore Roosevelt and the Progressive Movement* (Madison: University of Wisconsin Press, 1946), pp. 10–11; William H. Harbaugh, *Power and Responsibility: The Life and Times of Theodore Roosevelt* (New York: Farrar, Straus, & Cudany, 1961), p. 167.

assured. Roosevelt, like many Progressives, realized the dangers posed to democracy by extraordinarily wealthy and large labor-industrial organizations, especially industrial trusts. Years later he claimed that "of all the forms of tyranny the least attractive and the most vulgar is the tyranny of wealth." He warned big business to reform itself or face the consequences: "The turbulence and violence you dread is just as apt to come from an attitude of arrogance on the part of owners of property and of an unwillingness to recognize their duty to the public as from any improper encouragement of labor unions."[4] As early as 1902 he began a limited policy of breaking up large industrial combines by vigorous enforcement of the Sherman Anti-Trust Act.

Roosevelt's antitrust attitude was combined with a complex attitude of tolerance toward labor. He regarded unions as an inevitable creation of the times and, while favoring an open shop, he believed also in the right of employees to join a union if they chose. In principle, Roosevelt thought that union concerns should be heard and not ignored as if they were inherently without merit. Although on several occasions he opposed the positions of labor, he continued to maintain the right of unions to exist, and, in spite of the outcry of industrialists, he invited labor leaders Samuel Gompers and John Mitchell to the White House to discuss labor-industrial relations. Above all, he believed that social justice was the ultimate aim of the U.S. government. Concerning past tensions, he implied that businesses often brought on many of their own troubles by their "shortsighted, narrow-minded, greedy, and arrogant" attitudes. The president's goal was to give both business and labor a "square deal."[5]

The Anthracite Coal Strike of 1902

One of Roosevelt's first opportunities to put his ideas into action came shortly after 2 May 1902, when nearly 140,000 workers in the anthracite coal mines of five counties in eastern Pennsylvania walked off their jobs to go on a strike that lasted until late October. The Anthracite Coal Strike of 1902 presented the first clear indication that government policies toward military interventions in labor disputes were really changing.

For years George F. Baer, the president of the Philadelphia and Reading Railroad, a company owned by J. P. Morgan, had ignored union coal miners of the Knights of Labor and the United Mine Workers and their demands for a shorter workday, wage increases, and better living and working conditions. A strike in 1897, for example, was crushed by deputies and resulted in the deaths of twenty-four miners. Another strike in 1900, for the same demands, was successfully and rapidly ended when Ohio Republican Senator Marcus Hanna intervened with Morgan and succeeded in convincing him to grant a 10 percent wage increase. With Hanna's subsequent help the agreement reached in 1900 was extended twice until the spring of 1902. Not content, however, with small wage increases that did nothing to improve working conditions or gain union recognition, the UMW, under the leadership of John Mitchell, after repeatedly attempting to negotiate a settlement struck again in 1902. The miners vowed to stay out until Baer agreed to recognize and bargain

---

[4] Quotes from Mowry, *Roosevelt and the Progressive Movement*, pp. 10–11, 132. See also Harbaugh, *Power and Responsibility*, p. 167; Dulles, *Labor in America*, p. 184.

[5] Mowry, *Era of Roosevelt*, pp. 139, 141–42.

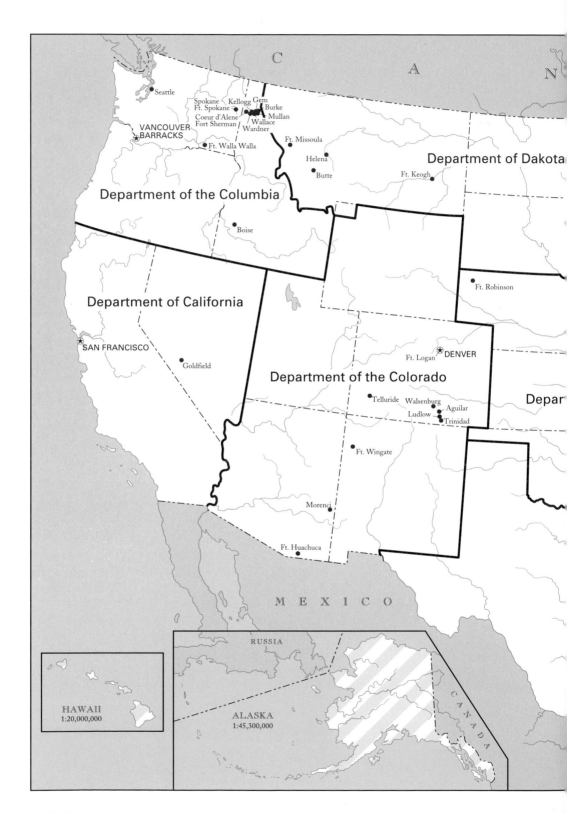

MAP 3

A   D   A

AUL

CHICAGO

Department of the Lakes

Missouri

Ft. Smith
Pairie Creek

ment of the Gulf

GOVERNORS ISLAND (NYC)

Department of the East

Washington, D.C.

Ft. Oglethorpe

ATLANTA

BAHAMAS

CUBA

Civil Disorders in the United States and Its Territories
1892–1916

•   Federal Intervention

⊛   U. S. Army Department Headquarters

━━━   U. S. Army Department Boundary

     Territory (as of 1916)

1:15,900,000

with the union. Oblivious to growing public toleration toward labor organizations, Baer denounced the UMW as "labor agitators" and urged workers to trust "the Christian men to whom God in his infinite wisdom has given the control of the property interests of the country." He took up the reins of industrial leadership and, representing the interests of his own firm and four others, refused to negotiate.[6]

The stubbornness of Baer and the miners' curtailed production caused a jump in the price of coal and threatened to expose eastern and midwestern cities to hardships in the winter from a lack of anthracite, used almost exclusively for heating. Roosevelt, in an effort to break the impasse, appointed Commissioner of Labor Carroll D. Wright to investigate the dispute. Wright recommended the organization of an anthracite miners' union, a nine-hour workday for a six-month trial period, and the creation of a union-operator mediation committee. Baer and Morgan rejected the recommendations, and subsequent efforts by Hanna to effect a settlement failed.[7]

At the urging of New York and Massachusetts officials, who feared massive riots and misery should the strike not be settled before winter, Roosevelt scheduled a meeting of cabinet members, mining officials, and union representatives on 3 October 1902 to discuss solutions for ending the strike. During that meeting John Mitchell, who "impressed Roosevelt deeply" with his sincerity and desire for compromise, proposed that the miners return to work immediately, while submitting their demands to an arbitration commission. Baer, however, refused to negotiate and insisted that Roosevelt prosecute the miners under the provisions of the Sherman Anti-Trust Act and Interstate Commerce Act.

Disgusted that Roosevelt would even meet with "a set of outlaws," Baer demanded that the president follow Cleveland's precedent set during the 1894 Pullman Strike of protecting strikebreakers and nonstriking miners with troops.[8] Then he launched into a diatribe claiming that free government was a contemptible failure if it could only protect lives and property and secure comfort of the people by compromise with the violators of law and instigators of violence and crime.[9] Roosevelt later wrote that the operators "came down in the most insolent frame of mind, refused to talk of arbitration or other accommodation of any kind, and used language that was most insulting to the miners and offensive to me." Efforts to have Mitchell call off the strike in anticipation of the creation of a commission failed, as Mitchell, knowing the attitude of the operators and Roosevelt's powerlessness to force them into arbitration, believed such unilateral actions inexpedient.[10]

Growing public indignation at the intransigence of the mine operators convinced Roosevelt to consider military intervention, but not in the manner Baer desired.[11] He

---

[6] Quote from Painter, *Standing at Armageddon*, p. 182, see also pp. 180–81; Edward Berman, *Labor Disputes and the President of the United States* (New York: Columbia University Press, 1924; reprint, New York: AMS, 1968), pp. 46–50; Yellen, *American Labor Struggles*, p. 160; Mowry, *Era of Roosevelt*, pp. 134–35.

[7] Yellen, *American Labor Struggles*, pp. 162–64; Berman, *Labor Disputes and the President*, pp. 50–51; Painter, *Standing at Armageddon*, pp. 182–83.

[8] Painter, *Standing at Armageddon*, p. 183.

[9] Yellen, *American Labor Struggles*, p. 160.

[10] Berman, *Labor Disputes and the President*, pp. 51–52; Mowry, *Era of Roosevelt*, pp. 136–37.

[11] See "Miners' Defense," *Nation* 74 (26 June 1902):499–500; "Miners' Demands," *Outlook* 72 (15 November 1902):619–20; "Miners' Evidence," *Outlook* 72 (20 December 1902):910; F. J. Warne, "Organized Labor in the Anthracite Coal Fields," *Outlook* 71 (24 May 1902):273–76, and "The Real Cause of the Anthracite Coal Strike," *Outlook* 71 (30 August 1902):1053–57; T. Williams, "General View of the Anthracite Coal Strike," *Review of Reviews* 26 (July 1902):64–66; M. G. McCunniff, "The Real Issues in the Anthracite

formed a plan, to go into effect if the operators continued to resist arbitration, by which Pennsylvania Senator Matthew Quay would convince Pennsylvania's governor to make a formal request for military aid. Roosevelt then would send a "first rate general," such as retired Lt. Gen. John M. Schofield, to the state, with enough troops to keep absolute order, taking any steps necessary to prevent interference by the strikers with men who wanted to work. That much of the plan suited the designs of the mine owners, but Roosevelt included a provision that was unacceptable. As he wrote later, "I would also instruct him [Schofield] to dispossess such operators and run the mines as a receiver until such time as the Commission might make its report."[12]

Concomitant with the formulation of these plans, Roosevelt, with the aid of J. P. Morgan, again sought to end the dispute without resort to military force. In early October 1902 Secretary of War Elihu Root met with Morgan on his yacht on the Hudson River and succeeded in convincing Morgan that arbitration was in the best interest of all parties, since a continued refusal of arbitration on the part of the operators would result in troops occupying the mines for an indeterminant period. Morgan contracted to help draft an agreement for arbitration that would gain operator approval. He was as good as his word; the operators accepted the arbitration agreement, and the first meeting of an arbitration commission was scheduled for late October. After Roosevelt's arbitration and secret military plans became public, attitudes softened on both sides. On 23 October 1902 the UMW ended its strike.[13]

ELIHU ROOT

Although Roosevelt considered using federal military force to settle the strike, deployment of regulars was unnecessary. Minor violence that did occur was adequately quelled by state National Guard forces. Increasingly during this period, local and state officials depended on a new, more professional National Guard as a force capable of suppressing disorder with a minimum of bloodshed. This growing sense of confidence in the guard was a direct result of its reforms of the previous years, which the legislature made formal and passed into law in January 1903.

Coal Strike," *World's Work* 4 (July 1902):2341–44; J. B. Bishop, "Coal Strike," *McClure's* 20 (December 1902):219–24; "Causes and Settlement of the Anthracite Coal Strike," *Review of Reviews* 26 (November 1902):515–17.

[12] Quotes from Theodore Roosevelt, *An Autobiography* (New York: Macmillan, 1916), pp. 489–90; Painter, *Standing at Armageddon*, pp. 184–85; Mowry, *Era of Roosevelt*, pp. 137–38; Berman, *Labor Disputes and the President*, pp. 56–58. General Schofield retired from the Army in September 1895.

[13] Berman, *Labor Disputes and the President*, pp. 54–56; Painter, *Standing at Armageddon*, pp. 183–86; Mowry, *Era of Roosevelt*, p. 139.

The Root Reforms and the National Guard

The Spanish-American War and Philippine Insurrection clearly had shown the government that state troops, as then configured, were unable to support adequately the Regular Army in an age of technological warfare and mass armies. The dubious performance of the various state National Guards in the labor disputes of the late nineteenth century had produced a similar negative impression among many Americans. Labor and industrial leaders, and a large portion of the public, viewed the National Guard as a tool of business and an antilabor strikebreaking force, a characterization the guard denied and sought to dispel. Yet by the turn of the century, many believed the time was appropriate for reform. The guard began actively to seek a position within the nation's military establishment similar to that held by their European counterparts: that of front-line reservists in time of war. The idea was unpopular with the Regular Army, whose leaders, heavily influenced by the ideas of the nineteenth-century theorist Emory Upton, favored forming an Army reserve force.[14] Regular Army officers thought generally that the guard was composed of amateurs who lacked the years of training and experience necessary to fulfill the nation's military needs as a global power. The National Guard could point to examples of distinguished service in the recent war, but more to the point politically, it enjoyed the support of the National Guard Association, a lobbying group that had sought recognition for the guard as a front-line reserve since the late 1870s.[15]

The responsibility for reforming the nation's military forces fell to Secretary of War Root, an attorney appointed by McKinley. President Roosevelt, himself a strong and enthusiastic supporter of military expansion and reform, asked Root to spearhead the reforms that he had first called for in 1901. Realizing that the depth of antimilitary feeling among Americans and the parsimonious attitude of Congress doomed any extensive addition to the nation's military forces as envisioned by the Regular Army, he worked with the National Guard Association to make reforms in the 116,542-man National Guard force.[16]

The result of Root's initiative was the Dick Militia Act of January 1903. This seminal piece of legislation met the main goal of the National Guard Association and recognized the guard as the nation's organized militia and primary reserve in time of war. The act mandated additional federal appropriations—nearly $4 million annually by 1908—to provide uniforms, armaments, and equipment similar to those of the Army. National Guard reorganizations were to take five years and would be supervised and inspected by the Regular Army until guard units met its standards of training, discipline, and organization. Guard

---

[14] For Upton, see Stephen E. Ambrose, *Upton and the Army* (Baton Rouge: Louisiana State University Press, 1964).

[15] National Guard Bureau, *A Brief History of the Militia and National Guard* (Washington, D.C.: National Guard Bureau, 1986), p. 24; Derthick, *The National Guard in Politics*, pp. 15–22; Riker, *Soldiers of the States*, pp. 67–69; Mahon, *History of the Militia and the National Guard*, pp. 138–53; Jerry M. Cooper, "National Guard Reform, the Army, and the Spanish-American War: The View From Wisconsin," *Military Affairs* 42 (January 1978):20–33. For Upton's view, see Emory Upton, *The Military Policy of the United States* (Washington, D.C.: Government Printing Office, 1880; 4th printing, 1917).

[16] U.S. War Department, *Annual Report of the Secretary of War, 1901* (Washington, D.C.: Government Printing Office, 1901), pp. 3–11, 21–23; Derthick, *National Guard in Politics*, pp. 22–24; Riker, *Soldiers of the States*, pp. 69–72; Russell F. Weigley, *History of the United States Army* (New York: Macmillan, 1967), pp. 321–22; Hill, *Minute Man in Peace and War*, pp. 186–89.

members were allowed to attend Army technical and leadership schools, and Army personnel were detailed to supervise enlisted training during summer encampments. Each guardsman was required by the new act to attend twenty-four drills per year, as well as one five-day annual encampment. Finally, the act of 1903 stipulated that all guard members were liable for up to nine months of federal service, if the president believed it to be necessary, although this service was not to entail duty outside the continental United States.[17]

The law clarified the role of Regular Army soldiers and guardsmen in civil disturbances. It also codified the presidential practice, operative since 1866, of using regular troops instead of federalized guardsmen to suppress domestic disorders. At the same time, both the state and federal governments were freed from the provisions of the obsolete Militia Acts of 1792, 1795, and 1834. Although governors could continue to employ guardsmen in local disturbances, Section 4 of the act ended the theoretical policy, enacted in 1792, of making the militia the president's sole military recourse for intervening to end disorders. The authority to call the National Guard into federal service contained in RS 5297 and RS 5298 remained in effect, because the guard was still legally defined as the organized militia. The provisions governing the domestic intervention of federal troops, or federalized National Guardsmen, as outlined in the *Revised Statutes of 1874* and the Posse Comitatus Act of 1878 remained in effect.[18]

The Dick Militia Act was amplified over the next thirteen years by legislation that shifted the National Guard toward a combined role as protector against civil disturbances and as a front-line reserve in time of war. The 1908 Militia Act disposed of many compromises in earlier legislation, increased federal appropriations, and provided that the guard now could be called to serve the federal government either inside or outside the United States, for any length of time the president believed to be necessary. This provision was nullified in 1912 but it was reinstituted and strengthened in the 1916 National Defense Act. The 1908 Act, like the Acts of 1903 and 1916, stipulated that the guard could be called into federal service when there was an invasion or danger of invasion, a rebellion or a danger of rebellion, or when the president was unable with Regular forces under his control to execute the laws of the United States.

Nevertheless, the National Guard remained under state control until such time as it was needed and federalized by the president for cases in which Regular troops were unable to meet an emergency alone. As before, after 1903 the guard was used by governors as their first reliance to quell disturbances stemming from labor disputes. Hence federal

---

[17] On the act, see *Secretary of War Report, 1901*, pp. 3–11, 21–23; Wilson, *Federal Military Aid in Domestic Disturbances*, pp. 253–55; Derthick, *National Guard in Politics*, pp. 22–24, 27; Robert W. Coakley, "The Federal Use of the Militia and the National Guard in Civil Disturbances," and Clarence C. Clendenen, "Super Police: The National Guard as a Law-Enforcement Agency in the Twentieth Century," both in Higham, *Bayonets in the Streets*, pp. 27–28 and 85–88, respectively; Hill, *Minute Man in Peace and War*, pp. 131, 186–89, 191; Millis, *Arms and Men*, pp. 173–80; *U.S. Statutes at Large, 1903*, vol. 32, pt. 2, p. 776; Ekirch, *The Civilian and the Military*, pp. 143–45; Riker, *Soldiers of the States*, pp. 69–72; "The Working of the New Militia Law" *Nation* 77 (3 September 1903):182, 218; Cantor, "The Creation of the Modern National Guard."

[18] "Working of the New Militia Law," pp. 182, 218; Coakley, "Federal Use of Militia," pp. 27–28; Clendenen, "National Guard as Law-Enforcement Agency," pp. 85–88; Hill, *Minute Man in Peace and War*, p. 131; Derthick, *National Guard in Politics*, pp. 22–24; *U.S. Statutes at Large, 1903*, vol. 32, pt. 2, p. 776. Although Adams used regulars in suppressing the 1799 Fries Rebellion, it was not until passage of the 1807 Act, during Jefferson's term, that presidents relied on regulars. After 1865, no president federalized the National Guard for use in a domestic disorder for nearly a century.

intervention increasingly took place only when guard forces were unavailable, or were unable to quell a disturbance.[19]

The 1916 National Defense Act reemphasized the role of the guard as the main Army reserve force. Provisions authorized its expansion from 100,000 to 400,000 men, set standards for officers and enlisted men similar to those demanded of Regular Army officers and troops, and required units to receive federal recognition and to meet Army standards. Further provisions improved National Guard training, enlistment, drill, and pay. By the time of the U.S. entry into World War I, the National Guard numbered over 132,000 men and had nearly completed the long transition from being a second-rate military and constabulary force to becoming a first-rate reserve capable of supporting Army field operations.[20]

The Root Reforms and the United States Army

Just as supporters of the National Guard sought reform and an improved reserve role as a combat force, so the Army sought also to effect major changes designed to transform the Regular Army from what many perceived as an Indian-fighting national constabulary into an efficient professional force capable of defending the nation from foreign armies either on the nation's borders and shores or on battlefields abroad. As the country advanced to a position of world leadership, forward-thinking people such as Roosevelt and Root realized that the United States needed a military force capable of meeting its missions. The National Guard reforms were part of a larger effort to reform the nation's military land forces begun as early as the 1880s. Most of the changes were based on the ideas of Bvt. Maj. Gen. Emory Upton, whose works, *The Armies of Asia and Europe*, published in 1878, and *The Military Policy of the United States*, published posthumously in 1904, influenced a generation of officers.[21]

Although Army reforms commenced as early as the 1880s, most efforts in the late nineteenth century remained small and underfunded by a recalcitrant Congress, reflecting the mood of an antimilitary public. With the advent of the Progressive era, however, reforms began in earnest. Root initiated a piece of legislation entitled "An Act To Increase the Efficiency of the Permanent Military Establishment of the United States," which passed into law on 2 February 1901. It prompted a reorganization and expansion of the

---

[19] Coakley, "Federal Use of Militia," pp. 27–28; Derthick, *National Guard in Politics*, pp. 28–29, 52–53; Riker, *Soldiers of the States*, pp. 72–73; Hill, *Minute Man in Peace and War*, pp. 203–04; Weigley, *History of the United States Army*, pp. 324–25. Note the change in the wording of the 1908 Act, which specifically referred to "Regular" rather than "other forces" as in the 1903 Act.

[20] National Guard Bureau, *Brief History of the Militia and National Guard*, pp. 30–31; Derthick, *National Guard in Politics*, pp. 33–38; Riker, *Soldiers of the States*, pp. 80–82; Weigley, *History of the United States Army*, pp. 348–49.

[21] For Army reform, see James E. Hewes, Jr., *From Root to McNamara: Army Organization and Administration, 1900–1963* (Washington, D.C.: U.S. Army Center of Military History, 1975); Weigley, *History of the United States Army*, pp. 313–15; Ekirch, *The Civilian and the Military*, p. 140; Ganoe, *The History of the United States Army*, pp. 356–57, 418; L. Buchanan, "Our Army and the Need of It," *World's Work* 13 (March 1907):8640–41; Barrie E. Zais, "The Struggle for a 20th Century Army: Investigation and Reform of the United States Army After the Spanish-American War" (Ph.D. diss., Duke University, 1981); William R. Roberts, "Reform and Vitalization, 1890–1903," and Timothy K. Nenninger, "The Army Enters the Twentieth Century, 1904–1917," both in Hagan and Roberts, *Against All Enemies*, pp. 197–218 and 219–34, respectively.

Army to 100,619 men, an increase in the officer corps, and the acquisition of updated equipment and weapons.[22]

A further target for reform was the Army high command, and in 1902 Root proposed a bill to create a general staff, based on German and French models. Under this plan the position of commanding general was dropped in favor of a new position of chief of staff of the Army, an officer selected by the secretary of war rather than by seniority. The chief of staff worked closely with the secretary and directed a general staff that developed war plans. Root's idea not only entailed centralization and reorganization, but also affirmed and reestablished strong civilian control by making the secretary of war the top military authority of the nation, subordinate only to the president. Congress passed the General Staff Bill in February 1903, despite the protests of Commanding General Miles and the Army bureaus, and established the Army general staff formally in August. Subsequent regulations called for creation of a separate War Department general staff.[23]

The area subjected to the greatest reform was the Army educational system. Root was amazed to discover that over one-third of the Army officers had no formal military education in spite of the pioneering work undertaken by Col. Arthur L. Wagner in the late 1880s. The Army established schools in the last quarter of the nineteenth century to impart scientific and technical training to current and future officers, but under the Root reforms the Army effected vast improvements in the number of schools and the intensity and quality of military education.[24]

When Root retired in 1904 he was replaced by William Howard Taft, who, although continuing to support Army reforms, was more concerned with colonial matters. During the second decade of the twentieth century, however, Root's reformist zeal persevered under Secretary of War Henry L. Stimson and Army Chief of Staff Leonard Wood.[25]

When World War I began in Europe in 1914, President Woodrow Wilson adopted a neutral foreign policy and initially discouraged sweeping changes in the Army lest the belligerent powers interpret such changes as hostile behavior. Nonetheless, in a quiet way earlier reforms were continued. The most significant military legislation of the period was the 1916 National Defense Act, which created a comprehensive military policy and completed the paper transformation of the Army into a world class military force. Spurred to passage on 20 May 1916 by the outbreak of troubles with Mexico, provisions of the act allowed for a peacetime strength of the Army of 175,000, increased the number and strength of all units, and allowed for an expandable strength of over 286,000 men. Under Secretary of War Newton D. Baker, the former Progressive mayor of Cleveland, the Army expanded to the unprecedented peacetime strength of 140,000 officers and men.[26]

---

[22] Weigley, *History of the United States Army*, pp. 317–18; Foner, *United States Soldier*, pp. 77–113; Ganoe, *The History of the United States Army*, pp. 355, 412–13; *Secretary of War Report, 1901*, pp. 3–11; "Secretary Root's Army Bill," *Nation* 70 (22 March 1900):217–18.

[23] Weigley, *History of the United States Army*, pp. 315–23; *Secretary of War Report, 1901*, p. 21; Spaulding, *The United States Army in War and Peace*, p. 396; Ekirch, *The Civilian and the Military*, p. 142.

[24] Weigley, *History of the United States Army*, p. 325; Ganoe, *The History of the United States Army*, pp. 363, 417–23; *Secretary of War Report, 1901*, pp. 14–21, 89–91; Spaulding, *The United States Army in War and Peace*, p. 394.

[25] Ganoe, *The History of the United States Army*, pp. 417–48; Weigley, *History of the United States Army*, pp. 322–35.

[26] Spaulding, *The United States Army in War and Peace*, pp. 406–08; Weigley, *History of the United States Army*, pp. 347–49.

The reforms were intended to reshape the Army for fighting a modern war, but they had a fundamental impact on domestic interventions. Still subject to the president's call to aid civil authorities during disorders, the reorganized Army proved to be a more efficient and capable force than its nineteenth-century counterpart, as evidenced by the interventions of 1914 to 1921. Although the Army sought to develop a mission that decreased its role in labor disputes, tensions between industry and labor necessitating military intervention did not disappear in the early years of the twentieth century. The unprecedented manner in which these disputes were resolved, however, indicated that significant changes in the federal attitude had taken place toward the domestic use of federal military force.

The Miners' Strike at Morenci, Arizona, 1903

Even as the era of reform began, in June 1903 a labor dispute between copper miners and the Phelps-Dodge Corporation over hours and wages compelled Roosevelt to dispatch federal troops to the town of Morenci, Arizona. There miners had recently attained a long-sought goal: a territorially mandated eight-hour workday. But mine operators had instituted a corresponding reduction of wages to reflect the shorter day. Miners protested and then struck. Violence erupted quickly, and the acting governor called in the territorial National Guard force on 10 June.

Along with the dispatch of territorial forces, the acting governor entered a formal request to Roosevelt under RS 5298 to send regulars should the situation deteriorate. Uncharacteristically, and without dispatching an investigator, Roosevelt immediately gave orders for regulars under Brig. Gen. Frank D. Baldwin to embark from Fort Huachuca for Morenci. When the regulars arrived, however, they discovered that territorial troops had the situation under control and that no real need had ever existed for federal intervention. The Regular Army troops left on 18 June 1903.

The incursion, although brief and seemingly insignificant, had a major impact on Roosevelt's subsequent military deployments. The mistakes he had made—not seeing the lack of a clear need, not requiring an independent confirmation of trouble, and sending the troops too hastily—convinced him that in the future more impartial intelligence was crucial, as was more time for reflection prior to the decision to deploy troops. In less than six months his determination to avoid a similar blunder became evident in Colorado.[27]

The Strike at Telluride, Colorado, 1903

On 16 November 1903 gold miners belonging to the Western Federation of Miners (WFM) went on strike against the Telluride Mining Association for an eight-hour workday in the Cripple Creek and Telluride Districts of Colorado. Mine operators in the state, like their eastern counterparts, stubbornly resisted the efforts of their employees to unionize and sought actively to prevent WFM organizers from campaigning for union recognition, shorter working days, and improved living and working conditions. The merest hint of labor unrest led successive governors to deploy the National Guard nine times during the decade

---

[27] Berman, *Labor Disputes and the President*, pp. 59–60; James W. Byrkit, *Forging the Copper Collar: Arizona's Labor Management War, 1901–1921* (Tucson: University of Arizona Press, 1982), pp. 28–29.

preceding 1903, at a cost of over $1 million. When the new unrest began, mine owners did not hesitate to bring in strikebreakers, nor did they hesitate to call on Colorado's Republican Governor James H. Peabody for military aid in breaking the strikes.

Although the conservative Peabody considered the AFofL–affiliated Western Federation of Miners a criminal organization, he did not immediately respond by sending the National Guard.[28] The cost of calling out the guard so frequently during the previous decade had strained the Colorado treasury. With the state facing labor troubles in both gold and coal fields, Peabody sought to call in Regular troops, whose expenses would be charged to federal rather than state revenues. He wired Roosevelt on 16 November, requesting that General Baldwin be ordered "to furnish me such aid as I may call for." On Roosevelt's behalf, Secretary Root immediately responded that the governor's request could not be honored, for it did not mention an insurrection against the state as required by RS 5297.[29]

After receiving Root's response, Peabody sent another wire declaring that the state had "exhausted every means at its command to enforce the law, suppress lawlessness, and protect life and liberty." Again he requested federal aid. Both his requests were meant to convince Roosevelt that National Guard troops were not available in sufficient numbers to handle the disturbances, although the guard had previously quelled any violence that had occurred and had yet to be deployed at Telluride. The lack of funds, however, not the lack of manpower, was the root of Peabody's difficulties. Since 1877, with some exceptions, presidents had usually taken governors at their word, but Roosevelt demanded solid factual evidence that the disorder was a genuine insurrection against state authority and that National Guard forces were either unavailable or unable to suppress it. Furthermore, as Root explained to Peabody, even if he furnished the proof required and the president sent troops, the regulars could not serve under state control.[30]

Meanwhile, Roosevelt departed from the usual practices of his post-Reconstruction predecessors by ordering a federal inquiry into the dispute. Maj. Gen. John C. Bates was to investigate, bearing "in mind that compliance with the governor's call must in every instance be based upon urgent necessity proceeding from open, organized, and armed opposition to the execution of the laws of the State which the State authorities, civil or military, are clearly unable to overcome." While on the scene, Bates was also to determine whether the strikers or the operators had violated any federal laws, which, independently of the governor's pleas, might justify intervention.[31]

After a hurried investigation, Bates reported that the Telluride disorder had indeed been an insurrection against the state government. The civil authorities had failed to maintain order, and the use of state troops would have been desirable. However, he added, lawlessness had subsided, making the use of federal troops unnecessary, unless Peabody was

---

[28] Rich, *President and Civil Disorder*, pp. 122–24; Berman, *Labor Disputes and the President*, p. 60; George G. Suggs, Jr., *Colorado's War on Militant Unionism: James H. Peabody and the Western Federation of Miners* (Detroit: Wayne State University Press, 1972), pp. 43–45, 118–22, and "The Colorado Coal Miners' Strike, 1903–1904: A Prelude to Ludlow?" *Journal of the West* 12 (January 1973):36–52.

[29] Quote from Rich, *President and Civil Disorder*, p. 123. See also Berman, *Labor Disputes and the President*, pp. 60–61; Suggs, *Colorado's War on Militant Unionism*, pp. 122–24.

[30] Quote from Rich, *President and Civil Disorder*, p. 123. See also Berman, *Labor Disputes and the President*, p. 61; Suggs, *Colorado's War on Militant Unionism*, p. 124.

[31] Quote from Rich, *President and Civil Disorder*, p. 124. See also Berman, *Labor Disputes and the President*, pp. 61–62.

FRANK D. BALDWIN

forced to deploy state forces in both gold and coal fields simultaneously. He reported further that at no time had either side violated federal law.

Forced to rely on his own resources, Peabody belatedly dispatched the Colorado National Guard to Telluride and Cripple Creek in late November 1903, funded by certificates of indebtedness purchased by the businessmen of the Telluride Mining Association. In response to the deployment of the National Guard and to what strike leaders perceived as legal harassment, WFM Secretary William D. Haywood and the federation's general counsel wrote separate communications to the president in early December asking for federal military aid to protect miners, who had been arrested and threatened with deportation on the grounds that such measures violated the miners' rights under the Fourteenth Amendment to the Constitution and other federal civil rights statutes, especially RS 5299. Roosevelt responded, as he had to Peabody, that under the circumstances presented to him by both sides, the federal government still lacked sufficient cause to intervene. He remained determined not to interfere in what he believed to be an entirely local matter.[32]

Although the crisis at Telluride continued, state and local forces were able to control events, and federal troops were not required in Colorado until 1914. In the Telluride disorder Roosevelt demonstrated that federal forces would be dispatched only when the circumstances surrounding the request were genuinely indicative of an armed insurrection against civil authority that state National Guard and/or law enforcement officials were clearly unable to handle. He reinforced his evenhanded policy four years later in another dispute in Nevada.

The Goldfield, Nevada, Mining Strike, 1907

In 1907 the Army became fully involved in its first major labor dispute of the century. On 27 November, within Brig. Gen. Frederick Funston's Department of California, 1,900 miners of Goldfield, Nevada, went on strike against the Goldfield Mine Operators Association, a trade association that dominated the economy of much of the southern portion of the state. The cause of the strike was the decision of the cash-poor mine operators' association to pay miners in scrip that could only be converted into cash at a substantial discount.

---

[32] Rich, *President and Civil Disorder*, p. 125; Suggs, *Colorado's War on Militant Unionism*, pp. 124–25, 127. William D. "Big Bill" Haywood later led the radical Industrial Workers of the World (IWW).

When the consortium vowed to bring in strikebreakers to reopen the mines and resume production, and in the process break the power of the local WFM, an apprehensive Governor John Sparks requested federal troops to prevent the violence that he felt was certain to result.

Roosevelt took steps to place federal forces in the vicinity, but with explicit instructions to take no action until the field commander had conducted an investigation of the circumstances surrounding the dispute, and to verify that a true disturbance existed. Receiving conflicting reports from Funston and the field commander, Roosevelt sent a commission to investigate the circumstances surrounding the dispute instead of risking the deployment of troops in a situation that was not beyond the control of local authorities. Their findings reflected the great complexity of such socioeconomic disputes.[33]

FREDERICK FUNSTON

Goldfield, the seat of Esmeralda County, had a population of between 15,000 and 20,000 people, mostly single males. Located in the mountainous region along Nevada's southwestern boundary, midway between Carson City and Las Vegas, the town was suitably named for the extensive gold mining that had flourished there since 1902. Like most mining towns, it consisted primarily of wooden frame buildings and small board shacks along unpaved, dusty streets. Two unions sought the miners' allegiance here, and property owners and businessmen considered both to be radical, criminal organizations: the Western Federation of Miners and the newer Industrial Workers of the World (IWW).[34]

Formed in 1905, the IWW was a heterogeneous group of Socialists, radical syndicalists, and industrial unionists. Popularly known as Wobblies, its organizers sought to supplant the AFofL's moderate philosophy and emphasis on skilled craft unions with a revolutionary philosophy and "One Big Union." Under its leader, the former WFM secretary, William D. "Big Bill" Haywood, the IWW followed an ideology closely resembling the European syndicalism of Georges Sorel.[35] Sorelians called for the abolition of the capitalist wage system and the organization of all workers, with no matter what degree of skill or

[33] Rich, *President and Civil Disorder*, pp. 125–26; Berman, *Labor Disputes and the President*, pp. 64–65.

[34] Rpt, Reynolds, 22d Inf, to AG, Dept of California, 11 Dec 07, Headquarters Document File, Dept of California, RG 393, Records of the U.S. Army Continental Commands, 1821–1920, NARA; Rich, *President and Civil Disorder*, p. 125. For the background, see Earl B. White, "Might Is Right: Unionism and Goldfield, Nevada, 1904–1908," *Journal of the West* 16 (March 1977):75–84. The WFM was the largest single affiliate of the IWW from 1906 to 1908, when it left the organization.

[35] For Haywood, see William D. Haywood, *Bill Haywood's Book: The Autobiography of William D. Haywood* (New York: International, 1929); Joseph R. Conlin, *Big Bill Haywood and the Radical Union Movement* (Syracuse: Syracuse University Press, 1969).

type of trade, into one large union called a *syndicat*. Syndicalists espoused the general strike to paralyze the state as a prelude to an anticapitalist revolution. Unlike the AFofL, which sought to share in the wealth created by capitalism, the IWW sought to overthrow the existing order, which it saw as beyond substantive reform. IWW strength was always greatest among workers the AFofL did not organize, mainly unskilled and migrant laborers—those with the least to lose by revolution.

Attempting to recruit workers who were inherently disorganized, largely uneducated, unskilled, and transient made the efforts of IWW organizers difficult, and the union never counted more than 100,000 active members. The presence of its activists in industrial areas, their militant and aggressive organization efforts, and their revolutionary rhetoric, however, may have affected nearly a million workers in mining, lumber, and farming areas employing migrant workers in the Far West. To mine owners who had already been grappling with the militant WFM for decades, the emergence of the even more militant IWW was ominous. In addition, the IWW did nothing to allay the fears of property owners and businessmen in the Far West, since Wobblies constantly and publicly espoused revolutionary solutions to the nation's ills.[36]

Soon after its founding, IWW members affiliated with the WFM. This radically tinged alliance organized Goldfield miners into Local 77, which between 1905 and 1907 became powerful enough to gain significant wage and hour reforms for its members. However, during the 1907 trial of several IWW leaders suspected of murdering former Idaho Governor Frank Steunenberg, mine owners in Nevada created the Mine Operators Association (MOA) for the avowed purpose of destroying the WFM in Goldfield and nearby Tonopah. Evidence suggests that the MOA conspired to provoke union members into illegal actions for which their leaders could then be arrested. Using the financial panic of 1907 as a pretext, the association announced a plan to suspend cash wage payments to miners. When operators began issuing company scrip instead of cash, the members of Local 77 denounced the scrip as "Christian Science money" and began a strike on 27 November 1907.[37]

Although sympathetic to the operators' efforts to provoke, disrupt, and, they hoped, disband the radical union locals, Governor Sparks recognized that Nevada lacked a National Guard or any means of civil law enforcement capable of protecting the mining companies from anticipated violence. Convinced by the mine owners that the union was hoarding dynamite and firearms, Sparks and the association contrived a scheme to request federal military aid on receipt of a coded message from the MOA. The message arrived on 3 December 1907, and Sparks wired Roosevelt for troops the next day, stating that "in the

---

[36] Patrick Renshaw, *The Wobblies: The Story of Syndicalism in the United States* (New York: Doubleday, 1967), pp. 22–23. For contemporary views, see V. Lee, "Sorel and the Syndicalist Myth," *Fortnightly* (London) 96 (October 1911):640–80; John G. Brooks, *American Syndicalism* (New York: Macmillan, 1913; reprint, New York: Arno, 1969). For the Wobblies, see Joseph R. Conlin, *Bread and Roses Too: Studies of the Wobblies* (Westport: Greenwood, 1969) and *At the Point of Production: The Local History of the IWW* (Westport: Greenwood, 1981); John S. Gambs, *The Decline of the IWW* (New York: Columbia University Press, 1932; reprint, New York: Russell & Russell, 1966); Philip S. Foner, *History of the Labor Movement in the United States*, vol. 4, *The Industrial Workers of the World, 1905–1907* (New York: International Publishers, 1965). Works by Wobblies include Ralph Chaplin, *Wobbly: The Rough-and-Tumble Story of an American Radical* (Chicago: University of Chicago Press, 1948); Fred W. Thompson and Patrick Murfin, *The IWW: Its First Seventy Years, 1905–1975* (Chicago: Industrial Workers of the World, 1976).

[37] Dubofsky, *We Shall Be All*, pp. 123–24; White, "Might Is Right," pp. 75–84.

near future . . . Nevada may expect serious labor troubles . . . which may result in violence and great destruction of property. . . . The sheriff of the county seems unable to cope with the situation." He explained further that Nevada lacked an organized National Guard and requested a small detachment of regulars. Nevada Senator George Nixon supported the request with another message to the president.[38]

Realizing that under ordinary circumstances Sparks' request was premature, Roosevelt understood also that Nevada's lack of an organized National Guard placed its citizens in greater peril of prolonged violence than residents of neighboring states. Alerting the Department of California to prepare two companies at Fort McDowell for immediate movement, he instructed Sparks to strengthen his request by citing instances of recent lawlessness and providing the statutory basis for federal intervention.[39]

WILLIAM D. "BIG BILL" HAYWOOD

After examining the *Revised Statutes of 1874*, Sparks forwarded a second request in which he confused the purpose of the three sections dealing with civil disturbances. Listing past instances of demolition of property, commission of felonies, and intimidation of company officials and nonunion employees, he correctly based his request upon the grounds enumerated in RS 5299: the existence of domestic violence and of unlawful combinations and conspiracies (the miners' union), which obstructed execution of state law and deprived a class of citizens of their civil rights (the MOA and the strikebreakers). In addition, he cited pertinent sections of RS 5297, concerning insurrections against the laws of the state, but then mistakenly cited RS 5298, concerning rebellion against federal authority, as further justification.[40]

Wishing to verify Sparks' statements, Roosevelt sent Brig. Gen. Frederick Funston to investigate. As Funston familiarized himself with the Goldfield dispute, he found that many of the Nevada strike organizers were members of the WFM and had participated in the earlier Coeur d'Alene disturbances. He noted also that most of the 1,000 striking miners were armed and that at least 300 of this number could be considered radical and dangerous

---

[38] Quote from Telg, Sparks to Roosevelt, 4 Dec 07, AGO File 1310155: Goldfield, Nevada, 1907, RG 94, Records of the Office of the Adjutant General, U.S. Army, NARA; Rich, *President and Civil Disorder*, p. 126. See also 22d Infantry Regimental History, 1907, RG 391, Records of U.S. Army Mobile Units, 1821–1942, NARA; Dubofsky, *We Shall Be All*, pp. 123–24; Berman, *Labor Disputes and the President*, p. 65.

[39] Telgs, AG to CG, Dept of California, and AG, Dept of California, to CO, Ft. McDowell, 4 Dec 07, both in HQ Doc. File, Dept of California, 1907, RG 393; 22d Inf Regt Hist, 1907, RG 391; Rich, *President and Civil Disorder*, p. 126.

[40] Rich, *President and Civil Disorder*, pp. 126–27; Telg, Sparks to Roosevelt, 5 Dec 07, AGO File 1310155, RG 94.

enough to blow up mining property and take the lives of nonunion, nonstriking workers. After speaking with mine owners, Funston reported that no violence would take place if the federal government would send troops. He advised Acting Secretary of War Robert S. Oliver that in view of the prevailing circumstances it would be wise to send a detachment from the 22d Infantry to Goldfield.[41]

Roosevelt approved the deployment to Goldfield of "a sufficient number of troops . . . wholly adequate to meet any emergency," remarking that "it is far better to avoid conflict by sending too many troops than too few and run the risk of inviting bloodshed." At 0800 on 6 December 1907, Col. Alfred Reynolds transported 250 men in five companies and a machine-gun platoon of the 22d Infantry by steamer to Oakland, California. There the regulars boarded trains of the Southern Pacific Railroad for the trip to Goldfield.[42]

The first company of troops arrived the next day and set up camp near the freight yards of the Tonopah & Goldfield Railroad. Ten hours later, a second group of four companies entered town and set up camp across town near the mines, one mile from their comrades. Telephones linked both camps. Although the altitude and primitive conditions created hardships for the troops, Reynolds had prepared for the extreme cold by bringing ample tents, stoves, rations, and warm clothing.[43]

Shortly after the Army troops' arrival, Oliver reminded Funston and Reynolds not to take any orders from Sparks "in any operations involving . . . military force. . . . It will be constantly bourne [sic] in mind that the duty of maintaining or restoring public order now rests in the president and officers acting under him." The president encouraged Reynolds to consult with Sparks about local conditions and measures to be used, but he expected Reynolds to be "guided solely by such instructions as he may receive from the president or Funston, and by his own judgment." If it became necessary to use troops to quell a riot, Reynolds was to inform the president, so that he could issue a proclamation as required by RS 5300.[44]

Oliver referred Funston to the tactical guidance on mob control contained in Section 489 of Army Regulations of 1904. After warning the crowds to disperse, the troops were to prod rioters with gun butts and bayonets. If they continued to resist and especially if they responded by throwing missiles or firing guns, the troops, at the discretion of the commander, were to act progressively with selective marksmanship, fire by volleys, machine-gun fire, and then, if necessary artillery.[45]

Perhaps fearful that the initial guidance might encourage Funston and Reynolds to be overly aggressive, Roosevelt subsequently advised them, in an excellent example of how restraint was now urged in federal military interventions, to "use utmost caution and good judgment in the very delicate and responsible situation which confronts you. . . . Anything

---

[41] Telg, AG to Funston, and reply, 5 Dec 07, HQ Doc. File, Dept of California, 1907, RG 393; see also 22d Inf Regt Hist, 1907, RG 391. Secretary of War William H. Taft was in Europe during the Goldfield crisis.

[42] Quote from Memo, Roosevelt for Oliver, 6 Dec 07; see also Telg, Funston to AG, 6 Dec 07; both in AGO File 1310155, RG 94. Rich, *President and Civil Disorder*, p. 127; 22d Inf Regt Hist, 1907, RG 391.

[43] See 22d Inf Regt Hist, 1907, RG 391; Rpt, Reynolds to AG, Dept of California, 11 Dec 07, HQ Doc. File, Dept of California, 1907, RG 393.

[44] Quote from Telg, Oliver to Funston, 7 Dec 07, AGO File 1310155, RG 94. See also *Regulations of the Army of the United States, 1904* (Washington, D.C.: Government Printing Office, 1905), par. 487, p. 78.

[45] *Army Regulations, 1904*, p. 78. This regulation was a restatement of Section 568 of *Army Regulations, 1901*, and Section 491, *Army Regulations of 1895*, both verbatim repeats of GO 23 of 9 July 1894.

FEDERAL SOLDIERS OF THE 22D INFANTRY AWAIT TRANSPORT TO GOLDFIELD, NEVADA

rash or impulsive is to be avoided. . . . The actions of the troops should make it evident to everyone that any difficulty that arises has not been provoked by the troops. . . . You should be especially conservative in speech and say nothing . . . not absolutely necessary in . . . carrying out your duty."[46]

Aware that the president had to issue a proclamation before troops could be used legally in a domestic disorder, on 7 December Oliver inquired of Funston whether such a proclamation was necessary. Although Funston anticipated no mob violence that would require military operations, he speculated that a prompt presidential proclamation would act as a strong deterrent. Nevertheless, he did not request such a proclamation pending receipt of Reynolds' next report.[47]

Impressed initially by the restraint of the striking miners, Reynolds recommended that the issuance of any proclamation be delayed for several days. The day after Reynolds entered town, however, the MOA reduced wages further and threatened to terminate the jobs of all members of the WFM. Despite such actions the miners refused to be provoked into attacks on company property or on nonunion or nonstriking employees. However, after talks with union officials that clearly displayed the miners' frame of mind, Reynolds

---

[46] Quote from Telg, AG, Dept of California, to Reynolds, 7 Dec 07, HQ Doc. File, Dept of California, 1907, RG 393. See also Rich, *President and Civil Disorder*, p. 127; Memo, Oliver for AG, 7 Dec 07, AGO File 1310155, RG 94.

[47] Telg, AG to Funston, and reply, 7 Dec 07, HQ Doc. File, Dept of California, 1907, RG 393; Wilson, *Federal Aid in Domestic Disturbances*, p. 310.

[48] Telgs, Reynolds to Funston, and Funston to AG, 9 Dec 07, both in HQ Doc. File, Dept of California, 1907, RG 393.

THE 22D INFANTRY CAMPS AT GOLDFIELD, DECEMBER 1907

predicted that violence would erupt on 12 December, the day mine owners intended to reopen the pits using strikebreakers.[48]

In a lengthy report to Funston, Reynolds criticized the MOA for using the presence of troops to support Draconian measures against the miners. He expressed strong reservations concerning the necessity and correctness of military intervention in Goldfield, stating that he did not "find that immediately previous to our coming the conditions contemplated by paragraphs 5297, 5298, and 5299 of the *Revised Statutes* existed. They certainly do not now." He continued, saying, "There is evidence of conspiracies to deprive individuals of their civil rights," but by the MOA not the WFM, and in his opinion there was no disturbance so extensive that it could not be controlled by civil authorities.[49]

Newspaper accounts and letters from mine owners and their friends had convinced Funston that Goldfield's civil authorities were sympathetic to the strikers and would take no action to avert violence directed toward the mine companies or strikebreakers. Therefore, he rejected Reynolds' implication that the 22d Infantry was no longer needed and that there had been no legitimate reason to send regulars. On 10 December he wrote in a letter to the War Department that Reynolds' reports were "too brief" to be useful and that he would go to Goldfield to collect intelligence on the situation. His intent was to assume "general" control of the troops in the area, while allowing Reynolds to continue to wield tactical control. He assured his superiors that he would take no "radical action" but would limit the duties of the regulars to the preservation of order and the protection of life and property. However, Funston mistakenly included in this definition an agreement he had made with Sparks to protect private mine property and strikebreakers.

[49] Rpt, Reynolds to AG, Dept of California, 11 Dec 07, HQ Doc. File, Dept of California, 1907, RG 393.
[50] Telg, Funston to AG, 10 Dec 07, HQ Doc. File, Dept of California, 1907, RG 393.

Funston's proposals, if Washington, D.C., had approved of them, would have placed federal troops in a clearly partisan position.[50]

As such, Funston's intentions ran contrary to Roosevelt's idea of the Army's mission in Goldfield. On 11 December, after conferring with Chief of Staff Maj. Gen. James F. Bell, the commissioner of corporations, and the assistant secretary of commerce and labor, Roosevelt telegraphed Funston: "The troops are not sent to take either side in a purely industrial dispute, as long as it is kept within the bounds of law and order. They are to be neither for nor against the strikers or the employers. They are to prevent riot, violence, and disorder, under and in accordance with the Constitution. . . . No man is to be interfered with so long as he conducts himself in a peaceful and orderly manner."[51]

Seeking to avoid any action that remotely implied partisanship, Roosevelt directed Reynolds to notify the adjutant general as soon as a presidential proclamation appeared necessary to suppress lawlessness or riot. Until that time the troops were not to be committed to any action. Reynolds was instructed strictly not to use his soldiers without explicit orders based on federal statute because, as the president said, "better twenty-four hours of riot, damage, and disorder than illegal use of troops."[52]

The president also had taken Funston's measure. Apparently dissatisfied with Oliver's ability to control the general's activities and utterances, on 13 December Roosevelt placed Secretary of State Root in charge of the Goldfield crisis. He directed Root to define clearly for Sparks the precise conditions under which Reynolds' troops could leave their encampments to assist civil law enforcement officials.[53]

Therefore, Root informed Sparks that before Roosevelt would order federal troops to intervene, the governor must prove that Nevada's legislature could not be convened in time to raise a sufficient National Guard force to deal with any disorder as specified in RS 5297. He noted further that Sparks had not demonstrated, as required by RS 5299, that a specific group of people were being denied constitutional guarantees of equal protection under the law.[54] Although the governor's request of 5 December for aid under RS 5297 was no less complete than those submitted by other state executives in earlier disturbances, granting federal military aid was steadfastly refused. In 1907 the Nevada governor was dealing with a president determined that military intervention, if it came, would be well informed, restrained, strictly legal, and above all else strictly neutral in its application and intent.

While Sparks pondered the contents of Root's telegram over the next three days, Funston reached Goldfield and sought evidence to confirm his fears of violence should the regulars depart. Writing to his superiors, he reiterated the contention of the MOA that civil authority had completely collapsed in Esmeralda County. Specifically, he repeated allegations that the sheriff was partisan and had recruited the majority of his deputies from the miners' union. He urged Root to retain at least two companies of troops and a

[51] Quoted in Telg, AG to Funston, 11 Dec 07, HQ Doc. File, Dept of California, 1907, RG 393. See also Rich, *President and Civil Disorder*, p. 129; Memo, Bell for Oliver, 11 Dec 07, AGO File 1310155, RG 94. For Bell, see Edgar F. Raines, "Major General J. Franklin Bell and Military Reform: The Chief of Staff Years, 1906–1910" (Ph.D. diss., University of Wisconsin, 1976).

[52] Memo, Bell for Oliver, 11 Dec 07, AGO File 1310155, RG 94.

[53] Rich, *President and Civil Disorder*, pp. 129–30.

[54] Telg, Root to Sparks, 14 Dec 07, AGO File 1310155, RG 94.

machine-gun platoon in Esmeralda County for an indefinite period as the only sure means of keeping the peace.[55]

Unimpressed, Roosevelt still wanted word from Sparks about whether the Nevada legislature could be convened to raise a National Guard force to relieve federal troops and perform "those ordinary duties of maintaining public order which rest upon the governor and the state." When Sparks equivocated and avoided a direct response, Roosevelt sent an investigatory commission to Goldfield. Composed of three high-ranking officials of the Department of Commerce and Labor, the group spent several days gathering evidence which showed that civil authority had not collapsed and that Sparks had bypassed civil officials and sought federal military aid directly as a first resort. The commission urged Roosevelt to present him with the choice of raising a National Guard force within ten days or facing the withdrawal of federal troops.[56]

Based upon information similar to that presented by the commission, the national labor press sought to depict the Army as an enemy of labor. One Socialist paper claimed that "it is clearly shown that neither riot nor insurrection occurred at Goldfield, nor was the situation beyond the control of the sheriff. Notwithstanding this, the federal troops were sent to the scene, ostensibly to protect life and order, but in reality to overawe the wage workers, and as an instrument with which to force upon labor the depreciated scrip which the domination of a master class makes possible."[57]

Undaunted by White House rebuffs and bad publicity, Sparks renewed efforts to keep federal troops in Goldfield. He reminded Roosevelt of the virtual "state of war" that had long existed in the county and that armed miners could easily overpower law enforcement officers at any time they chose to do so. He asked that federal troops be kept in Goldfield for at least three weeks until the legislature could be called. In response, Roosevelt promised that, if Sparks issued such a notice within five days, federal troops would stay for three more weeks; otherwise they would withdraw immediately. Sparks called for the legislature to convene on 16 January 1908 and, upon receiving word of the governor's actions, Roosevelt ordered Funston to retain two companies of troops in Goldfield. The remainder of Reynolds' 22d Infantry was to return promptly to Fort McDowell.[58]

The Nevada legislature convened as scheduled. After reiterating the familiar, if somewhat inaccurate, causes for the disorders in Esmeralda County and citing the lack of adequate protection for the citizens there, the legislature requested that Roosevelt leave the federal troops in Goldfield until a state constabulary could be organized and equipped. Roosevelt agreed to delay the withdrawal of federal forces an additional two weeks.[59] Within two weeks the legislature had voted to organize a Nevada state police, but it now required a further sixty days to make the unit operational. Roosevelt, having reached the limits of his patience, censured Nevada officials for their apparent stalling.

[55] Telgs, Funston to AG, 14 and 17 Dec 07, AGO Files 1310155A3 and 1310155A5, respectively, RG 94.

[56] Quote from Telg, Roosevelt to Sparks, 17 Dec 07, AGO File 1310155A15, RG 94. See also 22d Inf Regt Hist, 1907, RG 391; Rich, *President and Civil Disorder*, p. 131.

[57] Benton Harbor (MI) Socialist Party, 20 Dec 07, AGO File 1310155, RG 94.

[58] Telgs, Sparks to Roosevelt, 26 Dec 07, and Roosevelt to Sparks, 28 Dec 07, both in AGO File 1310155A18, RG 94. See also 22d Inf Regt Hist, 1907, RG 391; Telg, AG, Dept of California, to Reynolds, 31 Dec 07, HQ Doc. File, Dept of California, 1907, RG 393.

[59] Wilson, *Federal Aid in Domestic Disturbances*, p. 311. See also Telgs, Sparks to Roosevelt, 16 Jan 08, and reply, 17 Jan 08, AGO File 1310155A25, RG 94.

To him it seemed "quite unnecessary to delay. Surely with reasonable expedition the police force can be organized, armed, and equipped in a tenth of that time. . . . If there are any reasons why troops should remain beyond the fifteenth of this month, I should like to hear them at once."[60]

After consulting with the newly appointed captain of the state police, Sparks explained to Roosevelt that, although it would take thirty days to organize the police, it would take sixty days to ship the necessary arms and equipment to Nevada. Roosevelt accepted the explanation and made 7 March 1908 the final deadline for the withdrawal. The last federal troops departed as scheduled without having had to intervene actively and without serving any purpose other than ensuring the maintenance of public order.[61]

By his admirable patience and self-restraint, Roosevelt not only restored a measure of trust among labor groups in the capacity of the federal government to oversee their interests in a neutral manner, but helped also to erase somewhat the antilabor stigma and deflate the charges of militarism that the Army had to bear since the labor troubles of the late nineteenth century. The Progressive policies and processes that Roosevelt began continued through the administration of his Republican successor, William Howard Taft, and into that of President Woodrow Wilson after 1912.

---

[60] Telgs, Sparks to Roosevelt, 1 Feb 08, and Roosevelt to Sparks, 4 Feb 08, AGO Files 1310155A26 and 1310155A27, respectively, RG 94.

[61] Telgs, Roosevelt to Sparks, 6 Feb 08, and reply, 7 Feb 08, AGO Files 1310155A28 and 1310155A32, respectively, RG 94; Telg, Funston to AG, 7 Mar 08, HQ Doc. File, Dept of California, RG 393.

CHAPTER 9

Woodrow Wilson and the Coal Mine Wars, 1914–1915

My constitutional obligations with regards to the maintenance of order in Colorado are not to be indefinitely continued by the inaction of the state legislature. The federal forces are there only until the state of Colorado has time and opportunity to resume complete sovereignty and control in the matter. I cannot conceive that the state is willing to forego her sovereignty or throw herself entirely upon the Government of the United States and I am quite clear that she has no constitutional right to do so when it is within the power of her legislature to take effective action.
—President Woodrow Wilson to Governor Elias M. Ammons, 1914.

The seeming decline in public fears of labor radicalism and the growing public toleration, if not grudging acceptance, of labor unions evident during the Republican administration of Theodore Roosevelt continued throughout the first term of Democratic President Woodrow Wilson after 1912. Like his predecessor, Wilson, through the "new freedom," displayed a more tolerant attitude toward organized labor than his nineteenth-century counterparts and also sought to limit the frequency and scope of federal military interventions in labor and industrial conflicts.[1] In 1914 a coal strike in southeastern Colorado demonstrated clearly how the Army could serve as a neutral and constructive force in labor-related civil disturbances when deployed by a reform-minded administration that was confident of its policies, knowledgeable of the local labor and industrial situation, and certain of the goals federal military intervention was to obtain.

The Colorado Coal Strike, 1914

Since the 1880s, labor unions in southeastern Colorado had waged an unavailing struggle to achieve recognition and better living and working conditions. While major strikes occurred about every ten years, they routinely failed, often disastrously. The state's chief coal firm, the Rockefeller-owned Colorado Fuel and Iron Company, dominated both its smaller competitors and its employees, and like its corporate counterparts elsewhere it repeatedly ignored miner demands. Moreover the company's domination spread far beyond

---

[1] For Wilson's labor policies, see John S. Smith, "Organized Labor and Government in the Wilson Era, 1913–1921: Some Conclusions," *Labor History* 3 (Winter 1962):267; Dallas L. Jones, "The Wilson Administration and Organized Labor, 1912–1919" (Ph.D. diss., Cornell University, 1955).

the mining industry. Controlling 300,000 acres in the richest mining areas of the state, the company wielded social, economic, and political influence throughout Colorado. According to federal investigators, the company used its power to obtain advantages for the corporation and to ruthlessly suppress attempts at union organization. It engaged in wholesale political corruption on local and state levels and blatantly denied miners their basic civil rights.[2]

For many years the 30,000 miners in southern Colorado endured deplorable working and living conditions. During 1901–1902 they suffered 128 fatal and 186 crippling accidents. Owners ignored state-mandated safety regulations and statutes governing mine operations; state mine inspectors, who were few in number and often in the pay of mine managers, rarely enforced safety regulations governing mine operations. Conditions outside the mines were little better. Workers and their families lived in company housing on company land in isolated camps. Housing was substandard and described by one social worker as consisting of "hovels, shacks, and dugouts that are unfit for the habitation of human beings and are little removed from the pigsty make of dwellings."[3] Typhoid and other diseases associated with unsanitary living conditions were common. Independent home ownership was discouraged, and since the company owned all land surrounding the mines few laborers were able to move from the area. The company owned and controlled schools, hospitals, and churches and deductions from miners' wages maintained these, rather than state or local taxes on company property. Workers were paid in scrip that devalued if converted to cash; company stores charged excessive prices for food and other necessities. These company stores were the only such establishments for miles around. Employers controlled nearly every aspect of the lives of miners and their families; immediate dismissal and eviction were the fate of workers found in violation of any policy, in or out of the mines.[4]

Although absentee officials including John D. Rockefeller, Jr., were largely ignorant of the conditions in which their employees worked and lived, they were adamant in their refusal to recognize the unions through which miners hoped to better their lot. Since 1900 the United Mine Workers (UMW) had attempted to gain a foothold in the Colorado camps but was repeatedly thwarted by violent company opposition. On 13 September 1913, the union again voted to go out on strike, following the refusal of coal operators to negotiate reforms that included recognition of the UMW, a 10 percent pay increase, an eight-hour workday, liberation of miners from dependence on company stores and doctors, strict enforcement of Colorado mine laws, and abolition of the mine guard system.[5]

---

[2] Berman, *Labor Disputes and the President*, pp. 76–77; Rich, *President and Civil Disorder*, p. 136; Graham Adams, Jr., *The Age of Industrial Violence, 1910–1915* (New York: Columbia University Press, 1966), pp. 148–51.

[3] Quote from Adams, *Age of Industrial Violence*, pp. 148–51. See also Suggs, "The Colorado Coal Miners' Strike," pp. 36–37. For earlier troubles, see Suggs, *Colorado's War on Militant Unionism*.

[4] Adams, *Age of Industrial Violence*, pp. 148–51; Suggs, "The Colorado Coal Miners' Strike," pp. 36–37.

[5] Ltr, Maj Nathaniel F. McClure, 5th Cavalry, to AG, 31 May 14, Records of the Office of the Adjutant General, U.S. Army, File 2154620: Colorado Coal Field Disorders, RG 94, NARA; Berman, *Labor Disputes and the President*, pp. 77–78; Priscilla Long, "The Voice of the Gun: Colorado's Great Coalfield War of 1913–1914," *Labor's Heritage* 1 (October 1989):4–23; "Colorado Strike," *Survey* 31 (20 December 1913):333–34; Wilson, *Federal Aid in Domestic Disturbances*, p. 312.

The federal government had already taken note of rising tensions in Colorado and attempted to avert a strike. A week before the UMW strike vote, mediator Ethelbert M. Stewart of the Department of Labor had called on Colorado Fuel and Iron Company owner John D. Rockefeller, Jr., in his New York City office in an attempt to reach a settlement.[6] On vacation, Rockefeller instructed a subordinate to meet Stewart and to inform him that New York corporate officials did not interfere with the policies of the local mining executives. Rebuffed but undaunted, Stewart traveled to Colorado to meet with L. M. Bowers, the company superintendent. Bowers adamantly refused to deal with the UMW or hear any talk of mediation, telling Stewart that the company would resist union demands "until our bones are bleached as white as chalk in these Rocky Mountains." Rockefeller agreed publicly with these sentiments. Further efforts by Stewart to bring the dispute to a quick and just conclusion failed as other Colorado mine owners followed Bowers' lead.[7]

JOHN D. ROCKEFELLER, SR., AND JOHN D. ROCKEFELLER, JR., *at the time of the Ludlow Massacre.*

Ten days following the initial strike vote, some 10,000 men put down their tools, collected their families, and moved out of their company-owned housing into tent colonies off company land. In all, thirteen camps were created, the largest of these being located near Ludlow, south of the Arkansas River and east of the Sangre de Cristo Mountains. Ludlow contained about 500 men and 700 women and children. Over twenty-one nationalities were represented among the inhabitants of the camp, although most were Mexicans and southern Europeans. Ethnic animosities and economic grievances led to confrontations between the predominantly Anglo-Saxon company guards, who flooded into the area in large numbers in response to mining company recruitment, and the miners of southern European extraction. Violence intensified, resulting in the deaths of several strikers.[8]

---

[6] The Department of Labor was created in 1913 when the ten-year-old Department of Commerce and Labor was divided and made into two cabinet-level agencies. The first labor secretary was William B. Wilson, a former UMW member. See Roger Babson, *W. W. B. Wilson and the Department of Labor* (New York: Bretano's, 1919). For the efforts made to avoid a strike, see Billie B. Jensen, "Woodrow Wilson's Intervention in the Coal Strike of 1914," *Labor History* 15 (1974):63–77.

[7] Berman, *Labor Disputes and the President*, pp. 79–80.

[8] Ltr, McClure to AG, 31 May 14, File 2154620, RG 94; Wilson, *Federal Aid in Domestic Disturbances*, p. 312; Alvin R. Sunseri, "The Ludlow Massacre: A Study in the Misemployment of the National Guard," *American Chronicle* 1 (January 1972):23.

WILLIAM B. WILSON

In response, Democratic Governor Elias M. Ammons, who had also failed to persuade the mine companies to settle, decided to intervene. In late October 1913 he called out the Colorado National Guard and sent his adjutant general, Maj. Gen. John Chase, to the strike area with instructions to use any means deemed necessary and proper, either in cooperation with or independent of civil authorities, to enforce obedience to the constitution and laws of the state. Chase interpreted the phrase "independent of civil authorities" as giving him the unilateral authority to declare martial law and he immediately set up a "Military District of Colorado" in Huerfano and Las Animas Counties, designating himself as its commanding general.[9]

Initially, Chase used his command of 700 men to disarm troublemakers among the ranks of both striking miners and company men, and to deny strikebreakers entry into the region. Most of the weapons were taken from company guards, for the miners were very reluctant to surrender what they believed to be their only protection. Nonetheless, according to Chase's testimony, the guardsmen apparently were welcomed by both sides. His personal sympathies, however, and those of the majority of his command soon changed, at least in part because no public funds were available to pay them and because of ethnic differences with the striking miners. The Colorado National Guard on duty in the Ludlow area was gradually transformed into an antilabor force; imported strikebreakers were protected by guardsmen at the direction of company managers, and large numbers of strikers were arbitrarily arrested and held incommunicado without benefit of legal counsel.

The next development occurred when state troops—mainly professionals, college students, and businessmen—began to return to civilian status after completing their tours of duty. Many were replaced by adventurers, soldiers of fortune, or full-time mine guards, simultaneously in the pay of the Colorado Fuel and Iron Company and the state of Colorado. These newer troops watched passively as detectives harassed strikers and the residents of the tent colonies. State troops were not only financed by the Colorado

---

[9] Wilson, *Federal Aid in Domestic Disturbances*, p. 312; George S. McGovern and Leonard File Guttridge, *The Great Coalfield War* (Boston: Houghton Mifflin, 1972), p. 134; Adams, *Age of Industrial Violence*, pp. 152–54. On the Colorado National Guard, see John Case, "The Military Occupation of the Coal Strike Zone of Colorado by the Colorado National Guard, 1913–1914" (Denver 1914), in Leon Stein and Philip Taft, eds., *Massacre at Ludlow: Four Reports* (New York: Arno, 1971); Alan M. Osur, "The Role of the Colorado Guard in Civil Disturbances," *Military Affairs* 46 (February 1982):19–24; "Colorado Coal Strike," *Literary Digest* 48 (7 February 1914):247–48.

Fuel and Iron Company but were housed in company buildings, allowed free use of company-owned horses and vehicles, and issued supplies from company stores. "The Colorado Fuel and Iron Company actually paid the National Guard from $75,000 to $80,000 on certificates of indebtedness bearing interest collectible from the State," serving as "both commissary and paymaster."[10]

Still short of funds and encouraged that no large-scale violence had occurred, Ammons began to withdraw his forces in April 1914, amid heavy criticisms concerning Chase's increasingly Draconian tactics. Two hundred guardsmen were left behind to maintain the uneasy peace. But Ammons' plans for restoring order in southeastern Colorado with the limited number of state troops still there failed as new violence erupted in the so-called Ludlow Massacre of 20 April 1914.[11]

Acting on an anonymous tip that a nonunion miner was being held hostage by strikers in the Ludlow colony, a guard commander, Maj. Patrick Hamrock, ordered 1st Lt. Karl E. Linderfelt to take forty men to the colony to investigate. On arrival, Linderfelt, fearful that his men would be overrun in any attack, ordered soldiers to man a machine gun on a hilltop overlooking the Ludlow colony. Mistaking this show of force as preparation for an assault, the strikers grabbed their rifles and scattered to the cover of nearby ditches and boulders.[12] In turn, this movement by the miners was misinterpreted by the guardsmen, who were now convinced that an attack upon them was imminent. No one knows who fired the first shot; but as sporadic gunfire broke out and several explosions accompanied it, Linderfelt ordered the machine gunners to open fire. A day-long gun battle resulted. Vastly outgunned, the miners were eventually overwhelmed by the guardsmen and forced to flee their colony. The guard swept in, setting fire to the tents in an effort to drive into the open any armed strikers who remained. Amid widespread looting by guardsmen, the fires spread rapidly and, in one case, asphyxiated a group of women and children huddled for safety in a pit beneath the floor of a flaming tent. Estimates of the number of dead ranged from 16 to 77, including Louis Tikas, the strike leader, with over 200 miners and members of their families missing. A subsequent report by a state military commission disclosed numerous cases of brutality, arson, and looting by guardsmen, most of whom were also employees of the Colorado Fuel and Iron Company.[13]

When word of the Ludlow Massacre spread to surrounding communities, enraged miners attacked mining company property and employees throughout the region. Armed groups of workers seized control of the communities of Ludlow and Trinidad and burned and dynamited all mine property in sight. For ten days in late April hundreds of miners, company guards, and state troops clashed at Forbes, Delagua, Aguilar, Hastings, and Black

---

[10] Quote from Sunseri, "Ludlow Massacre," pp. 24–25. See also McGovern and Guttridge, *Great Coalfield War*, p. 134; Rich, *President and Civil Disorder*, p. 137.

[11] McGovern and Guttridge, *Great Coalfield War*, p. 134; Rich, *President and Civil Disorder*, p. 137.

[12] McGovern and Guttridge, *Great Coalfield War*, pp. 210–31; Wilson, *Federal Aid in Domestic Disturbances*, p. 312; Adams, *Age of Industrial Violence*, p. 157.

[13] McGovern and Guttridge, *Great Coalfield War*, pp. 210–31; Jensen, "Woodrow Wilson's Intervention," p. 70; Sunseri, "Ludlow Massacre," p. 27. See also Ltr, McClure to AG, 31 May 14, File 2154620, RG 94; Adams, *Age of Industrial Violence*, pp. 160–61. For contemporary views, see "Tent Colony Swept by Machine Guns," *Survey* 32 (2 May 1914):108–10; "Colorado Slaughter," *Literary Digest* 48 (2 May 1914):1033–34; "Comment on Colorado by Those Who Know," *Literary Digest* 48 (16 May 1914):1163–65; "Colorado Puzzle," *Nation* 98 (7 May 1914):517–18; "Hitch in Colorado Peace Plan," *Outlook* 107 (9 May 1914):49.

Hills in gunfights that claimed the lives of at least eleven mine guards and strikebreakers. Anarchy and violence threatened to engulf the entire state.[14]

The deaths at the hands of the Colorado National Guard and the outbreak of open warfare deeply shocked the citizens of the state.[15] On 25 April 1914, 1,000 members of the Women's Peace Association marched to the Denver State House and demanded that Ammons call for federal troops to restore order. He made the request that night, based upon Article IV, Section 4, of the Constitution, as defined by RS 5297. He stated that over 3,000 armed men were transforming parts of Colorado into a no-man's-land and that he could not hope to restore order with the meager law enforcement resources at his disposal. The state legislature could not be convened in time to take action, he continued, and federal cavalry and infantry units were urgently needed.[16]

President Wilson had troops available, but revolution and civil war had been raging through Mexico for over a year and threatened not only U.S. interests but also U.S. borders. Marines had already occupied Vera Cruz, and Army commanders in the Southwest were seeking reinforcements to thwart forays by bandits and revolutionaries, such as Pancho Villa, fearing a general uprising by Mexican-Americans on the northern side of the border.[17] Hence Wilson made an effort to end the crisis without military action. In late April he met with Congressman Martin Foster of Illinois, chairman of the House Committee on Mines and Mining, and with Colorado's congressional delegation. Wilson asked Foster to speak to Rockefeller about possible company concessions that might end the disorders. The magnate, however, flatly refused to consider any type of negotiated settlement involving union recognition. His attitude finally convinced Wilson that federal troops had to be dispatched to Colorado.[18]

Upon learning of Ammons' request, Secretary of War Lindley M. Garrison offered Wilson some practical advice on how to employ the regulars. He believed that the commander should be instructed to observe strict neutrality between the belligerents and to take vigorous measures for speedy results. Above all, he told Wilson, the federal commander should relieve the state National Guard, which "tended to provoke rather than allay disorder." To avoid wounding sensibilities concerning state sovereignty, however, Garrison advised Wilson to say only that such action was taken because "it would be confusing to have two military forces operating under separate sources of control."[19]

On 28 April Wilson decided on federal military intervention under authority granted by Article IV, Section 4, of the Constitution, and RS 5297 and informed Ammons later that day

---

[14] McGovern and Guttridge, *Great Coalfield War*, pp. 210–31; Ltr, McClure to AG, 31 May 14, File 2154620, RG 94; Adams, *Age of Industrial Violence*, pp. 160–61.

[15] See Elias Ammons, "Colorado Strike," *North American Review* 200 (July 1914):35–44; "Colorado Labor Conflict," *Independent* 79 (6 July 1914):37; C. Holmes, "Colorado Plays the Red Game," *Technical World* 21 (July 1914):648–53.

[16] McGovern and Guttridge, *Great Coalfield War*, pp. 251–52; Wilson, *Federal Aid in Domestic Disturbances*, pp. 312–13; "Colorado Appeals to President for Help," *Current Opinion* 56 (June 1914):413–16. Ammons did not mention that partisan actions by the National Guard, such as at Ludlow, had largely been responsible for triggering the violence.

[17] Telg, Bliss to Garrison, quoted in Ltr, Garrison to Wilson, 23 Apr 14, in Letterbook, item 77, RG 107, Records of the Office of the Secretary of War, NARA. See also Clarence C. Clendenen, *Blood on the Border: The United States Army and the Mexican Irregulars* (London: Macmillan, 1969), pp. 180–82.

[18] Rich, *President and Civil Disorder*, p. 140; Berman, *Labor Disputes and the President*, pp. 87–89.

[19] McGovern and Guttridge, *Great Coalfield War*, p. 262.

that troops were being sent. He advised Ammons that the regulars would neither take sides in the controversy nor permit anybody to contribute to the disorder. If the strike was defeated, it would not be because of the activities of federal troops. He made it known further to the UMW and the Colorado Fuel and Iron Company that they would be held strictly accountable for criminal acts by their agents. Following the dispatch of his message to the governor, Wilson issued the required proclamation warning lawless parties against aiding, countenancing, abetting, or taking part in such unlawful proceedings and ordering such persons to disperse and retire peaceably to their respective abodes on or before 30 April.[20]

Agreeing with Garrison's assessment that Colorado National Guardsmen tended to provoke hostilities rather than allay them, Wilson asked Ammons to withdraw all state forces from the strike area as soon as federal

LINDLEY M. GARRISON

troops arrived. He also followed Garrison's advice and explained that it was "disadvantageous to have two military forces under separate sources of control within the same localities." Wilson, like all his predecessors since the Civil War, with the exception of Hayes, apparently never considered the possibility of federalizing the Colorado National Guard for further duty in the strike zone. His decision was both political and military, fully supported by a Supreme Court decision, *in re Debs* (1894), that when the president accedes to a formal request for military aid he assumes full power to restore order by any and all means he may deem necessary. He continued the trend, in effect since the Civil War, of relying on the more disciplined regular forces in domestic disorders, rather than state forces of unknown quality.[21]

Wilson intended to send troops from the newly organized Central Department. In 1913 the Army's more then 92,000 troops had been reapportioned among six continental and overseas departments—Central, Eastern, Southern, Western, Philippine, and Hawaiian. From his headquarters in Chicago, the commander of the Central Department held responsibility for all the midwestern states, including the two Dakotas, Missouri, Kansas, Wyoming, and Colorado. At the time of the Ludlow Massacre, however, the commander of the Central Department was absent, and control of Colorado operations rested in the hands of the Army chief of staff, Maj. Gen. W. W. Witherspoon.[22]

---

[20] The proclamation is found in Wilson, *Federal Aid in Domestic Disturbances*, app. B, p. 319. See also Telg, War Dept to Postmaster, Trinidad, Colo., 28 Apr 14, File 2154620, RG 94, NARA; Rich, *President and Civil Disorder*, p. 141.

[21] Rich, *President and Civil Disorder*, p. 146.

[22] U.S. War Department, *Annual Report of the Secretary of War, 1913* (Washington, D.C.: Government Printing Office, 1913), GO 9, 9 Feb 13, p. 223; Telg, AG to McClure, 28 Apr 14, File 2154620, RG 94, NARA.

COLORADO NATIONAL GUARDSMEN OUTSIDE A LUDLOW SALOON

Witherspoon promptly recommended to Garrison that Maj. Willard A. Holbrook, 10th Cavalry—a trusted former subordinate temporarily in command of the Army Service Schools at Fort Leavenworth, Kansas—be appointed to lead the Army expedition into Colorado. Impressed by Holbrook's previous record as a provincial military governor in the Philippines, Garrison approved the choice.[23]

Holbrook was ordered to take the 2d Squadron, 5th Cavalry, and two troops of the 12th Cavalry from Fort Leavenworth and secretly proceed to Trinidad, Colorado, a town thirteen miles south of Ludlow. A smaller force, commanded by Maj. Nathaniel McClure, 5th Cavalry, was to proceed from Fort Russell, Wyoming, to Cannon City, Colorado, another trouble spot in the mining district. Holbrook's command numbered 350 men, McClure's 150.[24]

Lacking an experienced commander to oversee what could become a politically explosive situation, Secretary Garrison decided to manage the crisis personally. The mountainous terrain of the strike zone also dictated control from Washington, for isolated units were able to communicate faster by telegraph with Washington, D.C., than with each other by means of horses or vehicles, especially after spring thaws transformed mountain roads into muddy quagmires. Thus Garrison bypassed the traditional chain of command, communicating directly with the local field commanders and allowing them to exercise the same privilege in return.[25]

---

[23] Telg, AG to CO, Ft. Leavenworth, 28 Apr 14, File 2154620, RG 94, NARA.

[24] Memo, CofS, USA, for AG, USA, 28 Apr 14, and Telg, AG, USA, to CO, Ft. Leavenworth, 28 Apr 14, both in File 2154620, RG 94, NARA.

[25] Ltr, Garrison to Dir, U.S. Commission on Industrial Relations, 15 Jul 15, File 2154620, RG 94, NARA; Wilson, *Federal Aid in Domestic Disturbances*, pp. 312–13.

Above all, Garrison wanted to keep control of the situation and not exacerbate tensions by injecting a new armed force. On 28 April he instructed Holbrook, McClure, and their subordinate commanders to suppress domestic violence by disarming belligerents and ejecting troublemakers on both sides and to report the names of potential troublemakers to Washington. However, they were to await more precise instructions before conducting any large-scale operations. Regarding measures taken thus far in the crisis by state civil and military authorities, Garrison gave local Army commanders wide latitude to enforce or ignore them, telling the officers that "the measure of your authority is what necessity dictates."[26]

As General Schofield had done in 1894, Garrison conscientiously and clearly explained to his military subordinates the nature of the civil-military relationship in the disorders. Whenever possible the military was to act in support of civil authorities—for example, turning suspects the military had apprehended over to civil authorities for incarceration and trial. However, should the state begin releasing known troublemakers, the Army was to halt further transfers of custody. If the state courts issued writs of habeas corpus ordering release of such prisoners, the commanders could ignore those writs. The same privilege did not pertain with respect to federal writs.[27]

Meanwhile, sleet covered Trinidad, as Holbrook's squadron entered town. Holbrook welcomed the dismal weather, believing that it would "dampen the fervor of the strikers . . . and provide a breathing spell." To his complete surprise, however, many Trinidad citizens and strikers from Ludlow braved the weather to welcome the arriving troops. Both sides had grown tired of the violence and looked to Holbrook's force to restore peace. Capitalizing on this initial display of goodwill, Holbrook met with strike leaders, mine owners, civic officials, and, by telephone, with Ammons. In each case he promised, as a neutral intermediary, that he would restore order.[28]

Within five days federal units moved to most of the sixty-odd mines surrounding Trinidad and Ludlow, replacing Colorado National Guard units that were still on duty in the mining camps. In some cases, acting under recall instructions from Ammons, National Guardsmen had been withdrawn before the federal troops had even arrived, while elsewhere Holbrook's men relieved units of the guard whose usefulness had been compromised by the Ludlow Massacre. From the beginning the policy of replacing the guardsmen, rather than working with them, did much to reassure the strikers of Army efforts to guarantee neutrality.[29]

Without Colorado guardsmen, however, Holbrook and McClure faced the nearly impossible task of policing 400 square miles of rugged terrain with less than 500 men. Mountains made joint assistance between troops at mining camps difficult; even when two mines were only a couple of miles distant by air, they might be fifteen miles apart by road.

---

[26] Quote from Wilson, *Federal Aid in Domestic Disturbances*, p. 313. See also McGovern and Guttridge, *Great Coalfield War*, p. 267; Rich, *President and Civil Disorder*, pp. 141–43; Telg, AG to CO, Ft. Logan, Colo., 2 May 14, File 2154620, RG 94, NARA.

[27] Ltr of Instruction (LOI), Garrison to CO, Colo. (accompanying proclamation and letter to Ammons), 28 Apr 14, File 2154620, RG 94, NARA.

[28] Ltr, Holbrook to AG, 30 Apr 14, File 2154620, RG 94, NARA.

[29] Telg, Holbrook to AG, 2 May 14, File 2154620, RG 94, NARA; see also Rich, *President and Civil Disorder*, pp. 142, 150.

On 1 May 1914, Holbrook estimated that at least 500 additional troops would be needed. In response, Garrison ordered the entire 11th Cavalry, over 800 men commanded by Lt. Col. James Lockett, from Fort Oglethorpe, Georgia, to Colorado. New disorders north of Denver further prompted Garrison to call in an additional five troops of cavalry and a machine-gun platoon from Fort Robinson, Nebraska, and Fort Wingate, New Mexico. Within two weeks over 1,700 federal troops from the 5th, 11th, and 12th Cavalry regiments were on duty in Colorado coalfields.[30]

Federal commanders in Colorado were given wide latitude by Wilson and Garrison to effect policies that would quickly restore order. They were authorized to aid in the enforcement of state martial law, already declared by Ammons, by disarming belligerents, closing saloons, and rigidly controlling the admission and movements of union agitators and company strikebreakers. Disarming potential opponents, however, was the most difficult task faced by the Army. Holbrook's Trinidad District alone contained 1,300 armed company guards and nearly as many armed strikers. Past dealings with the Colorado National Guard and company guards made miners most reluctant to give up their arms, even to a federal force, the neutrality of which the strikers acknowledged.[31]

As the first troops arrived, Garrison provided their commanders with the text of Wilson's proclamation and with instructions to inform the affected populace that the president was calling for all individuals, firms, associations, and corporations to deliver their arms to local military headquarters in Trinidad, Cannon City, or Louisville, north of Denver. All weapons collected were labeled as to ownership and shipped to Fort Logan, Colorado, for storage and eventual return to the owners. By 3 May the miners had surrendered a sizable number of old weapons that were quickly replaced with newer models, especially in the Trinidad-Ludlow region. Holbrook asked Garrison to use the Secret Service or "some agency more sophisticated [in detecting smuggling operations] than the Army . . . to stop the flow of arms." The secretary, however, preferred to keep non-Army agencies out of the Colorado operation and denied the request.[32] To counter the claims of mine company paymasters and strikebreakers that they must carry weapons in the strike zone on payday, Holbrook assigned troops to guard payroll shipments and offices. He recommended also to Garrison that after a certain date troops should be permitted to disarm anyone openly carrying arms. Garrison promised to consider the suggestion.[33]

Leading the 11th Cavalry from Fort Oglethorpe, Georgia, on 5 May Lockett entered Trinidad and assumed overall command of federal forces. When Holbrook explained to him that most miners still had weapons despite the 5,000 turned in, Lockett issued a new proclamation demanding that all parties surrender their weapons, for "the president of the United States must be obeyed. We have soldiers and officers to see that he is obeyed." In

---

[30] Wilson, *Federal Aid in Domestic Disturbances*, pp. 313–14; see also Memo for CofS, USA, 31 Jul 14, File 2154620, RG 94, NARA; McGovern and Guttridge, *Great Coalfield War*, p. 267; William Grimes, "The Cavalry on Strike Duty in Colorado," *Cavalry Journal* (1915):473.

[31] Wilson, *Federal Aid in Domestic Disturbances*, pp. 313–14; Rich, *President and Civil Disorder*, pp. 141–43, 209–10.

[32] For quote, see Telg, Holbrook to Garrison, 3 May 14; see also Telg, Garrison to McClure, 1 May 14; Memo, Bliss, ACofS, for Garrison, 12 Mar 15; Telg, Wood to Greene, Central Dept, 4 May 14. All in File 2154620, RG 94, NARA.

[33] Telgs, Holbrook to Garrison, 3 May 14, and Wood to Greene, Central Dept, 4 May 14, both in File 2154620, RG 94; Telg, McClure to AG, 5 May 14, quoted in Ltr, Garrison to Wilson, Ltrbk, item 77, RG 107.

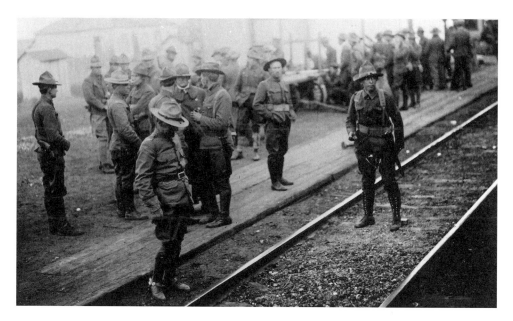

JAMES LOCKETT *(left foreground)* WITH TROOPS OF THE 11TH CAVALRY

support, Garrison approved McClure's prior suggestion and authorized disarmament of all persons openly carrying arms.[34]

Following the new proclamation, Holbrook took pains to explain the government's policy to miners at Trinidad and nearby Starkville. Strike leaders in return assured him of their goodwill and willingness to comply, and in proof of their good faith they signed an order to have 300 rifles and 60,000 rounds of ammunition coming by rail from New York turned over to Army officials. Despite their leaders' promises of cooperation, many miners continued to keep weapons, apparently still fearing reprisals from state troops and company guards after the Army withdrew. Lockett, unwilling to make exceptions or tolerate defiance of federal orders, sought permission from Garrison on 11 May to search houses and other buildings suspected of concealing arms caches. The secretary, however, was certain that such actions would result in claims from labor leaders that federal troops, like the Colorado National Guard before them, were taking sides against strikers, and denied the request. Though Holbrook and the other commanders had failed to effect total disarmament, their efforts were not entirely in vain. Both sides hid their weapons and adopted a far more peaceable demeanor than they had shown before the arrival of the regulars.[35]

While steadfast in his refusal to allow troops to search private dwellings for arms, on 7 May Garrison did respond favorably to Army requests for authority to close saloons and

---

[34] Quote from Rich, *President and Civil Disorder*, p. 144. See also Memo, CofS for AG, 2 May 14; Telgs, Lockett to AG, and McClure to AG, 5 May 14; all in File 2154620, RG 94, NARA. Wilson, *Federal Aid in Domestic Disturbances*, p. 314.

[35] Telgs, Lockett to Garrison, 6 and 11 May 14; Ltr, C. A. Frederick, the *Montezuma Journal*, Cortez, Colo., to Garrison, 12 May 14; Telgs, Holbrook to Garrison, 18 May and 20 Jul 14; all in File 2154620, RG 94, NARA.

OFF-LOADING EQUIPMENT IN TRINIDAD, COLORADO, MAY 1914

hotel bars. From May until December 1914, soldiers forbade liquor sales, inventoried liquor stocks, posted security seals upon doors of saloons, and prevented owners from removing stock. When a saloon keeper complained to President Wilson in September that he saw no connection between such actions and the coal strike, Garrison reminded the president that Ammons had previously instituted prohibition as a short-term method of defusing tempers and preventing violence on both sides. The liquor ban remained in effect.[36]

The government's neutral approach to affairs in Colorado was effectively displayed when mining companies decided to reopen the pits with strikebreakers. Such an event, Garrison was convinced, would immediately bring miners into bloody confrontations with strikebreakers and company guards, risking the collapse of everything gained thus far. Lockett recommended a possible solution when he suggested that all mines idled when the strike began—primarily mines where union activity had been the strongest—should not be reopened. He recommended reopening only those largely nonunion mines that were in operation on 20 April 1914, where nonunion workers had been driven off at gunpoint by strikers irate over the Ludlow Massacre. Garrison did not share Lockett's optimism that such a plan would work and took a simpler line. In a decision that greatly displeased the Colorado Fuel and Iron Company, he refused to allow any mines to reopen and forbade strikebreakers to enter the region. Seeking to maintain complete neutrality, he also angered strikers by forbidding union organizers to enter the coalfields. On 11 May Lockett carried out both decisions by drawing up a list of miners who had been working when the strike

---

[36] Telg, Lockett to Garrison, 7 May 14; Ltr, G. Hall to Garrison, 9 Sep 14; Memo, CofS for AG, 27 Nov 14; all in File 2154620, RG 94, NARA. See also Ltr, Garrison to Wilson, 7 May 14, Ltrbk, item 77, RG 107.

FEDERAL CAVALRYMEN ON PATROL IN THE TRINIDAD AREA, C. MAY 1914

began in September 1913. Anyone not on the list who was found working in a mine or living in a tent colony was to be sent on the next train to Denver.[37]

Congressional spokesmen, in support of either labor or business interests, severely criticized the government policy. On 11 June, Oklahoma Democratic Senator Robert L. Owen relayed to Garrison the complaint of a labor leader that Lockett had refused six union organizers entry into the Trinidad area, news that indicated to the secretary that his orders were being carried out. Following further reports that union organizers might try to renew hostilities, Garrison became even more convinced that banning both labor organizers and strikebreakers from the region was a necessary and prudent policy that should be continued. Protests also continued: in early August Colorado Democratic Congressman George J. Kindel criticized the federal ban on new hiring by coal companies; later in the month, UMW's Frank Hayes similarly protested to the War Department that local Army commanders were allowing the Colorado Fuel and Iron Company to recruit and import nonunion workers. General Witherspoon denied Hayes' accusation, and the ban on activities by both sides continued in force.[38]

Yet the indefinite presence of the Army as a governing body in the strike-plagued mining districts made the administration increasingly vulnerable to criticism and made the president personally uneasy about the effects that the occupation could have upon the balance of power within the federal system. Wilson had no intention of leaving a permanent garrison in southeastern Colorado and, in late May, when a special session of the Colorado

---

[37] Memo for CofS, 31 Jul 14, File 2154620, RG 94; Rich, *President and Civil Disorder*, p. 145.

[38] Quote from Rich, *President and Civil Disorder*, p. 146. See also Ltrs, Owen to Garrison, 11 Jun 14, and McClure to Garrison, 28 Jul 14; Telg, Hayes to Garrison, 27 Aug 14, and reply, 4 Sep 14; all in File 2154620, RG 94, NARA. Wilson, *Federal Aid in Domestic Disturbances*, p. 315.

legislature prepared to adjourn without providing for resumption of state control, Wilson criticized Ammons and the lawmakers for undermining the sovereignty of their own state. In the strike zone at least one commander shared the president's concern. On 20 July Holbrook reported that his "troops had had no trouble with mobs, yet. . . . The Commonwealth of Colorado had apparently lost all pride of power and does not intend to assume charge of the strike situation so long as the United States can be induced to retain control." Holbrook foresaw prolonged military occupation because no progress had been made toward solving the main issue of the strike: miner demands for union recognition, higher wages, and better living and working conditions. Matters looked different from the viewpoint of harried state officials. The legislature approved a one-million-dollar bond issue to obtain the necessary funds to rebuild the Colorado National Guard and regain control of southern Colorado. But the bonds were slow to sell, and the state had no recourse other than to continue to rely on federal forces.[39]

Meanwhile, federally sponsored mediation efforts to settle the coal strike continued. On the day following the arrival of federal troops, Wilson sent the president of the Kentucky Coal Operators Association and a representative of the UMW to Colorado to study the situation and propose a settlement plan. Their proposal, submitted on 5 September 1914, called for a three-year truce, the enforcement of state mining laws, the rehiring of all employees on strike, the creation of employee grievance committees, the firing of mine guards, the end to strikes for the duration of the truce, and the prohibition of other demonstrations on the part of workers during the truce. While the report and its provisions were accepted in toto by a convention of striking miners in Trinidad, the mine operators, led by the Colorado Fuel and Iron Company, accepted only those parts covered by Colorado or federal statute and rejected the rest. By mid-October 1914 Wilson had given up all hope that the plan would be accepted.[40]

By then it had become apparent that the strike was weakening. Economically devastated and desperate miners deserted union ranks and returned to the mines. In October 1914 Ammons reported that he was working with the legislature to hasten the time when the Colorado National Guard could resume peacekeeping duties. Public desires for the withdrawal of federal forces grew in the late summer and early fall of 1914. The Oak Creek, Colorado, Chamber of Commerce telegraphed Garrison and declared that "the presence of Federal troops here is a detriment to the community. Everything here is peaceable. No danger [exists] of present or future trouble on account of coal miners' strike. . . . Request withdrawal of troops from Oak Creek as there is absolutely no necessity for them to remain."[41]

While Ammons reorganized the guard, replacing officers known to be resented by the strikers, on 30 November Wilson appointed another commission to arbitrate the disputes between the Colorado Fuel and Iron Company and the United Mine Workers. On 8

[39] Quote from Ltr, Holbrook to Garrison, 20 Jul 14, File 2154620, RG 94. See also Rich, *President and Civil Disorder*, p. 146; Berman, *Labor Disputes and the President*, pp. 92–93; "Colorado Asked To Pacify Itself," *Literary Digest* 49 (19 September 1914):498; "Colorado Problem," *Nation* 99 (1 October 1914):397; "Mining War in Colorado," *Outlook* 108 (30 September 1914):237.

[40] Berman, *Labor Disputes and the President*, pp. 93–96.

[41] Ltr, Holbrook to Garrison, 4 Aug 14; quote from Telg, C. B. Haffee, Oak Creek, Colo., Chamber of Commerce, to Garrison, 15 Oct 14; both in File 2154620, RG 94, NARA. See also Rich, *President and Civil Disorder*, pp. 148–49.

December, however, the UMW executive board voted to end the strike. Relieved, both Ammons and Wilson made preliminary plans for the phased withdrawal of federal troops. Each day between 5 and 10 January, federal military units broke camp and moved to railroad depots for the return to their home stations, first from Routt County and the Louisville District north of Denver, then from Cannon City, and finally from Trinidad.[42]

The most objective view of the Army's eight months in Colorado came during an investigation in 1915 by the U.S. Commission on Industrial Relations. In a letter to Garrison on 28 June 1915, Director Basil M. Manly admitted to having been "greatly impressed by the celerity with which the Federal troops established order in Colorado, and also by the fact that both parties to the dispute were apparently satisfied that the actions taken . . . were wise and impartial." Manly attributed the Army's success to the immediate closing of saloons and to restrictions on the movement of strikebreakers. Commenting on the extent to which the president had restored the Army's reputation for neutrality, Manly added that "this has not been true in all cases (especially under Presidents Cleveland and McKinley) in which Federal troops have been sent into the field in connection with industrial disputes."[43]

The Colorado Coal Strike of 1914 was noteworthy in the history of federal military intervention involving labor disputes in several respects. Partisan and unprofessional conduct on the part of an ill-disciplined Colorado National Guard force, although not without precedent, had culminated in the Ludlow Massacre and led directly to U.S. Army intervention. The Army, however, unlike in previous labor-related interventions, would not collaborate closely with the guardsmen who were often active antagonists in the disputes federal troops had been sent to quell. Hence, for the first time in a case in which the state asked for federal aid, federal commanders requested and effected the removal of state forces from an area of civil unrest. Once state troops had withdrawn, the Army set out to restore order on its own. Suppression of lawlessness in Colorado became strictly a federal matter.

Given the mountainous terrain, the conventional chain of command yielded to direct communications between small unit commanders and the War Department. In addition, and at a higher level, the president, the secretary of war, and representatives of the fledgling Department of Labor directly involved themselves in the settlement of the disputes and remained in touch with events until the strike and its attendant disorders ceased to exist. With the approval of the president, Secretary Garrison allowed local Army commanders to continue to implement the various police measures first imposed by Colorado National Guardsmen during the period of state-administered martial law. Under nonpartisan federal military control, the measures eventually succeeded. Finally, the federal policy of disarming all citizens and controlling entry into the troubled counties not only prevented confrontations, but served notice to both sides that the Army was neutral and objective

---

[42] Telgs, Breckenridge to Garrison, 29 Dec 14; and COs, Colo., to AG, 5–10 Jan 15; all in File 2154620, RG 94, NARA. See also Rich, *President and Civil Disorder*, p. 149; Berman, *Labor Disputes and the President*, pp. 96–97; Howard M. Gitelman, *Legacy of the Ludlow Massacre: A Chapter in American Industrial Relations* (Philadelphia: University of Pennsylvania Press, 1988); "J. D. Rockefeller, Jr., Puts Over His Industrial Peace Plan With Colorado Miners," *Current Opinion* 59 (December 1914):415–16.

[43] Ltr, Manly to Garrison, 28 Jun 15, File 2154620, RG 94, NARA. For the commission's findings, see George P. West, *Report on the Colorado Strike* (Washington, D.C.: U.S. Commission on Industrial Relations, 1915).

in all its dealings with both sides. The burden of martial law, however, even the undeclared, modified variety, bore heavily upon Wilson, who exerted substantial pressure on Ammons, with some success, to resume state civil government control.

Prairie Creek, Arkansas, 1914

While Regular Army troops restored order in southeastern Colorado, a new disturbance involving coal mines under federal receivership broke out in western Arkansas' Sebastian County. When the halfhearted efforts of local and state civil officials failed to protect mine property and operators from violence, President Wilson intervened without an official state request for troops. By the time federal forces reached Sebastian County, however, the disorder had lessened to the extent that only a small, short-term military presence was required.[44]

Near Prairie Creek, Arkansas, thirty-four miles south of Fort Smith, the Bache-Denman Mining Company, a corporation owning eight mines within a six-mile radius, had unilaterally discarded its closed-shop agreement with the UMW and reopened its mines with nonunion workers. When striking workers seized the financially troubled mines, on 15 May 1914 Judge Frank A. Youmans of the Western Federal District of Arkansas enjoined the UMW against continued interference with company operations. The miners ignored the court order, and in July they became involved in a gun battle with company guards that seriously damaged six of the eight mines and caused $400,000 in damage. Youmans responded by placing the now insolvent company in federal receivership.[45]

Undaunted by the ramifications of federal receivership, on 28 October 1914 striking miners assaulted nonunion workers and company guards. Two days after driving out nonunion workers and U.S. Deputy Marshal Thomas Black at gunpoint, the strikers converged on Hartford, Arkansas, where they forced Black to free the three prisoners most closely connected with the dispute. During this crisis, Arkansas Governor George W. Hayes did not send state troops, nor did he ask the federal government for help, claiming that he had received no such requests from county officials, the federal marshal, or his deputies.[46]

Informed of uncontrolled lawlessness in western Arkansas, Attorney General Thomas W. Gregory proposed federal military intervention as a solution to the crisis. Since Hayes had not requested aid to suppress insurrection or domestic violence, Gregory turned to another basis for intervention, RS 5298, concerning enforcement of federal laws. Ordinarily attacks upon private property were a state offense outside federal authority. However, when Youmans declared the Bache-Denman Mining Company to be under federal receivership, he transformed attacks against the company into attacks against the property of the federal government and therefore into violations of federal law. Gregory's action

---

[44] Ltr, G. W. Hayes, Little Rock, Ark., 4 Dec 14, Papers of Ethelbert Stewart Relating to the Arkansas Strike, 1914, RG 257, Records of the Bureau of Labor Statistics, NARA.

[45] "Why U.S. Troops Are Coming to Prairie Creek," *Fort Smith (Arkansas) Times Record*, 4 Nov 14; Ltr, McClure to AG, 11 Nov 14, File 2225415: Disturbance at Prairie Creek, Ark., Nov 1914–Feb 1915, RG 94, NARA.

[46] Ltr, McClure to AG, 11 Nov 14, File 2225415, RG 94, NARA; Ltr, Hayes to J. C. Clary, Comm of Labor, 4 Dec 14, Papers of Ethelbert Stewart, RG 257, NARA.

was neither unique nor unusual. The precedent for using federal troops for protecting property under federal receivership had a long history dating from the railroad labor disputes in 1877 and 1894.[47]

Since a federal receivership had already been established, Garrison informed Gregory that the next step in obtaining federal troops was to have deputy U.S. marshals in the afflicted area verify that they were unable to enforce the federal court injunctions. Garrison suggested that Gregory follow the procedure used in the 1894 Pullman Strike by having a local federal judge, a deputy U.S. marshal, and a representative of the attorney general's office jointly attest that court orders could not be enforced. Taking this advice, Gregory sent a special representative to Prairie Creek to meet with Youmans and the deputy U.S. marshal. By 2 November all three federal officials affirmed that the resistance of nearly 5,000 armed miners made the injunction unenforceable and recommended the deployment of federal troops.[48]

With the Colorado coalfields now quiet and under federal military control, Wilson approved Garrison's proposal to transfer the experienced Major McClure from Cannon City, Colorado, to Fort Smith, Arkansas. At Fort Smith, Garrison instructed McClure to take charge of the 1st Squadron, 5th Cavalry, and a machine-gun platoon sent from Fort Sheridan, Illinois. Once in Arkansas, McClure was instructed to assist the deputy U.S. marshal in protecting property "under the care of the United States District Court." After three days marked by logistical mishaps and communications breakdowns in Chicago, 12 officers and 270 men left for Arkansas. McClure's command met these troops at Fort Smith on 6 November.[49]

By 3 November President Wilson had already issued the proclamation required by RS 5300 to the residents of Sebastian County. Not since President Cleveland's 8 July 1894 proclamation to the city of Chicago during the Pullman Strike had a president issued so stern a warning. Like Cleveland, Wilson categorized those strikers who destroyed property under federal receivership as "public enemies." Like Cleveland, he also warned spectators to stay away from the riot areas or risk being mistaken for rioters by federal military and civil authorities.[50]

For two weeks after the arrival of federal troops at Fort Smith, strikers left the mines under receivership alone. The only difficulty McClure encountered was with the deputy marshal who implored him to post federal troops as sentries throughout Prairie Creek and surrounding regions with instructions to accompany deputies on demand when they made arrests. McClure, however, was determined to keep the federal military presence low-keyed and clarified his view of the military's mission by observing that "there should be at least one deputy for each mining village and mine under the protection of the court. As I understand it, the civil authorities are to continue to exercise their functions and call

---

[47] Memo, Garrison for Gregory, 4 Nov 14, File 2225415, RG 94, NARA.

[48] Ibid.

[49] Memo, Witherspoon for AG, 4 Nov 14; quote from Telg, Garrison to McClure, 3 Nov 14; Rpt, Lt Col A. W. Brewster, AG, to IG, 24 Nov 14; all in File 2225415, RG 94, NARA. See also Ltr, McClure to Parker, 19 Nov 14, 5th Cavalry Regimental History, RG 391, Records of U.S. Army Mobile Units, 1821–1942, NARA.

[50] Cleveland's proclamation is found in Wilson, *Federal Aid in Domestic Disturbances*, page 230, and Wilson's on page 321. See also *U.S. Statutes at Large*, art. 38, sec. 2035; Telg, Garrison to McClure, 3 Nov 14, File 2225415, RG 94, NARA.

upon me for assistance only in case they are unable to exercise their functions without molestation."[51]

The month that followed, however, convinced McClure that county authorities were open partisans of the miners. Some county officials acquiesced when miners attacked incoming trains of strikebreakers at the Prairie Creek Station, while others arrested strikebreakers and company officials on trumped-up charges. McClure's mandate limited him to protecting property in federal receivership and did not include protection of company officials and employees off company property. Frustrated by these indirect yet effective efforts to interfere with mining operations, McClure inquired of his superiors whether he should "allow these disturbances to continue, or am I justified in stopping those taking place at my very doorstep?" Fearing that continued restriction of troops to the protection of company property would only encourage lawlessness, McClure recommended that a deputy marshal be posted at the railroad station, a curfew enacted, or the township placed under martial law. He persuaded Garrison and Gregory to select the first option, with the provision that McClure be permitted to send troops to assist the deputy marshal if needed. Since McClure received prior approval through the chain of command culminating in the president, any subsequent request for federal troops by deputies would not constitute a violation of the Posse Comitatus Act.[52]

No further violence occurred, though one confrontation threatened to erupt between strikers and strikebreakers in the Prairie Creek area. On 11 December the lease of the Central Coal and Coke Company expired with direct ownership reverting to the bankrupt Bache-Denham Company. When nonunion laborers began to dismantle property at the mine, a gang of forty striking union men gathered and began to abuse the laborers. At the request of the sergeant posted at the mine, McClure immediately deployed three troops of cavalry to the surrounding hills, and the crowd dispersed without further incident.[53]

The question of troop withdrawals arose in January 1915 in conjunction with plans to sell the mines still in federal receivership. McClure notified Garrison that if the receivers sold the mines to another firm or reopened them under a union shop agreement with the United Mine Workers, the troops could be withdrawn. However, if the receivers continued to run the enterprise using nonunion workers, public safety would require an extended federal military presence. Finding Bache-Denman "hopelessly insolvent," Judge Youmans instructed the receiver to prepare to sell the mines by late February 1915. Allowing for protection of the property during transfer and the safety of nonunion workers as they departed Sebastian County, McClure recommended that federal troops stay until 1 March 1915.[54]

When the actual sale and transfer of ownership took place in early February, both Youmans and McClure advised Garrison to commence withdrawals, and Wilson approved. On 10 February McClure's troops boarded trains for Fort Smith. Secretary Garrison expressed his appreciation to McClure: "While it was fortunate that you were not required by circumstances to exercise military force, I esteem it fortunate that I had you on the

[51] Ltr, McClure to Parker, 19 Nov 14, 5th Cav Regt Hist, RG 391.

[52] Ltr, McClure to AG, 5 Dec 14, and Telg, McClure to CO, Prairie Creek, Ark., 17 Dec 14, both in 5th Cav Regt Hist, RG 391, NARA. See also Ltr, Gregory to Garrison, 12 Dec 14, File 2225415, RG 94.

[53] Telg, McClure to AG, 9 Jan 15, File 2225415, RG 94, NARA.

[54] Ibid., 21 Jan 15; Ltr, McClure to AG, 30 Jan 15, 5th Cav Regt Hist, RG 391, NARA.

ground to use your wise discretion and ripe experience. . . . I am much pleased at the conduct of this matter."[55]

Regarding the basis and nature of federal military intervention, the disorder at Prairie Creek resembled more closely the Pullman Strike of 1894 than the Colorado Coal Strike. Acting in strict accordance with legal precedent set twenty years before, President Wilson dispatched troops to Arkansas to enforce court orders protecting property under federal receivership, as authorized under RS 5298. Like President Cleveland in the 1894 strike, Wilson issued a proclamation in which he sternly warned spectators to avoid rioters and participation in lawlessness. Those who did not heed these instructions, the proclamation implied, risked being treated as public enemies, subject to the full might of the federal government. Finally, in its civil disturbance role in Prairie Creek, the Army not only emphasized its neutrality, but practiced tactical self-restraint and fidelity to the letter of the Posse Comitatus Act and other applicable federal statutes. The handling of the disorders in Prairie Creek showed that Wilson's neutrality contrasted markedly with the actions of President McKinley and Attorney General Richard Olney who used the same techniques for partisan ends. Wilson demonstrated that the law could be applied in a neutral manner and that Army interventions in civil disturbances could be nonpartisan, well coordinated, and smoothly executed.

Taken together, the interventions in Colorado and Arkansas demonstrated the impartial and restrained use of federal troops characteristic of the first years of the Wilson administration and of the first fifteen years of the twentieth century. Few charges of militarism or partisanship were leveled during Wilson's first four years in office. His position represented a major change from the attitudes and civil disturbance policies of his nineteenth-century predecessors who did not put such a strict emphasis on federal military neutrality and objectivity. In Colorado federal troops demonstrated tolerance and self-control and enforced observance of the law by both sides while maintaining a calm, steadfast neutrality, unlike the Colorado National Guard, which caused more fatalities and injuries in the Ludlow Massacre alone than federal forces inflicted in over seventy years of civil disturbance interventions. In the Prairie Creek episode, the nature of intervention—the enforcement of an injunction protecting mines in federal receivership—placed the Army on the opposite side of the strikers. The Wilson administration, however, still emphasized neutrality under the law and carefully limited military action to protecting the mines under federal receivership and providing assistance to deputy U.S. marshals within statutory requirements.

But the new era did not last long. Within two years of the carefully executed federal military interventions in Colorado and Arkansas, U.S. involvement in World War I, combined with new forces of worldwide political and social upheaval, created a climate of jingoism and intense antiradicalism that caused the wartime Wilson administration to take an entirely different and extreme course in dealing with labor disputes and civil disorders, real and imagined. Federal, state, and local governments, the U.S. Army, and the overwhelming majority of the American public accepted the concept of *inter arma silent leges*—"in time of war the laws are silent"—for the duration of active hostilities and beyond, and tolerat-

---

[55] Telg, McClure to AG, 4 Feb 15; Ltrs, Garrison to Gregory, 5 Feb 15, Gregory to Wilson, 6 Feb 15, Wilson to Garrison, 8 Feb 15, and Garrison to McClure, 10 Feb 15; all in File 2225415, RG 94, NARA.

ed the wholesale abuse of civil liberties by the federal government in the name of the war effort.[56] The government in turn used the soldiers of the U.S. Army to an unprecedented degree as its primary agent to carry out these policies and stifle dissent, break strikes, curb alleged threats posed by radicals, and maintain social and political stability.

---

[56] See Henry C. Black, *Black's Law Dictionary*, 4th ed. (St. Paul, Minn.: West, 1951), p. 948.

CHAPTER 10

Inter Arma Silent Leges
The Army and the Wartime
Campaign Against Labor Radicalism
1917–1918

The Constitution of the United States is a law for rulers and people, equally in war and in peace, and covers with the shield of its protection all classes of men, at all times, and under all circumstances.
—*Ex Parte Milligan*, 1866.

The U.S. declaration of war against Germany in 1917 began a period of unprecedented federal military intervention in domestic disorders. By consuming almost every moment of President Wilson's time between early 1917 and late 1919, the war and the subsequent peace settlement relegated domestic disturbances to a place of secondary importance. Disputes were handled by cabinet officials and military officers acting in the president's name, usually without his knowledge and explicit approval.

The mood of the country was also transformed. To many Americans the war represented the gravest threat the nation had ever faced, and prewar tolerance of dissent disappeared accordingly. Federal troops guarded industrial plants and utilities, quelled race riots, and suppressed dissenters, including labor groups thought to be radical. Strikes and work slowdowns that threatened war production were viewed as subversion. Strikers, radicals, recent immigrants, antiwar groups, and social critics became the targets of secret federal investigations. The legal framework—the Constitution, federal statutes, and Army regulations—that had restrained federal military action before the war were set aside. In its place the period of the emergency brought forth new and dangerous precedents that lingered to affect the postwar years.

Providing for the Common Defense

President Wilson's war message proclaimed that the wartime emergency necessitated a vast extension of federal power and authority to protect the nation from its foreign and domestic enemies and to ensure an Allied victory.[1] Although the German Empire was the main foreign enemy, Wilson's war proclamation defined what most Americans believed was a more clear and present danger—the many aliens and "undesirable" immigrants in American society, including union members and labor radicals. These groups, by nature of their ethnic background, affiliations, and past allegiances, were automatically suspected of disloyalty.

Wilson's call to arms prompted Congress to pass a series of laws intended to aid the president in protecting the nation by strictly controlling dissidents, radicals, and labor groups. Examples of legislation that restricted rights of free movement, free speech, free assembly, and antigovernment dissent included sections of the 1916 National Defense Act, the 1917 Deficiency Appropriations Act and its April 1918 amendments, the Lever Act, and the 1917 Food and Fuel Act.[2]

The most dramatic examples of restrictive legislation came in the form of sabotage, sedition, and espionage laws clearly aimed at radical labor groups, political dissenters, and immigrant groups. On 5 February 1917, Congress passed a new Immigration Act of which Section 19, the antiradical clause, called on the secretary of labor to deport potentially threatening aliens. The Espionage Act passed on 15 June 1917, contained even more sweeping powers. Maximum penalties up to twenty years imprisonment and/or a fine of $10,000 were provided for those who—among other vaguely defined crimes—interfered in any way with the operation or success of the nation's military forces or who interfered with the operation of dockyards, canals, factories, mines, and other facilities where materials for war were being made or were stored under contract with the government. The Espionage Act was bolstered by passage of the Trading With the Enemy Act on 6 October 1917, which gave the president authority to control broadly defined subversive literature and to censor communications through the postmaster general, and by the Sedition Act of 16 May 1918, which expanded the scope of the 1917 Espionage Act and created even more severe penalties for violators.[3]

Both the rhetoric and the actions of the federal government played on and fed public fears of radicalism, espionage, and subversion. The public mood became volatile, exhibiting extreme nationalism, jingoism, and xenophobia. Anti-German propaganda disseminated by the government's official information agency, the Committee on Public Information, purposely equated dissent or disagreement with government war policies to treason and implied that German designs were behind every unpatriotic gesture, such as

---

[1] U.S. War Department, *General Orders and Bulletins, 1917* (Washington, D.C.: Government Printing Office, 1918), GO 45, 23 Apr 17, and GO 48, 27 Apr 17; Proclamation of 16 Apr 17, in *U.S. Statutes at Large, 1917*, pp. 1650–52.

[2] For the National Defense Act, see 39 *U.S. Statutes* 166, 213; for the Deficiency Appropriations Act of 1917 and amendments, especially the "Emergency Shipping Fund" section, see 40 *U.S. Statutes* 182, 535, 1020, 2022; for the Lever Act and Food and Fuel Act of 1917, see 40 *U.S. Statutes* 276, 279, 284. See also John L. Blackman, *Presidential Seizures in Labor Disputes* (Cambridge: Harvard University Press, 1967), pp. 290–91.

[3] For the antiradical clause of the immigration act, see 39 *U.S. Statutes at Large*, 889; for the Espionage Act, see *General Orders and Bulletins, 1917*, GO 43, 19 Jul 17; for the Sedition Act, see Act of 20 Apr 18, *U.S. Statutes at Large*, 65th Cong., 1st sess., 1918, ch. 59, p. 533; U.S. War Department, *General Orders and Bulletins, 1918*, Bulletin 30, 5 Jun 18 (Washington, D.C.: Government Printing Office, 1919). For the effect of this legislation, see Harry N. Scheiber, *The Wilson Administration and Civil Liberties, 1917–1921* (Ithaca: Cornell University Press, 1960), pp. 11–28; Paul L. Murphy, *World War I and the Origins of Civil Liberties in the United States* (New York: W. W. Norton, 1979), pp. 80–84.

a strike, an industrial fatality, or an unmet production quota. The public quickly grasped this idea and, in an amazing turnabout from Progressive era attitudes, began to demonstrate a strong antipathy for labor organizations, especially labor radicals. These attitudes were not new but were now displayed with government approval and acquiescence to a degree unknown previously. Anyone not publicly and wholeheartedly behind the war effort was suspected of being an enemy agent and union member; foreign-born citizens, immigrants, and those espousing left-wing ideologies naturally came under suspicion. The public apparently came to believe that a large segment of the nation's foreign-born population actually took orders directly from the German kaiser and was bent on destroying the nation from within. Scores of patriotic organizations known as loyalty leagues were formed on national and local levels by those hoping to aid the war effort by suppressing all groups and individuals they considered as radicals, undesirable aliens, saboteurs, spies, or otherwise seditious influences. These organizations often took the law into their own hands and perpetrated acts of violence with hundreds of cases of mob violence being recorded in 1917 alone.[4]

Labor unions and especially labor radicals became a primary focal point for government and public attention. President Wilson and his advisers realized that the greatest American contribution to the Allied war effort would come in the form of war materials and manpower. To prevent debilitating labor problems and to mobilize the economy, the government created myriad civil agencies from 1916 on, including the Council of National Defense, the War Labor Conference Board, the National War Labor Board (NWLB), the War Industries Board, and thirteen adjustment agencies to govern the activities of each major industry involved in defense work.[5] These agencies established principles that were to guide industrial relations during hostilities in return for the prohibition of strikes and walkouts, including the right of both businesses and workers to organize or unionize without harassment or interference; the right of union workers to bargain collectively; the guarantee of continued existence for union shops; the establishment of the industry-wide eight-hour day and basic health and safety standards; and equal pay for equal work. The NWLB and the adjustment agencies were acceptable to most workers and indeed had been created

---

[4] Painter, *Standing at Armageddon*, pp. 334–35; Higham, *Strangers in the Land*, pp. 207–09, 211. See also Frederick C. Giffin, *Six Who Protested: Radical Opposition to the First World War* (Port Washington, N.Y.: Kennikat, 1977); Jules Witcover, *Sabotage at Black Tom: Imperial Germany's Secret War in America, 1914–1917* (Chapel Hill: Algonquin, 1989); Murphy, *World War I and the Origins of Civil Liberties*, pp. 87–89; H. C. Peterson and G. C. Fite, *Opponents of War, 1917–1918* (Madison: University of Wisconsin Press, 1957), p. 18; American Civil Liberties Union, *Wartime Prosecutions and Mob Violence Involving the Rights of Free Speech, Free Press and Peaceful Assemblage (From April 1, 1917 to May 1, 1918)* (Washington, D.C.: National Civil Liberties Bureau, 1918), p. 3; Joan M. Jensen, *The Price of Vigilance* (Chicago: Rand McNally, 1969); Leslie Fishbein, "Federal Suppression of Leftwing Dissidence in World War I," *Potomac Review* 6 (Summer 1974):48–49.

[5] For labor and the war, see Smith, "Organized Labor and Government in the Wilson Era," pp. 267–70; Simeon Larson, *Labor and Foreign Policy: Gompers, the AFL, and the First World War, 1914–1918* (Rutherford, N.J.: Fairleigh Dickinson University Press, 1975); William Preston, Jr., *Aliens and Dissenters: Federal Suppression of Radicals, 1903–1933* (New York: Harper & Row, 1963), pp. 36–38; Philip Taft, *The A. F. of L. in the Time of Gompers* (New York: Harper & Brothers, 1957), pp. 342–60; "American Labor and the War," *Outlook* (18 April 1917):689–90. For the NWLB and WIB, see Valerie J. Connor, *The National War Labor Board: Stability, Social Justice, and the Voluntary State in World War I* (Chapel Hill: University of North Carolina Press, 1983); Robert D. Cuff, *The War Industries Board: Business-Government Relations During World War I* (Baltimore: Johns Hopkins University Press, 1973).

Western Department

Ce

SAN FRANCISCO
Alameda

Everett
Seattle
Cle Elum
Wenatchee
Centralia
Yakima
Astoria
Vancouver Barracks
Portland
Walla Walla

Spokane
St. Maries

Eureka
Troy
Whitefish

Helena
Butte

Needles
Kingman
Jerome
Humboldt
Los Angeles

Phoenix
Globe
Miami
Ray
Morenci
Clifton
Ajo
Tucson
Bisbee
Douglas
Ft. Douglas
Hermanas
Columbus

Albuquerque

Southern Department

M E X I C O

SAN ANTONIO
FT. SAM HOUS

HAWAII
1:20,000,000

UNION OF SOVIET
SOCIALIST REPUBLICS

ALASKA
1:45,300,000

CANADA

MAP 4

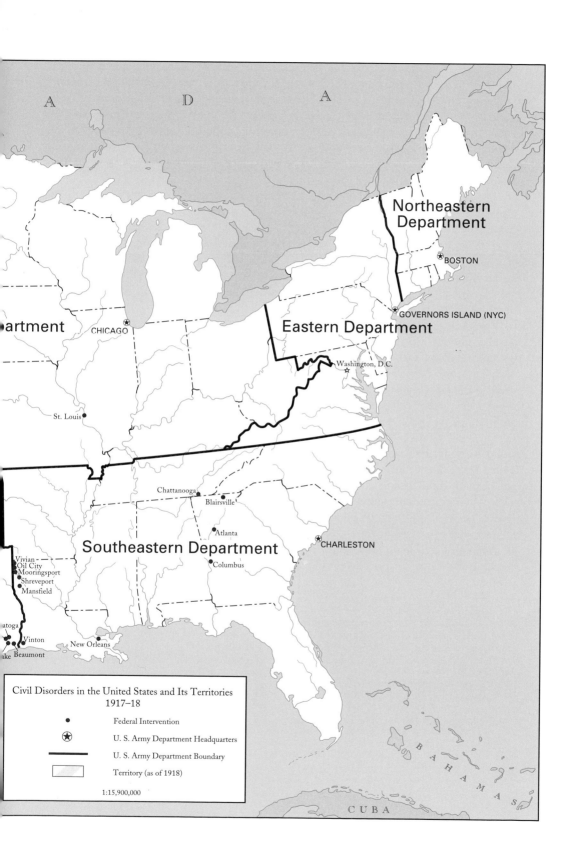

Civil Disorders in the United States and Its Territories
1917–18

- Federal Intervention
- ⊛ U. S. Army Department Headquarters
- ▬ U. S. Army Department Boundary
- ☐ Territory (as of 1918)

1:15,900,000

with organized labor groups, like the American Federation of Labor, in mind.[6] The AFofL responded to these federal programs that stressed mediation over confrontation by endorsing the war effort and agreeing to a truce with management for the duration, although it did not make an unequivocal no-strike pledge. In addition, the union promised to purge its ranks of enemies of the United States, be they pacifists, radicals, antiwar agitators, or left-wingers, and accepted lists from the government identifying such people to aid in this process. As a result, troops were sent less frequently into disputes involving the AFofL, although such interventions did occur.[7]

The same government policies that stressed cooperation and arbitration with the AFofL were not extended to groups defined as labor radicals, which were viewed as outlaw organizations. One such group was the Socialists; its American membership numbered in the hundreds of thousands, and it had issued an antiwar declaration in 1914. The movement split over the issue of U.S. participation in the war in April 1917, and with the exception of Eugene Debs, Morris Hillquit, Victor Berger, and a minority of the membership most American Socialists, like their European counterparts, supported the war effort in spite of contrary public perceptions.[8]

The radical group considered the most threatening was the Industrial Workers of the World. Although espousing revolution since its founding, by 1917 the Wobblies realized that the wartime American worker was anything but revolutionary and actually equated capitalism with patriotism and democracy. The IWW leadership believed the country would eventually enter the war, but felt it had no influence over U.S. foreign policy. Nonetheless, at their 1916 convention the IWW formulated a clear antiwar policy.[9] The primary aim of the union had always been the organization of a general strike in all industries, but in 1917 the IWW adopted new goals of organization and a continuation of the struggle for material improvements in working conditions. As an Immigration Bureau and Justice Department report stated, IWW writings "hinted at" resistance to the government but "contained nothing in direct advocacy of anarchism, active opposition to organized government or the destruction of property, public or private." Indeed, many Wobblies bought Liberty Bonds and 95 percent of those who were eligible registered for the draft, most serving when called.[10]

Yet Americans could not forget twelve years of IWW revolutionary rhetoric. Most people came to believe, deliberately encouraged by Creel's Committee on Public Information

---

[6] Berman, *Labor Disputes and the President*, pp. 137–42; Witte, *The Government in Labor Disputes*, pp. 247–48; Gordon S. Watkins, *Labor Problems and Labor Administration in the United States During the World War* (Urbana: University of Illinois Press, 1920); Grosvenor B. Clarkson, *Industrial America in the World War: The Strategy Behind the Lines, 1917–1918* (Boston: Houghton Mifflin, 1923).

[7] Taft, *The A. F. of L. in the Time of Gompers*, pp. 345–51; "American Labor's Protest Against War," *Review of Reviews* 50 (October 1914):509.

[8] Murphy, *World War I and the Origins of Civil Liberties*, pp. 141–44; Preston, *Aliens and Dissenters*, pp. 36–38; Dubofsky, *We Shall Be All*, p. 401. For socialism and the war, see Merele Farsod, *International Socialism and the World War* (Cambridge: Harvard University Press, 1935); Norman Bindler, "American Socialism and the First World War" (Ph.D. diss., New York University, 1970); James Weinstein, *The Decline of Socialism in America, 1912–1925* (New York: Monthly Review, 1967).

[9] Renshaw, *The Wobblies*, pp. 22–23; Robert L. Tyler, "The United States Government as Union Organizer: The Loyal Legion of Loggers and Lumbermen," *Mississippi Valley Historical Review* 47 (December 1960):432; Preston, *Aliens and Dissenters*, pp. 88–89.

[10] Preston, *Aliens and Dissenters*, pp. 90–91; Dubofsky, *We Shall Be All*, pp. 350–57, 376–79.

propaganda, that the union was in league with imperial Germany and guilty of espionage and sedition. Nationwide the public exhorted that the IWW be wiped out, even if evidence of treasonable behavior was lacking. While much anti-Wobbly activity was motivated by patriotic beliefs, many employers, especially in the West, used patriotism to justify attacks on all unions, including the AFofL, and "missed no opportunity to make profits compatible with patriotism and organized labor synonymous with treason." The war, to many business leaders, was the perfect opportunity to rid the nation of the IWW menace. In an early well-publicized incident, the Green Corn Rebellion, landowners linked an abortive antidraft march of 200 tenant farmers in Sasakwa, Oklahoma, with the IWW. From then on, antiwar actions, antigovernment agitation, and unpatriotic activities were connected, rightly or not, with the IWW. Although the union had deferred its revolution, however, it did conduct frequent strikes, lending weight to public suspicions. In the first six months of the war alone, the IWW initiated 116 strikes, idled 26,906 workers, and caused the loss of 1,001,364 workdays.[11]

The Ultimate Federal Response to Labor Radicalism: The Army and the National Guard

If legislative means failed to keep labor radicals from hindering the war effort through strikes, the National Guard and the Regular Army were available to aid civil authorities. Although the National Guard was customarily the first reliance of states in times of riot, it was not available to the governors when in federal service during times of national emergency. Therefore, federalized guard units could not be used to aid state or local authorities, except under the same legal conditions that applied to the Regular Army. The 1903 Dick Act gave the president added authority to federalize guard troops "to execute the laws of the union, suppress insurrection, or repel invasion" if regulars were unavailable, but this provision still failed to resolve the problem of finding sufficient numbers of men and the means to aid civil authorities once the guard was federalized.[12]

Just prior to the U.S. declaration of war against Germany, on 25 March 1917 Wilson called up 50,000 National Guardsmen to protect industrial, transportation, communication, and military facilities.[13] Although most enemy aliens lived in the East and Midwest, National Guardsmen in Washington State, Oregon, Idaho, Montana, and California were among the first units federalized and placed on guard duty at munitions plants, lumber mills, shipbuilding facilities, railroad trestles, and utilities. To many, this action meant that the threat posed by radical labor groups, also concentrated in the Northwest, was deemed as great by federal officials as that posed by Germany.[14]

When President Wilson federalized the entire National Guard in July 1917, he inadvertently deprived the states of sixteen National Guard divisions comprising 11,875 officers

---

[11] Quote from Renshaw, *The Wobblies*, pp. 219–20. For IWW strikes, see National Industrial Conference Board, *Strikes in American Industry in Wartime, April 6 to October 6, 1917* (Boston: National Industrial Conference Board, 1918), pp. 19–20.

[12] Dowell, *Military Aid to the Civil Power*, p. 203; 34 *U.S. Statutes at Large*, p. 402.

[13] The Army War College identified these sites, see Memo, Kuhn for CofS, 28 Mar 17, sub: Suppression of Lawlessness, RG 407, Records of the Adjutant General's Office, AG 370.6, NARA.

[14] Glasser Rpt, Lumber, p. 8, RG 60, Records of the Department of Justice, NARA.

and 361,294 enlisted men. The ramifications of these call-ups on the law enforcement capabilities of the states were immense, not only during the war, but afterward. According to
Section 111 of the 1916 National Defense Act, "all persons so drafted [into federal service]
shall from the date of their draft, stand discharged from the militia." Because discharged
guardsmen did not automatically resume membership in the organized militia, states would
have to rebuild their National Guard forces after the war. For the time being, until the states
could form home guard units to replace the National Guard units that were federalized, the
only forces available to control domestic disturbances (excepting local police forces) were
under federal control.[15]

Initiation of the Policy of Direct Access

Many state and local officials, especially those in the Pacific Northwest where IWW
activists were most prevalent, voiced their concerns about the absence of the National
Guard to federal authorities. In recognition of their problem, Secretary of War Newton D.
Baker unilaterally initiated a solution that constituted a drastic reversal of federal policy
concerning federal military intervention in domestic disorders. In instructions to Maj. Gen.
Tasker H. Bliss, the Army chief of staff, on 29 May 1917 he wrote that

in view of the fact that the National Guard is or will be in federal service, States will be deprived of
organized militia for preservation of public order and the suppression of riot . . . the Federal
Government should respond to calls from Governors and authorize the stationing of troops . . . in
such a way as to meet the necessities of such situations as they arise. . . . I therefore request you to
direct the commanders of the several depots to maintain relations of cordial cooperation with the
governors of the several states in their respective departments and to respond to any call for military
assistance from such governors for . . . maintaining the domestic peace."[16]

Thus Baker allowed local and state officials to request and obtain federal troops
directly from departmental Army commanders without going through the statutory procedure of a formal application to the president. One cabinet member had thus unilaterally
suspended several laws, including RS 5297, RS 5298, RS 5299, and the Posse Comitatus
Act, clearing the way for repeated legal violations in the years ahead. Use of troops under
any of these statutes requires the issuance, according to RS 5300, of a cease and desist
proclamation by the president.

This action also swept aside existing regulations that allowed commanders to order
troops to intervene in emergencies, but required them to inform the adjutant general
immediately for the purpose of seeking justification and approval for their actions from
higher authorities. Army officers, even when called to aid civil authorities, retained command of their troops and under no circumstances were to allow soldiers to be placed under
the control of a governor or any other state official, civil or military. Commanders were

---

[15] Ibid., Wartime Strikes and the Army, pp. 19, 75–76, and NW Lumber Strikes, 1917, pp. 42–49, RG 60. See
also U.S. War Department, *Report of the Chief of the Militia Bureau, 1917* (Washington, D.C.: Government
Printing Office, 1918); *General Orders and Bulletins, 1917,* GO 90, 12 Jul 17; Wilson, *Federal Aid in Domestic
Disturbances*, p. 317; Mahon, *History of the Militia and the National Guard*, pp. 154–57.

[16] Glasser Rpt, Wartime Strikes and the Army, pp. 25–28, and Memo, Baker for Bliss, 29 May 17, in
Introduction to Glasser Rpt, both in RG 60, NARA.

instructed, however, to "be in concert with the actions or views of duly constituted civil authorities."[17]

Commanding officers had often followed the suggestions, if not actual orders, of civil and even corporate officials while retaining direct control of their troops. Baker now explicitly gave high-ranking Army officers the authority to disregard the statutes governing the domestic use of federal military power and instructed them to allow their subordinates to do the same by directly responding to the calls for federal military aid of local officials and businessmen seeking to safeguard their communities. This authority was thus allowed to devolve to the platoon level, making lieutenants and their men available to local law enforcement officials in violation of the Posse Comitatus Act. For the first time since Reconstruction, commanders assumed jurisdiction where civil governments were

NEWTON D. BAKER

functioning and where peaceable strikes were in progress. Commanders were also authorized to make arrests, contrary to the Supreme Court doctrine set forth in *Ex Parte Milligan*.[18]

Such a sweeping revision of existing standards alarmed many in the Army. Queried whether the new policy placed its officers in danger of repeatedly violating the Posse Comitatus Act, the judge advocate general responded that

the history, the collocation and the context of the . . . statute conclusively demonstrate that its purpose was to prevent the use of the Army for the ends for which civil officers of the law are provided, either by way of assistance to such officers or of substitution for them. The Statute did not intend to limit the employment of the military forces of the nation in meeting an attack on the very nation itself—a duty which rests primarily on the military rather than on the civil power.[19]

Despite this line of reasoning, which had been clearly refuted by *Ex Parte Milligan* in 1866, the Army still attempted to keep military interventions under control. By General Order 147 of 20 November 1917, Army leaders were instructed that "department and other

---

[17] Quote from Dowell, *Military Aid to the Civil Power*, pp. 204–07. GO 49 was contained in art. 47, par. 484–89, "Employment of Troops in the Enforcement of the Laws," *Regulations for the Army of United States, 1913 (Corrected to 15 April 1917)* (Washington, D.C.: Government Printing Office, 1917), pp. 106–12. The current regulation is AR 500–50.

[18] Preston, *Aliens and Dissenters*, p. 105; Glasser Rpt, Wartime Strikes and the Army, pp. 25–28, and Memo, Baker for Bliss, 29 May 17, RG 60. Baker stated in 1920 that the direct access policy was "necessary in the public interest," see Ltr, Baker to CofS, 2 Dec 20, File 370.6, RG 407, NARA.

[19] Glasser Rpt, Lumber, pp. 7e–7f, and Memo, JAG for AG, 12 Mar 17, sub: Opinion on Legal Theory on Use of Troops in Civil Areas During War, both in RG 60.

commanders within the continental limits of the United States will, except in cases of unforeseen emergency, refer all requests for the use of troops . . . to the Adjutant General of the Army." In extreme emergencies, however, commanders were instructed to act on the requests of local and state officials at once, without seeking prior War Department approval. In practice the exception overwhelmed the rule. Nearly every subsequent deployment was perceived by local commanders to be a crisis justifying immediate intervention under the emergency provisions of Army regulations before informing the War Department or gaining a superior's prior approval.

Baker's policy, intended as an expedient to aid civil officials who were otherwise without means of enforcing their authority, had removed necessary and valuable restraints on the potential abuse of federal military power. Between July 1918 and September 1921, federal troops participated in twenty-nine domestic disorders. In only one instance was the required presidential proclamation issued. Not until early December 1919 did the War Department begin to advise commanders that they again follow the prewar statutes. The policy of doing so was not enforced until 1921.[20]

Although the legal framework had been set aside, the Army insisted officially that troops in any labor situation be impartial and not appear to be favoring employers over employees. Nonetheless, the presence of troops in areas of labor unrest usually served to intimidate workers and break strikes. Army intervention during the war was used by employers, local politicians, and ultrapatriotic citizens to destroy organized labor, radical labor, and radical political groups, as well as to stifle dissent, in essence a return to the tactics used on occasion by the federal government in the late nineteenth century. Officers sent troops on the request of civil officials to break strikes, disperse crowds and demonstrations, prevent labor meetings, and arrest, detain, and imprison workers without the right of habeas corpus. Troops often behaved in a manner resembling martial law, though martial law was never officially or legally declared. Army officers, in their dealings with labor disputes involving radicals, often received their briefings on local situations from employers or from private detective agencies employed as strikebreakers. In many cases they accepted housing and other gratuities from companies that had requested their aid in breaking strikes. According to Edward S. Corwin, a historian on the Constitution, the period was characterized by "the most complete, sustained, and altogether deliberate neglect of the formalities required by Article IV and the supplementary Acts of Congress that has thus far occurred." The goodwill earned by the Army among labor during the Progressive era was largely spent during the domestic interventions of World War I.[21]

The Military Intelligence Division

Troops' actions were not the only form of military intervention in civil affairs. In early May 1917 Lt. Col. Ralph A. Van Deman formed the Foreign Influence Branch (MI–4) of the Army Military Intelligence Division (MID) to deal with domestic counterintelligence.

---

[20] *General Orders and Bulletins, 1917*, GO 147, 20 Nov 17; Memo, E. D. Anderson for to AG, 29 Sep 19, Glasser File: Gary, Ind., RG 60; Wilson, *Federal Aid in Domestic Disturbances*, p. 317; Berman, *Labor Disputes and the President*, p. 207; Rich, *President and Civil Disorder*, p. 152.

[21] Corwin, *The President: Office and Powers*, pp. 165–66. See also Preston, *Aliens and Dissenters*, pp. 105–09, 244–45.

The Labor and Sabotage subsection of this branch handled "all matters relating to the prevention or delay of deliveries of war material by immobilization of resources, control of factories, or raw materials, subversion or intimidation of labor or physical damage to plants or products."[22] Although strikes were not specifically mentioned, the activities of radical labor groups were prime targets of subsequent MID investigations. By July 1917 MID had branches in New York City, Chicago, Philadelphia, St. Louis, Seattle, and New Orleans, and 500 smaller units at various Army posts, airfields, arsenals, and industrial plants nationwide. All told, 1,300 people were involved in its domestic surveillance work. In the majority of labor disputes prompting federal military intervention, Army officers drew intelligence from MID investigations.[23]

RALPH A. VAN DEMAN

MID was not alone in conducting domestic investigations and cooperated with the Office of Naval Intelligence; the U.S. Secret Service; the Bureau of Investigation (later the FBI); the War Trade Intelligence Board; the Department of Labor; the Plant Protection Service; state, county, and local law enforcement agencies; and volunteer groups, especially the American Protective League (APL). The APL received help in conducting its investigations and carrying out antisubversive activities from the Department of Justice and Bureau of Investigation and received badges that read "Auxiliary to the United States Department of Justice." By mid-June 1917 the APL had six hundred branches and a membership of 100,000, soon to peak at well over 250,000. Its membership assisted MID in its surveillance of radicals, aliens, and labor groups and was commended by the Army chief of staff in 1919.[24]

By the end of 1917 the government, through the Labor, Justice, and War Departments (including MID), had developed the policy and means to deal with real and perceived threats

[22] U.S. War Department, *Report of the Chief of Staff, United States Army to the Secretary of War, 1919* (Washington, D.C.: Government Printing Office, 1919), p. 109 (hereafter cited as *Chief of Staff Rpt, 1919)*; quote from Bruce W. Bidwell, History of the Military Intelligence Division of the Army General Staff, 1775–1945, study in U.S. Army Center of Military History, pp. 235, 247–51 (hereafter cited as History of MID); Marc B. Powe, *The Emergence of the War Department Intelligence Agency, 1885–1918* (Pittsburg: Kansas State University Press, 1975). For Van Deman, see Ralph E. Weber, ed., *The Final Memoranda of Major General Ralph H. Van Deman, Father of the United States Military Intelligence* (Frederick, Md. : University Publications of America, 1987); Jensen, *Price of Vigilance*, pp. 86, 97, 101, 117–124, 248, 301, 315.

[23] Bidwell, History of MID, pp. 235, 247–51; *General Orders and Bulletins, 1918*, GO 80, 26 Aug 18; Joan M. Jensen, *Army Surveillance in America, 1775–1980* (New Haven: Yale University Press, 1991).

[24] Murphy, *World War I and the Origins of Civil Liberties*, pp. 89–90; Jensen, *Price of Vigilance*, pp. 119, 123; Bidwell, History of MID, pp. 380–85, 428–31; *Chief of Staff Rpt, 1919*, p. 104; Higham, *Strangers in the Land*, pp. 211–12.

to the national security posed by aliens, by enemy spies or saboteurs, and by labor and radical organizations. The machinery of repression, however, was still incomplete when labor disputes racked the lumber-producing regions of the Northwest in the early spring of 1917.

Lumber, 1917–1918

The lumber industry of the Pacific Northwest had a long history of labor troubles. Since 1878 timber companies had successfully prevented attempts of unions to organize or bargain for improved wages and conditions. By 1917 the AFofL, despite numerous failures, had formed two unions—the International Shingle Weavers Union and the International Timber Workers Union. Neither was large, and the power of the AFofL received a serious setback as a result of a failed strike in 1915. Company union-busting now opened the way for more aggressive and radical groups like the IWW. In an effort to retrieve their waning influences, in March 1917 both AFofL unions decided to launch a strike the following month.[25]

Meanwhile, the IWW's Lumber Workers Industrial Union No. 500 had become the strongest in the Pacific Northwest with 3,000 members and 7,000 supporters. Like the AFofL, it encountered stiff and violent opposition. When 200 Wobbly organizers landed by ship in Everett, Washington, in November 1916, for example, they were met by the local sheriff and a hail of gunfire. The "Everett Massacre" left 7 dead and 50 wounded. The IWW persisted, however, and by the spring of 1917 had gained a foothold in, among other places, Eureka, Montana. Having failed to reach an agreement for concerted action with the AFofL, the IWW decided in March of 1917 to launch its own strike for the same objectives.[26]

The IWW strike began as planned during the mid-April logging drives. When nearly 200 members of LWIU No. 500 struck at the Eureka Lumber Company, the citizens and businessmen of Lincoln County immediately requested help from the governor, the state attorney general, and the U.S. district attorney. IWW members began riding the trains to and from Eureka. They picketed the right of way to prevent the arrival of strikebreakers, but threatened no violence against nonstriking employees and company officials or property.

Governor Samuel V. Stewart, however, wired the commanding general of the Western Department, Maj. Gen. James Franklin Bell, for troops on 16 April. Bell failed to respond directly, suggesting that he, like other officers, was confused by the lack of a clear policy regarding procedures for obtaining troops. Before 1917 Stewart's request would have gone directly to President Wilson. But in the hectic weeks following the declaration of war, the governor, ignorant of the correct procedure or anticipating bureaucratic delay, appealed directly to the Army. Without awaiting a response from Bell, on 17 April Stewart wired Secretary Baker for troops, several days before the strike became effective. He requested troops to prevent IWW interference with the nearby Great Northern Railroad, a strategic transcontinental line protected by federal railway acts, alleging that in an effort to prevent trains from bringing strikebreakers to Eureka, armed Wobblies might demolish railroad

---

[25] Glasser Rpt, NW Lumber Strikes, 1917, pp. 1–2, 6–9, 18–19, RG 60; Robert E. Ficken, "The Wobbly Horrors: Pacific Northwest Lumbermen and the Industrial Workers of the World, 1917–1928," *Labor History* 24 (Summer 1983):325–41.

[26] Glasser Rpt, NW Lumber Strikes, 1917, pp. 1–2, 6–9, 18–19, 36, RG 60. For the Everett Massacre, see Hofstadter and Wallace, *American Violence*, pp. 348–50.

bridges and other property.[27] Since the union posed no obvious or significant threat to the railroad at that time, one may assume that Stewart hoped to divert the troops sent to protect the Great Northern against the IWW at Eureka.

Two days later, Secretary Baker wired General Bell to make "adequate arrangements to protect the property of the Eureka Lumber Company and the nearby section of the Great Northern Railroad." Bell was also instructed to cooperate fully with state authorities. Discretion regarding the number of troops to use and how to deploy them was left to Bell and Governor Stewart. Because no actual disorder existed, they sought no presidential proclamation, nor did they conduct an independent investigation to substantiate the validity of Stewart's claims, or to determine the nature of the IWW threat.[28]

Bell ordered four companies of the 2d Regiment of the federalized Montana National Guard, stationed at Fort William Henry Harrison, to Eureka, the first company arriving on 20 April. Forty men were stationed in town, and the remainder were spread along the rail route between Whitefish and Troy.[29] On arrival, the troops under Col. John L. Hayden found that no threat existed. Hayden learned, however, that Wobblies were gathering to prevent strikebreakers from starting the logging drive on the following day. He quickly asked for clarification of his instructions and Bell told him to thwart "prearranged plans contemplating violence" by breaking picket lines and arresting strikers. Thus Hayden's mission changed from protecting the transcontinental railway to strikebreaking. Hayden and the guard followed their instructions without deviation, and the IWW strikers, prevented from picketing, returned to work but vowed to strike on the job.[30]

The IWW continued its efforts to organize the lumber industry, working now in Washington State. Employee living conditions there, as elsewhere in the Northwest, were abominable. The work was seasonal and migratory. In camp, loggers lived in crude, dirty huts that were too poorly constructed to withstand the rigors of the climate. The levels of hygiene and comfort were primitive and the food barely edible. The isolated camps did not accommodate the families of married men or anyone else except the loggers themselves. Stiff resistance from the logging companies had met attempts by labor in the previous four decades to remedy these conditions. The European war, combined with the organization efforts of the AFofL and IWW, created, however, conditions favorable to improvement. It also increased the probability of federal military intervention.

In spite of the failure of the Eureka strike, both the AFofL and the IWW were determined to continue their endeavors in the Pacific Northwest. State authorities knew this in advance, and Washington Governor Ernest Lister decided to seek federal help before the fact. He had recently been informed by the Council of State Defense that IWW activities threatened to curb the salmon output and interfere with the wheat harvest and the functioning of irrigation dams, tunnels, and flumes. On 2 July he asked Baker to continue an

---

[27] Glasser Rpt, NW Lumber Strike, 1917, RG 60. See also Telg, Stewart to Baker, 17 Apr 17, File 258862, RG 407, NARA.

[28] Glasser Rpt, NW Lumber Strike, 1917, p. 34, RG 60; Telg, AG to Western Dept, 19 Apr 17, File 370.6, RG 407, NARA. Baker had yet to establish the direct access policy when Stewart requested federal military aid from Bell. It is probable that Baker's actions here were the first steps toward the formal establishment of the direct access policy one month later.

[29] Glasser Rpt, Lumber, p. 30, RG 60; Telg, Bell to AG, 20 Apr 17, File 370.6, RG 407, NARA.

[30] Telg, Bell to AG, 21 Apr 17, Glasser File: NW Lumber Strike, 1917, RG 60, NARA.

HUNTER LIGGETT

existing policy by which federal troops provided protection against sabotage of utilities and to extend it to food crops and irrigation systems. In response Baker authorized the new commander of the Western Department, Maj. Gen. Hunter Liggett, to see Lister and "find out what to do and do it." Thus a soldier was allowed an extraordinarily wide latitude to use federal military forces as he saw fit.[31]

Liggett promptly carried out his instructions. After consulting with state and local officials, he sent troops to the Yakima Valley towns of Cle Elum, North Yakima, and Wenatchee. The troops actively searched for persons believed to be a threat to farming, fishing, or lumber enterprises. On 7 July soldiers in Yakima arrested 38 Wobblies on charges of possessing pistols and allegedly advocating sabotage and arson. Four days later, troops in Ellensburg arrested 50 to 60 Wobblies for supposedly interfering with crop harvests and lumber operations. Regulars acted to protect the fruit crop in North Yakima from a threatened IWW strike; further arrests took place also in Walla Walla. In Aberdeen, regulars guarded a local lumber mill and kept pickets away from company property. "Prisoners," according to a later report, "were held under military authority, but federal and state civil authorities would take over all prisoners who had violated specific statutes." U.S. attorneys in Washington conferred with Governor Lister and agreed that federalized guardsmen should be used to break picket lines, arrest union agitators, and detain them for trial in state and federal courts.[32]

From mid-July until mid-August regulars and federalized guardsmen arrested strikers—fundamentally on misdemeanor charges. Taking advantage of the itinerant status of many of the workers, troops helped local police pick up IWWs for vagrancy. Mere possession of an IWW membership card offered a cause for arrest. When raiding IWW meeting halls and freight train boxcars, federalized guardsmen routinely seized strikers to question them about their social, political, and economic views; authorities granted release only to those who agreed to return to work or who were not considered a "menace to the best interests of industry."[33]

---

[31] Telg, Lister to Baker, 2 Jul 17, File 370.6, RG 407, NARA. See also Glasser Rpt, NW Lumber Strike, 1917, p. 54, RG 60; Cletus E. Daniels, "Wobblies on the Farm: The IWW in the Yakima Valley," *Pacific Northwest Quarterly* 65 (October 1974):166–72.

[32] Quote from Glasser Rpt, NW Lumber Strikes, 1917, pp. 22–24, 54, RG 60. See also Telg, C. E. Dentler, CO, 1st Dist, Western Dept, to AG, 3 Oct 17, File 370.6, RG 407, NARA.

[33] Quote from Preston, *Aliens and Dissenters*, p. 106. See also Glasser Rpt, NW Lumber Strikes, 1917, pp. 55–56, RG 60.

The preoccupation of federalized guardsmen with strike duty, however, troubled Baker and the Army general staff. Many of the units involved had had no combat training above the regimental level, and divisional training was essential for anticipated combat duty with the American Expeditionary Forces in France. To relieve guard units for this purpose, Baker ordered General Liggett to notify Lister that beginning 1 August 1917 federal forces in the region would guard only major utilities, with protection of all other facilities devolving upon state and municipal governments. In reiterating the list of utilities—tunnels, bridges, locks, arsenals, depots, critical water supply systems, munitions plants, and so forth—Baker omitted any mention of lumber camps. But he temporarily withdrew the order when Lister appealed to him, explaining that federalized guardsmen had made a large number of arrests and were holding prisoners until the state could organize and outfit sixteen companies of state guards.

By late August 1917 Army and federalized National Guard units had participated in the arrest of over 140 persons, primarily Wobblies and suspected radical agitators. The arrests and harassment provoked IWW leaders into calling a general strike for 20 August against all industries in the state to effect the release of what they termed class war prisoners. State officials once again predicted dire consequences for the government's war effort and for the supply of fish, other foods, and lumber to the local population. In a preemptive move, the Army raided the IWW headquarters in Spokane on 19 August and arrested 27 Wobblies. These new arrests and rapidly dwindling funds forced the IWW to call off the strike. The IWW leadership ordered the rank and file to return to work and to strike on the job by slowdowns and acts of petty sabotage.[34]

The Loyal Legion and the Spruce Production Division

Despite the use of federal troops, the labor unrest in the Pacific Northwest caused a drastic decline in the production of lumber needed by the federal government, especially Sitka spruce essential for manufacturing aircraft. Between April and October the Army practice of rushing federalized guardsmen back and forth between idle camps and mills proved futile in forcing strikers back to work. Although federal intervention kept the peace, worker productivity and lumber output decreased steadily. The Army, therefore, stepped in and sent Col. Brice P. Disque, a Signal Corps officer in the Division of Military Aeronautics of the War Department, to investigate the causes of the strikes and to do whatever was necessary to resume the output. The role Disque played and the conclusions he rendered were unprecedented in the history of military intervention in labor disputes.

Colonel Disque arrived in Seattle in November 1917 for extensive talks with business and civic leaders and took an illuminating tour of the lumber camps. After witnessing "dangerously exposed saw blades, . . . repellent, greasy stew," and squalid bunkhouses, Disque commented, "We treated captured Moros better in the Philippines. . . . These conditions . . . not Wobbly ideology or sympathy were the major causes of unrest in the lumber industry."[35] Similar conditions were also uncovered by a presidential commission sent

---

[34] Telgs, McCain to Liggett, 14 Jul 17; ASW to Gregory, 30 Jul 17; Lister to Baker, 30 Jul 17, and reply, 2 Aug 17. All in file 370.6, RG 407, NARA.

[35] Telg, Dentler to AG, 3 Oct 17, File 370.6, RG 407. See also Glasser Rpt, NW Lumber Strikes, 1917, pp. 70–71, RG 60; Preston, *Aliens and Dissenters*, 107–08; Dubofsky, *We Shall Be All*, p. 403.

BRICE P. DISQUE

to the Northwest lumber camps during the fall of 1917: "efforts to rectify evils through the trade-union movement have largely failed. . . . Operators claim that the nature of the industry presents inherent obstacles to unionization. But a dominant reason is to be found in the bitter attitude of the operators toward any organization among their employees. The hold of the IWW is riveted instead of weakened by unimaginative opposition on the part of employers to the correction of real grievances."[36] Convinced that the legitimate grievances of the lumber workers had to be dealt with in any effort to mobilize the industry, Disque proposed to bring owners, operators, and workers together by creating an Army-sponsored company union called the Loyal Legion of Loggers and Lumbermen.

Disque organized the legion into seven districts and provided Army officers, under his supervision, acting as "district supervisors," to visit each locale on a regular basis, advise its executive committee, and enroll new members. By placing the Army between loggers and lumbermen with him in overall charge, he hoped to effect collective bargaining that would improve working conditions, eliminate threats of sabotage and sedition, and, most important, increase lumber production. To ensure success, he counted on federal troops.[37] Secretary Baker, weary of the endless and indecisive confrontations and strikes in the Northwest, gave his support to the scheme. Disque was supplied with 100 officers to act as union organizers.

The first local of the Loyal Legion of Loggers and Lumbermen, known as the 4 L, was created in Wheeler, Oregon, on 30 November 1917. Early in 1918 Disque began earnest reforms, in March gaining industry-wide approval of the eight-hour workday, a minimum hourly wage of forty cents for unskilled and ninety cents for skilled loggers, and vastly improved living conditions. In return for these reforms, the loggers allowed Disque to form the nonaffiliated—with the AFofL and the IWW—Loyal Legion in their camps, which implied compulsory membership and a no-strike policy. With the 4 L, Disque closed the woods to outside labor organizations. Army officers acted both as recruiters and as a police force to drive away other union organizers. According to critics, the 4 L was a union-busting arrangement that kept loggers on the job and productive, while offering a semblance of the industrial democracy they sought. Yet it grew rapidly, counting 35,000 members by

---

[36] Quote from Harold Hyman, *Soldiers and Spruce: Origins of the Loyal Legion of Loggers and Lumbermen* (Los Angeles: University of California Press, 1963), p. 110; Tyler, "U.S. Government as Union Organizer," pp. 337–41; "Tying Up Western Lumber," *New Republic* 12 (29 September 1917):242–44.

[37] United States, President's Mediation Commission, *Report of the President's Mediation Commission, January 9, 1918* (Washington, D.C.: Government Printing Office, 1918), p. 14.

the end of 1917 and 120,000 members, in twelve districts and a thousand locals, by Armistice Day 1918. The Loyal Legion was so successful that the rank and file voted to keep it in existence after the war.[38]

The creation of the 4 L did not guarantee, however, the unimpeded supply of Sitka spruce; hence Disque also created the U.S. Army Spruce Production Division. This innovative and unprecedented organization, made up of soldiers with lumber backgrounds, began with 10,000 men of the Signal Corps stationed at Vancouver Barracks, Washington, and later expanded to include 115,000 men. Uniformed soldiers lived and worked in the lumber camps for civilian wages, less Army pay. In addition to guaranteeing the production of vital lumber, the soldiers upgraded working and living conditions in the camps to military standards, provided security for company resources, and maintained a clear anti-radical, antiunion presence.[39]

Initially, Disque's officers evinced a natural respect for company officials who, like themselves, were middle- or upper-level managers. In return, the managers showed every hospitality and courtesy to the officers whose troops protected their plants and mills. Enlisted members of the Spruce Production Division, however, felt no similar bond with the lumbermen. To minimize any worker resentment toward the Army, Disque increased worker representation in the committees at the local, district, and central levels of the union. At the highest level, though, Disque retained the right of veto, ensuring that the committee did not pass measures detrimental to production.[40]

Because Disque's Loyal Legion and Spruce Production Division brought about needed reforms, workers were expected to make certain concessions. Continued membership in other unions was discouraged, and these organizations were soon no longer in the camps. At the outset of the legion's recruiting drive, Disque invited members of the IWW to put aside their differences and join his organization. This not only weakened IWW's image as the only resort for the disgruntled lumber worker, but it also enabled Disque's men to scrutinize the activities of those who joined. To assist him, MID personnel and agents from the American Protective League conducted investigations and provided information on rival organizations and their members. A favorite ploy was to disenroll Wobblies from the 4 L and report them to the local draft board, which, under existing employment laws, could induct men who were without jobs into military service. Together with the Loyal Legion, the American Protective League, and the Military Intelligence Division, the Spruce Production Division broke radical and organized labor in the Northwest. Most employers preferred the Loyal Legion to the independent radical unions, and many dismissed workers who refused to join. Disque's work boosted spruce production from a low of 200,000 board feet of lumber in August 1917 to 22 million board feet per month by November 1918—more than enough to fill aircraft production needs of the Allied Powers.[41]

Federal military intervention in the Northwest lumber camps effectively ended labor disputes in that region and in the lumber industry for the remainder of the war and beyond.

---

[38] Hyman, *Soldiers and Spruce*, pp. 112–14, 237.

[39] Tyler, "U.S. Government as Union Organizer," pp. 337–41; Dubofsky, *We Shall Be All*, pp. 413–14. The 4 L was abolished in the 1930s.

[40] Hyman, *Soldiers and Spruce*, pp. 110, 115–16, 307; Glasser Rpt, NW Lumber Strikes, 1917, p. 73, RG 60; "Spruce and the IWW," *New Republic* 14 (23 February 1918):99–100.

[41] Hyman, *Soldiers and Spruce*, pp. 239–43.

More important, the lumber strikes and Army interventions against the Industrial Workers of the World during the summer and early fall of 1917 provided the federal government and the War Department with valuable lessons on how to deal with labor disorders in industries such as mining and petroleum.

Mining, 1917–1919

Copper ranked high on the list of vital resources. In the mining industry, however, both the Industrial Workers of the World and the American Federation of Labor had been active in the prewar years and became more so as the war progressed. The copper mines of Arizona, concentrated in the central and southeastern counties of the state, produced almost 400,000 tons of copper in 1917, about twice that of Montana, their nearest competitor. This production was valued at $200 million annually and employed 23,000 men, nearly 10 percent of the state's work force. Recognizing the importance of this commodity, President Wilson authorized military commanders to protect copper-producing regions from the threat of sabotage, especially that posed by the alien-dominated IWW.[42]

In 1916 and 1917 the AFofL and the IWW had vied for control of the Arizona unions. At its convention in 1916, the AFofL–affiliated Western Federation of Miners changed its name to the International Union of Mine, Mill, and Smelter Workers (IUMMSW). Simultaneously, it repudiated radical unionism because its previous affiliation with the IWW had gained it the unpopular reputation of being a syndicalist organization. Many of its rank-and-file members, however, disagreed with the more moderate stand and drifted into the IWW, which took over several IUMMSW locals and created the Metal Mine Workers (MMW) Union No. 800 in January 1917. Even in areas where AFofL unions still existed, the IWW set up shop with the hope of taking over the rival organizations. By April, because of IWW's organizing skills, the MMW had over 6,000 members in the copper regions of Arizona and effectively dominated the industry.[43]

By the end of June 1917 the IWW was ready to test its strength and called a strike for better living and working conditions and higher wages. Most miners were painfully aware of the rising cost of living caused by wartime economic dislocations and believed that increased profits were going into the pockets of the mine owners at their expense. In some cases wage reductions had been imposed while profits were at an all-time high. The strike began as scheduled; miners left pits in Bisbee, Globe, Miami, and Swansea, Arizona, and the smaller and weaker IUMMSW, not to be outdone by the IWW, called out its locals. Within five days 25,000 strikers had closed every major copper mine in the state. The strike was 90 percent effective in Bisbee and 100 percent effective in the Clifton-Morenci district where the IWW and IUMMSW joined ranks in an uncharacteristic example of

---

[42] Ibid., pp. 224, 239–43, 253, 263–64, 307–09, 328; Tyler, "U.S. Government as Union Organizer," pp. 442–47. For blacklisting efforts and Army intervention in an IWW labor dispute in Idaho, see W. H. Urmy to C. P. Howard, 18 Feb 19; E. P. Marsh to C. P. Howard, 12 Feb 19; Memo, JAG for CofS, 10 Apr 18; Telg, HQ, San Francisco, to AG, 16 Mar 18; Memo, JAG for AG, 10 Apr 18; all in Glasser File: St. Maries, Idaho, RG 60, NARA. See also "Colonel Disque and the IWW," *New Republic* 14 (6 April 1914):284–85.

[43] Glasser Rpt, Arizona Copper Strikes, 1917–1918, pp. 1–2, RG 60, NARA. For labor disputes, see Byrkit, *Forging the Copper Collar*; Dubofsky, *We Shall Be All*, p. 370.

labor solidarity.[44] Local officials, management, and the press, however, immediately labeled the strike a "pro-German plot to disrupt the war effort." President of the Phelps-Dodge Corporation Walter Douglas vowed, "we will not compromise with rattlesnakes; this goes for the International, the AFofL organization, as well as for the IWW." On 28 June Arizona Governor Thomas E. Campbell appealed to the federal government for mediators and for an investigating officer from the Army's Southern Department to determine whether a need existed for military intervention.[45]

His request met with a favorable response. Secretary Baker ordered the Southern Department commander, Maj. Gen. James Parker, to send "a suitable officer and keep a suitable force in readiness." On 29 June Parker dispatched Lt. Col. James J. Hornbrook from Fort Douglas to the Copper Queen Consolidated Mine

JAMES PARKER

Company, which had 2,500 workers on strike. Hornbrook left a squadron of the 17th Cavalry in readiness at Fort Douglas, made a brief survey, and reported that no violence or disorder existed, although the two largest companies were operating with only 40 to 50 percent of their labor force. However, he reported also that the IWW grievances were without merit and suggested a wider movement on the part of labor to lower production and thus embarrass copper producers. The sheriff of the locality was pessimistic and had deputized many mine workers to assist nonstriking laborers coming off their shifts. Hornbrook believed that the citizens had backbone, and, although his troops would expedite production, their presence could not be justified on the grounds of disorder. Finally, he predicted that the presence of a large number of anti-Wobbly vigilantes made any future violence on the part of the union unlikely.[46]

Maj. Charles M. Bundel, 10th Field Artillery, who was sent to Globe to consult with Governor Campbell and local authorities about the labor situation there, made a similar report the following week. Like Hornbrook in Bisbee, he believed the situation was acute, but expected no violence. He wanted, however, to aid civil authorities with federal troops

---

[44] Dubofsky, *We Shall Be All*, p. 370; Meyer Fishbein, "The President's Mediation Commission and the Arizona Copper Strike, 1917," *Southwest Social Science Quarterly* 30 (December 1949):175; Douglas D. Martin, *An Arizona Chronology: Statehood, 1913–1936* (Tucson: University of Arizona Press, 1966).

[45] Dubofsky, *We Shall Be All*, pp. 368–72. For a description of the Arizona mining industry, see Works Progress Administration, Federal Writers Project, *Arizona: A State Guide* (New York: Hastings House, 1940), pp. 90–93.

[46] Quote from Fishbein, "President's Mediation Commission and Arizona Copper Strike," pp. 176–77. See also "Arizona Copper Strike," *Outlook* 116 (18 July 1917):434; Telg, Campbell to Baker, 28 Jun 17, as quoted in Telg, AG to CG, Southern Dept, 29 Jun 17, File 370.6, RG 407, NARA.

should violence on the part of the strikers occur. The War Department approved, especially if public utilities—which it defined to include mines—were in danger of sabotage or destruction by "mobs . . . under leadership and control of aliens hostile to the United States."[47]

As matters developed in the mines, the fears of the military authorities that striking miners might commit violence and disorder proved to be misdirected. The true danger, which ultimately required Army intervention, came from nonstriking workers and citizens of the region. In Jerome a Loyalty League was organized and, supported by local businessmen and leading residents, within a week took the law into its own hands. On 10 July hundreds of miners and others armed with rifles or pick handles cleared the town of the "agitators who they considered undesirable." The objects of their wrath, mainly strikers, were loaded on a train and removed to Needles, California, where other irate armed citizens refused to let them disembark. The train then returned to Arizona, dumping its cargo in Kingman. Most of the alleged agitators were IWW members, but the Jerome Loyalty League also threatened members of the IUMMSW with deportation unless they obeyed the mine owners.[48]

Events at Bisbee, population 8,000, were more violent than those at Jerome. Soon after the strike began, Sheriff Harry Wheeler contacted Governor Campbell to request federal aid in suppressing the strike because he anticipated bloodshed and a great loss of life. In addition, he stated, the majority of the strikers seemed "foreign," and the entire situation appeared pro-German and anti-American. He stressed the importance of the copper mines of Bisbee to the war effort and the tragedy that could result if they were to cease production. Before the governor could act, however, Bisbee citizens who were members of the Bisbee Workman's Loyalty League and Citizen's Protective League took the law into their own hands. With the blessing and perhaps connivance of Sheriff Wheeler, who had organized a posse, telegraph and telephone communications with the outside world were broken. Two thousand vigilantes under the supervision of Phelps-Dodge and Calumet & Arizona Mining Company executives then proceeded to round up 1,300 strikers and put them on railroad cattle cars belonging to the El Paso & Southwestern Railroad, a subsidiary of Phelps-Dodge, for removal. After a harrowing trip in hot, unsanitary, and overcrowded conditions, without food or water, the strikers arrived in Columbus, New Mexico, only to find aroused citizens blocking their departure. The train then proceeded to the small desert town of Hermanas, New Mexico, where the strikers were dumped in the desert without food, water, or shelter.[49]

Such deportations were illegal in every particular. At Bisbee the sheriff and the mining company officials failed to consult state or federal attorneys. The vigilantes seized and transported the strikers without warrant across a state boundary in violation of the constitutional rights of these people. Army personnel observing the event made no effort

---

[47] Quotes from Telg, Hornbrook to AG, 30 Jun 17; File Arizona (Copper IWW, 1917–18–19) and Arizona Copper Strike, 1917, pp. 2–4; both in Glasser Papers, RG 60. See also Telg, AG to CG, Southern Dept, 29 Jun 17, File 370.6, RG 407.

[48] As quoted in Telg, AG to CG, Southern Dept, 6 Jul 17; Telg, Parker to AG, 4 Jul 17; both in Glasser File: Arizona (Copper IWW, 1917–18–19), RG 60, NARA.

[49] Fishbein, "President's Mediation Commission and Arizona Copper Strike," p. 178; Dubofsky, *We Shall Be All*, pp. 384–85; John A. Lindquist, "The Jerome Deportation of 1917," *Arizona and the West* 11 (February 1969):233–40.

to protect the strikers, quell the vigilantes, or prevent the deportations. On the contrary, Colonel Hornbrook described the act as an "orderly procedure" and referred to the vigilantes as a "posse" and the strikers as "undesirables."[50]

In Washington, D.C., the events were viewed differently. President Wilson wired Governor Campbell and instructed him to take firm measures against vigilantism: "May I not respectfully urge the great danger of citizens taking the law into their own hands. . . . I look upon such actions with grave apprehension."[51] Campbell, however, mistook this concern for an offer of military aid and asked General Parker to post four companies at Bisbee and one each at Kingman, Jerome, Humboldt, Clifton, Morenci, Ajo, and Ray. Although federalized National Guard units were already at Bisbee and Ajo, Parker refused to act upon Campbell's request until the governor formally applied to the president for aid under RS 5297. (Parker's punctiliousness in observing traditional prewar requirements was admirable but unnecessary, under the direct-access dispensation given all state governors by Baker on 29 May.)[52] Nevertheless, Campbell submitted his application to President Wilson later that day, explaining that the federal status of the Arizona National Guard effectively denied him the means to protect strikers from attacks by vigilantes. Secretary Baker agreed and directed Parker to use as much force as necessary to protect lives and property but not to give the appearance of partisanship. Parker subsequently ordered the commanders of the Arizona and El Paso districts, respectively responsible for Arizona and New Mexico, to protect strikers and Wobblies from further mob violence.[53]

Baker also intervened directly. Bypassing Parker and the two district commanders, the secretary ordered the acting post commander at Fort Douglas to send Hornbrook's squadron of the 17th Cavalry to Hermanas to escort the strikers back to Columbus—a violation of the chain of command that Parker later protested.[54] Hornbrook's squadron did as ordered, returning the men to Columbus on 14 July and placing them in protective custody. He refused, however, to release any of the men, and recommended to his superiors in vain that all 1,200 strikers be held indefinitely on the grounds that "they do not want to work, and they influence other [nonstrikers] for the bad." But on Baker's orders he released 200 men on 21 July.[55]

The freed men promptly spread the word of their comrades' plight. Samuel Gompers spoke personally to President Wilson, and the Mexican ambassador lodged a protest with the Department of State because some 300 Mexican citizens were among the strikers. After Secretary of State Robert Lansing interceded with Baker on 7 August 1917, Hornbrook received orders to conduct a census of the strikers. Of the 1,000 men still being detained, over twenty nationalities were represented, including 199 Americans, 141 Britons, 82 Serbians, 179 other Slavs, 268 Mexicans, and nearly 200 enemy aliens from Germany or Austria-Hungary. In addition 700 strikers were foreign born, but 468 were American citizens, 472 had registered under the selective service law, 433 were married with families,

---

[50] Fishbein, "President's Mediation Commission and Arizona Copper Strike," p. 178; Glasser Rpt, Arizona Copper Strike, 1917, pp. 5–9, RG 60; Dubofsky, *We Shall Be All*, pp. 385–87; Philip Taft, "The Bisbee Deportation," *Labor History* 13 (Winter 1972):3–40.

[51] Glasser Rpt, Arizona Copper Strike, 1917, pp. 9–10, RG 60.

[52] Quoted in *Tucson Citizen*, 13 Jul 17; reprinted in Glasser Rpt, Arizona Copper Strike, 1917, p. 10, RG 60.

[53] Telg, Parker to AG, 12 Jul 17, File 370.6, RG 407, NARA.

[54] Telgs, AG to CG, Southern Dept, 12 Jul 17; Parker to AG, 13, 14 Jul 17, all in File 370.6 (Arizona), RG 407.

[55] Telg, Parker to AG, 14 Jul 17, Glasser File: Arizona (Copper IWW, 1917–18–19), RG 60, NARA.

426 were members of the IWW, 351 were members of the AFofL, and 360 were nonunion workers. Embarrassingly, 62 were military veterans, 205 owned liberty bonds, and 520 had subscribed to the Red Cross and were Bisbee property owners. The group did not seem revolutionary and seditious. Hornbrook released the Mexican nationals immediately and discharged the other prisoners between 9 August and early October.[56]

But the furor over the deportations continued. Pressures mounted until Wilson ordered the Council of National Defense, chaired by Baker, to investigate labor conditions in Arizona and in troubled areas of Montana, Idaho, Texas, Louisiana, Washington, and California as well. On 20 September 1917, the council appointed a commission led by Secretary of Labor William B. Wilson, consisting of J. L. Spangler, a coal-mine operator; Verner Z. Reed, a Colorado entrepreneur; John H. Walker, a UMW member; E. P. Marsh, a moderate Socialist and president of the Washington State AFofL; and Felix Frankfurter, the future Supreme Court justice. The group, known as the President's Mediation Commission, visited the Arizona copper districts in October 1917, hoping to adjust "the outstanding controversies which touch war industries, and to leave behind such a state of feeling that no conflict involving a stoppage of work would occur for the duration of the war."[57]

Its report, issued on 6 November, was surprising in its moderation:

Neither sinister influences nor the IWW can account for these strikes. The explanation is to be found in unremediated and remediable industrial disorders. The overwhelming mass of the laboring population is in no sense disloyal. With the exception of the sacrifices of the men in the armed service, the greatest sacrifices have come from those at the lowest rung of the industrial ladder. It is upon them that the war pressure has borne most severely. Labor at heart is as devoted to the purpose of the government in the prosecution of this war as any other part of society. Too often there is a glaring inconsistency between our democratic purposes in this war abroad and the autocratic conduct of those guiding industry at home. Personal bitterness and more intense industrial strife inevitably result when the claim of loyalty is falsely resorted to by employers and their sympathizers as a means of defeating sincere claims for social justice, even though such claims be asserted in time of war.

The commission condemned "the so-called 'loyalty leagues' [which] only serve to intensify bitterness, and, more unfortunately, to the minds of the worker in the West, served to associate all loyalty movements with partisan and anti-union aims."[58] It recommended that federal arbitration replace strikes for adjustment of grievances; that future working conditions be agreed upon by committees free of company influence; that employees be allowed to organize unions; and that all workers be rehired excepting those guilty of seditious utterances, inefficiency, or membership in organizations opposed to the recommendations.

---

[56] Ibid., 17 Jul 17, File 370.61 (Bisbee), RG 407, NARA.

[57] Fishbein, "President's Mediation Commission and Arizona Copper Strike," pp. 179–80; Telgs, L. Sigal, AF of L, to Wilson, 25 Jul 17; Y. Bonillas, Mexican Ambassador, to F. Polk, Acting Secy of State, 26 Jul 17; CG, El Paso Dist, Ft. Sam Houston, to AG, 7 Aug 17; Lansing to Baker, 7 Aug 17; Bliss to AG, 9 Aug 17. All in File 085–IWW, RG 407, NARA. See also Renshaw, *The Wobblies*, p. 235; United States, President's Mediation Commission, *Report on the Bisbee Deportations* (Washington, D.C.: Government Printing Office, 1918), p. 5; Byrkit, *Forging the Copper Collar*.

[58] Glasser Rpt, Arizona Copper Strike, 1917, pp. 16–17, RG 60; Dubofsky, *We Shall Be All*, p. 415; "President's Commission at Bisbee," *New Republic* 13 (8 December 1917):140–41. For a biography of Frankfurter, see Melvin Urofsky, *Felix Frankfurter: Judicial Restraint and Individual Liberties* (Boston: G. K. Hall, 1991).

Finally, the commission encouraged the attorney general to institute criminal proceedings against Sheriff Wheeler and the vigilantes for grossly misrepresenting the intentions of the strikers and forcibly deporting innocent men. As a result, a federal grand jury indicted Wheeler and twenty-four others for conspiring to "injure, oppress, threaten, and intimidate . . . a large number of citizens in the exercise of their federal and constitutional rights."[59]

No disciplinary action was taken against Army departmental or local commanders for their failure to prevent the mob actions at Jerome and Bisbee, yet there was much to criticize in their inactions. Ordered by Secretary Baker to protect lives and to avoid taking sides, both Parker and Hornbrook had badly misinterpreted the true situation in Arizona and had failed to protect workers who were exercising their right to conduct a nonviolent strike. Even

SAMUEL GOMPERS

greater criticism might well be directed at Secretary Baker and the Wilson administration for creating the conditions and formulating policies that allowed the officers to act without reference to existing laws and regulations.

Arizona: Continuing Tensions, 1917–1920

In spite of the commission's recommendations and the end of the strikes, labor tensions persisted. Troops stayed in the Globe, Miami, Ray, and Ajo districts through the remainder of 1917 and into early 1918. During this time the Arizona political climate changed significantly when a prolabor governor, George W. P. Hunt, was placed in office by court order on Christmas Day 1917, replacing his fraudulently elected predecessor. In February 1918 Hunt wrote to Baker that a federal arbitrator had advised him "that the labor situation would not be disturbed in any manner if troops were sent elsewhere." He recommended that the troops in all districts, with the exception of Ajo, be withdrawn because they caused "a certain measure of resentment on the part of workers, who, in the main, are thoroughly patriotic and who naturally feel the presence of the troops places them inferentially under suspicion." Their presence, he concluded, "proves an invitation to trouble rather than a precaution against it."[60]

---

[59] Quote from Fishbein, "President's Mediation Commission and Arizona Copper Strike," pp. 179–80; *Rpt of President's Mediation Commission,* pp. 4, 6, 19–20.

[60] Glasser Rpt, Arizona Copper Strike, 1917, pp. 16–17, RG 60; *Rpt of President's Mediation Commission,* pp. 6–7, 19. An Arizona federal district court acquitted all defendants, a decision upheld by the U.S. Supreme Court in December 1920. See *U.S.* vs. *Wheeler* in 254 Fed. 611 254 U.S. 281; Preston, *Aliens and Dissenters,* p. 119.

Hunt's prolabor and, to critics, pro-IWW reputation caused alarm on the part of company officials and military authorities. The War Department avoided the entire issue of the federal military presence awaiting a further Labor Department report. Before any federal action could be taken, Hunt's term ended and he was replaced by the now legally elected Thomas Campbell, who preferred that the troops stay indefinitely. In March 1919 the War Department informed him, however, that as soon as peace was formally declared the Army would withdraw troops from the six mines they still occupied in Arizona.[61]

Nevertheless, most federal troops remained until 23 January 1920, when the Army withdrew them for recuperation and instruction; one unit, a company of the 19th Infantry at Globe, remained until the summer of 1920. Even then mine owners protested, but the Army assured them that the soldiers could easily return in an emergency.[62] Federal troops had occupied the Arizona mining regions for three years after the strikes of 1917, and for one and one-half years after the armistice. As in the Northwest lumber strikes, federal action (or in the case of Arizona the lack of Army action to protect union members) had hampered labor organizations, moderate or radical, long after the war effort that provided the reason for intervention was over.

Butte, Montana, 1917–1921

Living and working conditions in Butte were in many ways worse than those in Arizona. Montana copper companies refused to recognize unions, paid subsistence wages, and required miners to labor under unsafe conditions. The Butte International Union of Mine, Mill, and Smelter Workers, like its Arizona counterpart, was extremely weak since its defeat in a 1914 strike and could not hope to persuade the copper companies to improve the lot of its members voluntarily. Although tensions had existed for years prior to the war, they increased with the Speculator Mine disaster of 8 June 1917. Here a fire broke out at the 2,400-foot depth and spread quickly to other areas of the mine. Improper safety precautions and a lack of escape routes resulted in the deaths of 164 miners.[63]

In the wake of this calamity, miners agreed to strike under the leadership of Tom Campbell and Joe Shannon, both members of the Industrial Workers of the World. The two formed a new organization, the Metal Mine Workers Union, in an effort to transcend the old rivalry between the IWW and the AFofL. The proposed strike was intended to obtain better working conditions, a $6 minimum daily wage, union recognition, and the abolition of the practice of blacklisting union members. The strike began on 12 June 1917.[64] Mine owners had little to fear because elements of the federalized Montana National Guard had been posted at the mines as utility guards since March. A supplemental force of the 2d Montana Infantry arrived the day before the strike began, bringing the total number of federalized guardsmen in Butte to over 200. The lack of any form

---

[61] Ltr, Hunt to Baker, 9 Feb 18, Glasser File: Arizona (Copper IWW, 1917–18–19), RG 60, NARA.

[62] Telg, R. C. Cabell, Southern Dept, to Campbell, 26 Mar 19, Glasser File: Arizona (Copper IWW, 1917–18–19), RG 60, NARA.

[63] Telg, Dickman to AG, 23 Jan 20, Glasser File: Arizona (Copper IWW, 1917–18–19), RG 60, NARA.

[64] Arnon Gutfield, "The Speculator Mine Disaster in 1917: Labor Resurgence at Butte, Montana," *Arizona and the West* 11 (Spring 1969):27–38.

of labor violence indicated that the troops were primarily intended to protect the mines from sabotage and to break potential strikes. On 10 August, and each day thereafter, two or three companies of troops were ordered to patrol mine approaches to intimidate strikers and to assure that nonstriking workers were allowed entrance. When the federal military presence failed to prevent another strike against the Anaconda Copper Company, however, company officials took matters in their own hands and closed all its operations in the area.

The ripple effect of this action immediately put 15,000 miners out of work. The company strategy worsened the already desperate financial plight of miners in the region and convinced the smelter workers to reach a quick settlement for slightly higher wages on 11 September. The scheduled reopening of the smelters and mines a week later brought federal troops to Anaconda "to prevent violence and disorder and interference with the rights of individuals to work unmolested." The lack of worker solidarity, company strength, and the presence of federal troops caused the labor action to collapse. The mines reopened without violence, ending the three-month strike.[65]

But the region was far from quiet. The following spring, in the midst of another IWW mine strike, a local Butte workingman's group, the Irish-American Pearce-Connally Club, requested permission from the local Army commander, Capt. Omar N. Bradley, commander of Company F, 14th Infantry, to conduct a parade down Butte's Main Street on St. Patrick's Day. Although Bradley's authority to grant permission for such activity was uncertain, he consented to the march provided it did not turn into an unpatriotic antiwar demonstration. Local citizens, however, strongly objected to the display and persuaded the mayor and State Council of Defense to prohibit the parade on the grounds that the Pearce-Connally Club was anti-British and allegedly dominated by the IWW. The real purpose of the parade, the council maintained, was to demonstrate IWW power and to intimidate nonstriking miners. Trouble was expected if the march occurred. The matter was referred to Governor Samuel Stewart, who contacted Maj. Gen. Arthur Murray of the Western Department to seek his approval to use Bradley's 14th Infantry to enforce the parade ban. Murray concurred and ordered Bradley to cooperate fully with state, city, and county officials in enforcing law and order in Butte. Bradley, after meeting with the mayor, agreed to station his troops along Main Street to disperse would-be marchers.[66]

Late on Sunday morning, 18 March 1918, Company F drilled in town to dissuade the club from attempting to march at noon. When the scheduled parade time passed without incident, Bradley ordered all his men back to camp, except for a five-man patrol. Sometime after 1600, a member of the patrol informed him that a crowd of between 5,000 and 7,000 men had gathered along Main Street. Bradley ordered two squads, numbering 25 men, to the scene to reinforce the patrol and soon joined them, accompanied by the local chief of police and the chief of detectives. In a matter of minutes the soldiers had cleared Main Street, except for a hard core of hangers-on who had to be moved with rifle butts and bayonets. In the process Bradley's troops helped local police arrest over 100 men. The city police charged 56 with being drunk and disorderly and remanded 46 others—"aliens, disloyal persons, or draft

[65] Dubofsky, *We Shall Be All*, pp. 366–67.

[66] Quoted in Glasser Rpt, Butte Mine Strike, pp. 51–58, 68, RG 60. See also C. Merz, "The Issue in Butte," *New Republic* 12 (22 September 1917):215–17.

ARTHUR MURRAY

dodgers"—to the custody of federal officials for probable trial on sedition charges.[67]

Bradley had carried out his instructions without bloodshed. Murray, however, had failed to observe the order issued by Baker on 20 November 1917, requiring that all requests for troops be made through the War Department unless an emergency situation existed. On learning of the oversight the acting judge advocate general, Samuel T. Ansell, in spite of the policy of direct access, reminded the acting chief of staff, Brig. Gen. Lytle Brown, that the governor of a state had absolutely no legal authority to make a request directly to an officer of the Army. Brown turned aside Ansell's objections, arguing that General Murray had acted in accordance with a provision of Army regulations covering cases of "emergency so imminent as to render it dangerous to await instructions requested through" usual channels. He concluded that Bradley had "acted entirely within the law and . . . [had] shown commendable good sense." Thus an incident, minor in itself, served to reinforce the wartime policy.[68]

Labor disputes continued in Butte through the remainder of 1918, but none required federal action. Bradley's 14th Infantry left in September 1918 and was replaced by a company of United States Guards. This force, created by the War Department in December 1917 to protect war utilities within the United States, formed a special unit of the Militia Bureau, National Army, and eventually comprised forty-eight battalions of 26,000 officers and men. Its existence freed Regular Army and National Guard units for service overseas and more vital war duties; its recruits were either volunteers too old or too young for the Army or draftees physically unqualified for overseas duty. The federal equivalent of a home guard, United States Guards were stationed at over 300 locations in 32 states between 1917 and the armistice.[69]

This replacement of regulars with United States Guards produced an abrupt transformation in attitudes toward union members, strikers, and radicals. "The troops in Butte changed from a fair, restrained body of men to an unfair, unrestrained, vicious, and violent

[67] Rpt, Bradley to CG, Western Dept, 19 Mar 18, File 370.6, RG 407, NARA; Glasser Rpt, Butte Mine Strike, pp. 81–83, RG 60. For a history of the Irish in Butte, see David M. Emmons, *The Butte Irish: Class and Ethnicity in an American Mining Town, 1875–1925* (Urbana: University of Illinois Press, 1990).

[68] Glasser Rpt, Butte Mine Strike, pp. 81–83, RG 60. See also Rpt, Bradley to CG, Western Dept, 19 Mar 18, File 370.6, RG 407; Preston, *Aliens and Dissenters*, p. 112. For Bradley's memories of his Butte posting, see Omar N. Bradley and Clay Blair, *A General's Life* (New York: Simon and Schuster, 1983), pp. 43–44. Several in the mob suffered bruises, but no serious injuries were reported.

[69] Preston, *Aliens and Dissenters*, p. 112. Ansell claimed Murray violated GO 147. Brown upheld Murray's actions under par. 487 of Army regulations.

body, carrying on a veritable reign of terror," said Attorney General Thomas Watt Gregory in October 1918 when he wrote Secretary Baker to demand that the force in Butte be kept within legal bounds. Yet the problem was not only with the guards. In July the War Department had issued special regulations intended to provide the Army greater leeway in dealing with labor radicals who disrupted production in the copper mines and lumber camps of the Far West. The new orders virtually made any agitation for strikes or strike activity synonymous with treason. Gregory protested that "the crime of treason is defined so broadly that a person not a lawyer and not familiar with the [court] decisions might conclude that any strike in a war industry plant or any promotion or agitation of such a strike would constitute the grave crime of treason. Wage earners very naturally resent having a strike, which they deem justifiable, treated as the gravest of all crimes."[70] The offend-

THOMAS WATT GREGORY

ing regulation was rescinded on 23 October 1918 and by the following February the overzealous United States Guards in Butte had been replaced by Regular Army troops. Nonetheless labor tensions continued, and MID investigations increased even as wartime repression seemed to ease.

Oil, 1917: Texas, Louisiana, and Oklahoma

Union activity began in the oil fields of East Texas and West Louisiana soon after the first gushers occurred in 1901. Locals of the AFofL–affiliated Brotherhood of Oil and Gas Well Workers formed in Spindletop, Batson, Sourlake, Saratoga, and Humble, Texas, by 1902. Although oil producers resisted attempts at union organization and refused recognition, the fledgling labor movement managed through well-timed and coordinated strikes to prevent the producers, such as the J. M. Guffey Petroleum Company (later renamed the Gulf Oil Corporation), from cutting wages in 1905 and 1907. Most oil-field workers ("roughnecks"), however, failed to see the need to support unions in noncrisis times. Consequently unions were very weak in the petroleum-producing regions of the nation on the eve of World War I.[71]

The rising wartime cost of living, continued poor working conditions, and paternalistic company policies caused an increase in union activity, especially in the Goose Creek,

---

[70] U.S. War Department, *Report of the Chief of the Militia Bureau, 1919* (Washington, D.C.: Government Printing Office, 1919), pp. 18–20; *General Orders and Bulletins, 1917*, GO 162.

[71] Quotes from Glasser Rpt, Butte Mine Strike, pp. 1, 78, 120, RG 60. The regulation in question was *Army Special Regulation 101* of 26 June 1918. See also Preston, *Aliens and Dissenters*, pp. 112–13.

Texas, oil fields in late 1916 and early 1917. Managers turned down requests by union leaders, speaking on behalf of all oil workers, to meet with producers for the redress of grievances in October 1917. The producer spokesman, Ross Sterling of the Humble Oil and Refining Company, echoing the sentiments of the oil producers, saw "no reason why we should confer with outsiders or strangers upon matters which concern our employees and ourselves." In response, the AFofL oil unions presented formal demands that included an eight-hour workday, a minimum daily wage of $4, a revised bonus system, and union recognition. When the producers refused to consider these demands, nearly 6,000 union members voted to strike. The first major labor action in the petroleum industry in a decade began on 1 November 1917, when 10,000 oilmen in seventeen fields in Texas and Louisiana left their jobs.[72]

Texas Governor William P. Hobby had already wired Secretary of War Baker, informing him that oil unions planned strikes throughout Texas, and warned him that federal troops were necessary to protect the oil fields against sabotage. Louisiana Governor Ruffin G. Pleasant repeated Hobby's admonition regarding the oil fields in his own state. On Baker's request the War Department issued instructions to department commanders that all possible cooperation was to be given civil authorities in protecting the oil fields, and troop deployments began immediately on orders from Maj. Gen. John W. Ruckman, commanding general of the Southern Department.[73]

On 3 November three companies of the 19th Infantry under the command of Maj. John McE. Pruyn left Fort Sam Houston for the oil fields in Damonmound, Texas. Other troops were stationed at the Goosecreek oil fields, forty miles north of Houston; two companies of the 132d Infantry guarded the oil fields in Sourlake; one battalion of the 131st Infantry controlled the situation in Humble, twenty miles north of Houston; and one officer and twenty-four military policemen of the 33d Division guarded the oil fields in Englewood, six miles from Houston. All locations were reported quiet when the federal troops arrived.

In Louisiana, Maj. Gen. William P. Duvall of the Southeastern Department ordered companies of the 1st Mississippi Infantry to Mansfield, Oil City, Crichton, Edgerly, and Vinton. They arrived without mishap, and all locations were reported as quiet.[74] The commanding officer in Shreveport reported that the oil-field workers were anxious to return to work and that company officials believed additional troops could convince 90 percent of their employees to resume work in forty-eight hours. The situation was serious but quiet. In Edgerly, also, the Army reported that the situation was calm and that the strike would last no longer than fifteen to thirty days. Over a hundred wells and power plants were still operating; only drilling had been suspended, and more troops were unnecessary. The strike in Oil City, however, showed signs of violence—unconfirmed reports claimed that a laborer had been shot from ambush. The following day the commanding officer informed his superiors that the oil companies would attempt to operate the fields with nonunion labor and requested more

---

[72] James C. Maroney, "The Texas-Louisiana Oilfield Strike of 1917," in Gary M. Fink and Merle E. Reed, eds., *Essays in Southern Labor History: Selected Papers, Southern Labor History Conference, 1976* (Westport: Greenwood, 1977), pp. 161–62; William L. Greer, "The Texas Gulf Coast Oil Strike of 1917" (M.A. thesis, University of Houston, 1974).

[73] Maroney, "Texas-Louisiana," p. 163.

[74] Telg, Hobby to Baker, 31 Oct 17, Glasser File: Tex., La., Okla. (Oil, Nov 1917), RG 60, NARA.

troops to prevent anticipated bloodshed. The remaining members of the 1st Mississippi Infantry at Vicksburg were sent to Vivian, Lewis, and Mooringsport, Louisiana, to protect the oil fields and strikebreakers. The soldiers of the 155th Infantry replaced these Mississippi troops and, in turn, the 3d Battalion of the 43d Infantry replaced the 155th in Oil City, Mooringsport, Mansfield, Vinton, and Shreveport, Louisiana, on 18 January 1918.[75]

WILLIAM P. DUVALL

By late November the Army had deployed 2,500 men in the oil fields of Texas and Louisiana. In addition, troops of the 19th Infantry were held in readiness at Fort Sill, Oklahoma, in case strikes taking place there went beyond the control of civil officials. Initially, Army relations with the strikers were good, although the presence of soldiers left the impression in the minds of most striking oilmen that the government agreed with oil company charges of striker disloyalty and subversive tendencies. While most officers and their men remained neutral and objective, others were openly hostile to the strikers, such as Col. J. D. Baker, 57th Infantry. He characterized the strikers "as Americans of the irresponsible type which, when it feels itself aggrieved is prone to violence and disorder," and warned that "there is much latent hostility to the operators which, whatever the outcome of the strike . . . must be for some time taken into account and guarded against." In Washington similar feelings were reflected in a Justice Department request that federal troops remain in the oil fields beyond the end of November and only be withdrawn gradually thereafter.[76]

As with other wartime labor disputes, the oil producers were quick to label the strikers as treasonous subversives. One group informed Attorney General Gregory that IWW agents and German spies had infiltrated the petroleum unions and that these outside agitators had caused the strike. Workers were reported to be afraid of returning to work because of IWW intimidation. However, little evidence existed of IWW influence in the strike. More important than company propaganda was the hostility of the public and the press to the strike. Even refinery workers, deemed crucial to the strike's success, failed to support it, although they sympathized publicly with their fellow workers.

As the strike entered its second month with no sign of a settlement, President Wilson ordered the Presidential Mediation Commission to investigate the troubles in the oil fields.

---

[75] Telgs, Ruckman to AG, 2, 3 Nov 17; see also Telg, Duvall to AG, 2 Nov 17; both in Glasser File: Tex., La., Okla. (Oil, Nov 1917), RG 60, NARA.

[76] The account of the strike given here is drawn from Maroney, "Texas-Louisiana," pp. 164–65, except as otherwise noted. See also A. Bruce Bielaski, Dept of Justice, to AG, 23 Nov 17, Glasser File: Tex., La., Okla. (Oil, Nov 1917), RG 60, NARA.

Although the strikers welcomed the commission, producers held it in contempt. They had the upper hand and hoped to use federal military assistance to break the oil unions. The commission's report infuriated the producers by calling for an industry-wide, eight-hour workday, union recognition, and an end to discriminatory hiring practices and systematic intimidation of union members. The commission chided the oil companies for dealing with their workers in a heavy-handed and uncompromising manner, implying that producers alone were responsible for their current troubles.

Bolstered by the commission report, which held the promise of an objective hearing of grievances and fair settlement, the unions ended their strike in late December 1917. Their hopes were short lived. On 2 January 1918, 241 oil producers representing 95 percent of the region's petroleum production met in Houston, denounced the findings of the commission, and refused to implement any reforms. With the strike over and production nearing prestrike levels, operators had no reason to change since the commission's recommendations were not binding. The government initiated no further movement for reforms, either during the war or in the years immediately thereafter. The operators, however, had gained in sophistication, founding company unions that provided many of the same material benefits but none of the independence that characterized AFofL unions. Independent unions were gradually pushed out of the oil fields. Subsequent attempts by the AFofL to form a new petroleum workers' union in the summer of 1918, while initially successful, ultimately failed when opposed by a strong and united oil industry.[77]

Conclusion

The use of federal military forces in labor disputes between 1917 and 1918 produced both immediate and long-range effects on the government, the labor and business community, and society at large. The government met its primary goals of obtaining vital war supplies, protecting industrial plants and resources, and maintaining domestic social and political stability. With a submissive, nonradical work force, business and industry collected profits previously unmatched in American history, giving in return only temporary concessions to workers. The abrogation of constitutionally guaranteed civil and political rights and processes and of the federal statutes concerning the domestic use of Regular Army troops was justified on the grounds of the wartime emergency and the lack of adequate local and state forces necessary to quell disorders. Yet the wartime practice of giving local and state officials direct access to troops marked a complete departure from prewar policies and procedures. In not one instance between April 1917 and November 1918 did federal civil or military authorities follow statutory procedures for summoning troops to aid civil authorities, even when local and state authorities did adhere to prewar procedures. These soldiers were repeatedly used by corporate leaders and civil officials whenever the first indications of labor unrest became apparent. Rarely were officials required to go farther than their nearest garrison or department commander to obtain federal forces, either Regular Army or federalized National Guard units, and rarely if ever were their requests questioned.

---

[77] For the later strike, quelled by U.S. Guards, see Telg, Holbrook to AG, 12 Aug 18, Glasser File: Tex., La., Okla. (Oil, Nov 1917), RG 60, NARA.

In most instances during the wartime emergency the Army acted as a strikebreaking force. On numerous occasions commanders ignored injunctions to remain neutral, while the work of the Military Intelligence Division was consciously antiradical and antilabor. The responsibility for determining when troops could intervene in a civil disturbance shifted from the president, the sole legally constituted authority in such matters, to civilians in the War Department and their military subordinates who made and enforced extralegal policies in the president's name without his direction or explicit approval. Lacking the background to handle the complicated issues involved in wartime civil disorders, Baker and others ignored important safeguards and protections built into the law over the previous fifty years to prevent the domestic abuse of federal executive and military power. The liberties taken by local, state, and federal authorities proved difficult and costly to repair in the years following the war. Indeed the "return to normalcy" announced by the new president in 1921 took years to effect.

Although federal mediation agencies had been created during the war that settled hundreds of disputes, the 1917–1918 period also produced a record number of strikes and military interventions. While some labor organizations grew and prospered because of federal intervention, others, especially in the South and West, were crushed by business and government actions. The lumber and oil industries broke the unions and weakened those unions in mining, shipping, and transportation. Federal executive and judiciary power was used deliberately to destroy organizations like the Industrial Workers of the World. Although moderate unions like the AFofL proved more robust, serious labor setbacks in many key industries required years of renewed organization to overcome. The AFofL, having promised to work through the system during the war, declared in the aftermath that the bill for its cooperation was coming due and that if its demands remained unmet larger strikes could be expected.

Active hostilities ended in November 1918, but the wartime regulations regarding the domestic use of federal military troops remained in effect amid increasing indications that even greater labor-management tensions lay ahead. In addition to new labor unrest, racial violence touched off by wartime social changes and the ideological challenges presented by Russian bolshevism promised greater internal turmoil in the future.

CHAPTER 11

The Army and Continued Labor Unrest, 1919–1920

It is quite likely that great numbers of immigrants will be led by the IWW's, the Russian Reds, and others . . . to join forces . . . to overthrow our government. . . . We shall be swamped by this class. They will assimilate us by sheer overpowering majority. . . . It seems as if the uncoordinated misfits and pent up passions and hates of the old world are being mobilized in this country. . . . The new type of immigrant, as distinguished from those who came before the 1880s, has seemingly come to our shores to use it as a battleground to fight out their feuds or to substitute the red flag for the stars and stripes.
—Lt. Col. Dennis P. Quinlan, Judge Advocate General's Office.

The armistice of 11 November 1918 that ended active hostilities in Europe had no effect on government policies regarding the domestic use of federal military troops against radicals or in labor disputes. The wartime policy of direct access remained in force for two more years. Federal mediation agencies, restrictive legislation rigidly enforced, and military interventions during 1917 and 1918 had effectively controlled dissenters, radical political and labor groups, and organized labor and had guaranteed the continued production and flow of materials to Allied armies. Such actions, however, had done little to alter the underlying causes of labor unrest or to alleviate labor concerns about the purposes of federal military intervention.

Following the armistice federal military intervention often exacerbated labor relations that were already tense because of military and industrial demobilization.[1] More than ever, to many labor groups federal action seemed intended to support the aims and goals of business and industrial interests over labor's.

The United States was still officially at war with the Central Powers in 1919 and remained so until formal peace declarations were pronounced by Congress and the president in 1920. Pending these developments, official wartime policies toward labor organizations, radicals, dissenters, and "undesirables" in American society continued in force. The public was instructed to stay vigilant and prepared to defend the home front against foreign radical ideologies and German militarism should the armistice break down and fighting resume.

---

[1] On demobilization, see Benedict Crowell and Robert Wilson, *Demobilization: Our Industrial and Military Demobilization After the Armistice, 1918–1920* (New Haven: Yale University Press, 1921); Jack S. Ballard, "The Shock of Peace: Military and Economic Demobilization After World War I" (Ph.D. diss., University of California in Los Angeles, 1974); E. T. Good, "Labor and Trade After the War: Boom or Slump?" *Living Age* 299 (9 November 1918):362–64.

The National Guard Gap

The problems related to the lack of adequate state military forces were also left unresolved at the end of hostilities in Europe. When federalized National Guardsmen were mustered out of national service in 1918 and 1919, they were by law under no further military obligation to the government or to their respective states. Time was needed for the states to re-create National Guard units, a situation made more difficult by the dearth of state revenues, the lack of immediate federal financial and military aid, and the general war-weariness among males of military age. Furthermore, many state and local officials aware of the costs of re-creating guard units found it cheaper, more convenient, and politically expedient to rely on federal troops as they had under the wartime policy of direct access. Therefore, the Army, also facing congressionally mandated retrenchments, continued to perform a massive internal defense role after 1918.

Lacking state troops, officials used federal military forces to quell a race-related civil disturbance during a sawmill strike in Bogalusa, Louisiana, in late November 1919, which typified the problem. Conflict between black and white workers and between union labor and the Great Southern Lumber Company had caused the death of four strikers. The mayor of Bogalusa, who was also the general manager of the company, requested aid from Governor Ruffin G. Pleasant. Because no state troops were available to prevent further bloodshed, Governor Pleasant requested regulars from Fort Morgan, near Mobile, Alabama. The commander of the Southeastern Department in Charleston, South Carolina, Maj. Gen. Henry G. Sharpe, ordered 5 officers and 100 enlisted men to Bogalusa. When this force arrived on 26 November 1919, however, the situation had stabilized and civil authorities were in control. Federal troops stayed, nonetheless, for another month. Sharpe was highly critical of the use of regulars in this situation and reported that "indications are that this call for troops was unnecessary and undoubtably would not have occurred had the states possessed units of the National Guard."[2]

The "Red Menace"

In many respects government policies toward labor organizations and radicals became more harsh after the armistice because of widespread perceptions of the existence of a new evil, bolshevism, and its influence on the American working man, which after 1918 replaced German militarism as the primary threat to the American way of life and social stability. To the Army this threat was particularly acute. Putting aside feelings of personal distaste for intervention in labor disputes, many officers saw their role in dealing with civil disturbances as a necessary means of protecting both the nation and the Army. Without concrete proof, many officers, like members of the middle and upper classes from which they came, attributed recent domestic disturbances—the IWW strikes, urban race riots, and industry-wide strikes—to the spread of the "red menace." Their readiness to intervene prompted critics to accuse them of playing on public fears as a means to escape the perennial slash of the budget cutter's knife.[3]

---

[2] Quote from Telg, Sharpe to AG, 25 Nov 19; Telgs, Sharpe to AG, 28 Nov 19; Shipman to AG, 20 Dec 19; all in RG 60, Records of the Department of Justice, Glasser File: Bogalusa, La. (Sawmill, Nov 1919), NARA.

[3] For Army officer views, see Richard C. Brown, "Social Attitudes of American Generals, 1898–1940" (Ph.D. diss., University of Wisconsin, 1951). See also "The Infantry in West Virginia," *Infantry Journal* 19 (November

Although the extent of antiradicalism within the Army in the early 1920s cannot be gauged precisely, two Army school texts devoted considerable space to the topic, suggesting it was one of the major problems the service had to face in the postwar period. In a text he prepared for officers at Camp Dix, Lt. Col. Dennis P. Quinlan allotted over thirty paragraphs to a discussion of the threat to the United States posed by foreigners from the poorer, undemocratic nations of Europe.[4]

Another work, by Maj. Cassius M. Dowell, was less impassioned and more influential, reflecting also the antiradicalism that affected the Army during the 1920s. In this 1924–1925 work, Dowell claimed the number of radicals and sympathizers in the United States to be 1,042,000, accounting for about 20 percent of the manpower in such industries as coal mining, shipbuilding, textiles, lumber, railroads, and metal working. These people, he observed, tended to concentrate in the cities where they could exert a choke hold on the nation's industry and commerce: Chicago, Cleveland, New York, Seattle, San Francisco, Boston, New Haven, Buffalo, Philadelphia, Pittsburgh, Detroit, Dayton, and Baltimore. While conceding that the radicals had thus far limited their activities to local disturbances, he predicted that a major catastrophe, for example a new war or a depression, might encourage these people to lead large-scale urban insurrections like those that shook Germany in 1918–1920. This emphasis on the alleged threat of revolution posed by labor radicals of foreign origin had changed little since the rail strikes of 1877 and 1894, indicating a continuity of thought regarding labor-related civil disorders. Such analyses totally ignored domestic causations, such as recalcitrant management and unremedied social and labor ills, preventing the creation of a realistic doctrine on the Army's role in dealing with domestic disorders until the late 1930s and early 1940s.[5]

Dowell's viewpoint was shared by the Army's Military Intelligence Division (MID). According to the MID office in Seattle "the signing of the Armistice has removed the checks imposed by the war and labor now feels it is safe to go as far as it likes." This was not only true of radical labor organizations like the now depleted Industrial Workers of the World but also of main-stream organizations like the American Federation of Labor, which one Army intelligence officer referred to as being "semi-radical." MID reported in late November 1918 that "there is very good reason to think that the AFofL may cause trouble shortly, for the leaders seem to have that desire and they have the strength." Indeed, MID now believed the AFofL to be a bigger threat than the IWW, which no longer had "a sufficient hold on the great body of labor." Nonetheless, the IWW was not thoroughly discounted. One MID officer, Capt. F. W. Wilson, reported in late 1918 that "the IWW is dangerous as a revolutionary movement . . . they consider themselves brothers to the Bolsheviki and now the German Reds. The Bolshevik element in this district [Seattle] are closely allied to the IWW's and

---

1921):576–78; "A National Police," *Army and Navy Register* 76 (17 September 1921):268; Scheips, Some Aspects of the Federal Response to Civil Disorder, pp. 48–49.

 [4] Dennis P. Quinlan, *Military Protection: Employment of the Army in Aid of Federal Civil Authorities in the Execution of Federal Laws* (Camp Dix, N.J., 1922), pp. 39–43. For further information on Quinlan, see James R. Woolard, "The Philippine Scouts: The Development of America's Colonial Army" (Ph.D. diss., Ohio State University, 1975), pp. 83–85.

 [5] See the following by Cassius M. Dowell: *Confidential Supplement to Military Aid to the Civil Power: Additional Legal Aspects, Organization, Equipment, Training, Tactics, and Formulation of Plans* (Fort Leavenworth, Kans.: General Service School, 1925), pp. 2–3, 11, *Military Aid to the Civil Power*, pp. 183–84, and Domestic Disturbances, Monograph, General Service School, Fort Leavenworth, Kans., 1922, pp. 2–3.

Socialists."[6] The IWW, considered a pro-German tool of an imperial military power prior to the armistice, was less than three weeks later regarded as a tool of the Russian and German Bolsheviks. What endured was MID's perception of American labor organizations as being under the influence of foreign radicals and their philosophies.

American Labor After the Armistice

Government and military concerns about the postwar behavior of labor groups were not totally unfounded. Organized labor definitely had a different view of what postwar America should be like when compared to the outlooks of government and corporate officials. Although the IWW had largely been destroyed by the combined actions of the War, Labor, and Justice Departments, the AFofL had grown in size and prestige during the war years. Samuel Gompers had served as a member of the Council of National Defense and developed close relationships with many government leaders, including President Wilson. With a few notable exceptions, the national AFofL union supported the war effort and cooperated with government labor mediation organizations in settling disputes. This attitude, however, did not imply that the AFofL supported all government policies or that postwar strikes were not planned. The AFofL was opposed to compulsory government arbitration of disputes, and it repeatedly criticized Wilson's reluctance to push AFofL–favored legislation, such as the bills that restricted immigration.[7]

To Gompers and other AFofL leaders, wartime cooperation had a price—a new recognition of the role of labor unions in America. In his view the rising cost of living, the end of war production in major industries, and the economic ground allegedly lost by workers during overseas hostilities made post-armistice strikes likely, if government and employer cooperation were not forthcoming.[8] Further, the victory won by the democracies in the war became intermingled in the minds of many workers with the initial idealism of Russia's Bolshevik Revolution and the alleged triumph it represented over wealth, privilege, and autocracy. These events raised the hopes and ambitions of many American laborers for the future of unionism in the United States. But widespread fear of labor radicalism blocked the best efforts of labor leaders to unionize unorganized workers and industries in the immediate postwar years.[9]

By contrast, the American business community, traditionally conservative and antiunion, was content with the policy of direct access. Wartime federal military interventions

---

[6] Quote from Wilson to Intelligence Officer, Western Dept, 22 Nov 18, Glasser File: Seattle, RG 60. See also Bruce W. Bidwell, *History of the Military Intelligence Division, Department of the Army General Staff: 1775–1941* (Frederick: University Publications of America, 1986), p. 279; "The IWW as an Agent of Pan-Germanism," *World's Work* 36 (October 1918):581–82.

[7] Glasser Rpt, Butte Mine Strike, pp. 140–44; Peterson and Fite, *Opponents of War*, p. 286; Smith, "Organized Labor and Government in the Wilson Era," p. 271. Although Labor Secretary Wilson was a member of AFofL's United Mine Workers' Union, his cabinet status did not assure prolabor policies.

[8] Glasser Rpt, Butte Mine Strike, pp. 140–44, RG 60; see also Peterson and Fite, *Opponents of War*, p. 286; Smith, "Organized Labor and Government in the Wilson Era," p. 271.

[9] For the revolution's effect on labor, see the following works: Philip S. Foner, *The Bolshevik Revolution: Its Impact on American Radicals, Liberals, and Labor* (New York: International, 1967); "American Labor and Bolshevism," *Literary Digest* 61 (21 June 1919):9–11; "Red Forces Disrupting American Labor," *Literary Digest* 63 (25 October 1919):11–14, "Red Hysteria," *New Republic* 21 (28 January 1920):249–52; "Red Threats of Revolution Here," *Literary Digest* 63 (8 November 1919):15–19.

had helped to produce a submissive work force, and managers were slow to adjust to the loss of direct access to federal troops when the government began steps to rescind that policy. In many instances, businessmen fed the fears of labor extremism to those in the government, military, and general public who would listen. Through the remainder of the Wilson administration and into the presidency of Warren G. Harding, the government and the Army continued to intervene in labor disputes, although signs of a transition back to prewar procedures began to appear as early as November 1919. Until September 1921, however, no presidential proclamation was issued before the troops intervened in domestic disturbances, and these interventions generally followed the pattern of 1917–1918. Only gradually did Harding's emphasis on a "return to normalcy" succeed in restoring prewar policies and procedures regarding the domestic use of restricting federal military power.

Butte, 1919–1920

The armistice caused a resurgence of labor troubles in the copper mining industry in the spring of 1919. The end of the fighting caused a drop in the demand for raw materials, including copper, the price of which fell from a wartime high of 26¢ per pound to the March 1919 low of 15¢ per pound. This caused a corresponding, precipitous drop in wages from $5.75 to $4.75 per day, in spite of the rising cost of living and huge wartime profits accrued by the copper companies. Miners who were financially pressed during the war found that the new cuts made life increasingly difficult. In response, and taking advantage of the situation caused by the AFofL shipyard strike and general strike in Seattle, the Metal Mine Workers' Union in Butte, supported by both the IWW and AFofL, decided to strike on 7 February 1919. Mine operators immediately labeled the strike as Bolshevik and IWW initiated. One Army officer concurred, declaring that poor living conditions, the rising cost of living, and the cut in wages were merely "an excuse by agitators" to create unrest for political purposes.[10]

The original garrison at Butte, the 44th Infantry under Capt. William B. Wilson, which had remained after the earlier troubles, was insufficient to meet the impending crisis, and another company of the 44th was ordered from Fort George Wright, Washington, under Maj. Albert M. Jones. Because of the policy of direct access and since federal troops were already in Butte, the statutory procedures for calling forth federal military aid, including the issuing of a presidential proclamation, were ignored. When Jones arrived on 9 February he took command of all federal troops. The only major disturbance during the strike took place the following day, when a hostile mob marched to the office of the supposedly antilabor *Butte Daily Post* newspaper and prevented street sales. The mob was dispersed by federal troops and several rioters were allegedly bayoneted. On that same day, streetcars ceased to run because their union was considering joining the strike that already included several AFofL unions. Local officials, however, claimed that strikers had intimidated the drivers.[11]

---

[10] Quote from W. H. Germer to Dalrymple, MID, 25 Feb 19; see also Glasser Rpt, Butte Mine Strike, p. 143; both in Glasser File: Butte (Feb, Nov 1919), RG 60.

[11] Glasser Rpt, Butte Mine Strike, pp. 157–60; Telg, F. B. Watson to CG, Western Dept, 4 Mar 19, Glasser File: Butte (Feb, Nov 19); both in RG 60.

Jones relinquished his command to Maj. George M. Halloran, who arrived in Butte on 12 February with two more companies of the 44th Infantry and promptly reported to the commander of the Western Department, Maj. Gen. John F. Morrison, that no disorder existed. When Morrison himself arrived in Butte from Seattle the next day, he was satisfied with the handling of the affair by Halloran and determined that a declaration of martial law was unnecessary. He did, however, report a tense situation to his superiors.

The situation here is serious. Civil government [is] apparently helpless, but the radicals are afraid of the troops and so far have not gone to extremes but are threatening. It is not so much a strike as an effort at revolution. The radicals openly preach Bolshevism. There are troops enough here for the present, but will send more if necessary. Believe this situation could be solved by the prompt deportation of undesirable aliens, mostly Finns and Irish with a few other nationalities. Even if a few of the worst are promptly deported the effect would be excellent.[12]

No opportunity to expel undersirables presented itself. On 17 February the strike collapsed, work resumed, and three of the four companies of the 44th Infantry were withdrawn. Despite much fearsome rhetoric, the troops played no role except to guard the local water and electric works. Yet they remained in Butte for another sixteen months to maintain order, which meant in fact keeping labor on the job and peaceable until sufficient state forces could be organized to perform the same function. Final orders for moving out the last soldiers from Butte were received on 29 December 1920, ending a total of forty-two months of federal military occupation.[13]

Seattle

The first large-scale labor disputes of the immediate postwar period, the Seattle shipyard and general strikes, took place in January and February 1919 and were directly related to circumstances created by the war and the end of active overseas hostilities. The immediate motivating factors behind the AFofL strike were union dissatisfaction over a wage settlement imposed by the government during the war and expected wage decreases and employee layoffs caused by the end of wartime ship orders.[14] When efforts of the AFofL to reach a new wage settlement failed, the unions called a strike. On 21 January 1919, approximately 35,000 shipyard workers in Seattle and Tacoma walked off their jobs. Simultaneous labor difficulties with IWW and AFofL mining unions in Butte heightened public worries and confirmed the worst fears of conservatives about radical labor and the menace of revolution.[15]

---

[12] Glasser Rpt, Butte Mine Strike, pp. 160–63, RG 60.

[13] Rpt, Dept CO to AG, 6 Mar 19; Memo, CofS for AG, 29 Dec 20; both in Glasser File: Butte (Feb, Nov 1919 and Apr, May 1920, respectively), RG 60, NARA.

[14] For other wartime shipbuilding labor disputes involving federal military intervention, see Berman, *Labor Disputes and the President*, pp. 132–34. See also Glasser Files: Astoria, Oregon (Shipbuilders, Oct 1917), and California (Bethlehem Strike, 1918), RG 60, NARA. For wage settlements, see V. E. Macy, "Labor Adjustments Under War Conditions," *Proceedings of the Political Science Academy* 7 (February 1918):785–91; "Labor View of the Shipbuilding Program," *New Republic* 14 (23 February 1918):111–12.

[15] Robert L. Friedheim, *The Seattle General Strike* (Seattle: University of Washington Press, 1964), pp. 55–58, 62–69, 75 and "The Seattle General Strike of 1919," *Pacific Northwest Quarterly* 52 (July 1961):81–98; Robert L. Friedheim and Robin Friedheim, "The Seattle Labor Movement, 1919–1920," *Pacific Northwest Quarterly* 55 (October 1964):146–56. See also C. Piez, "Labor and Ships," *North American Review* 209 (March 1919):352–61; T. S. McMahon, "Strike in Seattle," *Survey* 41 (8 March 1919):821–23.

The strike was immediately labeled as Bolshevik inspired. Although MID agents reported a lack of violence, they described the speeches they heard at union meetings as clearly radical. Agents grew more alarmed when members of organizations like the IWW and Socialists were invited by AFofL locals to join the strike. One special agent reported to his superiors that a group of prominent Socialists and IWWs, including Max Eastmann, Eugene Debs, and Fred Hegge, were plotting to gain control of the AFofL for the Bolsheviks and were receiving support from European Reds.[16]

Within days even more ominous news was forthcoming. MID received reports of an intended general strike, set for 6 February by all labor organizations (AFofL, IWW, and Socialist) in the Seattle area. MID agents pointed out that, although the national organization of the

JOHN F. MORRISON

AFofL forbade general strikes, it appeared that radicals, IWWs, and Bolsheviks had gained such a degree of control of the AFofL locals that they voted for a general strike in spite of the national organization's opposition. According to MID, decent organized labor was anxious to be divorced from this radical element. In fact, many AFofL locals, notably those in Seattle, were more radical than their national organization. They favored general strikes and hoped eventually to persuade the national organization of their utility. The conflict within the union later caused the censure of the locals in Seattle by the national AFofL.[17]

The Seattle General Strike began on 6 February 1919 as 40,000 more workers left their jobs, bringing the total number on strike in the region to over 70,000. Nearly every facet of life in the Seattle area was affected, including transportation, light and power, food shops, storage houses, express companies, and other services. Although no violence of any kind occurred, the city faced an emergency of the first order. The mayor of Seattle, Ole Hanson, had already wired Secretary of War Baker the previous day that the general strike constituted "a revolution against the United States government" instigated by the IWW and Bolsheviks. Not one national or international labor organization had endorsed the strike, he claimed. Implying that the strike was illegal, he requested that

---

[16] Telgs, Duncan to Mil Staff, 4 Feb 19; Wilson to Dir, MID (Military Intelligence Division), 21 Jan 19; Rpt, Special Agent W. R. Thayer to Capt Hayes, MID, 23 Jan 19; all in Glasser File: Seattle (Gen Strike), RG 60, NARA. See also Friedheim, *Seattle General Strike*, pp. 75–78.

[17] Rpt, Agent C-371 to OCofS, MID, 1 Feb 19; Rpt, J. Fisher to Dir, MID, 12 Feb 19; Telg, M. A. Matthews to Secy Wilson, 12 Feb 19; all in Glasser File: Seattle (Gen Strike), RG 60, NARA. See also Friedheim, *Seattle General Strike*, pp. 81–84, 139–40, 152–53.

OLE HANSON

federal troops be sent to the city to protect government assets and prevent "enormous suffering."[18] Baker had received a similar telegram from Washington Governor Ernest Lister, requesting federal troops because the National Guard of the state had been federalized during the war and the one regiment of infantry since reorganized was insufficient to cope with the situation. He asked Maj. Gen. John F. Morrison to have the 1st Infantry at Camp Lewis put at his disposal. Although he did not intend to use these troops unless life or property was in danger, he wanted to be prepared and have troops alerted so that they could reach Seattle and Tacoma in half an hour. In addition, Lister requested that Baker ask Secretary of the Navy Josephus Daniels to authorize the use of U.S. Navy and Marine personnel at Seattle and Bremerton stations for possible riot duty in Seattle.[19]

Army Chief of Staff Peyton C. March promptly approved Lister's request without seeking a presidential proclamation, in keeping with the direct access policy, and promised additional federal military aid from the Army, Navy, and Marine Corps. Morrison received orders to deploy troops in Seattle to guard government property and assist in suppressing disorder.[20] The military force collected for duty in Seattle would become one of the largest yet gathered in the immediate postwar period.

On the very day that the general strike began Col. John L. Hayden, commanding the 13th Field Artillery Brigade, arrived in Seattle with one provisional machine-gun company composed of elements of the 37th, 38th, and 39th Machine Gun Battalions and the 1st and 3d Battalions of the 1st Infantry regiment from Camp Lewis. Simultaneously, Brig. Gen. Frank B. Watson, commanding officer of the 26th Infantry Brigade, arrived in Tacoma with another battalion of the 1st Infantry and one provisional machine-gun company. By 7 February a total of 1,500 regulars were deployed in the Seattle area.[21]

---

[18] Telg, Hanson to Baker, 5 Feb 19, Glasser File: Seattle (Gen Strike), RG 60, NARA. See also Ole Hanson, "Fighting the Reds in Their Home Town," *World's Work* 39 (December 1919–March 1920):123–26; "Mayor Ole Hanson Who Sat Tight at Seattle," *Literary Digest* 60 (8 March 1919):47–50; P. C. Hedrick, "The IWW and Mayor Hanson," *Unpartizan Review* 12 (July 1919):35–45; Friedheim, *Seattle General Strike*, pp. 123–25, and 173–76, for Hanson's run for the presidency and for his denouncement by Clarence Darrow as being a "cheap poseur, a cheap vaudevillian, and a professional patriot."

[19] Telg, Lister to Baker, 5 Feb 19, Glasser File: Seattle (Gen Strike), RG 60, NARA.

[20] Telgs, March to Camp Lewis, 6 Feb 19, and Maj Gen J. D. Leitch to AG, 7 Feb 19. Both in Glasser File: Seattle (Gen Strike), RG 60, NARA.

[21] Telg, Leitch to AG, 7 Feb 19, and Rpt, Leitch to AG, 3 Mar 19, RG 60, Glasser File: Seattle (Gen Strike), RG 60, NARA.

Upon the arrival of federal units, Army headquarters was established in the Seattle Federal Building, and troops were billeted in the state armory. Units were immediately deployed to protect piers, offices, warehouses, the quartermaster depot, the Fisher-Lilly Flour Mills, the Galbraith Bacon Company, Ballard Dock, Puget Sound Traction Light and Power Company, U.S. Appraisers Store, and the U.S. Immigration Station. Naval forces, consisting of 350 sailors from the 13th Naval District and 501 sailors and 150 marines from the Puget Sound Navy Yard, were placed under the Army's command. Part of this force was sent to protect the Kilbourne and Clark Manufacturing Company, which was under contract to produce radio sets for the military. In addition, Maj. Clyde A. Malone, adjutant of the North Pacific Coastal Artillery District, reported that four provisional companies of 60 men at Fort Worden were ready for deployment. A further three companies of the 44th Infantry at Fort Lawton were also available to military authorities.[22]

General Morrison gave all his troops strict and explicit orders that they were not to act as policemen or to interfere in any way in disputes between employees and employers. The mission of federal military forces was to maintain order and support local authority, not to act as labor arbitrators or partisan agents for one or the other side. In addition sentinels were not to be posted in public view but were to remain out of sight at guard locations and to act as a reserve to local and private security personnel. Off-duty personnel were required to stay within the confines of the armory and were not permitted on the streets of Seattle. If violence and disorder occurred, however, the troops were to take any means necessary to protect the property in their charge.[23]

On Saturday, 8 February, Morrison arrived in Seattle and took command of the forces in the city. On the following day the mayor of nearby Everett, Washington, requested troops, which caused the deployment of one company of the 1st Infantry with two machine guns to that city under command of Maj. Ambrose R. Emery to deal with "serious threats made by agitators." By the time the troops arrived, however, the alleged threat had disappeared, and the troops returned to Seattle.

The presence of overwhelming numbers of federal military forces, stiff business and public opposition, and a lack of labor unity brought an end to the general strike on Tuesday, 11 February 1919. The first detachment of federal forces left Seattle three days later, and the remainder returned to Camp Lewis by 20 February. Federal troops, most of whom remained in their camps during their entire deployment, had succeeded so well in maintaining order and preventing any violence that a military presence was not needed for the last three weeks of the shipbuilding dispute. The strike continued until 11 March, when striking workers realized that further resistance was futile. They returned to their jobs without having gained either improvement in wages or working conditions or a guarantee of continued employment. The end of wartime ship orders and the failed general strike speeded the decline of both the shipping industry and the labor movement in the area. According to one historian of the strike, by 1921 Seattle had become "an industrial ghost town," which "retrogressed almost to the point of its pre-war economic position." The local shipbuilding economy, shorn of war orders for troop transports and merchant vessels, like the

---

[22] Friedheim, *Seattle General Strike*, pp. 128–29; Rpt, CO, U.S. Military Forces, Seattle, to Leitch, CO, Camp Lewis, 20 Feb 19, Glasser File: Seattle (Gen Strike), RG 60, NARA.

[23] Rpt, CO, U.S. Military Forces, Seattle, to Leitch, CO, Camp Lewis, 20 Feb 19, Glasser File: Seattle (Gen Strike), RG 60, NARA.

ineffective local labor movement, ultimately collapsed. Not until World War II did Seattle recover its economic position lost in 1919.[24]

In his final report on the military's actions during the strike, General Morrison stated that "the situation was undoubtedly serious at first due to the large number of ultra-radicals who seemed to have gotten control of the situation. The presence of a strong military force had a calming effect. Although troops were not used, the belief was practically universal that their presence in force was what made their use unnecessary."[25] Morrison was in turn informed by one of his Seattle MID agents that "agitators are going to continue to talk strike to 'save their faces' and to retain prestige . . . but the Bolsheviki movement is no longer of immediate concern. . . . It will take a long time for the leaders to again 'educate' the honest laboring man to the point of forfeiting several weeks pay. This last experience has hit hardest the laborers with whom the agitators have failed to make good their promises and as a result he [sic] is wary."[26]

MID analysts, who were very active in the prestrike period, concluded that the strike failed for many reasons. The privations and loss of wages shook striker unity and resolve. In essence, the strike boomeranged and the workers, because of the ongoing general decline of the shipbuilding industry, were worse off than before. Fewer government ship orders meant that many strikers would not be rehired. The general strike was a rash act, and the goals of the strikers—increased wages and guarantees of no layoffs—were impossible and unrealistic demands at that time and place. A further factor was the lack of popular support for the strikers who were blamed for disrupting, if not actually endangering, the lives and health of tens of thousands of innocent urban residents by their strike actions. The most important factor for the strike's failure, however, was the inability of workers to paralyze the city and intimidate its leaders into meeting their demands because of the civil and military forces in the city that opposed their methods and goals.[27]

The Great Steel Strike, 1919–1920

In 1919 a primary target of the AFofL was the steel industry, in particular the United States Steel Corporation. AFofL leaders reasoned that if antiunion, conservative U.S. Steel, which controlled half of the steel industry in the nation, could be organized, the entire industry would follow in a major triumph for labor. The AFofL had just successfully organized Chicago packinghouse workers, and the time seemed right to challenge those whom many union men perceived as the "steel barons."

At its convention in June 1918 the AFofL passed a resolution calling for a campaign to unionize steelworkers. Plans and strategy were completed during the winter, and in May 1919 union representatives approached Chairman of the Board of U.S. Steel Elbert H.

---

[24] Quote in Friedheim, *Seattle General Strike*, pp. 134–46, see also pp. 161–65; Rpt, CO, U.S. Military Forces, Seattle, to Leitch, 20 Feb 19, RG 60; Berman, *Labor Disputes and the President*, p. 208.

[25] Rpt, Morrison to AG, 28 Feb 19, Glasser File: Seattle (Gen Strike), RG 60, NARA.

[26] Memo, F. Wilson to Morrison, 11 Mar 19, Glasser File: Seattle (Gen Strike), RG 60, NARA.

[27] Rpt, J. Fisher to Dir, MID, 12 Feb 19, Glasser File: Seattle (Gen Strike), RG 60, NARA. See also "Strike That Oiled Its Own Troubled Waters—Seattle Strike," *Literary Digest* 61 (12 April 1919):90–92; W. Woehlke, "Revolution in America: Seattle Crushes the First Soviet Uprising," *Sunset* 42 (April 1919):13–16; W. MacDonald, "The Seattle Strike and Afterwards," *Nation* 108 (29 March 1919):469.

Gary, requesting negotiations leading to union recognition and eventual organization of U.S. Steel workers. Gary, a long-time union opponent, refused this request, and a similar one made in July.[28]

After Gary's second refusal, the union developed formal demands. These included (1) the right to collective bargaining; (2) reinstatement of all men discharged for union activity with lost pay; (3) an industry-wide eight-hour day; (4) one rest day in seven; (5) abolition of 24-hour shifts; (6) increased wages; (7) a standard wage scale; (8) double pay for overtime, Sundays, and holidays; (9) implementation of a seniority system in maintaining, reducing, and increasing the work force; and (10) abolition of the company account. When these demands were placed before the AFofL membership, 98 percent approved them and voted to strike if no agreement could be reached with U.S. Steel. In August 1919 Gary refused for the third time either to consider AFofL demands or even to recognize the right of unions to exist at U.S. Steel plants, espousing the open shop and claiming that union officials were outside agitators who did not represent mill employees.[29]

In late August union representatives turned to President Wilson, hoping he would intervene on their behalf and convince Gary to meet with them. Although Wilson agreed to try to arrange such a conference, he was involved in his western tour to garner public support for the Treaty of Versailles and the League of Nations. Twice in September inquiries were sent to him by union officials, and twice Presidential Secretary Joseph Tumulty responded that Wilson was continuing to arrange a conference. On receipt of the second reply the union, fearing independent action by its locals and foot-dragging by Wilson, voted to strike. Upon hearing of the union's decision, Wilson again requested patience until a conference could be arranged in Washington, D.C., in early October. Knowing that the steel companies were making major preparations to defeat any strike and were continuing to fire employees discovered to be union members, the AFofL National Committee ignored Wilson's request and confirmed 22 September as the starting day for a nationwide strike. The decision was a fateful one that gave the public the impression that the union was rash and provocative in refusing Wilson's request. The actions of the union further made Gary appear as a patriotic businessman attempting to protect his property and his employees from arbitrary labor radicals.[30]

The strike began as planned when 365,000 steelworkers walked off their jobs in fifty cities in ten states. The walkout was conducted in an orthodox fashion under AFofL guidelines and the strict leadership and control of Gompers and other top leaders. The

---

[28] Interchurch World Movement, *Report on the Steel Strike of 1919* (New York: Harcourt, Brace & World, 1920), p. 5; Berman, *Labor Disputes and the President*, pp. 166–67; Colston Warne, ed., *The Steel Strike of 1919* (Lexington: Heath, 1968), pp. i, vii; David Brody, *Labor in Crisis: The Steel Strike of 1919* (Philadelphia: Lippincott, 1965). For Elbert Gary, see Ida M. Tarbell, *The Life of Elbert H. Gary: The Story of Steel* (New York: D. Appleton, 1925).

[29] U.S. Congress, Senate, Committee on Education and Labor, *Investigation of the Strikes in the Steel Industry*, 66th Cong., 1st sess., pp. 9, 11; Berman, *Labor Disputes and the President*, pp. 166–68; J. A. Fitch, "Closed Shop and Other Issues of the Steel Strike," *Survey* 43 (8 November 1919):53–56. For U.S. Steel's policies and labor conditions, see J. A. Fitch, "U.S. Steel Corporation and Labor," *Annals of the American Academy of Political and Social Science* 42 (July 1912):10–19, and *The Steel Worker* (New York: Charities Publications, 1910; reprint, New York: Arno, 1969).

[30] Berman, *Labor Disputes and the President*, pp. 168–70; "Mr. Gary Moralizes," *Nation* 109 (11 October 1919):488. See also Melvin Urofsky, *Big Steel and the Wilson Administration* (Columbus: Ohio State University Press, 1969).

steel companies, however, joined the press in denouncing the strike and asserting that the union's objectives were alien, revolutionary, and Bolshevik inspired. Strikers were labeled disloyal and radical. The catchwords of the time—red, alien, Bolshevik, un-American— were used to prejudice public opinion.[31] Numerous press reports alleged that the strike had been caused by Germans to regain trade lost during the war, or else to disrupt the peace. Newspapers, especially in Pittsburgh, went to great lengths to convince the public that the strike was connected with radical organizations like the IWW. Even major news-papers like the *New York Times* reported that "radical leaders planned to develop the . . . steel and coal strike into a general strike and ultimately into a revolution to overthrow the government." Some allegations were "plants" by the steel companies; others were fabri-cations by the newspapers.[32]

Having learned from its wartime experiences, the AFofL was quick to disassociate its strike from any connection with the IWW or any foreign ideology or radical group. An independent investigation of the causes of the steel strike concluded "that while radicals sympathized with the strikers, as was natural, they were eventually debarred by the strike leaders and that far from having influence in it, they often denounced and opposed those who conducted the strike." Such was the case with the IWW, which not only did not sup-port the steel strike but actively labored against it, telling workers not to join the action because the AFofL always lost. In turn, AFofL leaders were quick to expel members thought to have IWW affiliations or sympathies.[33] A Senate investigation, however, cited William Z. Foster, the chairman of the National Committee of the AFofL, as evidence of radical influences. Foster had been an IWW member and a radical author who changed his affiliation because of the IWW's extremist reputation. A Senate committee insisted he was "wholly antagonistic to American labor unions, especially the AFofL," and had at one time stated he could prevail by "boring from within" and joined the AFofL solely to undermine the organization.[34]

Gary, Indiana, and Federal Military Intervention

Although violence accompanying the strike kept state and local civil and military author-ities busy, only one locale required federal military assistance. Gary, Indiana, contained one

---

[31] Interchurch World Movement, *Public Opinion and the Steel Strike of 1919* (New York: Harcourt, Brace & World, 1920), pp. 101, 103, 109; "Nationwide Steel Strike," *Current History* 11 (November 1919):200–203; M. H. Vorse, "Behind the Picket Line: The Story of a Slovak Steel Striker," *Outlook* 124 (21 January 1920):107–09, and "Civil Liberty in the Steel Strike," *Nation* 109 (15 November 1919):633–35; Philip C. Ensley, "The Interchurch World Movement and the Steel Strike of 1919," *Labor History* 13 (Spring 1972):217–30.

[32] *New York Times* as quoted in Interchurch World Movement, *Report on the Steel Strike*, p. 31. See also Berman, *Labor Disputes and the President*, p. 171; William Scheuerman, "The Politics of Protest: The Great Steel Strike of 1919–1920 in Lackawanna, New York," *International Review of Social History* 31 (1986):121–46; C. Merz, "Pittsburg: Is It Revolution?" *New Republic* 20 (8 October 1919):293–94.

[33] Interchurch World Movement, *Report on the Steel Strike*, pp. 155, 247. The UM workers at their September 1919 convention, for example, banned IWW members from joining UMW locals. Other AF of L unions followed a similar policy. See David J. McDonald and Edward A. Lynch, *Coal and Unionism: A History of the American Coal Miner's Union* (Indianapolis: Cornelius, 1939), p. 141.

[34] Senate, *Investigation of Strikes in Steel Industry*, 66th Cong., 1st sess., p. 16. William Z. Foster's book is entitled *The Great Steel Strike and Its Lessons* (New York: Viking, 1920). Foster was later prominent in the Communist Party, USA. See Taft, *The A. F. of L. in the Time of Gompers*.

of the largest steelmaking complexes in the nation—a U.S. Steel plant that had been the scene of bitter labor and racial disputes in the past. The frustrations of strikers triggered violent confrontations with local loyalty leagues and police. On 4 October, after attending a mass meeting, an estimated 5,000 strikers marched down Broadway, the main thoroughfare of the city. Here they encountered a streetcar carrying a group of strikebreakers to one of Gary's many steel mills. Surrounding the streetcar, the mob assaulted and slightly injured a black strikebreaker. In the melee several strikers were also injured. During the next two days, Gary experienced increased racial tensions and sporadic, violent clashes between strikers and nonstrikers, and between whites and blacks. The efforts of city police and the recently reconstituted Indiana National Guard did little to calm the situation. Fearing that local authorities were losing control, Mayor William F. Hodges informed Governor James P. Goodrich that federal troops were needed to restore order.[35]

Maj. Gen. Leonard Wood, commander of the Army's Central Department, received a telephone call from Goodrich on Monday afternoon, 6 October. Wood had anticipated such a request and was maintaining part of the 4th Division, 105 officers and 916 enlisted men, in a high state of readiness at Fort Sheridan, Illinois. Alerted by Central Department headquarters, the troops filed aboard buses and were on their way to Gary within fifteen minutes. The following day Wood diverted a further provisional battalion of the 6th Division, 18 officers and 512 enlisted men, en route from the race riot at Omaha, Nebraska, from their station at Camp Grant, Illinois, to Gary for strike duty.[36] The deployment followed the wartime policy of direct access and the emergency provision of Army regulations.

Wood, a medical doctor, Indian fighter, "Rough Rider," Medal of Honor winner, former military governor of Cuba, commander of the Philippine Division, and Army chief of staff, was at this time interested in seeking the Republican Party's presidential nomination on a strong antiradical and antialien platform.[37] His campaign claimed to embody "Americanism," an extreme nativistic and nationalistic appeal that equated change with radicalism, demanded total loyalty, and subordinated the wishes of individuals to the national interest. Above all, followers of Wood's Americanism advocated conformity to their definitions of proper citizenship and, if necessary, forceful coercion of dissenters. Wood saw all issues in light of this simplistic philosophy, believing that labor troubles were the result of alien agitation. Internationalism to him was merely a Bolshevik plot to substitute loyalty to humanity for loyalty to the nation. The disturbances at Omaha and Gary, he stated publicly, were clear evidence that conspiratorial forces were attempting to disrupt American society. As he wrote later, "The gravity of the situation at Gary is found in the presence of a dangerous and extremely active group—the Red Anarchistic element—which is striving to bring about extensive disturbances against law and order. These elements are working against everything which this country stands for." To Wood, the best thing for labor was a stable economy that encouraged business production.

---

[35] "Police Riot Guns Pacify Strikers in Gary Streets," and "New Riots Begin in Gary at Night," *New York Times*, 5 and 6 Oct 19, respectively; and *New York Times*, 7 Oct 19.

[36] General Leonard Wood Diary, Leonard Wood Papers, Library of Congress, Washington, D.C. See also Rpt, W. S. Mapes, CO, Gary, 19 Oct 19; Telgs, Wood to AG, 6 and 7 Oct 19, all in Glasser File: Gary (Steel Strike), RG 60, NARA. For the Omaha race riot, see Chapter 12.

[37] For a sympathetic biography, see Joseph H. Sears, *The Career of Leonard Wood* (New York: Appleton, 1919).

LEONARD WOOD

Strikes created instability and a poor business environment, which was detrimental to business, labor, and ultimately America. Stability was created through an adherence to the principles of Americanism and law and order.[38]

By the late fall of 1919 General Wood had become the law and order candidate, with the firm support of conservative and patriotic organizations like the American Legion and the National Security League. The situation in Gary alarmed his political advisers, however, who thought his involvement might damage his campaign. Not all voters adhered to his Americanist principles or thought force was the only remedy for labor disputes. Wood ignored their advice.[39]

Arriving in Gary around 2000 on 6 October, Wood immediately met with municipal and union leaders. He told the gathering plainly that "the military forces are in Gary not in the interest of the steel operators and not in the interest of the strikers, but to maintain law and order."[40] His real views were not so evenhanded; in his report he wrote that "the strikers, mainly aliens, many not speaking English, paraded the public streets and declared their intentions to continue to parade in defiance of the Mayor's order. The worst influence comes from Red agitators who desire to foment trouble. The best labor element stands for law and order."[41]

Wood's tendency to see foreign radicals at work in the strike may have been reinforced by the reports of the Military Intelligence Division and the Justice Department, whose agents were convinced that the strike was a sinister Bolshevik plot to destroy the nation. Army investigators claimed that 90 percent of the strikers were alien and were therefore subject to influence from outside "red" agitators. One report went so far as to claim that "IWW, Socialist, Communist, Anarchist, Russian Union of Workingmen, and other radical organizations are cooperating to one end: the establishment of the soviet republic in the

---

[38] Quote from Jack C. Lane, *Armed Progressive: General Leonard Wood* (San Rafael, Calif.: Presidio Press, 1978), pp. 235, 237–38. See also Rich, *President and Civil Disorder*, pp. 156–57; Higham, *Strangers in the Land*, pp. 204–07; E. J. David, "Leonard Wood on Labor Problems," *Outlook* 124 (25 February 1920):326–28; J. A. Ryan, "Americanism in Industry," *Annals of the American Academy of Political and Social Sciences* 90 (July 1920):125–30; "Americanism in the Present Crisis," *New Republic* 20 (12 November 1919):302–05.

[39] Wood Diary; Herman Hagedorn, *Leonard Wood: A Biography* (New York: Harper Brothers, 1931), 1:335; Lane, *Armed Progressive*, pp. 235–238. Wood declared his candidacy for the Republican presidential nomination in January 1920.

[40] Hagedorn, *Leonard Wood*, pp. 334–35.

[41] Telg, Wood to AG, 7 Oct 19, Glasser File: Gary (Steel Strike), RG 60, NARA.

United States by resort to force," and "are pursuing a policy of strike promotion, trusting that the resultant chaos will ultimately produce revolution."[42]

Following his meeting with city officials, Wood declared qualified martial law and issued a proclamation to the people of Gary outlining the new rules of military occupation. His proclamation placed the city under military control and made the local government an agency of the military authorities. It prohibited public meetings and parades, bearing of arms, and wearing of military uniforms by civilians. On the other hand it allowed the movie houses, theaters, and lecture halls to remain open and initially permitted picketing and indoor union meetings. This highly unusual and technically illegal action represents one of the few times that martial law had been declared in American history except for the period of the Civil War and Reconstruction. Nonetheless, Wood recounted, the grateful mayor "literally fell on his knees and approved everything we suggested."[43]

The first troops of the 4th Division arrived in Gary three hours after Wood, bringing with them an impressive array of arms and equipment and ample supplies of ammunition. The troops rapidly occupied positions in various parts of the city.[44] Within hours Wood felt satisfied that the situation was under control, and before returning to Chicago he placed Col. William S. Mapes, who had served with him in the Philippines, in command of the forces. Wood's sojourn in Gary satisfied both his military responsibilities and the dictates of his presidential campaign—he was in the city long enough to appear the decisive leader, but not long enough to risk damaging his presidential hopes.[45]

On the day that Wood left, a second provisional battalion of the 6th Division arrived, giving Mapes a total strength of 123 officers and 1,428 enlisted men. With the additional regulars the situation in Gary quickly calmed down, although no major outbreaks of rioting had occurred since the incidents on 4 October. Mapes organized his command to conduct patrolling, always maintaining a visible presence on the streets of the city. He also kept one infantry battalion, one machine-gun platoon, and one shotgun platoon in reserve and held a 37-mm. gun at headquarters "for any contingency warranting their employment."[46] But no such contingency arose in the three months that federal forces

---

[42] Rpt, J. B. Campbell to D. C. Van Buren, 5 Oct 19, File: Gary, Indiana (Steel Strike 2); Rpt, Campbell, Janovsky, and Rowans, 27 Sep 19; Rpt, T. B. Crockett, 30 Oct 19, File: Gary, Indiana (Steel Strike 3); all in Glasser Papers, RG 60, NARA.

[43] Proclamation, Gen Wood, 6 Oct 19, Glasser File: Gary (Steel Strike), RG 60, NARA. For further reference to this proclamation and for the above quote, see Wood Diary, 6 Oct 19. Although martial law was declared on a few occasions during the Civil War and Reconstruction, its first post-Reconstruction mention in Army regulations is in AR 500–50, 17 July 1945. Wood clearly exceeded his authority in Gary and directly violated the legal doctrine set forth in *Ex Parte Milligan* in 1866. See Richard Stockman and Dickinson Sackett, *Troops on Riot Duty* (Trenton: Military Publishing, 1912), p. 129; Dowell, *Military Aid to the Civil Power*, pp. 230–48. The applicable regulation during the Gary intervention was *Regulations for the Army of the United States, 1913 (Corrected to 27 November 1917)* (New York: Military Publishing, c. 1918), art. 47. See also AR 500–50, 6 Jun 23; AR 500–50, 17 Jul 45, sec. 4, par. 9, for the first discussion of martial law in regulations. Henry Steele Commager, ed., *Documents of American History*, 2 vols. (Englewood Cliffs, N.J.: Prentice-Hall, 1973), doc. 256, *Ex Parte Milligan*, 1:472.

[44] Memo, Col R. E. Wylie, 5 Nov 19, and Mapes Rpt, 19 Oct 19, both in Glasser File: Gary (Steel Strike), RG 60, NARA.

[45] Wood Diary; Hagedorn, *Leonard Wood*, 1:335; Lane, *Armed Progressive*, pp. 235–38, and see also pp. 240–47 for Wood's continued run for the presidency.

[46] Mapes Rpt, 19 Oct 19, RG 60.

occupied Gary. Mapes and his command faced periods of heightened tension, but never had to contend with a serious disturbance. Apart from routine patrolling, the units in Gary frequently aided MID and Justice Department agents in carrying out raids on suspected radicals, often identified by MID officers on the basis of anecdotal or hearsay evidence.[47]

Civil-military relations were apparently good on the whole. Maj. Jesse A. Ladd, the acting Army morale officer, stated that the people of Gary "seemed to recognize the fairness of the troops and only in isolated instances were there indications of hostility." Ladd's report also discussed the attitude of the regulars toward strike duty, noting some grumbling among the troops who did not like the idea of "bucking the working man," but he stressed that this sentiment of the soldiers disappeared once they arrived in the strife-torn city. The effect of radical labor propaganda, Ladd further explained, appeared negligible. The adjutant general's report for 1920 echoed these sentiments, claiming that "law and order was maintained at Gary, and the strikers, as well as the property owners and workers of the steel mills, were satisfied with the absolute fairness, to all concerned, with which the federal troops conducted the policing of the city whenever the civil police was inadequate to meet the special situations."[48] Mapes attempted to maintain this happy situation by evenhandedness, reminding his troops that "all soldiers are urged to constantly remember that we are not here in the interest of any party or faction" and that their sole duty was the "unprejudiced administration of justice." In a similar vein he informed the public that "no more force will be used than necessary."[49]

Not everyone, however, shared the Army's interpretation of fairness, restraint, and neutrality. Army-supported raids and arrests against strikers and union sympathizers produced a negative backlash and a gradual erosion of public confidence in the impartiality of both federal troops and the government. This was especially true of the strikers themselves, who had initially welcomed the troops as a neutral force that would prevent extreme reactions by strike opponents, but who later perceived that some Army activities—breaking up picket lines and arresting strikers suspected of radical or Bolshevik affiliations—were directed solely at labor. Strikers contended that the extended stay of troops in Gary, long after any actual violence or threat of violence existed, was proof that the Army supported the steel companies and intended to be there until the strike collapsed. After several clashes between troops and strikers, including the frequent stoning of Army vehicles, it became evident that the soldiers had lost their popularity. Furthermore, legal and constitutional questions arose from raids supported by the Army that were conducted on private homes without warrants. These kept War and Justice Department investigative and claims officials busy for months after the troops left.[50]

The nationwide steel strike faded by 15 October, and the situation was stable enough for the Army to begin withdrawing troops. A further reason for the withdrawal was the need for federal military intervention in nationwide coal strikes, which also started in

---

[47] Rpt, Maj J. A. Ladd, 3 Jan 20, RG 60, Glasser File: Gary (Steel Strike), RG 60, NARA.

[48] Ibid.; *AG Annual Rpt, 1920*, 22 Aug 20, Glasser File: Gary (Steel Strike 2), RG 60, NARA.

[49] Proclamation, 10 Oct 19, Glasser File: Gary (Steel Strike), RG 60, NARA.

[50] Rich, *President and Civil Disorder*, p. 157; Berman, *Labor Disputes and the President*, pp. 172–73; Interchurch World Movement, *Report on the Steel Strike*, pp. 240–42; G. Taylor, "At Gary: Some Impressions and Interviews," *Survey* 43 (8 November 1919):65–66.

September. The provisional battalion of the 6th Division, 568 officers and enlisted men, the first group to leave Gary, embarked on the Pennsylvania Railroad for Camp Grant, Illinois. The remaining troops of the 4th Division stayed on—continuing their duties as before—amid worsening relations with the public. A pool room brawl between soldiers and civilians on Christmas Night convinced Mayor Hodges that the time had come for federal troops to leave the city. At his request the first of the remaining soldiers left at midnight on 1 January 1920. Only a small detachment remained to settle civilian claims stemming from the prolonged troop deployment.[51]

The weakening of the steel strike in Gary was part of a general weakening of the AFofL work stoppage nationwide. By 8 January 1920, it was evident to union leaders that the strike had failed. The steel companies had recruited enough strikebreakers to replace three-fourths of the striking workers and continued to produce steel at 60 to 70 percent of the normal output. AFofL attempts throughout the fall and early winter to effect a settlement with U.S. Steel Chairman Gary foundered on Gary's adamant refusal to deal with any labor organization. The workers returned to their jobs without gaining any of their demands.

The 1919 strike collapsed for several reasons. The size, strength, and power of U.S. Steel, and the steel industry in general, was a primary factor, as was the hostile attitude of the press. The most important factor, however, was quick action by local and state law enforcement groups to contain and suppress strike activities, supported as in Gary by federal troops.[52]

The Knoxville Streetcar Strike, 1919

The American street railway industry was heavily regulated during World War I, and most regulations, especially those regarding wages, remained in effect afterward. Federal control was never popular with the national AFofL or its locals, and federal intervention during wartime street railway labor disputes favored transit companies over the unions.[53] When the war ended, street railway unions, like those in other industries, attempted to make up economic ground lost in 1917–1918 due to federal regulation, usually through strikes against transit companies that sought to maintain the wartime regulations that held down costs and wages. Strikes against federally controlled industries assured federal military intervention, often on a repeat basis.

Thus troops were summoned to quell a streetcar strike at Knoxville, Tennessee, in October 1919. Governor A. S. Roberts initially requested authorization to use the local Knoxville Army Recruiting Detachment and two companies at Fort Oglethorpe, Georgia, to maintain order. Federal military authorities hesitated to act on his request because they knew that the Tennessee National Guard had been reorganized to the strength of at least one regiment of 800 men and that this force had been used in Knoxville the previous month to quell a race riot. Although the necessity of federal military aid to suppress any alleged

---

[51] *AG Annual Rpt, 1920*, 22 Aug 20; Telgs, Wood to AG, 15 Oct 20; Devore to AG, 13 Jan 20; all in Glasser File: Gary, Indiana (Steel Strike 2), RG 60, NARA. See also Rich, *President and Civil Disorder*, p. 157.

[52] Berman, *Labor Disputes and the President*, p. 174.

[53] For military intervention in wartime street railway strikes, see Glasser Files: Chattanooga, Tenn. (Streetcar, Sep 1917), and Columbus, Ga. (Cottonmill/Streetcar, Aug 1918, Feb 1919), RG 60, NARA.

disturbance was doubtful, Roberts' request was inexplicably honored following the policy of direct access.[54]

At midnight on 28 October a composite riot unit, consisting of two rifle companies and one machine-gun company, 20 officers and 273 enlisted men, left Camp Gordon, Georgia, for Knoxville. The riot unit, commanded by Col. Robert H. Peck, 11th Infantry, was part of the 5th Division commanded by Maj. Gen. Edward M. Lewis.[55] The troops arrived early the next morning and immediately made camp on the courthouse lawn in the town center. Lewis met with state and local officials, who informed him that striking workers wanted both strikebreakers and federal troops to leave the city and threatened to orchestrate a general strike if they did not. Lewis believed that local officials were afraid that the streetcar strike would spark a coal strike, which would bring huge numbers of lawless elements into the city. He noted that while conditions were peaceful on 28 October, and twenty-five streetcars operated by strikebreakers were running on schedule, the cars were not well patronized by the public.[56]

Despite the ominous predictions, the only significant disturbance during the Army's time in Knoxville took place five days later when twenty-five to thirty striking streetcar workers began to interfere with trolley service. Two squads of troops were sent to aid the six policemen on duty in the affected area, but the crowd had dispersed before the troops arrived. The federal troops had such a calming effect on the city that the expected general strike did not take place, although an unrelated coal strike did begin on 1 November. Apparently this disruption had the common effect of stimulating antiunion sentiment among Knoxville citizens. One MID officer reported that the Knoxville city police had "been severely criticized because of their affiliation with the AFofL, and their failure to properly perform their duties by arresting strikers and sympathizers who have interfered with non-union men." As a result, he reported, the police union voted to surrender their charter and withdraw from the AFofL.[57]

Within two weeks the situation was under the control of the state military and civil authorities. Federal troops withdrew from Knoxville, except for one company that remained for another week at the request of the governor, primarily to show a federal military presence in the region where all the local coal miners were on strike. As the coal strike spread, the federal troops in Knoxville received reinforcements from Camp Gordon.[58] Such quiet duty hardly prepared federal troops for the next streetcar strike, a riotous episode in Colorado.

[54] Telgs, Roberts to CG, Southeastern Dept, 26 Oct 19; and Lt Col M. D. Wheeler to Dir, MID, 27 Oct 19, Glasser File: Knoxville, Tenn. (Streetcar, Oct–Nov 1919), RG 60, NARA. For the Knoxville race riot, which did not involve federal troops, see Lee E. Williams and Lee E. Williams II, *Anatomy of Four Race Riots: Racial Conflict in Knoxville, Elaine (Arkansas), Tulsa, and Chicago, 1919–1921* (Jackson: University Press of Mississippi, 1972), pp. 28–34.

[55] Telgs, Lewis to AG, 28 Oct 19, and F. G. Potts to Dir, MID, 28 Oct 19, Glasser File: Knoxville, Tenn. (Streetcar, Oct–Nov 1919), RG 60, NARA.

[56] Lewis to CG, Southeastern Dept, 29 Oct 19, Glasser File: Knoxville, Tenn. (Streetcar, Oct–Nov 1919), RG 60, NARA.

[57] Rpt, Capt R. Willard to Intelligence Officer, Southeastern Dept, 3 Nov 19, Glasser File: Knoxville, Tenn. (Streetcar, Oct–Nov 1919), RG 60, NARA.

[58] Telg, Brig Gen W. P. Richardson to CG, Southeastern Dept, 12 Nov 19, File: Knoxville, Tenn. (Streetcar, Oct–Nov 1919); and Telg, Bennett to AG, 2 Nov 19, File: Coal (Stearns Papers), both in Glasser Papers, RG 60, NARA.

Denver, 1920

The largest and most violent labor dispute involving transportation workers and federal troops took place in Denver in August 1920. Here, as in Knoxville and elsewhere, streetcar workers' wages were still controlled and determined by federal boards instituted during the war. In July 1918 the Denver streetcar workers organized an AFofL–affiliated union, the Amalgamated Association of Street and Electric Railway Employees of America, in the hope of obtaining better working conditions and higher pay. Within a year the War Labor Board raised wages and granted an eight-hour day, indicating that union representation could produce tangible benefits. In July 1919, however, the Denver Tramway Company violated the board's ruling and cut wages, precipitating a four-day strike. Arbitrators found in favor of the union and awarded the streetcar workers a higher wage than before. Shortly afterward, however, alleging an inability to pay, the company again reduced wages. The union obtained a court injunction to prevent this new cut and, at the same time, presented new demands for higher wages.

By this time feelings were hard on both sides of the dispute. Union leaders publicly stated that they were not interested in the company's ability to pay, demanded a "living wage" for streetcar workers, and announced their intention to strike should their demands not be met. This time the company obtained an injunction and simultaneously contacted the Jerome Detective Agency of Los Angeles, California, seeking to hire guards and strikebreakers. On 1 August 1920, AFofL leaders called a strike in defiance of the recent injunction.[59]

The walkout immediately snarled the transportation system of the city and turned the majority of the public against the union. As soon as striking workers left their jobs the company replaced them with strikebreakers, many of whom were armed. Their employment caused a violent reaction on the part of the strikers. On 4 August a mob of 2,000 people attacked trolley cars and strikebreakers and wrecked the offices and plant of what strikers termed the unfriendly antilabor *Denver Post*. The riot left 2 people dead and 33 wounded, including the Denver chief of police. Five additional major riots occurred on the next evening, and a clash on the following day left 3 people dead, 1 fatally injured, and 11 wounded. The situation in Denver, bordering on open warfare, was clearly beyond the control of local officials.[60]

As the strike reached the end of its first week and as the violence showed no signs of abating, Governor Oliver H. Shoup requested troops from the commander of the Central Department, General Wood, to restore order and prevent further loss of life and destruction of property. Wood later reported that the direct cause of the violence was the introduction of several hundred armed, professional strikebreakers—a surprising analysis from an officer who, only the fall before, had blamed radical labor for most of the ills in American society.[61]

---

[59] Intelligence Officer to CofS for Intelligence, Central Dept, Chicago, 19 Aug 20, Glasser File: Colorado (1920), RG 60, NARA. The agency, under "Black Jack" Jerome, was well known for its strike-breaking activities.

[60] Telg, Maj W. A. Fortmeyer, Ft. Logan, to Intelligence Officer, Wash., 6 Aug 20, Glasser File: Colorado (1920), RG 60, NARA.

[61] Wood's changed perception was possibly the result of the Republican presidential nomination going to Warren G. Harding rather than to him the previous June, thus ending his presidential hopes and any need to continue espousing "Americanism."

No militia, Wood added, was available for service in the city. Under the policy of direct access and Army emergency regulations, he gave orders for 250 soldiers under the command of Col. Charles C. Ballou to be sent to Denver from Fort Logan, Colorado, and for 500 federal troops to be sent from Camp Funston, Kansas. In the meantime, local authorities swore into service 500 men from the eleven posts of the Denver area American Legion to patrol residential areas and maintain order. Army officials were told that the legionnaires "have stated they will stay absolutely neutral, but will maintain law and order," and Wood later asserted that the Legion was "of very material assistance in the maintenance of law and order and the protection of property."[62]

On arrival, federal troops immediately disarmed the strikebreakers of the Jerome Detective Agency and placed soldiers on each operating streetcar. These actions had an instant salutary effect on the level of violence in Denver. Within days the situation cooled, although workers were still on strike and the Denver Tramway Company still refused to deal with the AFofL union or meet their demand that all striking workers be rehired. By 9 September 1920, federal troops were no longer required to maintain order and returned to their stations.[63]

In Denver, more so than elsewhere during the immediate postwar period, the prompt, informed, and intelligent actions of Army commanders quickly extinguished a civil disturbance of large proportions by removing the main cause of disorder, in this case armed and bellicose strikebreakers brought in from out of state. Army actions provided a breathing space that allowed both parties to attempt a peaceful solution to the strike, avoiding continued bloodshed and violence.

Conclusion

In the two years following the end of the war in Europe, the United States struggled with many problems of demobilization and conversion back to a peacetime social and economic structure. The transition brought much social, racial, and economic dislocation. The year following the armistice produced more widespread and violent labor disputes than the nineteen months of war, leading anxious people to believe that American society was careening toward collapse and that not only the United States but the world as well had permanently changed for the worse.

The Russian Revolution and the general social upheavals in central and eastern Europe seemed to pose a more immediate threat to the United States in a visibly shrunken environment. The federal government and the Army soon discovered that the policies adopted and the responsibilities undertaken in wartime were not easy to relinquish. This was especially true of the wartime policy of direct access. Federal civil and military leaders found that the public, local and state officials, and business and industrial leaders were unwilling to give up the degree of security that the rapid and easy access to federal troops provided. The desire to cling to wartime norms was all the more strongly felt because so

---

[62] Telgs, W. A. Fortmeyer to Intelligence Officer, Wash., 7 Aug 20, and Wood to AG, 11 Aug 20, both in Glasser File: Colorado (1920), RG 60, NARA. For a history of this veterans organization, see William Pencak, *For God and Country: The American Legion, 1919–1941* (Boston: Northeastern University Press, 1989).

[63] Memo, G. Johnston, G-2, for CofS, Glasser File: Colorado (1920), RG 60, NARA. See also Berman, *Labor Disputes and the President*, p. 208; "Denver Tramway Strike," *Survey* 44 (15 September 1920):702.

many Americans saw themselves faced by a resurgent radicalism, militant unionism, and alien revolutionary ideologies summed up in the popular image of bolshevism.

In each example of federal military intervention between Armistice Day and the summer of 1920, the Army was called in under the wartime policy of direct access. In each disturbance, alien, radical, or Bolshevist threats were cited by the federal government as the reasons and the justification for federal military intervention, rather than unremediated social and economic ills. Yet normalcy did assert itself gradually. In spite of demagogic exaggerations and the fact that most states were only slowly re-creating National Guard forces, in late 1920 the federal government and the Army began to return responsibility for quelling disturbances to state authorities. Similarly, the War Department took steps to halt the easy and nearly unrestricted access to federal troops that had allowed civil authorities during the war to entangle the Army in incessant labor-related riot duty. The transition to peacetime procedures, however, would require months to take effect and would prove difficult to implement with any degree of precision.

CHAPTER 12

The Race Riots of 1919–1920

Surely, in the face of the recent assaults upon the law and the courts, from the East St. Louis riots down to this orgy of fire and blood in Omaha, the time has come when it is incumbent upon the Federal Government to assume jurisdiction and set its hand to the task of stamping out the spirit of outlawry with which the state and local authorities have manifested their inability to contend.

—The Atlanta *Constitution*, October 1919.

Amid postwar labor upheavals and the "red scare," the United States was forced to confront racial disorders of a magnitude not seen since the end of Reconstruction.[1] Changes in American society, however, were transforming the racial tensions that had once been almost exclusively confined to the south into a nationwide phenomenon. In the course of 1919 alone, between twenty and twenty-five separate outbreaks of rioting and racial violence marked what one prominent journal labeled "our own race war." Once again, as in the anti-Chinese incidents of 1885 and 1886, the Army was called to restore order, this time between two groups of citizens who had developed into two separate, unequal, and sometimes hostile societies.[2]

The Background of the 1919 Riots

World War I caused many social and economic changes within the United States, especially in regard to the 10 percent of the population that comprised the black minority. Black America emerged from the war as a community with rising expectations. No longer willing to accept passively the indignities and abuses of Jim Crow laws and other

---

[1] Two major and especially violent race riots occurred in Brownsville and Houston, Texas, several years before the outbreaks of 1919. Although both were disturbances in which the Army was involved, neither was a case of federal military intervention under the laws. For the Brownsville riot, see Ann J. Lane, *The Brownsville Affair: National Crisis and Black Reaction* (Port Washington, N.Y.: Kennikat, 1971); John D. Weaver, *The Brownsville Raid* (New York: Norton, 1970); Emma Lou Thornbrough, "The Brownsville Episode and the Negro Vote," *Mississippi Valley Historical Review* 44 (December 1957):469–93; Lewis N. Wynne, "Brownsville: The Reaction of the Negro Press," *Phylon* 33 (Summer 1972):153–60; James A. Tinsley, "Roosevelt, Foraker, and the Brownsville Affray," *Journal of Negro History* 41 (January 1956):43–65; U.S. Congress, Senate, Committee on Military Affairs, *Affray at Brownsville, Texas*, doc. 402, 60th Cong., 1st sess., pt. 2. For the Houston Riot, see Robert V. Haynes, "The Houston Mutiny and Riot of 1917," *Southwestern Historical Quarterly* 76 (April 1973):418–39, and *A Night of Violence: The Houston Riot of 1917* (Baton Rouge: Louisiana University Press, 1976); Edgar A. Schuler, "The Houston Race Riot of 1917," *Journal of Negro History* (29 July 1944): 300–338.

[2] "Our Own Race War," *North American Review*, 210 (1919):436–38; Allen Grimshaw, "Actions of the Police and Military in American Race Riots," *Phylon* 24 (Fall 1963):271; "Facing the Negro Problem," *Missionary Review of the World* 42 (November 1919):818–19.

forms of racial discrimination practiced in the south, blacks showed a new determination to gain a practical realization of constitutional and civil rights granted a generation earlier in the years following the Civil War. World War I gave birth to what scholars have often referred to as the "New Negro," more aware of discrimination and more active in opposition to it.

The industrial expansion brought on by the war, and the concomitant drop in the numbers of white workers and European immigrants, meant more jobs in northern industries for blacks and a corresponding expansion of employment opportunities in areas from which they had previously been excluded. The prospect of a better way of life, steady employment and increased financial opportunity, and an atmosphere incorrectly thought relatively discrimination-free spurred a mass migration of southern blacks to northern industrial cities between 1914 and 1919, most being actively recruited by northern industries seeking cheap labor to fill war orders. Almost 500,000 blacks moved north between 1916 and 1918 alone.[3]

The wartime military service of some 380,000 other blacks stood as a source of immense pride and satisfaction to many in the minority community. Over 140,000 black servicemen went to France, and of this number 42,000 served in two all-black combat units, the 92d and 93d Infantry Divisions. The vast majority, however, had noncombat roles in supply, stevedore, engineer, and labor battalions, in a marked and unwelcome departure from the elite black units of earlier wars. Of the black combat troops, only half served with the American Expeditionary Forces, and the four regiments of the 93d were put exclusively under French command and control.

The large number of blacks serving in the Army brought many whites into close contact with them for the first time. As a result, their military service caused much discussion within the Army, with conclusions that were in general unflattering. Black units serving in the AEF were frequently criticized as lacking motivation, determination, efficiency, and courage. According to a publication of the Army War College, blacks were deemed "unfit for command in combat," while most black units were declared to be "inferior in combat to a corresponding white unit." A representative white officer, Col. Charles C. Ballou, writing of his wartime experiences with blacks in command positions, termed black officers "slothful and negligent" and "prone to leave the frontline trenches and loaf around the kitchens." Front-line service under black officers, he maintained, "was a farce."[4] By con-

---

[3] On blacks during this period, see Joseph A. Alvarez, *From Reconstruction to Revolution: The Black's Struggle for Equality* (New York: Atheneum, 1971), pp. 86–87; William M. Tuttle Jr., *Race Riot: Chicago in the Red Summer of 1919* (New York: Atheneum, 1980), pp. 208–41; Emmett J. Scott, *Negro Migration During the War* (New York: Oxford University Press, 1920); Joseph Boskin, *Urban Racial Violence in the Twentieth Century* (Beverly Hills, Calif.: Glencoe, 1976), p. 86; Herbert J. Seligmann, "What Is Behind the Negro Uprisings?" *Current Opinion* 67 (September 1919):154; John Hope Franklin, *From Slavery to Freedom: A History of Negro Americans* (New York: Knopf, 1974), especially ch. 24.

[4] Quotes from Negro Manpower in the Military Service, 18 Oct 25, Army War College, pp. 401–02; Martin Binkin, Mark J. Eitelberg, Alvin J. Schneider, and Marvin M. Smith, *Blacks in the Military* (Washington, D.C.: Brookings Institution, 1982), pp. 17–18; Bernard C. Nalty and Morris J. MacGregor, Jr., eds., *Blacks in the Military: Essential Documents* (Wilmington, Del.: Scholarly Resources, 1981), pp. 73–90; Richard O. Hope, *Racial Strife in the Military: Toward the Elimination of Discrimination* (New York: Praeger, 1979), pp. 15–23; Bernard C. Nalty, *Strength for the Fight: A Study of Black Americans in the Military* (New York: Free Press, 1986), pp. 107–14; Jack D. Foner, *Blacks and the Military in American History: A New Perspective* (New York: Praeger, 1974).

trast, the more racially tolerant French frequently commended and praised the members of the 93d Division for their discipline, high morale, and bravery under fire. The 8th Illinois, the only regiment with all-black officers in the U.S. Army at that time, won numerous battle honors during its service under French command in the sectors surrounding Verdun, and sixty-eight of its soldiers received the Croix de Guerre for valor.

Wherever they served, their contribution to the struggle to "make the world safe for democracy" led blacks to demand a greater degree of equality at home after the war. NAACP (National Association for the Advancement of Colored People) leader W. E. B. DuBois stated that "if the black man could fight the Kaiser . . . he could later present a bill for payment due to a grateful white America." Although DuBois told blacks to "forget . . . special grievances," and to "close . . . ranks shoulder to shoulder with our own white fellow citizens and the allied nations . . . fighting for democracy," he also predicted that blacks fighting for democracy expected their "full share of the fruits thereof."[5]

But the coming of peace did not produce the changes blacks sought. Instead, the period was marked by increased white hostility, violent outbursts against black civilians and soldiers, and acts of mob violence that included lynchings. In 1918 alone, sixty-three black men and women were lynched by mobs, leading many prominent Americans to compare the racial violence in America to the massacres of ethnic minorities in the Balkans, Turkish Armenia, and revolutionary Russia.[6]

At the root of the trouble lay racism and antiradicalism, combined with the whites' economic fears. The wartime gains resulting from the migration of blacks into the northern industrial cities created new arenas of interracial competition for jobs. White servicemen, newly returned from France, faced the possibility of unemployment in an economy not yet converted to peacetime production and blamed blacks for their economic woes. Some whites demanded that blacks return to the south and relinquish their new jobs, homes, and lives.[7] Black strikebreakers further inflamed tensions, especially in areas such as in East St. Louis, Illinois, where whites striking for higher wages and better conditions saw their jobs filled with blacks hired by antiunion employers.[8]

---

[5] DuBois quote in Tuttle, *Race Riot*, pp. 216–19. See also Nalty and MacGregor, *Blacks in the Military*, pp. 82–85; Stephen E. Ambrose, "Blacks in the Army in Two World Wars," in Stephen E. Ambrose and James A. Barber, Jr., eds., *The Military in American Society* (New York: Praeger, 1972), pp. 178–79; Edward M. Coffman, *The War To End All Wars: The American Military Experience in World War I* (New York: Oxford University Press, 1968), pp. 69–73, 216–19, 231–33. Not all blacks flocked to the colors, see Theodore Kornweibel, Jr., "Apathy and Dissent: Black America's Negative Response to World War I," *South Atlantic Quarterly* 80 (Summer 1981):322–38, and *Federal Surveillance of Afro-Americans (1917–1925): The First World War, the Red Scare, and the Garvey Movement* (Frederick, Md.: University Microfilms of American, 1987).

[6] NAACP, *Thirty Years of Lynching in the United States, 1889–1918* (New York: Negro Universities Press, 1919), pp. 7–10, 36–37, 43; "Mob-Rule as a National Menace," *Literary Digest* 63 (18 October 1919):9; Seligmann, "Negro Uprisings," p. 154. The total for lynchings in 1919 was even greater. See "63 Persons Are Lynched in the US in Ten Months," *New York City Call*, 12 Nov 19.

[7] Tuttle, *Race Riot*, pp. 210–16; Boskin, *Urban Violence*, pp. 40, 43; Seligmann, "Negro Uprisings," p. 154. On blacks and the labor movement, see Julius Jacobson, ed., *The Negro and the American Labor Movement* (Garden City, N.Y.: Anchor, 1968); Philip S. Foner, *Organized Labor and the Black Worker, 1619–1973* (New York: International, 1967). For a contemporary view, see J. L. Sewall, "The Industrial Revolution and the Negro," *Scribner's Magazine* 69 (March 1921):334–42.

[8] This riot, one of the nation's worst, did not involve federal troops. See W. E. B. DuBois and Martha Gruening, "Massacre at East St. Louis," *Crisis* 14 (1917):222–38; Elliot M. Rudwick, *Race Riot at East St. Louis, 2 July 1917* (New York: World, 1964); U.S. Congress, House, *Report of the Special Committee To Investigate the East St. Louis Riots*, H. Doc. 1231, 65th Cong., 2d sess., 15 July 1918.

C   A   N

Everett
Seattle
Ft. Lewis

Ft. Geo. Wright

Great Falls
Sandcoulee

Butte

Roundup

Red Lodge   Billings
                Bear Creek

IX Corps

Rock Springs

Ft. D. A. Russell

Salt Lake City
Ft. Douglas
            Helper

SAN FRANCISCO

Denver
Ft. Logan

Raton

Gallup

VIII Corps   Ft

El Paso

M E X I C O

SAN ANTON

UNION OF SOVIET
SOCIALIST REPUBLICS

HAWAII
1:20,000,000

ALASKA
1:45,300,000

C A N A D A

MAP 5

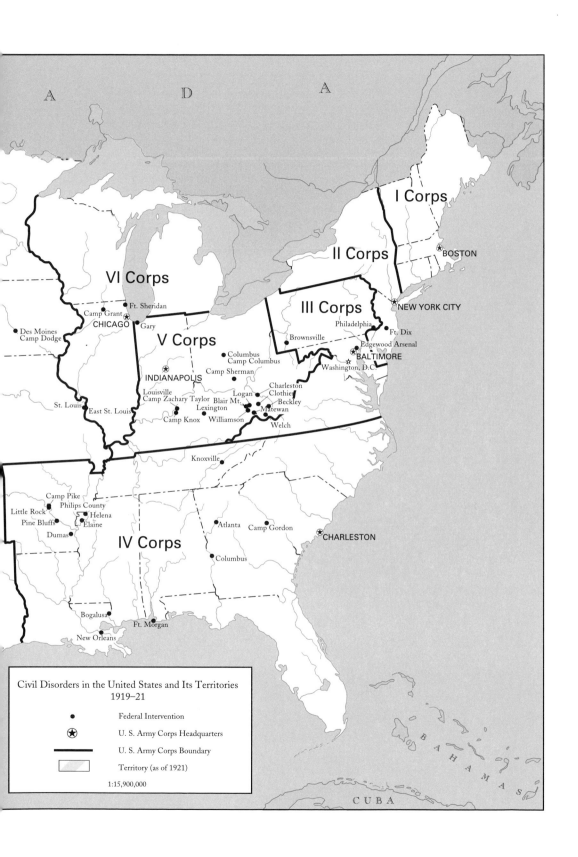

A D A

I Corps

II Corps

● BOSTON

VI Corps

● Ft. Sheridan

Camp Grant ●⊛
CHICAGO ● Gary

Des Moines ●
Camp Dodge

III Corps

● NEW YORK CITY

V Corps

Philadelphia ●
● Ft. Dix
Brownsville ● Edgewood Arsenal
● BALTIMORE

Columbus ●
Camp Columbus
Camp Sherman ●
Washington, D.C. ☆

St. Louis ● ⊛
INDIANAPOLIS

Louisville ●
Camp Zachary Taylor
Lexington ●
East St. Louis ● Camp Knox ● Williamson ●

Logan ● Charleston ●
Clothier ●
Blair Mt. ● Beckley ●
Matewan ●
Welch ●

Knoxville ●

Camp Pike ●
Philips County
Little Rock ● Helena ●
Pine Bluffs ● Elaine ●
Dumas ●

Atlanta ● Camp Gordon ●

⊛ CHARLESTON

IV Corps

Columbus ●

Bogalusa ●
Ft. Morgan ●
New Orleans ●

B A H A M A S

Civil Disorders in the United States and Its Territories
1919–21

●   Federal Intervention

⊛   U. S. Army Corps Headquarters

━━━   U. S. Army Corps Boundary

     Territory (as of 1921)

1:15,900,000

C U B A

Both riots and charges of subversion brought the federal government into the conflict. Of twenty-five major racial disorders in the two years following the armistice, six resulted in calls for the Army to restore order. In only one could racial violence be equally attributed to the actions of both sides. The remainder originated from provocative and hostile actions of whites, often caused by off-duty soldiers, sailors, and marines. Although the attitudes of the officers and men of the predominantly white Regular Army toward blacks were conventional for the times, the Army quelled the disorders in a neutral manner, but not bloodlessly. Nonetheless, Army discipline and adherence to orders proved to be the key to quelling disturbances that otherwise could have degenerated into widespread, open racial warfare.[9]

Washington, D.C.

In July 1919 more than 1,200 officers and enlisted men from the numerous military posts in the Washington area were summoned by civil authorities to restore law and order to the city of 401,000, which was wracked by mob violence and interracial strife. Ironically, the riot was precipitated by uniformed members of the armed forces, whose actions resulted in considerable injury and loss of life.[10]

In late June and early July of 1919 several attempted rapes of white women were reported in the District of Columbia and surrounding areas. Police officials within the 804-member city police department became convinced by eyewitness reports that one black was responsible for several of the crimes. Many whites, however, believed that a premeditated epidemic of sexual assaults by blacks upon area white women was under way. Although suspects were arrested, most were released amid strong press criticism of the district government for lax law enforcement. In particular, the *Washington Post* ran a sensational campaign about a "crime wave" in the city, highlighting rapes both actual and imaginary. The stories were picked up by Washington's other daily newspapers, the *Washington Times*, the *Washington Herald*, and the *Washington Evening Star*, generating outrage within the white community.[11]

Late in the evening of 18 July the wife of a sailor on her way home from work was jostled by two black men. Although frightened, the woman was not assaulted. On the following evening, several hundred off-duty white soldiers, sailors, and marines entered a black residential area in southeast Washington to avenge the incident. In route the mob assaulted several blacks and laid siege to the home of a black family. The city police and the military provost guard intervened and broke up the mob, but they were too late to prevent other clashes. Racial partisanship was an old tradition among the metropolitan police, who arrested eight blacks but only two white sailors. When policemen tried to arrest a black man later that night, he wounded one of them—the first sign that racial conflict in the nation's capital would not be a one-sided affair.[12]

---

[9] For government involvement, see Weber, *The Final Memoranda*, pp. 33–34; William Cohen, "Riots, Racism, and Hysteria: The Response of Federal Investigative Officials to the Race Riots of 1919," *Massachusetts Review* 13 (Summer 1972):373–400; "Has the Negro Gone Bolshevik?" *World Outlook* 5 (October 1919): 12–13.

[10] For the history of race relations in Washington, see Constance M. Greene, *The Secret City: A History of Race Relations in the Nation's Capital* (Princeton: Princeton University Press, 1967).

[11] For the press role in the riots, see Peter Perl, "Nation's Capital Held at Mercy of the Mob," *Washington Post Magazine* (16 July 1989), pp. 20–21.

[12] Arthur I. Waskow, *From Race Riot to Sit-In, 1919 and the 1960s* (New York: Doubleday, 1966), pp. 21–24; Boskin, *Urban Violence*, pp. 45–46. Whites on the District police force outnumbered blacks by twenty-seven to one.

The situation remained tense throughout the next day. By nightfall on 20 July violence erupted with greater intensity in the vicinity of 7th Street and Pennsylvania Avenue. As police attempted to arrest a black man, a group identified by witnesses as "soldiers, sailors, and marines" intervened, assaulting blacks who were returning home from work. The incident provoked an immediate response by blacks. Scattered rioting lasted throughout the night and into the early morning of 21 July.[13]

Attempts to calm the situation were unsuccessful. The Washington branch of the NAACP requested that Secretary of the Navy Josephus Daniels restrain the sailors and marines in the Washington area. Daniels did nothing, however, apparently blaming most of the trouble on the blacks and making no effort to protect them. Black leaders then sent a delegation to meet with Commissioner Louis P. Brownlow and other city officials on Monday, 21 July. Reports of police beatings of black prisoners had spread, and the delegation predicted that mounting black frustration could explode into greater violence. One member told Brownlow that the black people of Washington were "determined not to stand up and be shot down like dogs," but they were "prepared to protect their families and themselves and would do so at all hazard." The role of servicemen in the early stages of the riot did little to engender the trust of the black residents of the city. The black community leaders asked Brownlow if black soldiers would be included among any federal troops assigned to the police force. Upon being informed by Brownlow that all colored soldiers had been discharged, the black leaders bluntly told the assembled city officials that the black community believed that they would not receive a "square deal" from the white soldiers.[14]

After his meeting with the black leaders, Brownlow quickly met with Secretary of War Baker and Army Chief of Staff March at the War Department, requesting the help of any available federal forces to end the cycle of violence. The Navy Department agreed to supply 400 marines, and the War Department promised troops to reinforce the police. The special legal status of the District of Columbia ensured prompt help from the federal government, so shortly after the meeting several police precincts were reinforced with mixed military detachments equipped with motor transport.[15] A unit of five officers and ninety men of the 3d Cavalry under the command of Lt. Col. William O. Reed also made ready to supply the police with reinforcements if called. Yet the night of 21 July brought renewed strife.

The new violence reversed the pattern of the earlier clashes. Now the majority of assaults were directed by blacks against white citizens and police. Black men in automobiles mounted hit-and-run attacks, while Army cavalry detachments repeatedly charged surging white mobs that were attempting to break a police cordon around black neighborhoods. In contrast to the previous nights, military personnel were no longer a source of the interracial violence; the only service personnel involved were those assigned to riot duty.

---

[13] "Service Men Beat Negroes in Race Riot at Capital," *New York Times*, 21 July 1919; Waskow, *From Race Riot to Sit-In*, p. 24.

[14] Rpt of Meeting Between Black Leaders and City Officials, 21 Jul 19, NAACP MS, series G, container 34.

[15] Waskow, *From Race Riot to Sit-In*, pp. 23–26; Rpt of Meeting Between Black Leaders and City Officials, 22 Jul 19, NAACP MS, series G, container 34. The executive branch of the federal government could intervene in Washington, D.C., more easily than in the states, although under some conditions RS 5300 had to precede intervention. See also Military District of Washington Emergency Plan White, 6 Jan 45, pp. 5–6, RG 407, Records of the Office of the Adjutant General, U.S. Army, RG 407, NARA. For Brownlow, see *The Autobiography of Louis Brownlow*, 2 vols. (Chicago: University of Chicago Press, 1955–1958).

WILLIAM G. HAAN

Dozens of blacks and whites were injured; 15 were killed, and over 300 were arrested.[16]

The violence of the night of 21 July prompted a full-scale intervention by the federal government. Baker, acting under instructions from President Wilson and working with Navy Secretary Daniels, ordered additional forces sent to Washington to restore public order. Under the wartime policy of direct access, no presidential proclamation was issued. All federal forces were placed under the command of Maj Gen. William G. Haan, director of the Army's War Plans Division of the War Department General Staff. An artillery officer who excelled in organizational matters, Haan had combat experience in the Philippines and during World War I had commanded the 32d Infantry Division. His forces included 1,000 soldiers and U.S. marines from nearby Camp Meade and the Quantico Marine Base and 85 cavalrymen. In addition, MID agents in civilian clothes mingled with the populace seeking information, and the police enlisted 1,000 special deputies.[17]

With ample power at hand, Haan quickly set about to restore order in the district. Instead of acting simply in support of the district police, federal troops assumed primary responsibility for law enforcement. The creation of a unified command placed all law enforcement forces under Army direction and control. The centralization of authority in the hands of one commander produced an immediate and dramatic change in the city. Although a few incidents and casualties marred the first day of the military law enforcement, in general the saturation of trouble spots with federal troops quickly succeeded in restoring order.[18] By Thursday, 24 July 1919, rioting in Washington, D.C., had ended, and the Army indicated its strong desire to return law enforcement responsibilities to the district police. Larger federal units left Washington, D.C., on 27 July, while a smaller Army detachment of thirty-five officers and men of the 63d Infantry remained in the city to support police forces until the following day, when they too were withdrawn.[19]

---

[16] Memo for Maj Gen Haan, 22 Jul 19, Records of the War Dept General Staff–Military Intelligence Division, File 2198: Office of the Chief of Staff, War Plans Division, RG 165, NARA; Waskow, *From Race Riot to Sit-In*, pp. 26–28; "Capital Clashes Increase," *New York Times*, 22 Jul 19.

[17] Memo by Maj Gen Haan, 22 Jul 19, File 2198, RG 165; Memo for the AG, H. Jervey, 21 Jul 19, Glasser Papers, RG 60, NARA. See also "Home Guard Is Shot," *New York Times*, 23 Jul 19; Rich, *The President and Civil Disorder*, p. 153.

[18] "Capital Kept Calm by Federal Troops," *New York Times*, 24 Jul 19; Waskow, *From Race Riot to Sit-In*, p. 29.

[19] GO 2, 27 Jul 19, File 2198, RG 165; "Regulars Leave Capital," *New York Times*, 28 Jul 19; Rich, *President and Civil Disorder*, p. 154.

The participation of soldiers, sailors, and marines in attacks against the black populace on the nights of 20 and 21 July had been confirmed by many reports in the press and those presented to War and Navy Department officials. Although initially showing no concern, Secretary of the Navy Daniels later instructed the chief of naval operations to "direct officers in the district to spare no effort to prevent participation of men wearing the uniform." He further ordered that all commanding officers in or near Washington report the names of men in the Navy or Marine Corps so offending. Although the *New York Times* stated on 21 July that "several hundred soldiers, sailors, and marines participated in the rioting," Haan later denied that any soldiers still in the Army had any part in this mixup. He attributed the presence of men in uniform to the large number of recently discharged soldiers who were legally allowed to wear their Army uniforms. However, his request that the War and Navy Departments deny passes to enlisted personnel wishing to visit the city demonstrated his concern that servicemen might either take part in the disturbances or become victims of them. In any case he found the performance of federal military personnel on riot duty worthy of praise and requested that Baker dispatch a suitable letter of commendation for Marine and Navy units that served in the city.[20]

The Washington, D.C., race riot evoked a mixed response from the political and military figures most actively involved in its suppression. For Secretary Daniels, a southerner, the race riot deserved no more than a passing mention in his diary, and the role of marines and sailors in the outbreak of the disorder received no comment. Secretary Baker, on the other hand, was rare among government officials of his day in holding progressive views regarding racial problems. Reporting on the situation to President Wilson, he praised the "attitude of the colored people, particularly their leaders" who helped to ease the great interracial tension in the city.[21] General Haan did not attribute the origin of the trouble to the general population, either black or white. Instead, he placed the blame on the newspapers wholly. As he informed one of his military colleagues, "things quieted down as soon as I got control of the newspapers. It was merely a newspaper war. When I got them to agree to say approximately what I wanted them to say, which was the truth, then soon everything was over." Perhaps the most significant insight into Haan's thinking can be gained from a letter he wrote on 5 August. Dismissing the importance of the riot, he stressed that it was just a "short mopping up affair," and expressed the opinion that had troops been committed earlier in the race riot in Chicago that summer more lives could have been saved. For him, the safeguarding of human life by prompt military intervention was the central factor in dealing with a civil disturbance.[22]

---

[20] Quote from "Capital Clashes Increase." See also Ltr, Haan to Baker, 24 Jul 19, and Memo for the Dir, Operations Div, 22 Jul 19, both in File 2198, RG 165; Ltr, Baker to Daniels, 29 Jul 19, Glasser Papers, RG 60, NARA; Waskow, *From Race Riot to Sit-In*, p. 28.

[21] E. David Cronon, ed., *The Cabinet Diaries of Josephus Daniels 1913–1921* (Lincoln: University of Nebraska Press, 1963), p. 427; Ltr, Baker to Wilson, 23 Jul 19, Papers of Newton D. Baker, Library of Congress, Washington, D.C. For contemporary views, see H. J. Seligmann, "Race War in Washington," *New Republic* 20 (13 August 1919):48–50; "Riots in Washington and Chicago," *Current History Magazine* 2 (September 1919):453–54; "Washington Riots," *Nation* 109 (9 August 1919):173; J. E. McCulloch, "Another View of the Washington Riots," *Outlook* 123 (3 September 1919):2341–44.

[22] Ltrs, Haan to Maj Gen T. H. Barry, 30 Jul 19, and to Brig Gen C. R. Boardman, 5 Aug 19, both in William G. Haan Papers, State Historical Society of Wisconsin. For the Chicago riots, which did not involve federal troops, see Carl Sandburg, *The Chicago Race Riots, July 1919* (New York: Harcourt Brace & Howe, 1919; reprint, New York: Harcourt Brace & World, 1969); William M. Tuttle, Jr., "Labor Conflict and the Black Worker

The Army's principal aim had been that of upholding the law and restoring order with as little bloodshed as possible. To deal with the causes of the trouble was outside its mission and perhaps, given contemporary attitudes, beyond anyone's power. A member of the British embassy in Washington offered some insightful comments on the race riot. In a report to the Foreign Office, he noted that the disturbance reflected "deep underlying conditions for which there is no remedy at hand." He expressed relief also that "there has so far been none of those disgraceful outbursts of savagery which sometimes characterize riots in places where the race question is more acute than in Washington."[23] Within a month, however, the Army was called to intervene in a area where such savagery was clearly evident.

Omaha, Nebraska

As in Washington, D.C., the rape of a white woman by a black man was the cause of a racial disturbance in Omaha that required federal troops to quell. On 25 September 1919 a 19-year-old white woman, Agnes Loebeck, was allegedly assaulted at gunpoint by a black male in south Omaha. The assault was witnessed by Millard Hoffman, described by the newspapers and subsequent reports as "a crippled friend" of Loebeck's. The following day police arrested a 41-year-old black man, Will Brown, who was known by many to be living with a white woman. The victim identified Brown as the perpetrator of the assault, although the police and Army intelligence later reported that the identification was not positive. In the local *Omaha Bee*, however, the incident was cited as only one further example of unpunished depredations committed upon white women by blacks. Here, too, local politics was a factor. The newspaper was controlled by a recently ousted political machine that was highly critical of the new reform-minded city administration. Over the course of several months it had published a series of articles highlighting alleged instances of black criminality to embarrass city officials.[24]

The first attempt by a mob to lynch Brown was unsuccessful, but two days after his arrest rumors began to circulate that another attempt would be made on the his life. On the afternoon of Sunday, 28 September, a group of approximately fifty youths from age fourteen to twenty, reputed to be friends of Loebeck's, gathered at the Bancroft School in south Omaha and began a one-mile march to the downtown Douglas County Court House. By 1600 this group had been joined by a much larger crowd. Although initially good humored, the mob turned rapidly hostile, demanded that the prisoner be surrendered to them, and stoned the building, breaking all the windows on the first and second floors. These actions

---

in Chicago, 1894–1919," *Labor History* 10 (Summer 1969):425; Waskow, *From Race Riot to Sit-In*; Alma Herbst, *The Negro in the Slaughtering and Meat-Packing Industry in Chicago* (Boston: Houghton Mifflin, 1932; reprint, New York: Arno, 1971).

[23] Ltr, R. C. Lindsay to Curzon, 25 Jul 19, Great Britain, Public Record Office, Foreign Office Records, FO371/4247-112139.

[24] Quote from Rpt of Capt H. T. Lewis, Intelligence Officer, Ft. Omaha, 27 Oct 19, hereafter cited as Lewis Rpt, File 10218-371-11, MID, RG 165, NARA. See also Rpt, Col Alexander L. Dade to CG, Central Dept, 15 Oct 1919, hereafter cited as Dade Rpt, Glasser Papers, RG 60, NARA. See also Ltr, J. Hale-Moss to J. L. Shillady, 21 Aug 19, NAACP MS, series G, container 13. "The Real Causes of the Two Race Riots," *Crisis* 19 (December 1919):62. This *Crisis* article alleges a much closer and more intimate relationship between Loebeck and Brown and contains many illuminating comments regarding the former's character and the municipal political situation in Omaha. For an overview of the riot, see Clayton D. Laurie, "To Protect the Citizens and Property of Omaha: The U.S. Army and the Omaha Race Riot of 1919," *Nebraska History* 72 (Fall 1991):135–143.

forced the forty-five Omaha policemen present to retreat to the third and fourth floors. The county jail was on the fifth floor. The mob then stormed the building. The police opened fire, killing two, but only succeeded in delaying the mob temporarily. Within minutes the situation had escalated far beyond the capacity of the police to control. The Army later estimated that by 1945 the crowd numbered some 5,000 people.[25]

Throughout the confrontation, Omaha Mayor Edward P. Smith refused resolutely to surrender Brown, an effort that nearly cost him his life. As the mob surged onto the fourth floor of the courthouse, Smith, who was trying to calm the crowd, was seized, dragged from the building, and hoisted up a nearby trolley pole the mob intended to use as a makeshift gallows. The timely intervention of two police detectives, who cut the critically injured mayor down and rushed him away in a waiting automobile, saved him from certain death. Still intent on reaching the prisoner, the mob broke into hardware stores and pawnshops, seizing firearms and ammunition. By 2030 several rioters had looted a nearby gasoline station and seized fuel which they promptly used to set fire to the first several floors of the courthouse, hoping to burn out the police and Brown. Attempts by the fire department to extinguish the flames were thwarted. As the heat and smoke became intense, police authorities moved Brown and the other prisoners to the roof. At this point the mob finally captured Brown. The actual sequence of events remains unclear, but one account maintains that the prisoners on the roof, in spite of police efforts, surrendered Brown to save their own lives.[26]

The mob then took Brown to the corner of 16th and Harney Streets, near the courthouse, hanged him, mutilated and riddled his body with bullets, dragged it through the streets of the city at the end of a rope, and burned it. Still not satisfied, the mob ransacked more stores in search of arms and then went to the nearby police station to lynch blacks being held there. After Brown was murdered, however, the police captain on duty at the jail released the other black prisoners, an action that undoubtably saved their lives. Mob violence at the courthouse ended abruptly around 2230 when the first federal troops arrived. The local Army commander, acting without prior War Department authorization, had decided to intervene under Army regulations allowing the deployment of troops in an emergency situation.

Omaha municipal officials had already directed requests for aid both to local posts and to the War Department in Washington, D.C. Because of this dual approach, Army intervention proceeded slowly at both levels.[27] Lt. Col. Jacob Wuest, commanding officer at Fort Omaha, was the closest to the riot and first received news of the mob's formation in the early evening. To a telephone call from a captain of the Omaha police requesting aid, he replied (erroneously, in view of the emergency) that he could not deploy troops without the authority of the War Department. A short time later, the federal marshal in Omaha also requested troops. Again Wuest refused to act without permission from Washington. He received additional calls from various local authorities but remained firm, informing local, state, and federal civil officials that "federal troops could not be used as a posse comitatus" without authorization from higher authority.[28]

[25] Dade and Lewis Rpts.

[26] Lewis Rpt; Waskow, *From Race Riot to Sit-In*, p. 112.

[27] Rpt, Lt Col Jacob W. S. Wuest, CO, Ft. Omaha, 2 Oct 19, hereafter cited as Wuest Rpt, Files 10218-371-4 and 10218-317-11, RG 165, NARA. See also Dade Rpt.

[28] Quote from Wuest Rpt. See also Dade and Lewis Rpts.

Wuest's initial inaction clearly demonstrated a lack of knowledge of both Army regulations concerning emergency situations and of the direct access policy that had been in effect for two years. He did, however, monitor the developments at the courthouse throughout the evening, sending his adjutant to observe events and to make regular telephone reports. Other officers were sent into Omaha to collect all personnel on leave. In the meantime, Wuest ordered machine guns to be taken out of storage, ammunition to be made ready, and units to prepare for action. If he hoped to avoid federal action he was soon disillusioned. At 2045 he learned from the Nebraska adjutant general that National Guard troops were unavailable, because the closest unit, at Benson, west of Omaha, had been disbanded. Soon afterward, Wuest received a report that the mob had set the courthouse ablaze. After waiting a further hour and a half, during which time Brown was lynched, Wuest decided to intervene without orders from Washington. Later he explained that "the situation at this time had become so acute that it was evident that any further delay would be disastrous [*sic*] and that in order to protect the lives and property of the citizens of Omaha prompt action would have to be taken without [any] longer awaiting instructions from Washington." Lynching alone was evidently, to his mind, insufficient reason for risking action that might subsequently have been determined by Army authorities to be an unjustified or an illegal usurpation of civil authority.

Once in action, he moved decisively. He assembled his command by 2225 and ordered a group of 6 officers and 206 men into Omaha. Dividing the force, he sent the 27th Balloon Company, under the command of Maj. Henry C. White, to disperse the mob at the courthouse, while the 17th Balloon Company under Maj. Clarence H. Maranville proceeded to the black district to protect the populace from further violence. The 17th reached its station on commandeered streetcars, amid reports of the imminent arrival of the mob. The two detachments deployed with five machine guns to supplement their already substantial firepower. At 2245 Wuest received instructions from Secretary Baker directing him to offer all possible assistance to Omaha authorities.

Major White's force arrived in the vicinity of the courthouse in time to prevent any further loss of life or property. His unit quickly succeeded in dispersing groups milling around the charred building. Apart from breaking up small gatherings of rioters and putting an end to scattered looting, White's troops experienced no trouble. Meanwhile, Maranville's force found the black community tense. Several soldiers reported exchanging shots with snipers on rooftops, but no casualties were incurred by either side. At midnight, a second detachment of 108 troops arrived to reinforce the 17th Balloon Company. Early the next morning, Wuest's units reported that the city was quiet. On the morning of 29 September, Col. John E. Morris assumed command of the troops in Omaha. With Morris came sizable reinforcements from Camp Dodge, Iowa; Camp Grant, Illinois; and Camp Funston, Kansas. The largest detachment, from Camp Dodge, consisted of a provisional machine-gun company of 11 officers and 152 men with ten heavy machine guns.[29]

The Omaha Army commanders quickly published emergency orders to prevent a repetition of the previous day's events. Colonel Morris had the newspapers in Omaha publish a proclamation warning that any citizen bearing arms faced immediate arrest, and a further

---

[29] Wuest Rpt.

FEDERAL TROOPS MAN A MACHINE GUN AND CANNON IN OMAHA

proclamation ordering blacks to remain indoors. In the afternoon the Army launched an observation balloon in west Omaha, providing a panoramic view of the entire black neighborhood. A thunderstorm aided the Army in keeping people off the streets; by nightfall of 29 September the city was reported quiet and under control.[30]

While the troops spent an uncomfortable night in the rain, the Central Department commander, Maj. Gen. Leonard Wood, who had just arrived in Bismarck, North Dakota, received news of the disturbance. The call from Omaha triggered a flurry of activity. Wood immediately called the Army chief of staff, Maj. Gen. Peyton March, who granted him authority "to call upon any troops within the limits of the department."[31] Although troops had initially intervened under the conditions outlined by Army regulations that had been in effect before the outbreak of World War I, Wood assumed command under authority of the wartime policy of direct access formulated in 1917. This policy was reaffirmed by both Army officials and Secretary Baker on 3 and 15 October 1919, respectively. President Wilson was not consulted, but Wood did issue a proclamation informing Omaha citizens of the arrival and mission of the Army, and added that the governor of the state had called upon the president requesting federal aid. The general then set off for Omaha from Bismarck by rail, an uncomfortable journey in a caboose where, he noted, "we were in the air about as much as we were in our seats."[32]

---

[30] Ibid.

[31] Wood Diary, Leonard Wood Papers, Library of Congress.

[32] Proclamation of 30 Sep 19 in Wood Diary. See also Rich, *President and Civil Disorder*, p. 155; Waskow, *From Race Riot to Sit-In*, pp. 129–30; Hagedorn, *Leonard Wood*, p. 333; Lane, *Armed Progressive*, pp. 234–35. In actual fact Lt. Gov. P. A. Burrows made the request.

Arriving late in the evening of 30 September, Wood immediately met with Nebraska Governor S. R. McKelvie, Acting Omaha Mayor Ure, and Colonel Morris. He approved Wuest's earlier troop dispositions and ordered additional deployments to prevent any further outbreaks of rioting. Then he created a strong reserve at the city auditorium —a provisional battalion, company, and machine-gun company—capable of being thrown quickly into any trouble spot. Three other company-size detachments were deployed at 24th and Lake Streets, in the black neighborhood, the courthouse and city hall, in the city center, and in south Omaha at 24th and O Streets. Each soldier received a rifle, bayonet, and 200 rounds of ammunition, and each machine-gun unit was ordered to keep at hand 6,000 rounds per gun. The *New York Times* quoted Wood as warning that "those who attempt to interfere with the military authorities will find themselves fighting the United States Army."[33]

Wood next issued a proclamation outlining the reasons for the federal military presence. He also prohibited public gatherings and carrying of firearms by all people except the police and military. Drawing on community support to help with local policing, he approved the deputizing of 200 men of the American Legion. The legionnaires made a favorable impression upon Wood, who later deputized men from this private, patriotic veteran's organization in other civil disorders that the Army was ordered to quell. He observed in his diary that the legionnaires "have done good work and have shown what can be done with them in case of civic emergency." On the following day, 1 October 1919, Wood declared modified martial law in Omaha.[34]

Drawing on his previous civil experiences, Wood set out to rebuild the law enforcement agencies in the city to prevent any future repetition of the recent mob violence. In virtually all after action reports, Army officers criticized the performance of the Omaha Police Department. Wuest, for example, noted that "the police on duty made no effort to disperse the crowds when opportunity offered to do so."[35] The cornerstone of Wood's plan was to revitalize the Omaha police force by adding 100 carefully selected men and by purchasing an array of modern weapons including .45-caliber revolvers, riot guns, and .30-caliber machine guns. His request that these items be supplied from federal arsenals, however, was rebuffed by the War Department, citing statutes that forbade the sale of federal arms to municipalities.[36]

Undaunted, Wood went on to other matters. He had spent a great amount of time and energy dealing with the investigation and arrest of mob ringleaders, interviewing several participants himself. On the basis of photographs, the Army detained a number of people, arresting 100 men by 2 October on charges that ranged from arson to murder. Pending trial, the accused were held in Army custody. Omaha police compiled further lists of 300 people being sought for questioning in connection with the riot, including Agnes Loebeck's crippled friend, her brother, and a suspected ringleader named William Francis, all of whom had disappeared.[37]

---

[33] "Gen Wood Orders Arrest of Omaha's Rioters," *New York Times*, 1 Oct 19.

[34] *Secretary of War Report, 1920,* pp. 68–69. Wood's declaration of modified martial law in Omaha was no more legitimate than his declaration of the same in Gary, Indiana, five days later. For an account of this, see Chapter 11.

[35] Lewis, Wuest, and Dade Rpts.

[36] Wood Diary. For telegrams concerning arms, see Glasser Papers, RG 60, NARA. Arrangements were later worked out that allowed the use of federal property.

[37] Wood Diary; "Gen Wood Orders Arrest of Omaha's Rioters"; "Another Woman Attacked in Omaha," *New York Times*, 2 Oct 19; Waskow, *From Race Riot to Sit-In*, pp. 114–16.

Although racial tension obviously caused the Omaha riot, Wood's publicly stated conclusions more closely fit the needs of his presidential aspirations than they did reality. Much of his strategy for capturing the Republican Party's presidential nomination rested on "Americanism" and a staunch opposition to radicals and aliens. Hence, Wood concluded that the Industrial Workers of the World was behind the violence in Omaha. Two days after he arrived in the city, he recorded in his diary that "there were a number of requests for IWW meetings and one Russian soviet, all of which were declined." A passage in his diary on 2 October further reflected his belief that "every day demonstrates more and more the fact that preparations have been made by the IWW or some other organized element of disorder, to create very serious trouble and probably burn a good section of the city."[38] On the eve of his departure he addressed the Omaha University Club, categorically blaming the IWW for the trouble in the city. Wood exhorted his listeners to stand up to this threat, declaring that "there will be no red flag where there are brave public officials." His speech reflected the "red scare" hysteria that was sweeping the nation, but in the case of Omaha there was a significant gap between his campaign rhetoric and the actual measures he took. Wood's actions in deploying troops, rebuilding the Omaha police force, investigating the riot, and arresting the ringleaders of the lynch mob indicated that he had a better understanding of the situation than his public utterances revealed.[39]

The Army's efforts in Omaha involved the largest contingent of federal troops deployed to meet a racial disturbance during 1919–1920, 70 officers and 1,222 enlisted men. By early October the initial emergency had passed, and by midmonth only two companies of regulars remained in the city. The last troops departed Omaha on 15 November.[40] Although more prompt action by Wuest on the evening of 28 September could probably have saved Will Brown's life and prevented massive property loss in downtown Omaha, federal troops stopped additional violence and protected the black community from further mob actions. Wood's way of seizing and exercising authority marked another departure from prewar procedures for using the military in domestic disorders, and his analysis of the riot's origins were obviously flawed. Yet, the overall performance of the Army in Omaha represented a fair and effective effort.

Elaine, Arkansas

Army intervention in a racial disturbance in Phillips County, Arkansas, differed greatly from other similar situations. Here the setting was southern, rural, and agricultural. Furthermore, the events surrounding the Elaine disorder are still a matter of great controversy. The various interpretations of what transpired range from a white pogrom to a black uprising.[41]

---

[38] Wood Diary.

[39] "Wood Accuses the IWW," *New York Times*, 5 Oct 19; Lane, *Armed Progressive*, pp. 233–34; "Omaha," *Nation* 109 (11 October 1919):491; "Omaha: Riots in the Nebraska City," *Literary Digest* 63 (11 October 1919):16.

[40] Waskow, *From Race Riot to Sit-In*, pp. 115–17; *Secretary of War Report, 1920*, pp. 68–69.

[41] The major writings include B. Boren McCool, *Union, Reaction, and Riot: A Biography of a Rural Race Riot* (Memphis: Memphis State University, 1970); Waskow, *From Race Riot to Sit-In*; J. W. Butts and Dorothy Jones,

These interpretative differences extend to the Army intervention. Depending on the viewpoint accepted, federal troops are seen as either defenders of public order who saved a community terrorized by black agitators or as props of a local racist regime. Most interpretations, however, miss the fundamental reason for federal military intervention—to support lawful authority and to restore and maintain order. In performing its constitutional role the Army was duty bound to support a legally constituted, yet predominantly white, government unsympathetic to the blacks of Phillips County.

Phillips County lies in the southeastern corner of Arkansas, along the Mississippi River. Helena is the county seat, and Elaine, the closest settlement to the disturbance, is twenty miles farther south. In 1919 the rich alluvial soil supported an agricultural, cotton-based economy. The county population was about 45,000, with blacks forming 75 percent of that total. Typical of the southern socioeconomic order of the time, most real property, financial holdings, and political power were controlled by whites. The overwhelming black majority consisted of poor farmers, tenants or sharecroppers, who worked for a subsistence income. In 1919 a poor crop due to bad weather created special hardship among them. The despair of the black farmers and the growing activism by blacks nationwide awakened new demands for reform of the tenant-landlord relationship, under which sharecroppers were compelled to make all purchases from commissary stores operated by landowners and receive such credit for their cotton as the landlord decided to allow them.

This awareness by blacks found expression in Phillips with the formation of the Progressive Farmers and Household Union of America led by Robert Lee Hill, a 26-year-old black man. In spite of white threats, Hill succeeded in mobilizing black tenant farmers and channeling their grievances into an organization capable of extracting concessions from local white landlords. Many whites viewed these developments with resentment and alarm, seeing in them the initial signs of a racial uprising. New and sudden refusals of black men and women to pick cotton or to work as domestic servants convinced whites that the union was bent on their destruction.[42]

On 30 September 1919, black efforts to organize a union collided with white fears. In Hoop Spur Church, a few miles from Elaine, a group of blacks met to make final arrangements for a class-action lawsuit directed against their landlords. Fearing white interference, they came to the meeting armed. Meanwhile, Deputy Sheriff Charles Pratt and W. A. Adkins, a special agent for the Missouri Pacific Railroad, along with two other persons, left Elaine ostensibly to investigate a nearby marital disturbance. When they noticed activity in the vicinity of the Hoop Spur Church, the deputy sheriff and his companions went to investigate. What followed cannot be accurately ascertained and is still subject to dispute, but a violent confrontation took place that resulted in Adkin's death and the wounding of

---

"The Underlying Causes of the Elaine Riot of 1919," *Arkansas Historical Quarterly* 20 (1961):95–103; O. A. Rogers Jr., "The Elaine Riots of 1919," *Arkansas Historical Quarterly* 19 (1960):142–50; Ralph A. Demarais, ed., "Military Intelligence Reports on the Arkansas Riots, 1919–1920," *Arkansas Historical Quarterly* 33 (1974):175–91; Lee E. Williams and Lee E. Williams II, *Anatomy of Four Race Riots* (Jackson: University and College Press of Mississippi, 1972). For a contemporary view, see W. F. White, "Race Conflict in Arkansas," *Survey* 43 (13 December 1919):233–34.

[42] McCool, *Union, Reaction, and Riot*, pp. 1–7, 12–20; Butts and James, "The Underlying Causes of the Elaine Riot of 1919," pp. 100–101; Williams and Williams, *Anatomy of Four Race Riots*, pp. 39, 42–43; "The Real Causes of the Two Race Riots," *Crisis* 19 (December 1919):56–57.

Pratt. During the exchange of gunfire the others in the ill-fated party fled to a nearby town and notified authorities in Helena.[43]

Expecting further trouble, both black and white communities began amassing men and weapons. Black farmers gathered near Hoop Spur; the whites formed posses. Late on 1 October a posse arrived in Hoop Spur Church, recovered Adkin's body, and sent Pratt off for medical attention. The posse searched the surrounding area and by late morning located the farmers in a thicket, southwest of Hoop Spur. In the ensuing exchange of gunfire a member of the posse was killed, another wounded, and a black farmer injured. Not expecting such determined resistance, the posse retreated and requested help from Governor Charles H. Brough in dealing with what they termed a "negro uprising."[44]

Upon receiving news of the racial strife, Brough contacted Secretary of War Baker requesting federal troops. In a further telegram, he warned Baker that "negroes [are] said to be massing for attack." Baker responded by giving him verbal permission to use any available federal troops to suppress the disturbance, under the policy of direct access. A delay resulted because the commander of Camp Pike, Arkansas, Brig. Gen. Samuel D. Sturgis—confused about procedures to obtain military aid—refused to honor the request until orders arrived from Washington.[45]

The flurry of telephone calls and telegrams demonstrated anew the uncertainty of some officers about the procedure for summoning federal troops to deal with a civil disturbance. Apparently Sturgis was ignorant of Army regulations regarding emergency situations and the policy of direct access to federal forces. Baker gave his permission presumably on behalf of the president, and subsequent orders confirmed this presumed delegation of authority in its opening phrase "by direction of the President."[46] Whether Baker actually consulted with the president is unclear; Wilson had suffered a stroke on 25 September, while on a nationwide whistle-stop promotion tour for the Treaty of Versailles and the League of Nations, and for the next two weeks was close to death. Nor is it clear why Baker felt obliged to consult Wilson in what amounted to a *pro forma* effort to comply with normal prewar procedures. The best estimate is that the troop commitment was actually made under the wartime procedure of direct access. That evening the War Department confirmed Brough's authority to summon regular troops, and Sturgis responded by ordering Col. Isaac C. Jenks to lead a force to Elaine.[47]

Shortly after midnight, Jenks and 583 officers and men departed Little Rock, Arkansas, on a special train for Elaine. Brough accompanied the troops. Jenks' command consisted of six provisional companies reinforced by a machine-gun unit with twelve guns, an ammunition train, and a medical detachment. The federal force arrived around 0900 and found Elaine in chaos.[48] "On arrival," Jenks reported later, "we found the town in [a] great state of excitement. Hundreds of white men, all carrying firearms, were on the streets, near

[43] McCool, *Union, Reaction, and Riot*, pp. 21–24; Waskow, *From Race Riot to Sit-In*, pp. 124–26; Butts and James, "The Underlying Causes of the Elaine Riot of 1919," p. 102; Williams and Williams, *Anatomy of Four Race Riots*, pp. 44–45.

[44] McCool, *Union, Reaction, and Riot*, pp. 24–28.

[45] Telgs, Brough to Baker, 1 Oct 19, and Sturgis to AG, 1 Oct 19, both in Glasser Papers, RG 60, NARA.

[46] SO 264, HQ, Camp Pike, 1 Oct 19, Glasser Papers, RG 60, NARA.

[47] Telg, AG to Sturgis, 1 Oct 19, File 370.6, Elaine, RG 407, NARA.

[48] Rpt, Jenks to Sturgis, 14 Oct 19, hereafter cited as Jenks Rpt, File 370.61, Elaine, RG 407, NARA. See also Demarais, "Military Intelligence Reports," pp. 181–85.

the station and in groups all over town." He acted quickly to bring the population under control by ordering that anyone carrying a weapon, either black or white, be immediately disarmed. White officials in Elaine were all too willing to brief Army personnel on black activities. According to Jenks' adjutant, Capt. Edward G. Passailaigue, a committee of civilians met the train claiming that "negroes of the surrounding country had assembled and were killing the whites." Moreover, the committee told Jenks that "a large party of negroes were reported in a wood west of Elaine."[49]

Acting on this information, Jenks decided to investigate the reports of black outlaws in the woods. Dividing his command, he left Maj. John R. Baxter in Elaine with two companies and orders to collect all weapons and to unload the equipment from the train. Jenks took with him four companies under the command of Maj. Nathaniel E. Callen. Less than a half hour after arriving in Elaine, these regulars left for Hoop Spur, accompanied by civilian guides and Governor Brough. After traveling a mile and a half, the column discovered a black woman, lying on her doorstep, shot through the neck by persons unknown. Although medical attention was rendered, the woman died soon afterward. When the battalion reached the vicinity of Hoop Spur, the troops began to reconnoiter the surrounding countryside, which consisted of open fields interspersed with woods and canebrakes. Callen deployed three companies in a loose skirmish line. One company was placed in reserve and followed 200 yards behind the leading elements. The sweep progressed uneventfully until the regulars reached a canebrake, where they encountered a group of armed black men.[50]

The sequence of events is unclear. There is no indication that the blacks were given the opportunity to surrender, nor is there any indication of which group precipitated the subsequent action. In an exchange of gunfire, Cpl. Luther Earles was fatally wounded and Sgt. Pearl B. Gay suffered minor injuries. The official reports do not mention black casualties, but troops did take some fifty prisoners. Many fled and escaped in the dense underbrush.[51] The battalion completed its search of the area and turned back toward Elaine with their prisoners. En route the party came upon a farmhouse containing sixty-five white women and children, guarded by ten men with shotguns, who had fled there in fear of the "negro outlaws." Passailaigue reported that "had troops not arrived, the fate of that party would have been disastrous." Jenks stationed men in outposts here and at Hoop Spur to calm the fears of the whites in the area and dispatched one company with two machine guns to Helena, the county seat, "to prevent disorder and to protect the prisoners in the city jail from mob violence." This detachment, commanded by Capt. Herbert H. Lewis, prevented a lynching on the night of 2 October. At the same time, Jenks sent twenty-five men to the town of Millwood, Arkansas, presumably to disarm whites patrolling the streets.[52]

---

[49] Considerable confusion exists in the documentary and secondary records concerning the correct spelling of this officer's name. It is variously spelled as either Passialaigne, Passailaigne, or Passailaigue. No officer of this name is found in any of the *Army Registers* for the years 1918–1920. The latter name above is in official reports. Jenks Rpt; Demaris, "Military Intelligence Reports," pp. 181–85.

[50] Demarias, "Military Intelligence Reports," pp. 181–85; Jenks Rpt. Records do not specify the size of this group.

[51] Jenks Rpt; Demarais, "Military Intelligence Reports," pp. 181–85.

[52] Ibid.

A U.S. Army Soldier Escorts Sharecroppers Into Detention, Elaine, Arkansas

Jenks' troops engaged in mopping-up operations, and military patrols combed Phillips County, arresting blacks suspected of a role in the Farmers and Household Union movement or the recent hostilities. With the immediate threat neutralized, Jenks outlined five objectives for his command that he deemed essential for the restoration of order: to guard inhabitants of outlying localities where danger seemed imminent; dispatch strong patrols to apprehend ringleaders and to obtain evidence; prevent any shootings, lynchings, or other disorders in the area to "relieve the mental distress of the people . . . protect the colored people from any kind of violence and enable them to resume their work."

During rural sweeps between 3 and 6 October, the Army arrested several hundred blacks, taking the majority to Elaine for questioning. The interrogations were a joint local police and Army effort conducted by Lt. George S. Deaderick, whom Jenks praised for his "remarkable energy in his work." Most of the black prisoners were soon released, but many made accusations later that during the interrogations they had been maltreated and tortured by Army and law enforcement personnel for the purpose of extracting confessions and other evidence.[53]

Besides those allegations, other troubling questions lingered after the disorders in Phillips County. It was never definitely established how many fatalities occurred, and whether they resulted from the actions of whites, blacks, or federal troops. Captain

---

[53] Jenks Rpt; Waskow, *From Race Riot to Sit-In*, pp. 132–34.

Passailaigue noted that "to the best of my knowledge about twenty negroes were killed by soldiers for refusing to halt when so ordered or for resisting arrest. In all cases, all of the negroes were armed." Yet another intelligence report from Maj. Eugene E. Barton, an officer at Camp Pike, put the total number at 14 dead for blacks. Jenks made only passing reference to an incident in which 2 black men were machine-gunned and killed by troops on outpost duty guarding women and children. Other sources put the total of blacks killed in the Phillips County disturbance as high as 200; more reasonable estimates range from 50 to 73. Despite the infrequency of fatalities resulting from federal military interventions, no Army investigations were conducted into the validity of these figures or into the circumstances surrounding the 2 to 20 civilian deaths attributed to federal forces. Even without exact confirmation, Elaine was the bloodiest disturbance involving federal troops since 1894.[54]

After all the bloodshed, normal conditions were quickly restored in Phillips County. Governor Brough, satisfied that his presence was no longer needed, returned to Little Rock on 3 October. Four days later the local sheriff supported by a white citizens' committee issued a proclamation "to the Negroes of Phillips County." Blacks were exhorted to "Stop Talking! Stay at home—Go to work—Don't Worry!" After consulting with Brough, Jenks returned to Camp Pike on 9 October, leaving behind 53 men under the command of Capt. David E. Lane. They stayed in Elaine and Helena guarding prisoners until 15 October, when they returned to Camp Pike.[55]

In assessing the cause of the disturbance in Elaine, the officers involved firmly maintained that the black community of Phillips County was responsible. Their view reflected the opinion of local whites on racial disorders—and, indeed, the prevailing view of most whites nationwide. Jenks cited intelligence information that supposedly revealed that members of the black community, and especially the Farmers and Household Union, "plotted to kill twenty-one of the leading landowners." Furthermore, he maintained that the "negroes placed the whites at a considerable disadvantage, before the arrival of the troops." Passailaigue was more emphatic about the so-called black plot in Phillips County: "Upon examination, negroes confessed that they had planned to kill all the whites they saw in the outlying districts and then march on and 'Clean up' the town of Elaine. The attack on Elaine was planned for Thursday morning. The whites in that section are out-numbered 5 to 1 and to my mind, had troops not been sent to quell the disorder, the negroes would have succeeded in carrying out their murderous plans." How much of this information originated from the panic-inspired perceptions of the white community or from black confessions obtained under duress is unknown. Who fired the first shot it is impossible to say, but an exploitative social and economic system lay at the root of the trouble in the county.[56]

Although peace had returned to Elaine, the white communities in the plantation counties along the Mississippi River continued to fear the possibility of a black uprising. Such was the case in Desha County, south of Elaine. When Deputy Sheriff J. H. Breedlow and

---

[54] Waskow, *From Race Riots to Sit-Ins*, p. 128; Jenks quote in Jenks Rpt. Barton and Passailaigue quoted in Demarais, "Military Intelligence Reports," pp. 181–86.

[55] McCool, *Union, Reaction, and Riot*, pp. 32–33. See Rpt, Lane to Sturgis, 27 Oct 19, and proclamation and handbill, all in File 370.61, Elaine, RG 407, NARA.

[56] Quote from Demarais, "Military Intelligence Report," pp. 181–186. See also Jenks Rpt; Waskow, *From Race Riot to Sit-In*, pp. 131–34.

two other whites attempted to arrest Doc Hays, a black man accused on 21 January 1920 of stealing hogs, they met unexpected resistance. Ten armed black men objected to the arrest and freed Hays after a brief struggle with the deputy and his men. Local officials, fearing the clash was a portent of another rebellion, requested help from the governor.[57] Brough responded to the request by making a telephone call to Camp Pike, seeking federal troops to prevent a race riot. The post commander complied by sending a detachment of 130 men under the command of Maj. Austin F. Preston, who hastened to Dumas by special train the next day. Upon arrival Preston quickly discovered that a black uprising was not in the offing, and two days later the troops returned to Little Rock. Brough was quite satisfied, for in his opinion the "presence of troops in Desha . . . prevented the development of race feeling, which might have had a serious result."[58]

Lexington, Kentucky

The next racial disturbance grew out of an explosive situation in Lexington, Kentucky: the trial of a black man accused of raping and murdering a ten-year-old white girl. The trial was a cause celebre in Fayette County, Kentucky, and contained all the elements necessary to produce a lynch mob. Long before the guilt or innocence of the accused had been established, local whites arrived at their own verdict. Local law enforcement authorities were aware of the danger and took elaborate precautions to ensure that the decision of the court would not be preempted by a mob. The recently reconstructed Kentucky National Guard, commanded by Adjutant General J. M. DeWeese, reinforced the local authorities, who added fifty men to their own police force. Rope and wire barriers were erected around the courthouse to control crowds, and the accused was held in the state penitentiary at Frankfort to ensure his safety, pending trial.[59]

On the morning of 9 February 1920, a special train brought the defendant to Lexington, where the court, after a trial lasting forty minutes, sentenced him to die in the state's electric chair. Security precautions had seemed to work, for the prisoner had arrived safely at the courthouse to be tried and to hear the jury's verdict and the judge's sentence. During the proceedings, however, a hostile mob collected outside and gave every indication of becoming increasingly impatient with the seemingly slow course of justice. Suddenly, at 0930 the mob stormed the courthouse with the intent of lynching the prisoner. Police and guardsmen deployed in close formation with their backs to the entrance. After issuing several warnings for the crowd to disperse, DeWeese gave the signal to open fire at point-blank range. As a result five members of the mob fell dead or were dying, and eighteen others were wounded. Although this action halted the mob's attack on the courthouse, the mob then turned to looting hardware stores and pawnshops in search of weapons. With the situation rapidly moving beyond their control, the authorities requested outside help.[60]

---

[57] Demarais, "Military Intelligence Report," p. 179.

[58] Rpt, Maj Robert O. Poage, Intelligence Officer, to Dir, MID, 24 Jan 20, File 10218-372, MID, RG 165, NARA.

[59] "Troops Kill Five in Kentucky Mob Out To Get Negro," *New York Times*, 10 Feb 20.

[60] The suspect confessed to the crime, see "Troops Kill Five in Kentucky Mob Out To Get Negro"; Rpt, Maj G. F. Cornish, Intelligence Officer, Provisional Regiment, to MID, 10 Feb 20, hereafter cited as Cornish Rpt, Glasser Files, RG 60, NARA.

Using the wartime policy of direct access, Governor Edwin P. Morrow made a request to General Wood, commander of the Central Department, for federal troops. Wood immediately deployed troops on his own initiative, afterward informing the War Department as outlined in Army regulations regarding emergencies.[61] At Wood's direction the 1st Division staff at Camp Zachary Taylor near Louisville alerted 2d Brigade units to prepare for riot duty. Within minutes past noon, troops had boarded a special train supplied by the Louisville & Nashville Railroad Company and started the seventy-mile three-hour journey to Lexington. A provisional unit of the 28th Infantry followed under the command of Brig. Gen. Francis C. Marshall. A graduate of West Point, Marshall was a cavalry officer who had served with the AEF in France. Upon arrival, he immediately got off the train with his command at Water Street, two blocks from the courthouse. Several hundred local citizens who were gathered at the station immediately dispersed when the troop train arrived. Marshall's major concern was the mob, estimated at 10,000 people, milling outside the courthouse. His first action was to issue a proclamation placing Fayette County under martial law, "assuming all functions both civil and military in said County." Later on the same day he issued another proclamation stating that he, having declared martial law, was now empowering "the civil and criminal authorities in this County and State to assume and administer their usual functions excepting in cases wherein I may deem it necessary to assume jurisdiction."[62]

Next Marshall set out to raise the siege of the courthouse. So that troops might converge from two directions simultaneously, he divided his command. He led two platoons from the east along Main Street, while Patterson took a second group to the rear of the courthouse. The formations mixed sound riot tactics with the patriotic air of a Fourth of July parade: "Sergeants, unarmed, preceded the detachment by thirty feet. General Marshall marched immediately in front of the flag, also unarmed. Two squads, deployed as skirmishers, followed the flag at thirty feet; two columns of files on either side of the street followed the line of skirmishers. The rear guard was composed of one squad deployed as skirmishers."[63]

The summary report prepared by Maj. George Cornish offers considerable insight into the situation in Lexington and the Army's response. In dispersing the mob on 9 February, he noted that "no overt act of violence was shown the United States troops." He attributed the moral effect of federal forces to the citizenry's acceptance of the rule of law: "The general sentiment of the mob was that the United States Government as represented by its troops stood for law and order and had to be respected."[64]

The troops quickly cleared the streets adjacent to the courthouse. Marshall then issued orders that anyone caught loitering after 1700 would be arrested. By the appointed hour

---

[61] *Secretary of War Report, 1920*, p. 70; Telg, Wood to AG, 10 Feb 20, Glasser Papers, RG 60, NARA.

[62] Cornish Rpt. In this situation Marshall, like Wood in Gary and Omaha, greatly exceeded his authority. President Wilson gave no such direction, and regulations did not at this time, nor later, authorize any military commander to unilaterally declare martial law without presidential approval and direction. Marshall's actions were without any statutory authorization whatsoever and clearly violated the doctrine of *Ex Parte Milligan* set down in 1866. See Stockman and Dickinson, *Troops on Riot Duty*, p. 129; Dowell, *Military Aid to the Civil Power*, pp. 230–48; *Regulations for the Army of the United States, 1913*, art. 47; AR 500-50, 6 Jun 23; Commager, *Documents of American History*, doc. 256, *Ex Parte Milligan*, 1:472.

[63] Cornish Rpt.

[64] Cornish quote in Cornish Rpt. See also Telg, Wood to AG, 10 Feb 20; Rpt, Lt Col W. R. Scott to MID, 9–10 Feb 20, Glasser Papers, RG 60, NARA.

the mob had dispersed, and soon after a
train arrived carrying a provisional company of the 26th Infantry and a section of the
3d Machine Gun Battalion. With these
additional forces Marshall was able to
divide Lexington into four military districts
and implement a pass system to discourage
people from gathering near the courthouse.
Key installations, such as the building holding the condemned man and the arsenal at
the University of Kentucky, were placed
under heavy guard. In the very early morning of 10 February, a third troop train
arrived with the 1st Infantry Brigade. This
unit relieved the 2d Brigade of its responsibilities, and that same evening the 2d
Brigade left Lexington, escorting the condemned prisoner to the state penitentiary in
Eddyville, Kentucky.[65]

FRANCIS C. MARSHALL

With the condemned man out of town,
the threat of further mob action was greatly
diminished. Within a week Marshall left
Lexington with all but seventy-one soldiers under command of Lt. Col. G. W. Maddox,
who remained to protect local officials and a grand jury that had been convened to investigate the original mob action. Three weeks later, after the dismissal of the grand jury, the
last of the regulars departed Lexington.[66]

The Army intervention in Lexington lasted two weeks and involved 1,000 officers and
men. Besides two provisional infantry regiments and machine-gun battalions, detachments
of sanitary, signal, field artillery, and motor transport corps units participated in the operation. On the racial issue, Cornish's report reflected the mood then prevalent in white
America. He concluded: "There are no evidences of a race riot in Lexington. White civilians state that the negroes themselves wish to see the negro [William] Lockett lynched."
Discounting MID's concern about radicals in America, Cornish reported that no radical
influence was evident and that "there were no evidences of any foreigners in the mob." The
major noted that the troops showed no inclination to fraternize with either rioters or radicals and that the 20 percent of foreign-born troops employed in the upheaval in Lexington
were "absolutely trustworthy."[67] Perhaps because of the commander's attitude, the Army
troops in Lexington maintained strict neutrality and successfully aided local officials in
keeping order, although Marshall had no legal authority to declare martial law. The presence of troops in Lexington, more than any other factor, broke the will of a lynch mob and

[65] Cornish Rpt. Lockett, the convicted man, was to be executed in March 1920. Army records do not indicate
whether the sentence was carried out.

[66] Rpt, Maddox to the Intelligence Officer, Central Dept, 17 Feb 20, File 10218-389, MID, RG 165,
NARA.

[67] Cornish Rpt.

provided a decisive end to a stormy period. The Lexington riot was the last racial incident that required federal military involvement in the immediate post–World War I years.[68]

The Military Intelligence Division and "Negro Subversion"

The Army's Military Intelligence Division (MID) continued to play a key role in domestic surveillance operations between its creation in 1917 and 1921 by monitoring the racial situation. It amassed vast quantities of information on racial disturbances and the black community at large. MID's reports, however, tended to indicate more about prevailing American racial attitudes, especially those of its own officers, than about the causes and possible solutions of the race problem.[69]

Soon after the war, MID relied on two specialists on blacks in America, whose reports were subsequently read widely by military officials faced with racial disorders. Maj. Elbert Cutler, a white man with a doctorate from Yale, had a deep interest in sociology, then an emerging academic field. The MID director, Brig. Gen. Marlborough Churchill, described him as an "absolutely impartial expert in sociology." Cutler's colleague was Maj. W. H. Loving, a black man who had served honorably in the Philippine Constabulary. General Churchill portrayed him as one of the best types of "white man's negro."[70]

Cutler outlined his views in a 1919 memorandum entitled "The Negro Situation." From Cutler's point of view, a clear link existed between radicalism and the new black activism. "The doctrines preached by IWW agitators and radical socialists," he warned, "are daily winning new converts among the negroes." To him, black insistence on equal rights was a dangerously radical concept, and the NAACP a source of insidious propaganda. Hence, he believed it was a great mistake to allow the "negroes to arm themselves." Though Cutler, for all his education, viewed racial matters in the same way as many of his fellow soldiers and other less educated whites, he did hold a few progressive ideas. He deplored lynching, terming it a national disgrace, and believed that police forces in communities containing sizable black populations should exercise complete neutrality in upholding the law: "It is essential that a police department be alive to the importance of giving proper protection to both whites and colored when they are conducting themselves as law-abiding citizens and that an even-handed control be exercised over whites and colored who are inclined toward antagonistic conduct." The thrust of his thinking aimed at the maintenance of law and order and interracial peace. He disapproved of social equality but accepted the need for legal equality, provided it supported the status quo.[71]

Major Loving wrote the "Final Report on Negro Subversion" on the eve of his retirement in August 1919. In it he offered a thorough survey of the principal black newspapers, organizations, and personalities of the time, including DuBois' NAACP and Marcus

---

[68] A major race riot not involving federal troops took place in Tulsa, Oklahoma, in 1921, which left 270 dead. See Scott Ellsworth, *Death in a Promised Land: The Tulsa Riot of 1921* (Baton Rouge: Louisiana State University Press, 1982); Walter F. White, "Eruption of Tulsa," *Nation* 112 (29 June 1921):909–10; Loren L. Gill, "The Tulsa Race Riot" (M.A. thesis, University of Tulsa, 1946); "The Untold Story of One of America's Worst Race Riots," *Washington Post*, 12 Sep 82.

[69] Cohen, "Riots, Racism, and Hysteria," pp. 373–400; Kornweibel, "Apathy and Dissent".

[70] Cohen, "Riots, Racism, and Hysteria," p. 386.

[71] Ibid.

Garvey's Universal Negro Improvement Association. Emphasizing the theme of radicalism, Loving supported the notions of his white colleagues and countrymen. He emphasized that "until about four years ago radical sentiment among Negroes was of a moderate character and confined to resentment of lynching, disfranchisement, Jim Crowism, etc." The turning point, he argued, came in 1915 when young blacks flocked to the "torch of Socialism." The growth in popularity of socialism among blacks was rapidly creating a crisis, according to Loving, shown in IWW recruitment of "thousands of Negro laborers."[72]

To remedy the situation, he proposed reform of some of the major irritants to the black community. Like Cutler, he believed that Jim Crow laws needed to be eliminated to stem the tide of black radicalism. He suggested no concrete formula for effecting these changes, however. Although both officers attempted to shed light on the causes of the racial problems plaguing the nation, neither produced a valid assessment of the cause, let alone a workable policy for dealing with them.

The Army's involvement in quelling race riots in 1919 and 1920 revealed that it was not immune from the pervasive racism of white America, and yet that it could frequently perform nonpartisan duty in racial disturbances, protecting both black and white communities. In Omaha, Lexington, and Washington, D.C., the Army played a positive and key role in protecting both black and white lives and property. But the events in Elaine and Dumas emphasized that performing its duty of restoring law and order often necessitated upholding a political, social, and economic structure, the injustice of which to blacks helped to cause the initial disturbances. The events in Elaine, when contrasted with those in Omaha, demonstrate how difficult intervention could be for the predominantly white Army, whose members held the same racial views as other whites, and for the Army's reputation for fairness and neutrality under such circumstances. Finally, the Army's role in suppressing race riots was remarkably similar to its role in quelling violence arising from labor disputes. The same causations and policies were cited for interventions; the same procedures were followed once troops were deployed; and adherence to the same policies of neutrality and restraint were attempted, although, as evidenced in Elaine, not always achieved.

---

[72] Memo, Maj W. H. Loving for Dir, MID, 6 Aug 19, File 10218-361, MID, RG 165, NARA.

CHAPTER 13

The West Virginia Coal Mine Wars and the Return to Normalcy 1919–1921

The rule to be followed is that the public military power of the United States should in no case be permitted to be substituted for the ordinary powers of the States, and should be called into service only when the State, having summoned its entire police power, is still unable to deal with the disorder.
—Secretary of War Newton D. Baker, December 1920.

Authorities have not taken sufficiently active measures . . . [and] for purposes of both politics and economy, they have decided to rely on federal protection.
—Maj. Charles F. Thompson, 16th Infantry, May 1921.

The coal industry was afflicted by few labor difficulties during World War I, for production was strictly regulated by the Federal Fuel Administration, created by the Lever Act of August 1917. Through the efforts of the Fuel Administration, in October 1917 the bituminous coal operators and the AFofL's United Mine Workers (UMW) reached an agreement that granted wage increases to miners in return for a government-mandated increase in the price of coal and contract clauses preventing strikes and lockouts for the duration of hostilities. The agreement was not to remain in effect for more than two years beyond April 1918. Through this process of compromise and negotiation, and because of the increased profits going to mine owners, the UMW managed to improve the wages of its members nationwide in both bituminous and anthracite coalfields. Labor stability and heightened demand for coal resulted in a gigantic increase in coal production. In a 5-year period, 1913–1918, nearly 3 billion tons of coal were extracted—almost one-third as much as all the coal mines had produced in 106 years, from 1807 to 1913.[1]

Yet the wartime calm was an exception to the usually turbulent labor situation plaguing the industry during the previous forty years. The richest coal-mining areas, such as Appalachia, had only recently been developed. Little use had been made of the deposits until the American industrial takeoff in the late 1880s and 1890s, and until railroads provided both a demand for coal and the means to transport it to market. Then mine development brought

---

[1] David J. McDonald and Edward A. Lynch, *Coal and Unionism: A History of the American Coal Miner's Union* (Indianapolis: Cornelius, 1939), pp. 129–30, 136; Berman, *Labor Disputes and the President*, pp. 129–30.

a massive influx of people into a region that previously had been bucolic and sparsely popu-lated. Early mine owners had no state or federal laws to guide their operations and were free to conduct business as they saw fit, usually in a manner guaranteed to assure the largest prof-its. Cheap, plentiful labor was available from the cotton regions of the south and from the large immigrant populations jamming the eastern cities. Alluring offers of free transporta-tion, steady work at good wages, and company houses in which to live produced a stream of workers, even though mining coal—largely dug and loaded by hand using a pick, augur, black powder, and shovel—was extremely difficult and dangerous.

In most areas the promises of coal operators went unfulfilled. Miners claimed that operators robbed them of a large part of their earnings by paying them in company scrip, which was devalued if converted to cash; by charging excessive prices for electricity, coal, and sundries in company stores, which miners were compelled to patronize as a condition of their employment; and by demanding exorbitant rents for company-owned housing. By the early twentieth century the majority of coal operators, especially in West Virginia, had succeeded in putting into place a strict, paternalistic, and autocratic employment system, having near-feudal control over miners and their families, who lived in hundreds of isolat-ed mining villages throughout the state.[2]

Efforts to organize unions met fierce resistance from coal operators, who used evic-tion, termination, blacklisting, court injunctions, and outright coercion as weapons. In the eastern United States in particular, they influenced strongly both local and state govern-ments on policies that ensured high profits, prevented labor organization, and guaranteed a passive work force. Such tight control was necessary, coal operators maintained, because of the "boom and bust" nature of the industry, the instability of consumer demand, and the constantly fluctuating prices.[3] Except for a brief period during the Anthracite Coal Strike of 1902, when the federal government openly sided with labor against coal operators, the coal companies had been successful in their struggles with labor.

Some miners, however, had gone against the tide, forming unions as early as the 1860s. None of these early unions gained national following, company recognition, or large mem-berships until all merged in 1890 to form the AFofL–affiliated United Mine Workers. Although the UMW initially favored arbitration rather than strikes, resistance on the part of coal operators compelled it to adopt strikes as the primary means of achieving its goals. Union demands included the right of workers to join a union, thereby ending yellow-dog con-tracts; the right of free speech and assembly, especially during strikes; the outlawing of crib-bing, blacklisting, and antiunion espionage; the installation of scales to weigh coal; the hir-ing of weighing officials acceptable to the miners; the firing of all company-paid mine guards; safer working conditions; and a check-off system for the deduction of union dues.[4]

---

[2] Howard Lee, *Bloodletting in Appalachia: The Story of West Virginia's Four Major Mine Wars and Other Thrilling Incidents of Its Coalfields* (Morgantown: West Virginia University Press, 1969), pp. 4, 8; *AF of L: History, Encyclopedia, Reference Book: Prepared and Published by Authority of the 1916 and 1917 Conventions*, 4 vols. (Westport, Conn.: Greenwood, 1977), 2:364; A. Gleason, "Company-Owned Americans: Mine Workers of West Virginia," *Nation* 110 (12 June 1920):794–95.

[3] Lee, *Bloodletting in Appalachia*, p. 12.

[4] Ibid.; Anna Rochester, *Labor and Coal* (New York: International, 1931), pp. 163, 177. "Cribbing" refers to the company practice of building a crib-like structure on the sides of standard coal cars. These cars were used to figure miner production and wages. A cribbed car held more coal, but miners still received the same pay per car as if the crib did not exist.

Little progress was made in achieving any of these demands before World War I. In 1918, however, mine union membership grew to an all-time high. Yet miners believed that their wages remained out of alignment with the rising cost of living and with increases granted in other industries. After World War I, the UMW members, like other workers of the time, were determined to maintain the gains made during the war and to make new advances in the immediate postwar period.[5]

Not unexpected, the armistice brought major changes to the coal industry that threatened to undo union advances. In November 1918 the nation had an enormous surplus of coal, which caused an immediate drop in price, demand, and therefore production. Mining companies, facing postwar cutbacks, refused to consider voluntarily maintaining wartime labor agreements favoring workers. The Federal Fuel

JOHN L. LEWIS

Administration (FAA), which had settled disputes during the war, continued to function after the armistice, but only in cases in which both sides were willing to submit their grievances to the National War Labor Board if labor-management arbitration efforts failed. Increasingly, as in other industries, coal operators were unwilling to acknowledge the federal government as a neutral arbitrator, and the effectiveness of the labor board declined until its dissolution in August 1919.

Yet the federal government and the mine operators continued to hold the unions to wartime contracts. No new agreements would be considered by the mine operators, they stated publicly, until a peace treaty was signed and the war was declared over. Increased demands by the UMW—for renegotiation of all wartime labor contracts, to include a 30 percent increase in wages; nationalization of coal mines; and democratic management of the mines—were interpreted by many operators, and by many in the government as well, as indications of the extent that wartime radicalism and foreign ideologies had affected the miners. Although Secretary of Labor William B. Wilson had met with operators and miners for three weeks of negotiations in Washington, D.C., beginning in late October 1919, no progress resulted. UMW President John L. Lewis, against the advice of Secretary Wilson, declared that all contracts then in existence for the duration of the war would terminate on 1 November 1919 and that in the event no new contract was signed by that date a national coal strike would automatically ensue.[6] President Wilson, when

---

[5] McDonald and Lynch, *Coal and Unionism*, pp. 136, 141.

[6] Ibid., pp. 138, 140, 144–45; Berman, *Labor Disputes and the President*, pp. 141–42. For Lewis, see Robert H. Zieger, *John L. Lewis: Labor Leader* (Boston: Hall, 1988). See also S. Kopald, "Behind the Miner's Strike," *Nation* 109 (22 November 1919):656–58.

informed of the impending strike, declared it "not only unjustifiable but unlawful," reminding the miners that the Lever Act was still the law of the land, regardless of the state of European hostilities.

The Coal Strikes of 1919

Despite a prior injunction issued against the strike by a federal judge in Indianapolis, over 70 percent of the nation's soft-coal miners in fourteen states left their jobs on 1 November 1919. Already facing a nationwide steel strike, race riots, and a somewhat vague and murky threat of foreign radicals and Bolsheviks, the War Department alerted commanders to be prepared to respond to any civil disorder. Although the Wilson administration was moving to rescind the policy of direct access during early November, several requests by governors were honored in the last two months of that year, and most deployments were effected either under the wartime policy of direct access or the emergency provision of Army regulations. Army officials informed W. A. Marshall, president of the Wholesale Coal Trade Association, that "in the matter of protection of mine properties and miners desiring to work, the War Department is co-operating by furnishing troops wherever the state authorities are unable, with the means at their disposal, to cope with the situation and request federal aid."[7] The Army, already deployed for race riots and steel and transportation strikes, now undertook another major intervention in coal labor disputes from coast to coast, beginning in the Far West.

The first deployments were small. On the evening of 30 October, 100 men of the 21st Infantry under Col. George L. Byram left Fort Douglas, Utah, and Camp Kearny, California, to arrive at the town of Helper, Utah, at the request of Governor Simon Bamberger, to protect property and nonstriking miners and to keep order. When the troops arrived in Helper all was quiet, and the mines were operating with close to normal strength.[8] Reports that labor violence threatened the coal mines in and around Rock Springs, Wyoming, brought troops from Fort D. A. Russell and Fort George Wright on 27 October. Additional reinforcements of federal troops bolstered the garrisons at Fort Russell and Fort McKenzie in preparation to crush strike-related violence and remained until late December, although the Wyoming strikes were settled the month before.[9]

Federal troops were also requested by New Mexico's governor during the first week of November to deal with threatened labor violence in the coal regions of that state. In response, the Army dispatched a provisional squadron of the 8th Cavalry from El Paso, Texas, to Gallup, New Mexico, for protection of property and preservation of order. The mayor of Gallup did not approve of the governor's actions, however, requesting on two sep-

---

[7] Quote from Memo, Actg Dir of Opns, GS, for Marshall, Glasser File: Coal, RG 60, NARA. See also Rochester, *Labor and Coal*, pp. 200–201; Berman, *Labor Disputes and the President*, p. 185; "Injunction Against the Miners," *New Republic* 20 (12 November 1919):307–08; "Courts and the Coal Strike," *Nation* 109 (20 December 1919):787.

[8] Telgs, Bamberger to AG, 30 Oct 19, and Liggett to AG, 31 Oct 19, 1 Nov 19, and 4 Nov 19, all in Glasser File: Coal, RG 60, NARA. See also *Secretary of War Report, 1920*, p. 69.

[9] Telgs, Brennan to Warren, 25 Oct 19; Warren to Baker, 27 Oct 19; AG to CG, Western Dept, 1 Nov 19; Liggett to AG, 15 Nov 19, all in Glasser File: Coal, RG 60, NARA. *Secretary of War Report*, p. 69.

arate occasions that the troops be removed "as there is no need for them. . . . The miners are peaceful, and there is no intimidation or armed resistance." He believed that "it only aggravates the situation to have troops here." The regulars arrived on 3 November, and, although most left about one month later, the last of them did not return to their stations until January 1920. Other troops, the 3d Squadron of the 12th Cavalry and two companies of the 24th Infantry, were dispatched under command of Col. G. W. Bugler to Raton, New Mexico, on 3 November. These troops, like their counterparts in Gallup, returned to their stations in late December, having encountered no major disturbances.[10] In similar fashion 38 officers and 660 men of the 7th Division were sent to Pittsburg, Kansas, at the request of that state's governor. The troops, from Fort Leavenworth and Camp Funston, arrived on the last day of the month and returned to their stations only two weeks later; the coalfields remained quiet throughout the brief occupation.[11]

In neighboring Oklahoma, state and local officials were heartened by news that federal troops were on their way to protect volunteers and prison convicts who were mining coal in strike-idled mines. Threats of violence by strikers had convinced Governor J. B. A. Robertson to request federal military aid directly from the War Department. One squadron of the 13th Cavalry from Fort Clark, Texas, and two companies of the 24th Infantry from Columbus, New Mexico, were scheduled to arrive in McAlester, Oklahoma, as soon as they could find transportation. The relief of the local populace, however, turned to anger when they discovered that the 24th Infantry troops were black. Senator Thomas P. Gore of Oklahoma contacted Secretary Baker and complained that he did "not approve of sending Negro troops to Oklahoma" and that such an action would only make matters worse. Echoing Gore's sentiments, the chairman of the State Council of Defense, J. A. White, wired Oklahoma's other senator, Robert L. Owen, and informed him that Oklahoma was refusing the assistance of black troops—they need not be sent to McAlester, or anywhere else in the state. In response to the outrage of the state's white residents and the racial tensions nationwide, the 24th Infantry did not deploy; instead, the white 13th Cavalry under Maj. R. B. Harper deployed and remained in McAlester for three weeks in December.[12]

Unlike the Oklahomans, Montana residents and mine owners gladly welcomed any type of federal military assistance. On 6 December, by request of Governor Samuel V. Stewart, a total of 13 officers and 379 men of the 1st and 35th Infantry regiments from Camp Lewis, Washington, deployed to guard coal mines in Sandcoulee, Roundup, Red Lodge, and Bearcreek, Montana. A further company of the 1st Infantry had already traveled from Camp Lewis to Bayne, Washington, on 20 November to protect nonstriking miners and mine property. The federal troops stayed in Bayne for eight days.[13]

---

[10] Telgs, Dickman to AG; Gallup Mayor to Baker; Harris to CG, Southern Dept, all 3 Nov 19, Glasser File: Coal, RG 60, NARA. *Secretary of War Report, 1920*, p. 69.

[11] *Secretary of War Report, 1920*, p. 70; F. C. Trigg, "Kansas Gets Coal," *Outlook* 123 (17 December 1919):498; C. M. Harger, "Kansas' Volunteer Coal-Digging Army," *Outlook* 123 (24 December 1919):538–39.

[12] Telgs, Oklahoma Governor to Baker, 28 Nov 19; CG, Ft. Sam Houston to AG, 3 Dec 19; Gore to Baker, 4 Dec 19; White to Owens, 4 Dec 19; all in Glasser File: Coal, RG 60, NARA. *Secretary of War Report, 1920*, p. 70.

[13] Telg, Liggett to AG, 6 Dec 19, Glasser File: Coal, RG 60, NARA; *Secretary of War Report, 1920*, p. 69.

In the eastern United States, 21 officers and 526 enlisted men were already deployed in Knoxville, Tennessee, and 55 officers and 795 soldiers of the 1st Division from Camp Zachary Taylor, Kentucky, had occupied Charleston, Beckley, and Clothier, West Virginia, since the last day of October. When locks on the Monongahela River were allegedly threatened by striking miners, a detachment of 132 federal troops of the 22d Infantry under command of Col. File D. Evans arrived from Fort Niagara, New York, to perform guard duties at Brownsville, Pennsylvania. The War Department alerted other troops for possible riot and guard duty in the coal areas of Alabama, Arkansas, and Colorado.[14]

Meanwhile, in Washington, D.C., negotiations between mine owners and miners had resumed under the direction of Secretary of Labor Wilson and A. H. Garfield, former fuel administrator. Garfield told miners that they were entitled to a 14 percent wage increase to cover the rising cost of living, but Wilson favored a 31 percent increase. The miners rejected Garfield's proposal; mine operators rejected Wilson's. The talks broke down on 28 November. The federal government had persuaded John L. Lewis, however, that a state of war continued to exist and that the coal strikes were illegal, a betrayal of all the government had attempted to do for miners during the war. In return for a guarantee of a 14 percent wage increase and a promise by Attorney General A. Mitchell Palmer and presidential private secretary Joseph P. Tumulty to appoint a presidential commission to investigate the coal industry, Lewis, who was facing possible prosecution and a prison term, ordered miners back to work in late November. Most responded immediately, but some miners in many regions continued to strike until early December. With two exceptions, federal troops had returned to their stations by early 1920; only in West Virginia did regulars see further service.[15] As the government had intended, federal military intervention prevented the 1919 coal strike from becoming a violent and destructive affair. U.S. Army intervention, although it was useful in aiding civil authorities to reestablish order permanently in the coalfields in most areas, had little long-term effect on the tensions existing in the coalfields of West Virginia.

The West Virginia Coal Mine Wars, 1920–1921

The final instances of federal military intervention in labor disputes immediately after the war formed a sharp contrast to the quiet collapse of the nationwide coal strike. One of the largest deployments of federal troops for riot duty in history took place when regulars were called to West Virginia during 1920–1921 to deal with violence stemming from a series of local coal strikes. These so-called coal mine wars represented a turning point for American labor and for the Army's civil disturbance role.

---

[14] Telg, CG, Central Dept, to AG, 21 Nov 19, Glasser File: Coal, RG 60, NARA. See also *Secretary of War Report, 1920*, p. 69.

[15] McDonald and Lynch, *Coal and Unionism*, pp. 146–47; Rochester, *Labor and Coal*, pp. 200–201; "Compulsory Conferences and the Coal Strike: The Administration and Its Handling of the Industrial Problem," *New Republic* 20 (12 November 1919):310–12; "Who Won the Coal Strike?" *Literary Digest* 63 (20 December 1919):11–13; Berman, *Labor Disputes and the President*, p. 206. The promised commission first met in January 1920 but made no substantial progress. Most miners were left to negotiate individually with employers and received only small wage increases. See also Telg, CG, Central Dept, to AG, 21 Nov 19, RG 60.

The conflict originated in efforts by local UMW leaders to strengthen their union in a period of decline. Although half the coal mines in West Virginia were unionized, most of these operations were in the northern half of the state. Therefore union leaders launched a new recruiting drive in two antiunion strongholds, Mingo and Logan Counties, located in the southwestern corner of the state across the Tug River from Kentucky. They faced strong opposition. Coal operators counted upon their political connections in the state capital and in the county sheriffs' offices to resist unionization by mobilizing the machinery of local law enforcement. If those conservative methods failed to confound unionization, brute force was often the next recourse.[16]

Sheriff Don Chafin of Logan County, a popular figure to all except miners and union men, embodied both the conservative legal and the violent aspects of the opera-

JOHN J. CORNWELL

tors' antiunion campaign. In the pay of the operators, Chafin used his deputies to assault and evict union organizers as soon as they set foot in the county. Provoked by this opposition, in September 1919 the local branch of the UMW, District 17, organized several thousand miners for a march on Logan County to unseat Chafin. Taking advantage of the wartime arrangement for direct access to federal troops, West Virginia Governor John J. Cornwell asked General Wood, who was then simultaneously dealing with troop deployments to Gary, Indiana, and Omaha, Nebraska, for a force to intercept and disperse them. Wood consented and began to gather a force of 1,600 men. His actions were consistent with existing policy and the emergency provisions of Army regulations. The march ended quickly when the miners were confronted by state-recruited sheriff's posses, but the force

---

[16] See Daniel P. Jordan, "The Mingo War: Labor Violence in the Southern West Virginia Coalfields, 1919–1922," in *Essays in Southern Labor History: Selected Papers, Southern Labor History Conference, 1976,* eds. Gary M. Fink and Merl E. Reed (Westport, Conn.: Greenwood, 1977), pp. 102–03; Richard D. Lunt, *Law and Order Versus the Miners: West Virginia, 1907–1933* (Hamden, Conn.: Archon, 1979), pp. 12, 15–16; Rich, *President and Civil Disorder,* p. 159; Merle T. Cole, "Martial Law in West Virginia and Major Davis as Emperor of the Tug River," *West Virginia History* 43 (Winter 1982):125. See also Lee, *Bloodletting in Appalachia,* pp. 85, 87; Michael Meador, "The Redneck War of 1921," *Goldenseal* 7 (April–June 1981):44; Lon Savage, *Thunder in the Mountains: The West Virginia Mine War, 1920–1921* (Elliston, Va.: Northcross House, 1986); V. B. Harris, *Kanawha's Black Gold and the Miner's Rebellion* (Ann Arbor: Braun-Brumfield, 1987); David A. Corbin, *Life, Work, and Rebellion in the Coalfields: The Southern West Virginia Miners, 1880–1922* (Urbana: University of Illinois Press, 1981); Clayton D. Laurie, "The U.S. Army and the Return to Normalcy in Labor Dispute Interventions: The Case of the West Virginia Coal Mine Wars, 1919–1921," *West Virginia History* 50 (1991):1–25; Annual Rpt, Cmdr, Fifth Corps Area, Ft. Harrison, to AG, 9 Jul 21, and Memo, CofS, G2, Fifth Corps Area, for CG, Fifth Corps Area, 23 May 21, both in Records of the Adjutant General's Office, U.S. Army, WD File: Mingo County, RG 407, NARA.

Wood had assembled was sent to Kanahwa City, Clothier, and Beckley to keep order during the nationwide coal strike then in progress.[17]

By late 1919, however, the Wilson administration had decided to restore the prewar policies and to decrease the frequency of federal military intervention in labor disputes. The first indication of this change came on 3 November, when Secretary Baker, in a strange and inexplicable reversal of his wartime policies, flatly turned down a request for federal troops from the governor of Georgia, explaining that

> it should be borne in mind that our Regular or permanent Army is designed to resist and overcome enemies of our government and is provided for strictly federal use. . . . The protection of private property, rights, and liberties, and lives of the inhabitants of any state is primarily the duty of the individual concerned. . . . Use of federal troops for this class of duty has heretofore always been the last resort. . . . Our Constitution contemplates such force only when all other forces of a locality or state have been exhausted . . . or [are] insufficient to meet the emergency.

Baker's line of reasoning was clear: he severely limited the possible number of situations in which states could obtain rapid and direct military aid, but reiterated his willingness to aid the governors to organize, equip, and train a National Guard. The change in Army policy affected only the states like Georgia that had organized National Guard units or constabulary forces. West Virginia lacked both. Until such time as state forces could be re-created or raised, the burden of quelling civil disorder in West Virginia remained a federal military responsibility.[18]

Meanwhile, in January 1920 the UMW moved its unionization campaign from Logan to Mingo County. During the nationwide walkout in the coal industry the previous fall, while unionized mines were idle, the nonunionized mines of southern West Virginia had continued to produce cheap coal, undermining the strike. John L. Lewis and the union officials in West Virginia were determined that this situation would not recur. A massive effort to organize miners in Mingo County began with a visit and speech by labor agitator and union celebrity Mother Jones. The coal companies responded with wholesale firings of union miners and increased harassment of organizers. However, when operators hired detectives of the Baldwin-Felts Agency of Bluefield, West Virginia, to evict the families of fired miners from company housing and tent colonies near the town of Matewan, West Virginia, the detectives encountered resistance from prolabor Chief of Police Sid Hatfield.

Tension between the detectives and Hatfield continued through the spring, until a confrontation took place on the main street of Matewan on 19 May. When Hatfield tried to arrest the detectives for evicting miners from their camps and for illegally carrying weapons in his jurisdiction, a gunfight ensued. Hatfield was assisted by a number of armed miners who had been waiting in ambush for the detective force. In the shoot-out 10 people died, including Matewan Mayor Cable C. Testerman, Lee and Albert Felts, 5 other Baldwin-Felts employees, and 2 miners. The "Matewan Massacre" made Hatfield a hero to miners throughout the state and a national celebrity. On 1 July emboldened miners initiated strikes all along the Tug Valley in West Virginia and Kentucky. Incidents of violence

---

[17] Lee, *Bloodletting in Appalachia*, pp. 88–91; Lunt, *Law and Order*, p. 122; Cole, "Martial Law," pp. 125–26; Savage, *Thunder in the Mountains*, pp. iii–iv.

[18] Ltr, Baker to Dorsey, 3 Nov 19, File: Mingo County, RG 407, NARA.

among miners, company guards, and detectives multiplied, and by midsummer coal production in the region had halted.[19]

On 28 August, in response, Governor Cornwell asked the new commander of the Central Department, Maj. Gen. George A. Read, for a battalion of troops to guard the mines of southern West Virginia. Read ordered in the 2d and 40th Infantry regiments from Camp Sherman, Ohio. Troops under command of Col. Samuel Burkhardt were dispatched under the policy of direct access and arrived in Williamson, West Virginia, the next day. This force of 500 regulars kept the peace by conducting squad-size patrols near the coal mines and saw action soon after its arrival, employing classic infantry tactics on two occasions when fired upon by sizable groups of armed miners. The exchange of gunfire produced no casualties on either side.[20]

Despite these confrontations, relations between the regulars and the local populace were generally friendly. Both sides in the strike seemed to welcome the troops as a neutral intermediary, offering a chance for ending the decades-old conflict between operators and miners. Most residents were law-abiding and peaceable citizens before, during, and after the soldiers' arrival. The children of Mingo County found the men on duty in their mining camps a curiosity. Soldiers courted the local women, and one, a school teacher, married a federal soldier from Massachusetts. Troops provided food, clothing, and shelter to miners made homeless by evictions, and shared in local celebrations. Miners in return helped troops in moving heavy military vehicles over the muddy and often nearly impassable mountain tracts, as well as cooperating with them in other ways.[21]

The relative calm was disturbed in mid-September 1920 when the coal operators attempted to import strikebreakers into the region. Rioting broke out at Williamson, and officials summoned troops to protect strikebreakers and their families as they arrived, and to escort the strikebreakers to the coal tipples for work. The presence of the troops allowed the owners to reopen several mines, and the coal operators were further strengthened by a court injunction that forbade the UMW from interfering with mining operations. Gradually the various strikes in the region weakened, and by 4 November violent incidents had fallen to such a low point that federal troops began to withdraw at Cornwell's request.[22]

Although violent incidents had decreased, the desire among miners and operators to settle old scores had not. Less than four days after the departure of federal troops, new violence demonstrated the inability of the meager force of deputy sheriffs and state constables to maintain peace in Mingo County. As new violence erupted, Governor Cornwell quickly called upon the V Corps Area commander for the third time, on 28 November. Tiring of sending the troops to put down unrest that immediately began again after the

---

[19] Savage, *Thunder in the Mountains*, pp. 9–20.

[20] Annual Rpt, Fifth Corps Area, 1921, pp. 1–5, File: Mingo County, RG 407, NARA. See also Lunt, *Law and Order*, pp. 97–99, 105, 110, 113; Cole, "Martial Law," pp. 127–28; Lucy L. Fisher, "John L. Cornwell: Governor of West Virginia, 1917–1921," *West Virginia History* 24 (July 1963):381; Savage, *Thunder in the Mountains*, pp. 23–28; Berman, *Labor Disputes and the President*, p. 209; *AG Annual Rpt, 1921*.

[21] Interv, author with Howard Radford, 23 Aug 88, Matewan, W. Va.; Ltr, J. C. Ferrell to author, 8 Aug 88. See also R. B. Adams, "Blair Mountain From the Other Side," *Goldenseal* 13 (Fall 1987):70; Savage, *Thunder in the Mountains*, pp. 23, 28, 30; Cole, "Martial Law," pp. 128–30.

[22] Annual Rpt, Fifth Corps Area, 1921, pp. 1–5, RG 407. See also Lunt, *Law and Order*, pp. 97–99, 105, 110, 113; Cole, "Martial Law," pp. 127–28; Fisher, "John L. Cornwell," p. 381; Savage, *Thunder in the Mountains*, pp. 23–28; Berman, *Labor Disputes and the President*, p. 209; *AG Annual Rpt, 1921*, p. 58.

troops' withdrawal, Read urged the governor to submit a request for aid to the president, according to RS 5297, stipulating that the legislature could not be convened in time to submit its own request. In this way Read hoped to receive a presidential proclamation for lawless elements to cease, desist, and disperse. In his opinion, the unorganized and leaderless miners were likely to ignore the proclamation, and he would be empowered not only to declare martial law and to deploy the troops near the mines, as in the past, but also to assist law enforcement officers in arresting union members, thereby ending the strike.[23]

But Secretary Baker, although he approved Cornwell's request for military aid on behalf of Wilson, refused to recommend a presidential proclamation. In 1917 his original intent in launching the policy of direct access had been to avoid the delays that resulted from presidential involvement. Thus when Read sent a provisional battalion of the 19th Infantry, commanded by Col. Herman Hall, from Camp Sherman into Mingo County on 28 November, it went with no more authority than its predecessors—that is, authority under the direct access policy and paragraph 487 of Army regulations. In an effort to comply with federal wishes, however, Governor Cornwell proclaimed a state of martial law on 27 November, placing all members of the sheriff's department and the small state constabulary under Hall.

In Mingo County the gesture proved meaningless. Many of the law enforcement officials, like Sid Hatfield, sympathized with the miners or feared them. In either case, local officials were incapable of handling the situation. Hoping to counter the uncooperative lawmen and restore order, Read requested a presidential proclamation and martial law powers from Secretary Baker.[24] The secretary, though he was rapidly losing patience with the state of West Virginia, refused Read's request on the grounds that "the rule to be followed is that the public military power of the United States should in no case be permitted to be substituted for the ordinary powers of the States, and should be called into service only when the State, having summoned its entire police power, is still unable to deal with the disorder."[25]

Nevertheless, he took one decisive step. Baker explained that during the recent war, when National Guard units under federal control were no longer available to the states, he had suspended prewar laws and procedures for obtaining troops to aid civil authorities. However, two years after the war had ended the states no longer had an excuse for not reconstituting their guard units or fully resuming normal police functions. Therefore, he rescinded the policy of direct access, reaffirmed the Posse Comitatus Act, and ordered that henceforth all requests for federal troops be made through the War Department to the president. Prewar procedures outlined in the 1874 *Revised Statutes* would be followed unless the danger was so immediate as to warrant emergency intervention under paragraph 487 of Army regulations. Meanwhile, he instructed Read to begin an immediate withdrawal of the 19th Infantry from West Virginia.[26]

---

[23] Lunt, *Law and Order*, pp. 114–15; Annual Rpt, Fifth Corps Area, 1921, pp. 2–3, RG 407; Telgs, Read to AG, 24, 25, and 26 Nov 20, and Cornwell to Baker, 25 Nov 20, all in File: Mingo County, RG 407, NARA. The six continental military departments were redivided and reorganized into nine continental corps areas on 20 August 1920.

[24] Telgs, Read to AG, 24, 25, and 26 Nov 20, RG 407.

[25] Memo, Baker for CofS and Corps Area Comdrs, 2 Dec 20, File: Mingo County, Item 23-a, RG 407, NARA.

[26] Ibid.

This was unwelcome news to the governor. Faced with the likelihood of new trouble in January, when Sid Hatfield and other participants in the Matewan Massacre were to stand trial for the murder of the Felts brothers and other Baldwin-Felts detectives, Cornwell asked Baker to delay troop withdrawals at least until the legislature could reconstitute its National Guard units. Assured of West Virginia's intent to assume responsibility for maintaining law and order, Baker agreed to gradual withdrawals. In mid-January 1921 three companies of federal troops returned to Camp Sherman. The last company and the regimental headquarters, however, remained in Mingo County until 16 February.[27]

The shaky peace lasted for only three months. In the spring of 1921 a series of events changed the balance of power in southern West Virginia. In May Ephraim P. Morgan, an antiunion politician, took over the office of governor, and in Washington, D.C., the newly elected Republican President Warren G. Harding entered the White House, launching an administration that was to be generally unsympathetic to labor. A national recession only made the situation worse, creating a general labor surplus in the northeast.[28] Expecting no sympathy from the governments of West Virginia or the United States, the UMW chose once again the tactics of confrontation as it renewed its drive to organize Mingo and Logan counties. Soon rumors spread that the union was smuggling weapons to miners on both Kentucky and West Virginia sides of the Tug River. To investigate, Governor Morgan sent the constabulary captain, James R. Brockus, with sixty constables to Mingo County. From 12 to 14 May defiant miners greeted them with sporadic rifle fire up and down the banks of the Tug, an incident referred to by historians as "The Three Days Battle." Skirmishes between miners and constables, company guards, and nonunion strikebreakers raged along the river and the surrounding hills near the villages of Merrimac, Rawl, Sprigg, and Matewan, West Virginia, and McCarr, Kentucky, resulting in at least four people dead and many more wounded.[29]

Despite Cornwell's promise to Baker two months earlier that West Virginia would reestablish a National Guard, the state legislature had only begun to take steps in that direction. Perhaps hoping that new Secretary of War James W. Weeks would permit direct access one more time, on 12 May Governor Morgan asked Read for 500 soldiers "to prevent wanton slaughter of innocent citizens." The next day Governor Edwin P. Morrow of Kentucky, whose state also suffered from intermittent gunfire along the Tug River, made a similar request. Read declined to send troops to either state pending approval by President Harding. Anticipating such approval, Read, on his own authority, alerted the 19th Infantry for a return to Mingo County and dispatched his intelligence chief, Maj. Charles File

---

[27] Telgs, Cornwell to Read, 21 Dec 20; Read to AG, 23 Dec 20; Actg AG, Fifth Corps Area, to CO, Williamson, W. Va., 31 Dec 20; Read to AG, 14 Jan 21; Actg AG, Fifth Corps Area, to CO, Williamson, 17 Jan 21; Read to AG, 10 Feb 21; Fiske, Ft. Harrison, to AG, 15 Feb 21, all in File: Mingo County, RG 407, NARA; *Annual AG Rpt, 1921*, p. 58. Hatfield was acquitted of murder charges stemming from the Matewan Massacre in March 1921.

[28] For Harding's views, see S. Rogers, "Senator Harding on Labor," *Outlook* 125 (18 August 1920):668–70.

[29] Lunt, *Law and Order*, pp. 117–18; Cole, "Martial Law," pp. 129–30; Savage, *Thunder in the Mountains*, pp. 38–39; W. D. Lane, "Conflict on the Tug," *Survey* 46 (18 June 1921):398–99; Testimony of J. Brockus, in U.S. Congress, Senate, Committee on Education and Labor, *West Virginia and the Civil War in its Coalfields, Hearings Pursuant to Senate Resolution 8*, 67th Cong., 1st sess., 1921–22, hereafter cited as Senate, *West Virginia Coalfields*, p. 273.

NEWTON D. BAKER WITH JAMES W. WEEKS *(seated)*.

Thompson, to Charleston to determine the extent of the emergency and whether the two states had ample forces to deal with the troubles.[30]

After consulting with Governor Morgan, local officials, and Mingo County coal operators, but apparently making no effort to learn the miners' side of the controversy, Major Thompson decided that lawless miners had caused a serious disorder warranting some form of military intervention. However, he went on to investigate the military capability of the governments of Kentucky and West Virginia, seeking to discover whether the available state forces could end the troubles. Clearly Kentucky needed no help from the federal government. The state boasted 300 deputy sheriffs, a fully organized National Guard force comprising five companies of infantry and three troops of cavalry. In fact, 150 guardsmen had already been sent to the Kentucky side of the Tug River and had reported the situation there as improving. West Virginia, on the other hand, having temporized with the organization of its National Guard, had raised only a relatively small volunteer state police force made up of "respectable Mingo County citizens." Thompson concluded that in the cases of both Kentucky and West Virginia "Authorities have not taken sufficiently active measures . . . [and] for purposes of both politics and economy, they have decided to rely on federal protection."[31]

---

[30] Annual Rpt, Fifth Corps Area, 1921, p. 3; Telgs, Morgan to Read, 12 May 21; Morrow to Read, 13 May 21; Read to AG, 12 May 21; Sturgis, CO, 19th Infantry, Camp Sherman, to CG, Fifth Corps Area, 13 May 21; all in File: Mingo County, RG 407, NARA; Rich, *President and Civil Disorder*, p. 159; Savage, *Thunder in the Mountains*, p. 39.

[31] Memo, CofS, G2, Fifth Corps Area, for Read, 16 May 21, sub: Conditions in Mingo County, 13–15 May 1921, File: Mingo County, RG 407, NARA. See also Savage, *Thunder in the Mountains*, p. 39.

Apart from West Virginia's unwillingness to shoulder responsibility, Thompson recommended against a third deployment for an even more compelling reason. In 1919–1920 the War Department had limited the troops in West Virginia to guarding mines and exerting moral force. In each case the troops had no sooner left than the lawlessness recurred. Thompson concluded that only if the president declared martial law—giving troops the power to make arrests, to hold prisoners, and to supersede uncooperative officials—would a further deployment produce lasting results. In full accord, Read endorsed and forwarded this recommendation to Secretary Weeks on 16 May 1921. The following day President Harding made an important decision that indicated what his administration's policy regarding the domestic use of federal military force would be by informing Morgan that no regulars would go to West Virginia until he was "well assured that the State had exhausted all of its resources in the performance of its functions."[32]

Governor Morgan had exhausted his resources. After declaring martial law in Mingo County on 19 May, he placed Brockus' constabulary at the command of the county sheriff. In the decision *Ex Parte Lavinder*, however, the West Virginia Supreme Court ruled that there could be no martial law that depended upon a civil officer, such as a sheriff, for enforcement. Martial law could only be enforced by a state militia, which West Virginia lacked. Therefore Morgan resorted to the expedient of calling part of the untrained, unorganized, enrolled militia of Mingo County to active duty. The Mingo Militia, made up of coal company management, strikebreakers, and nonunion and antiunion men, promptly and enthusiastically began to enforce the provisions of state imposed martial law—against miners. Sniping and bombing incidents and more bloodshed followed the mass arrests. Instead of quelling violence as intended, martial law and its partisan enforcement heightened the tensions. The new outbreaks increased the calls within the state and the federal government for a congressional investigation of the violence in the coalfields.[33]

On 14 July 1921, the Senate Committee on Education and Labor, chaired by Iowa Republican Senator William Kenyon, began a three-month-long investigation of the recurring crises. Interviewing scores of witnesses, including Sid Hatfield, union officials Fred Mooney and Frank Keeney, and James Brockus, the Kenyon committee hearings aired innumerable abuses by the operators and kindled short-lived hopes among the miners for reform. In its report of October 1921 the committee condemned, among many other things, the practice in Logan County of paying the sheriff and his deputies from funds contributed by the coal operators instead of exclusively from the public treasury. No immediate reforms were forthcoming, however.[34]

During the Washington proceedings Sid Hatfield learned that he had been indicted by a West Virginia grand jury along with thirty-five other miners for their alleged role in an attack on a nonunion mining camp the previous summer. Although Hatfield suspected the

---

[32] Quote from Rich, *President and Civil Disorder*, p. 160. See also Memos, CofS, G2, Fifth Corps Area, for Read, 16 May 21; Read for AG, 16 May 21; both in File: Mingo County, RG 407, NARA. For Harding's reaction, see "President Withholds Troops From West Virginia," *Army and Navy Journal* 58 (21 May 1921):1021.

[33] See Rich, *President and Civil Disorder*, p. 161, for 88 W. Va. 713 S. E., 428 (1921); Senate, *West Virginia Coalfields*, pp. 273–77; Memo, Thompson for Read, 23 May 21, File: Mingo County, RG 407, NARA. See also Cole, "Martial Law," pp. 138–40.

[34] Jordan, "The Mingo War," p. 110; Lee, *Bloodletting in Appalachia*, pp. 92, 191; Lunt, *Law and Order*, p. 99; Savage, *Thunder in the Mountains*, pp. 48–50.

charges were trumped up by the state at the urging of the Felts family, who still sought vengeance for Hatfield's role in the Matewan Massacre, he returned to West Virginia to stand trial. On the steps of the McDowell County Courthouse in the town of Welch on 1 August 1921, gunmen of the Baldwin-Felts Agency avenged the deaths of Albert and Lee Felts and their colleagues by shooting to death, in cold blood, the unarmed Sid Hatfield and his associate Ed Chambers, as they and their wives prepared to enter the court building. The death of the popular prolabor chief of police enraged grief-stricken union miners and their sympathizers throughout southern West Virginia. That none of the perpetrators of the crime were ever punished for their deeds made the injury more grievous.[35]

Capitalizing on the miners' outrage, Frank Keeney, the president of UMW, District 17, organized a rally in Charleston and called for a march against the coal operators. On 7 August, 1,000 miners presented Governor Morgan with a resolution calling for an end to martial law in Mingo County. By that date, nearly 130 miners had been arrested and held without charges. When the governor refused to rescind martial law, Keeney called upon the miners to assemble within two weeks at the town of Marmet, just south of Charleston. From that location, along the banks of Lens Creek in Kanawha County, Keeney hoped to march thousands of miners sixty-five miles to Logan County and from there to Mingo County. Keeney's objectives remain uncertain, but evidence supports the idea that he hoped a gun battle would ensue that would eliminate 34-year-old Logan County Sheriff Don Chafin and enough mine company guards and private detectives to open the area for union organizers. If that failed, at least the march and ensuing violence would force federal intervention that, from the miner's point of view, was preferable to bossism or state-enforced martial law.[36]

Nearly 5,000 miners, armed with rifles and a machine gun with 3,000 rounds of ammunition, had assembled at Marmet by 10 August. Their commander, "General" Bill Blizzard, a 28-year-old man of proved leadership abilities, formed the men into a column and began marching toward Logan. Along the way new recruits swelled the column until it reached a total of 15,000 to 20,000 men. Informed of "Blizzard's army," on 23 August, Secretary Weeks directed General Read to place the 19th Infantry in readiness, and sent Major Thompson to Charleston to investigate. Realizing that two years of cumulative insurrectionary fury were about to explode in the coalfields, Governor Morgan asked Harding for 1,000 troops and military aircraft, claiming that "the miners had been 'inflamed and infuriated by speeches of radical officers and leaders.'" Learning, however, that Governor Morgan had taken what appeared to the president as only slow and halting steps to organize a National Guard, Harding withheld aid pending reports from his military advisers. Initial reports from Thompson played down the need for troops, but in face of continued requests for help Weeks determined that further information was needed.[37]

[35] Savage, *Thunder in the Mountains*, pp. 51–53; Lee, *Bloodletting in Appalachia*, pp. 96–98; Lunt, *Law and Order*, p. 125.
[36] Rich, *President and Civil Disorder*, p. 161; Lee, *Bloodletting in Appalachia*, pp. 96–98; Lunt, *Law and Order*, p. 125.
[37] Senate, *West Virginia Coalfields*, p. 681; Memo, Jervey, CofS, Opns Div, OCofS, for AG, 23 Aug 21, and Telg, Harris, WD, to CG, Fifth Corps Area, 25 Aug 21, both in File: Mingo County, RG 407, NARA; Lee, *Bloodletting in Appalachia*, pp. 98–99; Corbin, *Life, Work, and Rebellion*, pp. 195, 218–19; Rich, *President and*

Secretary Weeks, with the approval of President Harding, sent a more senior officer, Brig. Gen. Henry H. Bandholtz, to investigate the West Virginia troubles. A former provost marshal for the American Expeditionary Forces in France and in 1921 the commander of the Military District of Washington, the 56-year-old general carried with him a mandate to determine whether the use of troops was necessary, or whether the mere threat to use federal military force would suffice to restore order. After his train arrived in Charleston in the early morning hours of 26 August, Bandholtz immediately conferred with Thompson, Morgan, and UMW officials Keeney and Mooney. Armed with the moral authority of the White House and the War Department, he wasted little time in exerting pressure.[38]

HENRY H. BANDHOLTZ

Bandholtz made clear to Governor Morgan, and later to the two union leaders, that he was indifferent to the merits of the dispute and was concerned only with the president's directive to restore law and order without delay and preferably without bloodshed. During his meeting with Bandholtz, Morgan claimed that the southern counties were at the mercy of an armed rabble, and he insisted that Army intervention alone would prevent loss of life and destruction of property. Finally convinced that the miners were in the wrong, Bandholtz warned union leaders Keeney and Mooney that he considered them personally responsible for the march, for any property damage or loss of life caused by the miners, and for whatever consequences might ensue if the Army stepped in. "These are your people," Mooney reported Bandholtz as saying, "I am going to give you a chance to save them, and if you cannot turn them back, we are going to snuff them out like that." As Bandholtz snapped his fingers under Keeney's nose, he declared that "this will never do, there are several million unemployed in this country now and this thing might assume proportions that would be difficult to handle."[39]

For his part, Keeney conceded that Blizzard's army might become violent if it met resistance, but he assumed that the marchers would disperse if promised federal protection against reprisals by Chafin or mine guards. After Keeney and Mooney agreed to disband

---

Civil Disorder, p. 162; Savage, *Thunder in the Mountains*, pp. 64–65. Legislation re-creating the West Virginia National Guard took effect on 27 July 1921, and the first unit, Company I, 150th Infantry, was activated on 21 August. By October, eleven companies were created, see Cole, "Martial Law," pp. 139–40.

[38] Senate, *West Virginia Coalfields*, p. 1032; Rich, *President and Civil Disorder*, 162; Mauer Mauer and Calvin F. Senning, "Billy Mitchell, the Air Service, and the Mingo County War," *West Virginia Historian* 30 (October 1968):342.

[39] Lunt, *Law and Order*, p. 126; Rich, *President and Civil Disorder*, p. 162.

EPHRAIM MORGAN AND BANDHOLTZ

the miners, Bandholtz gave them a handwritten ultimatum to convince skeptics that he meant business. Confident that the marchers would yield, Bandholtz nonetheless requested permission from Weeks to continue preparations for the deployment of troops equipped with mortars and tear-gas shells.[40]

From Washington, Deputy Chief of Staff Maj. Gen. James G. Harbord wired Bandholtz, complimenting him for his great skill in handling matters in West Virginia. He directed Bandholtz further to have Governor Morgan rewrite the formal request for military aid, originally submitted on 25 August, to include a statement that he would try to convene the state legislature, including a list of measures that he would use to reassert state authority. This would place Governor Morgan in compliance with RS 5297. General Harbord warned, however, that West Virginia's "egregious failure" to accept federal money available to the states for the establishment of a National Guard might hinder federal efforts.[41]

Meanwhile, preparations to intervene went forward. Harbord sent Bandholtz to prepare for infantry operations and instructed Maj. Gen. Charles T. Menoher, chief of the Army Air

---

[40] Cabell Philips, "The West Virginia Mine War," *American Heritage* 25 (August 1974):90; Senate, *West Virginia Coalfields*, p. 1033.
[41] Telg, Harbord to Bandholtz, c/o Morgan, 26 Aug 21, File: Mingo County, RG 407, NARA.

Service, to examine Kanawha Field, outside Charleston, to determine its suitability for use in either reconnaissance or tactical air support operations. Later in the day, the commander of the 1st Provisional Air Brigade, Brig. Gen. Billy Mitchell, personally led a flight of three olive-drab De Haviland bombers (DH–4B) from Bolling Field in Washington, D.C., to execute Harbord's orders. Upon landing, Mitchell, never one to mince words about air power, commented to the press that the Air Service by itself could end the disturbance by dropping canisters of tear gas upon the miners. If that failed, however, he recommended the use of artillery by the ground forces to bring the crisis to a speedy conclusion.[42]

Mitchell lost the opportunity to demonstrate what tear gas or artillery could do to the mountaineers, miners, and immigrants causing the disorder. As soon as union leaders Keeney and Mooney read Bandholtz's

James G. Harbord

note and addressed the crowd, the miners decided to call off the march. The two men impressed the group with the seriousness of the situation and appealed to their loyalty and patriotism. If the march continued, they stated, it would be done so against the direct orders of the president of the United States. The miners would then face the fearsome might of the federal government and the U.S. Army. For the first time many miners realized that their march was interpreted by federal authorities as a rebellion against the West Virginia and federal governments and not as a justified and righteous struggle against what miners perceived as greedy coal operators, corrupt sheriffs, and ruthless Baldwin-Felts "thugs." As the marchers began to disperse, Keeney and Mooney hurriedly made arrangements with local railroads to return the miners to their homes.[43]

Upon learning of these events, Bandholtz, accompanied by a group including Major Thompson and Bill Blizzard, visited the positions previously occupied by the miners. Satisfied that the emergency was over, Bandholtz wired the War Department that all alerted units could stand down but remain prepared for future action if the need arose. He had no confidence in the ability of Governor Morgan and the legislature to maintain order, observing that "the State had made only a feeble attempt to check the growth of the insurgent movement or to keep reasonable touch with its progress." Bandholtz boarded a train for Washington, and Mitchell flew back to Bolling Field. Despite the outward appearance of calm, however, actions by state authorities immediately stirred further unrest.[44]

---

[42] Mauer, "Billy Mitchell, Mingo County War," pp. 339–43; Savage, *Thunder in the Mountains*, pp. 87–88.

[43] Mauer, "Billy Mitchell, Mingo County War," p. 343; Savage, *Thunder in the Mountains*, pp. 66–68.

[44] Senate, *West Virginia Coalfields*, p. 1033; Rich, *President and Civil Disorder*, p. 163; Mauer, "Billy Mitchell, Mingo County War," p. 343; Savage, *Thunder in the Mountains*, pp. 92–93.

FEDERAL TROOP ENCAMPMENT, BOONE COUNTY, WEST VIRGINIA

At midnight, 27 August 1921, in an ill-advised move to arrest leaders of the miners' march and union miners involved in a recent fracas with state police, a posse of 70 to 100 deputies and state police led by Chafin and Brockus went to Sharples, a small miners' community north of Blair Mountain near the Boone County line. A confrontation with miners resulted in a gunfight that left at least 2 miners dead and 2 others wounded. From positions on adjacent hillsides, miners fired at the police forces, who quickly withdrew. Within forty-eight hours, 5,000 miners streamed back into the area to defend their homes against what they saw as a new and unwarranted attack by those in league with the coal operators. Miners awaiting trains to return to their homes from the aborted march on Logan County now refused to board, resuming their march. Chafin and Brockus, in an effort to contain and combat the new uprising, gathered a volunteer force of approximately 3,000 antiunion, antiminer "militiamen," and took up positions near the summit of nearby Blair Mountain. With the miners deployed along a ten-mile front at the base of the mountain determined to wipe out all impediments to their march, on 29 August Governor Morgan renewed his application to President Harding through Secretary Weeks for federal troops, citing an insurrection fanned by the influx of "Bolshevist" outsiders from Indiana, Ohio, and Illinois. The next day he appended to his request a statement that the legislature could not be convened in time to avert bloodshed.[45]

The ineptitude and insensitivity displayed by West Virginia officials during the raid at Sharples convinced President Harding and his principal advisers that Governor Morgan and county officials were obviously too much a part of the problem to share in its solution. On 30 August the president issued a cease and desist proclamation as the first step toward

---

[45] Philips, "West Virginia Mine War," p. 91; Senate, *West Virginia Coalfields*, pp. 682, 1034; Lunt, *Law and Order*, pp. 130–31; Lee, *Bloodletting in Appalachia*, pp. 99–100; Savage, *Thunder in the Mountains*, pp. 94–96; Telgs, Thurman to W. Goodykoontz, House of Reps, 31 Aug 21, and Morgan to Weeks, 30 Aug 21, both in File: Mingo County, RG 407, NARA.

federal intervention to protect West Virginia from domestic violence and insurrection. The proclamation called for both the miners and the Logan County force to disperse by noon of 1 September 1921.[46] It was the first such presidential proclamation regarding a civil disorder issued since the American entry into World War I, nearly four and one-half years before, and it finally and formally put to rest the wartime policy of direct access.

Accompanied by his chief of staff, Col. Stanley H. Ford, and judge advocate, Col. Walter A. Bethel, General Bandholtz returned to Charleston on 30 August. Secretary Weeks had ordered him to investigate compliance with the proclamation and to provide guidance for the Army in the event that neither side dispersed. Neither complied immediately. With the broad mission of suppressing domestic violence, dispersing lawbreakers, and maintaining order, Weeks gave Bandholtz some leeway as to the tactics and the degree of force to be employed by stating that "necessity is the measure of your authority." Weeks informed Morgan of these instructions the next day, writing, "I very earnestly hope that it may not become necessary to employ federal troops. If they are used it will be to restore peace and order in the most effective and prompt way. The problem will be regarded by the military authorities purely as a tactical one."[47]

Support for civil authorities was contingent upon the inability of local and state forces to suppress violence and restore order efficaciously. If General Bandholtz determined that civil officials demonstrated negligence by releasing prisoners who they knew would contribute to new disorder, he was to retain the prisoners in his custody "as long as necessity exists," under the provisions of the *Court Martial Manual*. In each individual case, however, Weeks required Bandholtz to forward a full report of the circumstances. If both sides continued to refuse compliance, and if state and local authorities were unable to restore order, a declaration of martial law would be considered.[48]

By 1 September private airplanes had dropped copies of Harding's initial cease and desist proclamation on the belligerents. Both sides, now totaling an estimated 10,000 to 20,000 men, refused to comply: the Logan County force was unwilling to relinquish the commanding heights of Blair Mountain, and the miners feared that their withdrawal would precipitate new raids by Chafin and Brockus. Arriving in Charleston, Bandholtz carried with him a second proclamation reflecting the belated realization of President Harding and Secretary Weeks that the decision in *Ex Parte Milligan* after the Civil War prohibited "Martial law . . . where the courts are open and in the proper and unobstructed exercise of their jurisdiction." A full declaration of martial law, placing all civil law enforcement powers under federal control, required this second proclamation, under RS 5301, which declared a state of nonintercourse in areas thus far not in compliance with the initial cease and desist proclamation.[49]

---

[46] Rich, *President and Civil Disorder*, p. 163; Lunt, *Law and Order*, pp. 131, 140; Proclamation, Harding to the Citizens of West Virginia, 30 Aug 21, File: Mingo County, RG 407, NARA. See also *Secretary of War Report, 1920*, p. 204. For Harding's proclamation, see Dowell, *Military Aid to the Civil Power*, pp. 199–200.

[47] Ltr, Weeks to Morgan, 31 Aug 21, File: Mingo County, RG 407, NARA; Senate, *West Virginia Coalfields*, p. 1033; Rich, *President and Civil Disorder*, pp. 163–64; Savage, *Thunder in the Mountains*, pp. 101–02; LOI, Weeks to Bandholtz, c. 30 Aug 21, in Dowell, *Military Aid to the Civil Power*, p. 200.

[48] LOI, Weeks to Bandholtz, c. 30 Aug 21, in Dowell, *Military Aid to the Civil Power*, p. 200.

[49] *Ex Parte Milligan* (4 Wallace 2, 1866). See also Telgs, Morgan to Harding, 31 Aug 21, and Petry to Harding, 31 Aug 21, both in File: Mingo County, RG 407, NARA. See also Rich, *President and Civil Disorder*, pp. 164–66; Lunt, *Law and Order*, p. 132; Senate, *West Virginia Coalfields*, p. 134.

Over the next two days intermittent skirmishing took place. While the miners probed the positions of the defending force, their opposition, not content with rifle and machine-gun fire, sought to drive them off by arranging for commercial aircraft to drop homemade bombs filled with nails and metal fragments. The bombs missed their targets or failed to explode, but the incident gave rise to a short-lived rumor that the Army had bombed the miners. In fact, the chief factor in preventing casualties was the incompetence of both sides in the fighting. A member of Bandholtz's staff compared the Battle of Blair Mountain—with its considerable expenditure of ammunition, interrupted by frequent breaks for coffee, lunch, liquor or rest—to comic opera. However, on the third day, 3 September, the miners did make serious and prolonged efforts to overrun the militiamen, without success, due largely to the lack of miner organization, leadership, and a common tactical goal.[50]

Meanwhile, General Harbord ordered to West Virginia four units previously selected for the task. By rail from Camp Sherman and Columbus Barracks, Ohio, came 11 officers and 201 enlisted men of the 19th Infantry and 15 officers and 224 enlisted men of the 10th Infantry. The first troops of the 19th Infantry arrived on 2 September. From Camp Knox, Kentucky, Bandholtz ordered 36 officers and 384 men of the 40th Infantry to West Virginia, while further orders prompted the dispatch of 47 officers and 158 enlisted men of the 26th Infantry from Camp Dix, New Jersey. In addition, a detachment of Chemical Warfare Service troops equipped with tear gas was dispatched from Edgewood Arsenal, Maryland. All told, Bandholtz commanded 2,106 men. To supplement this federal force Morgan directed that all "state and county officers . . . deputies, assistants, and other subordinates" cooperate with and obey Bandholtz.[51]

While orders went out to the infantry regiments, Harbord directed General Menoher to have Billy Mitchell send twenty-one aircraft of the 88th Aero Squadron, commanded by Maj. Davenport Johnson, to Kanawha Field. In light of Mitchell's earlier comments, his reputation as a zealous booster of air power, and his proclivity for stealing the show, he was ordered to relinquish command of the squadron to Bandholtz and by no means accompany the unit to West Virginia.[52]

On 1 September De Haviland (DH–4B) bombers, each equipped with front- and rear-mounted machine guns and carrying tear gas and fragmentation bombs, began the 320-mile flight from Langley Field to Charleston. After spending the night at Roanoke, Virginia, the planes crossed over the Appalachians, and by late afternoon 11 had landed at Charleston's Kanawha Field. Of the 21 planes requested, only 17 were in satisfactory condition and managed to take off from Langley Field. Two planes experienced mechanical difficulties at Roanoke and 1 crashed there on takeoff. Another bomber experienced engine difficulty over West Virginia and crash-landed near Beckley, while 2 others became lost in dense fog and landed eventually in Mooresburg, Tennessee. Four aircraft, twin-engine "box-like Martin bombers," from Aberdeen, Maryland, were also ordered to Kanawha

---

[50] Lee, *Bloodletting in Appalachia*, pp. 100–101; Lunt, *Law and Order*, p. 137.

[51] Annual Rpt, Fifth Corps Area, 1922, File: Mingo County, RG 407, NARA. See also Mauer, "Billy Mitchell, Mingo County War," p. 348; "Federal Troops in West Virginia," *Army and Navy Journal* 59 (3 September 1921):12; Lunt, *Law and Order*, p. 138; Rich, *President and Civil Disorder*, p. 165; Senate, *West Virginia Coalfields*, p. 1032; Savage, *Thunder in the Mountains*, p. 121; *Secretary of War Report, 1921*, pp. 204–05.

[52] Rad, Menoher to CO, 1st Prov Air Bde, Langley Field, 1 Sep 21, File: Mingo County, RG 407, NARA. See also Mauer, "Billy Mitchell, Mingo County War," pp. 339, 344–46; Savage, *Thunder in the Mountains*, p. 127.

Field, 3 surviving the flight and arriving safely in Charleston. By Friday the total number of Army aircraft in West Virginia stood at 14. The bombers and their crews became an instant sensation with the local population, who had never seen so many military aircraft at one time in one place. Although neither the De Havilands nor the Martins ever used their armaments during this situation, their pilots performed several reconnaissance missions and enjoyed the unique distinction of being the first air unit to participate in a military operation to control a civil disturbance. (Mitchell subsequently boldly stated that the "'Mingo War' provided an excellent example of the potentialities of air power.")[53]

Bandholtz deployed his ample forces on 3 September 1921. From headquarters in the Chesapeake and Potomac Telephone Company building in Charleston, he divided the area around Blair Mountain into three operational zones and began a classic pincer movement around the two civilian forces. The first group of regulars, under the command of Col. C. A. Martin and Maj. Charles T. Smart, 19th Infantry, were ordered to advance southeast by rail along the Coal River, aiming at the rear of the miners' army. The 40th Infantry, in a second column under command of Col. G. A. Shuttleworth, would take up positions across Blair Mountain from the miners, and behind the army raised by Chafin. The remaining federal troops, regulars of the 26th Infantry, would reinforce the remaining units of the 19th Infantry at Madison, with additional companies positioning themselves along the Kanahwa River.

As the first two columns began their double envelopment of the Blair Mountain area, Bandholtz ordered a cease-fire. In compliance with Morgan's order to obey Bandholtz, the sheriff's deputies and the volunteers of the Logan force immediately disbanded. The miners, reassured then that they would not be attacked and unwilling to resist so many regulars and the power of the national government, surrendered to the federal troops or simply went home. Although casualty figures were not kept by either side, best estimates put the death toll during the Battle of Blair Mountain at 16, all but 4 of the dead being miners. No casualties were caused by federal troops.[54]

Between 4–8 September, Bandholtz's troops disarmed and sent home without incident nearly 5,400 miners. Having dramatically restored peace and order, virtually without firing a shot and without Army-induced bloodshed, General Bandholtz refused Governor Morgan's subsequent request for military posses to help civil authorities arrest miners wanted for violations of state laws. The maintenance of long-term order in West Virginia and the arrest of suspects, in Bandholtz's mind, was not an Army job. MID agents, however, did investigate union headquarters and meeting halls for evidence linking the marchers to a radical conspiracy. The agents found almost no radical literature, despite coal operators' claims, and determined that a mere 10 percent of the miners were foreign nationals, ". . . who will believe anything that they are told." One MID officer stated in his report, "I cannot find that any organization except the UMW are [*sic*] operating in this

---

[53] Telgs, AG to Menoher, 9 Sep 21; Menoher to AG, 12 Sep 21; Mitchell to AG, 17 Sep 21; all in File: Mingo County, RG 407, NARA. See also Mauer, "Billy Mitchell, Mingo County War," pp. 349–50; Savage, *Thunder in the Mountains*, pp. 125–28. The return flight was marred by tragedy. See Richard A. Andre, "Bomber No. 5," *Wonderful West Virginia* 48 (1984):21–23.

[54] Rich, *President and Civil Disorder*, pp. 165–67; Lee, *Bloodletting in Appalachia*, p. 101; Savage, *Thunder in the Mountains*, pp. 129–31, 134, 140; Lunt, *Law and Order*, p. 138; Mauer, "Billy Mitchell, Mingo County War," p. 348; Senate, *West Virginia Coalfields*, pp. 1034–35.

field." Although the authorities expected trouble prior to the arrival of soldiers in West Virginia, reports stated that during the entire deployment the miners perpetrated no violence against federal troops.[55]

For the next three months, withdrawals of Army troops proceeded piecemeal in the face of strong political opposition. General Bandholtz first recommended a partial withdrawal of regulars on 7 September; the next day Secretary Weeks ordered the return of the 26th Infantry to Camp Dix, the 88th Aero Squadron to Langley Field, and the Chemical Warfare Detachment to Edgewood Arsenal. Three days later, however, West Virginia Republican Senator Howard Sutherland began to press Weeks to retain a federal force near Charleston as a deterrent to future mining disorders.[56]

Like Bandholtz, Weeks opposed detaining troops for police duty, especially when congressionally mandated budget cuts made the immediate return of all regiments to their home stations desirable. Nevertheless, bowing to the senator's request, Secretary Weeks placed Bandholtz's remaining 1,300 men under Col. Carl A. Martin, the commander of the 19th Infantry. Martin's force was ordered to withdraw in phases over several weeks, a period deemed sufficient for Governor Morgan to replace it with units of the West Virginia National Guard. On 3 November a board of Army officers from the V Corps Area met with Morgan's adjutant to draw up a schedule for the deployment and allocation of the guard units throughout the state. One month later the last federal unit, a battalion of the 10th Infantry, boarded a train for Columbus Barracks, Ohio, quietly ending the Army's involvement in the coalfield wars.[57]

Conclusion

In the course of three months the Army had successfully fulfilled its mission by restoring order. But the fundamental issues that initially caused federal military intervention remained unresolved. Strikes continued into 1922, for the miners' old grievances were exaggerated by the indictment of local union leaders for offenses against state law in connection with the march on Logan County and the Battle of Blair Mountain. Although most escaped conviction, the influence of federal military intervention upon the United Mine Workers was unintentionally devastating. Clearly, the union could not accomplish its aims by peaceful means in the face of the tactics adopted by the coal companies, and the federal government had necessarily closed off the option of violence. In October 1922 the UMW ended its 18-month-long strike, which had cost District 17 over $2 million and the

[55] Telg, Bandholtz to William, Office of the Deputy Chief of Staff, 4 Sep 21, File: Mingo County, RG 407, NARA; Savage, *Thunder in the Mountains*, p. 141; Lunt, *Law and Order*, pp. 138–41. For contemporary views, see "Blame for West Virginia's War," *Literary Digest* 70 (10 September 1921):16–17; Heber Blankenhorn, "Marching Through West Virginia," *Nation* 113 (14 September 1921):288–89; "The War in West Virginia," *Independent* 106 (17 September 1921):121–22; W. D. Lane, "West Virginia: The War in Its Coal Fields," *Survey* 47 (29 October 1921):177–83.

[56] Ltrs, Sutherland to Weeks, 10 Sep 21, and reply, Weeks to Sutherland, 12 Sep 21, File: Mingo County, RG 407, NARA. See also Rich, *President and Civil Disorder*, p. 166; Senate, *West Virginia Coalfields*, p. 1034; Mauer, "Billy Mitchell, Mingo County War," p. 350.

[57] SO 240, HQ, Fifth Corps Area, 14 Oct 21; Proceedings of the Board of Officers, Fifth Corps Area, 3 Nov 21; both in File: Mingo County, RG 407, NARA. Lunt, *Law and Order*, pp. 142–43; "Federal Troops in West Virginia," *Army and Navy Journal* 59 (17 September 1921):54.

lives of at least twenty people. Thereafter, the UMW suffered a national decline lasting into the early 1930s. Not until a federally mandated organization campaign was launched under the New Deal would miners' unions begin a nationwide resurgence. In West Virginia, the UMW nearly faded into oblivion. State membership dropped from 50,000 miners in 1921 to a mere 600 by 1932.[58]

An important consequence of the upheaval was the federal government's return to prewar standards for the use of armed intervention in domestic disputes. In this respect the West Virginia disturbances marked a major change. The transition had been slow in coming; nearly two years had elapsed since the 1918 armistice and one year following the congressional and presidential proclamations officially declaring the war at an end. As was demonstrated in West Virginia, the policy of direct access, so easily formulated and implemented in 1917, was not so easily revoked. Conservative state governments had become dependent upon federal troops as a cheap and convenient means to suppress labor trouble. Only after substantial cajoling and large-scale troop deployments were federal officials both able to quiet the disorders and to convince state officials of the importance of re-creating a National Guard force capable of quelling future disturbances. By early 1922 the goal of returning primary responsibility for handling domestic disturbances to the states had been successfully accomplished by federal officials and the Army. Future major disturbances, with the exception of the 1932 Bonus March, would be dealt with in the first instance by new state police and National Guard forces that had been established nationwide.

Yet the Army's concern with the nation's internal security did not end with the final withdrawals of regulars from West Virginia. The strikes and race riots of World War I had already convinced the Army that labor radicals and foreign revolutionaries and ideologues were growing in strength and becoming more threatening. Army leaders, especially in MID and the War Plans Division of the War Department General Staff, realized that the establishment lacked comprehensive contingency plans to deal with domestic threats to the nation.

---

[58] Senate, *West Virginia Coalfields*, p. 671; Rich, *President and Civil Disorder*, p. 167; Lunt, *Law and Order*, pp. 141–43; Jordan, "The Mingo War," pp. 118–19; Savage, *Thunder in the Mountains*, p. 144.

CHAPTER 14

Interwar Civil Disturbance Contingency Planning, 1919–1941 The Army Prepares for Civil War

In order to provide the basis for action of the War Department in cases of internal disorder in which the Federal Government may be required to act, a plan, which will hereafter be referred to as 'War Plan White,' is being prepared in the War Department.

—Secretary of War Newton D. Baker, May 1920.

The federal intervention in the West Virginia coal mine wars in 1920 was the last use of Regular Army troops in a labor-related civil disturbance during the immediate postwar period and the last major domestic intervention until the Bonus March of 1932. Yet military leaders believed that civil disorders, and Army intervention to quell them, would increase during the coming decade of the 1920s. Hence it was during this relative quiet that the Army turned for the first time toward the creation of specific contingency plans and a specific doctrine for the use of military forces in domestic disorders. In particular, the six years of intense planning and doctrinal development between 1919 and 1925 reflected the incorrect belief within the Army that radical or Bolshevik revolutions, such as those seen in Europe, were possible and even imminent in the United States.

Therefore the scope of its contingency planning anticipated unrest of a scale that went well beyond the bounds of any disorder previously encountered. The planners approached the subject as they did the prospect of war against a foreign enemy. In fact, in the minds of many, rioters and enemy soldiers were synonymous, and Army contingency plans seemed more like preparations to fight a second civil war than those developed merely to restore law and order. By the time the plans had been completed in the late 1930s, most of them had become obsolete and unrealistic, despite periodic revisions. Most were never used or were so drastically revised to fit specific situations as to be unrecognizable.[1]

---

[1] Conf, Col John M. Dunn and Subsection Chs, M.I.2, and Other Officers, MID, 29 Jul 20, RG 165, Records of the War Department General Staff, Military Intelligence Division (MID), 1917–1941, File 242–13, NARA.

The Color Plans: War Plan White, 1919–1920

Army contingency plans for dealing with a leftist-radical insurrection originated in the autumn of 1919. The responsibility for preparing the first plan fell to the War Plans Division of the War Department General Staff (WDGS). At this time the Army was embarking on an ambitious program of contingency planning for possible future conflicts against foreign powers—the so-called color or rainbow plans. Among the more important, Orange signified Japan; Red represented Great Britain; and Blue stood for the defense of the continental United States against an outside aggressor. The War Plans Division designated White as the color of its first plan to meet a domestic emergency.[2]

The War Department's perception of the world situation undoubtedly influenced its decision to press immediately ahead with War Plan White. After four years of conflict, the possibility of war with one of the European nations seemed highly unlikely; nonetheless the War Department made plans involving each major power. To Army planners the most probable and realistic threat appeared to be posed by revolutions against the established order in the industrialized countries. Postwar Europe seethed with unrest. In Russia, Red and White armies were locked in open warfare, the turmoil spilling over that country's borders into Poland and leading to the employment of U.S. troops in northern Russia and Siberia. In Germany the Weimar Republic had weathered the Spartacist putsch in Berlin, but faced further threats from other groups of the revolutionary left and reactionary right. To the south a Communist government under Bela Kun succeeded for a time in holding sway over Hungary until the military of neighboring Romania ousted Kun. Such events confirmed the sense of danger first provoked by the postwar violence in the United States.[3]

Perhaps nowhere in the War Department were the revolutionary and radical threats viewed as more menacing than in the Military Intelligence Division (MID) of the general staff. MID produced a weekly intelligence summary that was meant for a select distribution that included the president, the secretary of war, the secretary of state, the Army chief of staff, and the MID director. The summaries, based on intelligence gathered by Army agents and their paid informants, revealed a disturbing picture of "radical activities," "labor unrest," and "negro subversion" in the United States.[4]

By the end of October 1919 the weight of the information gathered by the Intelligence Division and the intensity of domestic unrest convinced Brig. Gen. Marlborough Churchill, MID director, that the country was on the brink of a Bolshevik revolution. In a memorandum sent to Maj. Gen. William G. Haan, director of the War Plans Division,

---

[2] Summaries on Different Color Plans, 10 Jan 27, RG 407, Entry 365, NARA. See also Maurice Matloff and Edwin M. Snell, *Strategic Planning for Coalition Warfare, 1941–1942* (Washington, D.C.: U.S. Army Center of Military History, 1953), pp. 5–10; Marvin A. Kreidberg and Merton G. Henry, *History of Military Mobilization in the United States Army, 1775–1945* (Washington, D.C.: Department of the Army, 1955; reprinted, U.S. Army Center of Military History, 1984), pp. 385, 396–409; Louis Morton, "Germany First: The Basic Concept of Allied Strategy in World War II," in Kent Roberts Greenfield, ed., *Command Decisions* (Washington, D.C.: U.S. Army Center of Military History, 1960), pp. 12–23; Mark S. Watson, *Chief of Staff: Prewar Plans and Preparations* (Washington, D.C.: U.S. Army Center of Military History, 1950).

[3] Memo, Gen Simonds, CofSA, 19 Apr 19, WPD; Memo, Maj Gen W. G. Haan for Comdt, General Staff College (GSC), 20 Apr 19, WPD; both in File 111–A–2, pp. 1–30, Military History Research Collection, U.S. Army Military History Institute (MHRC, USAMHI), Carlisle Barracks, Pa.

[4] Weekly Intelligence Summaries, Sep–Oct 1919, Woodrow Wilson Papers, Library of Congress, Washington, D.C.

Churchill warned of an imminent outbreak of rebellion. According to him, the "first step in this process is scheduled to take place November 1, 1919," with the initiation of a nationwide coal miners' strike. Radicals were poised to launch an attack on the foundations of American society: "All evidence indicates that the impending situation is one in which the radical rebel groups of the country are attempting to capitalize on the economic situation for the purpose of accomplishing their ultimate objective—that of the overthrow of the constitutional government."[5]

The scenario he outlined was familiar: radicals exploited the strike, causing a halt in railroad transportation to disrupt the system of food distribution. The resulting famine would drive the urban populace into the arms of the revolutionaries. Impressed by events in Russia in 1917 and 1918 that had come to his attention, Churchill, still

MARLBOROUGH CHURCHILL

largely unaware of Russian history, saw starvation as the crucial element in the revolutionaries' plans for seizing power. The road to revolution passed not through the hearts and minds of average Americans, but through their stomachs. "It is realized that the foregoing sounds extremely foreign to American conditions," he wrote, but "Americans can starve just as quickly as any other people."

According to Churchill, the guiding hand behind this elaborate plot to overthrow the constitutional order of the United States was a dedicated, as yet unidentified, cadre of Red radicals within the nation itself. It should "be remembered," he stressed, "that the history of successful radical revolutions shows that the radical leaders created a small corps de elite or praetorian guard of their immediate henchmen whose loyalty is insured through the limitations of civil law and through having accorded them unlimited liberty for loot and rapine." He urged that steps be taken immediately to forestall such a revolution but did not propose any specific solutions, simply noting that the success of radicals increased "in inverse ratio to the preventative measures taken to meet the situation."

The Churchill memorandum initiated a stream of reports from the offices of the Military Intelligence Division to the highest levels of the government. Political and military leaders, shocked by repeated upheavals, could not dismiss Churchill's alarms or his call for immediate preparations. As a result, work on War Plan White began in earnest in the winter of 1919–1920, with MID playing a prominent role by accumulating and presenting the intelligence necessary to create the plans. Surveillance of suspect citizens and

---

[5] Memo, Churchill for Dir, WPD, 27 Oct 19, MID, RG 165, File 1835, NARA. Unless otherwise stated, the following is from the same source.

resident aliens provided much of the information. Although Churchill declared later that "secret service methods carried on by military agencies" could "not be justified in times of peace" and that the MID had not engaged in such activities since the armistice, subsequent evidence suggests that his statements were false.[6]

On 24 May 1920, Secretary Baker authorized the chief of staff to proceed with development of a comprehensive plan to deal with domestic insurrections. Three days later the departments, to be called corps areas after 20 August 1920, were instructed by the chief of staff to begin work on a domestic war plan "to provide the basis for action of the War Department in cases of internal disorder in which the Federal Government may be required to act."[7]

Responsibility for preparing War Plan White was divided between the War Department and the headquarters of each of the nine corps areas. Overseas commands, such as those in the Hawaiian Islands, the Panama Canal Zone, and the Philippine Islands, in keeping with normal staff procedure, were also to prepare their own white plans adapted to local conditions. The division of labor in drafting War Plan White made the corps areas and overseas commands responsible for detailed planning based on local conditions, although the War Plans Division retained overall control "with the duty of coordination of the works to the end of securing harmonious action and an effective plan."[8]

The Military Intelligence Division occupied a prominent place in the development of the white plan because it supplied a rationale through its supposed expert knowledge of radicalism. Whether it did so in an accurate and objective manner is another question. Gross exaggerations and estimates featuring vast and unsubstantiated numbers were characteristic of its style. One intelligence estimate that MID produced in the spring of 1921 claimed that there were 322,284 Red radicals, 914,854 Socialists, 42,950 Socialist labor, and 2,475,371 "unorganized Negroes" currently in the United States. Where these figures were acquired and by what means is not evident from surviving records. The ranks of Red radicals and their camp followers supposedly numbered 3,755,459, but MID emphasized that the Army could muster only 160,000 men. MID charged that "the headquarters and principal hotbed of every degree of radicalism in the United States . . . may be found in New York City," and that other important radical centers included Chicago, Denver, and Seattle. According to MID, the only areas free of radical contamination were the Deep South (a surprising choice, since it was home to many blacks), parts of the mid-Atlantic states, and California. Since all these areas at some time in the previous seventy years had experienced violent labor unrest, the reason for exempting them was no more clear than the source of the radical census elsewhere.[9]

Despite its questionable claims, MID practically predetermined the content and scope of the local white plan by the intelligence estimates it provided to corps area intelligence

---

[6] See Marlborough Churchill, "The Military Intelligence Division, General Staff," *Journal of the United States Artillery* 52 (April 1920):295.

[7] Ltr, OCofS, WPD, AGO, to CG, II Corps Area, 27 May 20, RG 394, Records of the U.S. Army Continental Commands, 1920–1942, Entry 37, NARA (hereafter cited as Directive WPW [war plans white]). See also Memo, CofS, WPD, for Baker, 24 May 20, RG 165, File 242–13, NARA. Army Chief of Staff, WPD, Simonds claimed that planning began in the fall of 1919; see Digest of Emergency Plan White (EPW), 19 Apr 30, WPD, MHRC, File 111–A–2. The records of I and II Corps Areas (CA) indicate, however, that planning began much later.

[8] Directive WPW, and Memo, CofS, WPD, for Baker, 24 May 20. None of these early white plans have survived.

[9] MID Estimate of the Military Situation, 3 May 21, RG 165, File 242–13, NARA.

officers. Around these estimates, corps area planning officers later drafted their versions of the plan. The process had not been intended to work this way; in 1920, when planning began, MID asked local intelligence officers for information on the estimated cause, intensity, location, and objectives of any civil disturbance in each corps area. The first drafts of the corps area intelligence figures reached Washington, D.C., just as the worst postwar civil disturbances were ending, and these drafts failed to satisfy MID. Thus the VII Corps Area effort was "wholly inadequate," a complaint that drew a tart reply from the corps area intelligence officer, Maj. Hu B. Meyers. Complaining to Maj. Charles H. Mason, the war plans reviewer, Meyers wrote that MID in Washington, D.C., operated in a vacuum: "you people who have been in the Intelligence Branch for a long time, perhaps do not realize the amount of technical stuff with which you have surrounded yourselves, [or] know how hard it is for an officer to come in from the outside and, with no instructions whatever— no guidance at all—march in step with you." The result was that corps area planning officers, unable to form accurate or independent estimates of the local radical threat on their own, made increasing demands on MID for information with which to draw up their plans. Often they requested detailed intelligence about radical leaders and organizations in their areas from the central MID registry. Increasingly they came to rely almost entirely on MID estimates, which entered the planning process from subordinate echelons as well as through MID's influence on the Army staff.[10]

At the top echelons the division's influence was increased by bureaucratic infighting. In late July 1920 the question arose over which organization, the Military Intelligence Division or the Morale Branch of the War Plans Division, had the ultimate responsibility for countering radical propaganda directed against Army troops. At a conference, one MID officer confidently asserted that the division knew "the big plan more than anybody else." Apparently the chief of staff agreed. The Intelligence Division won the task of preparing the basic counterpropaganda plan for War Plan White, and the Morale Branch had the unenviable task of trying to interpret and execute MID's strategy.[11]

The Intelligence Division was also very successful in acquiring contingency plans from foreign powers and from other U.S. government departments. Through its contacts with British military intelligence, MID gained a copy of a massive plan to meet a general strike in Britain and in turn sent each corps area a copy of the full fifteen volumes. In a cover letter, Maj. James L. Collins of MID instructed the corps area commanders that the plans were "extremely comprehensive," adding that MID did not endorse "either the form or the voluminous detail of these papers," but he thought "that they may be of assistance to you in suggesting methods and measures for War Plans White."[12]

The standing liaison arrangements that had developed between the Intelligence Division and other U.S. government agencies by late 1920 had strengthened the cooperation on such matters. MID officers maintained close and constant contact with officials in the Interior, Treasury, Justice, Labor, Commerce, Navy, and Post Office Departments

---

[10] Suggested Form for Intelligence Estimate of Situation, Corps Area EPW, n.d., and Memo, Mason, MID, for WPD, 18 Jan 21, sub: WPW of the VII Corps Area, MID, both in File 242–13–235; Ltr, Myers to Mason, File 242–13–26; and Ltr, Russell to ACofS, MID, 6 Aug 20, File 13–647. All in RG 165, NARA.

[11] MID Conf With Section Chs, 29 Jul 20, RG 165, File 242–13–15, NARA.

[12] Ltrs, Collins to ACofS, to All Corps Areas, 28 Dec 20, and Haan to Dir, MID, 15 Oct 20, RG 165, File 242–13–203, NARA.

concerning joint measures that could be undertaken with these federal departments in the event of an emergency requiring the use of the White Plan.[13] By exaggerating the danger of revolution and by making itself a center for the exchange of information, the division inflated its own importance and made its view of the world basic to the planning for domestic disturbances.

The War Department War Plans Division carefully delineated the types of emergencies to be considered and the mission of the Army should these situations develop. "There are two classes of emergencies," a departmental directive stated, "in which the Federal Government may be required to act: (a) Minor Emergencies, or localized disturbances, in which the Federal Government may be called upon for assistance by competent state authorities"; and "(b) Major Emergencies, or general disturbances developing from a series of minor emergencies in which interstate commerce, mails, or functions of government are interfered with. In such cases direct action by the Federal Government will be required." Although these instructions appeared to cover only situations that allowed federal intervention after a request by state or local authorities, the memorandum from the chief of staff of 24 May 1920 foresaw the wider use of troops under all applicable articles of "the Constitution and the Revised Statutes, especially Sections 5297, 5298, and 5299, as published in Article 47, Army Regulations." Under these statutes, the president was legally authorized to intervene to enforce federal laws in a state or locality without its request. Army planners, however, could not realistically conceive of any situation during this tense period when the states would not be willing to initiate action against domestic revolutionaries.[14]

The directive provided a further, practical definition of minor and major emergencies for the corps area commanders. "In a minor emergency, the troops available, and as at present distributed in your department, will be adequate," but a major emergency would exist when the corps area commander believed that troops available in his department were inadequate in strength, or that the situation would require new and special organizations, or that circumstances would demand changes in the distribution of troops. The commander's mission varied with the type of emergency. In minor emergencies, commanders were ordered "to suppress localized disorders, to restore order and to protect the interests of the government," after having been called upon to do so by competent state authorities, and in major emergencies the president would order commanders to perform similar duties.

The legal framework for Army intervention in minor emergencies under War Plan White took into account the direct access policy introduced in 1917, because the directive had been issued before that wartime expedient was revoked. This directive instructed corps area commanders that troops could be deployed by request of a state's executive or legislature without prior reference to the War Department, and without prior authorization. In major emergencies, the directive emphasized that Army action would be on the basis of presidential proclamation, a procedure in keeping with the Constitution and federal statutes.

All the assumptions in the white plans, however, were totally outside the legal framework as it had existed before the war, which said nothing about major or minor emergencies

---

[13] Ibid.
[14] Directive WPW; and Memo, CofS, WPD, for Baker, 24 May 20.

but did distinguish between state requests (RS 5297) and execution of the laws of the Union (RS 5298, RS 5299). Either the War Department planners were ignorant of the laws governing the domestic use of federal military power or chose to ignore them, to facilitate making neat plans for surprising and crushing a revolution in its incipient stages.

Among the miscellaneous items covered in the directive to the corps areas was the matter of interservice cooperation. The mission of the Navy in the event of the emergencies contemplated by War Plan White was to safeguard all naval stations, magazines, utilities, and so forth. Furthermore, the Navy would station naval vessels in all important coastal towns and would cooperate with local Army commanders. Under the terms of tacit interservice agreements, sailors and marines surplus to the above missions were to be placed at the disposal of the Army. In outline form, the directive listed sixteen points for inclusion in the White Plan ranging from troops required on D-day to cooperation with state and municipal authorities and agencies.

At the corps area level it is possible to identify only some of the primary concerns of the early Army planners, for none of the original plans have survived. Planners viewed the railroads as the key to the success of any radical coup, and because of Churchill's emphasis on food as a crucial weapon, officers expended a great deal of hypothetical planning effort to keep foodstuffs moving into cities. For example, the II Corps Area—responsible for a geographical region encompassing major urban centers such as New York City—drew up elaborate plans to commandeer privately owned trucks and organize them into convoys to ensure the delivery of essential supplies.[15] The location of railroad lines and Army garrisons made cooperation between the corps areas imperative in any emergency. Since each corps area essentially represented a bureaucratic fiefdom, the formulation of workable plans required detailed negotiation.[16]

At the War Department level, the War Plans Division not only had to act as a coordinating agency among the tiers of Army commands responsible for the white plans, but also had to grapple with legal and policy issues and harness the technical support necessary to make the plans work. One of the fundamental questions facing the planners, who appeared unfamiliar with the provisions of the unrepealed Posse Comitatus Act, was the legality of Army operations under War Plan White. The directive ordering corps areas to proceed with detailed planning stated that in a minor emergency federal troops could intervene directly at the request of "competent State authority." In late 1920, however, the commanding general of the V Corps Area questioned whether troops could be employed legally in a minor emergency without a presidential proclamation as required under RS 5300—although such commitments of federal troops had taken place without such a proclamation on repeated occasions since mid-1917. The query prompted the War Plans Division to relay the matter to higher authority. A memorandum to the chief of staff outlined the question and requested a legal opinion from the judge advocate general for the secretary of war. The War Plans Division, with great understatement, suggested that the policy of allowing direct access to federal troops for civil disturbance intervention needed revision: "United States troops have been employed in the past under conditions which might have involved the use of

---

[15] Memo, Wallace, II Corps Area, for CofS, 2 Feb 21, RG 394, Entry 37, NARA.
[16] Ltrs, Hall to CG, I Corps Area, 27 Sep 20; CG, II Corps Area, to CG, I Corps Area, 22 Oct 20; III Corps Area to AGO, 3 Nov 20; all in RG 60, Glasser Papers, NARA.

force accompanied by loss of human life . . . had such loss of life occurred, the courts might have held that United States troops then employed were not authorized to use force and were therefore not employed in strict accordance with the law."[17]

The judge advocate general, who was more familiar with the laws, agreed. Brig. Gen. Edward A. Kreger declared that "it is the opinion of this office that the Constitution and laws of the United States do not authorize the employment of United States troops to quell domestic disorders in a State without proclamation by the President as required in Section 5300, Revised Statutes." The opinion undercut the original War Plan White directive, for it did not recognize any legal difference between a minor or major emergency, nor did it find any legal basis for the policy of direct access, except under very rare situations in which a military commander might intervene under the emergency provisions of Army regulations to prevent loss of life or property. The possibility of court action against the Army and the government may have helped to focus attention on the need to revise or terminate the policy of direct access. As early as 20 November the War Department began to require state officials to make requests for troops through the prewar statutory procedures. Regarding War Plan White, however, the judge advocate general's opinion had a two-pronged effect: it meant that sections of the White Plan dealing with major and minor emergencies had to be revised in keeping with the recent legal opinion, and it meant that elaborate explanations of the laws and the legal procedures that affected Army personnel on riot duty had to be included in the revision.[18]

Aside from dealing with policy issues, the War Plans Division relied increasingly upon the Army's technical services for vital support in the development and possible implementation of War Plan White. Although nearly every branch of the Army had a role in handling civil disorders, the Corps of Engineers and the Signal Corps were considered crucial. The Corps of Engineers had to maintain and operate all public utilities, such as water, light and power systems, mail, and water transportation, in the event of a revolutionary upheaval. The Signal Corps provided secure communications between the War Department and the corps areas should telephone and telegraph service be disrupted by revolutionaries. For the Signal Corps, the updating of War Plan White hastened the creation of the War Department Radio Net, the first part of a future worldwide Army communications system.[19]

Emergency Plan White, 1921–1923

By late 1921 the Communist scare had substantially subsided within the United States, due in large measure to public outrage at the tactics used by Attorney General A. Mitchell Palmer and the Justice Department to root out "subversives" and a spreading realization that Soviet and European Bolshevik leaders, in spite of their boasts, were too weak

---

[17] Memo, Haan, Dir, WPD, for CofS, 11 Dec 20, sub: Employment of U.S. Troops in Minor Emergencies Under WPW, RG 407, NARA.

[18] Ibid.; Memos, Kreger, JAG, for CofS, 6 Jan 21, sub: Employment of U.S. Troops to Quell Domestic Disturbances in a State; EPW, WD (General Policies and Instructions), 1923, Entry 365; all in RG 407, NARA.

[19] Memo, Connor, Supply Div, G–4, for AG, 28 Nov 21, sub: EPW (Engineers), RG 60, Glasser Papers, NARA. See also Dulany Terrett, *The Signal Corps: The Emergency (To December 1941)* (Washington, D.C.: U.S. Army Center of Military History, 1956), p. 49.

and isolated to export revolution. The Army, having completed the transition to a small peacetime establishment, began to revise the White Plan not only to reflect the decreased danger of domestic insurrections and the return to prewar concepts of domestic intervention and prewar legal procedures, but also to reflect its own reduced size. In the fall of 1921 Secretary of War Weeks issued a new directive that the White Plan was to be revised and renamed Emergency Plan White. The War Plans Division relinquished control of the plans to G–3, the Operations and Training Division of the War Department General Staff.[20]

A War Department directive of October 1921 on Plan White contained a mixture of old and new. The instructions to the corps areas still identified minor and major emergencies as the primary concern of planners. The new directive, however, elaborated on the Army's mission in a far more exacting and detailed manner. Corps area commanders were instructed "to take cognizance of the situation in their corps area with special reference to the economic, industrial, and radical conditions," watching for and investigating any potential disorders, while informing the War Department of their activities and any situation that might require federal action. Reflecting the demise of the wartime policy of direct access, the directive went on to say that "in minor emergencies, when the Federal Government has been called upon by competent State authorities for assistance," corps area commanders would "assume, in preparing . . . plans, that the proclamation by the President required in Section 5300, Revised Statutes" would be issued, and that they would "be directed to assume charge of the situation, to suppress localized disorders, to restore order, and to protect the interests of the government." The provisions for direct intervention by the president without a state request, as authorized by RS 5298 and RS 5299, were made more specific, reflecting the belated realization by Army leaders that states themselves could in theory refuse to intervene or to call for federal intervention in a civil disturbance despite federal perceptions of an existing threat.[21]

Provisions for the use of federalized National Guard units were to be included in the new corps area plans, although guardsmen had not been called into federal service to quell a domestic disorder since the 1860s. Whether regulars or guardsmen, federal troops were "to be employed in the most effective and energetic manner to the end that normal conditions be restored in the minimum time with the least possible disturbance of local civil institutions." If local and state authorities proved incapable of restoring order, however, Army commanders were to declare martial law, after receiving direction from the president and after he had issued a proclamation to that effect. They were to "assume charge of the affected area or areas, to administer such area or areas, to suppress disorders, to restore order, and to protect the interests of the United States." Should the situation warrant, the plan told commanders to assume that additional troops and materiel would be forthcoming. Troops and commanders were to cooperate and consult with the commanders of contiguous corps areas and, when the scope of the emergency encompassed more than one area, a single officer was to be placed in command of all forces.[22]

---

[20] Memo, Col Wells, WPD, for CofS, 19 Oct 21, sub: EPW, MID, RG 165, File 242–13–525, and Ltr, AG to CG, I Corps Area, 22 Oct 21 (hereafter cited as AGO Dir EPW), RG 394, Entry 12, both in NARA; Higham, *Strangers in the Land*, pp. 230–33.

[21] Basic Instructions Issued, 22 Oct 22, Appendix E, EPW, AGO, WD, RG 407, Entry 365, NARA (hereafter EPW–WD, 1923).

[22] AGO Dir EPW, 22 Oct 21.

These instructions moved Army activity under Emergency Plan White closer to the customary boundaries of the law, reversing the first directive issued in May 1920, which was heavily influenced by wartime procedures and the policy of direct access. In the new directive, corps area commanders had their attention specifically aimed at the "approved opinion of the Judge Advocate General, relative to the employment of United States troops in domestic disturbances," issued in December 1920. The adjutant general, however, authorized the corps areas to operate, in the event of an emergency, under the provisions of War Plan White until completion of the revised plan.[23]

The format was also revised, indicating an increase in professionalism, expertise, and sophistication. The basic plan was to consist of four major elements: 1) an estimate of the situation, 2) the respective missions of the corps areas and War Department in major and minor emergencies, 3) the corps area plan, and 4) a statement of standing policy concerning War Department conduct in the event of civil disorders. A lengthy set of annexes was to cover the activities of personnel (G–1), intelligence (G–2), operations and training (G–3), and supply and hospitalization (G–4). The basic plan was the permanent element of Emergency Plan White, with the annexes containing material that required periodic revision.[24]

Under Emergency Plan White, the division of labor between the corps areas and the War Department remained for the most part the same. Detailed planning remained in the hands of the corps areas, and the War Department concerned itself with general policies and instructions. The experience gained in creating War Plan White, however, made the drafting of Emergency Plan White a much less arduous exercise, and it proceeded at a less urgent pace. In part this was because of diminished government fears of a domestic radical revolution, the existence of fewer large and violent radical labor disputes, and the inertia inherent in a peacetime Army. Although the Army drew up War Plan White in approximately one year under the perceived threat of revolution at home and abroad, amid unprecedented numbers of violent race riots, strikes, and labor disputes, the succeeding Emergency Plan White took three years to complete.

The War Department's finished draft, "General Policies and Instructions," is the earliest known version to survive. Consisting of a short general section and a longer section of appendixes, the 1923 White Plan provides a unique view of the Army's approach to contingency planning for civil disorder.[25] It incorporated vastly expanded legal explanations of the circumstances and procedures for the involvement of the Army in quelling a civil disturbance, reflecting developing doctrine on domestic interventions. In classifying the types of civil disturbances, the Army dropped the previously used "major" and "minor" disturbances, and instead characterized disorders as those that are "primarily a function of the State" and those that are a "function of the Federal Government." The new categories were consistent with the constitutional and statutory formulas by which federal troops could be employed to suppress a civil disturbance. The 1923 plan stressed that the first responsibility for the suppression of disorder lay with state and local governments, and that federal help could come only after a state had "exhausted all means at its disposal for

---

[23] Ibid.

[24] Ltr, AG to CG, I Corps Area, 6 Dec 21, sub: Method of Preparation of EPW and Similar Plans, RG 394, Entry 12, NARA.

[25] Unless stated otherwise, this section is from EPW–WD, 1923.

quelling the disturbance," and had "acknowledged itself . . . unable to cope with the existing emergency." Thus the Army could intervene only as a last resort, although the president was still authorized by the Constitution to take direct action in the event of federal laws' being broken, or in the case of a rebellion against the federal government.

Once under way, an intervention brought the Army broad but not unlimited temporary powers. Federal troops assigned the task of quelling a civil disturbance were, according to the 1923 White Plan, "in no way restrained by any statute." But further instructions in the plan tempered this phrase that could have been construed as permission to use unrestricted force. The document emphasized that the issues to be decided by commanders were "tactical rather than legal, though life should never unnecessarily be taken," an emphasis harking back to *General Order 23* of 1894. Given the sweeping authority of the Army in the wake of a presidential proclamation, a declaration of martial law was rarely thought to be necessary unless civil courts and law enforcement agencies were unable to function. But in cases in which the president declared martial law and supplemented the declaration with additional presidential instructions, the Army could supplant civil officials, courts, and law enforcement personnel and set up a military government, taking over all functions and duties of the civil authority. The old and imprecise notion of qualified martial law used in 1919 by Generals Wood and Marshall disappeared. Instead, the plan stated that, in the absence of a presidential proclamation, Army activities would aid civil authorities by the "exercise of the regular police functions that have been rendered inoperative or ineffectual in the disturbed regions." Troops could arrest rioters with or without warrants and detain and guard them, pending civil action. The plan emphasized the doctrine set forth in *Ex Parte Milligan* in 1866 that martial law was not legally justified, except "in time of war, in the theater of war, where courts cannot exercise their jurisdiction," and was specifically not justified when troops intervened under RS 5297 and RS 5298. A declaration of "martial law on such occasions would be ineffective in law, would delude the public, and would merely add to the confusion and difficulty."[26]

In such passages the document read more like a legal tract than a military contingency plan. Substantial parts of it, however, addressed the more practical aspects of using federal troops to suppress domestic upheaval. The general section gave guidance to planning officers on how to estimate the number of troops required to resolve a civil conflict. Most important, the plan provided a comprehensive list of matters needing attention should Emergency Plan White have to be implemented. In keeping with Army concerns about the strict legal use of troops, the exact sequence of statutory measures to take prior to deployment was carefully outlined, citing pertinent Supreme Court and lower court rulings, the Constitution and federal statutes, Army regulations, and opinions of the judge advocate general. The six appendixes, comprising forty-one pages of the 1923 Emergency Plan White, supplied War Department officers with a compendium of documents, telegrams, legal opinions, statutes, and Army regulations related to the historical and legal context of previous Army efforts to quell domestic strife. The bulk of the appendixes consisted of forms, proclamations, telegrams, and orders that the planners now considered necessary to implement the plans legally and to control its course adequately if it ever was implemented. In keeping with previous formats, specifics regarding the locations of actual troop

---

[26] *Ex Parte Milligan.*

deployments, the weapons to be issued and used, and detailed logistical plans were not dealt with in the War Department's 1923 Emergency Plan White but were to be included in the individual corps area plans.

The culmination of the planning process begun in the fall of 1919, the 1923 plan was a great improvement over its predecessor, hastily written during the postwar Communist scare. The carefully crafted contingency plan intended to meet and crush a radical revolution remained in place for seventeen years, until the threat of World War II prompted a new round of intensive planning to meet a different kind of perceived threat. The influence of the plan was reflected in that corps area plans of the next two decades often repeated entire sections verbatim.

Contingency Planning and the Corps Areas

The primary responsibility for detailed operational planning and, in the event of an emergency, for actual operations under Emergency Plan White rested with the headquarters of the corps areas. No examples of the corps areas' plans survive from the immediate post–World War I period. However, a number of such plans from the second half of the 1930s have survived, providing a clear picture of Army contingency planning during the latter part of the interwar period.[27]

The plans' most striking features are their diversity, reflecting the widely differing characteristics of each corps area in terms of geographical size, population background and density, and economic activity. But inconsistent criteria used in their formulation also contributed to the outcome. In April 1936 the Operations Branch, WDGS, requested from the Intelligence Division a study of the corps areas' white plans. According to the division, its survey of the white plans revealed both widespread neglect in keeping the plans current and many inconsistencies in preparation. Some plans were comparatively simple, while others were elaborations or repetitions of the War Department plan. Several cited outdated concepts found in earlier white plans. Obscure and contradictory directions from higher echelons were part of the problem: the Military Intelligence Division recommended that the War Department issue unambiguous guidelines and that the new instructions order corps area planners to check revised contingency plans for consistency with the Army basic field manuals and regulations.[28]

The III Corps Area Emergency Plan White, 1934

The evolution of a plan can be studied in the two versions of the III Corps Area document that survived, giving guidance for handling disorder in the states of Maryland, Pennsylvania, Virginia, and Washington, D.C.[29] The first, drafted in 1934, displayed many of the characteristics later criticized by the Intelligence Division. Foremost was

---

[27] RG 407, Entry 365, NARA, contains surviving examples.

[28] Memo, Col F. H. Lincoln for CofS, 18 Jun 36, sub: EPW, RG 165, File 242–13, NARA.

[29] EPW, Jul 39, I Corps Area, RG 394, Entry 12, NARA. See also EPW, 1934 and 1941, III Corps Area (hereafter cited as IIICA–EPW); EPW, Dec 36, VI Corps Area; EPW, Nov 35, VII Corps Area; all in RG 407, Entry 365, NARA. Surviving corps area plans include I Corps (Jul 39), III Corps (1934 and 1941), VI Corps (Dec 36), and VII Corps (Nov 35).

the wholesale incorporation of large parts of the elaborate legal procedure and history sections of the 1923 War Department White Plan. Along with the legal section, the III Corps Area plan included the full range of forms for proclamations, telegrams, and orders.[30] Not all the plan, however, was simply a repetition of the War Department's model. The bulk of the plan consisted of essential information designed to enable officers to cope with potential operational problems. The most important was a careful assessment of the resources available within the area and a scheme to mobilize them to meet civil unrest. A comprehensive inventory of military forces provided extensive information on the strengths, locations, and service branches of Regular Army units, whether under the jurisdiction of the corps area commander or not, and similar data on National Guard units. Such hard data enabled the commander to coordinate the deployment of federal troops with the deployment of state forces in response to many different contingencies, selecting from a variety of military units, technical, combat, and administrative.

Despite the legal constraints and the increasing precision of information, the basic rationale harked back to the shopworn notion evoked in the Communist scare. Under the worst case scenario envisioned by Army planners, cities would be subject to the threat of starvation and cold-related illnesses as a result of the disruption of rail transport and of vital food and fuel supplies by radicals or revolutionaries. Army planners visualized many of the same threats that their immediate postwar predecessors had done. The types of disturbances believed to be most likely to occur were those resulting from "conflicts between capital and labor, which will ordinarily begin as strikes." The scenario, as always, was simple and uncomplicated by any mitigating factors. Strikes would follow radical propagandizing among dissatisfied and unemployed labor. Recurring strikes would take place in one or more branches of an essential industry, and eventually they would develop into a general sympathy strike by all workers. This, the Army believed, would then lead to the seizure of transportation lines, public utilities, and food supplies by radical elements; organization of local revolutionary councils; and displacement of local government by force. Unchecked minor crises, Army planners warned, could develop into major emergencies, if not a full-blown revolution.

The corps areas' emergency white plans were still war plans, in essence created to deal with a threat as dangerous to national peace and stability as any foreign army. As they would in wartime against a foreign enemy, engineering officers included in their plan a thorough survey of the railroad lines in their command areas, identifying essential corridors that had to be kept open and operational. The III Corps Area was responsible for nearly 5,000 miles of track, of which 2,890 miles were designated as "first priority" to be kept open. In a similar fashion, III Corps Area headquarters outlined plans for Army engineers to keep important highways and waterways open to traffic and to keep public utilities, such as electric power plants, water works, and sewer systems, secure and operational.

Even though some branches of the service were not required to alter their white plans, since their missions always remained the same, other branches found that their foreign and domestic roles were very dissimilar. In their versions of the White Plan, III Corps Area

---

[30] Unless otherwise stated, this section is from IIICA–EPW, 1934.

Ordnance and Signal Corps planning officers had to develop a list of a variety of specialized weapons suitable only for quelling civil disorders. The Ordnance Department reported that the commander of III Corps Area had in depots 1,000 riot shotguns, with 50,000 shells of double-ought buckshot, as well as large quantities of tear and irritant gas grenades. The Signal Corps supplied a detailed list of Regular Army and National Guard radio stations, with their call letters, and details on the types of transmitters at each. Signal Corps planners believed that their network was crucial to the successful coordination of Army operations in quelling a large-scale civil disturbance, because in that event "considerable sabotage of commercial communications structures will take place and ultimate dependence for communications between principal cities may be by radio nets." To guarantee secure communications, the Signal Corps took the precaution of issuing a cipher device for encoding radio transmissions to all Army and National Guard radios in the III Corps Area.

Separate appendixes provided instructions for other Army technical services in the event of a civil disorder, including the Quartermaster Corps, the Medical Corps, and the Chemical Warfare Service of the Ordnance Corps. The Quartermaster Corps, for example, was instructed "to set up, organize and operate the necessary . . . transport pools," to prepare for the procurement and issue of supplies and equipment, and to provide shelter and office and storage space for supplies and equipment. The plan detailed which quartermaster troops were to be mobilized and the location of supply and distribution points within the III Corps Area. An advance warning order of M-day (mobilization day) would be provided, circumstances permitting.

These emergencies would be caused by what the Army vaguely referred to as the "radical element." Although III Corps planners admitted that no actual, accurate estimate of the strength of radicals was possible in their area, they believed that such groups were small and unequally scattered across the region. Nonetheless, radicals were considered a greater threat than their hypothetical numbers would indicate. Some 80 percent were said to be foreign-born and were concentrated in communities where 50 percent of the population was alien. They were arbitrarily categorized into three distinct groups by III Corps Area planners. The first, "active radicals," consisted of those who advocated the destruction by force of the industrial or political system as organized in the United States. This group included active, well-organized cells of Communists and anarchists. The second group, "latent radicals," included "certain labor, civil liberty or pacifist groups," who were well intentioned but who unwittingly aided the causes of active radicals. The third group, called "political radicals," was a catchall that referred to "aliens, certain radical and criminal groups, pacifists and conscientious objectors, Negroes, the unemployed, and certain labor groups." Writing as they were during the Great Depression and in the wake of the Bonus March of 1932, III Corps Area planners were aware of the social, economic, and political instability caused by the 1929 economic collapse. In this context the planners saw danger in the beliefs of latent and political radicals, warning that if "the economic depression should continue indefinitely, with accompanying extreme unemployment, the possibility of a general strike . . . is a factor that should be considered" in III Corps Area.

A compound of the old and the new, III Corps Area Emergency Plan White of 1934 still divided potential civil disturbances into the outdated categories of minor and major emergencies. The plan did, however, begin to reflect more sophistication in the Army's legal and tactical attitude toward intervention in civil disorders. Continuing development of an even more sophisticated doctrine prompted another revision of all corps area emergency plans white in the late 1930s and early 1940s.

The III Corps Area Emergency Plan White, 1941

The 1941 revised and improved plan reflected changes in Army regulations, the attitudes and philosophy of the Roosevelt administration, and changes in public perceptions and attitudes toward labor, radical threats, and the role of the military in civil disturbance intervention. The most notable change was the deletion of the numerous examples of forms, historical telegrams, and sample proclamations included in the 1934 plan, most of which were now viewed as superfluous to any specific mission in the III Corps Area. The annexes in the new plan contained instead many practical documents of specific use to III Corps officers, such as Information on the Protection of Industrial Plants; Draft of Suitable Press Release To Be Issued by Local Commanders—Facts Concerning Tear Gas; Plan of Signal Communication; and Outline Report To Be Submitted by Corps Area Commanders to the War Department Covering Estimate of the Situation When Disorder Is Imminent.[31]

To guarantee closer cooperation and coordination among the services, planners also included documents on the role of naval forces in the III Corps Area during civil disorders. Four major naval commands were placed on the distribution list of the Army's 1941 plan; and naval commanders, who had their own basic emergency plan, were instructed by their superiors to cooperate with the Army in matters of communication and intelligence and in the preparation of plans and to assist in the suppression of internal disorder or insurrection.

As in previous drafts, the 1941 plan included a listing of the locations of vital utilities; railroad lines, transportation centers, and defense-related industrial plants needing immediate protection in case of civil disorder. Reflecting a change in technology, however, the 1941 plan also listed vital airfields, Army communication centers, Class I highways, gas plants, electric power lines, telephone and telegraph lines and exchanges, and oil and gas pipelines considered crucial to the security of the III Corps Area.

The numbers and locations of state, local, and federal civil and military forces were listed, as they had been in 1934, with special note on the larger numbers and better quality of most of these forces over those in existence in previous years. The detailed descriptions of police formations available to aid the Army in quelling disturbances indicated that civil disorders were increasingly being interpreted by the Army as violations of civil law rather than as military attacks on the nation. Clearly, the Army planners saw the change with relief, giving special praise to the Pennsylvania State Police, or state constabulary, an "excellent force of approximately fifteen hundred . . . so located that in case of necessity a mobilized force of one hundred well armed men can be placed in any part of the State within an hour." They noted further that Pennsylvania, historically the site of many violent civil disorders, had created a "secret police force dispersed throughout the

---

[31] Ibid.

state, organized by counties." Other civil law enforcement agencies in the III Corps Area, however, were not so warmly or confidently praised. Many were either too small or too biased by the influences of local sentiments or politics to handle other than the usual police duties. Yet even those forces were supposed to be increasing in size and competence.

Continuity between the two plans was evident, for the mission of the Army in the III Corps Area did not change substantially between 1934 and 1941. But the domestic situation in the United States had changed enormously. With the worst effects of the Great Depression over, the threat stemming from radical labor groups and from social unrest, although still considered by Army planners, were not believed to be acute—an estimate confirmed by the relative social and economic stability of the period. Instead, World War II, already two years old, raised new concerns about national unity; military and industrial preparedness; and Axis-initiated espionage, propaganda, sabotage, and other fifth column activities within the United States. Also, the ethnic makeup of the region spurred continued fear that blacks might be ready material for social unrest, for their "resentment of racial discrimination is probably more articulate than at any time in the past."[32]

In addition to renewed fears of racial disturbances, III Corps Area planners, as in previous studies, addressed the issue of radicalism. The categorization of the radical element changed in the seven years between 1934 and 1941 to reflect alterations in society and in world events, but Army attitudes regarding the nature of the threat remained the same. Radical groups were broken down into vaguely defined categories that included radical labor organizations, groups dominated by alien ideologies, and groups of miscellaneous semiradical organizations. Radical labor organizations, not specifically named or defined, were again, as in earlier plans, considered the most dangerous. Their numbers, location in industrial areas, and disruptive activities raised familiar alarms, because the Army had frequently intervened in civil disorders initiated by strikes. That the Army had not been called to quell a labor-related civil disturbance since 1921 produced no change in emphasis. The actual militancy of groups like the then recently formed Congress of Industrial Organizations (CIO) was vaguely associated with traditional fears of foreign agents: Communist, Socialist, or Fascist.

Under the label of "groups dominated by alien ideologies" the Army included groups on opposite ends of the political spectrum, such as Communists—believed to be primarily located in Pennsylvania near Philadelphia and Pittsburgh—and Nazis, located in the German districts of Scranton, Wilkes-Barre, Reading, Pittsburgh, and Baltimore. Communist and Nazi agents, allied by the August 1939 Soviet-Nazi Non-Aggression Pact, were thought to be in "the places in which damage by disaffected elements will be most effective in impeding industrial production for war." By early 1941 President Franklin Roosevelt had already declared the United States "the Arsenal of Democracy" and had undertaken to supply the various anti-Axis Powers with all material and economic aid short of a declaration of war. The protection of fledgling American war industries against Axis attack or disruption became a top Army domestic priority, for "attempts to slow down industrial production through sabotage methods may be expected on an increased scale from strategically placed Communists and Nazi sympathizers as the possibilities for war

---

[32] Ibid.

increase." Fascism of the Italian variety was the final "alien ideology" the planners addressed. Although many Italians lived in the III Corps Area, primarily in Pennsylvania and Maryland, they were not considered a threat, since "there has been detected among them very little sympathy with Fascism."[33]

As in the 1934 Emergency Plan White, all the other groups considered radical were thrown together into the miscellaneous category and were described by the planners as being "devoted to miscellaneous ideals, civil liberties, pacificism, etc." These "well inten tioned but impractical groups," were "led by their views to play more or less into the hands of the more extreme and more realistic radical elements." Although they were not specifi- cally mentioned, American isolationist groups, such as the America First Committee or the Islands for War Debts Committee, and others holding noninterventionist viewpoints were probably placed in this semiradical category. (Many interventionist-minded Americans, in the general public and in the military, viewed proponents of these views as treasonous at worst and, at best, as unwitting dupes of Axis propagandists and fifth columnists.)[34]

Army views of labor had undergone interesting changes. Although the planners still considered labor disputes to be the primary form of civil disturbance that would be encountered in the III Corps Area, they believed also that "there is, at present, no indica- tion or likelihood of civil disturbances within the III Corps Area of such magnitude to require intervention by Federal authority." The planners noted, however, that there was "a great migration of industry within the corps area accompanied by changes of population," and that "new and influential industries commanding large payrolls are expanding rapid- ly." For this reason, planners warned, the estimate of the situation should be constantly revised because the III Corps Area demographic, economic, political, and social situations were in constant flux.[35]

When the United States entered World War II in December 1941, the Army had full and complete contingency plans to guide and direct federal troops should they be called to intervene in civil disturbances resulting from labor disputes, racial tensions, or the machinations of foreign agents, saboteurs, or revolutionaries. Although the plans did not cover every possible contingency and often focused on outdated and unrealistic scenar- ios, their formulation had produced within the Army a heightened level of preparedness and an increased awareness of who potential domestic enemies were, where they could strike, and what targets potentially would need federal military protection. The

---

[33] Ibid. The fear of Axis and Communist "fifth column" activities had been greatly overstated. See the fol- lowing: Alton Frye, *Nazi Germany and the Western Hemisphere, 1933–1945* (New Haven: Yale University Press, 1967); Sander A. Diamond, *The Nazi Movement in the United States, 1924–1941* (Ithaca: Cornell University Press, 1974); Louis De Jong, *The German Fifth Column in the Second World War* (Chicago: University of Chicago Press, 1956); Geoffrey Smith, *To Save a Nation: American Counter-subversives, the New Deal, and the Coming of World War II* (New York: Basic, 1974); Clayton D. Laurie, "Ideology and American Propaganda: The Psychological Warfare Campaign Against Nazi Germany, 1941–1945" (Ph.D. diss., The American University, 1990), especially chs. 1 and 2. For the perceived Italian threat, see James Miller, "Carlo Sforza E L'Evoluzione Della Politica Americana Verso L'Italia: 1940–1943" [Carlo Sforza and the Evolution of American Policy Toward Italy, 1940–1943], *Storia Contemporia* [Italy] 7 (1976):825–53; idem, "A Question of Loyalty: American Liberals, Propaganda, and the Italian Community, 1939–40," *Maryland Historian* 9 (1978):49–71.

[34] IIICA–EPW, 1941. See also Wayne S. Cole, *Roosevelt and the Isolationists, 1932–1945* (Lincoln: University of Nebraska Press, 1983); Mark L. Chadwin, *The Warhawks* (New Haven: Yale University Press, 1957).

[35] IIICA–EPW, 1941.

Emergency Plan White represented the first detailed effort by the Army to delineate in advance standing operating procedures, specific explanations of legal and statutory guidelines, and detailed information concerning tactical and strategic deployments that were to be implemented in each geographic area of the nation in the event of a civil disturbance requiring federal intervention.

In addition, the plan strongly emphasized coordination between Army technical, combat, and administrative branches, ensuring more effective and efficient performance of a wide range of military functions in addition to simple crowd control. This emphasis extended to include the other military services and federal civil departments, clearly indicating the growth and interdependence of the various arms of the government. Any future sizable domestic disorder would be controlled by the combined efforts of myriad federal, state, and local agencies. Gone, at least in theory, were the unilateral and often ineffective efforts by any single agency to deal with civil disorders that federal forces had undertaken in the past.

The Emergency War Plan White gave the Army of the pre–World War II years a distinct advantage over federal military forces performing the same civil functions during the World War I era. Sophistication in data and organization, however, did not imply a more realistic analysis of the underlying causes of civil unrest. Army contingency planning, at times completely divorced from the legal and constitutional framework, continued to emphasize perceived threats by radical labor groups or by a Bolshevik-inspired revolution and clearly anticipated the need to prepare the military forces of the nation to fight a second civil war. The threat from Axis agents in the form of a shadowy fifth column, although intriguing to the public and to government civil and military leaders, was unsupported by concrete evidence and eventually proved to be more fiction than reality. On the other hand, the perception that racial conflict might develop proved only too accurate.

Concomitant with its war plans, the Army also began to create and make formal doctrine, and, as a result, regulations were devised to fit the plans that governed federal military forces involved in domestic disorders. By the opening of World War II, the Army possessed a doctrine that would remain largely unchanged through the conflict and well into the postwar years.

CHAPTER 15

The Development of Army Civil Disturbance Doctrine, 1894–1945

A mob, forcibly resisting or obstructing the execution of the laws of the United States . . . is a public enemy. It is purely a tactical question in what manner they [federal troops] shall use the weapons with which they are armed—whether by the fire of musketry and artillery or by the use of the bayonet and saber, or by both, and at what stage of the operations each or either mode of attack shall be employed. . . . They are not called upon to consider how great may be the losses inflicted upon the public enemy, except to make their blows so effective as to promptly suppress all resistance to lawful authority.

—*General Order 23*, 9 July 1894.

While the military commander is subject to no authority but that of his military superiors, he will bear in mind that the suppression of violence without bloodshed or undue violence is a worthy military achievement, and will employ only such force as is necessary to accomplish his mission.

—Section IV, Paragraph 8, *Army Regulation 500–50*, 17 July 1945.

Concomitant with the development of contingency plans for dealing with civil disturbances in the interwar years, the Army evolved a doctrine for those disturbances defining how troops could best be employed against mobs and domestic revolutionaries. Catalyzed by the Communist scare, the doctrine began essentially as a combat literature for civil disorders, the first such corpus of official thought in American history. But development continued during the interwar period, and by the early years of World War II plans and doctrine emphasized instead the use of nonlethal force in quelling civil disorders. By that time Army officers had come to consider the crowds encountered in civil disorders as something other than public enemies, and civil disturbance doctrine differed in kind as well as in tactical detail from their literature of combat.

The roots of Army thinking about domestic upheavals can be traced to the 1894 Pullman Strike. At that time the press and public alike criticized its actions and many saw in retrospect, without concrete evidence, troop reactions to mob violence as having been unduly harsh. Critics noted a high degree of disorganization, confusion within the high command regarding its proper role, and a lack of coordination between federal, state, and local forces.[1]

---

[1] Cooper, *The Army and Civil Disorder*, pp. 120–21, 149–50, 152; Lindsey, *Pullman Strike*, p. 258.

During the height of the Pullman strike the Army issued the first component of a formal doctrine, set forth in *General Order 23* of 9 July 1894. Subsequently issued as an Army regulation, the order essentially applied combat doctrine to riot duty against civilians. The Army denounced as a "public enemy" any group that forcibly resisted or obstructed federal law, or that threatened or destroyed private property or property under the protection of the government. Because such public enemies were similar to a hostile foreign military force, federal troops were to show little restraint. The troops were to be "governed by the general regulations of the Army and military tactics in respect to the manner in which they shall act to accomplish the desired end." The commander's choice of means was "purely a tactical question," as was the "manner [the troops] shall use the weapons with which they are armed—whether by the fire of musketry and artillery, or by use of the bayonet and saber, or . . . at what stage of the operations each or either mode of attack shall be employed."[2]

Mitigating such harshness was the observation that "in the first stage of an insurrection, lawless mobs are frequently co-mingled with great crowds of comparatively innocent people, drawn there by curiosity and excitement, and ignorant of the great danger to which they are exposed." Hence officers were instructed to hold the fire of their troops until the innocent could be given "timely warning" to separate themselves from the guilty. Under no circumstances were troops to fire without proper command, although specially selected sharpshooters could at will "shoot down individual rioters who may have fired upon or thrown missiles at the troops."[3] Some sections of the order appeared to envision a graduated use of force: "as a general rule the bayonet alone should be used against mixed crowds in the first stages. . . . But, as soon as sufficient warning has been given . . . the action of the troops should be governed solely by the tactical considerations involved." Ultimately, the Army's mission was to end the disturbance as quickly and as completely as possible without counting the costs. Troops "are not called upon to consider how great may be the losses inflicted upon the public enemy, except to make their blows so effective as to promptly suppress all resistance to lawful authority, and to stop the destruction of life the moment lawless resistance has ceased." However, the order concluded that "Punishment belongs not to the troops but to the courts of justice."[4]

Although *General Order 23* had been issued at the height of the Pullman strike, and therefore was not known to all Army personnel on riot duty that summer, it established the Army's first theoretical position on domestic conflict. The order reflected the antiradical and antilabor attitudes and fears of the majority of Army leaders, government officials, and the general public. Yet coming at the end of a period of violent confrontations, its effect was more rhetorical than real. *General Order 23* remained the official Army civil disturbance guidance through the end of the century, but its terms were never fully carried out in any labor or race-related civil disorder.

The Army regulations of 1901 and 1904, reflecting Progressive-era changes in American society and the beginning of such changes in the Army, republished this tactical doctrine in a shortened and less strongly worded version. The references to *public enemy* and to the words troops *are not called upon to consider how great may be the*

---

[2] *General Orders and Circulars, 1894*, GO 23, 9 Jul 1894.
[3] Ibid.
[4] GO 23; Schofield, *Forty-Six Years in the Army*, pp. 504–05.

losses inflicted upon the public enemy were eliminated. Nonetheless, the confusion between domestic agitators and foreign enemies lingered. Except for a few minor changes in later years, the new instructions governed Army civil disturbance actions through the early decades of the century, including the World War I period and interwar years, until further modified by the Army regulations of 1937.[5]

Because of a lack of any comprehensive detailed federal military doctrine on civil disturbance duty in the prewar and early World War I period, local police, state militia, home guard, National Guard, and even Regular Army units sought additional guidance from whatever manuals and treatises might be available. As a result, the World War I era saw the proliferation of privately published pamphlets, manuals, and guidebooks on civil disturbances that filled the gap. Most elaborated on existing federal military tactics and policies for the benefit of National Guard units. In time the contents of these guides found their way into later official Army doctrine. Many of these guides were written by regulars—such as Lt. Col. Byron L. Barger, Maj. Henry A. Bellow, and Capt. Richard Stockton—and from the beginning represented Army thought if not official doctrine.[6]

One of the first and most comprehensive of these early manuals was Richard Stockton's *Troops on Riot Duty*, a privately published, unofficial summation of thought on riot duty. Brig. Gen. E. S. Wedgewood, head of Utah's National Guard, introduced the work in a harsh and no-nonsense tone that characterized the entire volume. "I am firmly convinced that . . . the militia should not be called out until such time as . . . it is necessary and proper to declare martial law," Wedgewood wrote, "and that martial law should be declared the instant the troops go on duty." Bringing the military into riot duty "implies the use of force to the point of death if necessary, and it should never be brought on the scene until the necessity to use that force is imminent." Paradoxically, the book itself sought to teach National Guard and regular officers how to handle crowds much larger than their own commands without having to resort to lethal force from the first. Yet, as Wedgewood wrote, the mere presence of troops and the use of the rifle butt and the prod of a bayonet were limited in their effectiveness when facing large, violent, and perhaps armed mobs raging out of control.[7]

The sixteen chapters of Stockton's work were devoted to setting forth precise instructions on such topics as the assembly of troops, their conduct and appearance, how to meet and disperse a mob, how to defend and attack barricades, duties of civil authorities, how to prevent lynchings, general legal aspects, and martial law. His work failed to introduce any innovative ideas on how to quell a civil disorder quickly and bloodlessly by other than forceful means, and, although fulfilling its purpose as a handbook or manual, it provided its readers no insight into the causes behind the social, economic, or political unrest of the time, nor of the legal restraints on troop action. Nonetheless, its timely publication helped

---

[5] U.S. War Department, *Regulations for the Army of the United States, 1901* (Washington, D.C.: Government Printing Office, 1901), par. 568; ibid., *1904* (Washington, D.C.: Government Printing Office, 1904), par. 488; AR 500–50, 6 Jun 23, par. 8; AR 500–50, 5 Apr 37, which superseded the 1923 regulation and its three changes, none of which affected par. 8.

[6] Byron L. Barger, *The Law and Custom of Riot Duty: A Guide for National Guard Officers and Civil Authorities With Commentaries on Federal Aid* (Columbus: B. L. Barger, 1907); Henry A. Bellow, *Manual for Local Defense* (New York: Macmillan, 1918), and *A Treatise on Riot Duty for the National Guard* (Washington, D.C.: Government Printing Office, 1920); Stockton and Sackett, *Troops on Riot Duty*.

[7] Stockton and Sackett, *Troops on Riot Duty*, p. 5.

fill the gap in civil disturbance literature by having federal military policies and practices compiled in a single detailed volume, and its contents reappeared in official government manuals during World War I.

Yet the entry of the United States into the war found the Regular Army without official or written policies and procedures regarding civil disturbances beyond the regulations based on *General Order 23* of 1894. The federalizing of state guardsmen obliged the government to recruit several special units to take their place, the largest being the United States Guards. The U.S. Guards were charged with protecting industrial plants and aiding authorities in the prevention and suppression of domestic sabotage, strikes, and other forms of civil disorder. To provide them with instructions, the staff of the War Department began writing a comprehensive guide for use by all federal or federalized forces in dealing with civil disorders. The guide was completed in October 1918, then revised when the U.S. Guards were disbanded one month later, and ultimately published in July 1919 as *Military Protection, United States Guards: The Use of Organized Bodies in the Protection and Defense of Property During Riots, Strikes, and Civil Disturbances*. Based heavily on Army regulations and private and National Guard publications, especially Stockton's work, it sought to provide not only the rudiments of the legal foundations governing Army intervention in civil affairs, but also practical "how to" advice to officers and troops.[8]

The writers of *Military Protection, United States Guards*, recognized that "riot service is one of the most distasteful duties which soldiers are called upon to perform," but also that officers had to be well trained and fully prepared to handle such duty effectively when the need arose. Therefore, the War Department undertook to familiarize officers with such topics as the legal aspects of riot duty, assembling troops, transporting troops, and forming and using motor patrols. Procedures were outlined for marching through and clearing streets, meeting and dispersing a mob, and attacking cities when armed resistance was expected or when cities were in the enemy's possession. Military leaders learned how to carry out police functions outside their normal competence. *Military Protection, United States Guards*, served as the basis for civil disturbance troop training in the immediate postwar years and as a guide for the majority of civil disturbance manuals during the interwar period.

As with previous Army civil disturbance regulations and instructions, *Military Protection, United States Guards*, emphasized the need to end any civil disorder as rapidly as possible and restated the methods by which federal or federalized troops could be called to aid civil authorities. It stressed especially the emergency provisions of Army regulations and the wartime direct access policy. Underlying theory remained unchanged. Any riot considered serious enough to warrant federal intervention was to be dealt with like a military campaign against a foreign enemy.

Yet, the manual's thirty "Important General Rules of Riot Duty" indicated that Army doctrine was becoming more detailed and sophisticated, simply because specific guidelines were now enunciated. Provisions for the use of lethal force were given as usual: troops should never be ordered on riot duty without an ample supply of ball ammunition,

---

[8] U.S. War Department, Adjutant General's Office, *Military Protection, United States Guards: The Use of Organized Bodies in the Protection and Defense of Property During Riots, Strikes, and Civil Disturbances* (Washington, D.C.: Government Printing Office, 1919). Until otherwise stated, the following text is from *Military Protection*, pp. 7–19, 26, 32–42, 52, 67–70.

for live ammunition was expected by rioters and "from the first, moral effect is obtained; it will not have to be used more than once, if at all." Troops were ordered "never [to] fire over the heads of rioters. The aim should be low," to prevent casualties to innocent bystanders who are not involved in the disorder. "If anyone is hurt it should be the rioters." Soldiers were not to fear prosecution if rioters were killed, for "Most States provide that if it is not proven that the killing was through mere malice, wantonness, or cruelty, a soldier is not punishable for such an act." Yet, while commanders on riot duty should never be limited in their use of force—that could only be determined on the spot—troops "should be instructed to use whatever force may be necessary to carry out their orders," by responsible military officials acting under federal civil superiors.

In dealing with a civil disturbance, troops were warned, "temporizing with a mob" was considered poor judgment since it indicated weakness and harmed the discipline of the troops. Trying to bluff a mob was also considered poor policy. The manual advised, "never threaten to do things you do not intend to do or that you can not do" otherwise the mob would lose both its fear and its respect for the troops and become even more dangerous. "The mob shall not be trifled with," nor permitted "to seem to be victorious for a single day."

It was considered imperative that riots be quelled in their incipient stage. Neither officers nor their troops were to show any hesitation in confronting the mob and were to act as rapidly as possible with the maximum force needed, but only as necessary. "Crowds," the instructions read, "should not be allowed to form," nor should rioters "be permitted to throw missiles at troops, even though they may be of such a nature that they cause no serious injury."

Mobs and their composition were given thorough treatment in *Military Protection, United States Guards*. The manual stated that mobs are "peculiarly liable to dejection or elation; they sneak into their hiding places or swarm into the streets directly as they fail or succeed." This was due to their makeup, which usually consisted of "professional agitators . . . anarchists, socialists, thieves, cutthroats, vagabonds, and ruffians," who, like vultures, "will seek a field of prey," or "with the instinct of the rat, desert the sinking ship." Mobs were described as being composed of moral cowards, who were generally led by agitators in the rear of the mob," which should be the focal point of any Army attack. Such groups were to be dealt with sharply as "nothing emboldens a crowd as passive resistance." Any rioter, Army personnel were instructed, who fires a shot, throws a stone, or otherwise assaults a soldier "should be shot down by a sharpshooter."

The tactics to be used in quelling a civil disturbance depended on the type of disorder encountered. Officers were given specific descriptions of formations to be used and how to deploy troops in such formations. Included were the wedge, the diagonal, and the deployed line. The wedge, for example, was described in the manual as "the normal offensive formation for breaking up, splitting, or striking a crowd," and the diagonal and deployed line were used with or following the use of the wedge. Commanders were warned to keep as many men in reserve behind the wedge as were in the wedge itself for the purpose of containing the crowd should the formation be broken. The mob should always be attacked from two sides at once, the manual read, since "a line of bristling bayonets across a street from wall to wall backed up by disciplined men ready to fire possesses a moral strength that mobs rarely oppose." Other instructions were given on how to attack a house occupied by rioters, how to defend and attack barricades, and how to defend bridges, street railways, and railroads.

Intelligence data about the crowd and the specific civil disorder were considered to be of the utmost importance. The manual warned that a commander who does not acquire such intelligence will, "sooner or later . . . commit the unpardonable blunder of being caught by surprise." To prevent this, a commander was to keep informed of all activities in his command area through close contact with local police officials, federal and military secret service and intelligence agencies, cooperative public groups and individuals, and perhaps even through individual soldiers of his own command who, when out of uniform, could be sent to mingle and speak with members of the crowd, gaining their confidence and securing "information beyond the reach of uniformed men."

Weapons and equipment necessary to perform riot duty included special trains and automobiles for transporting troops to the riot area, automobiles and motorcycles for patrolling city streets once there, bayonets, hardwood nightsticks measuring thirty inches in length and one inch in diameter for clearing crowds, machine guns, rifles, shotguns— preferably sawed-off and loaded with no. 1 shot or buckshot—and, "in some emergencies, field guns with projectiles" for demolishing buildings occupied by rioters. Troops were advised not to "use the butt of the rifle against mobs" because of "the danger that the rifle may be seized and wrested from the grasp of the soldier." Commanders were told that "soldiers should be impressed with the idea that the business end of his weapon is the point of the bayonet and the muzzle, which should be kept toward the enemy." The brevity of the section on weapons was indicative; most of the weapons had traditional combat applications, and few were specifically targeted at riot control. No evidence suggests that such specialized weaponry was considered necessary at the time.

The information in *Military Protection, United States Guards*, was influential in the formation of subsequent doctrine on civil disorders. Following its publication, several training courses used it to instruct federal troops. Thus a course offered at Camp Dix, New Jersey, in 1922 made the *Military Protection, United States Guards*, manual the basis for its own work entitled *Military Protection: Employment of the Army in Aid of Federal Civil Authorities in the Execution of Federal Laws*. Developed by Lt. Col. Dennis P. Quinlan of the Judge Advocate General's Division of the War Department, the course sought to provide junior officers with a detailed and comprehensive description of their legal and military responsibilities and obligations should they be called to command troops in a civil disorder. In its fifty-eight pages, heavy emphasis was given to the United States Constitution, Army regulations, and statutes governing federal military intervention in civil affairs, with further sections on legalities that governed actions by local, state, and federal agencies. The goal of the Camp Dix program was to provide a course of instruction that would guide the actions of junior officers and their troops during a civil disorder from beginning to end, paying special attention to the legal intricacies and practical difficulties of Army involvement. The Fort Dix course represented one of the first efforts by the Army to translate doctrine into training.[9]

Uneasiness over the threat of a Bolshevik revolution prompted several reports, monographs, and memorandums warning of the dire consequences that could result from Army

---

[9] Quinlan, *Military Protection,* pp. 14–15, 39–40.

unpreparedness. One such monograph, prepared in 1919–1920 by Lt. Col. Conrad H. Lanza at the General Staff College, entitled *Communist Warfare*, spoke clearly of the perceived leftist threat. Developed from data procured from the War Department's Military Intelligence Division, *Communist Warfare* drew heavily on the experiences of the German government in suppressing leftist revolutionary attempts in the immediate post-armistice period. For his monograph, Lanza obtained additional information from books describing the Russian Revolution of 1917 and from press accounts of the uprisings in Germany, Russia, and Hungary during 1918–1920.[10]

The legal aspects of combating communism in the United States as outlined by Lanza reflected wartime procedures, including the still-extant policy of direct access, and indicated that the return to prewar constitutional and statutory procedures had not yet been effected and was not anticipated. In all other matters, however, his work endorsed and described the same procedures, tactics, weapons, and methods as other official and unofficial civil disturbance manuals of the period, except that the word *Communist* figured prominently throughout the work. No mention was made of other varieties of radicals or subversives— as if communism constituted the only danger to the security of the United States. A survey of chapter titles reveals topics such as Information Required in Communist Warfare, Offensive Action Against Communists, Action Against Cities Completely Held by Communists, and Actions Against Cities Partially Held by Communists. Many sections of *Communist Warfare* appear to have been lifted verbatim from *Military Protection, United States Guards*, with the word *Communist* being substituted throughout for *radical*, *rioter*, or *mob*, and in this respect brought its model up to date.

Perhaps the most valuable aspect of Colonel Lanza's work was his curiosity and willingness to learn about the experiences of foreign governments and the organization of their forces to deal with domestic disturbances. Though his work unfortunately ignored cultural, political, and historical differences between these nations and the United States, it did introduce a broader perspective and sought to satisfy the increased interest of the American officer corps in developments abroad.

Post-armistice Germany impressed many American military leaders as an example of how a revolution could be successfully suppressed without great loss of life and property. Others were following the same path. The German experience in the spring of 1919 was described in a memorandum by Capt. W. H. Dearden for the Military Intelligence Division. Dearden, basing his account on information he had gleaned from German newspapers and conversations with British and French officers on occupation duty with him in Germany, concentrated on descriptions of German riot control tactics, their evolution, and the procedures for retaking cities from Communist occupiers—all areas of intense interest to Army planners who were then drafting War Plan White.[11] His report and several German manuals on civil disturbances were forwarded to General Churchill, the MID director, who concluded that German civil disturbance methods were "so remarkably effective in quelling disturbances in a minimum time and with a minimum damage to life and property as to warrant close study and probable adoption by us. It is

---

[10] Conrad H. Lanza, General Service Schools, "Communist Warfare," General Staff College, 1919–1920, MID, RG 165, Records of the War Department General Staff, Military Intelligence Division, 1917–1941, Entry 65, File 2246–126–4, NARA.

[11] Memo, Dearden for Mason, 20 Mar 20, RG 165, Entry 65, File 242–18–2, NARA.

recommended . . . the pertinent data contained here be issued to the Service for its information and use." Radical or leftist uprisings, American military officers came to realize, did not have to follow the example of the 1917 Russian Bolshevik Revolution if proper and sufficient military force was quickly applied.[12]

Several Army leaders questioned the suitability of the stringent German doctrine for the United States. In a letter to an assistant chief of staff for intelligence in MID, Brig. Gen. H. E. Ely, commandant of the General Service Schools at Fort Leavenworth, Kansas, expressed grave doubts about German methods. His thoughts, though uncharacteristic for Army officers of that time who seemed to be planning arbitrary actions distinctly prohibited by the laws of the United States, foreshadowed later thinking concerning the moderate use of military power in civil disorders. He wrote, "the measures . . . which have been successfully employed by the Germans in the suppression of riots and incipient revolutions, are harsher and less politic than would be advisable in this country. Germany's centralized government permits arbitrary actions which are distinctly prohibited by the laws of the United States." Further, he added, German methods "for the tactical employment of troops . . . are also open to the objection that some are unnecessarily harsh." In conclusion, the commandant wrote that the documents had a "technical value as a reference, but would require considerable revision" before they could be used as regulations for American troops.[13]

The Military Intelligence Division sought further information on doctrine from other foreign nations. During the drafting of the Emergency Plan White in 1923, MID, acting on a request from the Chemical Warfare Service (CWS), solicited data from United States military attaches in ten European capitals for possible incorporation into Army plans and doctrine. The attaches were instructed to provide information on the domestic use of foreign military and police forces, their size and organization, and the types of weapons employed, including nonlethal gases and chemicals.[14]

Their information varied widely in quality and quantity. Lt. Col. Edward T. Donnelly, military attache in Rome, reported that "only armoured motorcars were employed for quelling riots" and that "no chemicals were ever used." The attache in Istanbul, Maj. Sherman Miles, responded that "there have been no riots or civil disturbances worthy of the name since the Armistice" and that police were armed with "ordinary 'nightsticks' and with revolvers (which they never use)."[15] Information from the American military attache in Paris, Col. T. Bentley-Mott, was far more complete. Mott informed the War Department that the French Army did not have "special instructions formulated by the military authorities for use against mobs," although such instructions had existed years before. Because of the 1907 date of issue, however, the instructions were no longer considered valid. Taking into account French history, with its numerous revolutions and challenges to civil authority, Mott reported that "Tradition and long custom govern the method of procedure and verbal instructions are found quite sufficient without the dissemination of anything like a handbook." French police and military forces favored preventive measures instead of waiting for

---

[12] Memo, Churchill for Haan, Dir, WPD, 24 Mar 20, RG 165, Entry 65, File 242–18–11, NARA.

[13] Ltr, Ely to ACofS, MID, 23 Dec 21, RG 165, Entry 65, File 2246–126–4, NARA.

[14] Ch, MID, to Military Attache, sub: Means Taken for Quelling Riots, RG 165, Entry 65, File 2612–13–1, NARA.

[15] Donnelly to CofS, MID, 9 Jul 23, File 2612–13–3; Miles to CofS, MID, 20 Jul 23, File 2612–13–4; both in RG 165, Entry 65, NARA.

a disturbance to start. "Prevention rather than suppression is the underlying principle of all police operations against mobs." Like the U.S. Army, the French military always sought an overwhelming numerical advantage over any adversary in a civil disorder. Mott wrote that "the number of men, soldiers or policemen, employed in such cases is always very large as compared with the size of the unruly element which at any time assembles."[16]

Despite France's history of civil disorder, Mott noted that the French did not possess any weapons specifically intended for riot control purposes. The use of nonlethal gases and chemicals was not contemplated by French authorities, and "no preparations had been yet made for placing at the disposal of the French police . . . the engines of gas warfare." The efficiency of this weapon for handling mobs, however, was acknowledged by French civil and military authorities. Other weapons used were "those which the police or soldiers habitually carry," such as revolvers or rifles. French civil disorders, if the military became involved, were usually handled by infantry and cavalry troops who relied upon the flats of their sabers, but very rarely upon firearms. Mott stressed "that there is a strong aversion on the part of all authorities in France to ever using the military forces of the nation against mobs, and while troops are sometimes ordered out in anticipation of disturbances it is more to make a show of force than with the idea they will be called upon to use their weapons." French riot duty, he maintained, was "entirely the business of the police," both local and national. One Army infantry officer had told him that in thirty years of service he had been put on riot duty only four times, and he had "never seen a soldier use his arms in any way against a rioter."[17]

Police and military forces in Spain followed tactics dissimilar from the French in many ways because of its different history and traditions. Spain did not have a history of labor-induced civil disorder and prevention did not appear to be as heavily emphasized. Maj. C. B. Hodges reported that Spanish officials sought to avoid "as far as possible the use of fire-arms, . . . instead . . . charges of cavalry, trumpet-calls of warning, and . . . streams of water from fire-hoses" were employed. In the majority of cases these tactics sufficed. "Only when the tumult is seditious and armed," he reported, "is rifle and machine gun fire resorted to." Spanish military and civil authorities, Hodges concluded, had not yet organized a gas corps, and appeared to have had little reason or need to do so.[18]

The most detailed information came from Maj. Oscar N. Solbert, the military attache in London. He reported that civil disturbances were primarily handled by local police, and that if they proved unable to quell the disorder they were authorized "to requisition the regular military forces." (The American Cushing Doctrine, abrogated by the 1878 Posse Comitatus Act, was based on this British practice.) Territorial troops—who were comparable to the U.S. National Guard—were authorized to aid civil authorities in quelling disorders, but like their American counterparts they were considered inexperienced, less capable, and more partisan in outlook. Calling out the territorials, therefore, was a last resort, when all other means short of calling regulars had failed.[19]

---

[16] Mott to CofS, MID, 23 Jun 23, File 2612–13–9, 28 Jul 23, File 2612–13–5, and MID, 9 Aug 23, File 2612–13–8, all in RG 165, Entry 65, NARA.

[17] Ibid., 9 Aug 23.

[18] Hodges to CofS, MID, 11 Aug 23, File 2612–13–7, RG 165, Entry 65, NARA.

[19] Until otherwise noted the following is from Rpt, Solbert to CofS, MID, 30 Jul 23, RG 165, File 2612–13–6, Entry 65, NARA.

The procedure for calling out regular troops in Great Britain was simple, the product of numerous precedents set over the course of centuries. As Solbert reported, "it is only necessary for a magistrate or chief constable to call upon a local commander for troops stationed in the district. . . . If no troops are quartered locally, the requisition is made direct upon the War Office, which has full authority to move troops." When called to duty in a civil disorder situation, soldiers carry the arms with which they are normally equipped. The "King's Regulations," he reported, "require that when firing is resorted to, troops must shoot with intent to kill." Lachrymatory gases, Solbert reported, had been carefully considered for use but were never adopted. Although British authorities believed nonlethal gas might be useful, its employment would so enrage the public, after the gas-related horrors of the Great War, that "it would only incite further and more serious disturbances."

Concerning legal requirements, the attache reported that "the law requires that the magistrate shall, before he calls on the officer commanding the troops to take action, read a part of the Riot Act" (on which the American presidential proclamation required by RS 5300 is based), which orders all rioters to disperse within one hour. Prior to the reading of the Riot Act, members of the crowd are guilty only of a misdemeanor and are under local police jurisdiction. After reading of the act and expiration of the time limit, those who have not dispersed become felons subject to military action. Although the Riot Act is a necessary legal formality, failure to read it beforehand in no way limits military forces from acting on the request of civil authorities. The attache concluded that "only in rare cases have troops been required to fire upon rioters," because most Britons do not own firearms, and no police or military casualties caused by armed rioters had ever been recorded.[20]

The U.S. Army's attempt to find applicable information from foreign governments suitable for inclusion in its own civil disturbance doctrine was largely a failure. Reports from attaches indicated, more times than not, that foreign governments had even less well-defined policies for dealing with civil disorders than those developed by the U.S. Army prior to 1923. In addition, it was discovered that a government's policy on civil disturbance often depended on a variety of peculiar national factors such as precedent; tradition; social, economic, political, and legal structures; the type and severity of civil disorders; public attitudes about direct action; and the existence of various national police and military forces not present, or desired, in the United States. As a result of this failure to gain applicable insight from European experiences, the Army concluded that U.S. doctrine had to be tailored specifically to domestic situations, laws, and civil and military capabilities.

The definition of a clear American doctrine actually emerged from the work of other Army agencies. In 1922–1923, the U.S. Army Command and General Staff School at Fort Leavenworth, Kansas, issued a manual by Maj. Cassius M. Dowell, an infantry officer then assigned to the Judge Advocate General's Department. Dowell's manual was a remarkable document, which became the core of future texts for senior officers at the school, as did its subsequent confidential supplement. The manual dealt with all the same technical and tactical issues covered by earlier works, but in a more comprehensive manner. It emphasized

---

[20] Solbert appears to have been given a completely erroneous picture of both the number of civil disorders involving British regulars between the seventeenth and twentieth centuries and the scores of injuries and fatalities associated with their interventions. See Anthony Babington, *Military Intervention in Britain: From the Gordon Riots to the Gibraltar Killings* (New York: Routledge, 1990); and Geoffrey Marshal, "The Armed Forces and Industrial Disputes in the United Kingdom," *Armed Forces and Society* 5 (February 1979):270–80.

similarly "the ultra-radical element" as the primary cause for American domestic disorders, which was characteristic for manuals of the period.[21]

In 1925, after Dowell rewrote and revised this work, the Army published its more general and innocuous parts, with little mention of "ultra-radicalism." This new work, which included an appendix of sample civil disorder documents, was essentially a legal treatise entitled *Military Aid to the Civil Power*. At the same time it was published, however, the remaining parts of Dowell's endeavor, which the Army thought too sensitive for the general public, were collected as a *Confidential Supplement to Military Aid to the Civil Power*. The initial book contains no references indicating the existence of the *Confidential Supplement*, although the Army considered both to be parts of the same document.[22]

Dowell's published positions concerning radicalism were very different from his approach in the *Confidential Supplement*, which was strictly for internal Army use. In this supplement he was far more specific about the location and extent of the radical danger, although his conclusions in the *Confidential Supplement*, like his conclusions in *Military Aid*, were not supported by concrete evidence. Dowell believed that major cities, like Chicago, Cleveland, New York, Seattle, and San Francisco were likely soon to become scenes of violent revolutionary activities, with other, smaller cities subject to lesser risk. The evidence was "unmistakable," that "ultra-radical organizations" intended the "extermination of the so-called capitalistic class and the abolition of private property, nationalism, and religion." In response to the contention of liberals, civil libertarians, and Army critics that radicals were nothing but a harmless minority, Dowell cited the example of Russia, where it took but "a few months of radical misrule" by a minority party to bring her "to ruin and deep misery." Radical agitation, 90 percent of it traceable to aliens living in the United States, was not confined solely to "so-called 'economic ills'" but was also "directed towards racial prejudice."[23]

Referring to the commitment of federal troops, Dowell, in *Military Aid to the Civil Power*, described the policy that should govern Army actions. Although troops "should . . . move and operate with promptitude and efficiency," no more force than is reasonably required should be used, nor should disorderly elements be treated like an enemy in war unless the emergency demands extreme measures. Usually a display of force should be all that was necessary to accomplish everything desired.[24] Even though such statements emphasized using the minimum amount of force, Dowell's work also addressed emergencies that could require extreme measures, indicating an ambiguity that ran through the Army civil disturbance literature of that time. The 1894 *General Order 23* was still in effect, and now, in 1925 Dowell elaborated on it by declaring, as did the regulations, that "the equipment required by federal troops for duty in . . . the suppression of civil disturbances will not differ materially from that required for ordinary occasions of field service." In accord with this idea, Dowell wrote that machine guns, 37-mm. guns, and 3-inch mortars would be required, mortars ordinarily being more appropriate than artillery.[25] Other articles of equipment and weapons suitable for riot duty included tanks, airplanes, motorized and animal-

[21] Dowell, Domestic Disturbances.
[22] Dowell, *Military Aid to the Civil Power*, pp. 183–84, and *Confidential Supplement to Military Aid*.
[23] Dowell, *Confidential Supplement to Military Aid*, pp. 2–4.
[24] Dowell, *Military Aid to the Civil Power*, pp. 206, 210.
[25] Dowell, *Confidential Supplement to Military Aid*, p. 6.

drawn transport, riot cartridges or bird-shot, and shotguns. Armored vehicles, especially tanks, Dowell wrote, could certainly help disperse groups by their "moral effect," and airplanes were advantageous for reconnaissance purposes, for dropping proclamations, or for "keeping rioters off roofs by means of machine gun fire." They could even be used for bombing in certain cases. Armored cars, passenger cars, motorcycles with and without side-cars, and horses were all useful, as was mounting twin machine guns on trucks. Riot cartridges and buckshot should be included always in the inventory of munitions, because such "weapons will be used at short ranges only," and it was undesirable to have projectiles go much beyond the target.[26]

Although the Army's leaders doubted that "any ultra-radical element" could successfully keep plans of a potential nationwide uprising secret, let alone sufficiently equip a revolutionary force, Dowell envisioned situations in which revolutionaries could take up arms and challenge the authority of the United States. In such a contingency, he believed it advisable for the Army to study the successful tactics used by the Germans against the post-armistice Communist uprisings. These tactics were clearly a prescription for conquering a city by combat methods, by sheer weight of military force, and by deception as in a total war. Dowell suggested the use of "insincere negotiations" with adversaries for gaining time and the use of the maximum amount of military force, such as airplanes for machine-gunning rioters and trench mortars for hurling explosives into buildings occupied by mobs. Dowell believed "that the tactics employed were based on sound principles and, with some modifications, are applicable to an ordinary case in the United States where an uprising has assumed considerable proportions."[27]

In a separate chapter on tactics, Dowell differentiated between situations in which a small force would be sufficient and those disorders "requiring serious military operations." Due to the variety of possible civil disturbance situations, however, only general instructions could be given governing tactics, and all resembled those found in combat situations. Dowell dealt also with such topics as "Occupation of a City" and "Offensive Action Against a City," emphasizing the same combat themes of earlier sections. Of special note were his instructions for dealing with civilians while on civil disturbance duty. Civilians were to be treated with courtesy and fairness, and soldiers were instructed to "observe an air of dignified impartiality," to "avoid an overbearing manner or the use of excessive authority." In any domestic disorder troops should respect private property scrupulously and not accept favors, food, or drink from civilians.[28]

Despite the conventional views expressed in his works, Dowell also showed occasional insight into the future of riot control. Three years earlier, in preliminary drafts, Dowell had touched upon a weapon that was to become the central focus of Army civil disturbance doctrine in the interwar period, and the primary method used by federal and state military forces for controlling mobs in later years: tear gases and other chemicals. Debates over the use of nonpoisonous gases and chemicals indicated a significant philosophical move away from the use of lethal force, and increasingly influenced Army doctrine. The debate began before Dowell's writings appeared and continued well into the 1930s.

---

[26] Ibid., pp. 6–8, 28.
[27] Ibid., pp. 11–14.
[28] Ibid., pp. 15–23.

The military uses of gases and other chemicals as antipersonnel weapons were recent developments in the 1920s. Poison gases were used first with notable tactical success on the Western Front by German military forces against French colonial troops and Canadian units at Langemarck near Ypres, Belgium, on 22 April 1915. Soon it was clear, however, that gas failed to provide either side a clear advantage. Instead, the misery it caused the soldiers of all nations repelled and horrified public opinion on both sides of the conflict. Compounding its gruesomeness was its overwhelming military ineffectiveness. Despite the large number of horror stories in circulation during the immediate postwar years, only a small proportion of Great War fatalities were attributable to poisonous gas, far fewer than those caused by small arms, artillery, or machine guns. As a British general remarked, gas had "made war uncomfortable, to no purpose."[29]

This bad reputation was reflected insofar as the public very rarely made the distinction between poisonous gases that killed and less toxic varieties that merely incapacitated victims temporarily. The negative postwar public perception was shared by Secretary of War Baker, Army Chief of Staff General March, and former AEF Commander General John J. Pershing. Baker and March actually sought to dismantle American production facilities, destroy existing gas stocks, and abolish the Chemical Warfare Service shortly after the armistice. In regard to civil disturbances, and despite previous policy positions to the contrary, the use of lachrymatory or other neutralizing gases in dealing with mobs was disapproved by Baker in February 1919.[30]

This prohibition was repeated during the Gary, Indiana, steel strike in the fall of 1919, when General Wood requested both phosphorous and nonpoisonous gas grenades. All six Army departmental commanders, however, were told by the War Department that "you are confidentially informed that the Secretary of War does not desire the use of chemicals . . . or chemical filled artillery projectiles, or chemical projectors, or gas projectiles for mortars, or chemical drop-bombs, or of chemicals for the cloud gas attack against mobs composed of inhabitants of the United States, or of its possessions." All troops on strike duty were instructed to turn these weapons over to an arsenal or other Army post. For this reason nonlethal gas, though available, was not used during the labor and racial disturbances of 1919–1921.[31]

Within two years the Army completely reversed its policy. Most of the credit for the turnabout belongs to Brig. Gen. Amos A. Fries, the chief of the Army's Chemical Warfare Service. Fries believed that his service needed to define a peacetime role if it was to survive postwar retrenchments as a separate and viable branch of the Army. Developing the use of tear gases and chemicals for application in civil disorders, he believed, would assure the Chemical Warfare Service a permanent niche and ample appropriations in any future Army configuration. Simultaneously, he sought to maintain the nation's ability to wage gas warfare if necessary. Poisonous gases and chemicals were real, if odious, weapons of war that could not be uninvented. The relatively cheap and

[29] Edward M. Spiers, *Chemical Warfare* (Chicago: University of Illinois Press, 1986), pp. 15–17, 36–40; quote from p. 33.

[30] Memo for CofS, 5 Nov 19, sub: Use of Chemical and High Explosive Grenades by Troops on Riot Duty, RG 60, Glasser Files, NARA. See also Daniel P. Jones "Tear Gas—Adoption for Use in Civil Disturbances," *Technology and Culture* 19 (April 1978):152; Spiers, *Chemical Warfare*, pp. 15–17, 36–40.

[31] Memo, AG for CG, Northeastern Dept, 7 Nov 19, RG 60, Glasser Files, NARA; Jones, "Tear Gas," p. 156.

simple technology involved in gas manufacture, the prevalence of such technology among the major powers, and the stockpiles of existing chemical weapons led Fries to argue that such weapons could not be banned effectively. If the Army was to maintain a posture of readiness against potential enemies, gas technology, if not actual stockpiles, had to be developed, maintained, and eventually augmented. The Army could not risk a future chemical weapons gap.

Therefore, Fries launched an extensive public relations and lobbying campaign, eventually garnering the support of several American chemical companies and many influential congressmen. His arguments for tear gas were rational and effective. He went to great lengths to demonstrate to Congress, the public, and the Army that, although the effects of such chemicals were unpleasant, they were only temporary and that the extensive use of such agents would result in far fewer casualties during civil disturbances than the use of more traditional weapons. His efforts and those of congressional supporters were successful. The Chemical Warfare Service not only avoided abolition, but it was specifically singled out for retention as a distinct Army branch by the National Defense Act of 1920—despite increasing worldwide efforts to gain an agreement banning the use of all chemical agents by military forces.[32]

Triumphant in Congress, Fries continued to press his case on the Army. In an August 1921 memorandum for new Chief of Staff General Pershing, he described the various chemical agents available, their possible uses, and their potential effectiveness. "The perfectly safe and effective things," he wrote, "are the chloracetophenone candles and the chloracetophenone and carbon tetrachloride grenades. These are very powerful tear gases and will temporarily put out of action anybody coming in contact with their contents. The D. M. candles are still more powerful. Five of these put off to windward of any . . . crowd would absolutely disperse it." Furthermore, he added, "this stuff will go through any mask." Toxic smoke was "only very slightly poisonous," though in high concentrations it caused very serious headaches, vomiting, and coughing. "With an ugly mob it would be an excellent thing to use," said Fries. "The chances would be exceedingly small against hurting anybody seriously, though on the other hand there isn't any question but what it would put them out of action and if they get considerable of it, it would put them out of action for a day or two." Even chemicals delivered by mortar on a distant crowd would "cause much less loss of life than to fire at men with rifles or one-pounder guns." He closed by informing Pershing that the Chemical Warfare Service was ready "at all times for work at a moment's notice," and had on hand in its inventories ample supplies of gases that could be used for crowd control.[33]

Within two weeks of receiving Fries' memorandum the War Department informed the commanding generals of all corps areas that "the instructions with reference to the use of chemical warfare equipment contained in the telegram of November 7, 1919 . . . are hereby revoked in so far as they pertain to non-toxic gases." The Chemical Warfare Service immediately issued a manual which, although not an official training or policy-making document, outlined the proper procedures for using tear gases and chemicals in civil disturbances. This manual, *Provisional Instructions for the Control of Mobs by Chemical*

---

[32] Jones, "Tear Gas," pp. 157–59; Spiers, *Chemical Warfare*, pp. 37–38.
[33] Memo, Fries for Pershing, 25 Aug 21, RG 60, Glasser Files, NARA.

Warfare, was the first of its kind—in effect, not only a treatise on a new technology but, by implication, a statement of a new and practical philosophy for controlling mobs.[34]

To facilitate the use of gas against rioters, mobs were classified into three categories: well-disciplined organizations of a few hundred up to a few thousand members who carried arms; small groups with only a few arms, poorly organized and with little discipline; and mobs in which men were mixed with women and children, unorganized, excited, and irresponsible. The calculated best methods for handling each group differed greatly, as did the degree of force needed, but overall "the use of a tear gas is without doubt far more humane than clubs, rifle butts, bayonets, sabers, ball cartridges or machine guns." Troops were given detailed information in *Provisional Instructions* on the purpose, scope, and effectiveness of each type of gas or chemical and the means of delivery, including tear-gas hand or rifle grenades, white-phosphorus grenades, smoke candles, and aircraft-delivered gases and chemicals.

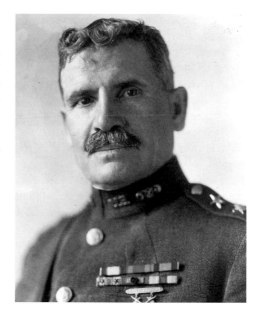

AMOS A. FRIES

Gas offered advantages both practical and psychological. Tear gas was far more effective than other means of riot control, because it "will fill cellars, hallways, mine shafts and extend in every direction in which a breeze is blowing." Rioters could not hide from its effects, the manual continued, because "when a cloud is turned loose," it covers "all areas with a speed which gives no time for aught but instant flight." The result would be "a stampede even in the most determined crowd." Hence, gas should be used on the edges of a mob, where flight would be possible, to cause disintegration in what would have been a compact and threatening body. Channels of escape should always be predetermined by officers before their troops use gas or chemical agents, to give crowds every possible means of dispersal and to prevent stampede injuries and extended exposure. (Massive doses against trapped individuals, as many CWS officers knew, could prove harmful if not fatal.) Properly used, gas seemed to its enthusiastic advocates the long-sought riot control panacea: "members of a mob once gassed and dispersed may recover from the effect within an hour, but will not attempt to withstand a gas cloud without protection. In addition to this, the news of the use of gas and its effects will have spread throughout the locality and no further organized resistance will be met with."

---

[34] Memo, AG for CGs, All Corps Areas, 7 Sep 21, sub: Use of Chemical Warfare Equipment for Riot Duty, RG 60, Glasser Files, NARA; U.S. War Department, Chemical Warfare Service, *Provisional Instructions for the Control of Mobs by Chemical Warfare* (Chemical Warfare Service, 21 November 1921), contained at U.S. Army Center of Military History, Washington, D.C. Unless otherwise stated this section is drawn from *Provisional Instructions*, pp. 2–4, 8–9, 11–18.

The final sections of the manual detailed the duties of the CWS staff officer and CWS troops in a civil disturbance situation. These troops were to be the sole dispersing agents of tear gases and chemicals and responsible for all matters pertaining to their use during any riot. Chemical warfare troops were to supply all forces with proper notification of the impending use of gases, with protective gear, and with information on the effects of the gases to be used on the targeted crowds. A final chapter entitled "Tactical Problems in Riot Duty" provided the work sheets, reports, and forms necessary for the legal and proper use of chemicals in any civil disorder.

Before the Chemical Warfare Service could actually begin to issue weapons and train troops, the Army once again reversed its position and prohibited the use of tear gases and chemicals against civil populations. This action resulted from the Washington Conference on the Limitation of Armaments, which, in January 1922, forbade "the use in war of asphyxiating, poisonous or other gases and all analogous liquids, materials or devices." Until the entire international legal issue concerning the use of gases and chemicals by military forces was resolved, the War Department stopped distribution of even nonlethal weapons to the corps areas. However the United States failed to ratify the treaty, and, as a result, in July 1922 the Army again changed its policy and authorized the use of tear gas in civil disorders.[35]

The War Department forwarded chemical weapons to each corps area from the Edgewood Arsenal near Baltimore. Commanders were instructed to begin immediate training not only of regular troops but also of National Guard units in their corps areas, who would probably be the first to arrive at any scene of disorder. The War Department further thought it prudent to require that a trained adviser from the Chemical Warfare Service be on hand whenever gas was requested, to ensure that it was being used in the proper quantities and places.[36] In one respect, Army instructions went one step further than any previously issued: before gas was used, corps area commanders were to announce publicly that tear gas was being employed in lieu of deadly weapons, that absolutely no permanent injury to health would result from gas exposure in the open, and that this course of action made it "possible for the military authorities to carry out the duty imposed on them of maintaining law and order without having to destroy the lives of our own citizens." Commanders were assured that the War Department would issue a similar statement after it was notified of the use of gas in a civil disorder.[37]

Rapid and contrary changes in Army policy regarding the use of gas were reflected in civil disturbance manuals and eventually in Army doctrine. In the first half of the 1920s considerable confusion existed as to what gases and chemicals could be used and under what circumstances, and even if their possession was allowable under international agreements. The League of Nations Geneva Conference in May 1925 renewed the questions regarding the use of gases that had been discussed at the Washington conference three years before. In June the league reaffirmed its earlier position favoring the prohibition of the use

[35] Jones, "Tear Gas," p. 164; Spiers, *Chemical Warfare*, pp. 40–44; AG to I Corps Area, 21 Jul 22, sub: Use of Tear Gas by Troops on Strike Duty, in Chemical Warfare Service Policy Book, 1921–1940, "Black Book," U.S. Army Chemical, Research, Development, Engineering Center Historical Office, Aberdeen Proving Ground.
[36] Chemical Warfare Service Policy Book; Spiers, *Chemical Warfare*, pp. 36, 43–44.
[37] AG to I Corps Area, 21 Jul 22, sub: Use of Tear Gas by Troops on Strike Duty.

of chemical agents, and adding the phrase "or other gases" to the earlier declaration. The United States was one of the forty-one powers that signed the protocol. Again facing the prospect of a total, worldwide ban of all chemical agents for antipersonnel purposes, Fries marshaled extensive opposition to the Geneva Protocol within the Senate and among private and public interest groups, including the American Legion, the Veterans of Foreign Wars, the Association of Medical Surgeons, and the American Chemical Society. Largely due to these efforts, the Geneva Protocol was withdrawn from Senate consideration and not ratified by the United States for decades. Riot-control gases, or such agents as those favored by the Chemical Warfare Service for use in domestic disturbances, were again entirely acceptable for the Army to use.[38]

The War Department had defined a gas policy by the time of the 1932 Bonus March, in which federal troops used chemical agents "somewhat indiscriminately" against the Bonus Expeditionary Force (*see Chapter 16*). The 1932 decision to use tear gas was significant; the Army had become convinced that use of nonlethal gases and chemicals was justified because they saved lives. In 1935–1936 the Army devoted considerable space in the domestic disturbance section of its basic field manual to the use of chemicals in civil disturbances. The manual emphasized that experiences of National Guard and police units had demonstrated the effectiveness of chemicals in handling mobs without loss of life. If the use of force was necessary, Army leaders were informed, "irritant chemical agents will frequently be more effective than firearms, will produce only temporary and non-injurious physical reactions, and may therefore relieve the responsible officer from the onus of having caused bloodshed." By the mid-1930s chemical riot-control agents had become important and standard weapons in the Army's arsenal for dealing with civil disturbances.[39]

The advent of tear gas slowly began to change general Army thinking about civil disorders. The decision to use tear gas and chemical agents before using deadly weapons indicated an increasing concern among many Army leaders about the need for more humane treatment of adversaries in a civil disorder—even those considered hard-core radicals. Many recognized that, whatever the political ideology of rioters or causes precipitating a civil disturbance, most radicals, striking workers, and members of the mob were American citizens whose injury or death would not necessarily improve chances for domestic stability or calm. Nevertheless, some officers still foresaw the possibility of a radical insurrection of such magnitude against the government that suppressing it would require full-blown combat tactics and the fullest possible use of lethal military force.

In the minds of many military leaders during the 1930s the phrase *domestic disorder* was still synonymous with radical insurrection and Communist revolution. This lingering concern was reflected both in Army civil disturbance doctrine and in the public and private statements of officers and enlisted men. As late as 1936 about one-half of the current field manual treating domestic disturbances was essentially a reissue of the information on

---

[38] Wil D. Verwey, *Riot Control Agents and Herbicides in War: Their Humanitarian, Toxicological, Ecological, Military, Polemological, and Legal Aspects* (Leyden, Netherlands: A.W. Sijthoff, 1977), pp. 225–28; Spiers, *Chemical Warfare*, pp. 44–46. The 1925 Geneva Protocol was eventually resubmitted to Congress by President Richard Nixon in 1970. It was ratified by the Senate in 1975, minus the tear gas proviso.

[39] Roger Daniels, *The Bonus March* (Westport: Greenwood, 1971), pp. 168, 303–06.

equipment, tactics, and offensive actions in urban areas that had been in various orders and regulations for the past forty years, and in Dowell's manuals for over a decade. Public, government, and Army concern for more prudent and humane actions was paradoxically combined in Army civil disturbance literature with a continuing fascination with the use of deadly force and, in extreme circumstances, of combat tactics.[40]

Given the types of weapons and tactics authorized for riot duty prior to the decision to use tear gases, and considering traditional, conservative Army attitudes toward labor organizations and what was vaguely termed *radicalism* by military and civilian leaders alike, it is a tribute to Army personnel that they showed such "respect for the principle that no more severe steps should be taken than are absolutely essential to end the disorder." The full might of federal military power rarely had been used against civilians in domestic disorders, although Army actions in the 1863 New York draft riots, 1894 Pullman Strike, and 1932 Bonus March came close to excess, indicating the latent desire among many in the military to use familiar combat tactics and lethal force instead of less practiced and less familiar nonlethal riot control measures.[41] The perception that crowds challenging civil authority were public enemies was evident during the Bonus March of 1932. Several Army participants in this incident gave weight to the suggestion that, although doctrine had changed toward the use of nonlethal force, attitudes of some military personnel had not substantially changed from those of their late nineteenth-century predecessors.

Maj. George S. Patton, Jr., wrote a paper in November 1932 after the summer dispersal of the Bonus Marchers that represented the older attitudes. Entitled "Federal Troops in Domestic Disturbances," Patton's paper was similar in tone and substance to Dowell's manuals of the 1920s and reminiscent of late nineteenth-century military works on civil disturbances. "A savage document," in the opinion of Patton's biographer, the paper argued that, if gas was ineffective against a mob, the troops should open fire and from nearby buildings sharpshooters should pick off mob leaders. "Always fire for effect," urged the future Third U.S. Army commander. "If you must fire do a good job—a few casualties become martyrs, a large number an object lesson." Even Patton, however, believed that breaking up the mob was the main Army objective: "When a mob starts to move keep it on the run, but always leave it a line of retreat—a cornered rat will fight desperately," he warned. But if any rioters resist, "they must be killed." Troops guarding buildings were urged to establish a deadline beyond which rioters would be shot. "Be sure to kill the first one who tries," Patton wrote, "and leave him there to discourage the others." Concerning legalities, Patton believed that "an armed mob resisting federal troops is an armed enemy. To aid it is treason. This may not be law, but it is fact. When blood starts running law stops, because, by the fact of bloodshed, it has demonstrated its futility."[42]

Patton's harsh opinions demonstrated the gap between the trend of Army policy toward the use of more prudent and humane nonlethal tactics and the hard, conservative opinions of many Army commanders. Such attitudes and opinions were still evident in official Army regulations, as indicated by the August 1935 *Basic Field Manual*, FM 27–15. Like its 1917–1918 predecessor, *Military Protection, United States Guards*, the manual was

---

[40] U.S. War Department, *Basic Field Manual (BFM), 1 March 1936*, vol. 7, *Military Law*, pt. 3, "Domestic Disturbances," pp. 7–8, 12–14, 16–24.

[41] Rich, *President and Civil Disorder*, p. 215.

[42] Martin Blumenson, *The Patton Papers, 1885–1940* (Boston: Houghton Mifflin, 1972), pp. 898–900.

extremely harsh in tone and substance, reflecting the hard-line views of Chief of Staff Douglas MacArthur, who figured prominently in its creation. An entire section of FM 27–15 dealt solely with domestic disturbances. It clearly delineated the responsibility of civil authorities in a civil disorder, constitutional and statutory provisions governing the use of federal troops, and the necessary procedures to be followed to apply for, and gain the aid of, federal troops in event of disorders beyond municipal and state control. Further sections addressed the legal and practical matters involved in the implementation and conduct of government by martial law and the civil liability of military personnel.[43]

Although tear gases and chemicals figured more prominently in the Army arsenal by 1935, many military officials, including the chief of staff, still considered the methods and means for quelling a disorder a tactical question best answered by the immediate commanding officer in a riot situation. The implication that full combat force was sometimes suitable for use against civilian crowds was evident in the statement that "the equipment required by Federal troops for . . . suppression of domestic disturbances will not differ materially from that required for ordinary occasions of field service." FM 27–15, like previous manuals, discussed the use of offensive combat weapons such as airplanes, armored cars, artillery, cavalry, hand grenades, machine guns, tanks, 37-mm. guns, and three-inch mortars against civilians, although considerably less space was devoted to the use and description of these traditional combat arms than in previous manuals. Officers were instructed that "as a rule rifle fire should be used against a crowd only as a last resort." But information was still included on how to engage in offensive actions against cities, how to occupy a center of domestic disturbance, how to use antimob tactical formations, and how best to attack or defend barricades and buildings.[44]

Despite the overwhelmingly harsh tone of FM 27–15, that part dealing with tear gases and chemicals showed the growing emphasis within the Army on nonlethal riot control methods. One entire chapter, comprising one-third of the civil disturbance portion, provided detailed descriptions of the types of chemicals and gases available, how best they were employed, and how military personnel could protect themselves against their effects while on duty. A special section detailed illustrative problems involving the use of gas, such as actions against riots in penal institutions, lynch mobs, or mobs barricaded in open country who were equipped with gas masks. Although neither Army regulations nor FM 27–15 suggested using gas as the initial means for quelling a civil disorder, the prominence given to the use of chemicals in the 1935 manual implied that it was the next best step if the mere presence of troops already on the scene failed to have the desired effect. Gas was certainly preferable to volleys of rifle fire.

The 1935 version of the Army's *Basic Field Manual* was available to the public through the Superintendent of Documents and aroused a storm of controversy and criticism, especially among liberals, civil libertarians, labor groups, and critics of the military. The manual and the attitude and philosophy behind Army civil disturbance doctrine that it

---

[43] U.S. War Department, The Judge Advocate General, *Basic Field Manual/FM 27–15*, vol. 7, *Military Law*, pt. 3, "Domestic Disturbances" (Washington, D.C.: Government Printing Office, 1935), pp. 1–22 (hereafter cited as *FM 27–15, 1935*). The Army revised and reissued *FM 27–15* in March 1936 and February 1941. Except for minor changes, such as a restricted classification, a further deemphasis on the use of combat weapons for riot control, and information about improved chemical weapons, these versions are similar to the 1935 edition.

[44] *FM 27–15, 1935*, 7:12–14, 17.

conveyed were denounced as reactionary, antidemocratic, antilabor, and fascist. Although the manual contained little that had not been printed in earlier manuals and civil disturbance literature, it was the first such official Army document regarding civil disorders available for purchase by the general public. The public outrage over the manual's contents gave a clear signal to many Army leaders that opinion on the proper role of federal troops in civil affairs, and especially on the use of lethal force and "shoot to kill orders" that allegedly allowed federal troops to shed blood with impunity, had changed dramatically since the Bonus March of 1932 and the advent of the New Deal. Groups and ideologies that had previously been considered serious threats to the nation's security and existence were now accepted entities. Army Chief of Staff General Malin Craig was forced to defend publicly the contents and wording of the document against press attacks in the *New York Post*, *New York World-Telegram*, the *Nation*, the *New Republic*, and *Women Today* and stated that "while some of the instructions . . . may seem over-drastic . . . it must be remembered that the regular Army is called on to suppress a riot only when police and national guardsmen have been unable to control it." Although Craig was supposedly more liberal than many of his Army colleagues, the chief of staff indicated that the Army had "no intention of remanding MacArthur's instructions" as outlined in FM 27–15.[45]

This determination did not last long. Bowing to public pressure in early 1936, Craig publicly ordered that the manual be withdrawn from circulation and use. All copies in the hands of individuals and on file in offices were ordered to "be secured and returned to this headquarters." The controversy over Army civil disturbance policy quickly subsided, and the manual was reissued in March 1936. In all respects, except for the addition of a Restricted classification that kept the manual from the hands of the public, the 1936 version was just the same as the banned 1935 version. It remained in force until superseded in 1941 by a new edition, which was also restricted to military personnel.[46]

The 1941 version of the *Basic Field Manual* represented the final revision to be undertaken prior to U.S. entry into World War II, and it guided Army riot-control actions on the home front throughout the war. Despite the earlier controversy, the new version differed only slightly from its predecessors. Except for a less detailed description of the combat weapons available for civil disturbance use and a short section entitled "Statutory Limitations and Authorizations," the revised manual was only a copy of its predecessors.[47]

By this time other moderating changes in doctrine had appeared. In 1937 the Army issued the first new regulations since 1923 covering the employment of federal troops in civil disorders. Tactical guidance on the use of musketry, artillery, bayonet, and saber, included in each set of regulations since 1894, was now omitted. The 1937 regulations began with a discussion of the legal restrictions governing the use of federal troops in a civil disturbance, and then they dealt with situations in which troops were legally authorized under the Constitution and by acts of Congress to combat civil disorders. Additional,

---

[45] George Seldes, *You Can't Do That: A Survey of the Forces Attempting, in the Name of Patriotism, To Make a Desert of the Bill of Rights* (New York: Modern Age, 1938), pp. 195–205, and *Witness to a Century: Encounters With the Noted, the Notorious, and the Three SOB's* (Boston: G. H. Hall, 1988), pp. 79–83.

[46] Seldes, *You Can't Do That*, pp. 202–03; U.S. War Department, *Basic Field Manual (BFM), 1 August 1935*, vol. 7, *Military Law*, pt. 3, "Domestic Disturbances," pp. 14, 30–67 at p. 3l; *BFM, 1 March 1936*, vol. 7, pt. 3, was marked "Restricted" but was otherwise identical to the 1935 *BFM*; *BFM (FM 27–15), 6 February 1941*. These appear to have superseded *Military Aid to the Civil Power* and its *Confidential Supplement to Military Aid.*

[47] *BFM (FM 27–15), 1941; FM 27–15* was superseded by *BFM 19–15* in July 1945.

special attention was given to the procedures that had to precede commitment of the Regular Army to any domestic disorder. All these updated instructions illustrated increased Army attention to legal procedures governing their domestic role and a decreased emphasis on the use of force, especially traditional combat weapons and tactics as in the past. These regulations served as a guide for federal intervention after 1937 and until further changes were made in July 1945.[48]

The creation and existence of a specific Army civil disturbance doctrine, supported by Army regulations, field manuals, and contingency plans, represented visible proof of the professional growth and maturation that took place in the Army during the interwar years concerning domestic disturbances. The differences in the Army's state of preparedness for dealing with domestic disorders in 1917 and in 1941 are striking. If the need arose, on the eve of World War II, federal leaders could call upon a professional military force, that in turn could consult a specific, detailed, and readily available corpus of regulations, manuals, and instructions to guide interventions in nearly any conceivable contingency. Of greatest importance to the future civil disturbance role of the Army by 1941 was the emphasis on the use of nonlethal force in quelling civil disorder and strict legal guidelines which assured that Army actions and procedures were within the letter of the law and authorized by the Constitution and federal statutes. This emphasis was perhaps the most enduring and beneficial legacy of Army doctrinal development during the interwar decades.

---

[48] Cf. AR 500–50, 6 June 1923, *Employment of Troops: Enforcement of the Laws*, paragraphs 1–7, 8, and AR 500–50, 5 April 1937, *Employment of Troops: Aid of Civil Authorities*, which omitted paragraph 8 in toto. There had been three changes to the 1923 regulation, the last being in 1933, but none affected the paragraph on tactics. See also AR 500–50, 17 July 1945, *Employment of Troops: Aid of Civil Authorities.*

CHAPTER 16

The Bonus March, 1932

The mob . . . was animated by the essence of revolution. The gentleness, the consideration with which they had been treated had been mistaken for weakness. . . . They were about to take over in some arbitrary way either the direct control of the government or else control it by indirect methods . . . a reign of terror was being started which may have led . . . to insurgency and insurrection.

—General Douglas MacArthur, 1932.

If during this operation a single shot had been fired, many would have died, for in the dark, on a flat plain, fire discipline could not have been maintained, and there was no cover.

—Maj. George S. Patton, 1932.

As government workers left their office buildings in downtown Washington, D.C., during the late afternoon of Thursday, 28 July 1932, they witnessed an unusual military procession. Led by a one-star general, a column of nearly 200 mounted cavalrymen, 300 infantrymen, and 5 tanks advanced southeast from the Ellipse, down Pennsylvania Avenue, toward 3d Street, Northwest, at the base of Capitol Hill. Instead of marching bands, colors with streamers, and dress uniforms, however, somber khaki uniforms, steel helmets, and grim expressions characterized the appearance of the troops. Accompanying the column in a staff car, Army Chief of Staff General Douglas MacArthur prepared to evict from the city a ragtag group of unemployed veterans known as the Bonus Expeditionary Force.

Not since the West Virginia coal mine wars of 1921 had so large and potent a federal military force taken to the field in a domestic disturbance. It would be the last major deployment of troops on riot duty before World War II. The fears of radicalism and urban insurrection, largely latent during the previous decade, resurfaced during the years immediately following the stock market crash of 1929 and the onset of the Great Depression. By 1932 the world had seen the consolidation of Mussolini's Fascist rule in Italy, Stalin's Communist rule in the Soviet Union, and increasingly successful attacks on the German Weimar Republic by Communists and Adolf Hitler's National Socialists. As the economic and social effects of the worldwide depression hit the United States, many Americans called for similarly drastic reactionary or radical changes. The public and many government leaders feared an attack against the American system by elements of both extreme left and extreme right wings. The advent of the 1932 Bonus March was to many a harbinger of revolution.

The Great Depression and the Background of the Bonus March

The Great Depression, the worst in American history, was three years old by 1932. Its effects on the nation were devastating. Industrial production had dropped to half the 1929 level, and construction of homes and office buildings had declined by over 80 percent. Banks foreclosed mortgages, eventually evicting more than a quarter-million families. At least 10 million people were unemployed by the end of 1931, a figure that had not yet peaked, with perhaps three times that number lacking steady employment. Of the unemployed, nearly 2 million drifted from city to city with their families, living in shanty towns called "Hoovervilles," a derisive reference to the Republican president who had been in office only six months prior to the stock market crash, but who was nonetheless blamed by many for the economic catastrophe and its continued ill effects on the nation.[1]

President Herbert C. Hoover tried seemingly proved techniques to move the economy back on track. He emphasized a limited and indirect governmental role, in keeping with a conservative Republican philosophy, and encouraged voluntary actions by private industry to maintain work forces and payrolls. Labor was similarly encouraged not to seek higher wages. Taxes were cut, credit was increased to banks, tariffs were raised, federal funds were grudgingly voted for entitlement and public works programs, and a moratorium was declared on war debts owed to the United States by foreign nations. In spite of these initiatives, most of which had little political or popular appeal, the economic situation worsened. Critics of the administration called for more direct and intensive government intervention in the economy, a course of action Hoover steadfastly refused to undertake.[2]

Although by 1932 many Americans were without hope, some veterans of World War I looked optimistically to an early payment of the Veterans' Compensation Certificate. In 1924 Congress had voted all veterans of World War I a bonus of $1.25 for every day served overseas or $1 for every day served within the United States—a lump sum of $2.4 billion, payable in 1945. In the spring of 1932 Congressman Wright Patman introduced a bill making the bonus payable at once. To help pressure Congress into passing it, Walter W. Waters, an unemployed former Army sergeant from Portland, Oregon, organized a band of 300 veterans to march in Washington, D.C. Within the next several weeks similar groups gathered in other cities. By May 1932 nearly 20,000 veterans, the so-called Bonus Expeditionary Force (BEF), boarded trains for the capital.[3]

The reception accorded the early contingents of the Bonus Expeditionary Force differed markedly from that given to Coxey's army forty years earlier. When Coxey and his followers had arrived in Washington, local citizens and government officials had greeted

[1] Irving Bernstein, *The Lean Years: A History of the American Worker, 1920–1933* (Boston: Houghton Mifflin, 1960), pp. 505–08; Oscar T. Barck, Jr., and Nelson M. Blake, *Since 1900: A History of the United States in Our Times,* 3d ed. (New York: Macmillan, 1959), p. 410; John Kenneth Galbraith, *The Great Crash, 1929* (Boston: Houghton Mifflin, 1955), pp. 173–74; William E. Leuchtenberg, *Franklin D. Roosevelt and the New Deal, 1932–1940* (New York: Harper & Row, 1963), pp. 1–3; Kevin McGoff, "The Bonus Army," *American History Illustrated* 12 (February 1978):29.

[2] Albert U. Romasco, *The Poverty of Abundance: Hoover, the Nation, and the Depression* (New York: Oxford University Press, 1965), pp. 13–23, 29–35, 182; Leuchtenberg, *Roosevelt and the New Deal,* pp. 13–14. See also Arthur M. Schlesinger, Jr., *The Age of Roosevelt,* vol. l, *The Crisis of the Old Order: 1919–1933* (Boston: Houghton Mifflin, 1957).

[3] Daniels, *The Bonus March,* pp. 46–64; McGoff, "The Bonus Army," pp. 29–30.

THE BEF CAMP AT ANACOSTIA FLATS

them with fear and hostility, reflecting strong public apprehensions of radicalism and the working class. But in 1932 city officials—many of them veterans, including Washington, D.C., Chief of Police Pelham D. Glassford—initially empathized with the marchers and helped the first contingents to set up temporary living quarters at twenty sites scattered throughout the city. Principal camps were located on Pennsylvania Avenue near 3d Street, Northwest, at 12th and C Streets, Southwest, and on the meadows east of the Anacostia River that were called the Flats.[4]

The relatively positive attitude held by local authorities toward the Bonus marchers was not shared by all officials in the Washington area. Some conservative officials, including high-ranking members of the War Department and the Army general staff, were opposed to the idea of allowing almost 20,000 unemployed veterans to camp in the city. The marchers aroused military concerns of radical activity, especially from the American Communist Party, which many officers believed might try to exploit discontent among the unemployed and recruit new members.[5]

---

[4] Rich, *President and Civil Disorder*, p. 168; Donald J. Lisio, *The President and Protest: Hoover, Conspiracy, and the Bonus Riot* (Columbia: University of Missouri Press, 1974), p. 107; McGoff, "The Bonus Army," p. 30; "The Human Side of the Bonus Army," *Literary Digest* 113 (25 June 1932):28.

[5] Thomas W. Collier, "The Army and the Great Depression," *Parameters* 18 (September 1988), p. 102; Memos, Glassford for Hurley, 28 May 32; Wright for MacArthur, 31 May 32; Payne for McSwain, 25 Jun 32; all in RG 407, Records of the Office of the Adjutant General, U.S. Army, Central Decimal Files, 1926–1939, AGO 240: Bonus March (5–28–32), NARA. See also *Report From the Chief of Staff, U.S.A., to the Secretary of War, on the Employment of Federal Troops in Civil Disturbances in the District of Columbia, July 28–30, 1932*, 15 Aug 32, World War Veterans Bonus March, Herbert Hoover Presidential Library (HPL), Iowa (hereafter cited as *Rpt, Chief of Staff*); Lisio, *President and Protest*, pp. 87–89, 105–06; D. Clayton James, *The Years of MacArthur, 1880–1941* (Boston: Houghton Mifflin, 1970), 1:382–83, 408.

American Communists did see an opportunity in the Bonus March and had already provided ample evidence of their intent to exploit it and the Great Depression for propaganda purposes. In early 1930 the Communists led demonstrations in Cleveland, Philadelphia, Chicago, Los Angeles, and New York City. In December 1931 about 1,500 unemployed workers, including many Communists, staged a hunger march in Washington, D.C., and a few weeks later 12,000 jobless men marched in Pittsburgh as a signal to Congress that labor expected new laws and new programs to end the depression. Occasional armed clashes gave the party other opportunities. In March 1932 policemen guarding the Ford Motor Company's River Rouge plant in Dearborn, Michigan, fired upon an angry, rock-throwing mob, killing 4 men and wounding over 50. During the funeral procession that followed, Communists unfurled red banners, and pictures of Lenin.[6]

The first rumor of an alleged Communist plan to subvert the BEF movement emerged in June 1932. A secret service agent who was present at a meeting of the John Reed Club in New York City reported to his superiors in Washington that Communist leaders had organized a "Workers' Ex-Service Men's League" to act as shock troops to train Communists in the capital for street fighting, culminating in a forced entry upon the grounds of the White House. Duly alarmed, Chief Glassford publicized the report, perhaps to lay the groundwork for an appeal to the president for federal military assistance. During the next several weeks, District police rigorously segregated the roughly "45 'actual communists' and 150 of 'their unintelligent followers'" from the Bonus marchers already present in the city, compelling the Communists to occupy a single encampment at 12th and C Streets, Southwest, far removed from the White House, the Capitol, and the main BEF camps. The Bonus army helped in the task by establishing its own "military police" to round up, interrogate, and—to Glassford's eventual alarm—physically abuse any Communists who entered the camps or attempted to distribute party literature.[7]

Though somewhat concerned about Communist activity, Hoover refused to be swayed by pressures from some congressmen to supplement city police with either federal deputy marshals or the Army. Barring solid evidence, such as an overt insurrection, he defended the rights of citizens, including Communists, to parade and peacefully protest government policies. Some Army officers, however, disagreed with their commander in chief. Standing in a long tradition of viewing with alarm the supposed schemes of European-bred radicals seeking to bring about revolution in American society, they connected the emotions of the Communist scare to the newer dangers of the depression. According to one biographer of MacArthur, "members of the General Staff probably viewed all outbursts of violence and unrest with red-tinted glasses."[8]

Perhaps the most ardent and influential anti-Communist in the high command was Maj. Gen. George Van Horn Moseley, MacArthur's deputy chief of staff. Moseley's rabid anticommunism dated back to the Bolshevik Revolution and Russia's betrayal of the Allied cause in World War I. Since then Moseley had believed in the existence of a ruthless and ceaseless Communist conspiracy to subvert Western democracies and overthrow capitalism. In 1932

---

[6] James, *Years of MacArthur*, 1:385–86; Daniels, *The Bonus March*, pp. 67–68, 212.

[7] Lisio, *President and Protest*, pp. 94–95, 102; Daniels, *The Bonus March*, pp. 108–09, 267–68; McGoff, "The Bonus Army," pp. 30–32.

[8] Quote from James, *Years of MacArthur*, 1:383–84; Lisio, *President and Protest*, p. 105; Daniels, *The Bonus March*, pp. 69–70.

Moseley had not yet become clearly and publicly aligned with American right-wing, anti-Semitic, and pro-Nazi groups as he did later, but he had long urged his confidants to support legislation calling for the deportation of foreign-born radicals and the outlawing of the Communist Party. In correspondence with several prominent Americans in May 1932 Moseley even advocated a military coup d'etat in the United States should the government prove unable to solve the nation's problems. When Wright Patman reintroduced the Bonus bill in 1932, Moseley adjudged the Bonus marchers as "veterans, Communists, and Bums" and offered his support to a conservative New York law firm in lobbying vigorously against passage of the bill.[9]

GEORGE VAN HORN MOSELEY

The Bonus March occurred at a time when anticommunism again permeated the thoughts of the public and segments of the Army general staff. Yet its leaders showed little interest at first, for they were struggling to counteract congressional budget slashing without assistance from their commander in chief. A Quaker by upbringing, President Hoover supported the objectives of the Geneva Disarmament Conference and supported congressmen seeking further cutbacks in an already meager Army budget. When General MacArthur became Army chief of staff on 21 November 1930, he devoted the limited funds available, and most of his subsequent efforts, to maintaining the Army at its manpower strength of 133,000, at the expense of equipment and weapons modernization and planning and doctrinal development. Preoccupied with more important things and content in the knowledge that the Army was prepared to cope with any disturbance in Washington as outlined in the Third Corps Area Emergency Plan White, MacArthur dismissed at first the Bonus March as a minor consideration.[10]

However, during its early weeks several factors changed his perspective. The growing number of unemployed veterans in the District of Columbia began to irritate both the members of Congress and the local populace. MacArthur thought that the eviction of the Bonus marchers from the city would demonstrate to Congress the Army's value as a

---

[9] Reference to Moseley's coup plot is in David Burner, *Herbert Hoover: A Public Life* (New York: Alfred A. Knopf, 1979), pp. 306–07, 408n.1. See also Ltrs, Moseley to the following: Van Ostrand, 19 Feb 32; ASW, 9 Oct 30; Grenville Clark, Law Firm of Root, Clark, & Buckner, New York, 3, 6, 7 Jun and 15 Jul 32; Pershing, 15 Jul 32; and Ltrs, Clark to Moseley, 6 Jun and 15 Jul 32; all in George van Horn Moseley Papers, Library of Congress, Washington, D.C. (hereafter cited as Moseley Papers).

[10] Lisio, *President and Protest*, pp. 90–92; Collier, "The Army and the Great Depression," pp. 102–08. For a contrary view, see John R. M. Wilson, "The Quaker and the Sword: Herbert Hoover's Relationship With the Military," *Military Affairs* 38 (April 1974):41–47.

guardian of the domestic peace and perhaps result in additional funding. Furthermore, nurtured by Moseley's antiradical jeremiads, MacArthur's own anticommunism received new impetus in June when he learned that Communists intended to lead a protest march on the White House. Given MacArthur's personality and ambition, it is possible to conclude that he saw in the efficient Army performance of an operation involving a civil disorder the kind of publicity that might be useful to a political aspirant. In any case, he came to believe that the presence of radicals in the march implied Communist domination of the Bonus Expeditionary Force.[11]

New Planning and Preparation

The Military District of Washington's version of Emergency Plan White had been drafted in the early 1920s. The plan's authors had not anticipated a disorder involving up to 20,000 military veterans, nor the alleged willingness of a revolutionary party to lead those veterans in a Communist insurrection. In May 1932 Moseley warned MacArthur that the plan should be revised and adapted to current events and Army capabilities. Appealing to his chief's vanity, he pointed out that in a crisis the country would look to the Army and, above all, to General Douglas MacArthur for strong, decisive, and effective leadership. MacArthur ordered the revision.[12]

The task devolved upon Brig. Gen. Perry L. Miles, commander of the 16th Infantry Brigade stationed at Fort Meade, Maryland. Newspaper and intelligence reports helped to shape his revisions. He believed that, although Communist leaders claimed credit for instigating the Bonus March, the overwhelming number of marchers had thus far resisted all Communist attempts at infiltration and control. Nonetheless the Communists could be expected to exploit every opportunity to provoke a violent confrontation between veterans and authorities. Before troops marched, therefore, the on-scene commanders should give the non-Communist veterans an opportunity to depart. Against those who remained, they should employ tear gas as a first resort. Meanwhile, the 16th Infantry Brigade should allot sufficient troops to guard the White House, the Treasury, and the Bureau of Engraving and Printing, the Capitol, and other critical points.[13]

Miles' revised plan comprised a detailed scenario for the concentration of troops, vehicles, and horses drawn from posts in the greater Washington area at the Ellipse behind the White House. From Fort Myer, Virginia, along the western boundary of Arlington National Cemetery, to the Ellipse, the 2d Squadron, 3d Cavalry, was to move by truck, except for one troop on horseback. The troopers were to bring a truck-mounted 75-mm. gun and a T–4 armored car on loan from the Aberdeen Proving Ground—a first-time, experimental use of these vehicles in a civil distrubance. With other trucks from

---

[11] James, *Years of MacArthur*, 1:386, 413–14; George H. Moseley, "The Bonus March," Military Rpts, Statements, and Notes, 1899–1938, pp. 1–2, and "One Soldier's Journey," 2:138–39, both in Moseley Papers. See also Lisio, *President and Protest*, p. 289.

[12] Lisio, *President and Protest*, p. 92; James, *Years of MacArthur*, 1:386, 413–14. See also Moseley, "The Bonus March," pp. 1–2, and "One Soldier's Journey," 2:138–39.

[13] Memo, Miles for MacArthur, 4 Jun 32, sub: Emergency Plan White for the District of Columbia, RG 394, Records of the U.S. Army Continental Commands, 1920–1942, Entry 321, File A46–485, Report of Operations Against the Bonus Marchers, Military District of Washington–III Corps Area, NARA.

Baltimore's Fort Holabird, troops of the 3d Battalion, 12th Infantry, were to drive from Fort Washington, located across the Potomac River from Mount Vernon in Virginia. The precise routes of approach were to be determined by the unit commanders. All troops were to be equipped with steel helmets, gas masks, and live ammunition.[14]

As an additional precaution, Army intelligence agents and District of Columbia police began coordinating their information and activities as early as 25 May. Col. Alfred T. Smith, the assistant chief of staff, G–2, War Department General Staff, synthesized intelligence and submitted daily reports to MacArthur. MacArthur decided to expand this intelligence network after a commencement speech he gave in Pittsburgh on 8 June was heckled by students when he declared that toleration of pacifism and radicalism would lead America to "dust and ashes." His belief that radicalism had now gained a hold on vast numbers of Americans probably intensified by pique, MacArthur ordered all corps area intelligence officers to begin collecting information on Communist infiltration of BEF groups passing through their areas.[15]

During the remainder of June and early July, however, corps area commanders failed to uncover any solid evidence of Communist direction or influence on the Bonus March movement. In addition, Smith and Glassford concluded that the BEF leaders were moderates who actually feared being branded as radicals by the press, public, and government. Far from plotting revolution, the two men concluded, the marchers merely wanted advance payment of the money they believed they had earned and had been promised by Congress and the nation. Both men agreed further that the only danger posed by the Communists to the city was that of inciting violent clashes between otherwise peaceful and law-abiding marchers and the police.[16]

The Democrat-controlled House of Representatives passed the Bonus bill by a vote of 209 to 176 on 15 June 1932, but under threat of a presidential veto the Republican-controlled Senate defeated the measure by 62 to 18. Convinced that Congress could be persuaded to reconsider, the veterans of the Bonus Expeditionary Force were determined to stay in the capital until their demands were met. Congress, however, adjourned on 16 July without having taken any further action on the bonus issue, except to vote $100,000 to help defray homeward travel expenses of the Bonus army. Though the marchers now had no reason to remain in the city, over 11,000 stayed on and were soon joined by more new recruits. In all probability they simply had no other place to go. However, the failure of the Bonus army to disperse convinced MacArthur more than ever of its sinister intent. His beliefs were reinforced when marchers conducted mass demonstrations in front of the White House on three occasions between 16 and 26 July.[17]

Even the moderate president was growing weary of the marchers. To Hoover the White House demonstrations—which in turn triggered other incidents of protest in the

---

[14] Memo, Miles for MacArthur, 4 Jun 32, sub: Emergency Plan White for D.C.; Ltr, Hof to CO, Aberdeen Proving Ground, 4 Jun 32, RG 394, Entry 321, File A46–485, NARA.

[15] Memo, Smith for AG, 10 Jun 32, RG 407, File 240, Bonus March, NARA; see also Daily Rpts, CofS, G-2, to MacArthur, 25 May to Jun 32, pts. 12 and 13, RG 165, Records of the War Department General Staff, Military Intelligence Division, 1917–1941, File 10110–2542: Bonus March, 1932, NARA.

[16] Ibid.

[17] *Rpt, Chief of Staff,* 15 Aug 32, HPL; Rich, *President and Civil Disorder,* pp. 169–70; Daniels, *The Bonus March,* p. 135; Lisio, *President and Protest,* pp. 154–55.

city—were a gratuitous provocation of the federal government. For two months he and Chief Glassford had resisted strong pressures to take more forceful measures in dealing with the marchers, had tolerated their presence, and had largely supported their rights. Their continued presence was irritating, unnecessary, and fruitless. From 21 to 27 July, therefore, he approved plans for U.S. Treasury agents to eject marchers from several abandoned buildings that they had occupied on Pennsylvania Avenue, ostensibly to clear the sites in preparation for constructing new offices for the Treasury Department. Evictions of marchers from Anacostia, 12th and C Streets, Southwest, and the numerous smaller camps by District police were scheduled to follow. Hoover had at last "flung down the gauntlet, apparently with backing from his cabinet members, generals, and the district commissioners."[18]

Escorted by 800 policemen, about half the District of Columbia's force, treasury agents began evictions on the morning of 28 July. Although many grumbled and 20 Communists verbally harassed police and threw bricks, the marchers left the 3d and Pennsylvania Avenue site without major resistance. A few persons were arrested in scuffles with police. But as the evictions continued into the early afternoon, violence increased. As police began to evict marchers from buildings in the next block, bricks were again thrown, and the police responded with nightsticks. In the ensuing melee several policemen were badly beaten, many marchers were injured, and two men were fatally wounded. The deaths signaled a dramatic escalation in the confrontation.[19]

Concentration and the Decision To Intervene

In the judgment of Chief Glassford, the violence of the morning left the police too exhausted to advance against other BEF campsites. He explained the situation to the city's Board of Commissioners, but they misinterpreted his request for a temporary delay in the evictions as a request for federal troops. Hoover received their telephone call for military aid in the early afternoon of 28 July. When he hesitated to dispatch troops solely on the basis of a verbal request, the commissioners forwarded a written memorandum that detailed the rioting and concluded: "it is the opinion of the [Police Chief], in which the Commissioners concur, that it will be impossible to maintain law and order except by the use of firearms which will make the situation a dangerous one; it is believed, however, that the presence of Federal troops in some number will obviate the seriousness of the situation and result in less violence and bloodshed. The Commissioners . . . request that they be given the assistance of Federal troops, in maintaining law and order in the District of Columbia."[20]

So formal a request was probably unnecessary. Under RS 5298 (now changed to Section 332, Title 10, *United States Code*), the president could have granted military aid

---

[18] Lisio, *President and Protest*, pp. 152–54; Minute Books of Commissioners' Orders, 21 Jul 32, RG 351, Records of the Government of the District of Columbia, NARA. See also James, *Years of MacArthur*, 1:395.

[19] Memo, Perry for Smith, 26 Jul 32, RG 165, File 10110–2542, NARA. See also Burner, *Herbert Hoover*, p. 310; James, *Years of MacArthur*, 1:396; Heaps, *Riots, U.S.A.*, p. 136; *Rpt, Chief of Staff*, 15 Aug 32, HPL.

[20] *Rpt, Chief of Staff,* 15 Aug 32, HPL; Daniels, *The Bonus March*, pp. 163–66; Lisio, *President and Protest*, pp. 183–85; Burner, *Herbert Hoover*, p. 31. For the request, see Ltr, Reichelfelder, Board of Commissioners, to Hoover, 28 Jul 32, RG 407, File 240, NARA.

once the commissioners reported to him that a mob was resisting the authority of a federal agency on federal territory and that the police and the courts were powerless to take action. Hoover's insistence upon a form prescribed for governors and state legislatures may have been motivated by the long-standing tradition against injecting military force into a civil matter without an array of preliminary steps as required under RS 5297 (now Section 331, Title 10, *United States Code*). The commissioners' request that the police "be given the assistance of Federal troops" had added significance. Since the courts and the police continued to function, the board was not asking that the civil power be supplanted by the military but rather reinforced, either by the mere presence of troops, serving as a moral deterrent, or by actual troop participation beside the police in operations to evict the marchers.

So modest a role, however, was less than MacArthur and his subordinates wanted. After reviewing Emergency Plan White for the District of Columbia, MacArthur, Moseley, and Maj. Gen. Blanton Winship, the judge advocate general, had concluded that once a riot erupted the president could and should declare martial law. Under such circumstances the Army was free to arrest and detain suspects without writs of habeas corpus. Although harsh for most situations, the generals believed such actions to be fully justified in the nation's capital, where the disruption of government operations could paralyze the country and encourage a Communist revolution. In this respect MacArthur's views harked back to those of General Hancock, who had commanded troops on riot duty during the Great Railway Strike of 1877, and of General Nelson Miles, who had commanded troops in the Pullman Strike of 1894. Although MacArthur sought more power during the Bonus March than his predecessors did in their respective situations, all three commanders shared the belief that once civil authorities called for federal military aid the resulting situation was fully a military matter in which civil officials should not subsequently interfere.[21]

The notion that the president might ignore Emergency Plan White and refuse to declare a state of insurrection apparently had never occurred to MacArthur, Moseley, or Winship. On 28 July Winship proposed an eleventh-hour modification of the revised Emergency Plan White indicative of the preponderant role the three generals expected the Army to play. Beginning with the mobilization of a sufficient force, Winship's revision assigned to MacArthur and his field commander, General Perry Miles, direction over Chief Glassford and the District of Columbia police force, an assignment which was not authorized under any existing federal statute or Army regulation. Once the troops had deployed to the areas of heaviest resistance, MacArthur was to offer BEF leaders the opportunity to depart in trucks operated and escorted by federal troops. Following the departures of those who accepted the offer, the chief of staff was to issue the president's proclamation to cease and disperse. If any marchers remained, the troops were to arrest and convey them under armed guard to their states of residence. Although MacArthur never concurred in full with this modification, he agreed with Winship that the crisis could not end while sizable numbers of marchers remained free to reassemble within or near the District.[22]

---

[21] Lisio, *President and Protest*, pp. 194–96; Memo, Winship for MacArthur, 28 Jul 32, app. 3, Container 375, Bonus Army, HPL.

[22] Memo, Winship for MacArthur, 28 Jul 32, app. 3.

Unaware of Winship's proposal and MacArthur's selective acceptance of it, Hoover approved the first step of the revised Emergency Plan White, the concentration of forces at the Ellipse. The movement began at 1340, minutes after the president had received the written request of the Board of Commissioners. Under the supervision of Miles, the 2d Squadron, 3d Cavalry, with an attached platoon of five tanks, and the 3d Battalion, 12th Infantry, moved by trucks from Fort Myer and Fort Washington to the Ellipse. The concentration took nearly three hours.[23]

For the 2d Squadron, the movement was uneventful, as recorded by its executive officer, Maj. George S. Patton, Jr.: "we moved in column of fours without security detachments; the tanks in trucks followed by themselves [at a distance] of about one mile. No outposts were established." Before crossing the Potomac River into the District of Columbia, the 3d Battalion, commanded by Lt. Col. Louis A. Kunzig, experienced mechanical difficulties with the trucks but reached the Ellipse shortly after 1600. When all units had assembled, supply clerks issued each man tear-gas grenades.[24] Though the troops were assembled, armed and ready, their concentration in no way committed Hoover to use them. As revised by Miles in June, Emergency Plan White had merely streamlined the process of intervention by pre-positioning the troops in case the president should exercise the option of using them.

Between 1340 and 1455 on 28 July, Hoover met with Secretary of War Patrick Hurley and General MacArthur. Despite Hurley's view that mob defiance constituted insurrection and that the marchers represented the vanguard of a Communist revolution, Hoover flatly refused to proclaim a state of insurrection or to declare martial law. Accepting the commissioners' view that troops were needed only to support the police, Hoover unequivocally ruled out a strictly military operation as unnecessary under the current circumstances.[25] Instead, by his direction, Secretary Hurley issued an order for MacArthur "to cooperate fully with the District of Columbia Police force which is now in charge." With this order the president officially sanctioned federal military intervention. MacArthur's troops were to surround the Bonus marchers at the 3d and Pennsylvania riot area, while District police cleared it. During the operation women and children were to be "accorded every consideration and kindness," and the troops were to "use all humanity consistent with the due execution of this order." Subsequently, MacArthur's men were to surround the other encampments, permitting the police to enter and arrest Communists and other agitators responsible for the riot earlier during the day on Pennsylvania Avenue. The troops were then to assist the police in turning over all prisoners to the civil authorities for prosecution.[26]

To his own political misfortune, Hoover failed to publicize his restrictions on the military. Indeed, during much of the crisis he shut himself in the White House and met only

---

[23] Rpt of Opns, MDW–III CA, 4 Aug 32; Message Center Record, Munitions Bldg, HQ, 16th Brigade, 4 Aug 32; both in RG 394, Entry 321, File A46–485, NARA.

[24] Blumenson, *Patton Papers*, 1:895; Rpt of Opns, MDW–III CA, 4 Aug 32; Rpt, Kunzig to Miles, 30 Jul 32, RG 394, Entry 321, File A46–485, NARA.

[25] Lisio, *President and Protest*, pp. 197–201, 268–71.

[26] Rpt of Opns, MDW–III CA, 4 Aug 32, and Memo, Hurley for MacArthur, 28 Jul 32, both in RG 394, Entry 321, File A46–485, NARA; Daniels, *The Bonus March*, p. 167; Lisio, *President and Protest*, pp. 190, 199–201; John W. Killigrew, "The Army and the Bonus Incident," *Military Affairs* (Summer 1962), p. 62; Rich, *President and Civil Disorder*, p. 171.

with his advisers, shunned the press, and gave the public the impression that he was aloof and unconcerned. Unaware of the narrow and explicit guidelines that the president had set, the public subsequently judged Hoover by what the Army actually did, not by what he had ordered it to do. Once Secretary Hurley relayed the president's order to intervene, MacArthur allowed no further interference from civil officials in an operation that he perceived as a strictly military matter.

Instead, the chief of staff inaugurated a plan based on assumptions about martial law that were implicit in Emergency Plan White but that clearly violated the presidential guidelines. Hoover had ordered support, not displacement, of the District police and had ordered the Army to aid in evictions only from the Pennsylvania Avenue site, scene of the violence earlier on 28 July. Hoover had given no autho-

PATRICK J. HURLEY

rization to MacArthur or any other Army commander to evict marchers elsewhere in the District of Columbia or to act independently of the police. Rather than accept a subordinate role to the District police force, MacArthur directed Miles to have his troops clear the Pennsylvania Avenue site; to clear the encampment at 3d and C Streets, Southwest, as well; to drive the marchers across the Anacostia River and clear the encampment there; and to conclude by driving all the marchers out of the capital. In short, MacArthur's objective was a rout by federal military forces of all Bonus marchers in the shortest time possible.[27]

Why MacArthur embarked on this course remains far from clear. He had confided his presidential ambitions to close friends and may have believed that a low-key form of military intervention, if it failed, would make him appear too weak and indecisive for the nation's highest office. Believing the rumors and reports of Communist revolutionary intent, MacArthur may have seen a complete rout of the marchers as the best way to prevent an uprising then or in the future. Finally, he may have hoped to convince Congress that in a world rocked by depression, dictators, and revolutionaries the Army was crucial to internal stability and therefore merited increased appropriations. His own subsequent explanation was couched in the lofty terms of preserving federal authority: "The issue had now become a broader one than that of the simple expulsion of recalcitrant persons from an illegally occupied area. . . . By their open and determined defiance of the Metropolitan police . . . the mob . . . had threatened the integrity of Federal authority within the confines of the Federally

---

[27] *Rpt, Chief of Staff,* 15 Aug 32, HPL; Lisio, *President and Protest,* pp. 192, 202–03; Daniels, *The Bonus March,* pp. 163, 170.

DOUGLAS MACARTHUR GIVES INSTRUC-
TIONS TO PERRY L. MILES, COMMANDER
OF THE 16TH INFANTRY BRIGADE

governed District of Columbia. . . . The dispersion and expulsion from the District became the only logical answer."[28]

Before operations commenced MacArthur met with Chief Glassford and outlined the Army's scheme to rout the marchers. "We are going to break the back of the BEF," he said bluntly. "Within a short time we will move down Pennsylvania Avenue, sweep through the billets there, and then clean out the other camps. The operation will be continuous. It will be done tonight." Impressed by the plan, and perhaps somewhat in awe of his former wartime commander, Glassford again repeated that the District police force was too exhausted to carry out the evictions single-handed, but that it could control traffic and crowds of curious spectators if the Army moved against the marchers. MacArthur accepted this proposal, which reversed the president's priorities, and asked the chief to warn all BEF leaders to prepare the marchers for immediate evacuation.[29]

Leaving his command post at the Munitions Building to meet with MacArthur at the State, War, and Navy Building next to the White House, Miles learned officially of Hoover's order to intervene. The chief of staff explained that, although Miles would actually command operations, MacArthur would accompany the troops in case a serious situation arose requiring decisions "beyond the purview of any subordinate commander and with the purpose of obtaining personal familiarity with every phase of the troops' activities."[30] A protest came from Maj. Dwight D. Eisenhower, MacArthur's military aide, who argued that "the Chief of Staff should not dignify the incident by going out himself." But MacArthur replied that the incident was "a very serious test of the full strength of the Federal Government." He sent for his Army uniform, which—contrary to press descriptions of a showy dress uniform festooned with glittering medals—was a comparatively sedate noncombat uniform complete with campaign ribbons

---

[28] Quote from Lisio, *President and Protest*, pp. 192–93, 289; James, *Years of MacArthur*, 1:408–14; *Rpt, Chief of Staff,* 15 Aug 32, HPL.

[29] *Rpt, Chief of Staff,* 15 Aug 32, HPL; Lisio, *President and Protest*, pp. 202–04, 272–74; Daniels, *The Bonus March*, p. 167.

[30] Rpt of Opns, MDW–III CA, 4 Aug 32; *Rpt, Chief of Staff,* 15 Aug 32, HPL; Moseley, "The Bonus March," p. 8.

to which its wearer was duly entitled.[31] He donned it because he thought it inappropriate for the Army chief of staff, although not in direct command, to be out of uniform while accompanying a military force on an operation.

The concentration of troops at the Ellipse concluded with the arrival of trucks bearing the 3d Battalion, 12th Infantry. That unit, along with the 2d Squadron, 3d Cavalry, which had arrived a half-hour earlier, was to bear the brunt of the subsequent operations. Both units had received special riot-control training, including briefings by Col. Dennis P. Quinlan, the judge advocate of III Corps Area and a leading expert on federal intervention in civil disturbances. Later during the day, the 1st Battalion, 12th Infantry, from Fort Howard, reinforced the first two units to a total of nearly 800 men. The 13th Engineer Regiment from Fort Humphreys (now Fort McNair) and a battalion of the 34th Infantry from Fort Meade—a total of 600 troops—acted as a reserve. In case 1,400 soldiers proved inadequate, Secretary of the Navy Charles F. Adams agreed to place the 6th Marine Reserves at Quantico, Virginia, on alert as well as Marine garrisons at the Washington Navy Yard and the 8th and I Streets Marine Barracks. The District of Columbia National Guard was not mobilized by President Hoover and played no part in the expulsion of the Bonus marchers.[32]

Operations: Pennsylvania Avenue, Southwest, and Anacostia

Once federal forces had concentrated, Miles prepared to go against the Bonus army occupying the vacant Treasury buildings on Pennsylvania Avenue, scene of the earlier clash between police and marchers. As conceived in the first phase of the scheme, the column was to march from the Ellipse southeast down Pennsylvania Avenue with the 2d Squadron in the lead, the 3d Battalion in the center, and Headquarters Company bringing up the rear. In the operations order, Miles directed Maj. Alexander D. Surles, the cavalry commander, to clear Pennsylvania Avenue of crowds as far as 3d Street. Then Colonel Kunzig, commander of the infantry, was to deploy his battalion facing south in the direction of the occupied buildings. With Surles' troops guarding the battalion's flanks, Kunzig was to evict the marchers and pursue them to Maryland Avenue, Southwest, the demarcation line of phase one.[33]

Taking heed of Hoover's instruction to treat women and children as humanely as possible, Miles cautioned Surles and Kunzig to use only such force as was necessary to accomplish their mission. With regard to the rioters they were to "avoid rushing tactics and use of any undue haste . . . likely to provoke useless conflict with the rioters." Miles believed that a demonstration of overpowering force, accompanied by ample time for marchers to withdraw, promised the "simplest and safest results." In the event of resistance,

---

[31] Raymond Henle, "Oral History Interview With General Dwight D. Eisenhower at Gettysburg, Pa., 13 July 1967," OH–106, Stanford, Hoover Oral History Program, Hoover Institution of War, Revolution, and Peace, pp. 2–3; Daniels, *The Bonus March*, p. 166. General staff officers in the capital area were then required to dress in mufti—that is, civilian clothing—while on duty.

[32] *Rpt, Chief of Staff,* 15 Aug 32, HPL; Rpt of Opns, MDW–III CA, 4 Aug 32; Ltr, Surles to Miles, 5 Aug 32; Rpt, Kunzig to Miles, 6 Aug 32; all in RG 394, Entry 321, File A46–485, NARA. See also James, *Years of MacArthur*, 1:398.

[33] Rpt of Opns, MDW–III CA, 4 Aug 32.

however, the troops were to use all the tear-gas grenades and candles necessary. Over 1,500 tear-gas grenades, bombs, and candles were eventually used.[34]

Shortly after receiving the operations order, Miles' force began to march down Pennsylvania Avenue. For twenty minutes cavalrymen with steel helmets, carbines at the sling, and sabers drawn rode through the spectators.[35] When the column reached 7th Street, it extended to cover the width of the avenue. Under the watchful eyes of the crowd and guards from the Headquarters Company, tanks were unloaded from the trucks and machine-gun detachments moved to the left and right flanks of the column. Behind the cavalry and the tanks followed three companies of the 12th Infantry. Miles then ordered the Bonus marchers and the crowds north of Pennsylvania Avenue to disperse. Despite his warning that gas would be used, many bystanders, apparently unaware of the gravity of the situation, did not move on.[36]

Following the clearing of the north side of the street, Miles ordered the crowd on the south side of the avenue to evacuate the buildings and grounds that they had named "Camp Glassford." By that time government offices had emptied, and many federal workers had mingled with crowds of Bonus marchers and innocent bystanders. As it grew, the entire crowd became surly and defiant, with some of its members shouting insults and throwing bricks at the federal troops. In response Kunzig ordered his soldiers to don gas masks and hurl tear-gas bombs. Coughing and weeping, the mob melted away, some taking refuge in nearby buildings, whence the infantry, moving forward with fixed bayonets, easily drove them out.[37]

Meanwhile the cavalry pushed the crowd to the next street south. But when the horsemen left their protecting infantry behind, the crowd turned to confront its pursuers. Joined by blacks living in the neighborhood, the crowd encircled the cavalry, shouting insults and throwing rocks. Thoroughly incensed, Surles' executive officer, Maj. George S. Patton, Jr., ordered a series of trotting charges. Amidst clouds of tear gas, the cavalrymen struck with the flat of their sabers, while the infantry, arriving at the scene, prodded the crowd with bayonets. Resistance collapsed in minutes. Troops of the 12th Infantry then turned to clear out the Communist encampment at 12th and C Streets, Southwest, near the Department of Agriculture. Accompanied by tanks, two companies of regulars reached the objective shortly after 1800 but found the encampment deserted.[38]

From the start of operations MacArthur had shown great confidence in the discipline of his troops and the effectiveness of their training. To display troop efficiency he had instructed Miles to permit reporters to accompany tactical units and had directed that Army spokesmen make no effort to coach the press. The reporters, favorably impressed that no one had been killed during the first two phases of the operation, responded with what

---

[34] Ibid.; *Rpt, Chief of Staff,* 15 Aug 32, HPL; Daniels, *The Bonus March,* p. 168.

[35] For a cavalryman's view, see Lucian K. Truscott, *The Twilight of the United States Cavalry: Life in the Old Army, 1917–1942* (Lawrence: University of Kansas Press, 1989), pp. 120–30.

[36] Rpt of Opns, MDW–III CA, 4 Aug 32; Rpt, Surles to Miles, 30 Jul 32; Rpt, Kunzig to Miles, 30 Jul 32; all in RG 394, Entry 321, File A46–485, NARA.

[37] Rpt of Opns, MDW–III CA, 4 Aug 32; Rpt, Surles to Miles, 30 Jul 32; *Rpt, Chief of Staff,* 15 Aug 32, HPL; Daniels, *The Bonus March,* p. 168; Killigrew, "The Army and the Bonus Incident," pp. 63–64.

[38] Rpt of Opns, MDW–III CA, 4 Aug 32; Rpts, Surles and Kunzig to Miles, both 30 Jul 32; Memo, Surles for Miles, 5 Aug 32; all in RG 394, Entry 321, File A46–485, NARA. Blumenson, *Patton Papers,* 1:896; *Rpt, Chief of Staff,* 15 Aug 32, HPL; Moseley, "The Bonus March," pp. 1–2.

TROOPERS OF THE 3D CAVALRY ADVANCE UP PENNSYLVANIA AVENUE

MacArthur termed a "very fair presentation of the facts." But the mood was already chang-ing. When the 3d Battalion and the tank platoon reached the Communist encampment, sev-eral fires were already burning. Arriving at 12th and C Streets soon after the troops, MacArthur ordered them to start counterfires to prevent a conflagration that could spread to other neighborhoods. Meanwhile, at Camp Glassford on Pennsylvania Avenue, several shacks built by the marchers also blazed against the evening sky. At the second site, reporters claimed to have seen soldiers in the vicinity helping police to set some of the fires and photographed an enlisted man actually setting one shack alight.[39]

A subsequent internal investigation by the Army revealed that many enlisted men were only carrying out orders from officers on Kunzig's staff in response to police requests for assistance "to destroy filthy, unsanitary shacks." Rather than admit any mil-itary connection with the fires, however, Secretary Hurley announced in a press confer-ence, even before the investigation had been completed, that defective tear-gas grenades

---

[39] *Rpt, Chief of Staff,* 15 Aug 32, HPL; Lisio, *President and Protest,* p. 215; Press Statement, Secy of War Hurley, 3 Aug 32, RG 407, File 240, NARA; Moseley, "The Bonus March," pp. 1–2; Rpt of Opns, MDW–III CA, 4 Aug 32; Rpt, Kunzig to Miles, 30 Jul 32; Memo, Miles for MacArthur, 23 Sep 32, RG 394, Entry 321, File A46–485, NARA.

SOLDIERS OF THE 12TH INFANTRY FIX BAYONETS, PENNSYLVANIA AVENUE

and "retreating radicals" accounted for most of the damage.[40] Hurley's disclaimer and his efforts to reinforce a BEF-radical connection backfired and opened a serious breach in the credibility of Army claims. Increasingly, too, the public began to see a wide disparity between the amount of force used to evict the marchers and the threat they supposedly represented. Although the Army did clear the downtown camps without bloodshed or serious injury, the use of so many heavily armed troops and mechanized vehicles, the widespread use of tear gas that affected scores of innocent bystanders, and the "occasional manhandling" of onlookers and reporters caused many to question Hoover's judgment in calling such a potentially lethal armed force into the city.[41]

In the early evening Glassford again met with MacArthur to ascertain Army plans for the next phase of operations. Here MacArthur reiterated his intention to send troops into Anacostia to clean out Camp Marks, and he asked Glassford to warn the marchers of Army intentions, giving them a chance to disperse. At Camp Marks, Eddie Atwell, a former military police sergeant acting as camp commander, received the warning at 2030.[42]

---

[40] Press Statement, Secy of War Hurley, 3 Aug 32; Rpt of Opns, MDW–III CA, 4 Aug 32; Memo, Miles for MacArthur, 23 Sep 32.

[41] Daniels, *The Bonus March*, pp. 169–70; John W. Price, "The Army Evicts the Bonus Marchers," *Military Review* 51 (May 1971):61, 63–64.

[42] Ibid.

The growing concentration of troops across from Anacostia prompted reporters to warn interested congressmen and President Hoover of MacArthur's evident intention to evict the marchers from the Flats. Disturbed by the election-year political implications of a complete rout of all veterans from the capital by federal troops, Hoover instructed Hurley to explicitly forbid MacArthur to send troops across the river. Although Hurley personally supported MacArthur's scheme to displace what both men believed were Communist radicals, the secretary duly sent General Moseley to deliver Hoover's message. Moseley accurately reported Hoover's order to MacArthur. But the chief of staff claimed that his hands were tied by a military operation already in progress that could not be halted. Meanwhile, Hoover ordered Hurley to repeat the president's instructions, so that MacArthur could not fail to understand. This time Moseley selected a member of his staff, Col. Clement H. Wright, to deliver the message. When Wright found MacArthur, the troops had already finished their suppers, left their bivouac, and were preparing to march to the bridge across the Anacostia River. MacArthur grumbled that he was too busy to stop an operation on the basis of an "alleged" order from someone pretending to come from the president.[43]

This extraordinary response reflected a fundamental misinterpretation of MacArthur's role. Evidence suggests that he, perhaps still influenced by Emergency Plan White, had intended from the beginning to treat the disorder as an insurrection, on the assumption that he knew better than the president how to deal with revolutionary rabble. Hoover's refusal to elevate the disturbance to that level, and his insistence that the military restrict itself to assisting police in evicting the marchers from Pennsylvania Avenue, had failed to deter the chief of staff. From the moment troops pushed marchers toward the river, MacArthur had violated the president's direct orders. His actions illustrated his view of the proper relationship between the civilian commander in chief and the military commander: civilian supremacy before and after a military operation, but complete military autonomy during it. Reinforcing his attitude was his overriding hatred of communism. According to one biographer, "Once MacArthur was convinced that the affair was a Communist assault against the federal government, he acted with overzealous determination and reckless impulsiveness." If Herbert Hoover had been of the same mettle as Harry S. Truman, the result might have been to end MacArthur's career two decades before his dismissal for another act of insubordination during the Korean War.[44]

At 2100, after informing Colonel Kunzig and Major Surles that "this command will proceed to Anacostia flats and evacuate Bonus Marchers from that property," Miles initiated phase three of MacArthur's plan. Ten minutes later federal forces began to move into Anacostia. Angry crowds jeered and jostled the troops as they marched from M Street toward the bridge. Headquarters Company suffered the brunt of the harassment. A civilian struck a sergeant, which led to several fist fights between other soldiers and civilians. With Kunzig's approval, the company's commander ordered his men to re-form

[43] Moseley, "One Soldier's Journey," 2:144–45; Interv, Donald J. Lisio with the Honorable F. Trubee Davison, Asst Secy of War for Air, Long Island, N.Y., 22 Apr 72; Daniels, *The Bonus March*, pp. 120–21, 170–71; Interv, Henle with Eisenhower, 13 Jul 67, pp. 2–3; Lisio, *President and Protest*, pp. 210–12; James, *Years of MacArthur*, 1:401–02.

[44] Quote from James, *Years of MacArthur*, p. 409. See also Lisio, *President and Protest*, p. 330; Daniels, *The Bonus March*, pp. 170–72.

AMID CLOUDS OF TEAR GAS, U.S. ARMY SOLDIERS CLEAR BEF ENCAMPMENTS, *Pennsylvania Avenue.*

and throw gas grenades. To help clear the crowd blocking the troops' access to the bridge, Chief Glassford personally led the police in a tear-gas assault. In the face of a combined effort by troops and police, the crowd yielded, and the column marched across the bridge.[45]

Reaching the east bank minutes before 2200, Miles planned to exert direct pressure on the Bonus marchers with infantry moving into Camp Marks, while the cavalry stood by to provide help if it was needed. Before either could go into action, however, Eddie Atwell, a Bonus March leader, with white flag in hand, met with MacArthur to ask for a one-hour delay while the marchers completed their evacuation. MacArthur consented and ordered Miles to halt for an hour. During the halt some soldiers along the river burned isolated sheds to illuminate the area of operation. Soon afterward several Bonus marchers set fire to their own dwellings and, possibly to spite the government, set fire to tents on loan from the District of Columbia National Guard. In the words of Eisenhower, an eyewitness during the episode, "the whole encampment started to blaze. Unquestionably the burning was started by the occupants themselves, but it was a very pitiful scene—those ragged, discouraged people burning their own little things."[46]

[45] Rpt of Opns, MDW–III CA, 4 Aug 32; Rpt, A. R. Bolling, HQ, to Miles, 30 Jul 32, RG 394, Entry 321, File A46–485, NARA; Blumenson, *Patton Papers*, 1:869.

[46] *Rpt, Chief of Staff,* 15 Aug 32, HPL. See also Rpts, Kunzig to Miles, 30 Jul and 6 Aug 32, both in RG 394, Entry 321, File A46–485, NARA; Price, "Army Evicts the Bonus Marchers," pp. 61, 65; Rich, *President and Civil Disorder*, p. 172; Lisio, *President and Protest*, pp. 212–16; Interv, Henle with Eisenhower, 13 Jul 67, p. 3.

FEDERAL TROOPS GUARD RUINS OF CAMP MARKS

As scheduled, Kunzig's battalion moved toward the encampment. While the four companies advanced in a line of skirmishers, policemen manning a fire truck played searchlight beams back and forth ahead of the troops. During the sweep through the smoldering ruins, the troops occasionally threw tear-gas grenades but met no resistance. Major Patton observed: "If during this operation a single shot had been fired, many would have died, for in the dark, on a flat plain, fire discipline could not have been maintained, and there was no cover." Patton attributed the lack of violence to the superb discipline of the troops and to the self-restraint exhibited by the marchers, of whom he noted: "had they really wanted to start something, they had a great chance, but refused."[47]

After reaching high ground south of Camp Marks, the Bonus marchers began to throw rocks at the regulars, who had just reached the base of the hill. While the three companies on the hill chased the band of rock throwers, a mob of nearly 2,000 marchers formed along the southern edge of the camp and began closing upon Kunzig's company. The troops, noticing the threat to the brigade commander, broke off their pursuit and formed a skirmish line around Kunzig. Under orders to avoid using tear gas for fear of injuring the women and children, the soldiers experienced some difficulty in moving the crowd, but ultimately prevailed. By 0200 the Bonus marchers had fled to other areas of Anacostia.[48]

[47] Blumenson, *Patton Papers*, 1:896–97.
[48] Rpt of Opns, MDW–III CA, 4 Aug 32; Rpt, Miles to MacArthur, 4 Aug 32; Rpt, Bolling, 1 Aug 32, RG 394, Entry 321, File A46–485, NARA. See also Killigrew, "The Army and the Bonus Incident," p. 63.

U.S. ARMY CAVALRYMEN GUARD WASHINGTON BRIDGE ACROSS ANACOSTIA RIVER

Leaving the mopping up to Miles, MacArthur accompanied Secretary Hurley to the White House for a meeting with the president. Many years later Hoover recalled how nervous MacArthur appeared. Not only had the general disobeyed two direct orders not to cross the Anacostia River to Camp Marks, but from the very beginning he had exceeded the written orders given him by the president through the secretary of war in a variety of ways: by supplanting rather than aiding the police; by clearing, rather than surrounding, the riot areas; and by failing to take prisoners for police interrogation. According to his own recollection, Hoover upbraided both Hurley and MacArthur, but he allowed himself to be soothed after the two men convinced him that the majority of loyal, law-abiding marchers had departed days earlier, leaving the remaining BEF members under control of troublemakers and Communists bent on taking over the city and the government. This, according to Hurley and MacArthur, justified the recent operations.[49]

Loyalty and expediency explain Hoover's refusal to discipline MacArthur. Impressed by the general's outstanding record and demonstrations of loyalty to the presidency, it is possible that Hoover repaid that loyalty by overlooking MacArthur's deliberate violation of direct orders on 28 July. A humanitarian, Hoover may even have nourished grudging admiration for the efficient and bloodless manner in which MacArthur had removed a very embarrassing problem from the capital. Inevitably, there were also political considerations: Hoover may have hesitated to chastise MacArthur publicly during an election year, especially in a period of depression when the public needed confidence in the stability and unity of the nation's leadership. However, the president's failure to divert blame

---

[49] Burner, *Herbert Hoover*, p. 311; Daniels, *The Bonus March*, pp. 167, 172, 173; Interv, Lisio with Davison, 22 Apr 72; Lisio, *President and Protest*, pp. 215–19.

from himself to MacArthur over the manner in which the BEF members had been dispersed assured that public criticism would fall directly on himself. Hoover, as one historian has written, "might have thrown the insubordinate MacArthur to the wolves," but instead he "did nothing to transfer the onus of the midnight rout from Anacostia onto the splendid scapegoat that his chief of staff could have provided." In the days and weeks following the events of 28 July, the president covered for MacArthur and publicly supported the actions of his chief of staff and the federal troops under his command. In a nation increasingly bitter and disaffected, Hoover's mistake or charity in dealing with MacArthur became a factor in making him "the most hated president in office since Andrew Johnson."[50]

Immediately following their tense interview with an angry commander in chief, MacArthur and Hurley gave a triumphant press conference. MacArthur described 90 percent of the marchers still in the area as nonveterans, criminals, and incipient revolutionaries: "The mob . . . was animated by the essence of revolution. The gentleness, the consideration with which they had been treated [by Chief Glassford] had been mistaken for weakness. . . . They were about to take over in some arbitrary way either the direct control of the Government or else control it by indirect methods . . . in the Negro section . . . a regular system of tribute was being levied . . . by this insurrectionist group; a reign of terror was being started which may have led to a system of Caponeism, and I believe later to insurgency and insurrection."[51]

While MacArthur painted a picture of dangerous desperadoes to the press, tired and frightened marchers from Camp Marks fled either to nearby Prince George's County, Maryland, or back into the District of Columbia. For those in Maryland, the governor provided trucks to transport them to the Pennsylvania state line. From there the marchers eventually returned to their homes, some finding shelter in shanty towns and missions, or melted into the general population of homeless drifters. Some returned to the District of Columbia, and Miles conducted a series of mopping-up operations on 29 and 30 July, until all stragglers had been apprehended and removed from the federal enclave.[52]

Before the last of the Bonus marchers departed on 29 July, Hoover sent a lengthy letter to the Board of Commissioners commending the Army for dissolving lawless mobs "without the firing of a shot or the loss of a life." Hoover reminded the board that he had never declared martial law and that the maintenance of order "still rests upon [the] commission and the police." Like MacArthur, Hoover now attributed the actions of the marchers who remained in Washington on 28 July to a desire to exploit the concessions hitherto given them by overconciliatory civil authorities. The president, who in support of MacArthur now believed the marchers to be Communists, nonveterans, and criminals, stated in his letter that "no group, no matter what its origins . . . can be allowed either to violate the laws of this city or to intimidate the government."[53]

District police began to replace federal troops on patrol and mopping-up activities on the morning of 29 July 1932. After making a last reconnaissance of all former BEF

---

[50] Ibid.

[51] Press Interv with Hurley and MacArthur, 29 Jul 32, RG 407, File 240, NARA; Lisio, *President and Protest*, pp. 219–20. "Caponeism" refers to the Chicago gangster Al Capone.

[52] Rpt of Opns, MDW–III CA, 4 Aug 32; *Rpt, Chief of Staff,* 15 Aug 32, HPL.

[53] Hoover to Reichelderfer, 29 Jul 32, RG 407, File 240, NARA.

campsites, Miles informed MacArthur that all troops would be relieved by nightfall. Actual withdrawals, however, started early in the afternoon of 30 July, and by 2 August the last federal forces had returned to their stations.[54]

Hoover's unwillingness to chastise MacArthur in public led many to conclude that the president either had condoned or had planned the complete rout of all marchers from the city. Twelve scholars, including two from the Brookings Institution, signed a protest accusing Hoover of manhandling veterans to develop a reputation for toughness conducive to campaign slogans such as "Hoover versus Radicalism." During the ensuing presidential campaign, Democrats nicknamed the president "Gas 'em out Hoover," and at various stops on the campaign trail, such as in Detroit, the president was greeted with taunts of "Down with Hoover, slayer of veterans." In the BEF *News*, a cartoon depicted a mustachioed Hoover as Kaiser Wilhelm II wearing the Capitol dome as his spiked, Prussian helmet. In a belated effort to cleanse Hoover from the stigma associated with the Bonus March, Republican campaign chairmen deleted the names of Hurley and U.S. Treasury Secretary Mills from the list of campaign speakers. [55]

The Army fared just as badly. As Major Eisenhower had predicted at the time, General MacArthur's grandstanding succeeded in making the Army appear equally responsible in the decision to drive the veterans out of the capital. The service, like the Republican president, became the target of liberals, veterans, and all people who were suffering during the depression and were happy to flay conservatives for fundamental violations of civil rights and to resurrect the historic American fear of militarism. Crying "Remember the Bonus March," many now accused the Army officer corps of eagerly and willfully hurling enlisted "Cossacks" against peaceful demonstrators. Although generally ignoring such criticism, MacArthur felt compelled to answer the accusation that he had forced the president into calling out troops by preparing contingency plans and by pre-positioning troops. In this case he was on firm ground, arguing that the Army must prepare in advance, rather than risk being found unready when called to intervene. MacArthur denounced the accusations of military interference in presidential decision making as either unfounded or as outright fabrications.[56] But in a presidential election year, his actions ensured that the Army would receive much stinging criticism, some fair and some unfair.

The controversy swirling around the rioting and intervention on 28 July also prompted an inquiry from the Justice Department. On 2 August 1932, Attorney General William D. Mitchell wrote MacArthur, asking specific questions concerning his use of troops. Mitchell wanted to know whether any District official had requested that MacArthur put

---

[54] Rpt of Opns, MDW–III CA, 4 Aug 32.

[55] Price, "Army Evicts the Bonus Marchers," pp. 62–63; Lisio, *President and Protest*, p. 221; Leuchtenberg, *Roosevelt and the New Deal*, pp. 16–17. For the aftermath, see the following: P. Y. Anderson, "Tear-Gas, Bayonets, and Votes," *Nation* 135 (17 August 1935):138–40; "Cowardice and Folly in Washington," *Nation* 135 (10 August 1932):116; "Bullets for the BEF: Hoover Relief, New Style," *New Republic* 71 (10 August 1932):328–29; "Victory of Anacostia," *New Republic* 72 (17 August 1932):20; "Official Misrepresentation of Eviction of Bonus Marchers," *New Republic* 72 (24 August 1932):29; "Causes of the Washington Disturbances," *Nation* 135 (24 August 1932):154; O. P. White, "General Glassford's Story," *Collier's* 90 (29 October 1932):10–11; F. C. Springer, "Glassford and the Siege of Washington," *Harper's Weekly* 165 (November 1932):641–55.

[56] Interv, Henle with Eisenhower, 13 Jul 67, p. 4; James, *Years of MacArthur*, 1:405; Killigrew, "The Army and the Bonus Incident," p. 65; Ltr, MacArthur to L. Richey, Secy to the President, 12 Aug 32, RG 407, File 240, NARA.

federal troops on alert prior to the time that Hoover authorized actual military intervention. MacArthur answered that Herbert Crosby, the commissioner of police and Glassford's immediate superior, had telephoned to say the rioting had got out of control and to recommend that troops be held in readiness. Mitchell asked whether the mob had actually committed acts of violence in the presence of federal troops and whether any police, soldiers, or citizens were injured after the Army began antiriot operations. MacArthur replied that although the mob had committed many acts of violence no serious injuries had resulted. Mitchell's final question had already been raised by others: Who set fire to the camps of the Bonus marchers? In view of an Army internal investigation, MacArthur equivocated, stating that "to the best of my belief, the camps were burned by the bonus marchers themselves. I issued no orders contemplating the burning of the camps."[57] Taking the chief of staff at his word, the attorney general took no further action.

An effort to explore the affair in Congress also came to nothing. In December 1932, after the presidential election, Senator Kenneth D. McKellar of Tennessee introduced a resolution calling for a committee to ask twenty-two questions, including the following: what were the lawful rights of the veterans; who was responsible for the riot; was it really necessary to call out the Army; who burned the shacks; and who ordered the routing of families in the middle of the night? The resolution was referred to the Senate Military Affairs Committee, and was there interred. By this time, however, it was clear that the United States would soon have a Democratic president, and the first months of his administration would set a course the effects of which were to transform Army plans and policies in handling civil disturbances.[58]

The New Deal, Labor, and the United States Army

By November 1932 the American public, having lost confidence in Herbert Hoover's ability to cope with the worsening depression, overwhelmingly elected Franklin Delano Roosevelt to the presidency.[59] Roosevelt proposed direct, massive federal intervention in society and in the economy, through a series of new, somewhat vague, ideas and programs. To Roosevelt the federal government was the only entity with sufficient resources and ability to bring the nation out of the depression, then entering its fourth year. His New Deal emphasized relief, recovery, and reform to rebuild the economy and bolster sagging public morale. By the time the United States entered into World War II in 1941, the social, political, and economic institutions of the nation had been reshaped, and the modern welfare state, necessitating heavy government involvement for continued successful operation, was an accomplished fact and a durable part of American society.

In an indirect manner the New Deal had a fundamental effect on the subsequent role of the Army in civil disturbances. Roosevelt's new labor legislation removed some major economic grievances, and labor disputes ceased to be a cause for massive internal strife; often the government backed unionization and was more likely to intervene legally against

---

[57] Mitchell to MacArthur, and reply, 2 Aug 32, RG 407, File 240, NARA.

[58] U.S. Congress, Senate, Senate Resolution 301 in *Congressional Record*, 72d Cong., 2d sess., 12 and 14 Dec 1932, pp. 304–05; Price, "Army Evicts Bonus Marchers," pp. 62–63.

[59] For Roosevelt's view of the march, see Rexford G. Tugwell, "Roosevelt and the Bonus Marchers of 1932," *Political Science Quarterly* 87 (September 1972):363–76.

employers than support them militarily. The programs of the New Deal, though unsuc-cessful in ending the depression entirely, helped to make the Bonus March of 1932 the last economically motivated domestic disorder requiring federal military intervention prior to the outbreak of World War II. This is not to say that conflict ceased to occur. During the 1930s the new administration successfully dealt with some of the most violent labor con-flicts of the century by throwing the full weight and power of the federal government into negotiated settlements. Just as important were ongoing local and state efforts to create or strengthen local police, state police, and constabulary forces to deal with civil distur-bances. Thus the role of the Army and the National Guard as keepers of the domestic peace, especially on the industrial front, steadily diminished.[60]

President Roosevelt did consider the domestic use of federal troops on several occa-sions in his first two terms of office. During this period, the increasing strength and mili-tancy of labor led to frequent strikes and to several violent disputes, such as those occur-ring in Minneapolis, San Francisco, and Toledo, Ohio, in 1934. Each required National Guard intervention, under state control. Even more violent labor confrontations took place in strikes against seventeen plants of General Motors in late 1936 and early 1937 and against the nationwide steel industry in 1937. But despite massive property damage and bloodshed, especially in the later strikes, Roosevelt refused to intervene with federal mil-itary forces and left the matter of quelling the violence to local and state governments, which similarly hesitated to employ National Guard forces and relied primarily on local and state police units.[61] Only after 1941, when the worst social and economic effects of the Great Depression were over, and when the nation faced an even greater threat from fascism and militarism abroad, did Roosevelt call on the Army to help maintain industrial produc-tion and keep the peace domestically. Army duty during the civil disorders of World War II, however, was markedly different from the Bonus March operation and the domestic mil-itary interventions of the World War I.

---

    [60] Arthur M. Schlesinger, Jr., *The Age of Roosevelt,* vol. 2, *The Coming of the New Deal* (Boston: Houghton Mifflin, 1958), 2:3–4, 20–23; Leuchtenberg, *Roosevelt and the New Deal*, pp. 18–19, 26–30, 33–34; Romasco, *The Politics of Recovery*, pp. 4–5.
    [61] Schlesinger, *Coming of the New Deal*, pp. 386–93, 403, 414–16; Leuchtenberg, *Roosevelt and the New Deal*, pp. 239–43. For a labor history of the period, see Bernstein, *The Turbulent Years*, and Nelson Lichtenstein, "Auto Worker Militancy and the Structure of Factory Life, 1937–1955," *Journal of American History* 67 (1980):335–53.

CHAPTER 17

Plant Seizures and Race Riots
1940–1945

Resolution of the basic dispute, and of related questions involving controversy between management and labor, is the function of the various civilian agencies created to deal with such problems. It is not the function of the War Department . . . the Army will not act as the arbiter or mediator of a labor dispute, or as an agency to solve specific controversies between labor and management.

—*Army Service Forces Plant Seizure Manual, September 1944.*

In the domestic use of federal troops, World War II differed sharply from World War I. Interventions were few and the World War I policy of direct access was not exhumed. The Army entered the war period equipped with plans and policies to deal with any kind of internal disorder, but found little use for them. The Soviet Union's position as an ally ensured that the Communist Party was a passionate supporter of the war effort, and the government saw no threat from political radicals. The only significant cases of actual troop intervention in domestic disorders during World War II were in a race riot in Detroit, Michigan, in 1943, and a race-related labor dispute in Philadelphia, Pennsylvania, in 1944.

Yet there was no absence of labor stoppages that threatened to interfere with the production and transportation of war materials. The number of strikes in American industry steadily increased throughout the late 1930s and early 1940s, reaching a peak in 1944.[1] In dealing with the problem of wartime strikes, as well as disputes and production bottlenecks caused by unenlightened and uncooperative management, the Roosevelt administration relied on federal mediation and arbitration agencies and, when these failed, on the expedient of plant seizures. Plant seizures in most cases ended labor disputes rapidly and peacefully on conditions favorable to the government and labor unions, and required only the smallest use of the federal military to implement and enforce. World War II, therefore, continued the new era in civil-military relations, and further reduced the role of the Army in domestic disorders.[2]

---

[1] Byron Fairchild and Jonathan Grossman, *The Army and Industrial Manpower* (Washington, D.C.: U.S. Army Center of Military History, 1959), pp. 62–63.

[2] For government labor policies, see Harry A. Millis and Emily C. Brown, *From the Wagner Act to Taft-Hartley: A Study of National Labor Policy and Labor Relations* (Chicago: University of Chicago Press, 1950); Howard S. Kaltenborn, *Government Adjustment of Labor Disputes* (Chicago: Foundation, 1943); Harold W. Metz, *Labor Policy of the Federal Government* (Washington, D.C.: Brookings Institution, 1945); U.S. Office of Education, Federal Security Agency, *The Worker, His Job, and His Government: An Introduction to Federal Labor Laws* (Washington, D.C.: Government Printing Office, 1942); Joel Seidman, *American Labor From Defense to*

By early 1942 the Army service commands—formerly corps areas—had definite missions governing the federal military role in the event of a civil disturbance. The white plans' detailed surveys of strategic locations, vital utilities, and transport facilities, with appropriate policies and legal guidelines, were available to meet any threat promptly, without confusion or duplication of effort. But by the early 1940s Army contingency planning showed a clear predilection for the use of tactical restraint. Civil disorders were now viewed as unique situations, not as civil wars in miniature.[3] As a result, the white plans were modified by special legislation and executive orders, which authorized the federal executive to meet internal threats to the nation by means other than large troop deployments.

The Army and Industrial Plant Seizures: The Legal and Historical Background

During the war the federal government seized sixty-four privately owned industrial plants, railroads, and municipal transportation systems. The great majority of seizures were precipitated by labor problems—conflicts between rival unions, or between management and unions, or between the races. The government acted only when such conflicts threatened to interrupt the production of war materials or public services that were essential to the war effort. Twenty-nine seizures were conducted by the War Department—more than any other agency—which affected two million workers. The other thirty-five were conducted by the Departments of Navy, Commerce, and Interior; the Office of Defense Transportation; the War Shipping Administration; and the Petroleum Administration.

The policy justifying seizures developed only gradually. Prior to June 1943 the War Department had taken control of only four plants. The legal questions involved were still being debated in Congress and the courts. In that month, however, Congress passed the War Labor Disputes (or Smith-Connally) Act, which gave President Roosevelt clear authority to seize industrial plants vital to the war effort. Thereafter the pace of plant seizures quickened, as twenty-five plants were taken over and operated by the federal government. In June, July, and August of 1945 alone, the various executive agencies of the federal government seized essential war plants at the rate of one per week. By that time the process was firmly established, and a score of seizures were averted only because the war ended.[4]

Reconversion (Chicago: University of Chicago Press, 1953); Fred Witney, *Wartime Experiences of the National Labor Relations Board, 1941–1945* (Urbana: University of Illinois Press, 1949); Nelson Lichtenstein, *Labor's War at Home: The CIO in World War II* (Cambridge: Harvard University Press, 1982).

[3] For the military and labor, see Paul A. C. Koistinen, *The Hammer and the Sword: Labor, the Military, and Industrial Mobilization, 1920–1945* (New York: Arno Press, 1979); Paul A. C. Koistinen, "Mobilizing the World War II Economy: Labor and the Industrial-Military Alliance," *Pacific Historical Review* 42 (1973):443–78. On 9 March 1942, Army administrative functions were divided among three commands: Ground Forces, Air Forces, and Service Forces (Army Service Forces [ASF]). The ASF was charged with supply, procurement, and "general housekeeping," and with the War Department's administrative bureaus: the Provost Marshal General's Office, the Adjutant General's Office, and the Judge Advocate General's Office. Its field organizations were the old geographic departments and more recent corps areas. As with prior departments and corps areas, service commands were further subdivided into districts.

[4] John H. Ohly, The Emergency Operation of Industrial Facilities by the War Department During World War II, 3 vols., manuscript in CMH files, 1: i–iii. See also John L. Blackman, Jr., *Presidential Seizures in Labor Disputes* (Cambridge: Harvard University Press, 1967), pp. 3–5; Fairchild and Grossman, *Army and Industrial Manpower*, pp. 74–84.

The government practice of seizing vital war plants and transportation facilities to ensure continued operation had a lengthy history. During the Civil War the federal government, acting under special statutory authority, took over several Northern railroads and some telegraph companies that controlled lines needed by the military. During World War I, the government seized the facilities and equipment of 385 major railroads, 855 smaller railroads, 4 steamship companies, the harbor facilities of New York, and the cable and telegraph facilities of 21 communications companies, as well as lesser industries and businesses nationwide. The large majority of these actions were preemptive, intended to forestall disruptive labor-industrial disputes that might have hindered the war effort.[5]

Only one major War Department seizure during World War I—that of the Smith and Wesson Company of Springfield, Massachusetts—was rooted in a labor dispute. Its immediate cause was a series of antilabor actions of plant managers who refused to abide by a National War Labor Board ruling. When the managers fired union organizers and unionized workers demanding higher wages, the War Department, the main customer for the pistols produced at the plant, tried and failed to mediate a settlement. The dispute was referred to the National War Labor Board, which decided in favor of a compromise settlement that entailed a partial increase in workers' wages and a recognition of workers' rights to bargain collectively. The Smith and Wesson directors then informed the War Department that the company had no intention of complying with the ruling. Under Section 120 of the National Defense Act of 1916, Secretary of War Newton D. Baker ordered the company to manufacture the goods that they were obligated to produce under Army contract. When the company indicated its intention to continue to refuse compliance, on 13 September 1918 the War Department took control of the plant. The employees then returned to work.[6]

Faced with the need to operate the factory, the War Department created the National Operating Corporation to run all firms seized by the government. The corporate directors were Army ordnance officers, and the company, ostensibly a private business, was entirely funded by the federal government, which controlled all facets of production, including work hours, wages, operating costs, and contracts. Employees were granted most of the demands they had sought in the original dispute, but were not brought into the federal work force. Under this arrangement the plant continued to fill its government orders for pistols until Smith and Wesson's contract with the Army expired. The plant was returned to its owners on 31 January 1919. The Smith and Wesson case was atypical for World War I and did not serve as a pattern for World War II plant seizures, but it did provide a striking example of the government's power to seize and run private enterprises engaged in war work.[7]

Both the National Defense Act of 1916 and the Selective Training and Service Act of 1940 empowered the president to seize any plant whose management refused to fulfill government contracts for necessary war supplies or equipment. Section 9 of the Selective Training and Service Act essentially restated Section 120 of the 1916 National Defense Act, which had been used in the Smith and Wesson case. These provisions, however, granted

---

[5] Ohly, Emergency Operation of Industrial Facilities, 1:2–6; Blackman, *Presidential Seizures*, pp. 257–58.
[6] Ibid.; Blackman, *Presidential Seizures*, pp. 20, 128, 150, 200–201, 258.
[7] Ibid.

MAP 6

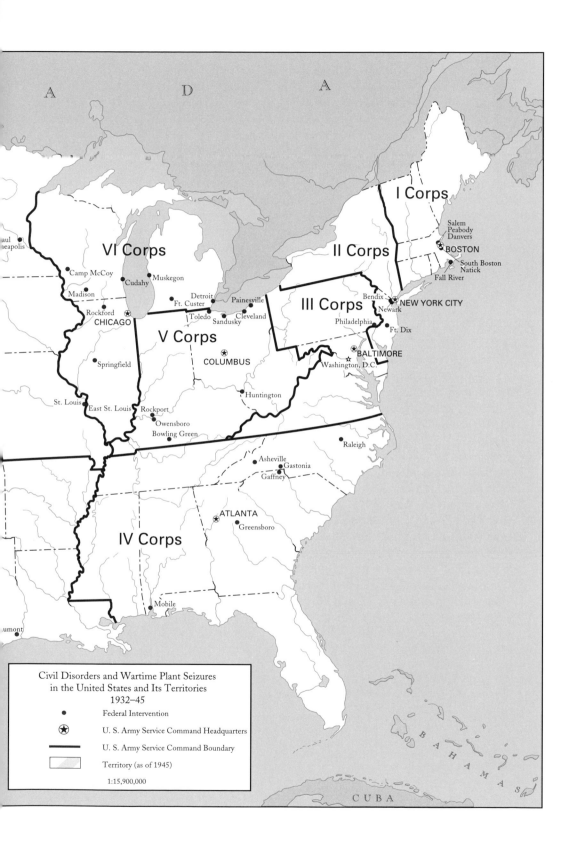

CANADA

I Corps

VI Corps

II Corps

III Corps

V Corps

IV Corps

aul
eapolis
• Camp McCoy
Madison •
Rockford •
⊛ CHICAGO
Muskegon
Cudahy •
Detroit
Ft. Custer
Toledo
Sandusky
Painesville
Cleveland
Bendix
Newark
⊛ NEW YORK CITY
Philadelphia
Ft. Dix
⊛ COLUMBUS
Springfield •
St. Louis
East St. Louis
Rockport •
Owensboro •
Bowling Green •
• Huntington
⊛ BALTIMORE
☆ Washington, D.C.
• Raleigh
Asheville •
Gaffney •
• Gastonia
⊛ ATLANTA
• Greensboro
umont
Mobile •

Salem
Peabody
Danvers
⊛ BOSTON
South Boston
Natick
Fall River

BAHAMAS

CUBA

Civil Disorders and Wartime Plant Seizures
in the United States and Its Territories
1932–45

•   Federal Intervention

⊛   U. S. Army Service Command Headquarters

⎯⎯   U. S. Army Service Command Boundary

▭   Territory (as of 1945)

1:15,900,000

authority for seizure only when management refused to fulfill a war contract. Until Congress passed the War Labor Disputes Act in June 1943, President Roosevelt was forced to rely on a variety of statutes and legal justifications, and ultimately to conduct most seizures by means of executive orders justified under his powers as commander in chief. No specific statutory authority empowered him to deal with nonfulfillment of war contracts caused by labor disputes, or management refusal to abide by War Labor Board orders.

Despite the lack of a firm statutory base, planning for probable plant seizures began in the War Department almost a year before Pearl Harbor. During the first six months of 1941, amid growing labor strife, the Labor Section in the Office of the Under Secretary of War gave considerable study to the thin World War I file on plant seizures. The various white plans dealt largely with widespread domestic insurrections and provided little guidance regarding possible plant seizures. No firm doctrine had emerged by June, when the War Department was faced with its first labor-management crisis requiring Army intervention. For the next two years, the department would operate largely ad hoc, through trial and error, and as a result each of its major plant seizures differed markedly from the others. In only four cases were federal troops used.[8]

The Initial Seizures, 1941–1942

The first use of federal troops arose in the seizure of North American Aviation, Inc., a large Inglewood, California, manufacturing company that produced almost 20 percent of U.S. military aircraft. In March 1941 a jurisdictional dispute began between the AFofL's Machinists Union and the CIO-affiliated United Auto Workers (UAW). In an election sponsored by the National Labor Relations Board, the CIO union gained a narrow victory and the right to act as the bargaining agent for all workers at the plant—a work force that had recently expanded by 4,000 workers. When the emboldened UAW local demanded higher wages, company officials refused, claiming that the new scale was out of line with the rest of the aircraft industry. The dispute was referred to the National Defense Mediation Board (later called the National War Labor Board). While mediation was in progress, on 5 June 1941 the leaders of UAW Local 683, claiming bad faith on the part of the board, suddenly called a strike without the authorization of the national leadership of the CIO or the sympathy and cooperation of the AF of L local. A picket line of 2,000 strikers shut the plant, putting 11,000 employees out of work. The timing of the strike was exceptionally poor, coming as it did ten days after President Roosevelt had proclaimed a national emergency. The striking workers appeared to be directly challenging his authority, and rumors of Communist involvement heightened the sense of public outrage and alarm. Roosevelt acted quickly and decisively. He drafted an executive order and, when it appeared that workers were going to continue their strike, authorized the War Department to begin preparations to seize the plant. Lt. Col.

---

[8] Ohly, Emergency Operation of Industrial Facilities, 1:4, 7–8, app. 3: F–3, X–1, X–2, X–3; 39 *U.S. Statutes at Large*, 213 (1916 National Defense Act); 54 *U.S. Statutes at Large*, 892 (1940 Selective Training Service Act). The President could also act under 39 *U.S. Statutes at Large*, 721 (1916 Adamson Act) for rail disputes, 40 *U.S. Statutes at Large*, 904 (16 July 1918 Joint Resolution) for communications company seizures, and other legal justifications such as federal receiverships, the power of eminent domain, statutes governing the regulation of interstate commerce, and legislation like the Sherman Anti-Trust Act, the 1917 Food and Fuel Act, or the 1916 and 1920 Transportation Acts. See Blackman, *Presidential Seizures*, pp. 18–20, 289–93.

Charles E. Branshaw, the West Coast Army Air Corps procurement chief, was designated the War Department's representative and was ordered to have federal troops ready to move by Monday morning, 9 June. In the meantime, the management of North American Aviation publicly announced its intention of reopening the factory on the same day with nonstriking employees.[9]

ROBERT P. PATTERSON

The atmosphere in the morning was tense. Fighting broke out when police used tear gas to force a lane through a mob of 1,000 strikers to admit nonstriking employees. Branshaw had nine Army investigators at the plant and an airplane overhead surveying both the emerging riot and the progress of troops to the scene. He concluded that the 100 policemen on duty at the plant had completely lost control of the situation and that Army intervention was required. At this particular point, 2,000 soldiers of the 15th Infantry arrived on the scene from Camp Hunter Liggett, California, accompanied by 500 men of the 3d Coast Artillery from Fort MacArthur, California. Roosevelt, who had been in constant contact with the military authorities, signed the executive order instructing the War Department to "take charge of the plant and remain in charge and operate the plant until normal production shall be resumed." Branshaw, notified by Under Secretary of War Robert P. Patterson to proceed with seizure operations, quickly deployed the forces under his command, armed with loaded rifles and bayonets. The troops, in a skirmish-line formation, dispersed the pickets within 30 minutes, causing only minor injuries. The gates of the factory were opened, and by noon 1,200 men were back at work.[10]

To prevent any violence against the nonstrikers, Branshaw had a military escort accompany them to and from the plant. Joint Army-police teams patrolled the working-class neighborhoods where many employees lived. Although federal troops arrested several strikers for

---

[9] The take-over was effected by Executive Order 8773 of 9 June 1941. On North American, labor, and the aircraft industry in World War II, see Rich, *President and Civil Disorder*, pp. 177–81; Ohly, Emergency Operation of Industrial Facilities, 1:14–17; Arthur P. Allen and Betty V. H. Schneider, *Industrial Relations in the California Aircraft Industry* (Berkeley: University of California Press, 1956); Martin Glaberman, *Wartime Strikes: The Struggle Against the No-Strike Pledge in the UAW During World War II* (Detroit: Berwick Press, 1980); Nelson Lichtenstein, "Defending the No-Strike Pledge: CIO Politics During World War II," *Radical American* 9 (1975):49–76; I. B. Holley, jr., "The Management of Technological Change: Aircraft Production in the United States During World War II," *Aerospace Historian* 22 (1975):161–65; Otto H. Reichardt, "Industrial Concentration in World War II: The Case of the Aircraft Industry," *Aerospace Historian* 22 (1975):129–34; James R. Prickett, "Communist Conspiracy or Wage Dispute? The 1941 Strike at North American Aviation," *Pacific Historical Review* 5 (May 1981):215–33.

[10] Rich, *Presidents and Civil Disorder*, pp. 181–82; Ohly, Emergency Operation of Industrial Facilities, 1:18–20.

trespassing on company property, few detainees were held for long. No violence against the soldiers or nonstriking workers was reported. Picketing, liquor sales, and the entrance into the plant area of anyone but workers was forbidden. Army patrols both inside and outside the plant enforced federal prohibitions, and military guards stood at the factory gates.[11]

Although seizing the plant and quelling violence proved to be relatively simple and familiar tasks for the Army, actual operation of the business was not. Many problems quickly appeared: how to put the plant back into full production, how to settle the original labor dispute, and how to define the new status of the company and its stockholders. Restoring production was comparatively easy, for the large majority of employees did not sympathize with the strike. The Army promised fair treatment to all workers who returned to their jobs as employees of the government, excluding strike leaders, who were ousted by their unions. Workers were frankly informed that no concessions would be given for their return to work, which must be totally unconditional.

To arbitrate the original dispute, War Department officials deferred to their civilian counterparts in the National Defense Mediation Board. Negotiations resumed between company officials and the new leaders of the reconstructed local. To settle the question of plant and stockholder status under government seizure, the War Department allowed the old managers to remain in place and to perform the same functions they had before. Indeed, from the outset North American Aviation continued to function in all business and financial matters as it had prior to federal control, except in labor matters and with the exception that the government held final authority over company policies affecting federal contracts.[12]

Under the circumstances production resumed quickly. The 2,000 federal troops on duty in the Inglewood area had returned to their home stations by 17 June 1941. On 2 July Roosevelt terminated the order authorizing government control of the plant, and the remaining 1,500 troops encamped near the plant left the next day. The actual use of troops at North American Aviation closely resembled strikebreaking tactics employed in earlier decades, and in that respect it did not provide a model for later plant seizures during World War II. The perception of the strike as an unprovoked and a Communist-inspired unpatriotic act probably explained why this seizure was conducted as a straight military operation.[13] Nevertheless, it left the War Department uneasy. Despite the Army's success in seizing North American, Army leaders considered themselves and their service ill suited to run war plants. Their forebodings were confirmed when administrative problems well outside military training and experience developed in the second and third plant seizures carried out by the War Department during 1941–1942.

The next facility seized, Air Associates, Inc., was a small, financially troubled manufacturer and jobber of aircraft parts. Five months after the events at Inglewood the company, headquartered in Bendix, New Jersey, fired a number of UAW members whose union had recently won an election designating the CIO as the bargaining agent for plant employees. Although company directors maintained that the layoff had been caused by a temporary lack of materials, the National Defense Mediation Board, in return for a termination of the

---

[11] Ohly, Emergency Operation of Industrial Facilities, 1:25–26, 40–42.
[12] Ohly, HPS, 1:24–36.
[13] Ibid., 1:40–42; Rich, *President and Civil Disorder*, pp. 182–83.

strike, ordered the directors to reinstate the workers. The company refused and another strike followed. Two top Air Associates officials, President Leroy Hill and Vice President H. I. Crowe, steadfastly refused either to abide by the National Labor Relations Board order or to deal with the union in good faith. Soon the company became delinquent on deliveries. The War Department intervened in late October. Its attempts to mediate the dispute failed, even though it offered to force the termination of strike breakers and effect the reinstatement of union employees. Continued equivocation on the part of company directors and the employment of nonstriking workers threatened to cause violence.

Local authorities informed Army officials that they feared they could not maintain order. On 28 October 1941 the War Department determined "that seizure of the facilities was the only satisfactory answer from the standpoint of the government, the public, the employees and management." On 31 October 1941 Roosevelt issued his executive order, seizing the plant and facilities of Air Associates. The president also sent a message "castigating the company for its failure to accept the recommendations of the Mediation Board and calling for an immediate return to work." On the same day, Col. Roy Jones, the chief of the Eastern Procurement District of the Army Air Forces, acting as War Department representative, seized the plant and positioned 2,000 federal troops on company property.[14]

At once Army officials undertook the difficult task of resuming production and finding a permanent solution to the conditions leading to the seizure. The first order of business was to rehire all striking workers as government employees and resume full production, a process completed within two days. All strikebreakers were fired. According to one historian, however, "the government withheld wage increases, imposed working rules, arrested and tried rank-and-file strike leaders, used troops as strike replacements or to preserve order, and obtained an injunction," to maintain peace and production at the plant.[15] Army officials also managed seven other Air Associates facilities nationwide. Convinced that President Hill and Vice President Crowe were the primary instigators of the problems at the plant, War Department officials pressured the board of directors to remove them, and the board complied on 18 November 1941. While Hill waged a press campaign against what he termed the arbitrary actions of the Army and of the federal government, War Department officials went ahead with efforts to return the now refinanced and restructured company to its new executives. Although the labor problems were not entirely settled, negotiations between company officials and union representatives were under way by early December. Following the conclusion of mutual release agreements between the Army and company officials, the government returned the firm to full private control on 29 December 1941.[16]

The third seizure was also complex, and far more protracted. In August 1942 the War Department seized the S. A. Woods Company of South Boston, Massachusetts, a firm that employed 1,000 people producing munitions for the American and British governments. Its owner and primary stockholder, H. C. Dodge, like his counterparts at North American Aviation and at Air Associates, was experiencing difficulties with unionized labor. When

---

[14] Ohly, Emergency Operation of Industrial Facilities, 1:46–55; Blackman, *Presidential Seizures*, p. 257. The take-over was effected by Executive Order 8928.

[15] Quote from Blackman, *Presidential Seizures*, pp. 91–92, see also pp. 128–29, 139–43, 184, 257.

[16] Ohly, Emergency Operation of Industrial Facilities, 1:68–73.

federal mediators ruled in favor of the local union, Dodge refused to comply with their orders. Meanwhile a worker slowdown jeopardized the timely delivery of munitions to the government. After state efforts to mediate the dispute failed, Roosevelt signed an executive order authorizing War Department seizure of the company. The order was carried out on 19 August 1942 by Maj. Ralph Gow of the Boston Ordnance District. Secretary of War Henry L. Stimson simultaneously issued a statement that "no company and no labor organization can be permitted to defy the mandate of this impartial tribunal [National War Labor Board] with impunity."[17]

Dodge's intransigence soon convinced the War Department that the only solution was to bypass company officials entirely and to assume control for the duration of the war. Federal troops provided security at the main plant, and workers were rehired as unclassified civil servants. For managers, the War Department turned to civilian experts in the field. Eventually the Murray Company of Dallas, Texas, a firm with labor policies above reproach, signed a contract to run all seized S. A. Woods Company plants. Under authority of the Second War Powers Act (56 Statute 176), the War Department canceled all its outstanding munitions contracts with S. A. Woods and condemned the property. Then it promptly let new contracts with the Murray Company, which leased the S. A. Woods property and equipment from the government. Operating under Army Ordnance Department supervision, the new management was required to abide by all National Defense Mediation Board orders previously handed down; labor troubles quickly ended, and full production resumed. The S. A. Woods seizure lasted longer than any other World War II takeover, and the property was not returned to the owners until 31 August 1945.[18]

The final major use of federal troops prior to 1943 was unique in that Army regulars actually operated a facility without a specific executive order. The Fairport, Painesville, and Eastern Railroad was a line only ten miles long that served thirteen defense plants located between Fairport Harbor and Perry, near Cleveland, Ohio. The railroad was the only means for bringing raw materials into the factories and for shipping finished goods out. The nature of the industries it served and the lack of adequate storage space prevented raw materials' being stockpiled. Consequently, when a dispute between the United Mine Workers (UMW) and the Brotherhood of Railroad Engineers and Firemen stopped railroad operations on 6 November 1942, the industries along the line were paralyzed within hours. The strike occurred suddenly, forestalling any government attempts to avert it, and President Roosevelt was unavailable to handle the dispute.

After Assistant Secretary of War John J. McCloy had discussed the problem with White House officials and had received their informal approval, Secretary Stimson invoked the Act of 29 August 1916 and Executive Order 8972 of 12 December 1941.[19] These laws authorized him to "establish and maintain military guards and patrols and to take other appropriate measures to protect from injury or destruction national defense materials, national defense premises and national defense utilities." The 730th Railway Engineer Battalion and the 735th Military Police Battalion moved to the area that same

---

[17] Ibid., 1:88–93; Blackman, *Presidential Seizures*, p. 261. This takeover was effected by Executive Order 9225.

[18] Blackman, *Presidential Seizures*, pp. 20, 91, 140, 234, 261; Ohly, Emergency Operation of Industrial Facilities, 1:93–110 passim, pp. 114–15.

[19] 39 *U.S. Statutes at Large*, 619, 645.

evening and began operating the railroad the following morning. As a result, the labor dispute ended suddenly, and federal troops withdrew on 10 November, the day after the War Labor Board, by War Department request, stepped in to conclude an agreement between the two contending parties.[20]

Seizures in the Later War Years, 1943–1945

The apparent inability of some union leaders to understand that strikes in wartime might be viewed as unpatriotic by many Americans led to continued disputes and ultimately to new legislation. The most sensational labor crisis took place in May 1943, when UMW President John L. Lewis led 530,000 coal miners off the job in nearly 4,000 hard- and soft-coal mines in twenty-two states. Although President Roosevelt seized the mines by an executive order, and government control continued until the fall of 1943, the public was outraged, and sentiment to curb wartime strikes became irresistible. Congress already had legislation under consideration, and on 25 June 1943 it passed the War Labor Disputes Act over President Roosevelt's veto. Though Roosevelt had opposed the act, favoring a weaker variant, he would use the enacted version nearly fifty times before his death in April 1945.[21]

The War Labor Disputes Act furnished clear statutory authority for seizing plants when labor disputes threatened war production and also settled a number of questions raised by earlier seizures. The act amended Section 9 of the 1940 Selective Service Act to allow seizure for labor-initiated disturbances as well as management noncompliance with federal orders. It also declared the terms of employment for workers in a seized plant to be "those which were in effect at the time possession was taken," meaning that workers would not, as in the past, become government employees upon seizure. Nor could they automatically expect concessions or changes in employment status as a result of a federal takeover. The act did allow the government-appointed agent at the seized plant, without the cooperation or agreement of company officials, to request from the War Labor Board wage increases and other changes in employee status to resolve the causes of the initial labor problem. Finally, the law made it a criminal offense to interfere with workers in a seized plant. (Although this section was aimed at labor leaders, its provisions would have been equally applicable to the activities of President Hill of Air Associates, after the government seizure of that plant.)

The War Labor Disputes Act "put the ordinary plant seizure beyond the probability of legal attack." After 1943, plant seizures took on such well-established patterns that they became routine. Those seizures involving labor or management noncompliance with War Labor Board orders became "almost token in character." Only when management refused to cooperate in running the business did seizure involve active control by the War Department.[22]

---

[20] Ohly, Emergency Operation of Industrial Facilities, 1:122–29; Blackman, *Presidential Seizures*, pp. 20, 160, 262, 290.

[21] Blackman, *Presidential Seizures*, pp. 262–63; Fairchild and Grossman, *Army and Industrial Manpower*, p. 78; Ohly, Emergency Operation of Industrial Facilities, 1:137. For the act, see 57 *U.S. Statutes at Large*, 163. The applicable Executive Order was 9340.

[22] Quotes from Ohly, Emergency Operation of Industrial Facilities, 1:130–144, pp. 159–60; Fairchild and Grossman, *Army and Industrial Manpower*, pp. 78–79; Blackman, *Presidential Seizures*, pp. 20–21, 68, 292.

Nevertheless, the administration still sought ways to minimize the need for intervention. Six weeks after the passage of the War Labor Disputes Act, the White House issued Executive Order 9370 to encourage labor unions and management to accept War Labor Board rulings. Under the executive order, the government could withhold or withdraw from companies materials, priorities, or contracts, and it could similarly withhold or withdraw benefits, draft deferments, and government support from unions or workers who refused to accept War Labor Board directives. The order, however, failed completely. It could not be used effectively against large contractors without severely handicapping or stifling war production. Furthermore, sanctions against recalcitrant managers would harm innocent employees, and vice versa. Finally, the executive order was of dubious legality and inherently difficult to administer. Executive Order 9370, therefore, was seldom applied and failed to become a substitute for the War Labor Disputes Act.[23]

The law also spurred the War Department to make new studies of plant seizures, to give its employees better training in such matters, and to reorganize its apparatus for carrying out the process. On 31 October 1943 the department issued a confidential manual that contained standard forms, texts of laws and executive orders, a description of the purpose, philosophy, and routine for future seizures, and a history of previous seizures. The manual, revised in 1944, represented "the first step in placing the handling of plant seizures on an orderly, methodical basis."[24]

Henceforth, plant seizures were carried out by specially created War Department teams. Each consisted of a team leader who acted as the primary executor of War Department policies, an executive officer, and various specialists in fiscal and legal matters and in public, labor, and industrial relations. For administration, supply, transportation, and troop assistance, the leader called upon the commander of the applicable Army service command. This commander, however, had no control over the seizure itself. Even the decision on whether to use troops was confided to the team leader, for, as John Ohly explains, "it was felt that the use of troops was incidental to the main mission [of restarting production] and that therefore the person primarily responsible for the mission should have the final say."[25] Army acceptance of this principle—that the primary purpose of military intervention was to maintain production and not to break strikes—represented a fundamental departure from the practices of the previous seventy years.

In this new conceptual and legal framework, seizures became a stylized procedure following predictable steps: the Labor Branch of the War Department monitored potential labor-industrial problems, potentially disruptive disputes were referred to the civilian War Labor Board, and the board recommended seizure to the president. When seizure became probable, the Labor Branch selected and briefed a seizure team, and the Army service command that controlled the area in which the targeted plant was located began to consider administrative, supply, and logistical details—travel orders, accommodations, printing needs, transportation, and so forth. The seizure team, furnished with copies of all pertinent documents, traveled to the scene a day in advance and held last-minute conferences with officers of the Army service command. Then, after a formal announcement from the White

---

[23] Ohly, Emergency Operation of Industrial Facilities, 1:154–57.

[24] Quote from Ibid., 1:152–54, 563 16n; U.S. Army, Office of the Judge Advocate General, *Emergency Operation of Industrial Facilities, 23 September 1944* (Washington, D.C.: TJAG, 1944).

[25] Emergency Operation of Industrial Facilities, 1:189, 197–200.

House, the team seized the targeted plant. The team leader visited top-ranking company officials, explained his mission, presented copies of the appropriate documents, and urged cooperation and approval of an operating contract. Meanwhile, other members of the team raised the American flag over the seized plant, posted notices of War Department possession and, in cases of strikes, sought to put idle workers back on the job.[26]

Old attitudes and habits among some Army officers favoring the rapid application of military force to labor disputes still persisted. In November 1943, while in the process of seizing the strike-idled Salem Peabody Leather Manufacturing Company in Massachusetts, the War Department representative supervising the operation had to convince the commanding general of the First Service Command that regular troops were not required and should not be called or used. On another occasion, the April 1944 seizure of the Ken-Rad Tube and Lamp Corporation because of management refusal to comply with War Labor Board orders, the War Department instructed its representative to withdraw if he met resistance, rather than provoke a confrontation requiring troop intervention. The War Labor Disputes Act and better organization of the War Department so completely obviated the need for armed intervention that combat troops were used on only one occasion after 1943, in a race-related transit strike in Philadelphia.[27]

The Philadelphia Transit Strike, 1944

The origins of the strike lay in a dispute between a CIO union, recently certified by the state labor relations board as the exclusive bargaining agent for transit workers, and a local independent union. The independent union refused to acquiesce in the state's decision and began to use racial issues as a means to undermine CIO support and regain control of the transit workers.[28]

The racial conflict was long-standing. On 27 December 1943 the federal Fair Employment Practices Commission had ordered the privately owned Philadelphia Transit Company to train black employees, previously limited to shop employment, for jobs as vehicle operators. The company, although fearful of the reaction of its white employees, finally accepted the order on 1 July 1944 and began training black operators one week later.[29] The new and inexperienced leaders of the CIO transit union, however, soon lost control of their membership amid increasing charges from the rival union that black operators were violating seniority rules and would deprive returning veterans of their transit jobs. The resulting strike, therefore, was as much a product of racial issues as it was of union jurisdictions.

White employees, inflamed by racist rhetoric, ignored appeals from CIO union officials and struck the system on 1 August, when the first blacks finished training and began

---

[26] Ibid., 1:427–38.

[27] Ibid., 1:172, 2:232–69.

[28] Ibid., 2:294–98; Allan M. Winkler, "The Philadelphia Transit Strike of 1944," *Journal of American History* 59 (1972):73–89.

[29] For the FEPC and wartime race relations, see Warren Schaich, "A Relationship Between Collective Racial Violence and War," *Journal of Black Studies* 5 (1975):374–94; James A. Nuechterlein, "The Politics of Civil Rights: The FEPC, 1941–1946," *Prologue* 10 (1978): 171–91; Tony Martin, "March on Washington Movement," *Journal of African Afro-American Affairs* 3 (1979):63–69; Merl E. Reed, "Black Workers, Defense Industries, and Federal Agencies in Pennsylvania, 1941–1945," *Labor History* 27 (Summer 1986):356–84.

PHILIP HAYES

to operate buses and trams. The existence of numerous defense and defense-related industries in the area, especially the Philadelphia Navy Yard, gave the federal government an immediate interest, especially when federal officials learned that absenteeism at these locations ranged from 50 to 70 percent on the first day of the strike. Interference with war production, however, was not the only concern of local, state, and federal officials. As the U.S. district attorney for Philadelphia stated, "if this strike is not settled immediately, Philadelphia will experience one of the worst race riots in the history of the country." Local officials promptly called out 10,000 auxiliary policemen, banned all liquor sales, and made appeals for calm over the radio and in local newspapers. The state guard was alerted for possible riot duty.[30]

At the federal level, on 2 August the War Labor Board admitted its failure to reach a settlement and voted to refer the dispute to President Roosevelt. It took until the following day, however, to wire a proposed executive order authorizing seizure of the transit system to the president, who was in Hawaii conferring with Army and Navy leaders. By then, the War Department, though hesitant to become involved, had already made plans to act. Because a large number of troops might be required, the department named Maj. Gen. Philip Hayes of the Third Service Command as its representative. Following presidential approval, the War Department seized the Philadelphia transit system on 3 August. On the following day many CIO-affiliated workers reported for work, but strikers threatened them, demanding a written guarantee that blacks would not be hired as operators. The War Department, in a tense meeting with transit union officials, emphasized its resolve to enforce the Fair Employment Practices Commission order at all costs. The strike continued among increasing signs of violence.[31]

Undeterred by striker recalcitrance, the Army moved ahead with its plans to make the transit system operational. On 5 August, Hayes implemented a comprehensive plan that shortly broke the strike and returned the system to full operation. First, he deployed 6,000 combat troops of the 102d Infantry Division from Fort Dix, New Jersey, who were waiting to embark overseas, at all car barns and on all buses and trains in the Philadelphia area. Second, he called a meeting of strike leaders and threatened them with arrest under the War Labor Disputes Act unless they promised prompt cooperation. Finally, he ordered an additional 2,000 combat troops to Philadelphia and began setting up a substitute transit system using Army vehicles, primarily for defense plant and Navy yard workers, while other sol-

---

[30] Ohly, Emergency Operation of Industrial Facilities, 2:294–98.
[31] Ibid., 2:299–305.

U.S. ARMY MILITARY POLICEMAN DIRECTS CONVOYS ARRIVING IN PHILADELPHIA

diers hurriedly underwent training to operate city buses and trolleys. On 6 August four strike leaders were arrested for violating the War Labor Disputes Act, as promised, and a federal grand jury was impaneled to investigate the causes of the strike and the culpability of union leaders. On the following day, just as the Army completed preparations to run the entire system itself, it became apparent that the strike was collapsing as 98 percent of the transit employees reported for work.

Later reports indicated that most employees returned to work not because of any patriotic feeling, but because they feared induction into the Army and the subsequent loss of their jobs. With the National War Labor Board now dealing with all sides in the dispute, with a federal grand jury investigation under way, and with the system fully operable, the War Department saw no further need for an Army presence. Between 10–17 August 1944, federal troops withdrew from the city, and the owners regained full control of the Philadelphia Transit Company.[32]

Coming after the most intense union organizing campaign in American history in the 1930s, World War II presented the federal government with a new set of labor-indus-

---

[32] Ibid., 2:305–17.

Federal Troops at 32d Street and Lancaster Avenue and *(below)* at Broad and Locust Streets in Philadelphia.

trial problems. The dream of the New Dealers featured strong unions able to bargain collectively with management to ensure the worker a fair share of the economic pie, with
the government acting as a neutral mediator of disputes. They did not foresee the possibility that jurisdictional disputes between competing unions, or the refusal of management or labor to accept the results of mediation, could cripple the entire system. In
addition, members of the Roosevelt administration did not foresee the possible disruption that such a system of labor-industrial-government relations might cause in wartime.
When war came and disruptive labor-industrial disputes did occur, the government
turned to the technique of plant seizures, rather than to the use of federal troops as in
the past. However, when necessary, as in Philadelphia, the administration was prepared
to use force. Plant seizures were not intended to be permanent, but rather were intended to restore production and buy time for federally sponsored mediation to succeed.
After 1943 the seizure process became an efficient, effective, and largely nonviolent
legal and bureaucratic procedure for solving industrial-labor disputes, in which the use
of federal troops was seldom required.

The 1943 Detroit Race Riot

World War II, like World War I, presented black Americans with the promise of
increased economic opportunity and the hope for social equality. As in the First World
War, industries met their manpower needs largely by recruiting labor from other areas,
especially the rural south where a labor surplus existed. Many of the 15 million people
who migrated north were blacks seeking relatively high-paying jobs in war plants. This
opportunity for economic advancement was coupled with a renewed black activism as
civil rights leaders sought to abolish social barriers to black equality, such as segregation in the armed forces. Like the World War I generation, in the early 1940s blacks saw
the war as an opportunity to fight for liberty, democracy, and social justice both at home
and abroad.

But one effect of the new activism was the heightened resistance by whites to the
very idea of black social and economic equality. By mid-1943 it was increasingly obvious to many blacks that they had not met their economic and social goals. Although
blacks as war workers earned higher wages than they ever had before, they still endured
crowded slum housing, held menial jobs, obtained only limited opportunities for
advancement, and faced continued segregation. As a result, racial violence exploded in
1942–1943 in Beaumont, Texas; Mobile, Alabama; Marianna, Florida; Los Angeles,
California; Newark, New Jersey; New York City; Philadelphia, Pennsylvania; and
Detroit, Michigan.

Wartime racial incidents varied in character and scale. In Beaumont, a race riot
delayed war production and left two people dead. Racial violence occurred on military
reservations in Mississippi, Georgia, Texas, California, New Jersey, and Kentucky. In
Mobile, white workers assaulted blacks employed at the defense-contracted Alabama
Dry Docks and Shipbuilding Company, and the ensuing race riot had to be suppressed
by forty Army military policemen dispatched from nearby Brookley Field. In Harlem a
serious race riot erupted briefly in August 1943. And meanwhile, the failure of the
Detroit police to respond quickly and effectively to a violent outbreak allowed racial

violence in that city to mushroom into one of the largest and bloodiest riots of twentieth century America.[33]

Wartime conditions exacerbated Detroit's existing racial problems. Once called "the
most beautiful in America," the city had been transformed during the early twentieth century by the automobile industry's demands for an increasing number of workers. Many
whites and blacks came from the south, where Detroit industries advertised lucrative
employment opportunities, such as Henry Ford's five-dollar-per-day wage. By 1920
Detroit's population had grown to 1.5 million, a fivefold increase since 1900. The flow of
migrants temporarily abated during the depression, only to rise again in the 1940s, when
wartime production once again attracted throngs of workers to the "Arsenal of
Democracy." In the fifteen months prior to the 1943 riot alone, 350,000 people had moved
to the city.[34]

As Detroit's population grew, its racial composition changed. A large majority of the
city's newcomers were blacks, whose numbers increased from 8,000 in 1916 to 85,000 in
1925. As jobs became less plentiful during the depression, blacks were forced to compete
with other minority groups, such as the Poles, who were already established in Detroit, and
southern whites who had also come north seeking employment. Inevitably, blacks became
the targets of racist organizations like the Ku Klux Klan, creating a foundation of hatred
upon which tensions would build. With the war production boom, blacks once again
migrated by the thousands to Detroit. By 1943, 200,000 blacks lived in the city, of whom
50,000 had established residency only since March 1942.[35]

This large and rapid influx of people put a heavy strain on the city's resources. A
severe housing shortage for everyone had existed before the war. Many blacks were
crowded into the city's old Jewish ghetto, an area known as Paradise Valley, where they
paid exorbitant rents for slums that were often inferior to the sharecropper shacks left
behind in the south. City recreation and transportation services were strained as well. Few
parks existed in Paradise Valley, and blacks often went to the only recreation area available to them on nearby Belle Isle, previously used exclusively by whites. To reach work
and recreation, blacks crowded the public transit system. Social and physical contact
between stressed and resentful individuals heightened tensions. Furthermore, blacks and
whites confronted each other in the work place, especially during unionization efforts.

---

[33] Merl E. Reed, "The FEPC, the Black Worker, and the Southern Shipyards," *South Atlantic Quarterly* 45
(1975):446–61; Thomas Sancton, "The Race Riots," *New Republic* 109 (5 July 1943):10–11; Dominic J. Capeci,
Jr., *The Harlem Riot of 1943* (Philadelphia: Temple University Press, 1977); Morris J. MacGregor, Jr., *Integration
of the Armed Forces, 1940–1965*, (Washington, D.C.: U.S. Army Center of Military History, 1981), p. 39; Jean
Byers, *A Study of the Negro in Military Service* (Washington, D.C.: U.S. Army Center of Military History, 1947),
pp. 53–70; Ulysses Lee, *The Employment of Negro Troops* (Washington, D.C.: U.S. Army Center of Military
History, 1966), pp. 348–79; for overseas difficulties, see Kenneth P. Werrell, "Mutiny at Army Air Force Station
569: Bamber Bridge, England, June 1943," *Aerospace Historian* 22 (Winter/December 1975):202–09; Rpt on
Riot Duty, Mobile, Ala., 25 May–5 Jun 43, Office of the Alabama AG, Internal Security Div, Emergency
Protection Branch, Records of the Provost Marshall General's Office, Race Riots Strikes, 1942–45, RG 389,
NARA.

[34] Robert Shogan and Tom Craig, *The Detroit Race Riot: A Study in Violence* (New York: Chilton, 1964), p.
19; Walter White, "What Caused the Detroit Riots?" pt. I of Walter White and Thurgood Marshall, *What Caused
the Detroit Riots?* (New York, 1943), as cited in *Afro-American History: Primary Sources* ed. Thomas R. Frazier
(New York: Harcourt Brace & World, 1970) pp. 5–16, George W. Beatty, *The Background Causes of the 1943
Detroit Race Riot* (Princeton: Princeton University Press, 1954).

[35] White, "What Caused the Detroit Riots?"

The organization of the Ford Motor Company by the UAW was delayed, according to many whites, by black workers who refused to join unions and remained devoted to "Uncle Henry" Ford, who often provided well-paid jobs to black strikebreakers. Black promotions also provoked white resentment. White anger led to a number of work stoppages and strikes immediately preceding the July riot, the most serious at the Packard Motor Company, involving 28,883 workers.[36]

Making a bad situation worse, racist organizations fueled white resentments, while the city's overt discrimination angered blacks. Demagogues such as Father Charles Coughlin and the Reverend Gerald L. K. Smith stirred up racial hatred, as did racist organizations like the Black Legion, the Development of Our Own, and the Ku Klux Klan. The NAACP and the black press contributed to the tension by keeping the race issue in the public eye. Segregation of public facilities was still commonplace in Detroit, despite state civil rights laws. Blacks were cared for in separate hospital wards; a third of Detroit's restaurants refused to serve blacks at all and another third served them sporadically. In February 1941, when a group of whites attempted to prevent blacks from occupying the federally funded Sojourner Truth housing project, over 1,700 city and state police were called to quell the riot. Clearly, Detroit was "a powder keg with a short fuse."[37]

The Riot Begins

Sunday, 20 June 1943, was a hot day marked by a number of minor fights between whites and blacks on Belle Isle. That night, among the cars lining the Belle Isle bridge, a more serious fight broke out between black men and white sailors from the nearby naval armory. The altercation soon escalated into a riot involving 5,000 people. The Detroit police restored order on the bridge by 0200, but not before rumors of the rioting and alleged atrocities had ignited outbreaks of violence in Paradise Valley and on Detroit's major thoroughfare, Woodward Avenue, two blocks west of and parallel to Paradise Valley. Rumors of the Belle Isle clashes inflamed the crowds at the all-night taverns in Paradise Valley, and by 0100 black rioters began to stone passing cars and break the windows of white-owned shops on nearby Hastings and Forest Streets. Mayhem soon spread through Paradise Valley as white pedestrians were beaten by blacks and parked cars were overturned and set aflame. By early the next morning, 21 June, gangs of whites randomly assaulted blacks traveling on Woodward Avenue. The police appeared openly biased; they physically attacked black rioters and merely ordered offending whites to disperse. Future U.S. Supreme Court Justice Thurgood Marshall, an investigator for the NAACP, charged that police treated whites with restraint, but blacks were accorded "the ultimate in force: night sticks, revolvers, riot guns, submachine guns, and deer guns."[38]

In response to the growing seriousness of the situation, Detroit Mayor Edward Jeffries convened a meeting of area military and law enforcement officials at 0400. In attendance

---

[36] Shogan and Craig, *The Detroit Race Riot*, p. 32; White, "What Caused the Detroit Riots?" p. 345.

[37] Beatty, *Background Causes*, pp. 50, 61–62, 79; Harvard Sitkoff, "The Detroit Race Riot of 1943," *Michigan History* 53 (Fall 1969):188; Domonic J. Capeci, Jr., *Race Relations in Wartime Detroit: The Sojourner Truth Housing Controversy of 1942* (Philadelphia: Temple University Press, 1984).

[38] Thurgood Marshall, "The Gestapo in Detroit," *Crisis* (August 1943), reprinted in Joseph Boskin, *Urban Racial Violence in the Twentieth Century* (Beverly Hills: Glencoe, 1976), pp. 232–33, 246.

were Col. August M. Krech, commander of District No. 1, Army Sixth Service Command; Capt. Milton R. Wortley, U.S. Navy, commandant of the Detroit Naval Armory; and Detroit Police Commissioner John H. Witherspoon. Among the topics they discussed were the procedures for obtaining federal military aid if necessary. Krech assured Jeffries that Military Police battalions stationed within the Detroit area could be committed within forty-five minutes after proper orders had been received from his military superiors in response to a request by the governor. Jeffries, confident that the worst of the rioting had passed, declared that the city police force was capable of dealing with the crisis and that no federal troops were required at that time.[39]

The military, however, had already begun to make preparations in expectation of a request by officials for federal troops. The Military Police detachment stationed at the Detroit police headquarters was already bringing in prisoners and injured persons two hours before the mayor's meeting was convened. The detachment's commander had telephoned the intelligence officer of District No.1 to report that a race riot was in progress; the intelligence officer had reported the situation to Krech, and Krech had alerted the 728th Military Police Battalion at Camp River Rouge Park, on the outskirts of Detroit near Dearborn Heights. For the time being, however, the military police waited as new violence broke out in the city.[40]

Contrary to Jeffries' hopes, the riot escalated after a predawn lull. Crowds on Woodward Avenue increased in size, and violence in Paradise Valley intensified. Several prominent citizens attempted to restore order, but their efforts failed. Even 3,500 city policemen, the largest force mobilized in Detroit to that time, could not control the rioting.[41] Realizing that his previous assessment was in error, the mayor called Michigan Governor Harry S. Kelly to request state troops. Kelly, attending a governors conference in Columbus, Ohio, called out the state police and state troops, the latter a force organized to replace federalized National Guardsmen. Then he telephoned Maj. Gen Henry S. Aurand, commanding general of the Sixth Service Command, to inquire about the use of federal troops in Detroit. (Kelly later asserted that he had meant this call to be an actual request for troops, but at the time the call was understood by Army officials to have been merely a "possible request for Federal Troops in Detroit.") In either case, the governor was not following accepted procedures, since a request for federal military aid had to be directed to the president, not to an Army commander. This confusion on the governor's part delayed commitment of the Army. Believing his duty completed, Kelly left for Detroit.[42]

In the meantime, the Army continued to prepare. At midmorning Aurand ordered Brig. Gen. William E. Guthner, director of the Internal Security Division of the Sixth Service

[39] Sitkoff, "The Detroit Race Riot of 1943," p. 190; Earl Brown, "The Truth About the Detroit Riot," *Harper's* (November 1943):496; Alfred McClung Lee and Norman D. Humphrey, *Race Riot* (New York: Dryden, 1943), pp. 29–30; Brig Gen William E. Guthner, CG, U.S. Armed Forces in Michigan, Commander's Estimate of the Situation for the Period Sunday, June 20, 10:30 P.M. (Eastern War Time) to Thursday, June 24, 12:00 Noon (EWT), n.d., p. 3, RG 389, NARA. Hereafter cited as Cmdr's Est 1. The Detroit metropolitan area fell within District 1 of the U.S. Army Sixth Service Command, headquartered in Chicago.

[40] Cmdr's Est 1, p. 2.

[41] Associated Press (AP) Rpt, 11:01 A.M., 21 Jun 43, RG 389, NARA.

[42] Cmdr's Est 1, p. 3; Memo, Michigan AG for Chief, National Guard Bureau, 9 Jul 43, RG 389, NARA. See also Shogan and Craig, *The Detroit Race Riot*, p. 74.

Command, to place all Military Police battalions in District No. 1 on alert. Guthner ordered the commander of Fort Custer, Michigan, to place the 701st Military Police Battalion (zone of the interior or ZI) on alert, and to create a provisional battalion of the 237th, 279th, and 280th Military Police Companies (ZI). Finally, Guthner ordered Krech to alert the 728th Military Police Battalion (ZI), which Krech had done already on his own authority. The 701st required two and one-half hours to prepare, with the provisional battalion, which required additional weapons, transportation, supply, and staff, taking almost three times as long. Aurand then ordered Guthner to fly from Chicago to Detroit, to make a survey of the situation, and to assume command of all federal troops in the area.[43]

Upon his arrival, Guthner ordered the 701st to Camp River Rouge Park and alerted the commander of Selfridge Field Air Base to ready the twelve-station complement squadrons for deployment. These units were undergoing home defense training and, as Guthner had previously recommended, training in potential labor or racial disorders that might affect war production in or around Detroit. Altogether, Guthner had 2,500 federal troops on alert. Aurand sought to supplement this number by requesting, from the deputy chief of staff for service commands, that steps be taken to obtain ground troops from the Second Army. ASF's Operations Plans Division responded by taking the necessary steps to have the 2d Infantry Division, without artillery, made available for his use. The size of the troop allotment was in accordance with the War Department's Emergency Plan White. All that was necessary for the commitment of federal troops to riot duty in Detroit was a formal request from Governor Kelly to President Roosevelt and the president's suitable response.[44]

The situation in Detroit worsened throughout the afternoon as rumors spread that hundreds of people had been killed. The crowds on Woodward Avenue increased in size, and public transportation was brought to a near standstill as whites pulled blacks off streetcars and assaulted them. The Detroit fire department reported receiving 125 calls, and the police department received 4,000. Absenteeism was high in many plants, although ironclad union discipline kept rioting from breaking out within the plants themselves. The closing of the high schools during the afternoon only made matters worse, because many youths rushed to swell the crowds.[45]

At 1500 another conference was called to discuss methods for quelling the violence. In attendance were Krech, Jeffries, Kelly, and local Navy, Marine, Army Air Forces, Coast Guard, FBI, and police officials. The meeting reviewed the military preparations that had been made, including the concentration of Michigan State Troops in Detroit. The military leaders again emphasized that no federal troops could be committed without General Aurand's orders. The conference centered, however, on the question of martial law. Kelly and Jeffries were both under the mistaken, but not unusual, impression that a declaration of martial law was needed before federal troops could be committed. Despite Jeffries' urging, Kelly did not want to request the troops, since martial law, with its accompanying suspension of civilian authority, implied state incompetence and failure. The governor intended

    [43] Military Ops from Cmdr's Est 1, pp. 3–4; Ltr, Aurand to Maj Gen Allen Gullion, 3 Jul 43, p. 1, RG 389, NARA.

    [44] Ltr, Guthner to Col H. G. Reynolds, Air Provost Marshal, 2 Jul 43; Col James M. Roamer, Summary of Events in the Detroit Race Riot, pp. 1–2; both in RG 389, NARA.

    [45] AP Rpt, 11:01 A.M., 21 Jun 43; Cmdr's Est 1, pp. 4–5.

instead to rely on state troops and state police, leaving the federal military option open if the situation did not improve substantially by evening.[46]

Army officials in Washington were kept informed about developments in Detroit, but they were slow to give assistance. Except for having seen some press releases, the Provost Marshal General's Office first heard of the riot about 1200 on 21 June. At that time Brig. Gen. Edward Greenbaum, executive officer to the under secretary of war, phoned Brig. Gen. Archer Lerch, the assistant provost marshal general, and told him that over 90,000 people were involved in the riot, which had started the day before "at some big celebration." So far, he continued, "four have been killed, 186 injured, three hundred of them jailed and stores [have been] smashed open."[47]

General Aurand's call requesting additional forces again raised the question among Washington officials of what procedures were required to commit federal troops in a civil disturbance. Since the governor of Michigan had not asked for troops, Army officials apparently were looking for some means of intervening without such a request. Maj. Gen. Allen W. Gullion, the Army's provost marshal general, discussed the matter with Col. James M. Roamer, an officer in G–2 of the War Department General Staff. Gullion recognized the seriousness of the situation and that "it comes closer to being an Emergency Plan White than anything we've had yet," but Roamer was unsure whether troops could be committed without presidential authority. However, the general informed him that Aurand could use federal troops in Detroit without specific presidential direction because General Aurand was "interested in the protection of the war effort and of these plants . . . he's not going in there to keep white people from killing black people or vice versa. . . . Now that's the ground on which he can use the troops. . . . And if incidental to protecting the plant he saves life well and good." (This pragmatic, but incorrect, principle was applied only once. A military guard was placed at the J. T. Wing Company, a Detroit retail outlet of the Defense Supplies Corporation, which stocked 4,800 weapons that many feared could fall into the hands of rioters.)[48]

In any case, the Provost Marshal General's Office decided not to act. General Lerch believed that they should "stand by in Washington and supply the help when the Service Commander asks for it without tying him down with instructions or any directions, because as soon as we give him any instructions or directions we'll furnish him with a first class alibi if things go wrong and he should be left a free hand until he asks for something and when he asks for something we should be ready to give it promptly." Any further action on the part of the War Department would come about only on Aurand's initiative, and he was still awaiting a formal request for troops from Kelly.[49]

Meanwhile, some twenty hours after the riot had started, Kelly at last declared a state of emergency in Detroit. In an 1800 radio broadcast he called upon the state armed forces to place themselves under civil law enforcement personnel to aid in implementing law and

[46] Memo, Michigan AG for Chief, National Guard Bureau, 9 Jul 43, p. 1; Cmdr's Est 1, p. 6. See also Sitkoff, "The Detroit Race Riot of 1943," p. 193.

[47] Log, Provost Marshal General's Office; Telecon, Brig Gen Lerch and Brig Gen Greenbaum, 12:30 P.M., 21 Jun 43; both in RG 389, NARA.

[48] Quote from Telecon, Gullion and Roamer, 1:45 P.M., 21 Jun 43; see also Telecon, Lt Col F. W. Reese and Col O. G. Miller, 4:30 P.M., 21 Jun 43; both in RG 389, NARA.

[49] Telecon, Lerch and Roamer, 4:25 P.M., 21 Jun 43, RG 389, NARA.

order throughout Wayne, Oakland, and Maycomb Counties. The governor banned the sale of alcohol, forbade public gatherings, closed all places of amusement, and imposed a 2200 curfew, which excepted only those traveling to or from work.

The proclamation cleared the way for the commitment of state troops already concentrated in Detroit and Highland Park. Shortly afterward, two detachments of state troops of the Michigan 31st Regiment began aiding city police. They soon proved to be entirely ineffective. An Army inspector general later declared that "these troops did not leave a favorable impression among the civilian population of Detroit. They were not dressed as soldiers, did not look like soldiers and were looked upon simply as additional police by the mobsters [rioters] who, it appears, had very little respect for police." Yet these were the last remaining state resource. Only federal troops remained now, the last resource for reestablishing control.[50]

HENRY L. STIMSON WITH LESLEY J. MCNAIR *(center)* AND BREHON B. SOMERVELL *(right).*

Even as the Michigan State Troops moved into Detroit, the Army increased its own involvement. At 1720 Aurand briefed Lt. Gen. Brehon B. Somervell, the ASF commander, and requested that the secretary of war ask President Roosevelt for a proclamation extending federal military aid to the governor of Michigan under RS 5297. Somervell informed Secretary Stimson and Lt. Gen. Joseph T. McNarney, Army deputy chief of staff, before calling a conference for 1800. In attendance were General Gullion and Colonel Roamer. They decided that the Provost Marshal General's Office, with the assistance of the Judge Advocate General's Office, would draft a proclamation for the president's signature. Two hours later Gullion had the proclamation—modeled on a sample form given in the Emergency Plan White—ready for the president's signature. Gullion and Somervell then took the proclamation to Stimson for final approval and transmission to the president.[51]

On the evening of 21 July the violence in Detroit peaked. Absenteeism forced many smaller plants to close completely and many others to reduce operations, leaving thousands of Detroit citizens idle and on the streets. Those injured in rioting were now arriving at Detroit's Receiving Hospital at the rate of one person every two minutes, while police forces were swamped with multiple calls for assistance from over 75 percent of the

---

[50] Memo, Michigan AG for Chief, National Guard Bureau, 9 Jul 43; Memo, Col J. R. Burney, IG Div, for IG, 30 Jun 43, RG 389, NARA.

[51] Cmdr's Est 1, p. 8. The account of the conference is taken from Roamer, Summary of Events in the Detroit Race Riot, p. 3; Log, Provost Marshal General's Office, p. 2.

metropolitan area. Rumors of atrocities and outrages committed by all sides abounded, and these fueled violence.[52] The situation convinced Aurand and Guthner to move federal forces to a forward assembly area near Fort Wayne. The 701st Military Police Battalion (ZI), which had already arrived at Camp River Rouge Park, was ordered to advance to Fort Wayne along with the Selfridge Field provisional battalion. One hour later Guthner assumed command of the U.S. Army forces in Michigan.[53]

Governor Kelly at last made an unofficial request for federal troops, but the intervention did not follow traditional procedure. Kelly made his request early on the morning of 22 July to Aurand, who in turn ordered Guthner to provide the needed assistance. He was to act with restraint in dispersing the rioters, relying as far as possible upon the moral effect of a display of force. But he was authorized to use chemical weapons and then gunfire if milder methods proved ineffective. He was to cooperate closely with city, state, and federal authorities but to accept orders only from his military superiors. He was not to permit local officials to interfere with the accomplishment of his mission. Acting on these instructions before the governor had spoken with Roosevelt and before a cease and desist proclamation had been issued, Guthner ordered troops onto the streets of Detroit.[54]

Federal Troops Intervene

Action began at a number of points. The 728th Military Police Battalion (ZI), under Lt. Col. Victor Colson and consisting of 18 officers and 450 enlisted men, moved to protect the federal building at Fort and Shelby Streets. The 701st Military Police Battalion (ZI), under Lt. Col. John Bagby and consisting of 28 officers and 714 enlisted men, took up a position two blocks away, at the corner of Woodward Avenue and Fort Street. The partially trained and partially equipped composite battalion from Fort Custer, consisting of 22 officers and 440 enlisted men, was still en route to Camp River Rouge Park. Finally, the provisional battalion from Selfridge Field was ordered to move forward to Fort Wayne along with three tanks.[55]

These forces faced not one but several mobs. A throng estimated at 15,000, not all of whom were rioters, had gathered on Woodward Avenue north of the Vernor Highway; another group of 5,000 milled about near City Hall and Cadillac Square. Near Adelaide Street serious rioting that involved 7,000 people was in progress, and other mobs were rioting at Third and Warren Avenues. Finally, smaller groups of both whites and blacks were roaming the city at will, especially in Paradise Valley, engaged in arson, fighting, and looting. The situation demanded that a major force be deployed down Woodward Avenue to disperse the larger crowds, while smaller Army patrols cleared the streets of roving bands. The troops were admonished to show restraint in dealing with the rioters and to resort to firepower only

---

[52] Ltr, Guthner to Reese, 2 Aug 43, RG 389, NARA. See also Gordon W. Allport and Leo Postman, *The Psychology of Rumor* (New York: Henry Holt, 1947), pp. 196–97.

[53] Telecon, Gullion and Guthner, 10:30 A.M., 25 Jun 43, RG 389, NARA; Cmdr's Est 1, pp. 8–10.

[54] Cmdr's Est 1, p. 10; Memo, Aurand for Guthner, 22 Jul 43, sub: Use of Troops in Connection with Domestic Disturbance in Detroit, Mich., RG 389, NARA.

[55] Cmdr's Est 1; Memo, Burney for IG, 30 Jun 43; and Guthner, Summary of Events and Cmdr's Est of the Situation for the Period Thursday, Jun 24, 1943, 1200 to Sunday, Jun 27, 1943, 0800," p. 5, RG 389, NARA, hereafter cited as Cmdr's Est 2.

FEDERAL TROOPS ON PATROL IN DETROIT

when "all other measures fail to control the situation, bearing in mind that the suppression of violence when accomplished without bloodshed is a worthy military achievement."[56]

In a short time, the military police were ready to deploy. Three hundred and fifty men of the 701st quickly dispersed the mob around City Hall and Cadillac Square and then proceeded up Woodward Avenue, scattering crowds as they went. This sweep completed, the companies formed a skirmish line and moved through Paradise Valley. The 728th was assigned to patrol duty, using jeeps, scout cars, weapons carriers, and small foot detachments. Although the troops used tear gas in a few instances, they fired few shots and killed no one. Throughout, they acted with firmness and restraint and were remarkably effective. Isolated outbreaks of violence persisted through the early morning hours, but by late that evening for all practical purposes the great Detroit Riot had ended.[57]

---

[56] Cmdr's Est 1, p. 11; Ltr, Aurand to Gullion, 3 Jul 43; Ltr, Guthner to Reese, 2 Aug 43, p. 2; and FO 2-A; all in RG 389, NARA.

[57] Ltr, Aurand to Gullion, 3 Jul 43; Memo, Aurand for Guthner, 22 Jul 43, sub: Use of Troops in Connection With Domestic Disturbance in Detroit, Mich.; Telecons, Guthner and Lt Col H. T. Loftin, 10:10 A.M., 22 Jun 43; Lerch and Aurand, 3:30 P.M., 23 Jun 43; Gullion and Guthner, 10:30 A.M., 25 Jun 43, and 5:10 P.M., 10 Jul 43; all in RG 389, NARA.

Ironically, the last act in the drama was the presidential proclamation. At 2210 Aurand had called Washington and reported Kelly's request for troops and his own decision to intervene. He requested permission to issue the still unsigned presidential proclamation. Colonel Roamer, at Somervell's direction, advised Aurand to have the governor call Roosevelt at Hyde Park immediately and request the proclamation personally. After locating the governor, Guthner, on Aurand's orders, had Kelly call Hyde Park. At 2315, the president signed the proclamation, ordering the rioters to "disperse and retire peacefully to their respective abodes immediately, and hereafter abandon said combinations and submit themselves to the laws and constituted authorities of said State [Michigan]." A few minutes later Aurand was authorized to issue the proclamation, which was then distributed to the press.[58]

The Armed Truce

The following day saw an armed truce in Detroit, with the Army fully positioned to prevent further violence. Federal troops were ordered to patrol all transportation lines, to ensure that workers could proceed safely to and from work, to disperse all crowds, and to quell any disorders that might break out. Patrols consisted of either four men on foot or one Army scout car and one jeep. About 2,400 Michigan State Troops joined the patrols on 24 June. According to the terms of the presidential proclamation, overall command of all troops in the city was transferred to General Guthner. Guthner used his forces with flexibility, augmenting the forty-four patrols as necessary in response to individual instances of racial violence that continued to occur sporadically. The patrols, he later commented, "did more to restore order than any other action."[59]

Although most of the violence had ended, additional federal troops soon arrived in Detroit. The 2d Division's 9th Infantry regiment, 3,600 strong, left Camp McCoy, Wisconsin, on 22 June and arrived in Detroit that night. Their arrival allowed Guthner to relieve fatigued Military Police units and to return others, such as the Selfridge Field provisional battalion, to their stations. On 28 and 30 June the federal forces were joined by another Military Police unit, the 792d Battalion (ZI) from Camp Maxey, Texas. This unit assumed patrol duties on 2 July.[60]

While Detroit grew quiet, its riot produced repercussions elsewhere in the nation. At Fort Custer, Michigan, black soldiers of the 543d Quartermaster Battalion seized trucks, 178 rifles, and thousands of rounds of ammunition in a vain attempt to aid blacks in Detroit. Five soldiers were subsequently arrested and charged with mutiny by military authorities. In Toledo, Ohio, police prevented 1,500 blacks from taking trains to Detroit, while other minor disturbances occurred in Muskegon, Michigan; Indiana Harbor, Indiana; and Springfield and East St. Louis, Illinois. These incidents prompted the Sixth Service

---

[58] Shogan and Craig, *The Detroit Race Riot*, p. 154; Roamer, Summary of Events in the Detroit Race Riot, p. 3; Log, Provost Marshal General's Office, p. 2.

[59] Ltr, Guthner to Reese, 2 Aug 43, p. 2; Cmdr's Est 1, p. 11; Memo, Michigan AG for Chief, National Guard Bureau, 9 Jul 43; Telecons, Reese and King, 11:10 A.M., 24 Jun 43; Guthner and Loftin, 10:10 A.M., 22 Jun 43; Log, Provost Marshal General's Office; all in RG 389, NARA.

[60] Telecon, Aurand and Maj McQuade, 8:30 P.M., 22 Jun 43, p. 2; Log, Provost Marshal General's Office; Ltr, Guthner to Col H. G. Reynolds, Air Provost Marshal, 2 Jul 43; all in RG 389, NARA.

Command in particular, and other Army service commands in general, to heighten their vigilance and to prepare for possible new outbreaks of urban interracial violence. The Sixth Service Command sent daily memorandums on Detroit race relations to the Military Intelligence Service (MIS) in the War Department for the remainder of the war, and kept up an active surveillance of other cities with large black populations, such as East St. Louis, Chicago, and Springfield, Illinois.[61]

In Detroit the trouble was over. The city had returned to relative normalcy by Thursday, 24 June. Citizens once again moved freely on the streets of Paradise Valley, and black absenteeism in the plants, which had run from 50 to 90 percent during the riot, declined to customary levels. Despite continued rumors, people returned to their usual routines. Hence, Governor Kelly lifted emergency restrictions in Oakland and Maycomb Counties and eased restrictions in Wayne County. Curfews were reduced, alcohol sales resumed, and places of amusement reopened, though only during daylight hours. Residents were still prohibited from assembling in large numbers and from carrying weapons, and federal troops continued their patrols to prevent any possible recurrence of violence.[62]

The Detroit riot had taken a significant toll in both material and human terms. Although there had been no racial violence within the war plants themselves, absenteeism had slowed output and resulted in the loss of over 2 million man-hours. Material damage to the city was extensive, with losses from looting, vandalism, and arson exceeding $2 million. The human cost was high as well. Final figures showed 34 dead, of whom 25 were blacks (16 of whom had been shot by police), and 675 of both races wounded. Hundreds were arrested. By 3 July 1943, the courts had already concluded proceedings in over 900 misdemeanor and 402 felony cases.[63]

Withdrawal of Federal Troops

Fears of renewed violence were quickly dispelled when the Fourth of July passed without incident. On the following day Kelly concluded that "the situation in Detroit is sufficiently in hand so that federal troops can be withdrawn from the streets and reduced in strength to the two battalions normally stationed in this area." Michigan State Troops ceased patrols on 5 July 1943, and federal troops ended their patrols the next day. Except for detachments guarding key bridges in Detroit and Port Huron, state troops were rapidly demobilized, and the 9th Infantry returned to Camp McCoy on 9 July. The 701st Military Police Battalion and the composite battalion followed, moving to their home

[61] Memo, Lt Col J. F. Perry for Col Harris, 23 Jun 43, sub: Racial Disturbances, Detroit, Mich., Sixth Army Service Command Army Intelligence Project, 1 Jul–31 Jul 43; Memo, Col W. L. Fubershaw for MIS, sub: Daily Summarization of Racial Situation and Coal Mining Situation in the Sixth Service Command; Memos, HQ, Sixth Service Command, for MIS, 12, 13, and 17 Jul 43; Memo, Perry, Chief, Evaluation Branch, CIG, MIS, for Col Harris; Telecon, Guthner and Aurand, 5:00 P.M., 22 Jun 43; all in RG 389, NARA. See also Lee and Humphrey, *Race Riot*, p. 43; Sitkoff, "The Detroit Race Riot of 1943," p. 196.

[62] Shogan and Craig, *The Detroit Race Riot*, p. 85; Cmdr's Est 1, p. 13.

[63] Director of Personnel Division, Race Relations Analyst Files, 1942–1946, p. 13; Memo, A. Luchek, War Production Board, for Joseph D. Keenan, Vice Chairman for Labor Production; both in Records of Headquarters, Army Service Forces, RG 160, NARA. See also Shogan and Craig, *The Detroit Race Riot*, p. 89; Guthner, Summary of Events Cmdr's Est of the Situation for the Period Wednesday, 30 Jun 43, 0800 to Saturday, 3 Jul 43, 0800, p. 2, RG 389, NARA, hereafter cited as Cmdr's Est 4.

stations the same day. Restrictions on local military personnel were lifted, and plant guards who had been placed under Guthner's control during the riot were released from military authority.[64]

Concerns that violence possibly would recur once troops had left Detroit, however, made Army officials keep the 728th Military Police Battalion at Camp River Rouge Park and the 792d Military Police Battalion at nearby Camp Waterloo, Michigan. When Guthner was replaced as commander of the Army in Michigan on 7 July, responsibility for these troops devolved upon Krech. At the same time, at Kelly's request, the previously issued presidential proclamation was extended until 2 August 1943, so that Army units could be redeployed in any new emergency in the Detroit area without another state request.[65]

Assessment of the Riot

Federal troops left with praise ringing in their ears from civilian authorities, the general public, and their military superiors. Governor Kelly told General Somervell that "your men are doing a marvelous job in our state." General Guthner commended the 9th Infantry and the Military Police battalions, and General Aurand declared that "the entire operation reflects great credit on the Military Police (ZI) and justifies their organization and existence." The Inspector General's Office, however, found some room for improvement in Military Police equipment and personnel. Common shotguns, furnished as substitutes for specialized riot guns, proved unsatisfactory, and a lack of radio equipment hindered communication among patrols, requiring military police to rely on the state police radio network. Furthermore, the poor physical condition of some of the military policemen, 60 percent of whom were limited service personnel, allegedly detracted from the impression that the Army made on rioters. The 9th Infantry, however, made a good impression, for it was "perhaps one of the best trained units in the army." On the whole the Army's performance had been effective and restrained.[66]

The experience in Detroit provided important lessons for federal troops who might draw riot duty in the future. Among these lessons were the usefulness of curfews; the need for cooperation with local police, especially for intelligence purposes; the importance of assembling an able operational staff quickly; the need to issue detailed instructions for commanders, and the value of an accurate log of events. Although none of the techniques was new, the riot had underlined their effectiveness in a highly charged situation. Guthner spoke highly of the effectiveness of patrols, of firm and restrained action, and of use of the bayonet. An officer from the Army's Inspector General's Office noted that traditional riot-control formations, such as the wedge and the diagonal, were not used to any great extent

---

[64] Ltr, Kelly to Somervell, 5 Jul 43, in Col Krech, Cmdr, All Armed Forces in Affected Areas, State of Michigan, Summary of Events and Commander's Estimate of the Situation for the Period Saturday, 3 Jul 43, 0800, to Friday, 9 Jul 43, 1201, pp. 8, 14, RG 389, NARA, hereafter Cmdr's Est 5.

[65] Cmdr's Est 5, pp. 12–15. See also Transcript of Conversation, Kelly and Somervell, 28 Jun 43, Classified File, 1943–1945: AG 291.2 (23 Jun 43), Records of the Office of the Adjutant General, United States Army, RG 407, NARA.

[66] Telecon, Kelly and Somervell, 28 Jun 43, RG 407, NARA; Ltr, Aurand to Gullion, 5 Jul 43, p. 2; Memo, Burney for IG, 30 Jun 43, p. 4.

because the fluidity of the Detroit situation made such slow-moving formations impractical. Instead, the situation had demonstrated the need for a flexible response, using small, highly mobile patrols to counter small groups of rioters. The lessons learned in Detroit in areas of planning, intelligence, training, operations, and communications were summarized in a memorandum prepared by Headquarters, Army Service Forces, which was subsequently distributed to Army service commands and to the Military District of Washington.[67]

While the Army evaluated its performance in Detroit, various civilian officials and groups examined the causes of the riot. Mayor Jeffries appointed an interracial committee to investigate Detroit's problems, while another fact-finding investigatory committee composed of state and city law enforcement officials was set up by Wayne County Prosecutor William Dowling. Both groups proved ineffective. The interracial committee recommended but could not implement reforms in the city's racial practices. The Dowling committee simply placed blame on the blacks, and ruled out charges that the riot was instigated by enemy agents or nativist groups. Most investigators developed explanations grounded in Detroit's demographic, economic, and social conditions. Despite protests on the part of Jeffries and Police Commissioner Witherspoon, the investigators, and the general public as well, found great fault with the Detroit Police Department. Thurgood Marshall stated that "much of the blood spilled in the Detroit riot is on the hands of the Detroit police department. In the past the Detroit police have been guilty of both inefficiency and an attitude of prejudice against Negroes. . . . In the June riot of this year, the police ran true to form." Similarly, Guthner concluded "that [the police] have treated the negroes terribly up there and I think they have gone altogether too far."[68]

Another controversy centered around the long delay between the start of the riot and the federal troop deployment. In a post-riot statement, Commissioner Witherspoon blamed the Army, claiming that Colonel Krech led the governor and city officials to believe that troops could be deployed in Detroit within forty-five minutes after the governor requested them from General Aurand. Krech replied that he had told the commissioner he could deploy troops once proper orders were received from his superiors. The misunderstanding lay in what procedures were needed before Krech could receive his orders.[69]

Once it became clear to civilian authorities that their mere verbal request to Aurand for troops had not fulfilled the legal requirements for the deployment of troops, they focused on the question of martial law. Both Kelly and Jeffries claimed that Aurand and Guthner had told them a declaration of martial law was necessary before the troops could be committed. The inspector general disagreed, noting that "General Guthner, upon his arrival in Detroit, took immediate steps to inform the Governor of the necessary steps to obtain Federal troops." The fact remains that neither Kelly nor Jeffries understood what procedures were involved in receiving aid from federal troops and that neither of the generals made these

---

[67] Ltr, Guthner to Reese, 2 Aug 43; Memo, Burney for IG, 30 Jun 43, p. 2. See also Memo, AG for CGs, First, Second, Third, Fourth, Fifth, Sixth, Seventh, Eight, and Ninth Service Commands, and MDW, sub: Plans for Action in Domestic Disturbances, RG 407, NARA.

[68] Investigations were conducted by the FBI, the Michigan Adjutant General, the prosecuting attorney of Wayne County, the Army, the NAACP, the National Urban League, the Federal Council of Churches, and Communist Party. Quotes from Allen Grimshaw, "Actions of the Police and the Military in American Race Riots," *Phylon* 24 (Fall 1963):271–89; Telecon, Reese and King, 11:10 A.M., 24 Jun 43.

[69] Memo, Burney for IG, 30 Jun 43, p. 8.

procedures clear in terms understandable to civilians. Why the governor's legal counsel did not inform him and why Aurand and Guthner were unable to communicate the information amply available in Army publications remains unclear.[70]

General Aurand's decision to commit troops before the issuance of a presidential proclamation did not indicate ignorance of the law on his part. In a post-riot statement, he said clearly that intervention came "upon request of the Governor of Michigan without waiting for the authorization of the President of the United States." Such an action was justified by paragraph 5b of AR 500–50, which allowed immediate federal intervention in cases of "sudden and unexpected invasion, insurrection, or riot, endangering the public property of the United States, . . . or other emergency so imminent as to render it dangerous to await instructions requested through the speediest means of communications." Once it was clear to Aurand that Kelly wanted and needed federal troops to restore order in Detroit, the general acted at once, with full knowledge of the law and Army regulations. Then, as prescribed, he promptly reported his actions to the War Department.[71]

Nevertheless, the controversy resulted in changes to Army regulations and the preparation of a memorandum on the subject for the Army service commands. AR 500–50 was rewritten to reflect the law more clearly, and President Roosevelt asked Secretary Stimson to make service commanders and state governors aware of federal military intervention procedures. The president's instructions were carried out by Acting Secretary of War Robert Lovett who, like his superiors, hoped that confusion could be averted in the future, and with it the loss of life caused by the equivocation of military and civil officials.[72]

V–J Day ended an era in American history that had seen repeated federal military interventions, especially in labor-related disputes. The Army's role had changed dramatically within the last years, in reference to new developments—plant seizures, federally sponsored labor legislation and arbitration, and the development of state and local forces to deal with strikes and labor-related violence. In the area of race relations as well, state and local forces would supplant the Army as the main keepers of the peace until they were overwhelmed by the conflicts associated with the civil rights movement of the 1950s and 1960s. The Army role in domestic disturbances changed and diminished, but it did not end; nevertheless, the Army's concept of its role, its doctrine and techniques of intervention, had been permanently transformed.

---

[70] Shogan and Craig, *The Detroit Race Riot*, p. 75; Memo, Burney for IG, 30 Jun 43, p. 8.

[71] USAMHI Aurand interview, p. 35; AR 500–50, p. 5. Italics added.

[72] Telecons, Lerch and Roamer, 1900, 10 Jul 43; Lerch and Pearson, 22 Jun 43; both in RG 389, NARA. See also Shogan and Craig, *The Detroit Race Riot*, pp. 155–59.

Conclusion

The sections of U.S. Army regulations issued in 1945 dealing with "Employment of Troops in Aid of Civil Authorities" stated that a military commander involved in a civil disorder "will bear in mind that the suppression of violence without bloodshed or undue violence is a worthy military achievement." Commanders were advised that they should employ only such force as is necessary to accomplish their mission of restoring order and maintaining lawful authority.[1] The wording of this regulation clearly reflected a true evolution and maturation of thought concerning the role of federal military forces in domestic disorders and the extent to which Army attitudes and policies had changed during the previous seventy years.

The United States had changed dramatically in the period 1877 through 1945. Although the nation had endured industrial and social upheavals that few could have predicted at the end of the Civil War, the federal military role during this era of transition was largely positive. Charged with maintaining the rule of law during a period of often troublesome economic and social adjustment, the Army helped keep the course of national development on an even keel. Despite the variety of complex situations necessitating federal military aid, in every instance (some 125 occasions) the Army successfully upheld legally constituted civil authority, restored or maintained law and order, and prevented or quelled violent labor-industrial disputes and race riots before major loss of life and property could take place. Simply put, the Army served as a brake on uncontrolled social and political change, providing stability and time for legal and democratic institutions and processes to cope with the deep transformations sweeping the country. The use of federal military forces by the various presidents to quell domestic disorders assured that changes in American institutions and ways of life were evolutionary and not revolutionary in nature. Federal military interventions quickly, effectively, and, in most cases, permanently ended civil disorders that might have had deeper and more tragic consequences if allowed to play themselves out.

The mission of maintaining domestic tranquility fell to the Army by default and was not a task of its own choosing. Yet the federal military was the only major armed force of order available to the federal executive in a disordered era—the only organization of sufficient size, power, and reliability capable of aiding civil authorities in times of crisis. The Army thus attempted to fulfill the difficult internal defense mission defined for it by the president and the Congress in a tactically restrained and nonlethal manner. In doctrine, training, and organization the Army was clearly suited for tactical operations against foreign armies, but in its internal defense role it was generally successful. With few exceptions officers and enlisted men adhered to the laws and provisions of the Constitution and

---

[1] U.S. War Department, *Regulations of the Army of the United States, 17 July 1945* (Washington, D.C.: Government Printing Office, 1945), AR 500–50, sec. IV, para. 8.

obeyed the orders of their military and civilian superiors without question. The enlisted ranks never mutinied even though they were often deployed against civilians of similar social and economic origins with whom at times they sympathized. Likewise, officers never refused to follow the orders of their superiors or ever attempted permanently to supplant or overthrow federal or state civil governments during times of domestic strife. In the context of the times, federal military interventions were legal and justified, nonpartisan, moderate, evenhanded, and for the most part bloodless, in stark contrast to those disputes quelled by state-controlled military and police forces. Federal troops were never even remotely responsible for civilian massacres such as those inflicted by their state militia and National Guard contemporaries, or by their Old World counterparts in nations such as Russia, Great Britain, and France. There are no "Bloody Sundays," "Peterloos," or "Paris Communes" in the history of U.S. Army domestic interventions. Nevertheless, the nature of the task often appeared to place the Army in a conservative political role, whatever the thoughts and inclinations of its leaders.

Army professionalism, restraint, and neutrality are best illustrated in the Nevada and Colorado labor disputes of 1907 and 1914. Here, during the terms of Presidents Theodore Roosevelt and Woodrow Wilson, Army officers were ordered explicitly to maintain a nonpartisan attitude toward both labor and management, reflecting the attitudes of two presidents who saw the military's role as one of strict neutrality, keeping violent adversaries apart until peaceful solutions could be found to labor-industrial disputes. Close presidential interests in the deployment of troops was generally accompanied by clear guidance to the responsible commander, accelerating a successful outcome. Both Roosevelt and Wilson saw limited civil violence as preferable to the hasty, and perhaps illegal, use of military forces as an antilabor constabulary.

On other occasions, government officials and military commanders alike deliberately allowed federal troops to be used as strikebreakers or to serve partisan ends. Such situations occurred in Lincoln and Johnson Counties, in the Chicago Pullman Strike, in the Coeur d'Alene mine wars, and during the World War I period. The partisan use of federal troops was purely unintentional in times such as during the 1877 Great Railway Strike or the anti-Chinese riots of 1885–1886. Although the passage of the 1878 Posse Comitatus Act had had a seminal effect on domestic interventions by placing restrictions on how and when federal troops could be used, and by whom, in times of crisis it was often ignored by both civil and military officials alike, was superseded by emergency, executive, or general orders, or otherwise circumvented for what was interpreted at the time as being the public good. The most notable examples took place during the World War I and the immediate postwar years. The strict regard for neutrality that had developed through a century of precedent-setting operations and which was clearly displayed during the terms of Roosevelt and Wilson ended, and interventions reverted to the pattern of the late nineteenth century. Antiradical, racist, and xenophobic fears resurfaced with a majority of Americans exhibiting an unprecedented degree of intolerance and xenophobia. Most Army interventions during this time reflected this mood, especially during the "red scare," the 1919 race riots, and the heightened labor unrest of 1919–1920. The initial lack of National Guard units or reliable local or state police forces to maintain domestic stability once again forced the Army to bear the primary burden for upholding law and order.

During the Great War years civil leaders were also distracted by foreign events, and responsibility for the domestic deployment of federal troops devolved to lower-level military and civil officials, often to states and municipalities. These individuals frequently used troops in a partisan fashion, creating policies without President Wilson's direct involvement or knowledge. Such was the case with Secretary of War Newton Baker's formulation of the direct access policy that allowed Army officers, often at the platoon level, to respond directly to the requests of civil officials for federal military forces to deal with threats to authority and security, real or imagined, without regard to prewar procedures. The result of this policy was a total and complete abrogation of the constitutional provisions and federal statutes intended to prevent the domestic misuse of federal military power. The period included the most widespread and intrusive domestic use of federal troops seen since Reconstruction.

Although critics often charged that federal military forces were used as strikebreakers or to stifle dissent, such use was as a rule unintentional, of short duration when it did occur, and did not constitute a behavior officially sanctioned by the federal executive in peacetime. Abuses were usually quickly identified and remedied, and officers suspected of partisanship and legal infractions were investigated and often replaced. There was, in fact, no clearly definable military mentality concerning civil disorders or the Army's internal defense role against groups perceived as threatening, be they immigrants, dissenters, labor radicals, other labor groups, or minorities. Army attitudes reflected those of civilian society, and military officers most usually deferred to the orders and directions of their civilian superiors, essentially sharing their attitudes however harsh they may have seemed to contemporary critics or latter-day observers.

Army domestic interventions between the late 1870s and the end of World War II were almost exclusively confined to labor disputes and economically related race riots that were episodic in nature. Army actions were initially unguided by any central planning or overall federal civil or military policy or doctrine. Each intervention had its own tenor, and Army actions and attitudes usually mirrored the views of government officials who generally sanctioned, when necessary, the use of overwhelming military firepower and force. Toward the latter part of the nineteenth century, however, more prudent individuals such as General John Schofield urged tactical restraint, and such moderating conduct was always practiced despite the existence within the service of stronger views. Although Schofield was the author of the first portion of what became a Draconian civil disturbance doctrine, his actions in the 1894 Pullman Strike were nonetheless moderate and pragmatic. The dichotomy of thought among soldiers like Schofield and others such as Nelson Miles, Leonard Wood, or Douglas MacArthur, who favored the application of overwhelming military force, was a microcosm of the larger and ever controversial philosophical conflicts between Army officers and civilian leaders that continued until the late 1930s.

As the federal government developed policies and legislation to deal with the upheavals occurring in American society, the Army similarly developed a doctrine to guide officers and enlisted men embroiled in these events. The creation of a doctrine and corpus of civil disturbance literature—with accompanying contingency plans—was the most significant and lasting development to come from the federal military interventions of the time. Soldiers ordered onto riot duty after the 1930s intervened with a set of clearly defined plans and regulations, assuring as far as possible that Army deployments were orderly, efficient, and above all nonviolent and legal. The gradual establishment of a civil disturbance doctrine diminished the perennial concerns of civil and military leaders regarding the legality of Army domestic interventions that were especially acute during the thirty years following the passage of the 1878 Posse Comitatus Act. Although soldiers throughout this entire era normally adhered to the provisions of this act and maintained their neutrality, the existence of regulations, contingency plans, and a variety of works on civil disorders greatly lessened the likelihood of excessive military force.

A final common factor in all major civil disturbances of the time was the general acceptance by civil and military leaders of the concept that federal troops always remained under the command and control of their federal civil and military superiors and were not subject to the control of local or state civil or law enforcement personnel. This principle was established by degrees, beginning in 1877, and became an integral part of Army doctrine by the end of the nineteenth century. Exceptions were few. The Coeur d' Alene mining wars were perhaps the clearest prewar examples of the partisan use of federal troops as a *posse comitatus* by openly antilabor Idaho state officials who wanted to destroy a radical labor organization. The actions of the federal military commander in Idaho, and his abject deference to the wishes of state authorities, reflected not only current public, military, and government views toward radical labor, but also the negative ramifications of allowing local authorities to control federal military forces. Precautions were taken to prevent a recurrence of the Coeur d' Alene situation in the future, although such safeguards ultimately required two decades to put into effect and were ignored during World War I.

During the 1920s the federal government returned to the policies and attitudes of the Progressive era, requiring rigid adherence to legal procedures and a strict neutrality in all domestic interventions. This renaissance was best exemplified by President Warren G. Harding's judicious, restrained, and careful use of federal troops in West Virginia in 1920–1921. His actions, and those of the Army, were divorced from the "red scare" hysteria of the times and were carried out as if the phenomenon did not exist. The West Virginia intervention also marked an increasing trend toward using state and local forces for maintaining order and quelling labor disputes.

Military attitudes, however, clearly were even less sympathetic to labor than they had been in the past. The depth of Army antiradical and antilabor thinking during the 1920s and early 1930s was most evident in the professional writings of officers and in the War Plans White, both based on a harsh civil disturbance doctrine that persisted in seeing lethal force as the only way to deal with civil disorders. These attitudes clearly were evident in the Army's gross overreaction to the challenge posed by the Bonus marchers of 1932, a reaction that shocked government officials and the public alike.

Federal civil and military attitudes changed significantly with the onset of the Great Depression, the New Deal, and World War II. These events repudiated much of the conservative and parochial thought that had dominated the nation since the late 1870s. With the New Deal acceptance of organized labor and intensive government intervention in social and economic affairs, the use of federal troops in labor disputes in essence came to an end. Legislative solutions were found to labor and racial problems that before seemed only to result in violence. At the same time, state and local civil law enforcement agencies, which had been small, ill-equipped, and disorganized in the late nineteenth and early twentieth centuries, began to take on peacekeeping functions once performed exclusively by the

Army. The end of the frontier constabulary mission had the same result. Thus by the time World War II began, the War Department had adopted a policy of leaving social, economic, and industrial problems to civil officials and agencies and restricted its own interventions in labor disputes to nonviolent, low-key war plant seizures accomplished through administrative procedures not involving combat troops. Except for troop interventions in Philadelphia and Detroit during World War II, when close adherence to legal guidelines was of paramount concern, the Army's role in domestic disorders involving labor-related disputes ended well before V–J Day.

Despite the decreased emphasis on the Army's role in labor disputes, the internal defense mission of the military did not end in 1945. Instead, a new host of problems appeared, beginning in the 1950s when the federal government was increasingly drawn into violent racial struggles involving civil rights. These struggles often escalated into violent interracial conflicts that necessitated using federal troops to prevent bloodshed and social chaos. Later, in the 1960s and 1970s, federal military forces were called upon to maintain law and order and civil authority during demonstrations protesting United States policies toward the war in Southeast Asia. Although the social and political situations precipitating these new domestic disturbances were unlike the race riots and labor disputes of the previous decades, the laws and military regulations, tactics and procedures, emphasis on tactical restraint, insistence on military command and control of federal troops, strict adherence to legal guidelines, and discipline and reliability proved during the period 1877–1945 would again provide valuable assistance.

Bibliography

Unpublished Sources

Iowa. Herbert C. Hoover Presidential Library. Herbert C. Hoover Papers.

Ohio. Rutherford B. Hayes Memorial Library. Rutherford B. Hayes Papers.

Washington, D.C. Library of Congress.

> Newton D. Baker Papers.
> Grover Cleveland Papers.
> George W. Getty Papers.
> Walter Gresham Papers.
> Benjamin Harrison Papers.
> Daniel S. Lamont Papers.
> William McKinley Papers.
> George Van Horn Moseley Papers.
> Richard Olney Papers.
> Elihu Root Papers.
> John Schofield Papers.
> Woodrow Wilson Papers.
> Leonard Wood Papers.

Washington, D.C. National Archives and Records Administration.

> Bureau of Labor Statistics (RG 257).
> Department of Justice (RG 60).
> Government of the District of Columbia (RG 351).
> Headquarters, U.S. Army Service Forces (RG 160).
> Office of the Secretary of War (RG 107).
> U.S. Army Adjutant General (RG 94).
> U.S. Army Adjutant General's Office (RG 407).
> U.S. Army Continental Commands, 1821–1920 (RG 393).
> U.S. Army Continental Commands, 1920–1942 (RG 394).
> U.S. Army Judge Advocate General, 1812–1939 (RG 153).
> U.S. Army Mobile Units, 1821–1942 (RG 391).
> U.S. Army Provost General's Office (RG 389).
> U.S. Army and Special Staffs (RG 319).
> War Department General Staff and Special Staffs (RG 165).

Wisconsin. State Historical Society of Wisconsin. William G. Haan Papers.

Published Sources

Reports, Documents, and Manuals

California. State Senate. Special Committee on Chinese Immigration. *Chinese Immigration: Its Social, Moral, and Political Effects*. Report to the California State Senate.

Sacramento, 1878.

Interchurch World Movement. *Public Opinion and the Steel Strike of 1919*. New York: Harcourt, Brace & World, 1920.

————. *Report on the Steel Strike of 1919*. New York: Harcourt, Brace & World, 1920.

National Association for the Advancement of Colored People. *Thirty Years of Lynching in the United States, 1889–1918*. New York: Negro Universities Press, 1969.

National Guard Bureau. *A Brief History of the Militia and National Guard*. Washington, D.C.: Office of Public Affairs, National Guard Bureau, 1986.

National Industrial Conference Board. *Strikes in American Industry in Wartime, April 6 to October 6, 1917*. Boston: National Industrial Conference Board, 1918.

"Special Report Concerning Chinese Labor Troubles (1885)." *Report of the Governor of Wyoming to the Secretary of the Interior, 1885*. Washington, D.C.: Government Printing Office, 1886.

"Special Report Concerning Chinese Labor Troubles (1886)." *Report of the Governor of Washington Territory to the Secretary of the Interior, 1886*. Washington, D.C.: Government Printing Office, 1886.

United States. Anthracite Coal Strike Commission. *Report to the President on the Anthracite Coal Strike of May–October 1902*. Washington, D.C.: Government Printing Office, 1902.

————. Civil Service Commission. *Official Register of the United States, 1941–1946*. Washington, D.C.: Government Printing Office, 1942–1947.

————. Congress. House. Coeur d'Alene Labor Troubles. H.R. 1999, 56th Cong., 1st sess., 1900.

————. House. Lawlessness in Parts of Arizona. Exec. Doc. 58, 47th Cong., 1st sess., 1882.

————. House. Message From the President of the United States in Relation to Disorders and Lawlessness in Arizona, April 26, 1882. Exec. Doc. 188, 47th Cong., 1st sess., 1882.

————. House. Report of Miner's Riot in the State of Idaho. 56th Cong., 1st sess., H. Docs., vol. 4, no. 2, pt. I, 1899.

————. House. Providing Indemnity to Certain Chinese Subjects. Exec. Doc. 2044, 49th Cong., 1st sess., 1885.

————. Congress. Senate. Committee on Education and Labor. Investigations of the Strikes in the Steel Industry. 66th Cong., 1st sess., 1920.

————. Senate. Committee on Education and Labor. West Virginia and the Civil War in Its Coalfields: Hearings Pursuant to Senate Resolution 8. 67th Cong., 1st sess., 1921–22.

————. Senate. Findings of the Senate Judiciary Committee. 47th Cong., 1st sess., *Congressional Record*, vol. 13.

————. Senate. Report of Brigadier General H. C. Merriam, on Miners' Riots in the State of Idaho. 56th Cong., 1st sess., S. Docs., vol. 4, no. 24, 1899.

————. Senate. Resolution 301 in *Congressional Record*, 72d Cong., 2d sess., December 12, 14, 1932.

————. Senate. Supplement to Federal Aid in Domestic Disturbances, 1903–1922. S. Doc. 263, 67th Cong., 2d sess., 1923.

_____. Senate. Wilson, Frederick T., Federal Aid in Domestic Disturbances, 1787–1903. 57th Cong., 2d sess. S. Doc. 209. Washington, D.C., 1903.

_____. Department of Justice. *Annual Report of the Attorney General for 1894 and 1896*. Washington, D.C.: Government Printing Office, 1894 and 1896.

_____. Department of Justice. *The Strike Files of the Department of Justice, Part I: 1894–1920*. Melvyn Dubofsky, ed. Bethesda, Md.: University Publications of America, 1990.

_____. Department of Labor. *Annual Report of the Secretary of Labor, 1918*. Washington, D.C.: Government Printing Office, 1919.

_____. Department of Labor. "Strikes in the United States, 1880–1936." no. 652 by Florence Peterson. Washington, D.C.: Government Printing Office, 1938.

_____. Department of State. *Foreign Relations of the United States, 1882, 1885, 1886*. Washington, D.C.: Government Printing Office, 1883, 1886, 1887.

_____. President's Mediation Commission. *Report on the Bisbee Deportations*. Washington, D.C.: Government Printing Office, 1918.

_____. President's Mediation Commission. *Report of the President's Mediation Commission, January 9, 1918*. Washington, D.C.: Government Printing Office, 1918.

_____. *Statutes at Large*.

_____. War Department. *Annual Report of the Secretary of War*. Washington, D.C.: Government Printing Office, 1876–1936.

_____. War Department. *Army Register*. Washington, D.C.: Government Printing Office, 1877–1945.

_____. Adjutant General's Office. *Annual Report of the Adjutant General, 1921*. Washington, D.C.: Government Printing Office, 1922.

_____. Adjutant General's Office. *Military Protection, United States Guards: The Use of Organized Bodies in the Protection and Defense of Property During Riots, Strikes, and Civil Disturbances*. Washington, D.C.: Government Printing Office, 1919.

_____. Chemical Warfare Service. "'Black Book', Chemical Warfare Service Policy Book, 1921–1940," U.S. Army Chemical, Research Development, and Engineering Center History Office, Aberdeen Proving Ground, Maryland.

_____. Chemical Warfare Service. *Provisional Instructions for the Control of Mobs by Chemical Warfare*. Chemical Warfare Service, November 1921.

_____. Chief of Staff. *Report of the Chief of Staff to the Secretary of War, 1919*. Washington, D.C.: Government Printing Office, 1919.

_____. Chief of Staff. *Report of the Chief of Staff, to the Secretary of War, on the Employment of Federal Troops in Civil Disturbances in the District of Columbia, July 28–30*. n.p., August 15, 1932.

_____. *General Orders, Bulletins, and Circulars*. Washington, D.C.: Government Printing Office, 1879, 1895, 1917, 1918, 1919.

_____. "Instructions and Information Pertaining to the United States Guards, National Army," July 26, 1918, Special Regulation no. 101.

_____. Judge Advocate General's Office. *Army Regulation AR 500–50, Employment of Troops: Aid of Civil Authorities*, 6 June 1923, 5 April 1937, and 17 July 1945.

_____. Judge Advocate General's Office. *Basic Field Manual FM 27–15*. Vol. VII, *Military Law*, Pt. III, "Domestic Disturbances," August 1, 1935, 1 March 1936, 6

February 1941.

_____. Judge Advocate General's Office. *Emergency Operations of Industrial Facilities* (ASF–EOIF–44), Revised: 23 September 1944. Washington, D.C.: Judge Advocate General, 1944.

_____. Militia Bureau. *Report of the Chief of the Militia Bureau, 1917, 1919*. Washington, D.C.: Government Printing Office, 1918 and 1919.

_____. *Regulations for the Army of the United States*. Washington, D.C.: Government Printing Office, 1881, 1889, 1895, 1899, 1901, 1904, 1913.

Books

Abbott, Carl J. *Urban America in the Modern Age, 1920 to the Present*. Arlington Heights, Ill.: Harlan Davidson, 1987.

Adamic, Louis. *Dynamite: The Story of Class Violence in America*. Gloucester, Mass.: Peter Smith, 1960.

Adams, Jr., Graham. *The Age of Industrial Violence, 1910–1915*. New York: Columbia University Press, 1966.

Allen, Arthur P. and Schneider, Betty V. H. *Industrial Relations in the California Aircraft Industry*. Berkeley: University of California Press, 1956.

Allport, Gordon W., and Postman, Leo. *The Psychology of Rumor*. New York: Henry Holt, 1947.

Altschuler, Glenn C. *Race, Ethnicity, and Class in American Social Thought, 1880–1940*. Arlington Heights, Ill.: Harlan Davidson, 1982.

Alvarez, Joseph A. *From Reconstruction to Revolution: The Black's Struggle for Equality*. New York: Atheneum, 1971.

Ambrose, Stephen E. *Upton and the Army*. Baton Rouge: Louisiana University Press, 1964.

_____. "Blacks in the Army in Two World Wars." In *The Military in American Society*. Stephen E. Ambrose and James A. Barber, eds., New York: Praeger, 1972.

_____. "The Armed Forces and Civil Disorder." In *The Military in American Society*. Stephen E. Ambrose and James A. Barber, eds., New York: Praeger, 1972.

Ambrose, Stephen E. and Barber, James A., Jr., eds. *The Military in American Society*. New York: Praeger, 1972.

American Civil Liberties Union. *Wartime Prosecutions and Mob Violence Involving the Rights of Free Speech, Free Press, and Peaceful Assemblage (From April 1, 1917 to May 1, 1918)*. Washington, D.C.: National Civil Liberties Bureau, 1918.

American Federation of Labor. *AF of L: History, Encyclopedia, Reference Book: Prepared and Published by Authority of the 1916 and 1917 Conventions*. 4 Vols. Westport: Greenwood, 1977.

Avrich, Paul. *The Haymarket Tragedy*. Princeton: Princeton University Press, 1984.

Babington, Anthony. *Military Intervention in Britain: From the Gordon Riots to the Gibraltar Killings*. New York: Routledge, 1990.

Babson, Roger. *W. W. B. Wilson and the Department of Labor*. New York: Bretano's, 1919.

Bagley, Clarence B. *History of Seattle From the Earliest Settlement to the Present Time*. 3 vols. Chicago: S. J. Clarke, 1916.

Bailey, Thomas A. *A Diplomatic History of the American People*. 3d ed. New York: F. S.

Crofts, 1946.

Baker, Ray Stannard. *The New Industrial Unrest*. New York: Doubleday, Page, & Co., 1920, reprint, New York: Arno Press, 1971.

Ball, Larry D. *The United States Marshals of New Mexico and Arizona Territories, 1846–1912*. Albuquerque: University of New Mexico Press, 1978.

Barck, Oscar T., Jr., and Blake, Nelson M. *Since 1900: A History of the United States in Our Times*. 3d ed. New York: Macmillan, 1959,

Barger, Byron L. *The Law and Custom of Riot Duty: A Guide for National Guard Officers and Civil Authorities with Commentaries on Federal Aid*. Columbus: Byron L. Barger, 1907.

Barnard, Harry. *Eagle Forgotten: The Life of John Peter Altgeld*. Secaucus, N.Y.: Lyle Stuart, 1938.

_____. *Rutherford B. Hayes and His America*. Indianapolis: Bobbs-Merrill, 1954.

Barnett, George E. and McCabe, David A. *Mediation, Investigation, and Arbitration in Industrial Disputes*. New York: Appleton, 1916, reprint, New York: Arno Press, 1971.

Barth, Gunther. *Bitter Strength: A History of the Chinese in the United States, 1850–1870*. Cambridge: Harvard University Press, 1964.

Baruch, Bernard. *American Industry in the War*. New York: Prentice Hall, 1941.

Beard, Mary R. *A Short History of the American Labor Movement*. New York: Harcourt, Brace & Howe, 1920, reprint, New York: Arno Press, 1969.

Beatty, George W. *The Background Causes of the 1943 Detroit Race Riot*. Princeton: Princeton University Press, 1954.

Bellow, Henry A. *Manual for Local Defense*. New York: Macmillan, 1918.

_____. *A Treatise on Riot Duty for the National Guard*. Washington, D.C.: Government Printing Office, 1920.

Bennett, David H. *The Party of Fear: From Nativist Movements to the New Right in American History*. New York: Random House, 1988.

Berman, Edward. *Labor Disputes and the President of the United States*. New York: Columbia University Press, 1924.

Bernstein, Irving. *The Lean Years: A History of the American Worker, 1920–1933*. Boston: Houghton Mifflin, 1960.

_____. *The New Deal Collective Bargaining Policy*. Berkeley: University of California Press, 1950.

_____. *The Turbulent Years: A History of the American Worker, 1933–1940*. Boston: Houghton Mifflin, 1970.

Bidwell, Bruce W. *History of the Military Intelligence Division of the Army General Staff, 1775–1941*. Frederick, Md.: University Publications of America, 1986.

Bing, Alexander. *Wartime Strikes and Their Adjustment*. New York: E. P. Dutton, 1921, reprint, New York: Arno Press, 1971.

Binkin, Martin, Eitelberg, Mark J., Schenider, Alvin J., and Smith, Marvin M. *Blacks in the Military*. Washington, D.C.: Brookings Institution, 1982.

Birkhimer, William E. *Military Government and Martial Law*. Washington, D.C.: James J. Chapman, 1892.

Black, Henry C. *Black's Law Dictionary*. 4th ed. St. Paul: West, 1951.

Blackman, John L. *Presidential Seizures in Labor Disputes*. Cambridge: Harvard

University Press, 1967.

Blumenson, Martin. "On the Function of the Military in Civil Disorders." In Handbook of Military Institutions. Roger W. Little, ed. Beverly Hills: Sage Publications, 1971.

_____. *The Patton Papers: 1885–1940*. 2 Vols. Boston: Houghton Mifflin, 1972.

Bodnar, John. *The Transplanted: A History of Immigrants in Urban America*. Bloomington: Indiana University Press, 1985.

Boskin, Joseph. *Urban Racial Violence in the Twentieth Century*. Beverly Hills: Glencoe, 1976.

Boyer, Paul. *Urban Masses and Moral Order in America, 1820–1920*. Cambridge: Harvard University Press, 1978.

Bracey, John H., Jr., Meier, August, and Rudwick, Elliott, eds. *Black Workers and Organized Labor*. Belmont, Calif.: Wadsworth, 1971.

Bradley, Omar N., and Blair, Clay. *A General's Life*. New York: Simon & Schuster, 1983.

Brecher, Jeremy. *Strike*. San Francisco: Straight Arrow Books, 1972.

Brissenden, Paul F. *The I.W.W.: A Study of American Syndalism*. New York: Columbia University Press, 1920.

Brody, David. *Labor in Crisis: The Steel Strike of 1919*. Philadelphia: Lippincott, 1965; reprint, Urbana: University of Illinois Press, 1987.

_____. "The American Worker in the Progressive Age: A Comprehensive Analysis." In David Brody, *Workers in Industrial America: Essays on the Twentieth Century Struggle*. New York: Oxford University Press, 1980. pp. 3–47.

_____. *Steelworkers in America: The Nonunion Era*. Cambridge: Harvard University Press, 1960.

Broehl, Wayne G., Jr. *The Molly Maguires*. Cambridge: Harvard University Press, 1964.

Bromley, Isaac H. *The Chinese Massacre at Rock Springs, Wyoming Territory, September 2, 1885*. Boston: Franklin Press; Rand, Avery, 1886.

Brooks, John Graham. *American Syndicalism*. New York: Macmillan, 1913, reprint, New York: Arno Press, 1969.

Brown, R. G., Chaffee, Zechariah, Jr., Frankfurter, Felix, et al. eds. *Report Upon the Illegal Practices of the United States Department of Justice*. Washington, D.C.: National Popular Government League, 1920; reprint, New York: Arno Press, 1969.

Brown, Richard M. *Strain of Violence: Historical Studies of American Violence and Vigilantism*. New York: Oxford University Press, 1975.

Brownlow, Louis. *The Autobiography of Louis Brownlow*. 2 vols. Chicago: University of Chicago Press, 1955–58.

Bruce, Robert V. *1877: Year of Violence*. Indianapolis: Bobbs-Merrill, 1959.

Buder, Stanley. *Pullman: An Experiment in Industrial Order and Community Planning, 1880–1930*. New York: Oxford University Press, 1967.

Bunting, David G. *Statistical View of the Trusts: A Manual of Large American Industrial and Mining Corporations Active Around 1900*. Westport: Greenwood, 1974.

Burbank, David T. *Reign of the Rabble: The St. Louis General Strike of 1877*. New York: Augustus M. Kelley, 1966.

Burner, David. *Herbert Hoover, A Public Life*. New York: Alfred A. Knopf, 1979.

Byers, Jean. *A Study of the Negro in Military Service*. Washington, D.C.: Office of the Chief of Military History, 1947.

Byrkit, James W. *Forging the Copper Collar: Arizona's Labor-Management War, 1901–1921*. Tucson: University of Arizona Press, 1982.

Calhoun, Frederick S. *The Lawmen: United States Marshals and Their Deputies, 1789–1989*. Washington, D.C.: Smithsonian Institution, 1989.

Cantor, Milton, ed. *American Workingclass Culture: Explorations in American Labor and Social History*. Westport: Greenwood, 1979.

————. *Black Labor in America*. Westport, Conn · Negro Universities Press, 1969.

Capeci, Domonic J., Jr. *Race Relations in Wartime Detroit: The Sojourner Truth Housing Controversy of 1942*. Philadelphia: Temple University Press, 1984.

————. *The Harlem Riot of 1943*. Philadelphia: Temple University Press, 1977.

Carlson, Paul H. *"Pecos Bill:" A Military Biography of William R. Shafter*. College Station: Texas A&M University Press, 1989.

Carwardine, William H. *The Pullman Strike*. Chicago: Charles H. Kerr, 1894; reprint, New York: Arno Press, 1969.

Case, John. "The Military Occupation of the Coal Strike Zone of Colorado by the Colorado National Guard, 1913–14." In *Massacre at Ludlow: Four Reports*. Leon Stein and Philip Taft New York: Arno Press, 1971.

Caughey, John W. *Their Majesties the Mob*. Chicago: University of Chicago Press, 1960.

Chadwin, Mark Lincoln. *The Warhawks*. New Haven: Yale University Press, 1957.

Chandler, Alfred D., Jr. *The Railroads: The Nation's First Big Business*. New York: Harcourt, Brace & World, 1965.

————. *The Visible Hand: The Mangerial Revolution in American Business*. Cambridge: Harvard University Press, 1977.

Clarkson, Grosvenor B. *Industrial America in the World War: The Strategy Behind the Lines, 1917–1918*. Boston: Houghton Mifflin, 1923.

Clendenen, Clarence C. *Blood on the Border: The United States Army and the Mexican Irregulars*. London: Macmillan, 1969.

————. "Super Police: The National Guard as a Law-Enforcement Agency in the Twentieth Century." In Robin D. Higham, ed. *Bayonets in the Street: The Use of Federal Troops in Civil Disorders*. Manhattan: University of Kansas Press, 1969, pp. 85–112.

Coakley, Robert W. "Federal Use of Militia and the National Guard in Civil Disturbances." In *Bayonets in the Street: The Use of Federal Troops in Civil Disorders*. Robin D. Higham, ed. Manhattan: University of Kansas Press, 1969, pp. 17–34.

————. *The Role of Federal Military Forces in Domestic Disturbances, 1787–1878*. Washington, D.C.: U.S. Army Center of Military History, 1989.

Coffman, Edward M. *The Old Army: A Portrait of the American Army in Peacetime, 1784–1898*. New York: Oxford University Press, 1986.

————. *The War To End All Wars: The American Military Experience in World War I*. New York: Oxford University Press, 1968.

Cole, Wayne S. *Roosevelt and the Isolationists, 1932–1945*. Lincoln: University of Nebraska Press, 1983.

Coleman, Walter J. *The Molly Maguire Riots: Industrial Conflict in the Pennsylvania Coal Region*. Washington, D.C.: Catholic University of America, 1936, reprint, New York: Arno Press, 1969.

Commager, Henry Steele, ed. *Documents of American History*. 2 vols. Englewood Cliffs,

N.J.: Prentice-Hall, 1973.

Commons, John R., et al. *History of Labor in the United States, 1896–1932*. 4 vols. New York: Macmillan, 1918–1935, reprint, New York: Augustus M. Kelley, 1966.

_____, et al. *A Documentary History of American Industrial Society*. 10 vols. New York: Russell and Russell, 1958.

Conlin, Joseph R. *Big Bill Haywood and the Radical Union Movement*. Syracuse: Syracuse University Press, 1969.

_____. *Bread and Roses Too: Studies of the Wobblies*. Westport: Greenwood, 1969.

_____. *At the Point of Production: The Local History of the IWW*. Westport: Greenwood, 1981.

Connor, Valerie J. *The National War Labor Board: Stability, Social Justice, and the Voluntary State in World War I*. Chapel Hill: University of North Carolina Press, 1983.

Constantine, J. Robert. *Letters of Eugene V. Debs*. 3 Vols. Urbana: University of Illinois Press, 1990.

Cooper, Jerry M. *The Army and Civil Disorder: Federal Military Interventions in Labor Disputes, 1877–1900*. Westport: Greenwood, 1980.

_____. "The Army's Search for a Mission, 1865–1890." In *Against All Enemies: Interpretations of American Military History From Colonial Times to the Present*. Kenneth J. Hagan and William R. Roberts, eds. Westport, Conn.: Greenwood, 1986.

Corbin, David. *Life, Work, and Rebellion in the Coalfields: The Southern West Virginia Miners, 1880–1922*. Urbana: University of Illinois Press, 1981.

Cornell, Robert J. *The Anthracite Coal Strike of 1902*. New York: Russell and Russell, 1957.

Cortner, Richard C. *A Mob Intent on Death: The NAACP and the Arkansas Riot Cases*. Middletown, Conn.: Wesleyan Press, 1987.

_____. *The Wagner Act Cases*. Knoxville, Tenn.: University of Tennessee Press, 1964.

Corwin, Edward S. *The President: Office and Powers, 1787–1948*. 5th rev. ed. New York: New York University Press, 1984.

Cosmas, Graham. *An Army for Empire*. Columbia, Mo.: University of Missouri Press, 1971.

Cronon, David E., ed. *Labor and the New Deal*. Chicago: Rand McNally, 1963.

Crook, George. *General George Crook, His Autobiography*. Norman: University of Oklahoma Press, 1946.

Cross, Ira B. *A History of the Labor Movement in California*. Berkeley: University of California Press, 1935.

Crowell, Benedict, and Wilson, Robert F. *Demobilization: Our Industrial and Military Demobilization After the Armistice, 1918–1920*. New Haven: Yale University Press, 1921.

Cudacoff, Howard P. *The Evolution of American Urban Society*. Englewood Cliffs, N.J.: Prentice-Hall, 1981.

Cuff, Robert D. *The War Industries Board: Business-Government Relations During World War I*. Baltimore: Johns Hopkins University Press, 1973.

Current, Richard N., Williams, T. Harry, and Freidel, Frank. *American History: A Survey*. New York: Alfred A. Knopf, 1975.

Dacus, J. A. *Annals of the Great Strikes*. Chicago: L. T. Palmer, 1877; reprint, New York: Arno Press, 1969.

Daniels, Roger. *Asian America: Chinese and Japanese in the United States Since 1850*. Seattle, Wash.: University of Washington Press, 1989.

_____. *The Bonus March: An Episode of the Great Depression*. Westport: Greenwood, 1971.

Davis, David Brion. *The Fear of Conspiracy. Images of Un-American Subversives from the Revolution to the Present*. Ithaca: Cornell University Press, 1971.

Davison, Kenneth E. *The Presidency of Rutherford B. Hayes*. Westport: Greenwood, 1972.

De Jong, Louis. *The German Fifth Column in the Second World War*. Chicago: University of Chicago Press, 1956.

Debs, Eugene V. *Writings and Speeches of Eugene V. Debs*. Introduction by Arthur Schlesinger, Jr. New York: Hermitage Press, 1948.

Degler, Carl. *The Age of Economic Revolution, 1876–1900*. Glenview, Ill.: Scott Foresman, 1967.

Derber, Milton and Young, Edwin. *Labor and the New Deal*. Madison: University of Wisconsin Press, 1957.

Derickson. Alan. *Workers' Health, Workers' Democracy: The Western Miners' Struggle, 1891–1925*. Ithaca, N.Y.: Cornell University Press, 1988.

Derthick, Martha. *The National Guard in Politics*. Cambridge: Harvard University Press, 1965.

Diamond, Sander A. *The Nazi Movement and the United States, 1924–1941*. Ithaca: Cornell University Press, 1974.

Diamond, Sigmund, ed. *The Nation Transformed: The Creation of an Industrial Society*. New York: George Braziller, 1963.

Donner, Frank J. *The Age of Surveillance: The Aims and Methods of American Political Intelligence Systems*. New York: Alfred A. Knopf, 1980.

Douglas, Paul H. *Real Wages in the United States, 1890–1926*. New York: Houghton Mifflin, 1930.

Dowell, Cassius M. *Military Aid to the Civil Power*. Ft. Leavenworth, Kans.: General Service School, 1925.

_____. *Confidential Supplement to Military Aid to the Civil Power: Additional Legal Aspects, Organization, Equipment, Training, Tactics, and Formulation of Plans*. Ft. Leavenworth, Kans.: General Service School, 1925.

Downey, Fairfax. *Indian Fighting Army*. New York: Charles Scribner's Sons, 1941.

Dubofsky, Melvyn. *Industrialism and the American Worker, 1865–1920*. Arlington Heights, Ill.: Harlan Davidson, 1985.

_____. *We Shall Be All: A History of the IWW*. New York: Quadrangle, 1969, Urbana: University of Illinois, 1988.

Dubofsky, Melvyn, and van Tine, Warren. *John L. Lewis*. New York: Quadrangle/New York Times, 1977.

Dulles, Foster Rhea. *Labor in America*. 2d ed. New York: Thomas Y. Crowell, 1960.

Dulles, Foster Rhea and Dubofsky, Melvyn. *Labor in America*. 4th ed. Arlington Heights, Ill.: Harlan Davidson, 1989.

Edwards, P. K. *Strikes in the United States, 1881–1974*. Oxford: Oxford University Press,

1981.

Eggert, Gerald G. *Railroad Labor Disputes: The Beginnings of a Federal Strike Policy.* Ann Arbor: University of Michigan Press, 1967.

Ekirch, Jr., Arthur A. *The Civilian and the Military: A History of the American Anti-Militarist Tradition.* Colorado Springs: Ralph Myles, 1972.

Ellsworth, Scott. *Death in a Promised Land: The Tulsa Riot of 1921.* Baton Rouge: Louisiana State University, 1982.

Emmons, David M. *The Butte Irish: Class and Ethnicity in an American Mining Town, 1875–1925.* Urbana: University of Illinois Press, 1990.

Fairchild, Byron and Grossman, Jonathan. *The Army and Industrial Manpower.* Washington, D.C.: Office of the Chief of Military History, U.S. Army, 1959.

Farsod, Merele. *International Socialism and the World War.* Cambridge: Harvard University Press, 1935.

Filippelli, Ronald L. *Labor in the U.S.A.: A History.* New York: Knopf, 1984.

_____. *Labor Conflict in the United States: An Encyclopedia.* New York: Garland, 1990.

Fink, Gary M., ed. *Biographical Dictionary of American Labor.* Westport: Greenwood, 1984.

Fink, Gary M. and Reed, Merle E., eds. *Essays in Southern Labor History: Selected Papers, Southern Labor History Conference, 1976.* Westport: Greenwood, 1977.

Fink, Leon. *Workingmen's Democracy: The Knights of Labor and American Politics.* Urbana: University of Illinois Press, 1983.

Fitch, John A. *The Steel Worker.* New York: Charities Publications, 1910, reprint New York: Arno Press, 1969.

Fligstein, Neil. *Going North: Migration of Blacks and Whites From the South, 1900–1950.* New York: Academic Press, 1981.

Fogel, Robert W. *Railroads and American Economic Growth: Essays in Econometric History.* Baltimore: Johns Hopkins University Press, 1964.

Fogelson, Robert M. *America's Armories: Architecture, Society, and Public Order.* Cambridge: Harvard University Press, 1989.

Folsom, Franklin. *Impatient Armies of the Poor: The Story of Collective Action of the Unemployed, 1808–1942.* Niwot, Colo.: University of Colorado Press, 1991.

Foner, Jack D. *Blacks and the Military in American History: A New Perspective.* New York: Praeger, 1974.

_____. *The United States Soldier Between Two Wars: Army Life and Reforms, 1865–1898.* New York: Humanities Press, 1970.

Foner, Philip S. *History of the Labor Movement in the United States.* 8 vols. New York: International Publishers, 1947–88.

_____. *Organized Labor and the Black Worker, 1619–1973.* New York: International Publishers, 1974.

_____. *The Bolshevik Revolution: Its Impact on American Radicals, Liberals, and Labor.* New York: International Publishers, 1967.

_____. *The Great Labor Uprising of 1877.* New York: Monad Press, 1977.

_____. *Fellow Workers and Friends: I.W.W. Free-Speech Fights as Told by Participants.* Westport, Conn.: Greenwood, 1981.

Foster, William Z. *The Great Steel Strike and Its Lessons.* New York: Viking, 1920.

Franklin, John Hope. *From Slavery to Freedom: A History of Negro Americans*. New York: Alfred A. Knopf, 1974.

Fraser, Steven. *Labor Will Rule: Sidney Hillman and the Rise of American Labor*. New York: Free Press, 1991.

Friedheim, Robert L. *The Seattle General Strike*. Seattle: University of Washington Press, 1964.

Frisch, Michael H. and Walkowitz, Daniel J., eds. *Working-Class America: Essays on Labor, Community, and American Society*. Urbana: University of Illinois Press, 1983.

Frye, Alton. *Nazi Germany and the Western Hemisphere, 1933–1945*. New Haven: Yale University Press, 1967.

Fulton, Maurice G. *History of the Lincoln County War*. Tucson: University of Arizona Press, 1968.

Galambos, Louis P. *The Public Image of Business in America, 1880–1940*. Baltimore: Johns Hopkins University Press, 1975.

Galbraith, John Kenneth. *The Great Crash, 1929*. Boston: Houghton Mifflin, 1955.

Galenson, Walter. *The CIO Challenge to the AF of L: A History of the American Labor Movement, 1935–1941*. Cambridge: Harvard University Press, 1958.

Gallup, George H. *The Gallup Poll: Public Opinion, 1935–1971*. 2 Vols. New York: Random House, 1971.

Gambs, John S. *The Decline of the IWW*. New York: Columbia University Press, 1932, reprint, New York: Russell & Russell, 1966.

Ganoe, William A. *The History of the United States Army*. New York: Appleton Century, 1943.

Gardner, A. Dudley, and Flores, Verla R. *Forgotten Frontier: A History of Wyoming Coal Mining*. Boulder, Colo.: Westview, 1989.

Gardner, Lloyd C. *Safe for Democracy: The Anglo-American Response to Revolution, 1913–1923*. New York: Oxford University Press, 1984.

Garraty, John A. *The New Commonwealth, 1877–1890*. New York: Harper & Brothers, 1968.

_____. *Labor and Capital in the Gilded Age*. Boston: Little Brown, 1968.

Giffin, Frederick C. *Six Who Protested: Radical Opposition to the First World War*. Port Washington, N.Y.: Kennikat Press, 1977.

Ginger, Ray. *Age of Excess: The United States From 1877 to 1914*. 2d ed. New York: Macmillan, 1975.

_____. *The Bending Cross: A Biography of Eugene Victor Debs*. New Brunswick, N.J.: Rutgers University Press, 1949, reprint, New York: Russell and Russell, 1969.

_____. *Altgeld's America: The Lincoln Ideal Versus Changing Realities*. New York: New Viewpoints, 1973; reprint, New York: M. Wiener, 1986.

Gitelman, Howard M. *Legacy of the Ludlow Massacre: A Chapter in American Industrial Relations*. Philadelphia: University of Pennsylvania Press, 1988.

Glaab, Charles N., and Brown, A. Theodore. *A History of Urban America*. 3d ed. New York: Macmillan, 1983.

Glaberman, Martin. *Wartime Strikes: The Struggle Against the No-Strike Pledge in the UAW During World War II*. Detroit: Berwick Press, 1980.

Gompers, Samuel. *Seventy Years of Life and Labor*. Nick Salvatore, ed. Ithaca: Cornell University Press, 1984.

Goodwyn, Lawrence. *Democratic Promise: The Populist Movement in America*. New York: Oxford University Press, 1976.

Gordon, David A., Edwards, Richard, and Reich, Michael. *Segmented Work, Divided Workers: The Historical Transformation of Labor in the United States*. New York: Cambridge University Press, 1982.

Green, James R. *World of the Worker: Labor in Twentieth-Century America*. New York: Hill and Wang, 1980.

Greene, Constance McLaughlin. *The Secret City: A History of Race Relations in the Nation's Capital*. Princeton: Princeton University Press, 1967.

Greenfield, Kent R., ed. *Command Decisions*. Washington, D.C.: U.S. Army Center of Military History, 1960.

Gregory, Charles O. and Katz, Harold A. *Policy Development Under the National Labor Relations Act*. Chicago: Industrial Relations Center, University of Chicago, 1947.

Grob, Gerald. *Workers and Utopia: A Study of Ideological Conflict in the American Labor Movement, 1865–1900*. Evanston, Ill.: Northwestern University Press, 1961.

Gross, James A. *The Making of the National Labor Relations Board*. Vol. 2: *The Reshaping of the National Labor Relations Board: National Labor Policy in Transition, 1939–1947*. Albany: State University of New York Press, 1981.

Grossman, James R. *Land of Hope: Chicago, Black Southerners, and the Great Migration*. Chicago: University of Chicago Press, 1990.

Grubbs, Jr., Frank L. *The Struggle for Labor Loyalty: Gompers, the AF of L, and the Pacifists, 1917–1920*. Durham: University of North Carolina Press, 1968.

Gutman, Herbert G. *Work, Culture, and Society in Industrializing America*. New York: Random House, 1977.

Hagan, Kenneth J. and Roberts, William R., eds. *Against All Enemies: Interpretations of American Military History From Colonial Times to the Present*. Westport: Greenwood, 1986.

Hagedorn, Herman. *Leonard Wood: A Biography*. New York: Harper Brothers, 1931.

Halseth, James A. and Glasrud, Bruce A. "Anti-Chinese Movements in Washington, 1885–1886: A Reconsideration." In *The Northwest Mosaic: Minority Conflicts in Pacific Northwest History*. James A. Halseth and Bruce A. Glasrud, eds. Boulder, Colo.: Pruett, 1977.

Harbaugh, William H. *Power and Responsibility: The Life and Times of Theodore Roosevelt*. New York: Farrar, Straus, & Cudany, 1961.

Harris, Vernon B. *Kanawha's Black Gold and the Miner's Rebellion*. Ann Arbor: Braun-Brumfield, 1987.

Hayes, Rutherford B. *Diary and Letters of Rutherford B. Hayes*, Charles Richard Williams, ed., 5 vols. (Columbus: Ohio State Archeological and Historical Society, 1922–1926.

Haynes, Robert V. *A Night of Violence: The Houston Riot of 1917*. Baton Rouge: Louisiana State University Press, 1976.

Hays, Samuel P. *The Response to Industrialism, 1885–1914*. Chicago: University of Chicago Press, 1957.

Haywood, William D. *Bill Haywood's Book: The Autobiography of William D. Haywood.* New York: International Publishers, 1929.

Heale, Michael J. *American Anti-Communism, 1830–1970.* Baltimore: Johns Hopkins University Press, 1990.

Heaps, Willard A. *Riots, U.S.A., 1765–1970.* New York: The Seabury Press, 1970.

Herbst, Alma. *The Negro in the Slaughtering and Meat-Packing Industry in Chicago.* Boston: Houghton Mifflin, 1932, reprint, New York: Arno Press, 1971.

Hewes, James E. Jr. *From Root to McNamara: Army Organization and Administration, 1900–1963.* Washington, D.C.: U.S. Army Center of Military History, 1975.

Hicks, John D. *The Populist Revolt.* Minneapolis: University of Minnesota Press, 1931.

Higham, John. *Send These to Me: Immigrants in Urban America.* Baltimore: Johns Hopkins University Press, 1984.

_____. *Strangers in the Land: Patterns of American Nativism, 1860–1925.* New York: Atheneum, 1963; rev. ed. Westport: Greenwood, 1981, and New Brunswick, N.J.: Rutgers University Press, 1988.

Higham, Robin, ed. *Bayonets in the Streets: The Use of Federal Troops in Civil Disorders.* Manhattan, Kans.: The University of Kansas Press, 1969.

Hill, Jim D. *The Minute Man in Peace and War: A History of the National Guard.* Harrisburg, Penn.: Stackpole, 1964.

_____. "The National Guard in Civil Disorders." In *Bayonets in the Street: The Use of Federal Troops in Civil Disorders.* Robin Higham, ed. Manhattan: University of Kansas Press, 1969.

Hoerder, Dirk, ed. *American Labor and Immigration History, 1877–1920.* Champaign: University of Illinois Press, 1983.

Hoffman, Charles. *The Depression of the Nineties: An Economic History.* Westport: Greenwood, 1970.

Hofstadter, Richard and Wallace, Michael, eds. *American Violence: A Documentary History.* New York: Alfred A. Knopf, 1971.

Holley, Irving Bainton, jr. *Buying Aircraft: Materiel Procurement for the Army Air Forces.* Washington, D.C.: Office of the Chief of Military History, U.S. Army, 1964.

Hope, Richard O. *Racial Strife in the Military: Toward the Elimination of Discrimination.* New York: Praeger, 1979.

Horan, James D. *The Pinkertons: The Detective Dynasty That Made History.* New York: Crown Publishers, 1967.

Horn, Calvin. *New Mexico's Troubled Years: The Story of Early Territorial Governors.* Albuquerque: Horn & Wallace, 1963.

Horowitz, Ruth L. *Political Ideologies of Organized Labor: The New Deal Era.* New Brunswick, N.J.: Transaction, 1978.

Huntington, Samuel P. *The Soldier and the State: The Theory and Politics of Civil-Military Relations.* Cambridge: Harvard University Press, 1957.

Hutton, May A. *The Coeur d'Alene or a Tale of the Modern Inquisition in Idaho.* Denver: Wallace, 1920.

Hyman, Harold M. *Soldiers and Spruce: Origins of the Loyal Legion of Loggers and Lumbermen.* Los Angeles: University of California Press, 1963.

Jacobson, Julius, ed. *The Negro and the American Labor Movement.* Garden City, N.Y.:

Anchor Books, 1968.

Jacoby, Sanford. *Employing Bureaucracy: Managers, Unions, and the Transformation of Work in American Industry, 1900–1945*. New York: Columbia University Press, 1985.

James, D. Clayton. *The Years of MacArthur*. Vol. 1: *1880–1941*. Boston: Houghton Mifflin, 1970.

Jensen, Joan M. *The Price of Vigilance*. Chicago: Rand McNally, 1969.

_____. *Army Surveillance in America, 1775–1980*. New Haven: Yale University Press, 1991.

Jensen, Vernon H. *Heritage of Conflict: Labor Relations in the Nonferrous Metals Industry up to 1930*. Ithaca, N.Y.: Cornell University Press, 1950.

Johnson, Clyde. "CIO Oil Workers' Organizing Campaign in Texas, 1942–43." In *Essays in Southern Labor History: Selected Papers, Southern Labor History Conference, 1976*. Gary M. Fink and Merl E. Reed, eds. Westport: Greenwood, 1976, pp. 173–88.

Johnson, Donald D. *The Challenge to American Freedom: World War I and the Rise of the American Civil Liberties Union*. Lexington: University of Kentucky Press, 1963.

Johnson, Virginia W. *The Unregimented General: A Biography of Nelson A. Miles*. Boston: Houghton Mifflin, 1962.

Jordan, Daniel P. "The Mingo War: Labor Violence in the Southern West Virginia Coalfields, 1919–1922." In *Essays in Southern Labor History: Selected Papers, Southern Labor History Conference, 1976*. Gary M. Fink and Merl E. Reed, eds. Westport: Greenwood, 1977.

Jordan, David M. *Winfield Scott Hancock: A Soldier's Life*. Bloomington: Indiana University Press, 1988.

Kaltenborn, Howard S. *Government Adjustment of Labor Disputes*. Chicago: Foundation Press, 1943.

Kaufman, Stuart B. *Samuel Gompers and the Origins of the American Federation of Labor, 1848–1896*. Westport: Greenwood, 1967.

Keleher, William A. *Violence in Lincoln County, 1869–1881*. Albuquerque: University of New Mexico Press, 1957.

Kennedy, David M. *The First World War and American Society*. New York: Oxford University Press, 1980.

Kinnear, George. *Anti-Chinese Riots in Seattle, 1885–1886*. Seattle: George Kinnear, 1911.

Klein, Maury D., and Kantor, Harvey A. *Prisoners of Progress: American Industrial Cities, 1850–1920*. New York: Macmillan, 1976.

Kluger, James R. *The Clifton-Morenci Strike: Labor Difficulty in Arizona, 1915–1916*. Tucson: University of Arizona Press, 1970.

Koistinen, Paul A.C. *The Hammer and the Sword: Labor, the Military, and Industrial Mobilization, 1920–1945*. New York: Arno Press, 1979.

Kornweibel, Theodore, Jr. *Federal Surveillance of Afro-Americans (1917–1925): The First World War, the Red Scare, and the Garvey Movement*. Frederick, Md.: University Microfilms, 1987.

Kraut, Alan. *Huddled Masses: The Immigrant in American Society, 1880–1921*. Arlington Heights, Ill.: Harlan Davidson, 1982.

Kreidberg, Marvin A. and Henry, Merton G. *History of Military Mobilization in the United States Army, 1775–1945*. Washington, D.C.: Department of the Army, Office of the

Chief of Military History, 1955; reprint, Washington, D.C.: U.S. Army Center of Military History, 1984.

Lane, Ann J. *The Brownsville Affair: National Crisis and Black Reaction*. Port Washington, N.Y.: Kennikat Press, 1971.

Lane, Jack C. *Armed Progressive: General Leonard Wood*. San Rafael, Calif.: Presidio Press, 1978.

Larson, Simeon. *Labor and Foreign Policy; Gompers, the AFL, and the First World War, 1914–1918*. Rutherford, N.J.: Fairleigh Dickinson University Press, 1975.

Laslett, John. *Labor and the Left: A Study of Socialist and Radical Influences in the American Labor Movement, 1881–1924*. New York: Basic Books, 1970.

Latham, Frank B. *The Panic of 1893: A Time of Strikes, Riots, Hobos, Coxey's "Army," Starvation, Withering Droughts, and Fears of "Revolution."* New York: Franklin Watts, 1971.

Lauck, William J. *The Causes of the Panic of 1893*. Boston: Houghton Mifflin, 1907.

Lavash, Donald. *Sheriff William Brady: Tragic Hero of the Lincoln County War*. Sante Fe, N.M.: Sunstone Press, 1986.

Lebegott, Stanley. "Wage Trends, 1800–1900." In *Trends in the American Economy in the Nineteenth Century*. Princeton: Princeton University Press, 1960.

Lee, Alfred McClung, and Humphrey, Norman D. *Race Riot*. New York: Dryden, 1943.

Lee, Howard B. *Bloodletting in Appalachia: The Story of West Virginia's Four Major Mine Wars and Other Thrilling Incidents of Its Coalfields*. Morgantown, W. Va.: West Virginia University Press, 1969.

Lee, Rose Hum. *The Chinese in the United States of America*. Hong Kong: Oxford University Press, 1960.

Lee, Ulysses. *The Employment of Negro Troops*. Washington, D.C.: Office of the Chief of Military History, 1966.

Leggett, Mortimer D. "The Military and the Mob." In *Sketches of War History, 1861–1865: Paper Before the Ohio Commandery of the Military Order of the Loyal Legion of the United States*, Vol. 1: *1883–1886*. Cincinnati: Robert Clark, 1888.

Lemann, Nicholas. *The Promised Land: The Great Black Migration and How It Changed America*. New York: Alfred A. Knopf, 1991.

Lens, Sidney. *The Labor Wars: From the Molly Maguires to the Sitdowns*. Garden City, N.Y.: Doubleday, 1973.

Leuchtenberg, William E. *Franklin D. Roosevelt and the New Deal, 1932–1940*. New York: Harper & Row, 1963.

Lewis, Austin. *The Rise of the American Proletariat*. Chicago: C. H. Kerr, 1907.

Lichtenstein, Nelson. *Labor's War at Home: The CIO in World War II*. Cambridge: Harvard University Press, 1982.

Lindsey, Almont. *Pullman Strike: The Story of a Unique Experiment and of a Great Labor Upheaval*. Chicago: The University of Chicago Press, 1942; reprint, 1967.

Lingenfelter, Richard E. *The Hardrock Miners: A History of the Mining Labor Movement in the American West, 1863–1893*. Berkeley: University of California Press, 1974.

Link, Arthur S., ed. *The Papers of Woodrow Wilson*. Vols. 1–69. Princeton: Princeton University Press, 1966–1993.

Link, Arthur S. *Woodrow Wilson and the Progressive Era, 1910–1917*. New York: 1954.

Link, Arthur S. and McCormick, Richard L. *Progressivism*. Arlington Heights, Ill.: Harlan Davidson, 1985.

Lipset, Seymour M. and Raab, Earl. *The Politics of Unreason: Right-Wing Extremism in America, 1790–1970*. New York: Harper & Row, 1970.

Lisio, Donald J. *The President and Protest: Hoover, Conspiracy, and the Bonus Riot*. Columbia, Mo.: University of Missouri Press, 1974.

Livesay, Harold. *Samuel Gompers and Organized Labor in America*. Boston: Little Brown, 1978.

Logan, John A. *The Volunteer Soldier of America*. Chicago: R. S. Peale, 1887.

Long, Clarence D. *Wages and Earnings in the United States, 1860–1890*. Princeton: Princeton University Press, 1960.

Long, Priscilla. *Where the Sun Never Sets: A History of America's Bloody Coal Industry*. New York: Paragon House, 1989.

Lovestone, Jay. *The Government—Strikebreaker: A Study of the Role of the Federal Government in the Recent Industrial Crisis*. New York, Workers Party of America, 1923.

Lunt, Richard D. *Law and Order Versus the Miners, West Virginia, 1907–1923*. Hamden, Conn.: Archon Books, 1979.

McCool, B. Boren. *Union, Reaction, and Riot: A Biography of a Rural Race Riot*. Memphis, Tenn.: Memphis State University, 1970.

McDonald, David J., and Lynch, Edward A. *Coal and Unionism: A History of the American Coal Miner's Union*. Indianapolis: Cornelius, 1939.

McGovern, George S., and Guttridge, Leonard F. *The Great Coalfield War*. Boston: Houghton Mifflin, 1972.

McKee, Irving. *"Ben Hur" Wallace: The Life of General Lew Wallace*. Berkeley: University of California Press, 1947.

McMurry, Donald L. *Coxey's Army: A Study of the Industrial Army Movement of 1894*. Boston: Little Brown, 1929; reprint, Seattle: University of Washington Press, 1968, and New York: Arno Press, 1970.

McQuaid, Kim. *Big Business and Presidential Power: From FDR to Reagan*. New York: William Morrow, 1982.

Mahon, John K. *A History of the Militia and the National Guard*. New York: Macmillan, 1983.

Marrill, Horace S. *Bourbon Leader: Grover Cleveland and the Democratic Party*. Boston: Little Brown, 1957.

Maroney, James C. "The Texas-Louisiana Oilfield Strike of 1917." In *Essays in Southern Labor History: Selected Papers, Southern Labor History Conference, 1976*. Gary M. Fink and Merl E. Reed, eds. Westport: Greenwood, 1977.

Martin, Douglas D. *An Arizona Chronology: Statehood, 1913–1936*. Tucson: University of Arizona Press, 1966.

Martin, Edward W. *The History of the Great Riots: Together With a Full History of the Molly Maguires*. Philadelphia: National, 1877; reprint, New York: Augustus M. Kelley, 1971.

Martin, Robert F. *National Income in the United States, 1799–1938*. New York: National Industrial Conference Board, 1939.

Matloff, Maurice and Snell, Edwin M. *Strategic Planning for Coalition Warfare, 1941–1942*. Washington, D.C.: U.S. Army Center of Military History, 1953.

Mattes, Merrill J. *Indians, Infants, and Infantry: Andrew and Elizabeth Bart on the Frontier*. Denver: Old West, 1960.

Meier, August, and Rudwick, Elliott. *Black Detroit and the Rise of the UAW*. New York: Oxford University Press, 1979.

Meltzer, Milton. *Bread - and Roses: The Struggle of American Labor, 1865–1915*. New York: Alfred A. Knopf, 1967.

Metz, Harold W. *Labor Policy of the Federal Government*. Washington, D.C.: Brookings Institution, 1945.

Miles, Nelson A. *Personal Recollections and Observations of General Nelson A. Miles*. Chicago: Werner, 1896, reprint, New York: DaCapo Press, 1969.

_____. *Serving the Republic: Memoirs of the Civil and Military Life of Nelson A. Miles*. New York: Harper & Brothers, 1911.

Miller, Stuart C. *The Unwelcome Immigrant: The American Image of the Chinese, 1785–1882*. Berkeley: University of California Press, 1969.

Millett, Allen and Maslowski, Peter. *For the Common Defense: A Military History of the United States*. New York: Free Press, 1984.

Millett, John D. *The Organization and Role of the Army Service Forces*. Washington, D.C.: Office of the Chief of Military History, United States Army, 1954.

Millis, Harry A. ed. *How Collective Bargaining Works*. New York: The Twentieth Century Fund, 1942, reprint, New York: Arno Press, 1971.

Millis, Harry A. and Brown, Emily Clark. *From the Wagner Act to Taft-Hartley: A Study of National Labor Policy and Labor Relations*. Chicago: University of Chicago Press, 1950.

Millis, Walter. *Arms and Men: A Study in American Military History*. New York: G. P. Putnam's Sons, 1956.

Mink, Gwendolyn. *Old Labor and New Immigrants in American Political Development*. Ithaca, N.Y.: Cornell University Press, 1990.

Mitchell, John. *Organized Labor*. Philadelphia: Amcrican Book and Biblc Housc, 1903.

Mohl, Raymond A. *The New City: Urban America in the Industrial Age, 1860–1920*. Arlington Heights, Ill.: Harlan Davidson, 1985.

Monkkanen, Eric H. *America Becomes Urban: The Development of United States Cities and Towns, 1780–1980*. Berkeley: University of California Press, 1989.

Montgomery, David. *Worker's Control in America: Studies in the History of Work, Technology, and Labor Struggles*. New York: Cambridge University Press, 1979.

_____. *The Fall of the House of Labor: The Workplace, the State, and American Labor Activism, 1865–1925*. New York: Cambridge University Press, 1987.

Morgan, Murry C. *Puget's Sound: A Narrative of Early Tacoma and the Southern Sound*. Seattle: University of Washington Press, 1979.

Morgan, Richard E. *Domestic Intelligence: Monitoring Dissent in America*. Austin: University of Texas Press, 1980.

Morsberger, Robert E. and Morsberger, Katherine M. *Lew Wallace: Militant Romantic*. New York: McGraw Hill, 1980.

Mowry, George E. *The Era of Theodore Roosevelt, 1900–1912*. New York: Harper & Row, 1958.

_____. *Theodore Roosevelt and the Progressive Movement*. Madison: University of Wisconsin Press, 1946.

Murphy, Paul L. *The Constitution in Crisis Times, 1918–1969*. New York: Harper & Row, 1972.

_____. *World War I and the Origins of Civil Liberties in the United States*. New York: W. W. Norton, 1979.

Murray, Robert K. *Red Scare: A Study in National Hysteria, 1919–1920*. Minneapolis: University of Minnesota Press, 1955.

Nalty, Bernard C. *Strength for the Fight: A Study of Black Americans in the Military*. New York: Free Press, 1986.

Nalty, Bernard C. and MacGregor, Jr., Morris, eds. *Blacks in the Military: Essential Documents*. Wilmington, Del.: Scholarly Resources, 1981.

Neely, Mark E., Jr. *The Fate of Liberty: Abraham Lincoln and Civil Liberties*. New York: Oxford University Press, 1991.

Nelson, Daniel. *Managers and Workers: The Origins of the New Factory System in the United States, 1880–1920*. Madison: University of Wisconsin Press, 1975.

Nenninger, Timothy K. "The Army Enters the Twentieth Century, 1904–1917." In *Against All Enemies: Interpretations of American Military History From Colonial Times to the Present*. Kenneth J. Hagan and William R. Roberts, ed. Westport: Greenwood, 1986.

_____. *The Leavenworth School and the Old Army: Education, Professionalism, and the Officer Corps of the United States Army, 1881–1918*. Westport: Greenwood, 1978.

Nevins, Allan. *Grover Cleveland: A Study in Courage*. New York: Dodd, Mead & Co., 1932.

Newton, Michael and Newton, Judy Ann. *Racial and Religious Violence in America*. New York: Garland, 1991.

Nolan, Frederick, ed. *The Life and Death of John Henry Tunstall*. Albuguerque: University of New Mexico Press, 1965.

Painter, Nell Irving. *Standing at Armageddon: The United States, 1877–1919*. New York: W. W. Norton, 1987.

Parker, James. *The Old Army: Memories, 1872–1918*. Philadelphia: Dorrance, 1929.

Pencak, Willaim. *For God and Country: The American Legion, 1919–1941*. Boston: Northeastern University Press, 1989.

Perlmutter, Philip. *Divided We Fall: A History of Ethnic, Religious, and Racial Prejudice in America*. Ames, Ia.: Iowa State University Press, 1990.

Peterson, H. C., and Fite, G. C. *Opponents of War, 1917–1918*. Madison: University of Wisconsin Press, 1957.

Phelps, Orme Wheelock. *The Legislative Background of the Fair Labor Standards Act: A Study of the Growth of National Sentiment in Favor of Government Regulation of Wages, Hours, and Child Labor*. Chicago: University of Chicago Press, 1939.

Ping Chui. *Chinese Labor in California, 1850–1880*. Madison: University of Wisconsin Press, 1963.

Pinkerton, Allan. *The Molly Maguires and the Detectives*. New York: n.p., 1906.

Pollack, Norman. *The Populist Response to Industrial America: Midwestern Populist Thought*. Cambridge: Harvard University Press, 1966.

Porter, Glenn. *The Rise of Big Business, 1860–1910*. Arlington Heights, Ill.: Harlan

Davidson, 1973.

Powderly, Terence. *Thirty Years of Labor, 1859–1899*. Columbus: Excelsior, 1889, reprint, New York: Augustus M. Kelley, 1967.

Powe, Marc B. *The Emergence of the War Department Intelligence Agency, 1885–1918*. Manhattan, Kans.: Military Affairs/Aerospace Historian Publishing, 1975.

Preston, William, Jr. *Aliens and Dissenters: Federal Suppression of Radicals, 1903–1933*. New York: Harper & Row, 1963.

Quinlan, Dennis P. *Military Protection: Employment of the Army in Aid of Federal Civil Authorities in the Execution of Federal Laws*. Camp Dix, N.J.: 1922.

Ramirez, Bruno. *When Workers Fight: The Politics of Industrial Relations in the Progressive Era, 1898–1916*. Westport: Greenwood, 1978.

Regan, James. *Military Duties in Aid of the Civil Power: For the Regular Army, National Guard, and Police Forces Generally*. New York: P. M. Fiske, 1888.

Renshaw, Patrick. *The Wobblies: The Story of Syndicalism in the United States*. Garden City, N.Y.: Doubleday, 1967.

Reynolds, Charles B. *Washington: A Handbook for Visitors*. Washington, D.C.: B. S. Reynolds, 1935.

Rezneck, Samuel. *Business Depression and Financial Panics: Essays in American Business and Economic History*. Westport: Greenwood, 1968.

Rhode, Robert B. *Booms and Bust on Bitter Creek: A History of Rock Springs, Wyoming*. Boulder, Colo.: Pruett, 1987.

Rich, Bennett. *The President and Civil Disorder*. Washington, D.C.: Brookings Institution, 1941.

Richardson, James D. *A Compilation of the Messages and Papers of the Presidents, 1789–1897*. 10 vols. Washington, D.C.: Library of Congress, 1900.

Riker, William H. *Soldiers of the States: The Role of the National Guard in American Democracy*. Washington, D.C.: Public Affairs Press, 1957.

Roberts, William R. "Reform and Vitalization, 1890–1903." In *Against All Enemies: Interpretations of American Military History From Colonial Times to the Present*. Kenneth J. Hagan and William R. Roberts, eds. Westport: Greenwood, 1986.

Rochester, Anna. *Labor and Coal*. New York: International Publishers, 1931.

Romasco, Albert U. *The Poverty of Abundance: Hoover, the Nation, and the Depression*. New York: Oxford University Press, 1965.

Roosevelt, Theodore. *An Autobiography*. New York: Macmillan, 1916.

Rosenblum, Gerald. *Immigrant Workers: Their Impact on Labor Radicalism*. New York: Basic Books, 1973.

Rosenfarb, Joseph. *The National Labor Policy and How It Works*. New York: Harper & Row, 1940.

Rosenzweig, Roy. *Eight Hours for What We Will: Workers and Leisure in an Industrial City, 1870–1920*. Cambridge: Cambridge University Press, 1983.

Rudwick, Elliott M. *Race Riot at East St. Louis, 2 July 1917*. New York: World, 1964.

Ryan, Garry D. and Nenninger, Timothy K. eds. *Soldiers and Civilians: The United States Army and the American People*. Washington, D.C.: National Archives and Records Administration, 1987.

Ryan, John A. *A Living Wage*. n.p., 1912, reprint, New York: Arno Press, 1971.

Salerno, Salvatore. *Red November, Black November: Culture and Community in the Industrial Workers of the World*. Albany: State University of New York Press, 1989.

Salvatore, Nick. *Eugene V. Debs: Citizen and Socialist*. Urbana: University of Illinois Press, 1982.

Sanborn, Henry R. *The Law and Tactics of Civil Commotion*. Henry R. Sanborn, ca. 1919.

Sandburg, Carl. *The Chicago Race Riots, July 1919*. New York: Harcourt, Brace & Howe, 1919, reprint, New York: Harcourt, Brace & World, 1969.

Sandmeyer, Elmer C. *The Anti-Chinese Movement in California*. Urbana: University of Illinois Press, 1973.

Savage, Lon. *Thunder in the Mountains: The West Virginia Mine War, 1920–1921*. Elliston, Va.: Northcross House, 1986.

Saxton, Alexander. *The Indispensible Enemy: Labor and the Anti-Chinese Movement in California*. Berkeley: University of California Press, 1971.

Scheiber, Harry N. *The Wilson Administration and Civil Liberties, 1917–1921*. Ithaca: Cornell University Press, 1960.

Schlesinger, Arthur M. *The Rise of the American City, 1878–1898*. New York: Macmillan, 1933.

Schlesinger, Arthur M., Jr. *The Age of Roosevelt*. 3 vols. Boston: Houghton Mifflin, 1958–1960; reprint, Boston: Houghton Mifflin, 1988.

Schofield, John M. *Forty-Six Years in the Army*. New York: Century, 1897.

Schwantes, Carlos A. *Coxey's Army: An American Odessy*. Lincoln: University of Nebraska Press, 1985.

————. *Radical Heritage: Labor, Socialism, and Reform in Washington and British Columbia, 1885–1917*. Seattle: University of Washington Press, 1979.

Scott, Emmett J. *Negro Migration During the War*. New York: Oxford University Press, 1920.

Scott, Hugh L. *Some Memories of a Soldier*. New York: Century, 1928.

Sears, Joseph H. *The Career of Leonard Wood*. New York: Appleton, 1919.

Seidman, Joel. *American Labor From Defense to Reconversion*. Chicago: University of Chicago Press, 1953.

Seldes, George. *You Can't Do That: A Survey of the Forces Attempting, in the Name of Patriotism, To Make a Desert of the Bill of Rights*. New York: Modern Age, 1938.

————. *Witness to a Century: Encounters With the Noted, the Notorious, and the Three SOB's*. Boston: G. K. Hall, 1988.

Shifflett, Crandall A. *Coal Towns: Life, Work, and Culture in Company Towns in Southern Appalachia, 1880–1960*. Nashville: University of Tennessee Press, 1990.

Shogan, Robert, and Craig, Tom. *The Detriot Race Riot: A Study in Violence*. New York: Chilton Publishers, 1964.

Skelton, William B. "The Army Officer as Organization Man." In *Soldiers and Civilians: The United States Army and the American People*. Garry D. Ryan and Timothy K. Nenninger, eds. Washington, D.C.: National Archives and Records Administration, 1987.

Smith, Geoffrey. *To Save a Nation: American Countersubversives, the New Deal, and the Coming of World War II*. New York: Basic Books, 1974.

Smith, Helena Huntington. *The War on Powder River*. Lincoln: University of Nebraska Press, 1967.

Smith, R. Elberton. *The Army and Economic Mobilization*. Washington, D.C.: Office of the Chief of Military History, U.S. Army, 1959.

Smith, Robert Wayne. *The Coeur d'Alene Mining War of 1892*. Corvallis: University of Oregon Press, 1961.

Sobel, Robert. *The Age of Giant Corporations: A Microeconomic History of American Business, 1914–1970*. Westport: Greenwood Press, 1972.

Spaulding, Oliver L. *The United States Army in War and Peace*. New York: G. P. Putnam & Sons, 1937.

Spiers, Edward M. *Chemical Warfare*. Chicago: University of Illinois Press, 1986.

Sproat, John G. *The Best Men: Liberal Reformers in the Gilded Age*. New York: Oxford University Press, 1968.

Stein, Leon and Taft, Philip, eds. *Massacre at Ludlow: Four Reports*. New York: Arno Press, 1971.

_____. *The Pullman Strike, 1894–1913*. New York: Arno Press, 1969.

_____. *Religion, Reform and Revolution: Labor Panaceas in the Nineteenth Century*. New York: Arno Press, 1969.

_____. *Wages, Hours, and Strikes: Labor Panaceas in the Twentieth Century*. New York: Arno Press, 1969.

Stockton, Richard, and Sackett, Dickinson. *Troops on Riot Duty: A Manual for the Use of the Troops of the United States*. Trenton, N.J.: Military Publishing Co., 1912.

Stolberg, Benjamin. *The Story of the CIO*. New York: Viking Press, 1938, reprint, New York: Arno Press, 1971.

Storti, Craig. *Incident at Bitter Creek: The Story of the Rock Springs Chinese Massacre*. Ames, Ia.: Iowa State University Press, 1990.

Suggs, George G., Jr. *Colorado's War on Militant Unionism: James H. Peabody and the Western Federation of Miners*. Detroit: Wayne State University Press, 1972.

Sung, Betty Lee. *Mountain of Gold: The Story of Chinese in America*. New York: Macmillan, 1967.

Taft, Philip. *The A. F. of L. in the Time of Gompers*. New York: Harper, 1957; reprint, New York: Octagon Books, 1970.

_____. *The A. F. of L. From the Death of Gompers to the Merger*. New York: Harper & Brothers, 1959.

Takaki, Ronald. *Strangers from a Different Shore: A History of Asian Americans*. Boston: Little Brown, 1989.

Tarbell, Ida M. *The Life of Elbert H. Gary: The Story of Steel*. New York: D. Appleton, 1925.

Taylor, George W. *Government Regulation of Industrial Relations*. New York: Prentice Hall, 1948.

Taylor, Philip. *The Distant Magnet: European Emigration to the United States of America*. New York: Harper & Row, 1971.

Terrett, Dulany. *The Signal Corps: The Emergency*. Washington, D.C.: U.S. Army Center of Military History, 1956.

Thompson, Fred W., and Murfin, Patrick. *The IWW: Its First Seventy Years, 1905–1975*. Chicago: Industrial Workers of the World, 1976.

Thrapp, Dan L. *The Conquest of Apacheria*. Norman: The University of Oklahoma Press, 1967.

Trachtman, Paul. *The Gunfighters*. New York: Time-Life Books, 1974.

Troy, Leo. *Trade Union Membership, 1897–1962*. New York: Columbia University Press, 1965.

Truscott, Lucian K. *The Twilight of the U.S. Cavalry: Life in the Old Army, 1917–1942*. Lawrence, Kans.: University of Kansas Press, 1989.

Tuttle, William M., Jr. *Race Riot: Chicago in the Red Summer of 1919*. New York: Atheneum, 1970.

Tyler, Robert L. *Rebels of the Woods: The IWW in the Pacific Northwest*. Eugene: University of Oregon Press, 1940.

Upton, Emory. *The Military Policy of the United States*. Washington, D.C.: Government Printing Office, 1880; reprint, Washington, D.C., 1917.

Urofsky, Melvin. *Big Steel and the Wilson Administration*. Columbus: Ohio State University Press, 1969.

_____. *Felix Frankfurter: Judicial Restraint and Individual Liberties*. Boston: G.K. Hall, 1991.

Utley, Robert M. *Billy the Kid: A Short and Violent Life*. Lincoln: University of Nebraska Press, 1989.

_____. *Four Fighters of Lincoln County*. Albuquerque: University of New Mexico Press, 1986.

_____. *Frontier Regulars: The United States Army and the Indian, 1866–1891*. New York: Macmillan, 1973.

_____. *High Noon in Lincoln: Violence on the Western Frontier*. Albuquerque: University of New Mexico Press, 1987.

Verwey, Wil D. *Riot Control Agents and Herbicides in War: Their Humanitarian, Toxicological, Ecological, Military, Polemological, and Legal Aspects*. Leyden, Netherlands: A.W. Sijthoff, 1977.

Wagoner, Jay J. *Arizona Territory, 1863–1912: A Political History*. Tucson: University of Arizona Press, 1969.

Walker, Samuel. *In Defense of American Liberties: A History of the ACLU*. New York: Oxford University Press, 1990.

Wallace, Lew. *Lew Wallace: An Autobiography*. 2 Vols. New York: Harper & Brothers, 1906.

Warne, Colston Estey, ed. *The Pullman Boycott of 1894: The Problem of Federal Intervention*. Boston: D.C. Heath, 1955.

_____. *The Steel Strike of 1919*. Lexington, Mass.: D.C. Heath, 1968.

Waskow, Arthur I. *From Race Riot to Sit-in, 1919 and the 1960s*. New York: Doubleday, 1966.

Waters, W. W. *BEF: The Whole Story of the Bonus Army*. New York: John Day, 1933.

Watkins, Gordon S. *Labor Problems and Labor Administration in the United States During the World War*. Urbana: University of Illinois Press, 1920.

Watson, Mark Skinner. *Chief of Staff: Prewar Plans and Preparations*. Washington, D.C.: Office of the Chief of Military History, U.S. Army, 1950.

Weaver, John D. *The Brownsville Raid*. New York: W. W. Norton, 1970.

Weber, Ralph E., ed. *The Final Memoranda of Major General Ralph H. Van Deman, Father of United States Military Intelligence*. Frederick, Md.: University Publications of America, 1987.

Webster's American Military Biographies. Springfield, Mass.: Merriam, 1978.

Weibe, Robert H. *Businessmen and Reform: A Study of the Progressive Movement*. Cambridge: Harvard University Press, 1962.

_____. *The Search for Order, 1877–1920*. New York: Hill & Wang, 1967.

Weigley, Russell F. *History of the United States Army*. New York: Macmillan, 1967.

Weinberger, Barbara. *Keeping the Peace? Policing Strikes in Britain, 1906–1926*. Oxford: Berg, 1990.

Weinstein, James. *The Decline of Socialism in America, 1912–1925*. New York: Monthly Review Press, 1967.

West, George P. *Report on the Colorado Strike*. Washington, D.C.: U.S. Commission on Industrial Relations, 1915.

White, Walter. "What Caused the Detroit Riots?" In *What Caused the Detroit Race Riots?* Thurgood Marshall and Walter White, eds. New York: 1943. Reprinted in *Afro-American History: Primary Sources*. Thomas R. Frazier, ed. New York: Harcourt, Brace & World, 1970.

William, T. Harry, ed. *Hayes: The Diary of a President, 1875–1881*. New York: David McKay, 1964.

Williams, Charles R. *Diary and Letters of Rutherford B. Hayes*. 5 Vols. Columbus: Ohio State Archeological and Historical Society, 1922–1926.

Williams, Lee E. and Williams, Lee E., II. *Anatomy of Four Race Riots: Racial Conflict in Knoxville, Elaine (Arkansas), Tulsa, and Chicago, 1919–1921*. Jackson, Miss.: University and College Press of Mississippi, 1972.

Wilson, Frederick T. *Federal Aid in Domestic Disturbances, 1787–1903*. Washington, D.C.: Government Printing Office, 1903.

_____. *Federal Aid in Domestic Disturbances, 1903–1922*. Washington, D.C.: Government Printing Office, 1922.

Witcover, Jules. *Sabotage at Black Tom: Imperial Germany's Secret War in America, 1914–1917*. Chapel Hill: Algonquin Books, 1989.

Witney, Fred. *Wartime Experiences of the National Labor Relations Board, 1941–1945*. Urbana: University of Illinois Press, 1949.

Witte, Edward E. *The Government in Labor Disputes*. New York: McGraw Hill, 1931; reprint, New York, Arno Press, 1969.

Wolff, Leon. *Lockout: The Story of the Homestead Strike of 1892*. New York: Harper & Row, 1965.

Wong, Karen C. *Chinese History in the Pacific Northwest*. Seattle: University of Washington Press, 1972.

Wu, Cheng-Tsu, ed. *Chink!: A Documentary History of Anti-Chinese Prejudice in America*. New York: World, 1972.

Wyman, Mark. *Hard Rock Epic: Western Miners and the Industrial Revolution, 1860–1910*. Berkeley: University of California Press, 1979.

Wynne, Robert E. *Reaction to the Chinese in the Pacific Northwest and British Columbia, 1850–1910*. New York: Arno Press, 1978.

Yellen, Samuel. *American Labor Struggles, 1877–1934*. New York: Monad Press, 1936.

Yellowitz, Irwin. *Industrialization and the American Labor Movement, 1850–1900*. Port

Washington, N.Y.: Kennikat Press, 1977.

Young, Richard W. *Legal and Tactical Considerations Affecting the Employment of the Military in the Suppression of Mobs Including an Essay on Martial Law*. New York: Public Service Publishing, 1888.

Zieger, Robert H. *American Workers, American Unions, 1920–1985*. Baltimore: Johns Hopkins University Press, 1986.

————. *John L. Lewis: Labor Leader*. Boston: G. K. Hall, 1989.

Journal Articles

Adams, R.B. "Blair Mountain From the Other Side." *Goldenseal* 13 (Fall 1987).

Andre, Richard A. "Bomber Number 5." *Wonderful West Virginia* 48 (1984).

Asher, Robert. "Union Nativism and the Immigrant Response." *Labor History* 23 (1982).

Beaumont, Roger A. "Constabulary or Fire Brigade? The Army National Guard." *Parameters* 12 (March 1982).

Bernstein, Samuel. "American Labor in the Long Depression, 1873–1878." *Science and Society* 20 (1956).

————. "American Labor and the Paris Commune." *Science and Society* 15 (Spring 1951).

Birdsall, William C. "The Problem of Structure in the Knights of Labor." *Industrial and Labor Relations Review* 6 (1953).

Black, Isabella. "American Labor and Chinese Immigration." *Past and Present* 25 (1963).

Blum, Albert A. "Work or Fight." *Industrial and Labor Relations Review* (April 1963).

Butts, J. W. and Jones, Dorothy. "The Underlying Causes of the Elaine Riot of 1919." *Arkansas Historical Quarterly* 20 (1961).

Capeci, Dominic J., Jr. "Black-Jewish Relations in Wartime Detroit: The Marsh, Loving, Wolf Surveys and the Race Riot of 1943." *Jewish Social Studies* 47 (Fall 1985).

Carroll, Murry L. "Governor Francis E. Warren, The United States Army, and the Chinese Massacre at Rock Springs." *Annals of Wyoming* 59 (Fall 1987).

Cary, Lorin Lee. "The Wisconsin Loyalty Legion, 1917–1918." *Wisconsin Magazine of History* 53 (Autumn 1969).

Chandler, Alfred D., Jr., and Galambos, Louis. "The Development of Large-Scale Economic Organizations in American History." *Journal of Economic History* 30 (March 1970).

Cherry, George L. "American Press Reaction to the Paris Commune of 1871." *Mid-America* 32 (January 1950).

Clinch, Thomas C. "Coxey's Army in Montana." *Montana* 15 (October 1965).

Coben, Stanley. "The American Red Scare of 1919–1920." *Political Science Quarterly* 79 (1964).

Coffman, Edward M. "Army Life on the Frontier, 1865–1898." *Military Affairs* 20 (Winter 1956).

————. "The Army Officer and the Constitution." *Parameters* 17 (September 1987).

Cohen, William. "Riots, Racism, and Hysteria: The Response of Federal Investigative Officials to the Race Riots of 1919." *Massachusetts Review* 13 (Summer 1972).

Cole, Merle T. "Martial Law in West Virginia and Major Davis as Emperor of the Tug

River." *West Virginia History* 43 (Winter 1982).

Collier, Thomas W. "The Army and the Great Depression." *Parameters* 18 (September 1988).

Cooper, Jerry M. "National Guard Reform, The Army, and the Spanish-American War: The View From Wisconsin." *Military Affairs* 42 (January 1978).

————. "The Army as Strikebreakers: The Railroad Strikes of 1877 and 1894." 18 *Labor History* (Spring 1977).

Cuff, Robert D. "American History and the Organizational Factor." *Canadian Review of American Studies* 4 (Spring 1973).

Crane, Paul and Larson, Alfred. "The Chinese Massacre." *Annals of Wyoming* 12 (1940).

Daniels, Cletus E. "Wobblies on the Farm: The IWW in the Yakima Valley." *Pacific Northwest Quarterly* 65 (October 1974).

Daniels, Roger. "American Labor and Chinese Immigration." *Past and Present* 27 (1964).

Demarais, Ralph A., ed. "Military Intelligence Reports on the Arkansas Race Riots, 1919–1920." *Arkansas Historical Quarterly* 33 (1974).

Douglas, Donald M. "Social Soldiers: The Winona Company and the Beginnings of the Minnesota National Guard." *Minnesota History* 45 (April 1976).

Dubofsky, Melvyn. "The Origins of Western Working Class Radicalism, 1890–1905." *Labor History* 7 (1966).

Eggert, Gerald G. "Coxey's March on Washington." *American History Illustrated* 12 (October 1977).

Elliott, Russell R. "Labor Troubles in the Mining Camp at Goldfield, Nevada, 1906–1908." *Pacific Historical Review* 19 (November 1950).

Engdahl, David E., "Soldiers, Riots, and Revolution: The Law and History of Military Troops in Civil Disorder." *Iowa Law Review* 57 (October 1971).

————. "The New Civil Disturbance Regulations: The Threat of Military Intervention." *Indiana Law Review* 49 (Summer 1974).

Ensley, Philip C. "The Interchurch World Movement and the Steel Strike of 1919." *Labor History* 13 (Spring 1972).

Ficken, Robert E. "The Wobbly Horrors: Pacific Northwest Lumbermen and the Industrial Workers of the World, 1917–1928." *Labor History* 24 (Summer 1983).

Fishbein, Leslie. "Federal Suppression of Leftwing Dissidence in World War I." *Potomac Review* 6 (Summer 1974).

Fishbein, Meyer. "The President's Mediation Commission and the Arizona Copper Strike, 1917." *Southwest Social Science Quarterly* 30 (December 1949).

Fisher, Lucy Lee. "John J. Cornwall, Governor of West Virginia, 1917–1921." *West Virginia History* 24 (July 1963).

Friedheim, Robert L. "The Seattle General Strike of 1919." *Pacific Northwest Quarterly* 52 (July 1961).

Friedheim, Robert L. and Friedheim, Robin. "The Seattle Labor Movement, 1919–1920." *Pacific Northwest Quarterly* 55 (October 1964).

Furman, H. W. C. "Restrictions Upon the Use of the Army Imposed by the Posse Comitatus Act." *Military Law Review* 7 (January 1960).

Galambos, Louis. "The Emerging Organizational Synthesis in Modern American History." *Business History Review* 44 (Autumn 1970).

Gates, John M. "The Alleged Isolation of United States Army Officers in the Late Nineteenth Century." *Parameters* 10 (March 1980).

Grimshaw, Allen. "Actions of the Police and the Military in American Race Riots." *Phylon* 24 (Fall 1963).

Grob, Gerald N. "Reform Unionism: The National Labor Union Movement." *Journal of Economic History* 14 (1954).

————. "Terence V. Powderly and the Knights of Labor." *Mid-America* 39 (1957).

————. "The Knights of Labor and the Trade Unions, 1878–1886." *Journal of Economic History* 18 (1958).

————. "The Knights of Labor, Politics, and Populism." *Mid-America* 40 (January 1958).

————. "The Railroad Strikes of 1877." *Midwest Journal* (Winter 1954–55).

Gutfield, Arnon. "The Speculator Mine Disaster in 1917: Labor Resurgence at Butte, Montana." *Arizona and the West* 11 (Spring 1969).

Gutman, Herbert. "Work, Culture, and Society in Industrializing America, 1815–1919." *American Historical Review* 78 (June 1973).

Hacker, Barton. "The United States Army as a National Police Force." *Military Affairs* 33 (1969).

————. "The Federal Policing of Labor Disputes, 1877–1898." *Military Affairs* 33 (1969).

Harris, William H. "Federal Intervention in Union Discrimination: FEPC and West Coast Shipyards During World War II." *Labor History* 22 (1981).

Haynes, Robert V. "The Houston Mutiny and Riot of 1917." *Southwestern Historical Quarterly* 76 (April 1973).

Hays, Samuel. "The Social Analysis of American Political History, 1890–1920." *Political Science Quarterly* 80 (September 1965).

Higham, John. "Origins of Immigration Restriction, 1882–1897: A Social Analysis." *Mississippi Valley Historical Review* 39 (1952).

Hill, Herbert. "Anti-Oriental Agitation and the Rise of Working-Class Racism." *Society* 10 (1973).

Hilton, O. A. "Public Opinion and Civil Liberties in Wartime, 1917–1919." *Southwestern Social Science Quarterly* 28 (December. 1947).

Hogg, J. Bernard. "Public Reactions to Pinkertonism and the Labor Question." *Pennsylvania History* 11 (1944).

Holley, Irving B., jr. "The Management of Technological Change: Aircraft Production in the United States During World War II." *Aerospace Historian* 22 (1975).

Hurley, Patrick J. "The Facts About the Bonus March." *McCall's* 77 (November 1949).

Jensen, Billie B. "Woodrow Wilson's Intervention in the Coal Strike of 1914." *Labor History* 15 (1974).

Jones, Daniel P. "Tear Gas—Adoption for Use in Civil Disturbances." *Technology and Culture* 19 (April 1878).

Jones, Okah L. "Lew Wallace: Hoosier Governor of Territorial New Mexico, 1878–1881." *New Mexico Historical Review* 70 (April 1965).

Karlin, Jules Alexander. "The Anti-Chinese Outbreaks in Seattle, 1885–1886." *Pacific Northwest Quarterly* 39 (1948).

_____. "The Anti-Chinese Outbreaks in Tacoma." *Pacific Historical Review* 23 (August 1954).

Killigrew, John W. "The Army and the Bonus Incident." *Military Affairs* (1962).

Kleiler, Frank. "The World War II Battles of Montgomery Ward." *Chicago History* 5 (1976).

Koistinen, Paul A. C. "Mobilizing the World War II Economy: Labor and the Industrial-Military Alliance." *Pacific Historical Review* 42 (1973).

Kornweibel, Jr., Theodore. "Apathy and Dissent: Black America's Negative Response to World War I." *South Atlantic Quarterly* 80 (Summer 1981).

Laurie, Clayton D. "The Chinese Must Go: The United States Army and the Anti-Chinese Riots in Washington Territory, 1885–1886." *Pacific Northwest Quarterly* 81 (January 1990).

_____. "Civil Disorder and the Military in the Rock Springs, Wyoming; The Army's Role in the 1885 Chinese Massacre." *Montana: The Magazine of Western History* 40 (Summer 1990).

_____. "The U.S. Army and the Return to Normalcy in Labor Dispute Interventions: The Case of the West Virginia Coal Mine Wars, 1919–1921." *West Virginia History* 50 (1991).

_____. "The Army and the Omaha Race Riot of 1919." *Nebraska History* 72 (Fall 1991).

_____. "Anti-Labor Mercenaries or Defenders of Public Order: The United States Army and the Chicago Pullman Strike." *Chicago History* 20 (Winter/Spring 1991–92).

_____. "Extinguishing Frontier Brushfires: The U.S. Army's Role in Quelling the Pullman Strike in the West, 1894." *Journal of the West* 32 (April 1993).

_____. "The U.S. Army and the Labor Radicals of Coeur d'Alene: Federal Military Intervention in the Idaho Mine Wars of 1892–1899." *Idaho Yesterdays* 37 (Summer 1993).

_____. "Filling the Breach: The United States Army and Frontier Law Enforcement in the Trans-Mississippi West." *Western History Quarterly* 25 (Summer 1994).

Lawson, Michael L. "Omaha, A City in Ferment: Summer of 1919." *Nebraska History* 58 (Fall 1977).

Lichtenstein, Nelson. "Ambiguous Legacy: The Union Security Problem During World War II." *Labor History* 18 (1977).

_____. "Defending the No-Strike Pledge: CIO Politics During World War II." *Radical American* 9 (1975).

Lindquist, John A. "The Jerome Deportation of 1917." *Arizona and the West* 11 (February 1969).

Lindsey, Almont. "Paternalism and the Pullman Strike." *American Historical Review* 44 (1939).

Lisio, Donald J. "A Blunder Becomes Catastrophe: Hoover, the Legion, and the Bonus Army." *Wisconsin Magazine of History* 51 (Autumn 1967).

Livingstone-Little, D. E. "An Economic History of North Idaho: Pt. V, Discovery and Development of the Coeur d'Alene Mines." *Journal of the West* 3 (July 1964).

Long, Priscilla. "The Voice of the Gun: Colorado's Great Coalfield War of 1913–1914." *Labor's Heritage* 1 (October 1989).

McBride, J. R. "Utah and the Mormons." *International Review* 181 (12 February 1882).

McClymer, John F. "Late Nineteenth Century American Working Class Living Standards." *Journal of Interdisciplinary History* 17 (Autumn 1986).

McGoff, Kevin. "The Bonus Army." *American History Illustrated* 12 (February 1978): 29.

McMurry, Donald L. "Federation of the Railroad Brotherhoods, 1889–1894." *Industrial and Labor Relations Review* 7 (October 1953).

————. "Labor Policies of the General Manager's Association of Chicago, 1886–1894." *Journal of Economic History* 13 (1953).

Mandel, Bernard. "Notes on the Pullman Boycott." *Explorations in Entrepreneurial History* 6 (1954).

Marshal, Geoffrey. "The Armed Forces and Industrial Disputes in the United Kingdom." *Armed Forces and Society* 5 (February 1979).

Marszalek, John F., Jr. "A Black Cadet at West Point." *American Heritage* 22 (August 1971).

Martin, Tony. "March on Washington Movement." *Journal of African-Afro-American Affairs* 3 (1979).

Mauer, Mauer, and Senning, Calvin F. "Billy Mitchell, the Air Service, and the Mingo County War." *West Virginia Historian* 30 (October 1968).

Meador, Michael. "The Redneck War of 1921." *Goldenseal* 7 (April–June 1981).

Meier, August, and Rudwick, Elliott. "Communist Unions and the Black Community: The Case of the Transport Workers Union, 1934–1944." *Labor History* 23 (1982).

Menard, Orville D. "Tom Dennison, The Omaha Bee, and the 1919 Omaha Race Riots." *Nebraska History* 68 (Winter 1987).

Miller, James. "Carlo Sforza E L'Evoluzione Della Politica Americana Verso L'Italia: 1940–1943" [Carlo Sforza and the Evolution of American Policy Toward Italy, 1940–1943], Storia *Contemporanea* (Italy) 7 (1976).

————. "A Question of Loyalty: American Liberals, Propaganda, and the Italian American Community, 1939–1940." *Maryland Historian* 9 (1978).

Molineux, Brig. Gen. E.L., New York National Guard. "Riots in Cities and Their Suppression." *Journal of the Military Service Institution of the United States* 4 (1883).

Murray, Robert K. "Communism and the Great Steel Strike of 1919." *Mississippi Valley Historical Review* 38 (1951).

Nolen, Russell M. "The Labor Movement in St. Louis From 1860 to 1890." *Missouri Historical Review* 34 (1940).

Nuechterlein, James A. "The Politics of Civil Rights: The FEPC, 1941–1946." *Prologue* 10 (1978).

Osur, Alan M. "The Role of the Colorado Guard in Civil Disturbances." *Military Affairs* 46 (February 1982).

Otis, Col. Elwell S., 20th Infantry, U.S.A. "The Army in Connection with the Labor Riots of 1877." *Journal of the Military Service Institution of the United States* 5 (September 1884), and 6 (June 1885).

Perl, Peter. "Nation's Capital Held at Mercy of the Mob." *Washington Post Magazine*, 16 July 1989.

Philips, Cabell. "The West Virginia Mine War." *American Heritage* 25 (August 1974).

Poe, Douglas A. "The Use of Federal Troops to Suppress Domestic Violence." *American*

Bar Association Journal 54 (February 1968).

Price, John W. "The Army Evicts the Bonus Marchers." *Military Review* 51 (1971).

Prickett, James R. "Communist Conspiracy or Wage Dispute? The 1941 Strike at North American Aviation." *Pacific Historical Review* 5 (May 1981).

Pryde, George B. "The Union Pacific Coal Co., 1868 to August 1952." *Annals of Wyoming* 25 (July 1953).

Quinn, Larry D. "'Chink, Chink, Chinamen': The Beginnings of Nativism in Montana." *Pacific Northwest Quarterly* 58 (April 1967).

Raphalides, Samuel J. "The President's Use of Troops in Civil Disorders." *Presidential Studies Quarterly* 8 (1978).

Reed, Merl E. "Black Workers, Defense Industries, and Federal Agencies in Pennsylvania, 1941–1945." *Labor History* 27 (Summer 1986).

_____. "The FEPC, the Black Worker, and the Southern Shipyards." *South Atlantic Quarterly* 74 (1975).

Reichhardt, Otto H. "Industrial Concentration in World War II: The Case of the Aircraft Industry." *Aerospace Historian* 22 (1975).

_____. "Industrial Concentration and World War II: A Note on the Aircraft Industry." *Business History Review* 49 (1975).

Reinders, Robert. "Militia and Public Order in Nineteenth Century America." *Journal of American Studies* 11 (April 1977).

Rezneck, Samuel. "Distress, Relief, and Discontent in the United States During the Depression of 1873–1878." *Journal of Political Economy* 58 (December 1950).

_____. "Unemployment, Unrest, and Relief in the United States During the Depression of 1893–1897." *Journal of Political Economy* 61 (August 1953).

Richards, Kent D. "Insurrection, Agitation, and Riots, The Police Power and Washington Statehood." *The Magazine of Western History* 37 (Autumn 1987).

Rogers, O. A., Jr. "The Elaine Riots of 1919." *Arkansas Historical Quarterly* 19 (1960).

Sancton, Thomas. "The Race Riots." *New Republic* 109 (5 July 1943).

Schaich, Warren. "A Relationship Between Collective Racial Violence and War." *Journal of Black Studies* 5 (1975).

Scheuerman, William. "The Politics of Protest: The Great Steel Strike of 1919–1920 in Lackawanna, New York." *International Review of Social History* 31 (1986).

Schubert, Frank N. "The Suggs Affray: The Black Cavalry in the Johnson County War." *Western Historical Quarterly* (1973).

Schuler, Edgar A. "The Houston Race Riot of 1917." *Journal of Negro History* 29 (July 1944).

Schwantes, Carlos A. "Patterns of Radicalism on the Wage Worker's Frontier." *Idaho's Yesterdays* 30 (Fall 1986).

_____. "Law and Disorder: The Suppression of Coxey's Army in Idaho." *Idaho's Yesterdays* 25 (Summer 1981).

_____. "The History of Pacific Northwest Labor History." *Idaho's Yesterdays* 28 (Winter 1985).

Sitkoff, Harvard. "The Detroit Race Riot of 1943." *Michigan History* 53 (Fall 1969).

Slaner, Philip A. "The Railroad Strikes of 1877." *Marxist Quarterly* 1 (April–June 1937).

Smith, John S. "Organized Labor and Government in the Wilson Era, 1913–1921: Some Conclusions." *Labor History* 3 (Winter 1962).

Suggs, George G., Jr. "The Colorado Coal Miners' Strike of 1903–1904: A Prelude to Ludlow?" *Journal of the West* 12 (January 1973).

Sunseri, Alvin R. "The Ludlow Massacre: A Study in the Misemployment of the National Guard." *American Chronicle* 1 (January 1972).

Taft, Philip. "The Bisbee Deportation." *Labor History* 13 (Winter 1972).

Thiessen, D. G. and Schwantes, Carlos A. "Industrial Violence in the Coeur d'Alene Mining District: The Visual Record." *Pacific Northwest Quarterly* 78 (July 1987).

Thornbrough, Emma Lou. "The Brownsville Episode and the Negro Vote." *Mississippi Valley Historical Review* 44 (December 1957).

Tinsley, James A. "Roosevelt, Foraker, and the Brownsville Affray." *Journal of Negro History* 41 (January 1956).

Todd, Frederick P. "Our National Guard: An Introduction to Its History." *Military Affairs* 5 (1941).

Tugwell, Rexford G. "Roosevelt and the Bonus Marchers of 1932." *Political Science Quarterly* 87 (September 1972).

Turnbaugh, Roy. "Ethnicity, Civic Pride, and Committment: The Evolution of the Chicago Militia." *Journal of the Illinois State Historical Society* 72 (February 1979).

Tuttle, William J., Jr. "Labor Conflict and the Black Worker in Chicago, 1894–1919." *Labor History* 10 (Summer 1969).

Tyler, Robert L. "The United States Government as Labor Organizer: The Loyal Legion of Loggers and Lumbermen." *Mississippi Valley Historical Review* 47 (December 1960).

————. "Violence at Centralia, 1919." *Pacific Northwest Quarterly* 45 (October 1954).

Utley, Robert M. "General Nelson A. Miles." *By Valor and Arms* 3 (March 1978).

Varg, Paul A. "The Political Ideas of the American Railway Union." *The Historian* 10 (1948).

Vaughn, William P. "West Point and the First Negro Cadet." *Military Affairs* 35 (October 1971).

Vivian, James F. and Jean H. "The Bonus March of 1932: The Role of General George Van Horn Moseley." *Wisconsin Magazine of History* 51 (Autumn 1967).

Voeltz, Herman. "Coxey's Army in Oregon, 1894." *Oregon Historical Quarterly* 65 (September 1964).

Wade, Louise Carroll. "Hell Hath No Fury Like a General Scorned: Nelson A. Miles, The Pullman Strike, and the Beef Scandal of 1898." *Illustrated History Journal* 79 (Autumn 1986).

Walker, Henry P. "Retire Peaceably to Your Homes: Arizona Faces Martial Law, 1882." *Journal of Arizona History* 10 (1969).

Weibe, Robert. "The Anthracite Coal Strike of 1902: A Record of Confusion." *Mississippi Valley Historical Review* 49 (1961–62).

Weigley, Russell F. "The Military Thought of John M. Schofield." *Military Affairs* 22 (Summer 1959).

Werrell, Kenneth P. "Mutiny at Army Air Force Station 569: Bamber Bridge, England, June 1943." *Aerospace Historian* 22 (Winter/December 1975).

Whelan, Christopher. "Military Intervention in Industrial Disputes." *Industrial Law Journal* 8 (December 1979).

White, Earl B. "Might Is Right: Unionism and Goldfield, Nevada, 1904–1908." *Journal of the West* 16 (March 1977).

White, W. Thomas. "Boycott: The Pullman Strike in Montana." *Montana* 29 (Autumn 1979).

————. "Race, Ethnicity, and Gender in the Railroad Workforce: The Case of the Far Northwest, 1883–1918." *Western Historical Quarterly* 16 (July 1985).

Williams, David. "The Bureau of Investigation and Its Critics, 1919–1921: The Origins of Federal Political Surveillance." *Journal of American History* 68 (December 1981).

Wilson, John R. M. "The Quaker and the Sword: Herbert Hoover's Relationship With the Military." *Military Affairs* 38 (April 1974).

Winkler, Allan. "The Philadelphia Transit Strike of 1944." *Journal of American History* 59 (1972).

Wish, Harvey. "The Pullman Strike: A Study in Industrial Warfare." *Journal of the Illinois State Historical Society* 32 (September 1939).

Wunder, John R. "The Chinese and the Courts in the Pacific Northwest: Justice Denied?" *Pacific Historical Review* 52 (May 1983).

————. "Law and Chinese in Frontier Montana." *Montana* 30 (1980).

————. "The Courts and the Chinese in Frontier Idaho." *Idaho's Yesterdays* 25 (1981).

Wynne, Lewis N. "Brownsville: The Reaction of the Negro Press." *Phylon* 33 (Summer 1972).

Wynne, Robert E. "American Labor Leaders and the Vancouver Anti-Oriental Riot." *Pacific Northwest Quarterly* 52 (July 1961).

Yearly, Jr., Clifton K. "The Baltimore and Ohio Railroad Strike of 1877." *Maryland Historical Magazine* 51 (September 1956).

Zickel, Lewis. "The Soldier and Civil Disorder." *Military Review* 57 (May 1977).

Theses, Dissertations, and Miscellaneous Sources

Auble, Arthur G. "The Depressions of 1873 and 1882 in the United States." Ph.D. diss., Harvard University, 1949.

Bindler, Norman. "American Socialism and the First World War." Ph.D. diss., New York University, 1970.

Brown, Richard Carl. "Social Attitudes of American Generals, 1898–1940." Ph.D. diss., University of Wisconsin–Madison, 1951.

Cantor, Louis. "The Creation of the Modern National Guard: The Dick Militia Act of 1903." Ph.D. diss., Duke University, 1963.

Davison, the Honorable Trubee F., Assistant Secretary of War for Air. Interview with Dr. Donald J. Lisio. Long Island, New York, 22 April 1977.

Dowell, Cassius M. "Domestic Disturbances," Monograph, General Service School, Ft. Leavenworth, Kansas, 1922.

Greer, William Lee. "The Texas Gulf Coast Oil Strike of 1917." M.A. thesis, University of Houston, 1974.

Henle, Raymond. "Oral History Interview With General Dwight D. Eisenhower, President of the United States, 1953–1961, at Gettysburg, Pennsylvania, July 13, 1967." OH–106 (Palo Alto, California: Herbert Hoover Oral History Program; Hoover Institution of War, Revolution, and Peace).

Holmes, Joseph J. "National Guard of Pennsylvania: Policemen of Industry, 1865–1905." Ph.D. diss., University of Connecticut, 1971.

Jones, Dallas L. "The Wilson Administration and Organized Labor, 1912–1919." Ph.D. diss., Cornell University, 1955.

Killigrew, John W. "The Impact of the Great Depression on the Army, 1929–1936." Ph.D. diss., Indiana University, 1960.

Laurie, Clayton D. "Ideology and American Propaganda: The Psychological Warfare Campaign Against Nazi Germany, 1941–1945." Ph.D. diss., the American University, 1990.

Leibowitz, H. "Unemployment Relief During the Depression of 1893–1894." M.A. thesis, Columbia University, 1936.

Meneely, Alexander H. "The Anti-Chinese Movement in the Northwest." M.A. thesis, University of Washington, 1922.

Phipps, Stanley S. "From Bull Pen to Bargaining Table: The Tumultuous Struggle of Coeur d'Alene's Miners for the Right To Organize, 1887–1942." Ph.D. diss. University of Idaho, 1983.

Raines, Edgar F. "Major General J. Franklin Bell and Military Reform: The Chief of Staff Years, 1906–1910." Ph.D. diss., University of Wisconsin–Madison, 1976.

Reichley, Martin S. "Federal Military Intervention in Civil Disturbances." M.A. thesis, Georgetown University, 1939.

Senior Officer Debriefing Program. Conversation Between General Aurand and Lieutenant Colonel William O. Morrison. United States Military History Institute, Carlisle Barracks, Pennsylvania, 1974, Section 2, p. 36.

Shuman, Howard H. "The Role of Seattle's Newspapers in the Anti-Chinese Agitation of 1885–1886." M.A. thesis, University of Washington, 1968.

Sneller, Maurice P., Jr. "The Bonus March of 1932: A Study of Depression Leadership and Its Legacy." Ph.D. diss., University of Virginia, 1960.

Somma, Nicholas A. "The Knights of Labor and Chinese Immigration." Ph.D. diss., Catholic University of America, 1952.

Weberg, Frank P. "The Background of the Panic of 1893." Ph.D. diss., Catholic University of America, 1929.

Wilson, John M. "Herbert Hoover and the Armed Forces: A Study of Presidential Attitudes and Policy." Ph.D. diss., Northwestern University, 1971.

Woolard, James R. "The Philippine Scouts: The Development of America's Colonial Army." Ph.D. diss., Ohio State University, 1975.

Zais, Barrie E. "The Struggle for a 20th Century Army: Investigation and Reform of the United States Army After the Spanish-American War." Ph.D. diss., Duke University, 1981.

Photograph Credits

Illustrations courtesy of the following sources

Index

ISBN 0-16-048983-0

9 780160 489839

90000

PIN: 074152-00(